Aging and the Law

Aging and the Law

An Interdisciplinary Reader

EDITED BY

Lawrence A. Frolik

TEMPLE UNIVERSITY PRESS

PHILADELPHIA

Temple University Press, Philadelphia 19122

Published 1999
Printed in the United States of America

∞ The paper used in this publication meets the requirements of American National Standard for Information Sciences—Permanence of Paper for Printed Library Materials, ANSI Z39.48-1984

Text design by Erin Kirk New

Library of Congress Cataloging-in-Publication Data

Aging and the law : an interdisciplinary reader / edited by Lawrence A. Frolik.

p. cm.

Includes bibliographical references and index.

ISBN 1-56639-652-2 (cl. alk. paper). — ISBN 1-56639-653-0 (pbk. alk. paper)

1. Aged—legal status, laws, etc.—United States. I. Frolik. Lawrence A.

KF390.A4A424 1999
346.7301'3—dc21 98-22615
CIP

To Maureen and Tom

who proceedeth before me.

Contents

Preface

Typically, reality outpaces law and legal institutions. Certainly that is the case with the aging of America. As the number of older Americans rises, both in absolute numbers and as a percentage of the population, society, acting through law and legal institutions, must respond. For the most part, however, the law has been playing a "catch-up" game. While the aging of America creates social, political, and legal problems, our laws and legal institutions respond only after the fact. Of course "the law" doesn't respond to anything; rather individuals, legislators, and policy-makers respond. Collectively we create the kind of law and society that we deserve. Thus, we are all to blame for our failure to create laws and social policies that deal forthrightly and effectively with the problems of older Americans.

This book is an attempt to help close the gap between reality and the law. I have gathered here portions of articles, essays, and books that address many of the social, political, and legal problems occasioned by having an increasing number of older Americans. My hope is not to persuade readers of this book to any particular solution, but only to convince them that the problems exist and will not disappear absent some action on our part. What solutions, what actions, I leave to the reader.

To be sure, aging is foremost an individual event, and each individual will respond differently. For society, however, our aging population creates social and political issues that must be addressed politically. This is not to say that society must, in fact, take action. It is possible to take a very libertarian approach and simply allow each individual to meet the problem of aging as best as he or she can. But for most of us, such a hands-off policy seems either impractical, immoral, or cruel. As a society we want to alleviate the problems of our older members and make their later years more comfortable. But we cannot do so unless we first understand the variety of economic, legal, political, and social issues that accompany aging. This book attempts to do that.

For the most part, I have let the writings speak for themselves, and so have provided only the briefest introductions. For some issues for which I was unable to find material that I could reprint, I have written short introductory essays.

While the book attempts to address many of the problems, space did not permit them all to be addressed. The book is only a beginning. Readers are urged to seek out the original sources of these articles to find the full import of the writers' thoughts. Moreover, this is an area in which articles are frequently published. Indeed, if the past is prologue, there will continue to be an outpouring of essays, articles, and books on the issue of aging and the law that will enrich our collective understanding of the area. Though they may yet be supplanted, I hope that these materials serve as a foundational introduction and put other readings in perspective.

The materials in this collection have been severely edited, though without, I trust, affecting their message. Some textual footnotes have been eliminated for the sake of brevity. The institutions listed to identify the authors are where the authors were located at the time of original publication.

For the past decade, I have found aging and the law to be a fascinating topic. I hope the reader of this material will also find it stimulating and yet unsettling, which is so often the case when law and public policy intersect.

Acknowledgments

The successful publication of a book requires the help of many persons. I would like to thank the many contributors to this volume for permitting me to reprint their articles. I also would like to express my appreciation to Doris B. Braendel of Temple University Press for her perception of the need for such a book and her assistance in its creation.

Several students at the University of Pittsburgh School of Law provided research assistance. The efforts of Julia M. Tedjeske, Carrie E. Matesevac, Jeannette L. Jang, and James C. English are gratefully acknowledged.

I thank my secretary, Patricia Szalla, for her conscientious assistance, and I particularly thank the University of Pittsburgh School of Law Document Technology Center, under the direction of LuAnn Driscoll, and her staff, Karen Knochel, Darleen Mocello, Carolyn Rohan, and Barbara Salopek.

Part I

Introduction

As recently as twenty years ago, lawyers did not refer to themselves as practicing elder law. They did not even perceive themselves as primarily serving an older population. A lawyer might have a number of older clients, particularly if he or she specialized in writing wills and probating estates, but such lawyers called themselves estate planners. In contrast, today there is a recognized field of elder law, a national association of elder law attorneys (the National *Academy of Elder Law Attorneys), and a law review devoted to elder law issues (the* Elder Law Journal*), and every year hundreds of law students take courses, seminars, and clinics in elder law. The how and why of this rapid growth of a new area of law is the subject of the following article, which was the first article in the initial volume of the* Illinois College of Law Elder Law Journal.

CHAPTER 1

What Is Elder Law?

Lawrence A. Frolik

The Developing Field of Elder Law: A Historical Perspective

* * *

Elder law owes its existence to the convergence of two social and intellectual forces: the desire of lawyers to create legal practices that have come to be called elder law, and the simultaneous growth of academic interest in the topic of the elderly and the law.[1] Of course, elder law would exist even if not identified as such. For example, tax attorneys and tax law would exist even if there were no collective name for them. The names are, after all, only shorthand descriptions of a number of complex tasks lawyers perform that are known as "tax law." Similarly, elder law exists whether or not it has a label.[2]

Most law practice labels arise naturally out of the lawyer's activity. Criminal and securities law arise, respectively, out of dealing with persons associated with crime and clients who have legal problems with securities. Occasionally, however, a particular constellation of legal work that lacks an obvious title nevertheless acquires a label. The term *estate planning*, for example, gradually became the umbrella description of activities that in an earlier time had been called "wills and trusts" or "probate work."[3] The term *estate planning* does not eliminate these older terms. Instead, it binds them together and identifies them as part of a larger practice. In a similar manner, the term *elder law*[4] bundles together a variety of legal work. The term, however, does not only aggregate a group of existing activities. It implies something more, a

The Elder Law Journal, Vol. 1, No. 1 (Spring 1993).

new kind of legal practice, a new way to perceive what the lawyer does. The term *elder law* is both a collective title for existing activity and a new category of legal work, which creates new practice possibilities for lawyers.

* * *

Elder law can be roughly divided into two categories: (1) health law issues and (2) income and asset protection and preservation. Older clients have a higher incidence of legal problems associated with their health than do younger persons for two reasons. First, they are in poorer health. In particular, the elderly suffer more chronic illness, and they suffer more severe incidents of acute illness than those younger.[5] In addition, the elderly suffer the inevitable physical decline associated with aging. Loss of aerobic capacity, muscle, and flexibility are unavoidable as one grows older.[6] Most older persons also experience a decline in their hearing and vision.[7] Perhaps most significantly, many elderly eventually require long-term care whether at home, in a personal care home, or in a nursing home.[8]

As a result of their medical needs, many elderly require legal assistance. They may need a living will or an advanced directive for health care, or they may require advice regarding how to make health care decisions for an incapacitated spouse. Payment for health care can cause problems with Medicare reimbursement.[9] Poor elderly clients may have Medicaid eligibility difficulties. Middle-class clients with concerns about paying for long-term nursing home care seek advice about how they can become eligible for Medicaid. Other clients need assistance in protecting the rights of a relative in a nursing home or advice on what to do about an elderly person who appears to be the victim of abuse or neglect. A decline in the mental capacity of a client may require an attorney to file a guardianship petition, represent an allegedly incapacitated person, or support or challenge the acts of a guardian or conservator.

The elderly also have financial concerns. Some elderly will think that they were the victim of age discrimination in their employment. Many have questions about their rights under an employer-provided pension plan, or they are concerned about the income and estate tax implications of their pension plan distributions. Lower income elderly may have difficulty establishing eligibility for Supplemental Security Income or may have questions concerning veterans' benefits. Of course, traditional client needs for testamentary planning are also part of an elder law practice. Estate planning, including tax planning, the traditional drafting of wills and trusts, and the newer drafting of durable powers of attorney, constitutes an important aspect of elderly legal needs.

Elder law, then, is a legal practice that combines something old (e.g., estate planning) with something new (e.g., Medicaid planning). By calling themselves "elder law attorneys," lawyers identify themselves with this particular legal practice. But why should a lawyer want to do so? Why are lawyers not content with being traditional general practitioners with a concentration on matters dealing with the elderly? The answers to these questions are found in the changing composition of private practice.

* * *

The practice of elder law benefits from specialization arising from advertising. Lawyers who want to advertise and distinguish themselves from other lawyers can use the description "elder law specialist" as a means of attracting attention and, hopefully, clients. Although somewhat limiting, the term is expansive enough to encompass a fairly broad spectrum of legal practice. Yet advertising oneself as an elder law attorney does not necessarily exclude younger clients. Once in the office, the lawyer can, in effect, advertise his or her general availability for all types of legal consultations.

Many elder lawyers, however, are in fact elder law specialists whose practice is limited to legal problems of the elderly. For these lawyers, the use of advertising is often critical. Although some specialists, such as tax attorneys, can depend upon referrals from other attorneys, accountants, individuals in corporations served by the firm, and former clients, elder law attorneys depend more upon direct contact with the potential client.

By its nature, the elder law practice often deals with individuals who have no "family" lawyer. Often the last time a prospective client saw a lawyer was when he or she bought a house. In need of legal advice, such people seek an attorney versed in the relevant law. Most likely, they quickly discover that many lawyers lack the necessary ability or skill to help them. For example, a lawyer who is a traditional estate planner may prove inadequate when trying to establish eligibility for Medicaid. Given the relatively small number of elder law attorneys compared to the total number of practicing attorneys, finding an elder law attorney is a daunting task.[10] That is where advertising comes into play. By targeting potential clients and advertising specialized knowledge of elder law, an attorney creates a practice by direct contact with potential clients.

* * *

Subject to practical realities, lawyers are free to choose the form of legal practice in which they engage. A lawyer must have the skill, the training, and the interest in the area of law in which he or she elects to practice. Even more fundamental to the practice of law, however, is the necessity of clients. Wanting to develop a practice is not enough; a sufficient number of potential clients who need that particular type of legal assistance must exist. No one, for example, can practice elder law unless clients who need an elder law attorney exist. The fact that clients do need an elder law attorney partly explains the growth of the field.[11]

* * *

For those lawyers who gravitate toward what is sometimes called "people law," elder law is a natural fit. By definition, it is the practice of solving an individual's legal problems that arise from elemental human experiences: aging, loss of loved ones, loss of health, and death. For some attorneys, this is why they went to law school: to help people, to be involved in their most intimate problems, and, most importantly, to solve those problems. The lawyer's self-image of being a savior-in-pinstripes is well served by the tasks of the elder law attorney. These lawyers, at the end of the day, reflect upon the "good" deeds that they have performed. They might, for example, have assuaged clients' fears about the future by drawing up an advance health care directive, a durable power of attorney, or a will, or more importantly, they may have helped preserve the family assets through timely transfers to qualify for Medicaid. In short, an elder law practice translates into doing "good" by being on the "right side of the law."[12]

Identifying elder law with the more idealistic aspects of law practice should not be discounted. The coming of age of elder law as the baby boomer lawyers entered maturity was not accidental.[13] Touched intellectually by the radical idealism of the late 1960s, often attracted to law as a perceived instrument of social change, the boomers, initially in law school and then in the "real world," met the reality of law, which was being transformed from a profession to a business. Far from being some sort of domestic Peace Corps,[14] the practice of law revealed itself to be "nasty, brutish, and short."[15] For some of these disillusioned lawyers, elder law appeared to offer a plausible mix of earning a living while doing good. Within an elder law practice, attorneys solved problems of the middle and working class (not the poor, however, for they could not afford an attorney). In addition, they had little affinity with the upper-class clients who were identified with traditional estate planning. They preferred to work for the middle class: fighting for statutorily-promised government benefits; assisting their clients through stressful times, such as physical infirmity, mental incapacity, or death of a loved one; and doing battle with "bad" institutions, such as nursing homes and bureaucratic, unresponsive public agencies. In short, the elder law attorney was on the side of the angels.[16]

In addition, elder law attracts those lawyers who prefer counseling to litigation. Emotionally, these lawyers are just not cut out to fight and scrap for their clients. The tumult of the courtroom, the frustration of litigation, or the anxiety of a trial is not for them. These lawyers measure success not in how many adversaries they vanquish but in how many satisfied clients they serve. The world of planning and advising, of helping clients avoid problems, of reducing stress rather than creating it, and of a future orientation rather than an attempt to rectify the past, typifies these attorneys. Elder law allows them to practice law in a manner that plays to their professional strengths, while avoiding what they perceive to be the less desirable aspects of legal practice.

Elder law also attracts less experienced lawyers who believe that the practice is dependent more on knowledge than experience. A lawyer's inexperience even may help by permitting the lawyer to be more open to the new realities presented by state and federal statutory entitlements and entrapments. A determined individual, even a sole practitioner, who is willing to master the arcane ways of bureaucracy can acquire the necessary knowledge.[17] Being tutored in an established law office, although desirable, is not required for an attorney who wishes to establish an elder law practice. Elder law can be learned on one's own, always an appealing prospect to an inexperienced attorney.[18]

Elder law may attract female attorneys, whose numbers have risen sharply over the last twenty-five years.[19] Perhaps because female attorneys, on the average, are less experienced than male attorneys, a less traditional practice may attract them more than one dominated by the "old guard."[20] Opportunities for professional success may appear greater in a developing field such as elder law. If, as it is suspected, women continue to be victims of sex discrimination in hiring and promotion, they well might prefer to strike out on their own. What better area of the law than one which is relatively "unoccupied territory"? Elder law also might appeal especially to women if it is true, as some claim, that women are more effective than men in skills such as reconciliation, counseling, and negotiation that are so essential for the elder law attorney.[21] Finally, women might prefer a legal practice that in theory allows them more control over their time. Unlike many other attorneys, particularly litigators, the elder law attorney should be able to control his or her calendar—even to the point, if desired, of limiting hours in order to attend to family responsibilities. Although female attorneys probably do not take advantage of that relative possibility of control any more than their male counterparts, the thought that they might be able to do so if they desire may attract some women to the practice.

Elder law should also attract those who come to the law as a second career. As any law professor can attest, many older law students come to law school after careers as nurses, social workers, doctors, stockbrokers, and any other number of occupations. Some attend law school with the desire to renounce completely their past and forge new lives as attorneys. Others prefer to make use of their past training and to integrate the practice of law with their professional experience. They see in the practice of elder law the opportunity to avoid a complete break with the past, to build upon it. For these older law students, elder law offers the hope of drawing upon and giving value to their work prior to attending law school. The former nurses and doctors perceive that they can rely upon their medical expertise in advising clients about health care decisions. Former social workers see continuity in advising clients faced with difficult life choices. The former hospital administrator realizes the value of his or her knowledge of Medicare and Medicaid. For these individuals, and many more, elder law offers a special opportunity.

Changes in the economics of law, legal work opportunities, and lawyers' emotional needs coincided with a sharp rise in the number of older Americans and in their corresponding need for legal assistance. The result of the emergence and convergence of all these factors was the rise of elder law.[22]

* * *

Notes

1. The rise of elder law obviously is also dependent upon the growth in the number and relative wealth of the elderly. My purpose in this essay is to consider the other, less obvious factors, that help explain the growth of elder law and, thus, this journal.

2. At a conference I attended a lawyer asked me what was *elder law*. After I explained the kind of practice to which I thought the term applied, she responded: "Oh, that's what I do. I guess that I've been an elder law attorney for years and never knew it."

3. I have not been able to discover just when the term *estate planning* came into general usage. Certainly it was well established by 1953 when James Casner published his widely influential volume, A. JAMES CASNER, ESTATE PLANNING, CASES, STATUTES, TEXT, AND OTHER MATERIALS (1953).

4. There is no common agreement on whether the preferred term is *elderly law* or *elder law*. One group, the National Academy of Elder Law Attorneys, selected the term *elder law*. Yet, some books that advise lawyers on how to assist older clients use the term *elderly*. *See, e.g.*, LAWRENCE A. FROLIK & MELISSA BROWN, ADVISING THE ELDERLY OR DISABLED CLIENT (1992); JOHN J. REGAN, TAX, ESTATE & FINANCIAL PLANNING FOR THE ELDERLY (1993). Others use a single-word term, *elderlaw*. *See, e.g.*, LAWRENCE A. FROLIK & ALISON P. BARNES, ELDERLAW: CASES AND MATERIALS (1992); and some authors still use the term *aging*. *See, e.g.*, PETER STRAUSS ET AL., AGING AND THE LAW (1990); The American Civil Liberties Union helped publish ROBERT N. BROWN ET AL., THE RIGHTS OF OLDER PERSONS (1979). The American Association of Law Schools has a section devoted to the issues of the elderly with the title, Aging and the Law. Time alone will determine the preferred term.

5. ROBERT C. ATCHLEY, SOCIAL FORCE AND AGING 91 (5th ed. 1988).

6. DAVID A. TOMB, GROWING OLD 15 (1984).

7. Lawrence A. Frolik & Alison P. Barnes, *An Aging Population: A Challenge to the Law*, 42 HASTINGS L.J. 683, 694–96 (1991).

8. *See generally* HOUSE SELECT COMM. ON AGING, EXPLODING THE MYTHS: CAREGIVING IN AMERICA, 100TH CONG., 2D SESS. (1988).

9. FROLIK & BROWN, *supra* note 4, at 9–18.

10. Although I live in Pittsburgh, individuals throughout Pennsylvania, including Philadelphia, call me seeking an expert in elderly legal affairs. They either ask to employ me (I usually decline), or they hope that I can refer them to a specialist or at least a knowledgeable attorney. With the exception of Philadelphia, I am often at a loss as to whom to refer them, not for the lack of capable attorneys, but because I simply do not know a qualified attorney in their area of the state. Like the client, often I have no way of locating elder law attorneys. With the exception of the members of National Academy of Elder Law Attorneys, I know of no list of lawyers who consider themselves to have expertise in the legal rights of the elderly.

11. [The rapid growth in the number of Americans age sixty-five or older supports the growth of elder law. In 1990, those age sixty-five or older constituted 12.6 percent of the population, up from 9.9 percent in 1970. The total number in 1990 was over 31 million out of a total population of approximately 248 million. U.S. BUREAU OF THE CENSUS, DEP'T OF COMMERCE, STATISTICAL ABSTRACT OF THE U.S., table no. 13, at 73 (111th ed. 1991).]

12. As Professor John Langbein wrote about the field of estate planning, "The notion that what you are doing is good for everybody you touch is tremendously gratifying." [John Langbein, *Taking a Look at the Pluses and Minuses of the Practice*, TR. & EST., Dec. 1989, at 10.]

13. The term *baby boomer* refers to the 69 million Americans born between 1943 and 1960. Neil Howe & William Strauss, *The New Generation Gap*, ATLANTIC, Dec. 1992, at 67.

14. One of my favorite cartoons from the mid-1960s showed two young white men lolling at the beach. By their appearances, they were college students, probably at some elite institution. One said to the other, "I'd like to be of service to humanity and still have a piece of the pie." I suspect that sentiment was shared by many would-be social activists who helped swell law school enrollments.

15. *See* THOMAS HOBBES, LEVIATHAN 91–100 (Richard Tuck ed., Cambridge Univ. Press 1991) (1651) (writing about life in a natural state).

16. This description will embarrass many elder law practitioners who would not put such a self-serving glow on their practices. Nevertheless, I think that many do believe it even if they would not feel comfortable expressing it in these terms.

17. If not a sole practitioner, perhaps a law firm's sole elder law attorney. In 1992, NAELA reported that out of a membership of nearly 1800, only 122 of its members belonged to a firm with two or more members of NAELA. Robert B. Fleming, *NAELA Membership Update,* NAELA NEWS (National Academy of Elder Law Attorneys, Tucson, Ariz.), Oct. 1992, at 15.

18. I stress *appears* to be masterable by the individual. As they gain experience, elder law attorneys soon learn just how complex and difficult a practice it can be.

19. By 1988, women constituted approximately 30 percent of all lawyers, up from 2.8 percent in 1970. [AMERICAN BAR ASS'N, LEGAL EDUCATION AND PROFESSIONAL DEVELOPMENT—AN EDUCATIONAL CONTINUUM, REPORT OF THE TASK FORCE ON LAW SCHOOLS AND THE PROFESSION: NARROWING THE GAP 18 (1992) [hereinafter LEGAL EDUCATION AND PROFESSIONAL DEVELOPMENT].]

20. Compare the make-up in 1992 of the Board of Directors of NAELA for 1992 (7 women, 8 men) with that of the ABA Real Property, Probate and Trust Council (9 women, 16 men).

21. This view of the different talents of women finds much of its basis in the work of the psychologist Carol Gilligan. She claims, *inter alia,* that by their nature women are nurturers and men are combative. *See generally* CAROL GILLIGAN, IN A DIFFERENT VOICE (1982).

22. The growth of interest in the practice of elder law, or at least of an interest in the legal problems of the elderly, is symbolized by the number of state bar journals that have dedicated an issue to the legal problems of the elderly. *See, e.g.,* J. KAN. B. ASS'N, May 1990; 69 MICH. B.J. 493–620 (1990); WIS. LAW., Aug. 1991. The July 1991 issue of *Trust & Estates* (a magazine directed to bank trust counsel) was devoted to the topic—Symposium, *Addressing the Problems of Elder Care,* TR. & EST., July 1991. At least two law reviews have put out special issues on elderly legal problems. Symposium, *Legal Issues Relating to the Elderly,* 42 HASTINGS L.J. 683, 683–937 (1991); Symposium, *Housing and Home Care for the Elderly,* 10 ST. LOUIS U. PUBLIC L. REV. 437, 437–564 (1991).

CHAPTER 2

Why Treat Older Persons as a Separate Category?

Categorizing older persons as a separate group for legal purposes is not intuitively obvious. Age has not traditionally been treated as a separate category in the common law. True, advanced age is certainly noted when relevant. In particular, the law has always assumed a nexus between advanced age and mental competency. In the past, guardianship could often be created if the person suffered from the "infirmities of old age." Wills written by the very old might be more easily challenged on the claim that the testator lacked mental capacity to write a valid will. Yet, despite the recognition that old age might be a signal of decreasing capability, the law in general did not treat older persons any differently than a competent adult of any age. However, national social programs such as Social Security, and more recently Medicare, have created special rights for older Americans in recognition of their unique needs.

Though it may seem natural to treat older persons as a distinct category, that categorization is a crucial decision and not one that should pass unexamined. In the past, age sixty-five was thought an appropriate point to involuntarily retire older employees. Today, however, the law forbids the use of an arbitrary retirement age. We might well ask why we continue to use age as the primary eligibility requirement for many government benefit programs such as Medicare and Social Security. Instead of using age as a surrogate indicator of need, why don't we use more direct indicia of need such as poverty or ill health? In the following articles Professors Barnes and Frolik detail the number of older persons and briefly discuss the shared effects that make old age appropriate to use as a legally recognizable category.

Lawrence A. Frolik and Alison P. Barnes

An Aging Population: A Challenge to the Law

* * *

A. General Trends

Examination of current and projected demographics in the United States reveals three significant trends. First, the absolute number of elderly individuals is increasing.[1] Second, the percentage of the total population that is elderly is increasing.[2] Third, the ration, the ratio of workers (those age twenty to sixty-four compared to those age sixty-five or older), has steadily fallen for the past fifty years and will continue to fall for the foreseeable future.[3]

Two reasons have been advanced to explain the significant growth in the number of elderly. First, the number of individuals who reach age sixty-five increases every year. In 1991 more Americans will celebrate their sixty-fifth birthday than did so in 1990. Between 1995 and 2005, however, the number of new sixty-five-year-olds will decline as a result of the lower birth rates during the Great Depression of the 1930s. But as the baby boomers age, the number of sixty-five-year-olds will increase again beginning in the year 2005.[4] After 2030, barring any extraordinary increase in immigration rates, the number of individuals turning sixty-five will decline again until the children of the baby boomers—the "baby boomers redux" born between 1985 and 2010—begin to age, in around 2050.

* * *

The fact that individuals live longer is the other major contributor to the increase of the elderly. Not only do more individuals survive until age sixty-five, they have a longer life expectancy once they reach that age. Life expectancy measures the number of years an individual is expected to live as measured from birth. Over the years, life expectancy in the United States has gradually increased; consequently, more individuals survive until age sixty-five and beyond. In 1950 the average life expectancy of a United States resident was 68.2 years; by 1985 that figure had increased to 74.9 years.[5]

Life expectancies can be broken down by race and by sex. In 1985, for example, white male Americans had an average life expectancy of 72.0 years, while their white female counterparts' average life expectancy was 78.9 years.[6] In 1985, nonwhite[7] males had a life expectancy of 65.5 years; nonwhite women had an average life expectancy of 73.6 years. Life expectancy figures such as these can be deceiving, however, because they merely predict the average (mean) age of death for "age cohorts"—all those born in the same year. When we say that American women born in 1990 have a life expectancy of "x" years, all we are saying is that if death rates[8] do not change, "x" years is the average number of years that this specific age-sex cohort is expected to live. Life expectancy tables have only modest predictive value because the death rate always has fallen from that projected. That is, the average life span of the age cohort increases over time.

In addition, more than half of the age-sex cohorts will live past the projected life expectancy age. If we say that life expectancy is "x" years, we only predict an average mean age of death for a cohort. Since some members of the cohort begin to die soon after birth, thereby greatly lowering the average age, many must live past the average age.

What is of more interest than an individual's life expectancy at birth is how long he can expect to live from today. If he is age sixty-five, for example, how much longer can he expect to live? As a person grows older, his life expectancy rises as his cohort group is redefined to include only those surviving. If he is age sixty-five, his life expectancy is based upon the average age of death for those who reach age sixty-five. That figure will be higher than at birth since it will not include those who died before they reached age sixty-five.[9]

Finally, the percentage of the population that is elderly increases in part because of falling birth rates. As individuals age, the elderly become a larger proportion of the population because there are relatively fewer young people. As fertility rates level off, the percentage of elderly in society will diminish even though their absolute numbers will continue to grow.[10]

B. Growth in the Over Age Eighty-Five Category

The elderly are by no means a homogeneous group. We would not think of lumping together any other age group that ranges over thirty-five years (e.g., age sixty-five to one hundred plus). In recognition of the wide age span, many observers now subcategorize the elderly into three groups: the young old, age sixty-five to seventy-five; the old, age seventy-five to eighty-five; and the old-old, age eighty-five plus. The utility of categorizing by age is debatable. It may be more sensible to group the elderly by physical and mental capability; for example, the well elderly, the frail elderly, and so on.

Be that as it may, the rapid rise in the numbers of persons age eighty-five or older is noteworthy. As of the last census in 1980 there were over 1.5 million women and 675,000 men eighty-five years old or older.[11] In terms of percentage growth, those over age eighty-five are the fastest growing age cohort.

Growth in the number of those over age eighty-five often is cited as cause for particular concern. It is claimed that this group will put particularly heavy demands on the health care systems, supported living arrangements, and nursing homes. Those who live past age eighty-five also may outlive their children, thereby raising personal assistance issues, emotional support problems, and concern for their financial well-being.[12] Certainly our current laws and government programs were created when the number of individuals in this age group was much lower. Whether those laws and programs will meet the needs and the problems of the old-old is problematical. The expected growth of this group alone gives good cause to examine the relationship between the elderly and the law.

C. Aging Patterns by Gender

Patterns of aging differ by gender. As was illustrated by some of the statistics discussed above,[13] women outlive men. The graying of America is in large part a female phenomenon.[14] The overwhelming ratio of elderly women to elderly men cannot be overemphasized. At every year past age sixty-five, women greatly outnumber men. When we refer to the elderly, we should visualize women. If the term "elderly individual" conjures up a picture of a man, bear in mind that he is a minority representative and a rather small minority at that.

For society, its policy, and policy makers, the preponderance of elderly women has profound significance. How society allocates its resources to assist the elderly should (but does not always) take into account that the elderly are mostly women.

* * *

D. Aging Patterns by Race

Nonwhite Americans do not live as long as white Americans. For a host of economic, health care, and cultural reasons, nonwhite Americans have a shorter life expectancy than whites. As a result the elderly are disproportionately white.[15] Although the life expectancy of minorities is increasing (as are the numbers of African American and Hispanic elderly), the gap between whites and minorities continues with no evidence that it is going to close soon.

For social policy planners, the shorter life expectancies of African Americans and Hispanics mean that benefit programs for the elderly disproportionately favor whites. For example, although all employees regardless of their race or gender pay Social Security taxes, because of their higher death rates, many minorities will not live long enough to collect retirement benefits. When the minimum age for collecting Social Security benefits is raised, all employees are disadvantaged, but minorities particularly are harmed because a greater number of them will not live long enough to collect retirement benefits.

* * *

Notes

1. P. ZOPF, AMERICA'S OLDER POPULATION 12 (1986).
2. *Id.*

3. [The ratio of workers (those 20 to 64) to elderly (those over 65) has declined steadily since 1950. In 1950 there were 7.1 workers for each elderly individual in the United States. By 1970 that number had dropped to 5.3 workers and by 1990 to 4.6 workers per elderly. The figure is expected to continue to decline in the future: by the year 2025 there will be only 2.9 workers for each elderly individual and by 2050 the number is projected to decline to 2.5. (P. ZOPF, *supra* note 1 at 47.)]

4. P. ZOPF, *supra* note 1, at 10.

5. [Longino, Soldo & Manton, *Demography of Aging in the United States,* in GERONTOLOGY: PERSPECTIVES AND ISSUES 19 (K. Ferraro ed. 1990) (hereinafter Longino).]

6. *Id.*

7. "Nonwhite" refers to anyone who would not declare his race to be white or Caucasian and therefore includes, *inter alia,* African Americans, Hispanics, and Asian Americans.

8. Death rates refer to the number of cohorts per thousand that died in a particular year. The projected death rate determines the life expectancy of the cohort. As the death rate declines (*i.e.,* fewer members of the cohort die in each year), the life expectancy of the cohort increases (*i.e.,* more years will pass before half of the cohort will have died).

9. Statistics illustrate that the additional life expectancy of those who reach age 65 rose between 1950 and 1985. Measured for the group as a whole, the life expectancy rose from 13.9 years in 1950 to 16.1 in 1970 and finally to 16.9 in 1985. Female life expectancies, as compared to male, were higher for each of these years with 15 years in 1950 (male 12.8), 18.1 in 1975 (male 13.8), and 18.6 in 1985 (male 14.8). *Id.* The life expectancies of the white male and female 65-year-old population for these years were essentially the same as those for the group as a whole. *Id.* (The fact that the life expectancy figures for whites are identical to those for the overall group indicates that nonwhites did not make up a significant part of the sample group.) Notably, the life expectancies of the nonwhite 65-year-old population were lower than those of the total in all years for both men and women. In 1985, for example, nonwhite male life expectancy at age 65 totalled 13.6 years and nonwhite female life expectancy totalled 16.9. *Id.* These figures clearly illustrate that those individuals who live until age 65 statistically have a number of years remaining to live.

10. I. ROSENWAIKE, THE EXTREME AGED IN AMERICA 6 (1985).

11. *Id.* at 7.

12. *See generally id.*

13. *See supra* note 9.

14. The so-called sex ratio confirms this. The ratio is the percentage of males to females at a given age. At age 5, the ratio is 105%. By age 60 the ratio is 88%; by age 65 the ratio is 83%; and at age 75 the ratio declines to 70%. P. ZOPF, *supra* note 1, at 57.

15. A few statistics are illustrative. In 1980 the percentages of white men surviving to ages 65, 75, and 85 were respectively 72.3%, 47.5%, and 18.3%. The survival rate of nonwhite males (African American, Hispanic, and those of and other races) for these same ages compared at 58%, 35.5%, and 13.9% respectively. Similarly, white females' survival rates also compared more favorably with survival rates of nonwhite women (African American, Hispanic, and those of other races) at ages 65, 75, and 85: 84.7% survival for white women to age 65 contrasted with 75% for women of other races; 68.5% survival to age 75 versus 55.7% for women of other races; and 38.4% survival to age 85 compared with 29.6% for females of other races. *Id.* at 33.

Alison P. Barnes and Lawrence A. Frolik

America the Aging: Changing demographics pose dramatic new challenges for our country and the courts

* * *

The Nature of Aging

Inevitable changes in appearance accompany growing older. Aging, however, is more than skin deep. Healthy aging, which begins early in life, involves loss of physical vigor; vision impairments, such as sensitivity to glare and impaired focus on moving objects; hearing losses at high and low frequencies and associated loss of balance; and more fragile bones due to loss of calcium. Aging may cause some memory loss, though severe loss is a symptom of illness.

Although older people generally tend to have fewer episodes of acute illness, once ill, they take longer to recover. More significantly, they generally suffer more from chronic (i.e., incurable, nonterminal) conditions such as diabetes, heart disease, and arthritis. In 1989, about one-fifth of individuals age seventy and older had some chronic condition that limited activity. About 10 percent were unable to carry out a major activity such as bathing or eating. (National Institute on Disability and Rehabilitation Research, *Digest of Data on Persons with Disabilities:* 1992 (Washington, D.C.).)

By the year 2020, the number of disabled elderly is conservatively projected to increase 84 percent, from 5.1 million to 9.4 million. By 2040, when the baby boomers reach their eighties and nineties, the number of disabled elderly is projected to range as high as 22.6 million. (Kunkel and Applebaum, "Estimating the Prevalence of Long-term Disability for an Aging Society," 47 J. of Gerontology S253–S260). As medical technology cures or arrests more serious illnesses, the likelihood increases that survivors will endure lasting impairments from illness (and treatment) and from aged-related chronic conditions.

One illness that becomes more prevalent with age is Alzheimer's disease, a form of dementia characterized by progressive mental, emotional, and intellectual decline. The diagnosis cannot be certain without an autopsy, though an experienced neurologist can distinguish conditions that mimic many symptoms of the disease. An Alzheimer's patient progresses over an average of eight years after diagnosis from mild forgetfulness to confusion of time and place to emotional disturbances. In time, the individual cannot identify familiar faces. Physical skills decline, and the power of speech is lost.

About 2.5 million Americans had Alzheimer's disease in 1990, and an equal number had other types of dementia, which progress at different rates for different reasons. Because incidence increases with age and the elderly population is growing, the number of people with severe symptoms of Alzheimer's disease is projected to increase to nearly 8 million by 2040.

Mental impairment need not be an irreversible symptom of physical illness, however; the most common psychological diagnosis among elderly people is depression. Living with the symptoms of chronic illness takes a toll on confidence and self-esteem. Some elderly people who cannot fully participate in daily life become isolated. Some express their loss of hope in apathy, leaving to others important decisions about their well-being and life-style.

The Need for Assistance

About half of the elderly require some degree of assistance with the activities of daily living. Assistance is traditionally provided by family members. Wives, in particular, care for their husbands, who tend to be slightly older and in need of help first. Most of the responsibility for a surviving spouse traditionally has been assumed by an adult daughter who often must delay her own life plans to care for a parent. (Marjorie Cantor, "Families and Caregiving in an Aging Society," *Generations,* Summer 1992 at 67.)

The tradition of family assistance is alive and well, but threatened by geographic mobility, work patterns, smaller families begun later in life, and by extended old age itself. The need for elder care may last for years, even decades, exceeding a family's financial and emotional resources. Some families live too far apart to be of practical assistance. Approximately 55 percent of women age fifty-five to fifty-nine, the principal caregivers for aged parents, are in the labor force. (Interview with Cynthia Taeuber, Chief of the Age and Sex Statistics Branch of the U.S. Census Bureau, Nov. 30, 1992, reported in *LTC News and Comment,* January 1993 at 3.) They may also have conflicting obligations; later childbearing has produced a population with simultaneous caregiving responsibilities to young and old: the so-called "sandwich generation." Divorce and remarriage, in either generation, may multiply the claims on a potential caregiver's time and energy.

In addition, there are fewer adult children to share the burden of care. The low birthrate throughout the 1930s has resulted in a cohort of octogenarians who are likely to have one or no surviving children. The current birthrate—below replacement level for two decades—assures that a similarly childless group will become elderly after 2020. A measure of the shift resulting from fewer children and longer lives is the "parent support ratio," which measures the number of persons age eighty-five to one hundred with persons age fifty to sixty-four, the age bracket of most adult children of very elderly parents. The parent support ratio will increase from 9 in 1990 to 28 in 2050. (*Sixty Five Plus in America* at 2–17.)

Elderly people who lack family assistance develop social support networks of neighbors, friends, and church members. African American elderly may more often rely on kin relationships with community and church members. As individuals become very old and impaired, however, nonfamilial support networks begin to fray. Few helpers are available among the elderly person's contemporaries, and gaps in assistance leave more and more needs unmet.

Formal assistance—home health workers, a housekeeper, a home repair business, a driver and companion—can be employed by some elderly persons to fill the gap. Though the median income of elderly individuals in 1989 was $9,422, only about half that of comparable younger adults, the median net worth of an elderly household totaled $73,471. (*Aging America* at xx.) About one third have assets exceeding $100,000.

The distribution of income and assets varies enormously, however, and those with the least resources are often the most in need of care. The median income for people age eighty-five and over was only three fourths that of younger retirees. Widowed individuals, usually women, had only 40 percent of the net worth of elderly married couples.

Twice as many women as men are poor; among the oldest women, one in five lives in poverty. The most costly item purchased by the elderly, other than shelter and food, is health care. In 1989, people over age seventy-five paid an average 15 percent of their income for health insurance premiums, copayments, and drugs. (*Aging America* at 79.)

Governmental Assistance

Though most elderly people do not depend on their children directly for financial assistance, almost all take advantage of public benefit programs that redistribute resources in the form of Social Society income payments and Medicare health insurance benefits. The elderly did contribute to the Social Security program during their working years; however, most receive benefits that far exceed the value of those contributions. Similarly, Medicare requires payments from beneficiaries but represents a significant subsidy for elderly participants.

These government programs were established on the premise that age is an appropriate substitute to a showing of need. In the past, age often did strongly correlate with poverty. Furthermore, governments, employers, and other institutions prefer such an inexpensive, "bright-line" test to a snarl of litigation over who is "needy." As our resources fail to keep pace with benefit payments, however, the government will be forced to adopt a new bright-line standard. It has already adopted new standards for Social Security payments, by gradually raising to sixty-seven (in the year 2008) the age at which a worker can begin collecting full retirement benefits.

Recently, some have questioned whether the elderly reap too many benefits. The charge results not only from the improved economic status of many elderly, but from the growth of societal needs for health care for uninsured workers and the poor, crime prevention, education, environmental protection, and infrastructure repairs. Though the assertion that the elderly are oversubsidized is debatable, the demands of society's most pressing needs cannot be ignored.

The larger issue is one of intergenerational justice: How much do the young owe to the old? Younger workers feel compelled to contribute through taxes to maintain the aging while forgoing retirement savings and borrowing to meet their children's college tuition needs. It is doubtful that under the rules of current benefit programs, workers will be able to support the elderly population in the future. The rising "economic support ratio"—the number of persons age seventy-five and older for every 100 persons age twenty to sixty-four—is projected to increase from 8.9 in 1990 to 22.4 in 2050. (*Sixty Five Plus in America* at 2–17.) In any case, some argue that it is an individual's responsibility to save for old age.

Perhaps the best response to the debate over the "worthiness" of the elderly to receive benefits from the working population is the observation that this is the first generation of elderly people for whom an extended old age is a widespread phenomenon. Many did save for the retirement they anticipated, but some have simply outlived their own expectations.

Furthermore, virtually all of today's beneficiaries (or their spouses) paid taxes into the Social Security trust fund and in turn were promised retirement income. Many who worked hard and continuously, including low-wage employees and agricultural workers, had little or nothing left to save beyond subsistence. The oldest elderly, who paid the least in taxes, are, by and large, the neediest.

The question, however, remains to be resolved: What does society owe the elderly, now and in the future? It must be answered in the context of massive federal deficits and strained state budgets.

* * *

The challenge to the law will be to move the arguments beyond mundane program details and immediate financial concerns to a meaningful examination of policy choices. Our ambivalence regarding the "worthiness" of the elderly to receive society's benefits must be resolved in large part in a legal arena. How we resolve the conflicts will be fundamental to the future of elder law. How we as a society treat the elderly will reveal much about us as a people. We may hope that what we learn is to our credit.

CHAPTER 3

Social Attitudes Toward the Elderly

The recognition that older persons are an appropriate category for the creation of a legal practice and for the determination of public benefits is not without its costs, however. The flip side of elder law is ageism, the pernicious belief that older persons are less capable, less deserving of respect, and less needful of personal independence and autonomy. In her article, Professor Whitton discusses how corrosive ageism and its companion, paternalism, are of the rights of older persons to a dignified, autonomous life.

Linda S. Whitton

Ageism: Paternalism and Prejudice

* * *

I. From Age Segregation and Youth Obsession to Gerontophobia—The Coming of Age of Ageism

The term "ageism," coined in 1968 by Dr. Robert N. Butler, the first director of the National Institute on Aging, was originally defined as:

> [A] systematic stereotyping of and discrimination against people because they are old, just as racism and sexism accomplish this with skin color and gender. Old people

46 *DePaul Law Review* 453 (1997). Reprinted by permission.

> are categorized as senile, rigid in thought and manner, old-fashioned in morality and skills. . . . Ageism allows the younger generation to see older people as different from themselves; thus they subtly cease to identify with their elders as human beings.[1]

Twenty years later, Dr. Butler noted that the current manifestations of ageism go beyond stereotyping and alienation and include both envy and resentment of the elderly—envy of affluent elderly for their economic successes and resentment of poor elderly for their ostensible burden on public benefits and tax expenditures.[2] Dr. Butler concluded that there is universal fear of the increasing older population based on notions that such a population "will become unaffordable, lead to stagnation of the society's productive and economic growth, and generate intergenerational conflict."[3]

* * *

A. Age Consciousness and Age Segregation

Although people have aged since time immemorial, chronological age has not always been the important means of social categorization and organization that it is today. Written accounts of life prior to the mid-nineteenth century are practically devoid of the mention of age as an organizing principle.[4] One explanation for the relative unimportance of chronological age in that era was the economic interdependence of multigeneration families. Prior to 1850, most families operated as self-reliant economic units in which individual family members of all ages, from small children to the elderly, contributed to the productivity of the collective.[5] Likewise, participation in education and community activities also tended to be age integrated.[6] So unimportant was chronological age to daily existence that most people did not even keep an awareness of their exact age.[7]

* * *

Several convergent trends in the mid- to late nineteenth century marked the emergence of chronological age as a new basis for categorizing individuals and the aging process. Although industrialization is usually cited as the most influential of these trends,[8] advancements in science and medicine were at least concomitant, if not integrally related, factors in the transition from an age-integrated to an age-conscious and age-graded society.[9] The production efficiencies of factories permitted families to live above the subsistence level and diminished the need for the labor of children and the elderly.[10] Not only was the labor of older workers considered less essential to family survival, writers in the early twentieth century argued that older workers were not as efficient as younger workers and should therefore retire.[11] During this same time period, science and medicine began using age to organize the study of physical and psychological development,[12] as well as pathology.[13] In medical circles, old age became synonymous with disease and degeneration,[14] leading to the conclusion that the illnesses of the elderly were the result of natural deterioration, and thus untreatable.[15] Old age also became more closely associated with death as improved health care lowered mortality rates and more individuals survived to an older age.[16]

By the turn of the century, the concept of age segregation had invaded education, industry, and family life.[17] The emphasis on rationality and efficiency produced a new system of education where students became segregated by peer groups, rather than abilities, and were advanced in lock-step fashion by age.[18] In the workplace, the rising prevalence of old-age pensions encouraged workers to accept age sixty-five as the appropriate end of productive life.[19] Even the age composition of families changed as the size of the average family decreased with the shift from agrarian to industrial life.[20] Preindustrial American families were typically composed of a large number of children spread over many years, and distinctions between generations were blurred by a broad age range among siblings.[21] In postindustrial families with fewer children, the gap between generations became greater because the ages between children were more compressed.[22] The combined result of these trends was a growing importance of peer associations and a decreasing significance of intergenerational relationships.[23]

* * *

B. The Obsession with Youth

The association between youth, new technology, and the future formed the foundation for what historian W. Andrew Achenbaum has described as the "youth cult."[24] The advent of this obsession with youth actually preceded the "baby boom" of the mid-twentieth century and is attributed to a cultural belief at the turn of the century that young people embodied the qualities necessary to advance society into a new progressive era.[25]

* * *

Of course, the strength in numbers of the baby boom generation intensified the cult of youth,[26] as is reflected by the focus of present-day popular media and marketing campaigns. Studies of prime time television dramas, commercials, magazines, and advertisements reveal very few images of older people.[27] When older Americans are featured, it is usually in the context of programs dealing with the "plight" of the elderly.[28]

* * *

Beyond the obvious impact on advertising content, erroneous notions held by advertising professionals have an even more pervasive effect on the content of media programming. Advertisers, relying on the advice of their advertising firms, generally believe that youth-oriented programs best attract the consuming public.[29] This orientation has produced a kind of "youth nepotism" in the film and television industry similar to that in the advertising industry. Young executives tend to be selected to produce youth-oriented programs, and these young executives tend to surround themselves with young writers, directors, and actors.[30]

* * *

As the "young is better" campaign has gained momentum, the negative stereotypes of old age that began with the biomedicalization of age in the early twentieth century[31] have become more entrenched. The typical negative stereotypes reported and studied by sociologists, psychologists, and gerontologists include beliefs that the old are impaired, incompetent, unproductive, depressed, disengaged, inflexible, and senile and lack sexual desire.[32] These stereotypes are based on the premise that physical and mental failure in old age is inevitable.[33]

* * *

II. Ageism and the Health Care Profession

Given that it was the medical community that generated the "decline and failure" model of aging, the presence of ageist attitudes and practices in the health care profession is not surprising. Professional ageism in health care parallels, to a certain degree, the general evolution of ageism in society, exhibiting characteristics of prejudice, paternalism, preference for youth, and gerontophobic concerns with generational equity. For example, ageist prejudice is apparent in the negative-treatment bias that some physicians have labeled "therapeutic nihilism"—the belief that medical interventions for the elderly are futile.[34] Paternalism, or "compassionate ageism," is detectable in the indifference of many health care professionals to participation by elderly patients in their own treatment decisions.

A preference for youth is also evident in the health care profession based on the shortage of health care professionals who are willing to specialize in geriatrics and long-term care.[35] In mental health services, the treatment bias toward younger patients is so strong that it has been given a name—the "YAVIS syndrome," representing the tendency of mental health professionals to treat primarily "Young, Attractive, Verbal, Intelligent and Successful" patients.[36] Finally, controversial proposals for age-based, health care rationing indicate that gerontophobia and the generational equity debate have also invaded the health care profession.[37]

Anecdotal instances of professional paternalism and prejudice toward elderly patients are legion.[38] Derogatory labels for elderly patients include "gomers" (an acronym for "Get Out of My Emergency Room"),[39] "crocks," and "dirt balls."[40] Patronizing language that infantilizes older patients is also common.[41]

Other forms of compassionate ageism are manifested in treatment protocols that encourage dependency and decrease autonomy. Classic examples are daily routines in long-term care facilities that provide few choices for residents regarding their schedules and activities,[42] or worse, the overuse of restraints.[43]

There may be only a fine line between compassionate ageism, which strips a patient of self-respect and autonomy, and "therapeutic nihilism," which results in undertreatment or nontreatment of the elderly. It has been estimated that between ten and thirty percent of treatable mental disorders are misdiagnosed as irreversible in elderly patients.[44] Two biases in particular are hypothesized to result in undertreatment of elderly patients who have mental disorders. One stems from the "decline and failure" view that senility in old age is both inevitable and untreatable,[45] and the other is based on overestimation of the prevalence of Alzheimer's disease.[46]

Notes

1. Robert N. Butler, *Dispelling Ageism: The Cross-Cutting Intervention*, ANNALS AM. ACAD. POL. & SOC. SCI., May 1989, at 138, 139 n.2 [hereinafter Butler, *Dispelling Ageism*]. Dr. Butler's Pulitzer prize-winning work in the mid-seventies was both the baseline and catalyst for subsequent scholarly interest in ageism. *See* ROBERT N. BUTLER, WHY SURVIVE?: BEING OLD IN AMERICA (1975) [hereinafter BUTLER, WHY SURVIVE].

2. Butler, *Dispelling Ageism*, *supra* note 1, at 140–41.

3. *Id.* at 142.

4. HOWARD P. CHUDACOFF, HOW OLD ARE YOU?: AGE CONSCIOUSNESS IN AMERICAN CULTURE 20–27 (1989). [*See, e.g.*, BILL BYTHEWAY, AGEISM (Brian Gearing series ed., The Open University 1995)] (noting that ancient Persians observed birthdays and Greek philosophers recorded chronological ages, but that in computing age "there was also a degree of latitude which permitted rounding, estimating, inconsistencies and forgetting").

5. CHUDACOFF, *supra* note 4, at 10–11; *see also* MICHAEL YOUNG & TOM SCHULLER, LIFE AFTER WORK: THE ARRIVAL OF THE AGELESS SOCIETY 1–2 (noting the philosophy that those "[w]ho would not toil, should not eat").

6. CHUDACOFF, *supra* note 4, at 15 (observing that before age-graded schools in the mid-nineteenth century, education followed "diverse and unsystematic paths. . . . There was no uniform age of entry into, or departure from, these schools, and it was not uncommon to see very young children in the same classroom with teenagers"); *see id.* at 16–18 (noting age-integrated work and social activities).

7. *See* THOMAS R. COLE, THE JOURNEY OF LIFE: A CULTURAL HISTORY OF AGING IN AMERICA 5 (1992) [hereinafter COLE, THE JOURNEY OF LIFE].

8. *See* YOUNG & SCHULLER, *supra* note 5, at 3 (noting that "[it] was the factory that put an end to the all-age family as the unit of production and brought into existence age-classes where there had been none before").

9. CHUDACOFF, *supra* note 4, at 5–6.

10. YOUNG & SCHULLER, *supra* note 5, at 3–4.

11. *See* W. Andrew Achenbaum, *The Obsolescence of Old Age in America, 1865–1914*, 1974 J. SOC. HIST. 48, *reprinted in* MILDRED M. SELTZER ET AL., SOCIAL PROBLEMS OF THE AGING: READINGS 26, 31 (Stephen D. Rutter ed., 1978) [hereinafter Achenbaum, *The Obsolescence of Old Age*].

12. *See, e.g.*, CHUDACOFF, *supra* note 4, at 55. According to Howard P. Chudacoff:

> The earliest and most important developments in this separation [of old people from the rest of society] occurred in medicine; indeed, just as the evolution of pediatrics reflected new conceptions of the distinctiveness of childhood, a parallel movement did the same for old age and paved the way for the establishment of a new medical specialty for the treatment of old people.

Id. at 55. The author also noted the development and impact of psychologist G. Stanley Hall's theories of child development. *Id.* at 66–67.

13. *See, e.g.*, Achenbaum, *The Obsolescence of Old Age*, *supra* note 11, at 30 (describing the work of Drs. Charcot and Loomis as laying the basis for a pathology of senility); CHUDACOFF, *supra* note 4, at 56 (same).

14. CHUDACOFF, *supra* note 4, at 56.

15. *Id.* at 58.

16. *Id.* at 13–14; COLE, THE JOURNEY OF LIFE, *supra* note 7, at 3–4.

17. CHUDACOFF, *supra* note 4, at 27–28, 65.

18. *See id.* at 35–36 for discussion of the evolution of graded common schools:

> Through the standardization of grades, educators thought they had found a means of bringing order to the socially diverse and seemingly chaotic environment of American schools. To achieve their goals of efficient management, reformers explicitly copied the new factory system, in which a division of labor was used to create a product, from raw material, in successive stages of assembly, each stage building upon the previous one.

Id. at 36.

19. *See* Achenbaum, *The Obsolescence of Old Age, supra* note 11, at 31.

20. *See* CHUDACOFF, *supra* note 4, at 93–95.

21. *Id.* at 93–94.

22. *Id.* at 95.

23. *Id.* at 97–98 (noting that "[t]he family, once generationally integrated in a functional and emotional sense, had become a way station for different peer groups").

24. Achenbaum, *The Obsolescence of Old Age, supra* note 11, at 32.

25. *Id.*

26. *See* CHUDACOFF, *supra* note 4, at 168–69.

27. *See* BETTY FRIEDAN, THE FOUNTAIN OF AGE 35–39 (1993). *But see Some Series Face Ageism Head-On,* NEWS & OBSERVER (Raleigh, N.C.), Mar. 19, 1995, at G10, *available in* 1995 WL 2662597 (discussing examples of popular sitcoms that deal with the topic of ageism).

28. FRIEDAN, *supra* note 27, at 39–41 (observing that a concomitant trend to the "pervasive media blackout of images of older people . . . in everyday American life" was increased "media attention to the 'plight' of the elderly, to age as a 'problem'" and citing programs on nursing homes, Alzheimer's disease, and the burdens of Social Security and Medicare as examples).

29. David Horowitz, *Advertisers, Retailers Need To Reconsider the Image of Aging—Ignoring Elderly Can Be Costly Mistake,* L.A. DAILY NEWS, Nov. 6, 1993, at L20, *available in* 1993 WL 3545774; *see* Nina J. Easton, *Hey, Babes! How Old Is Too Old for Hollywood?,* L.A. TIMES, Nov. 17, 1991, at 7.

30. *See, e.g.,* Easton, *supra* note 29, at 7 (noting that "young producers tend to staff shows with their peers—who are equally young"); Horowitz, *supra* note 29, at *2 ("Three-fifths of all TV writers are between ages 30 and 45.").

31. *See supra* notes 12–15 and accompanying text.

32. *See* BUTLER, WHY SURVIVE, *supra* note 1, at 6–10; [JACK LEVIN & WILLIAM C. LEVIN, AGEISM: PREJUDICE AND DISCRIMINATION AGAINST THE ELDERLY (Curt Peoples et al. series eds., Lifetime Series in Aging 1980); ERDMAN B. PALMORE, AGEISM: NEGATIVE AND POSITIVE (Bernard D. Starr series ed., Springer Series on Adulthood & Aging No. 25, 1990) [hereinafter PALMORE, AGEISM: NEGATIVE AND POSITIVE]; SHURA SAUL, AGING: AN ALBUM OF PEOPLE GROWING OLD 20–27 (1974); Mary Lee Hummert et al., *Judgments About Stereotypes of the Elderly: Attitudes, Age Associations, and Typicality Ratings of Young, Middle-Aged, and Elderly Adults,* 17 RESEARCH ON AGING 168, 175 (table summarizing stereotype trait sets). *But see* PALMORE, AGEISM: NEGATIVE AND POSITIVE, . . . (noting that ageism has also produced positive, but less common, stereotypes of old age, including the characteristics of "kindness, wisdom, dependability, affluence, political power, freedom, eternal youth, and happiness").

33. *See supra* notes 14–15 and accompanying text; *see also* BUTLER, WHY SURVIVE, *supra*

note 1, at 7 (describing among the common myths and stereotypes of old age the belief that an older person is "a study in decline, the picture of mental and physical failure").

34. *See id.* at 231; [Alvin J. Levenson, *Aging Gracefully with Ageism: Difficult at Best,* PERSPECTIVES ON MEDICAID & MEDICARE MGMT., Feb. 1981, at 55].

35. *See* PALMORE, AGEISM: NEGATIVE AND POSITIVE, [ERDMAN B. PALMORE, AGEISM: NEGATIVE AND POSITIVE (Bernard D. Starr series ed. Springer Series on Adulthood and Aging No. 25, 1990) [hereinafter PALMORE, AGEISM: NEGATIVE AND POSITIVE]. Palmore notes that it is not uncommon for medical school geriatric fellowships to go unfilled. *Id.* at 133.

36. *See* BUTLER, WHY SURVIVE, *supra* note 1, at 233 (attributing to William Schofield the origination of the acronym "YAVIS" and discussing supporting statistics for the "syndrome").

37. *Compare* DANIEL CALLAHAN, SETTING LIMITS: MEDICAL GOALS IN AN AGING SOCIETY (1987) (suggesting that health care priorities be reordered to guarantee a "minimal and common baseline of accessible health care up through a normal life span" for everyone; and arguing that although such a system would necessitate denying Medicare support for life-extending treatments beyond a certain age, the resources could be shifted to improve preventative health care and long term care), *with* TOO OLD FOR HEALTH CARE?: CONTROVERSIES IN MEDICINE, LAW, ECONOMICS, AND ETHICS (Robert H. Binstock & Stephen G. Post eds., 1991) (explaining that rationing health care should not be based on age alone).

38. *See, e.g.,* Robert N. Butler, *Ageism: A Forward, J. Soc. Issues,* 8, 9 (1980) [hereinafter Butler, *Ageism*]; [Robert N. Butler, *The Triumph of Age: Science, Gerontology, and Ageism,* 58 BULL. N.Y. ACAD. MED. 347, 349 (1982) [hereinafter Butler, *The Triumph of Age;* Alvin J. Levenson, *Aging Gracefully with Ageism: Difficult at Best,* PERSPECTIVES ON MEDICAID & MEDICARE MGMT., Feb. 1981, at 55; Jack Levin et al., *The Challenge of Ageism,* AM. HEALTH CARE ASS'N J., Mar. 1983, at 47]; John F. Peppin, *Physician Neutrality and Patient Autonomy in Advance Directive Decisions,* 11 ISSUES L. & MED. 13, 16–17 (1995). *See generally* FRIEDAN, *supra* note 27 (listing a selection of clippings and studies about age).

39. [Robert N. Butler, *The Triumph of Age: Science, Gerontology, and Ageism,* 58 BULL. N.Y. ACAD. MED. 347, 349 (1982) (hereinafter Butler, *The Triumph of Age*); Alvin J. Levenson, *Aging Gracefully with Ageism: Difficult at Best,* PERSPECTIVES ON MEDICAID & MEDICARE MGMT., Feb. 1981, at 55; John F. Peppin, *Physician Neutrality and Patient Autonomy in Advance Directive Decisions,* 11 ISSUES L. & MED. 13, 16–17 (1995)].

40. [Robert N. Butler, *The Triumph of Age: Science, Gerontology, and Ageism,* 58 BULL. N.Y. ACAD. MED. 347, 349 (1982) (hereinafter Butler, *The Triumph of Age*); Alvin J. Levenson, *Aging Gracefully with Ageism: Difficult at Best,* PERSPECTIVES ON MEDICAID & MEDICARE MGMT., Feb. 1981, at 55].

41. [Jack Levin et al., *The Challenge of Ageism,* AM. HEALTH CARE ASS'N J., Mar. 1983, at 47] (giving as an example—"The nurse who gives an 82-year-old woman a patronizing pat on the arm while saying, 'Good girl! You ate all your breakfast!'").

42. *See, e.g.,* Barry L. Hall & Jochen G. Bocksnick, *Therapeutic Recreation for the Institutionalized Elderly: Choice or Abuse,* J. ELDER ABUSE & NEGLECT, No.4, 1995, at 49 (identifying conflicts between residents' needs for self-determination, control and autonomy in program participation and recreational therapists' goals and expectations).

43. *See generally* Lois Evans & Neville E. Strumpf, *Tying Down the Elderly: A Review of the Literature on Physical Restraint,* 37 J. AM. GERIATRICS SOC'Y 65, 66 (1989) (indicating that between 25% and 84.6% of the American nursing home population is subject to physical restraints).

44. [*See, e.g.*, Robert N. Butler, *Ageism: A Forward*, J. Soc. Issues, 8, 9 (1980) (hereinafter Butler, *Ageism*)].

45. *See id.*

46. *See* [Margaret Gatz & Cynthia Pearson, *Ageism Revised and the Provision of Psychological Services*, 43 Am. Psychologist 184 (1988)] (finding that nearly half of all respondents to the Alzheimer's Disease Knowledge test overestimated the prevalence of the disease).

CHAPTER 4

Who Is Old?

The term "old age" is not self-defining. Old age, like any age categorization, is a social construct and indeed necessarily an arbitrary one. Yet we do age, and aging is truly accompanied by physical and possibly mental changes. It is this reality of the physiology of the aging person that is the foundation of the concept of old age and of elder law. In the following article Professors Frolik and Barnes outline the various ways of defining old age.

Lawrence A. Frolik and Alison P. Barnes

An Aging Population: A Challenge to the Law

* * *

I. Who Really is "Elderly"?

Statistics count who is old merely as a function of chronological age. But a more accurate description, reflecting how most of us naturally think, is to classify who is "elderly" by more than just one criterion. Typically before we think of a person as being old, we look at a combination of factors such as chronological age, functional capacity, social involvement, and physical and mental health.[1] As a result, we might say that a healthy, functioning sixty-three-year-old is not elderly, but that a poorly functioning, unhealthy sixty-year-old is elderly.[2] Yet at some point chronological age alone is enough for all of us to agree to and label an individual as elderly. For example, everyone would concur that an eighty-five-year-old is elderly. But not everyone would refer to all sixty-year-olds as elderly. For purposes of this essay, we shall use age sixty-five as the entry age for being classified as elderly. Although admittedly this is an arbitrary age, it is the "traditional" age of retirement and the age that most commentators use as delineating old age.

Before we simply say anyone over sixty-five is old, however, we really ought to ask, "Why do we care?" For if we classify people, we do so (or at least *ought* to do so) for some reason. We group and count individuals by race, for example, because we consider race relevant in many respects if only to ensure that race is not used as an irrelevant criterion. We do not classify people by eye color in any official manner because, although certainly a fact, it is not a relevant fact.

So, why do we so frequently group individuals by age, whether for official ends—such as eligibility for social security benefits—or in our day-to-day informal discussions? We do so, it seems, because the elderly have something in common that they do not share (or that they share to a much lesser extent) with the rest of the population. Just as we group babies together and teenagers together because of their respective shared characteristics (dependency in the case of the former, adolescence for the latter), so also do we group the old together.

But just what are the common characteristics of the old that differ from the rest of the population? It is conventional wisdom that the qualities of senescence distinguish the elderly from the young. Typically, we think of the loss of physical capacity and, to a lesser extent, the loss of mental capacity. Though most certainly not shared by all, it is the often experienced loss of mental alertness and agility and the even more common, if not universal, loss of physical strength, flexibility, and endurance, and the deterioration of the senses, that the elderly share to the exclusion of the non-elderly. Although many individuals who are not elderly suffer the loss of physical or mental capability, it is the inevitable loss of physical vigor and the increasing possibility of the loss of mental alertness that makes it sensible to label those over the age of sixty-five as elderly and to consider them as a group. It is not by chance that if younger persons suffer a permanent physical or mental ailment, we label them "disabled." Yet, should a similar affliction strike older individuals, we are likely merely to identify them as being "old."

All of this categorizing by age is in a way false. Merely being old in years does not signify that one has lost physical or mental capacity. As a generalization about the old, it is false as to many particular individuals and is, therefore, a particularly pernicious generalization. Labeling an entire group as "the elderly" merely because of the infirmities of some inevitably leads to the perception and widespread belief that all members of the group suffer from diminished physical and mental capacity. All become tainted with the problems of a minority. Still, if we keep in mind that not all the old have diminished mental capacity and that the extent of the loss of physical capacity varies greatly, it is useful to perceive that if many of the elderly did not so suffer, it is unlikely that we would group them together.

By grouping the chronologically old together and labeling them "elderly" we impute to them characteristics associated with the label. In general, if the characteristics truly reflect those possessed by the individual so labeled, all the better. The label serves as a shorthand manner of identifying characteristics of the individual to which we wish to call attention.

But if the generalized label misses the mark as to a particular individual and falsely attributes some of the group characteristics to the labeled individual, we are driven to ask why anyone would use a deceptive label. We do not, for example, similarly group together individuals between ages twenty and sixty. While we may speak casually of "yuppies" or "the middle-aged," no one knows of just whom we are speaking when these terms are employed. Are yuppies those aged twenty to thirty, or twenty-five to forty? Who is to say? Who exactly is middle-aged is even more difficult to pin down. When you are twenty you might think of anyone age thirty-five to fifty-five as middle-aged. But when you are thirty-five, you are more likely to see the middle aged as only including those age forty-five to sixty. When you are age fifty-five, you may well accept the title "middle-aged," but you may insist that it extends until age sixty-five. Perhaps the best distinction between middle age and old age was noted by Groucho Marx: "Middle age is when you think things will feel better in the morning. Old age is when you hope to wake up in the morning."

In cultural terms, old age seems fairly well set as beginning at age sixty-five.[3] This is not because physical deterioration and possible mental decline necessarily commence at that age. Age sixty-five has no particular physiological significance because old age has no sudden manifestation or appearance. After all, although most of us hate to admit it, we grow older every day of our lives. In reality, physical deterioration is steady and irreversible. Although keeping "in shape" may mask the trend by allowing the body to perform up to its potential, the inevitable decline in potential cannot be forestalled. What we choose to call "old age" is merely social convention. If we label someone at age sixty-five as "elderly," we do so not because they are elderly by innate characteristics, but rather because we choose to label them so.

Many who are past age sixty-five might object that they are not old. By that they mean that, though old in years, they are not old in body or spirit. Conversely, there are those who are not yet sixty-five whom we might think of as old. In a word, our chronological age is only a very rough indicator of "elderlyness" if we take that term to mean the relative state of an individual's physical or mental condition. So we have come full circle. We cannot generalize as to which individuals are old because the term is a measure of the individual's particular physical and mental condition.

But even after admitting that generalizations are spurious, and concentrating on the individual, it is difficult to say with certainty who is old and who is not. The state of being old has no bright line at which it commences. It is a condition that certainly exists, but we have no definition that crisply cleaves the old from the non-old. One cannot say, "Today I became old." At some point we will admit that we are old, but just when that occurred is unknown even to the individual. As white turns to gray and then to black, so does youth turn to middle age and then to old age. Though we know that it occurs, we do not know just when.

Why then do we choose to use a label that so falsely characterizes so many of those over age sixty-five? False labeling often indicates an intent to deceive or to confuse the true nature of the labeled individual. That motive, however, does not seem to be the reason that we label all those over sixty-five as elderly even though that population varies so greatly in characteristics. Rather we use the labels "elderly," "old," or "senior citizen" because it serves our purposes to do so. Even though by so labeling we draw into a common fold those of very disparate characteristics, we nevertheless bring together individuals with something in common that is of overriding importance to us. If we call all those over sixty-five old, it is because the fact that they are over sixty-five is more important for our purposes than is the fact that they are often very different in almost all other ways.

While admitting, then, that biological age—physical and mental condition—is only loosely related to chronological age, we cannot ignore the reality that societal institutions commonly use age sixty-five to mark the beginning of old age. For example, we favor the elderly with Social Security benefits, and until quite recently, we decreed that "normal" retirement should occur at age sixty-five.[4] The use of a precise chronological age in these contexts arises out of practical necessity. Governments, employers, and other institutions would rather not operate in a world of gray indeterminacy. They prefer bright-line tests. The government pays Social Security benefits not because one has deteriorated physically, but because one has reached age sixty-five and has retired. The employer's preference would be to retire employees at age sixty-five, and not have to rely on a more subjective, individualized critique of their abilities. The movie theater grants reduced admission to all "golden agers," and thus avoids requiring a demeaning showing of financial need.

When not using age criteria as a means of making distinctions, institutions perform rather poorly. When the government bases benefits upon a showing of disability, the result is a snarl of litigation as to just who is "disabled."[5] Employers who can no longer engage in mandatory retirement arrange pension benefits to encourage voluntary retirement in order to spare themselves the attempt at justifying forced retirement of a particular individual.

The use of chronological age, usually age sixty-five, as an indicator or monitor remains common and reinforces the general cultural sense that after age sixty-five one is old. Even as we use chronological age as a shorthand indicator of "oldness," we should not forget that it is only a rough indicator. In reality, being old or elderly is a state of being neither limited only to the group of individuals over age sixty-five nor universally applicable to that group.

Notes

1. Achenbaum, *Societal Perceptions of Aging and the Aged,* in HANDBOOK OF AGING AND THE SOCIAL SCIENCES 129 (R. Binstock & E. Shanas ed. 1985).

2. Try it. Think of an older colleague, one past age 60. Do you think of him or her as being

old? If not, why not? Who do you think of as old? Why? I was surprised, for example, to learn that our law school budget director was about to retire. I had never thought of this active, vigorous woman as old. Indeed she was; at least old enough to qualify for retirement.

3. Some might place it at an earlier age, age 60 or even age 55, a few try to move its onset upward to age 70 or 75. But in the main, our culture marks age 65 as the inception of old age. With the barring of mandatory retirement (which traditionally was set at age 65) and with the normal retirement age for Social Security benefits due to gradually rise to age 67, however, the universal acceptance of age 65 as the gateway to old age may be eroding. Walz, *Aging in the Twenty-First Century: Implications for the Profession of Law,* in AGING AND THE LAW: LOOKING INTO THE NEXT CENTURY 6 (P. Powers & K. Klingensmith ed. 1990) [hereinafter AGING AND THE LAW].

4. The reliance on age 65 is commonly attributed to Germany's Chancellor Otto Von Bismarck, who created the German social welfare system in 1889. Among the welfare programs was a forced retirement age and public pension program. Originally the retirement age was set at age 70, but in 1916 it was reduced to 65. At that time, Germany was fighting in World War I, so it seems probable that the lower retirement age was designed to elicit public support for the government. We will note that this certainly is not the last time that the onset of public benefits for the elderly was changed for political gain rather than as a result of a new insight into when people become old. *See* D. O'MEARA, PROTECTING THE GROWING NUMBER OF OLDER WORKERS: THE AGE DISCRIMINATION IN EMPLOYMENT ACT 342 n.4 (1989).

5. Murphy, *When the Government Ignores the Law: The Consequences of Relitigation,* 29 JUDGES J. 2, 3 (Summer 1990).

CHAPTER 5

Aging and Ethnicity

The old are not a homogenous group of individuals with largely overlapping characteristics and needs. Rather, older persons are as varied among themselves as are younger members of the population. Older persons are divided along lines of wealth and income, geography, urban and rural residence, religion, political beliefs, and social attitudes. One significant division occurs along racial and ethnic lines. Dr. Yee discusses how aging among members of minority groups is integrated into the family experience in ways that differ from the customs of the majority white population.

Barbara W. K. Yee

Gender and Family Issues in Minority Groups

* * *

Native Americans and Native Alaskan Eskimos

Diversity among Native American families is reflected in linguistic and cultural features (see Markides and Mindel, 1987; Gelfand and Barresi, 1987; Yee, 1989). The extended family model, as loosely defined, has been identified as one common thread found across a diversity of tribes. The exact form of the extended family takes many shapes, influenced as it is by urban or reservation residence, socioeconomic issues, acculturation factors, and family circumstances (see John, 1988).

Native American families are more interdependent than Anglo American families.

Generations, Vol. 14, No. 3, Summer. Reprinted with permission from *Generations,* 833 Market Street, Suite 511, San Francisco, CA 94103.

The elderly Native American has been portrayed as a family leader whose advice and social acceptance are sought by younger family members (Red Horse et al., 1978). Elders are an integral resource and play a central role in family life by providing guidance to younger family members for discipline (appropriate interpersonal behavioral training), spiritual guidance, and maintenance of cultural heritage. In ordinary times or during times of crisis, grandmothers will often provide needed childcare and perform household duties (Red Horse, 1980) or take complete childrearing responsibilities for their grandchildren (Shomaker, 1989).

In return for meeting these family responsibilities, Native American elders expect to be respected and cared for when they become too frail to care for themselves. In fact, the traditional Navajo practice of giving grandchildren to grandparents served this purpose (Shomaker, 1989).

It appears that social support for Native Americans increases with availability and proximity to family members. Thus, those on reservations provide more social support because of living arrangements that ensure there are more family members living nearby. At the same time, since unemployment and poverty are widespread on reservations and among urban Native Americans, the income from the elders' pensions or Social Security makes a significant contribution to the family's survival and thereby ensures interaction with family (Williams, 1980).

Elderly Native Americans are a source of strength for many families and are the recipients of support from their younger family members. Unfortunately, the family portrait is by no means rosy for the Native American population. Poverty, alcoholism, conflicts over acculturation, and despair wreak havoc all too frequently in the Native American family. Poorer health and mental health status of this population, coupled with fewer resources that could help them cope, make for greater stress (Yee, 1989). Despite the strengths of elderly Native Americans and their families, considerable outside resources and support are required to get this population closer to the quality of life many white, middle-class elderly have come to enjoy.

Native Americans have traditionally had rigid gender roles. Women had responsibility for expressive functions in the family such as "kin-keeping." In contrast, men were concerned with breadwinner activities such as employment. The oldest-old Native American still retains many traditional gender roles, but gender roles for the young-old are changing. For instance, among the Navajo, women are increasingly concerned with breadwinner activities while elderly men have lost their traditional roles but have not replaced lost roles. Middle-aged Native American women are taking on more tribal leadership positions than in the past (Hanson, 1980). Older Native American men have experienced the most role changes (John, 1988).

Asians and Pacific Islanders

The Asian and Pacific Islander population is a very diverse group (Markides and Mindel, 1987; Gelfand and Barresi, 1987; Yee, 1989). In many respects they do not constitute a group at all since they vary on a number of critical characteristics such as language, immigration history, American response to their arrival or presence, and resulting socioeconomic and social adaptation (Yee and Hennessey, 1982).

Immigration history itself promotes diversity in the Asian and Pacific Islander population in part because immigration laws regulated the number and types of people allowed in the United States. As a result, immigration laws have directly influenced Asian family patterns by restricting availability of marital partners or by creating quotas on the flow of Asians and Pacific Islanders. These waves of Asian immigrants and their American children have characteristics and needs that are quite diverse, including the ability to speak English and acculturation to a variety of American ways such as gender roles or family patterns (see Mindel et al., 1988).

Despite this diversity, Asian and Pacific islander families share some cultural themes, evidenced both in values and behavior, that have implications for the role of the elderly in the family. Individuals and their families express cultural themes in a variety of ways, depending on level of acculturation and a unique combination of other factors.

Confucian philosophy generates a specific role for each person in the family and society. Every person has a prescribed status, with all relationships of the subordinate-superordinate type: husband-wife, parent-child, or teacher-pupil. This implies that elders have more authority than younger members of the family and that women have a secondary role to men.

Asians who came to the United States as young or early middle-aged persons have grown old in this country and as a result have become acculturated toward less traditional family relationships (Yee, 1989). Moreover, their American adult children, while they have not completely adopted all American ways, are somewhere between the American norm and their more traditional ethnic counterparts—thereby creating a real gender gap (Osako and Liu, 1986). The generational gap is lessened, of course, for Asian and Pacific Islander families with longer periods of residence and acculturation in the United States—with traditional elders becoming less traditional, and adolescents or young adults adopting a more bicultural synthesis of both American and Asian values or behaviors (Ho, 1987).

Newly transplanted families, the Southeast Asian refugees being a prime case in point, must deal with the more egalitarian expectations between men and women, older and younger, as well as cope with the greater power of women and younger members of the family (that is, paycheck and duties in the household). This situation often bolsters the more egalitarian role of wives and younger family members but creates family conflicts at the same time (Yee, 1989).

Second, the needs of the family take precedence over the needs of a given individual, and interdependence or obligations and responsibilities are a lifelong characteristic of traditional Asian and Pacific Islander families. Divorce was relatively infrequent among Asian elders because keeping the family together was a more significant goal than spousal happiness. Since interdependence is a lifelong process, increasing dependency with old age is not frowned upon by traditional Asians (Liu,

1986). Thus, generational differences in gender and age roles or expectations within the Asian family could be a source of possible conflict.

African American Families

The black population is becoming increasingly diverse. There is a growing middle class that is highly educated and represented in the highest occupational ranks, while blacks are disproportionately represented among the poor and illiterate (see Markides and Mindel, 1987; Gelfand and Barresi, 1987; Yee, 1989). Black family patterns have been influenced by African cultural roots, socialization patterns developed under slavery, effects of racism and discrimination, current socioeconomic and social circumstances, and a whole host of other factors (see McAdoo, 1988).

The African family has traditionally been organized around kinship rooted in blood ties. In contrast, American family kinship revolves around marital ties between spouses. Stability of the African family was not dependent upon the stability of marriages, rather the family kept together by blood ties (Sudarkasa, 1988). Slavery served to modify certain aspects of African family traditions, but emphasis on blood ties, strong bonds of obligation among kinsmen (especially to the mother or grandmother), and strong role of family elders were maintained (McAdoo, 1988).

* * *

Jackson (1978) reports that grandmothers interact more with the grandchildren from their daughters than with the grandchildren from their sons. Younger grandparents were more likely to share residences with grandchildren than were older ones. Regardless of living arrangement, the majority of grandparents helped with childcare. In contrast to Hill and Shakleford (1978), Jackson (1978) found that grandparents preferred having their grandchildren living near but not with them. Perhaps a social class or regional sample difference could account for this disparity.

The grandparent factor in black life is thought to be critical. For instance, black women take in relatives at twice the rate of white age peers during the middle-age period (Beck and Beck, 1989). This suggests that black middle-aged women provide both economic and social support for younger as well as older relatives (Malson, 1983). Black middle-aged and elderly women over their lifetimes have been a significant source of strength and support for the black family.

Hispanic Families

The Hispanic populations share the Spanish language, but their migration histories differ (see Markides and Mindel, 1987; Gelfand and Barresi, 1987; Yee, 1989). For instance, there are generational differences in language and acculturation for Mexican Americans. The majority of Puerto Rican and Cuban elderly are foreign-born. Despite these differences, one noted gerontologist (Bastista, 1984) suggests that there are more similarities between the Mexican, Puerto Rican, Cuban, and other Hispanic groups than similarities between the Hispanics and the white middle-class population.

Three generalizations can be made about Hispanic families (see Applewhite, 1988). First, the Hispanic population as a whole has a very strong extended-family orientation. The family is viewed as a warm and nurturing place that offers security and a sense of belonging. The Hispanic family includes close friends and children's godparents, who traditionally share social support privileges and family responsibilities. Designation of specific functions and responsibilities among different generations by sex ensured survival of the family.

The second generalization is that there is sex grading. Machismo can take many forms, ranging from head of the household, breadwinner, major decision maker, and requiring total obedience by spouse and children to the man providing for protection and being responsible for dependent family members. Marianismo, the self-sacrificing mother and wife, is the complementary role traditional Hispanic women are often said to play. The extent to which elder Hispanics actually play these roles depends on individual personalities, acculturation, and period of the life cycle in which they find themselves.

* * *

Elders are viewed as wise, knowledgeable, and deserving of respect. Bacerra (1988) argues that these family roles resulted from the division of labor that occurred as a result of biological functions such as pregnancy and childrearing, for women, and protector for more physically powerful males working the fields or hunting. The elderly assumed their special roles after they could no longer do hard physical labor, taking on functions that helped assure family continuity by being transmitters of accumulated wisdom, nurturers of small children, religious teachers, or family historians. Respect was given to elderly members of the family in return for past labor and for maintenance of family continuity functions during their later years.

In a study of Mexican, Puerto Rican, and Cuban women fifty-five and older, Bastista (1984) found that there was an acceptance of aging and the realities of aging. Bastista also found consensus about the age and gender norms among Mexican, Puerto Rican, and Cuban women, with cultural sanctions for recognition of one's own aging and appropriate modification of one's attitudes and behavior so as to be consistent with and proper for one's age taking place sometime during the fifth and sixth decades of life. Age-inappropriate behavior and attitudes were more strictly sanctioned for women who deviated than for men. Bastista (1984) also observed that gender influenced the context of conversation, while age determined the content of conversation.

Conclusions

Two broad-ranging generalizations can be made regarding gender and family issues in minority groups. First, there is much diversity within each minority group. This diversity of family patterns has grown larger over the course of residency in the United States (Mindel et al., 1988). More egalitarian family patterns are typically seen among the young-old, who typically are American-born or else came to this country during their younger years, during which their job participation directly influenced their family roles. The second generalization is that the subgroups that make up each ethnic category share more similar life experiences with each other than with white, middle-class families (Bastista, 1984; Yee and Hennessey, 1982). Shared cultural roots and experiences with racism provide some bases for these similarities. Likewise, similarities may be produced across minority families as a result of their shared experiences as minority individuals in America.

References

Applewhite, S. R., ed., 1988. *Hispanic Elderly in Transition,* New York: Greenwood Press.

Bacerra, R. M. 1988. The Mexican American Family. In C. H. Mindel, R. W. Habenstein, and R. Wright, eds. *Ethnic Families in America: Patterns and Variations,* 3d edition. New York: Elsevier.

Bastista, E., 1984. "Age and Gender Linked Norms Among Older Hispanic Women." In R. Anson. ed., *The Hispanic Older Woman.* Washington, D.C.: National Hispanic Council on Aging, U.S. Government Printing Office.

Beck, R. W., and Beck, S. J., 1989. "The Incidence of Extended Households Among Middle-Aged Black and White Women." *Journal of Family Issues* 10:147–68.

Gelfand, D. E., and Barresi C. M., eds., 1987. *Ethnic Dimensions of Aging.* New York: Springer.

Hanson, W. 1980. "The Urban Indian Woman and Her Family." *Social Casework,* (Oct.) 476–83.

Hill, R., and Shakleford, L. 1978. "The Black Extended Family Revisited." In R. Staples, ed. *The Black Family: Essays and Studies.* Belmont, Calif.: Wadsworth Publishing Co.

Ho, M. K., 1986. *Family Therapy with Ethnic Minorities.* Newbury Park, Calif.: Sage.

Jackson, J., 1978. "Black Grandparents in the South." In R. Staples, ed., *The Black Family: Essays and Studies.* Belmont, Calif.: Wadsworth Publishing Co.

John R., 1988. In C. H. Mindel, R. W. Habenstein and R. Wright, eds., *Ethnic Families in America: Patterns and Variations,* 3d edition. New York: Elsevier.

Liu, W. T. 1986. "Culture and Social Support." *Research on Aging* 8:57–83.

McAdoo, H. P., ed., 1988. *Black Families,* 2d edition. Newbury Park, Calif.: Sage.

Malson, M., 1983. "The Social-Support System in Black Families." *Marriage and Family* Review 5:37–57.

Markides, K. S., and Mindel, C. H., 1987. *Aging and Ethnicity.* Newbury Park, Calif.: Sage.

Mindel, C. H., Habenstein, R. W. and Wright, R., 1988. *Ethnic Families in America: Patterns and Variations,* 3d edition. New York: Elsevier.

Osako, M. M., and Liu, W. T., 1986. "Intergenerational Relations and the Aged Among Japanese Americans." *Research on Aging* 8:128–55.

Red Horse, J. G., et al. 1978. "Family Behavior of Urban American Indians." *Social Casework* 59:67–72.

Red Horse, J. G., 1980. "American Indian Elders: Unifiers of Indian Families." *Social Casework* (Oct.) 490–93.

Shomaker, D. J., 1989. "Transfer of Children and the Importance of Grandmothers Among the Navajo Indians." *Journal of Cross-Cultural Gerontology* 4:1–18.

Sudarkasa, N., 1988. "Interpreting the African Heritage in Afro-American Family Organization." In H. P. McAdoo, ed., *Black Families,* 2d edition. Newbury Park, Calif.: Sage.

Williams, G. C., 1980. "Warriors No More: A Study of American Indian Elderly." In C. L. Fry, ed., *Aging in Culture and Society.* New York: Praeger.

Yee, B. W. K. 1989. "Loss of One's Homeland and Culture During the Middle Years." In R. A. Kalish, ed., *Aging in Culture and Society.* New York: Praeger.

Yee, B. W. K. 1989. *Variations in Aging: Older Minorities.* Texas Consortium of Geriatric Education Centers Publication.

Yee, B. W. K., and Hennessey S. T., 1982. "Pacific/Asian American Families and Mental Health." In F. U. Munoz and R. Endo, eds., *Perspectives on Minority Group Mental Health.* Washington, D.C.: University Press of America.

CHAPTER 6

Generational Justice

The phrase "generational justice" encompasses two concepts. First, it describes the relative justice in the distribution of wealth and income between living generations and, more particularly, what comprises justice between the young and the old. Income redistribution in the form of Social Security payments is often cited as raising serious issues of the justice of transferring income from the young to the old. Just how much do the young owe to the old? Or put another way, just how much can the old take before they do an injustice to the young?

Generational justice can also be used to describe what the living owe to those yet unborn. In this form, the phrase raises the question of what kind of legacy the living owe to their descendants. When the living pollute the environment, use scarce natural resources or destroy natural beauty, they are diminishing the quality of life for those to come. If the living spend all that they earn and leave no savings for their heirs, have the living transgressed some moral obligation? If an aging person spends all his or her accumulated wealth on end-of-life medical care, has that person selfishly consumed a legacy that might have provided vital support for a yet unborn grandchild?

There is no consensus as to what constitutes generational justice. As to the living, all agree that need should be the touchstone, yet there is no agreement as to who needs what. For example, Medicare is a federally subsidized acute care health insurance for those age sixty-five or older. Very few dispute the need for Medicare. Indeed, health insurance is almost universally praised. But if the question of how much the federal government should subsidize Medicare is raised, the consensus fractures. Some maintain that the only elderly who should be subsidized are the economically needy, because it is unfair to tax the working young with below-average incomes to assist older persons with above-average incomes. Others, who may agree that only those in need should benefit, nevertheless dispute how to measure need. Some want it to mean poor, others think need means merely below average, and still others maintain that almost anyone facing inordinate medical bills is in need. Others argue that Medicare should not be a needs-based program. They point out that the older population was once young, and they, too, paid taxes to support social programs for the elderly. Now that they are old, they deserve to be rewarded with benefits like those who went before them. Some may agree that Medicare should not be based on need but that the premiums charged to the older recipients should be fairly high (thereby lowering the federal subsidy), because older persons should be expected to lower their standard of living in light of their expensive medical needs. Others would not go that far but would base Medicare premiums on a sliding scale, charging more to the well-off elderly.

Quite naturally, there is no agreement as to what is just or unjust across generations. Yet public policy and governmental programs continue to be created and operated while the debate continues. Medicare reform, for example, is driven more by the need to balance the federal budget and the opposing need not to alienate older voters than by deeply reasoned concerns over justice. Still, the issue of generational justice exists and serves as a tool that can either be used to attack programs for the elderly or, conversely, to demand more aid for the elderly. As they say, it all depends on your point of view.

Regardless of how one comes out on the generational justice issue, the need for an accurate understanding of the relative economic well-being of older Americans is absolutely essential. The elderly comprise a group that stretches across thirty to forty years. Not surprisingly, the economics of that group vary considerably. What may not be so apparent, however, is that income and household wealth decline directly with age so that the oldest old, those over age eighty-five, are also the poorest. In the following material Daniel Radner examines the economic situation of older persons and demonstrates how income and wealth are inverse to advancing age.

Daniel B. Radner

Income of the Elderly and Nonelderly, 1967–92

The economic status of the aged in 1992, as measured by before-tax money income, was substantially better than in 1967, but was about the same as in 1984.

From 1967 to 1992, the real median income (adjusted for unit size and age) of elderly family units rose 69 percent. The median fell from 1989 to 1992; the 1992 median was slightly below the 1984 value. The real median adjusted income of nonelderly units rose 26 percent from 1967 to 1992.

The ration of the median adjusted income of aged family units to the median for the nonaged rose from 0.526 in 1967 to 0.710 in 1992. The 1992 ratio, however, was below the 1984 ratio. To a great extent, the rise in the aged/nonaged income ratio from 1967 to 1992 offset a decline in that ratio from 1947 to 1967.

58 *Social Security Bulletin* 82 (Winter 1995)

Despite substantial increases in income during the 1967–92 period, in 1992 the median adjusted income of units aged 85 or older was only 55 percent of the median for units of all ages. The corresponding value for 1967 was 38 percent (Table 1).

Income inequality for elderly units fell substantially from 1967 to 1992. Inequality rose sharply for the nonelderly during that period.

The poverty rate for aged persons fell sharply from 1967 to 1992, while the rate for nonaged persons rose. The rate for each detailed age group was higher in 1992 than that in 1989. In each year shown, poverty rates were lowest for middle-age groups and highest for the youngest and oldest groups. In 1967, the oldest age groups had the highest rates of any group; in 1992, the youngest age groups had the highest rates (Table 2).

The increase in total income for the aged from 1967 to 1992 was the result of large increases in mean Social Security benefits, property income, and pensions and other income, and a large decrease in mean earnings. The largest increase was in Social Security benefits. The composition of total income for the aged shifted in accordance with these changes.

* * *

The results shown in this article illustrate the important point that the incomes of all age groups have fluctuated over time. Both the elderly and nonelderly have experienced periods of income growth and income decline, and this pattern can be expected to continue in the future. The relationship between the incomes of the elderly and the nonelderly in the future is uncertain. That relationship is affected by the economy's level of activity, as well as by long-run trends. Fluctuations in property income, resulting primarily from changes in interest rates, can be expected to continue to play an important role in changes in the income of the aged.

* * *

Justice between the living and those yet to be born is often brought up in the debate over the environment and resource use. Who hasn't felt a twinge of guilt when another lovely farm is turned into a housing development? Who hasn't wondered what will happen when oil becomes a scarce commodity? Most of us merely shrug and admit that our need for affordable housing and cheap gasoline takes precedence over the needs of future generations. In his article, Professor Epstein argues that our concerns for the future are best met by relying on the market and the institution of private property. By extension, his reading would support the claim that public subsidies for the elderly may well be causing a misallocation of resources between generations.

Richard A. Epstein

Justice Across the Generations

The recent revival in ethical theory has led philosophers, political theorists, and even lawyers to think hard about justice across the generations.[1] The conceptual problems that lie in the path of this venture are difficult. As commonly phrased, the issue is often what duties do people alive today owe to unborn future persons? The normal modes of inquiry are effectively barred in dealing with this question. Democratic processes with universal suffrage cannot register the preferences of the unborn, and dialogue between generations is frustrated when future generations, or at least some future generations, are of necessity silent. The usual sources of information being closed, the analysis often proceeds by examining hypothetical situations, most of which ask a deceptively simple question: What would we want the present generation to do if we stood in the shoes of some future unborn generation?

For some, like John Rawls, the answer seems relatively straightforward: "Each generation must not only preserve the gains of culture and civilization, and maintain intact those just institutions that they have established, but it must also put aside in each period of time a suitable amount of real capital accumulation."[2] Rawls emphasizes collective determination, undertaken from behind a veil of ignorance, as to the optimal savings rate within each generation for the benefit of those who follow it. As stated, the principle anticipates a persistent increase of the savings rate with wealth until some kind of "steady state" is achieved, for "when just institutions are firmly established, the net accumulation required falls to zero."[3] The entire scheme essentially insists that the temporal priority of people alive in the present yields them no moral priority. The same sentiments are expressed by Bruce Ackerman, who has argued that "all citizens are at least as good as one another regardless of their date of birth."[4] Again, the clear implication is that some form of moral and, more importantly, legal constraint is necessary to protect the legitimate claims of future generations.

I confess that my moral intuitions on the grand scheme of things are not as well developed as either Rawls or Ackerman. Hard as I try, I cannot determine precisely what it was that my parents owed me, or what their generation owed my generation, or those yet to come. I am also somewhat overwhelmed by a similar inability to express what I owe my children, as opposed to what I hope to provide them with, or to determine, even globally, what my generation owes the next generation. I shall therefore attend to a more modest task. I propose to worry less about moral duties and more about real prospects. My thesis is that the debate on equity between the genera-

Published originally in 67 *Texas Law Review* 1465 (1989).

tions focuses too much on duty and too little on practice and incentive. Coercion and duty can do little specifically to ensure that the next generation receives its "fair share" of human and natural resources. If we continue along in an unreflective state to create sound institutions for the present, the problem of future generations will pretty much take care of itself,[5] even if we do not develop some overarching policies of taxation or investment that target future generations for special consideration.

* * *

I. The Self and the Future

The problem of equity between the generations presupposes that we can identify a conflict of interest between what people want today and what unborn people will want on some distant tomorrow. If one were to indulge for the moment in the assumption of a pie of constant size, then the argument is that each generation is entitled to only one slice of that pie, so that it is greed (or worse, theft)[6] if members of the present generation even nibble on a slice that in principle belongs to some future generation.[7] To understand how serious a risk this overconsumption might prove to be in practice, imagine a different kind of universe where the question of temporal preferences remains but where any conflict of interest between generations disappears. That world exists when there is a single person who has all present and future claims on a limited set of resources. No group of individuals living in succession over the same period of time could hope to do a better job allocating those resources than this single person.

But how long does that person live? If that person were immortal, then the question of asset use and conservation quite literally blows up before our eyes. It is quite impossible to have equal endowments of a finite asset that will last an infinite period of time. If any minimum level of asset consumption is required for each period, it cannot be satisfied for all periods simultaneously. The only distributions of finite assets that can last an infinite time are those that follow some exponential decay function. This situation rules out equal consumption over all relevant periods.[8]

* * *

Once we assume the existence of some fixed life, even one with an uncertain duration, the problem of resource allocation over time becomes tractable. The ordinary individual will have to decide the allocation between present and future consumption, and present and future labor, given his preferences (which may change) for both labor and consumption, subject to a scarcity constraint. The resources used today will not be available in future periods: those who work hard today must recuperate tomorrow. By the same token, the consumption enjoyed today cannot be had tomorrow. An individual of this type would face the problem of discounting future costs and benefits to their present value.[9] This discounting tendency suggests that it is better to advance consumption and to defer labor, but there is a countervailing tendency. The person's probable belief that there are diminishing returns to consumption in any given period will lead to some desire to equalize net consumption over different periods of time. There is thus some pressure to defer net consumption. Exactly how these two pressures balance out is hard to predict in the abstract.

One implicit assumption in this model is that individuals retain constant preferences over time, or more generally, that they will be the "same people" tomorrow that they are today. This proposition is not necessarily accurate. People may have preferences that change all the time, and in principle the changes could be large enough to constitute a radical change in personal identity. But denying the continuity of preferences and of persons has certain dramatic consequences for the way in which people undertake the ordinary business of life, even within the same generation, or on the same day. Taken to its extreme, the position could be that persons are reconstituted on a continuous basis.[10] The person who orders the ham sandwich at lunch is not the same person to whom it is served ten minutes later, who in turn is not the same person who pays for it ten minutes after that. (This is a fast food restaurant.)[11] People could be regarded as constant entities only over the smallest slivers of time, so that every case necessarily involves a temporal externality: the person who buys the sandwich at noon is allowed to bind the "different" person called upon to eat it at 12:10 p.m., and so on throughout the days, weeks, months, and years.

Thinking of this sort, however, is both ruinous and wrong. It is ruinous because it undermines the possibility of any social order. No set of long-term arrangements—no contracts, marriages, or friendships—could exist if individual personality was as plastic as this model of personal identity might suggest. Similarly, governmental regulation would be impossible, for no regulator could govern if his own preference structure and personal identity were as unstable as those of the public at large. No set of institutions can make sense if human preferences are radically discontinuous over time.[12] For governmental regulation to be possible, the internal transformations within the person must be ignored, even if personal identity is as unstable as this extreme illustration suggests. The ordinary presumptions have to be established the other way, and some special proof of mental disorder (such as addition to mind-bending drugs) must be necessary to overcome them.

* * *

This observation notwithstanding, individual preferences for work and consumption do evolve over time. Any person who has seen other persons at different stages of their lives knows that some demands change as people age. Yet, as long as the ordinary person is aware of the problem, he will probably want to invest his assets in ways that permit some flexibility in future use—at least with respect to those matters for which preferences are expected to change. Most people keep their pension funds in liquid and tradeable assets for good reasons. Although we know today that consumption at certain levels may be required in the future, a person can defer some consumption decisions until after obtaining better information, as by consulting with people who have already reached retirement age. A person need not choose a retirement home at age thirty-five, even if he sets aside retirement income at that time. There is certainly a mortality risk, but millions of people take advantage of simple lifetime annuities that allow them to keep a constant (or other desired) level of income over their lives. A great deal of difference exists between philosophical doubt about personal identity and imperfect information about future demands. The former, like assumptions of immortality, makes it impossible to think about routine transactions in a sensible way. The latter is an argument for private ordering. People probably have *better* knowledge of their own future than do others, even if both are mistaken. Insurance companies always worry about selection against the firm precisely for this reason: their customers know more about the true status of risk than they will reveal to an insurance carrier. But individuals have less incentive to conceal the truth from themselves. Where knowledge is imperfect, the costs of external regulation quickly outstrip the costs of self-regulation.

* * *

III. Public Investment and the Future

Another strategy that might be adopted to cope with the conflicts between generations, given the limitations of an estate tax, is to impose a system of income taxation coupled with public investment in projects, that have expected lives running over to the next generation. But again, there is strong reason to doubt that such a system will work.

* * *

The protection of future generations is very hard even when the political system, say, through the pressure of environmental groups, works to preserve long-term assets in their original form. The difficulty here is that one cannot determine the wealth of the next generation simply by counting the number of acres of virgin timber that have been purchased for national parks. The cutting of timber does not necessarily amount to a transfer from the future generation to the present generation; the uses to which that timber is put must also be taken into account. If the timber in question is used to build long-term assets, such as housing, it may well be that long-term values are diminished by nationalization as inefficient public uses are substituted for more efficient, private ones. Again, standing timber is often a wasting asset, so that the failure to harvest in a proper mode results in older trees with rotten wood crowding out the newer growths that might replace them.[13] The ability to make sense of the individual worth of the collective account makes it hard to determine the soundness of strategies endorsed even by persons whose concern for the future generation is unquestionable.

* * *

IV. Deficits

The problem that exists on the asset side of the ledger can exist as well on the liability side.

* * *

If there is a long-term debt for an asset with a short expected life, then some portion of the cost is externalized on the next generation in ways that cut against the goal of intergenerational justice. More to the point, public indebtedness today is not only incurred for long-term capital projects. Huge amounts of the deficit are incurred to generate short-term transfers to the present generation. It is no great news that the most powerful coalition in Washington today is the elderly and that social security benefits, including medical services, have increased far more rapidly than has the cost of living (and more than any other component of the welfare budget). These transfers systematically thwart any claims of intergenerational justice.

* * *

There is a built-in tendency to introduce methods for repayment that reduce the proponents' own fraction of the payment. One way to discharge the debt is through a progressive income tax. The shares of the indebtedness implicitly shift, as the poor pay less and the rich pay more. Alternatively, where the debt is refinanced by new borrowing the obligation remains constant across different classes of individuals. The total amount of indebtedness is not reduced by shifting between these payment methods, but the costs of trying to shift the incidence of debt, whether successful or not, result in some long-term social loss. An elimination of the progressive tax thus offers an important advantage: the choice between debt and tax financing will depend less on distributional consequences, thereby reducing the opportunities for strategic behavior and placing some gentle constraint against increasing the total amount of government expenditures.

* * *

Inflation presents yet another risk to long-term contracting. Since the government (at least the federal government) controls the printing presses, the temptation to discharge the public debt by increasing the money supply and inflating the currency is great. This stratagem reduces the real amount of fixed debt and effects a short-term implicit transfer from creditors to debtors. Arguably the strategy is self-defeating, because the public debt is "internal" in that we owe the money to ourselves, so that what we gain in one capacity we lose in the other.

Yet the fallacy of composition works in this area as well.[14] The argument about internal debt is correct only if every person has the identical interest as creditor (such as that of a lender of private money to the state) as he does as debtor (such as that of a citizen). But debt instruments are never held in precise proportion to wealth by all citizens. Some people are not creditors at all; some have extensive amounts of government paper. Much credit is held by foreign creditors, who are especially vulnerable to domestic manipulations of the money supply. Political coalitions do have incentives to change the value of money in order to alter the size of the debt. The creditor's gains are offset by the debtor's losses, but (as ever) the transaction is *not* an economic wash, because someone has to bear the costs of influencing the political process, while everyone has to bear the increased costs of uncertainty in the value of government bonds.[15]

To complete the picture, inflation also imposes risk on any long-term private indebtedness, for if private debtors can increase the rate of inflation, they can secure an implicit wealth transfer from their creditors. (The converse is true of deflation.)

* * *

The proof in this case is generally in the pudding. To be born in the future is to be born in a world that typically holds out the promise of greater comfort and happiness. Historically, future generations have received benefits from past generations that exceed the level of transfers stipulated under any of the standard theories of justice between the generations. We can keep it that way by observing the same principles of private and public law that work to promote justice in the present generation. Indeed, we could probably do nothing today to neutralize the power of the next generation if that generation decided to act in selfish and short-sighted ways. If we govern ourselves well, we can and will leave the blessings of liberty for our posterity. At that point, someone else has to carry the ball.

Notes

1. *See, e.g.*, B. ACKERMAN, SOCIAL JUSTICE IN THE LIBERAL STATE 107–221 (1980) (chapter entitled "Justice Over Time"); J. RAWLS, A THEORY OF JUSTICE 284–93 (1971) (chapter entitled "The Problem of Justice Between Generations").

2. J. RAWLS, *supra* note 1, at 285.

3. *Id.* at 287. The "steady state" seems to be remarkably static in that increased levels of productivity might call for a positive savings and investment rate.

4. B. ACKERMAN, *supra* note 1, at 203.

5. *See* Williams, *Running Out: The Problem of Exhaustible Resources,* 7 J. LEGAL STUD. 165, 182 (1978) ("Let future generations take their luck as past ones did.").

6. *See, e.g.*, B. ACKERMAN, *supra* note 1, at 203 ("So far as ideal theory is concerned, the bad trustee stands no better than any other kind of thief.").

7. Here I put aside the problem of an infinite number of future generations, so that no one generation could have a finite part of any pie, no matter how large. In the short run, this difficulty could be overcome by assuming an expanding output via improved production. But, in the long run, if resources are finite, then extinction is the necessary face of all living species, including man, so that equality between the generations could never be maintained.

8. *See* Williams, *supra* note 5, at 169–73. Williams demonstrates that the resource owner will diminish the consumption in each period by the real interest rate, which in turn reflects the price of deferred gratifications. The formula he derives is $x = S(1 - a)$ where S equals the amount of the original stock, a equals the fractional use that each period represents of the prior period, and x equals that portion of the stock consumed in the period. In order for the consumption to be equal in all periods, a has to be set equal to 1, which means that x, the amount consumed in the first period is zero. If x is a market basket of all goods and services, then there will be no second period. If there is some threshold x^* below which an individual or group cannot sustain itself, then human survival and equal consumption over all periods are not mutually compatible.

9. *See* Williams, *supra* note 5, at 170 (noting that a human preference exists for discounting the future to present value).

10. *See generally* D. PARFIT, REASONS AND PERSONS 302–06 (1984) (discussing the concept of "successive selves").

11. John Donne, both lawyer and poet, made the same point far more elegantly in *Woman's Constancy:*

Now thou hast lov'd me one whole day,
Tomorrow when you leav'st, what wilt thou say?

Wilt thou then Antedate some new made vow?
Or say that now
We are not just those persons, which we were?
Or, that oathes made in reverentiall fear
Of Love, and his wrath, any may foreswear?

J. DONNE, THE POEMS OF JOHN DONNE 9 (H. Grierson ed. 1912).

12. *See* North, *Institutions, Transaction Costs, and Economic Growth,* 25 ECON. INQUIRY 419, 421 (1987) (explaining that the complexity of stable institutions is limited by the stability of norms of behavior and common ideologies of the relevant population).

13. For a chronicle of difficulties with public management of forests, see FORESTLANDS: PUBLIC & PRIVATE (R. Deacon & M. Johnson eds. 1985).

14. We are committing the fallacy of composition when we argue from the premise that every man can decide how he will act to the conclusion that the human race can decide how it will act . . . ." [*See generally* R. HARDIN, COLLECTIVE ACTION 2–3 (1982) (explaining the concept of the prisoner's dilemma)] (quoting Mackie, *Fallacies,* 3 ENCYCLOPEDIA PHIL. 169, 173 (P. Edwards ed. 1967)). The fallacy applies to any movement from the single individual to any group, however small the group.

15. Uncertain levels of inflation convert any fixed income offering into a variable payment instrument whose maximum value (when inflation is always zero) is achieved when inflation remains at zero. The costs are that uncertainty simultaneously reduces the return to creditors and increases the costs to borrowers. The sum of those two costs acts as a wedge that prevents gainful transactions from taking place where the difference between what the debtor demands and what the creditor is willing to pay is smaller than the total level of uncertainty.

Part II

Work, Income, and Wealth

For many, old age is synonymous with retirement. After all, the average age of retirement is approximately sixty-three. Of course, not everyone retires. Many individuals continue working well past seventy. A few keep on going into their eighties. But on the whole, most of us accept old age as an appropriate time to leave the work force. Some, of course, have no choice. They cease to work because of ill health or because they lose their job and are unable to find work. Some find that their skills are no longer needed, and they either cannot or will not learn new ones. But most retirees leave the work force voluntarily. With mandatory retirement outlawed for almost all jobs, retirement today almost always reflects an individual choice. Often the retiree looks forward to retirement as an opportunity for a life free of the constraints of work, with time to devote to other activities including recreation, hobbies, volunteerism, family, or learning. Some may even retire in order to begin a new job or career.

CHAPTER 7

Retirement

Why do people voluntarily retire? This simple question has elicited a number of conflicting answers. Until recently most researchers believed that declining health was the primary reason for retirement, but now most believe that the primary reason is a desire for greater leisure coupled with more adequate retirement income. If so, this helps to explain why the age of retirement continues to decline despite improving health in the older population. Still, many retirees cite poor health as a reason for retirement because it is more acceptable than admitting to just wanting to take it easy. Actual ill health probably accounts for less than 15 percent of retirements.

Involuntary retirement based on a potential layoff or because of a plant closing is another cause of retirement. Many older workers choose to retire rather than be fired in a general reduction of force or in the face of a possible demotion, relocation, or transfer to a new job that would require learning a new skill.

The existence of Social Security also encourages voluntary retirement. The assurance of a pension that increases along with the cost of living is a strong inducement for many to leave the labor force. Studies indicate that there is a moderate increase in retirement at age sixty-two when workers first become eligible for benefits and, of course, a much larger departure rate at age sixty-five when retirees are eligible for full benefits. While Social Security may not reduce retirement age, it does cluster it at ages sixty-two and sixty-five. If so, the change in the eligibility age for retirement, which is now scheduled to move gradually to age sixty-seven, can be expected to reduce the number of retirements at age sixty-five and gradually increase the number of retirements at age sixty-seven.

Private employer-provided pensions are another strong inducement to retirement. Most pensions are available at a set age, typically age sixty-five. This means that many employees see the continued work after age sixty-five as working for less than full payment. For example, if a worker could receive \$40,000 a year while employed but \$25,000 a year as a retiree, by working the employee actually earns only \$15,000 a year since the other \$25,000 would have been received whether he or she worked or not. For white collar workers the incentive to retire can often be very high since they often have relatively generous pension plans. The movement away from defined benefit plans, which promise a set number of dollars per year, to defined *contribution plans, which merely assure that the worker will have a certain amount of dollars applied to a pension plan each year, may affect retirement rates because the value of the retirement plan will depend on the investment acumen of the employee during the years of employment. The more successful the retirement account investment portfolio, the larger the potential pension and the greater the inducement to retire.*

Interestingly, the higher an individual's pay, the less likely he or she is to retire. Lower paid workers are much more likely to retire at an early age than those earning higher wages. This results from a couple of factors. First, continuing to work produces less income for low-paid workers. Because of pensions and Social Security, termination of work often results in only a modest loss of income. Conversely, higher paid employers not only have more income to gain from continuing to work, they also often enjoy greater job satisfaction. Generally, low wages in this country are associated with repetitive or low status jobs while higher wages are usually associated with greater status and prestige. Individuals who have good incomes from their jobs may be reluctant to retire not only because of the loss of income, but also because of the loss of social status and prestige associated with their work.

It should be emphasized that the above discussion reflects the work experience of white male workers. There is a lack of information about subpopulations such as African Americans or Hispanic Americans, and there is even less understanding of how women respond to retirement incentives and opportunities. There is a good deal of speculation, for example, that women may retire earlier than men, but to date there is little data to support that belief.

CHAPTER 8

Age Discrimination in Employment

The increase in voluntary retirement is a consequence of federal and state laws that outlaw mandatory retirement on account of age. Though these laws prohibit age discrimination in employment, employer prejudice against older workers remains strong. As a result, many employers discriminate against older workers in the hiring process and some employers attempt to encourage their older workers to voluntarily retire.

Employers have long favored mandatory retirement as a means of ridding themselves of older, higher paid employees. Though an employer could terminate employees on an individual basis, the use of a mandatory retirement age, usually age sixty-five, was very popular because it spared supervisors from making the difficult decision to terminate an older employee. For example, a supervisor in a retail store would not have to fire the sixty-seven-year-old long-time sales clerk, Mary (much beloved by the other sales clerks), whose advanced age supposedly left her out of touch with the younger customers. Rather than giving Mary the bad news that she was fired, her supervisor could announce, "According to the company rules, Mary had to retire." Because both employer and employee knew the date the employee was going to retire, companies were able to create pension plans to provide income for retirees. Yet, while some workers did not mind being terminated by an arbitrary age limit, many felt that they were being unjustly stigmatized by being forced to retire. It was as if the sixty-fifth birthday signaled the end of productive and valued careers. The retiree was left with the empty feeling of being unwanted and, even worse, with a much emptier pocketbook.

Regardless of pension plans and Social Security, the overwhelming majority of retirees suffer a significant income loss upon retirement. Reacting to employee dissatisfaction with mandatory retirement, Congress in 1967 passed the Age Discrimination in Employment Act (ADEA). The history of the passage of the Act is succinctly described in the following student note published in the Cornell Law Review.

Toni J. Querry

Note: A Rose by Any Other Name No Longer Smells as Sweet: Disparate Treatment Discrimination and the Age Proxy Doctrine After *Hazen Paper Co. v. Biggins*

* * *

I. Background

A. Overview of the ADEA: Legislative History and Purpose

Enacted in 1967, the Age Discrimination in Employment Act was, in part, an outgrowth of the civil rights movement.[1] However, concern about age discrimination in employment was, by this time, nothing new. Legislative and executive initiatives to eliminate arbitrary age discrimination in employment appeared as early as the 1950s.[2] Among these early efforts to combat ageism[3] in the workplace were proposals to include protections for elderly workers in Title VII of the Civil Rights Act of 1964.[4] Although these proposals were ultimately rejected, Congress inserted a provision in the Civil Rights Act of 1964 instructing the Secretary of Labor to make a "full and complete study of the factors which might tend to result in discrimination in employment because of age" and to propose "recommendations for legislation to prevent arbitrary discrimination in employment because of age."[5]

In response to Congress's directive, then-Secretary of Labor W. Willard Wirtz issued a report entitled *The Older American Worker: Age Discrimination in Employment*,[6] detailing the problems older workers faced as they attempted to retain employment. The 1965 report documented the existence of widespread age discrimination in employment but noted that ageism was very different from other forms of workplace discrimination.[7] Age discrimination in employment, unlike race and gender discrimination, was not due to any dislike, intolerance, or "antagonism" toward older workers, but rather was based on inaccurate stereotypes about older workers' declining abilities and productivity.[8] The report distinguished "arbitrary age discrimination" from job-related "circumstances," such as health factor differentials, educational requirements, and changes in technology, "which [adversely] affect older workers more strongly, as a group, than they do younger workers,"[9] and from a range of "institutional arrangements that indirectly restrict the employment of older workers."[10] The report concluded that "decisions about aging and ability to perform in individual cases . . . may or may not be arbitrary discrimination on the basis of age, depending on the individual circumstances."[11]

Cornell Law Review, Vol. 81, 530 (1995–1996). Reprinted by permission.

Wirtz's 1965 report focused almost exclusively on discriminatory hiring practices and employers' customary imposition of arbitrary age limits on candidates for job openings—both of which had a marked effect on the employment of older workers.[12] Citing the nation's loss of productive manpower and the potential economic and psychological effects of arbitrary age discrimination on older workers, the report highlighted the injustice of judging workers based on group characteristics rather than on their individual abilities.[13] The report recommended legislative action to remedy this "arbitrary" age discrimination.[14]

Acting on Wirtz's recommendations, Congress enacted the ADEA in 1967.[15] Although the 1965 report was primarily concerned with discriminatory hiring practices, Congress went further with the ADEA, extending its proscription of arbitrary age discrimination in employment to all employment practices, including promotion, compensation, termination, and hiring decisions.[16] Specifically, the ADEA prohibits qualifying local, state, and private employers[17] from refusing to hire, discharging, or otherwise discriminating against older workers with respect to the compensation, terms, conditions, or privileges of employment "because of age."[18] Nor may a qualifying employer "limit, segregate, or classify his employees in any way which would deprive or tend to deprive an individual of employment opportunities or otherwise adversely affect his status as an employee, because of such individual's age."[19] In addition to these statutory prohibitions, Congress instituted an "education and information program" as part of a continuing effort to "reduc[e] barriers to the employment of older workers and [to promote] measures for utilizing their skills."[20]

Congress's purpose in enacting the ADEA is set forth explicitly in the Act's preamble: "to promote employment of older persons based on their ability rather than age; to prohibit arbitrary age discrimination in employment; to help employers and workers find ways of meeting problems arising from the impact of age on employment."[21] The general "theme of the ADEA is 'to shift [the] focus away from chronological age and age-related barriers.'"[22] The ADEA protects workers age forty and older from discrimination in the workplace "because of . . . age";[23] however, consistent with the recommendations made in the 1965 report, the ADEA proscribes only "arbitrary" age discrimination in employment.[24]

* * *

Notes

1. Joseph E. Kalet, Age Discrimination in Employment Law 1 (2d ed. 1990). The ADEA was preceded by the Equal Pay Act of 1963, Pub. L. No. 88-38, 77 Stat. 56 (codified at 29 U.S.C. § 206(d) (1994)), and Title VII of the Civil Rights Act of 1964, Pub. L. No. 88-352, 78 Stat. 265, (codified at 42 U.S.C. §§ 2000e to 2000e-17 (1994)).

The ADEA has often been called a "hybrid" piece of legislation. *See* Barbara L. Schlei & Paul Grossman, Employment Discrimination Law 485 (2d ed. 1983); Monte B. Lake, *Substantive Requirements Under the ADEA, in* ADEA: A Symposium Handbook For Lawyers and Personnel Practitioners 28, 35 (1983). Many of the ADEA's prohibitions parallel Title VII provisions. *Compare* 29 U.S.C. § 623(a) (1994) *with* 42 U.S.C. § 2000e-2(a) (1994). Other provisions, including the ADEA's "reasonable factors other than age" exception, 29 U.S.C. § 623(f)(1)

(1994), closely resemble Equal Pay Act (EPA) provisions, and the ADEA explicitly incorporates Fair Labor Standards Act (FLSA), enforcement mechanisms and procedures, leaving courts and commentators to disagree on the applicability of Title VII, EPA, and FLSA case law to ADEA claims. For a discussion of the dangers in "transplanting" precedent developed under these other statutes to claims arising under the ADEA, *see* DANIEL P. O'MEARA, PROTECTING THE GROWING NUMBER OF OLDER WORKERS: THE AGE DISCRIMINATION IN EMPLOYMENT ACT 82–96 (1989) (appraising the role of FLSA and Title VII case law as applied to the ADEA); *see also* Lorillard v. Pons, 434 U.S. 575, 584–85 (1978) (applying FLSA precedent in determining the availability of a jury trial under the ADEA, although acknowledging that "the prohibitions of the ADEA were derived in haec verba from Title VII"); Laugesen v. Anaconda Co., 510 F.2d 307, 312 (6th Cir. 1975) ("That the [ADEA] is embodied in a separate act and has its own unique history at least counsel the examiner to consider the particular problems sought to be reached by the statute."); Howard Eglit, *The Age Discrimination in Employment Act, Title VII, and the Civil Rights Act of 1991: Three Acts and a Dog that Didn't Bark,* 39 WAYNE L. REV. 1093 (1993); Mack A. Player, *Title VII Impact Analysis Applied to the Age Discrimination in Employment Act: Is a Transplant Appropriate?,* 14 TOLEDO L. REV. 1261 (1983).

2. *See Age Discrimination in Employment: Hearings Before the Subcomm. on Labor of the Senate Comm. on Labor and Public Welfare,* 90th Cong., 1st Sess. 23 (1967) (statement of Sen. Javits). On February 12, 1964, President Johnson issued an executive order establishing a "federal policy" against age discrimination in employment. The policy banned age discrimination in employment by federal contractors and subcontractors on account of age, providing that federal departments and agencies should "take appropriate action to enunciate the policy." Executive Order No. 11,141, 3 C.F.R. 181 (1964–1965). Because it neither provided a mechanism for its enforcement nor authorized a private cause of action for its violation, the executive order was largely ineffective. *See* Kodish v. United Air Lines Inc., 628 F.2d 1301, 1303 (10th Cir. 1980); 1 EGLIT, AGE DISCRIMINATION § 2.02, at 2–7 n.33 (2d ed. 1994). For a summary of early federal legislative and executive efforts to eliminate age discrimination in the workplace, see Richard L. August, Note, *Age Discrimination in Employment: Correcting a Constitutionally Infirm Legislative Judgment,* 47 S. CAL. L. REV. 1311, 1324–28 (1974).

3. "Ageism" has been defined as the "process of systematic stereotyping of and discrimination against people because they are old." *See* James E. Birren & Wendy L. Loucks, *Age Related Change and the Individual,* 57 CHI.-KENT L. REV. 833, 833 (1981) (quoting R. BUTLER, WHY SURVIVE? BEING OLD IN AMERICA 12 (1975)). Dr. Robert Butler is generally credited with coining the term. *Id.*

4. *See* 110 CONG. REC. 9911–16, 13,490–92 (1964) (Smathers amendment rejected in the Senate); 110 CONG. REC. 2596–99 (1964) (Dowdy amendment rejected in the House); 1 JOAN M. KRAUSKOPF ET AL., ELDERLAW: ADVOCACY FOR THE AGING § 3.31, at 77 n.2 (2d ed. 1993). This effort to include age discrimination among the practices prohibited by Title VII has been characterized by some commentators as a "disingenuous" attempt led by Southern opponents to Title VII to make the bill "so broad and 'unreasonable' as to keep it from passing . . . to load it up in order to sink it." O'MEARA, *supra* note 1, at 11–12.

5. Civil Rights Act of 1964 § 715, 42 U.S.C. § 2000e (1994).

6. U.S. DEP'T OF LABOR, THE OLDER AMERICAN WORKER: AGE DISCRIMINATION IN EMPLOYMENT (1965), *reprinted in* EQUAL EMPLOYMENT OPPORTUNITY COMM'N, LEGISLATIVE HISTORY OF THE AGE DISCRIMINATION IN EMPLOYMENT ACT 16–41 (1981) [hereinafter 1965 REPORT]. For a thorough analysis of this report and its role in the legislative history of the ADEA, *see* Alfred W. Blumrosen, *Interpreting the ADEA: Intent or Impact, in* AGE DISCRIMINATION IN EMPLOYMENT

ACT: A COMPLIANCE AND LITIGATION MANUAL FOR LAWYERS AND PERSONNEL PRACTITIONERS 68–115 (Monte B. Lake ed., 1982). Relying on the legislative history of the ADEA, Professor Blumrosen argues that intentional age discrimination "was the gravamen of age discrimination" and that actions which have a disparate impact on older workers were not intended to be prohibited under the ADEA. *Id.* at 73.

7. 1965 Report, *supra* note 6, at 2.

8. *Id.* at 5–6.

9. *Id.* at 11–14.

10. *Id.* at 15–17.

11. *Id.* at 5.

12. *Id.* at 6–10.

13. *Id.* at 18–19.

14. Secretary of Labor Wirtz was thereafter directed, under the Fair Labor Standards Act Amendments of 1966, to prepare and submit a legislative proposal addressing the problems of age discrimination in the workplace. Fair Labor Standards Act Amendments of 1966, Pub. L. No. 89-602, § 606, 80 Stat. 845. On January 23, 1967, President Lyndon Johnson delivered a special message to Congress in which he recommended that Congress enact "a law prohibiting arbitrary and unjust discrimination in employment because of a person's age." *Aid for the Aged,* 113 CONG. REC. 1087–90 (1967), *reprinted in* EQUAL EMPLOYMENT OPPORTUNITY COMM'N, LEGISLATIVE HISTORY OF THE AGE DISCRIMINATION IN EMPLOYMENT ACT 60–61 (1981). The next day, Wirtz submitted what was to become the Age Discrimination in Employment Act of 1967. *See* 113 CONG. REC. 1377 (1967). The bill was amended and ultimately signed into law on December 15, 1967. *See* Williams v. General Motors Corp., 656 F.2d 120, 126 (5th Cir. 1981), *cert. denied,* 455 U.S. 943 (1982); O'MEARA, *supra* note 1, at 14.

15. The ADEA went into effect on June 12, 1968, 180 days after its enactment. *See Williams,* 656 F.2d at 126; Hodgson v. First Fed. Sav. & Loan Ass'n, 455 F.2d 818, 820 (5th Cir. 1972).

16. *See* 29 U.S.C. § 623(a)(1) (1994).

17. The ADEA applies to employers "engaged in an industry affecting commerce" which employ at least 20 employees for 20 or more weeks annually. *Id.* § 630(b). Qualifying labor organizations and employment agencies are also bound by ADEA provisions. *See id.* § 630(c)–(d). The prohibitions imposed on employment agencies are set out at *id.* § 623(b), (d)–(e), and those imposed on labor organizations may be found at *id.* § 623(c)–(e).

The ADEA's protections also extend to most federal job applicants and employees. See *id.* § 633a. However, notwithstanding the ADEA, maximum hiring ages or mandatory retirement ages for certain federal employees are imposed by statute. *See* 1 KRAUSKOPF, *supra* note 4, § 3.33, at 79 n.4.

18. 29 U.S.C. § 623(a)(1) (1994).

19. *Id.* § 623(a)(2). The act also prohibits employers from reducing an employee's wages to comply with the ADEA. *See id.* § 623(a)(3).

The ADEA's prohibition of age discrimination in employment is not, however, absolute. See, for example, the exceptions embodied in *id.* § 623(f) (permitting age-based discrimination where age is a "bona fide occupational qualification" or where necessary "to observe the terms of a bona fide seniority system or . . . employee benefit plan") and in *id.* § 631(c) (permitting employers to impose mandatory retirement guidelines on "bona fide executives" or individuals in "high policymaking positions").

20. 29 U.S.C. § 622(a) (1994).

21. *Id.* § 621(b).

22. Evan H. Pontz, Comment, *What a Difference ADEA Makes: Why Disparate Impact Discrimination Theory Should Not Apply to the Age Discrimination in Employment Act*, 74 N.C. L. REV. 267, 272 (1995) (footnote omitted from title) (quoting Steven J. Kaminshine, *The Cost of Older Workers, Disparate Impact, and the Age Discrimination in Employment Act*, 42 FLA. L. REV. 229, 235 (1990)).

23. 29 U.S.C. § 631(a) (1994). As originally enacted, the ADEA applied only to employees age 40 to 65. Age Discrimination in Employment Act of 1967, Pub. L. No. 90-201, § 12, 81 Stat. 607. In 1978, Congress amended the ADEA, extending the upper age limit to 70. Age Discrimination in Employment Act Amendments of 1978, Pub. L. No. 95-256, § 3, 92 Stat. 189. The 1986 amendments to the ADEA eliminated the age ceiling altogether. Age Discrimination in Employment Act Amendments of 1986, Pub. L. No. 99-592, § 2(c), 100 Stat. 3342.

24. Unlike Title VII, the ADEA prohibits only "arbitrary" discrimination in employment. Although "arbitrary" is mentioned no less than three times in the Act's preamble, 29 U.S.C. § 621 (1994), nowhere does the ADEA specify what types of discrimination are considered "arbitrary" or what in fact constitutes "discrimination" under the ADEA. The ADEA's sparse legislative history likewise provides little guidance. However, in his 1965 report, *The Older American Worker: Age Discrimination in Employment*, Secretary of Labor W. Willard Wirtz described "arbitrary discrimination" as the "rejection [of older workers] because of assumptions about the effect of age on their ability to do a job *when there is in fact no basis for these assumptions.*" 1965 REPORT, *supra* note 6, at 2.

The following article describes the protections offered by the Act.

George J. Tichy, II

The Age Discrimination in Employment Act of 1967

Introduction

The Age Discrimination in Employment Act of 1967 (ADEA), as amended, prohibits discrimination against employees age forty or over on the basis of age. In addition, the ADEA also prohibits employers from discriminating on the basis of age between two individuals, both of whom are within the protected age group.[1] For example,

The Catholic Lawyer, Vol. 34, 373 (1991). Published by The St. Thomas More Institute for Legal Research of St. John's University School of Law. Reprinted by permission.

it is a violation under the Act for an employer to hire a forty-five-year-old applicant as opposed to a fifty-year-old applicant on the basis of the difference in age between them.

The prohibitions against age discrimination found in the ADEA forbid discrimination in hiring, discharges, promotions and all other terms or conditions of employment. Generally, the approach used in Title VII litigation to establish discrimination is followed in ADEA litigation.[2] Some courts have relied on the similarity between the two statutes to analogize cases arising under the ADEA to case law established under Title VII. Courts generally have found a plaintiff makes out a prima facie case of age discrimination by demonstrating: (1) the plaintiff was in a protected age group; (2) the plaintiff was qualified; (3) the plaintiff was nevertheless adversely affected; and (4) the defendant sought someone else with similar qualifications to perform the work.

* * *

I. Areas Affected by Age Discrimination Laws

A. Promotions

It is not unlawful for an employer to either: (1) limit eligibility for promotions to those employees in an existing work force, or to give preference in selection for promotion to an incumbent employee; or (2) to promote a candidate under age forty in preference to a candidate over age forty based on the younger candidate's superior experience, or other work-related qualifications. However, an employer may not base his refusal to select a candidate for promotion solely on the fact that the individual is over age forty.

The ADEA permits an employer to "observe the terms of a bona fide seniority system" in hiring or promoting a younger employee with a greater number of or a higher amount of years of seniority over an older employee with less seniority.[3]

An employee cannot make out a claim for age discrimination merely because he has reached the top of the salary range for his classification and a cap on that salary range forestalls the prospect of future raises, nor because the employer fails to create new positions with the promise of more money for senior employees.[4]

B. Medical Examinations

An employer is permitted to require applicants age forty or over to take a medical examination if it is directly related to employment standards reasonably necessary for the specific work to be performed. However, the requirement of a medical examination must be uniformly and equally applied to all applicants for a particular job category, regardless of age; employees over the age of forty may not be "singled out" for such examinations.

C. Mandatory Retirement

Employers are prohibited from requiring employees within the protected age group from retiring because of their age. Thus, no seniority system or employee benefits plan can permit the forced retirement of any individual because of age. The law's prohibitions extend to all new and existing systems and plans that force or permit involuntary retirement.

* * *

1. Early Retirement is Lawful if Voluntary

The prohibition against mandatory retirement because of age encompasses a prohibition against giving employees an ultimatum that they either accept retirement under a special early-retirement plan or be subjected to adverse treatment such as demotion, reduction in pay, or diminished chance of career advancement.[5] However, early retirement programs that are purely voluntary, and are offered to reduce costs, are lawful.[6] In *Cipriano v. Bd. of Education*,[7] a federal court held that employer costs can be relied on as a justification for voluntary retirement incentive plans under the ADEA. The court held that an employer may lawfully offer an early retirement incentive plan under Section 4(f)(2) of the ADEA if all employees eligible for retirement are offered an opportunity to voluntarily participate in the plan and a legitimate reason exists for structuring the plan with specific age limitations. The court noted that cost justifications would be insufficient if a retirement plan was involuntary, but that such justifications can be used to support a voluntary plan. The court concluded that legitimate incentive plans may provide a less harmful method than layoff for implementing work force reductions and corporate layoffs while allowing the employer to save more money per employee by eliminating higher-paid senior positions or replacing the retired workers with lower-paid workers.[8]

* * *

In a layoff situation, in order to prove age discrimination, the plaintiff must produce circumstantial or direct evidence from which a fact finder might reasonably conclude that the employer intended to discriminate in laying off the older employee rather than a younger employee.[9] Moreover, the fact that an older employee is laid off and is eventually replaced by a younger employee is not enough to establish that the employer's reasons were pretextual.[10]

Courts have permitted layoff schemes based on qualifications and performance. In *Arnell v. Pan American World Airways, Inc.*,[11] the court upheld the layoff of employees under a peer review system that assigned points according to qualifications, abilities, and productivity; age and salary levels had no influence in the scores. Based upon these scores, the company decided whom to lay off and whom to retain.[12] Similarly, in *Zick v. Verson Allsteel Press Co.*,[13] the court granted summary judgment in favor of the employer, finding that although the plaintiff had a good performance record, all of the employees had good performance records. The ADEA does not guarantee continued employment to those over age forty, and an employer is not required to place an older employee in any job for which he or she is qualified, nor does the older employee have the right to move into a younger employee's job simply because the older employee is also qualified to perform that job.[14]

* * *

II. The Bona Fide Occupational Qualification (BFOQ) and Other Defenses

The ADEA contains five specific exemptions to its prohibition against age discrimination. Thus, it is not unlawful for an employer to take any action (1) where age is a bona fide occupational qualification (BFOQ) reasonably necessary to the operation of business, (2) where the action is based on reasonable factors other than age, (3) where the action is in observance of a bona fide seniority system, (4) when the action is in observance of a bona fide employee benefit plan, or (5) where the employer has good cause to discipline or discharge the employee.[15]

An employer therefore will not be in violation of the ADEA if its job classifications or qualifications are based on bona fide occupational qualifications. In order to successfully show that a job qualification is a BFOQ, an employer must prove: (1) the age limit is reasonably necessary to the essence of the business, and either (2) that all, or substantially all, individuals excluded from the job involved are in fact disqualified or (3) that some of the individuals so excluded possess a disqualifying trait that could not be ascertained except by reference to age.[16]

Many of the decisions involving the assertion of a BFOQ to an age discrimination claim involve public safety jobs, such as pilot and police officer. An employer who asserts that the reason for making age a factor in an employment decision is public safety, must successfully prove that the elimination of those individuals who are within the protected age group does in fact effectuate the stated goal of public safety and that no available alternative to advance the goal of public safety exists that has a lesser discriminatory impact. For example, in *Western Air Lines, Inc. v. Criswell,*[17] the Supreme Court found that Western violated the ADEA by refusing to allow flight captains aged sixty years and over to downbid to the position of flight engineer and by requiring flight engineers to retire at age sixty. The court held that the restriction was not a BFOQ, since it was not reasonably necessary to ensure safe transport of passengers, and rejected the airline's contention that the restriction should be upheld as reasonable in light of the safety risks. Instead, the Court noted that modern medical techniques allowed individual appraisals of a particular employee's capabilities. The Court also noted that other airlines did not have such a requirement and that Western allowed flight captains under sixty years of age who were incapacitated for other reasons to downbid to the flight engineer position.[18]

Similarly, in *Tullis v. Lear School Inc.,*[19] the Lear School terminated the employment of a bus driver because the school's insurance carrier would not insure any drivers over age sixty-five. The school contended that requiring that bus drivers to leave employment at age sixty-five was a BFOQ. The Eleventh Circuit Court of Appeals, however, rejected the school's defense because the school had not shown that it had either a factual basis for believing that all or substantially all persons over age sixty-five would be unable to perform a bus driver's job safely, or that it was impossible or highly impractical to deal with older employees on an individualized basis. A gerontologist who testified on behalf of the bus driver stated that tests were available to determine on an individual basis whether a bus driver was capable of performing his job safely.[20]

* * *

An employer may take action where differentiation between employees is based on "reasonable factors other than age." However, an employer may not differentiate between employees on the grounds that it costs more to employ older workers. Similarly, an employee's eligibility for pension benefits cannot be a "reasonable factor other than age" in selecting employees for layoff, since that criterion is closely associated with age and would have a much greater impact on older employees.[21]

* * *

III. Bona Fide Executives and Other Exemptions

An exemption exists in the ADEA to the general limitation against mandatory retirement. The ADEA permits compulsory retirement for certain executives and individuals in high policy-making positions provided three requirements are met. First, the employee must be at least sixty-five years of age. Second, the employee must have been employed for the two-year period immediately before retirement in a bona fide executive or high policy-making position. And third, the employee must be entitled to an immediate nonforfeitable annual retirement benefit from the pension, profit sharing, savings or deferred compensation plan of at least $44,000 a year.[22]

* * *

IV. Willful Violations of the ADEA, Liquidated Damages, and Statute of Limitations

Section 7(b) of the ADEA provides that a prevailing plaintiff may be entitled to double damages in cases of willful violations of the Act.[23] In *Trans World Airlines, Inc. v. Thurston,*[24] the United States Supreme Court explained what constitutes a "willful" violation. An employer's conduct is willful, the Court declared, if it knows or shows reckless disregard for whether its conduct is prohibited by the ADEA.[25]

* * *

The ADEA provides for a two-year statute of limitations in which an age discrimination complaint may be filed, and a three-year statute of limitations in the case of "willful" violations. However, Section 7(e)(2) of ADEA allows for a tolling of this limitations period while the EEOC attempts voluntary conciliation of a finding of age discrimination.[26] Many courts have interpreted this tolling period to only apply to cases where the EEOC subsequently filed a lawsuit against the employer. However, the EEOC has since amended its regulations to explicitly provide that this tolling period also could be relied upon when private litigants file the lawsuits.

V. The Older Workers Benefit Protection Act Signed into Law

On October 16, 1990, President Bush signed into law the Older Workers Benefit Protection Act.[27] Title I of this legislation clarifies that Employee Retirement Income Security Act (ERISA) plans are subject to the Age Discrimination in Employment Act (ADEA). Title II of this legislation imposes stringent requirements on employers seeking to negotiate and prepare employment severance and settlement agreements. In such agreements, employers typically insist upon a waiver of claims by the employee. In order for an individual to waive his or her rights to bring a claim under the federal ADEA, a waiver must now include, at a minimum, the following seven elements:

1. The waiver must be part of a written agreement between the employee and the employer that is written in a clear, understandable manner;
2. The waiver must specifically refer to claims arising under the ADEA;
3. The employee must not waive the right to claims which may arise after the date on that the waiver is signed;
4. The employee must be given "consideration" (something of value) in exchange for the waiver of ADEA age discrimination claims in addition to that to which the employee is entitled;
5. The employee must be advised in writing to consult with an attorney prior to signing the waiver;
6. The employee must be given at least twenty-one days in which to consider the proposed waiver; and
7. The employee must be given seven days after signing the waiver in which to revoke it.[28]

* * *

Notes

1. 29 U.S.C. § 621.

2. *See* Foster v. Arcata Associates, Inc., 772 F.2d 1453, 1458–59 (9th Cir. 1985), *cert. denied,* 475 U.S. 1048 (1986).

3. *See* Dalton v. Mercer County Bd. of Educ. 887 F.2d 490, 492 (4th Cir. 1989).

4. *See* Genoar v. Clorox Co., 51 Fair Empl. Prac. Cas. (BNA) 240, 241 (N.D. Ill. 1989), *aff'd,* 54 Fair Empl. Prac. Cas. (BNA) 1560.

5. *See* Ackerman v. Diamond Shamrock Corp., 670 F.2d 66, 70 (6th Cir. 1982); Kneisley v. Hercules, Inc., 577 F. Supp. 726, 729 (D. Del. 1983).

6. *See* Coburn v. Pan Am. World Airways, Inc., 711 F.2d 339, 343 (D.C. Cir.), *cert. denied,* 464 U.S. 994 (1983).

7. 700 F. Supp. 1199 (W.D.N.Y. 1988).

8. *See generally id.*

9. *See* Hollry v. Sanyo Mfg., Inc., 771 F.2d 1161, 1164 (8th Cir. 1985); Williams v. General Motors Corp., 656 F.2d 120, 129 (5th Cir. 1981), *cert. denied,* 455 U.S. 943 (1982).

10. *See* Chappell v. GTE Prods. Corp., 803 F.2d 261, 267 (6th Cir. 1986), *cert. denied,* 480 U.S. 919 (1987).

11. 611 F. Supp. 908 (S.D.N.Y. 1985).

12. *Id.* at 909.

13. 644 F. Supp. 906 (E.D. Ill. 1986), *aff'd,* 819 F.2d 1143 (7th Cir. 1987).

14. *Id.* at 913; *accord* Ridenour v. Lawson Co., 791 F.2d 52, 57 (6th Cir. 1986).

15. 29 U.S.C. § 623(f).

16. 29 C.F.R. § 1625.6(b).

17. 472 U.S. 400 (1985).

18. *Id.* at 407.

19. 874 F.2d 1489 (11th Cir. 1989).

20. *Id.* at 1491.

21. *See* EEOC v. City of New Castle, 32 Fair Empl. Prac. Cas. (BNA) 1409 (W.D. Pa. 1983), *aff'd,* 740 F.2d 956 (3d Cir. 1984).

22. 29 U.S.C. § 631(c)(1).

23. 29 U.S.C. § 626(b).

24. 469 U.S. 111 (1985).

25. *Id.* at 128.

26. 29 U.S.C. § 626(e)(2).

27. *Id.* § 621.

28. *Id.* § 626(f)(1)(A)–(G).

If employers discriminate against older workers, perhaps it is because employers believe that younger workers provide better value. In some cases it may reflect an employer belief that younger workers are more productive, perhaps because they are stronger, have more energy, are more easily motivated, have better skills, have more relevant skills such as knowledge of computers, or are easier to train. Alternatively, the employer may simply want to terminate an older, higher paid employee and hire a younger, less costly one. Why should an employer be denied the right to hire the most productive or least costly employee? Professor Jolls addresses that question in the following article.

Christine Jolls

Hands-Tying and the Age Discrimination in Employment Act

Title VII's prohibitions on discrimination based on race, gender, religion, and national origin are typically justified on grounds other than economic efficiency. These prohibitions reflect, for many of us, a basic normative judgment that different outcomes for equally qualified employees of different races or other protected categories are simply wrong, wholly apart from their efficiency.[1] This argument is more difficult to sustain with regard to age discrimination, the subject of the Age Discrimination in Employment Act of 1967 (ADEA).[2] As the Supreme Court noted in *Massachusetts Board of Retirement v. Murgia*,[3] holding that age is not a suspect classification under the Equal Protection Clause: "[O]ld age does not define a 'discrete and insular' group . . . in need of 'extraordinary protection from the majoritarian political process.' Instead, it marks a stage that each of us will reach if we live out our normal span."[4] Old age has a temporal and, most critically, a universal element (almost universal at least) that is lacking in the categories covered by Title VII. These features mean that distributive or other gains for older workers are likely to come at the expense of these same workers in earlier years, making rules against age discrimination difficult to justify on traditional distributive or rights-based grounds.

* * *

The efficiency argument developed below arises out of the difficulty of achieving desirable "hands-tying" in the employer-employee relationship. Hands-tying refers to a commitment not to engage in behavior that is attractive in the short term but ultimately destructive of long-term goals.[5]

* * *

The hands-tying perspective on the ADEA is grounded in a striking empirical regularity in the ADEA cases: older workers are often terminated or otherwise disfavored because they command higher wages than younger workers capable of performing the same job. . . . The empirical regularity in the cases seems to put the efficiency costs of the Act (interpreted to prohibit the employer's behavior) in stark relief: society is forced to pay more for goods and services than in the absence of the prohibition. As Part I argues, however, this perspective on cost-based decisions about older workers fails to ask the obvious question raised by the pattern observed in the cases and corroborated by empirical evidence in the economics literature: *Why* do older workers tend to be paid more than younger workers capable of performing the same jobs? Wages, after all, are determined in the market, not handed down from above. Yet higher pay based on age—wholly apart from either productivity or seniority at a particular firm—seems to be a fairly robust empirical fact about our economy. Why does the market produce such a situation, and what, if anything, does the answer suggest about the ADEA?

Part II sketches an answer to the first of these questions, concerning why the market might produce wages that rise with workers' age. The first and most familiar explanation for age-based wages (which I treat fairly briefly on that account) links such wages to incentive problems in the employment relationship. On this view, rewarding employees with higher wages later in life is desirable because it encourages them to work hard even when their efforts cannot be directly monitored. A second explanation for rising wages focuses on individuals' psychological preference for improvement in their earnings over time. Here rising wages are better than flat ones even if total earnings across the life cycle are the same in present value terms; people like to feel that they are doing better over time. These two theories together seem to explain at least part of the rise in wages with workers' age.

The fact that age-based wages may be desired by labor market participants leads naturally to the question of whether these parties face limits on their ability to put such wages into practice. If they do not, then legal intervention, including the ADEA, would be difficult to justify on efficiency grounds. As Part III explains, however, private solutions may be limited by employers' inability to *commit* to plans of rising wages, where the incentive to renege in the high-wage phase is great. Explicit or implicit contracts may help to mitigate the commitment problem, but in a world in which individuals often change jobs over the course of their working lives, contractual solutions are likely to be imperfect. As explained below, job mobility, though valuable in many respects, creates a species of inter-employer externality that cannot readily be solved by conventional private contracts. Legal limits on cost-based decisions about older workers represent a possible solution to this externality problem; such limits tie employers' hands and prevent them from reneging on the payment of age-based wages. Evidence on wages negotiated by unions—entities that may help to address the contracting barriers created by job mobility—seems to provide some support for the view that legal limits on cost-based decisionmaking may help to replicate the arrangements parties would choose in the absence of contracting barriers.

Part IV examines the implications of the hands-tying analysis for the ADEA. It explains that hands-tying considerations argue in favor of ADEA liability for cost-based decisions about older workers.

Notes

1. Title VII may also be efficient. *See* John J. Donohue III, *Is Title VII Efficient?*, 134 U. PA. L. REV. 1411, 1430–31 (1986).

2. 29 U.S.C. §§ 621–634 (1994).

3. 427 U.S. 307 (1976).

4. *Id.* at 313–14.

5. *See* Henry Hansmann & Reinier Kraakman, *Hands-Tying Contracts: Book Publishing, Venture Capital Financing, and Secured Debt*, 8 J.L. ECON. & ORGANIZATION 628, 629 (1992); Christine Jolls, *Contracts As Bilateral Commitments: A New Concern About Contract Modification*, 26 J. LEGAL STUD. 203 (1997).

The Age Discrimination in Employment Act of 1967 had two goals: to reduce discrimination in the hiring of older workers (and thereby reduce poverty among the elderly) and to eliminate mandatory retirement based on an arbitrary age requirement. Most commentators believe that the ADEA has had little effect on the hiring of older workers. The prejudice against hiring older persons is invidious and not easily overcome. There are very few lawsuits by older rejected job applicants claiming a violation of the ADEA, probably because proving such a case is extremely difficult. Absent a "smoking gun" such as an intra-office memo stating that the company does not want to hire older applicants, it is very difficult for a rejected job applicant to prove that age was the reason for the failure to hire. Because hiring decisions are often based on subjective factors such as compatibility, apparent ambition, a willingness to work hard, or the ability to get along with others, it is easy for the employer to claim that the failure to hire was due to factors other than the age of the applicant.

The ADEA has been much more successful in combating mandatory retirement based on age. Except for the few companies that can sustain a BFOQ exemption, such as a mandatory age limit for pilots, mandatory age retirement requirements no longer exist. To be sure, a few highly placed executives such as CEOs can still legally be required to retire at a set age, but overwhelmingly employees no longer face mandatory age-based retirement. Of course, they can be terminated if they can no longer perform their job, but most employees retire voluntarily.

Still, not all retirement is voluntary. Though age-based retirement is almost always illegal under either federal or state law, white collar workers, in particular the so-called middle managers, often find themselves facing a choice of either retiring—often with a healthy bonus or other incentives—or facing possible termination because of corporate downsizing. Professor Harper describes how so-called "exit incentives" are used to defeat the intent, if not the letter, of the Age Discrimination in Employment Act.

Michael C. Harper

Age-Based Exit Incentives, Coercion, and the Prospective Waiver of ADEA Rights: The Failure of the Older Workers Benefit Protection Act

* * *

I. The Effect of Conditional Age-Based Exit Incentive Windows: The Case for Regulation

A. Conditional Age-Based Exit Incentives and the ADEA

Any pension plan that provides retirement benefits solely to employees who have attained some minimum age encourages only older workers to exit from employment and thus is in some tension with the ADEA's goal "to promote employment of older persons based on their ability rather than age."[1] An employer who wants to limit the number of employees above a certain age in its workforce can be confident of doing so without discharging any older worker by offering sufficiently attractive retirement benefits to any worker above that age to induce most, or at least many of them, to choose retirement over work.

Yet the antidiscrimination commands and purposes of the ADEA need not and should not be read to condemn all retirement pensions.[2] It is certainly clear that Congress never intended such a broad reading. The legislative history of the development of the ADEA indicates that Congress has been concerned about encouraging the employment of older Americans who prefer a continuation of their employment to the retirement options available to them. Congress has been concerned about the inability of older workers who are displaced from jobs in which they are productive to find alternative employment that utilizes their skills.[3] Congress has also asserted the goal of avoiding public support of older workers who could effectively support themselves if judged fairly as individuals rather than on the basis of their age.[4] Yet this goal has never moved Congress to attempt to restrict retirement opportunities that older workers prefer to continued work. This is confirmed by Congress's continued support of the public Social Security system, which, like any private pension plan, encourages at least some older workers to retire.[5]

* * *

In contrast to the typical age-based pension plan, however, the use of conditional age-based exit incentive programs does not simply enable employers to encourage

Virginia Law Review, Vol. 79, 1271 (1993). Reprinted by permission, Virginia Law Review Association and Fred B. Rothman & Co.

older employees to leave their jobs by making the alternative of retirement more attractive than continued employment. Rather, employers can use these conditional incentive windows to induce older workers to leave jobs they would prefer to the retirement promised by the incentive benefits. Thus, conditional age-based exit incentives can be used to achieve precisely what the ADEA seeks to eradicate: the age-based elimination of productive older workers who would prefer continued employment to retirement.

B. Coercion and the Operation of Conditional Age-Based Exit Incentives

Conditional age-based exit incentives can be surprisingly effective in coercing older workers who may prefer to continue to work into accepting early retirement. However, the use and effects of these incentives are considerably more subtle than outright threats of discriminatory discharges based on age.

1. The Use of Conditional Exit Incentives to Induce Retirement To understand how conditional exit incentive offers can be used to induce retirement from employees who would prefer continued employment, consider how a typical offer of this type would be weighed by an offeree. Assume that an employer announces to its workforce that because of general recessionary conditions or deep cuts in the demand for its particular product, employment will have to be cut by thirty percent over the next four months. The employer also announces at the same time that in order to avoid as many involuntary layoffs as possible, it will offer retirement incentives to all employees over the age of fifty-five. These incentives might include some significant lump sum payment; they might include continued health insurance coverage during at least some years of retirement; or they might consist of the allowance of earlier or greater pension benefits, perhaps by crediting all those who accept the offer with additional years of service or additional years of age to make them eligible for increased retirement benefits under the employer's defined benefit pension plan.[6] The offer is conditional, however, because the benefits will only be granted to those who voluntarily retire within the next two months.[7] Those offerees who are involuntarily laid off, or those offerees who decide to retire after the expiration of the two-month period, will not obtain the benefits. Finally, assume that the employer does not specify how it will determine who will be laid off to achieve the necessary residual amount of reductions in staff after the closure of the voluntary retirement window.

A post–fifty-five-year-old offeree in this typical exit window scenario might well rationally accept early retirement even though she prefers continuing employment. The reason is that the offeree must include in her calculations the chance that she will be terminated without the extra benefits offered for voluntary retirement. Thus, an offeree who prefers employment to retirement with increased benefits might prefer the latter to the perceived chance of continued employment plus the perceived chance of termination without enhanced benefits.[8] Clearly it is the conditional nature of the retirement incentive that makes the two preferences consistent, that, in other words, makes it rational for an offeree to accept the incentive even though she prefers continued employment.[9]

This is highly significant for an employer wanting to rid itself of more older workers than could be justified by individualized comparisons of the productivity of all its workers. For instance, assume an employer wanted to cut a section of its workforce in half and that one half of the employees in this section were over fifty. Assume further that the employer could eliminate half of these post–fifty-year-old employees on the basis of individualized analyses of relative productivity. Also, assume that by offering a conditional incentive, the employer could convince three-fourths of the post–fifty-year-olds to accept retirement, even though many of these employees would prefer continuing to work. Even if none of the other one-fourth who declined retirement were vulnerable to discharge, the employer increased by 50 percent (from 50 to 75 percent) the proportion of its older workforce that it could displace. If the one fourth of the older workers who declined the retirement incentive were as likely to be vulnerable to termination based on their relative productivity as the three-fourths that accepted the offer, the employer could increase from 50 to 80 percent (a 60 percent increase) the proportion of terminations in its workforce reduction drawn from its older workers.[10]

An employer is thus able to use an age-based retirement plan to eliminate significantly more older workers than it could terminate by individualized consideration of their productivity, despite the fact that many of these older workers prefer continued employment.[11] It is the critical interaction between the offer of additional benefits and the threat of termination without these benefits that enables conditional age-based exit incentives to eliminate older workers who could not be induced to exit by either the offer of retirement incentives in traditional pension plans or the threat of forced terminations.[12]

* * *

C. Conflict with the Principles of the ADEA

Second and more important, even if age-based conditional exit incentives are not viewed as coercive, they still undermine fulfillment of the antidiscrimination purposes of the ADEA. Acceptance of conditional age-based exit incentives enable employers to achieve something condemned by the antidiscrimination provisions of the ADEA—the elimination of employees because of age from jobs they wish to continue to hold.

1. Age Discrimination The condemnation by the ADEA's antidiscrimination principles of even noncoerced acceptance of conditional age-based exit incentives should be especially clear to the extent that such offers are driven by age-based categorizations or stereotypes. We often regulate exchanges driven by preferences that our society wishes to condemn,[13] and the ADEA certainly reflects our society's collective judgment that we should not honor preferences driven by age-based stereotypes for the retirement of older workers.

* * *

3. "Rational" Age Discrimination: Economic Justifications Moreover, further analysis suggests that employers have strong reasons for wanting to displace older workers, especially during periods of substantial force reductions. Admittedly, most managerial decisionmakers are not likely to have the kind of animus toward older workers that has fueled racism and sexism at all levels of our society.[14] Managers are likely, however, to be influenced by the stereotypes regarding the capabilities of older workers that were the primary concern of the Congress that enacted the ADEA.[15] Many of these stereotypes are more powerful because they may contain an element of truth: for many jobs, at least at some age, average productivity starts to decline.[16]

In some situations it therefore may be economically rational for an employer to use age as a proxy for productivity, rather than to incur the costs of individual evaluations, including those costs engendered by employee anxieties. It may also be economically rational for an employer to want a reduction in force to remove productive older workers rather than equally productive younger workers, because both the projected future average productivity and the projected future average job tenure of the younger workers may be higher. Job tenure may be especially important if training and other turnover costs are significant. An employer may be particularly concerned that a reduction in force by reverse seniority resulting in the displacement of only younger workers could generate especially high turnover costs when the remaining older workers later retire during the same period.

Some might argue that our society should not condemn such economically rational "statistical" discrimination against older workers.[17] Permitting employers to justify age-based generalizations because they are economically rational would seriously compromise the ADEA's promise of individualized consideration regardless of age, however. Therefore, it is not surprising that the ADEA, like Title VII, has been read to condemn all decisionmaking that is unnecessarily based on stereotypes or generalizations, whether economically rational or not.[18] It is inconsistent to condone incentives that induce unwanted retirement even if they have such a rational basis.

An economically rational employer may also want to get rid of older workers whose productivity is equal to that of younger workers because the average pay of the older workers is higher. Older employees may have generally higher wages relative to marginal productivity because there is an implied "life-cycle" agreement to pay wages above marginal productivity, as well as above the opportunity wage in the external labor market, at the end of a long tenure to compensate for wages below marginal productivity paid in the earlier stages of employment.[19] Such long-term implied contracts may be attractive to employers because they discourage "worker shirking and malfeasance," and because they induce commitments to the firm that reduce personnel turnover costs and encourage interemployee cooperation and training.[20] They may be attractive to employees who appreciate being able to rely on a rising wage curve as they age and who may share in the returns from their workforce's greater efficiency. Such long-term commitments traditionally have not been enforceable in court, but worries about reputational costs and incumbent employee morale normally deter employers from opportunistic breaches.[21] Such concerns may not be sufficient deterrence, however, during reductions in force when employers need to be less sensitive to their external reputations and when incumbent employees are focused on job preservation rather than promises of wage enhancement. During such periods employers may want to take the opportunity to eliminate higher paid older workers.[22]

Doing so by laying off older workers without individualized consideration of their productivity relative to their wage, however, clearly contravenes the antidiscrimination commands of the ADEA.[23] Whether or not it should be illegal for an employer to impact older workers disparately by discharging everyone in a particular job making more than some set figure, there is no authority to support the legality of discharging everyone beyond some maximum age because of the average wage of workers beyond that age.[24] Any calculated effort to use conditional exit incentives to achieve the same result should also be unacceptable under the ADEA.

* * *

Notes

1. 29 U.S.C. § 621(b).

2. Sections 4(a)(1) and (2) of the ADEA provide:

It shall be unlawful for an employer—

(1) to fail or refuse to hire or to discharge any individual or otherwise discriminate against any individual with respect to his compensation, terms, conditions, or privileges of employment, because of such individual's age;

(2) to limit, segregate, or classify his employees in any way which would deprive or tend to deprive any individual of employment opportunities or otherwise adversely affect his status as an employee, because of such individual's age. . . .

29 U.S.C. § 623(a).

3. See, e.g., The Older American Worker: Age Discrimination in Employment, Report of the Secretary of Labor to the Congress Under Section 715 of the Civil Rights Act of 1964 (June 1965), *reprinted in* EEOC, Legislative History of the Age Discrimination in Employment Act 5 (1981) [hereinafter Wirtz Report] (report of then Secretary of Labor Wirtz, which led to the original passage of the ADEA, noting that age discrimination wastes a "wealth of human resources"); id. at 18–19 (asserting that unemployment rates rise with age); see also S. Rep. No. 723, 90th Cong., 1st Sess. 4 (1967) (setting forth views of leading ADEA sponsor, Senator Javits); 113 Cong. Rec. 34,742 (1967) (statement of Rep. Matsunaga).

4. See, e.g., Select Comm. on Aging, 95th Cong., 1st Sess., Mandatory Retirement: The Social and Human Cost of Enforced Idleness 23 (1977) (expressing concern that society will not be able to support its retired members if the trend toward early retirement continues); 113 Cong. Rec. 34,744 (1967) (remarks of Rep. Hawkins); id. at 34,745 (1967) (remarks of Rep. Eilberg).

5. Recent amendments to the Social Security law, however, have been framed to encourage longer employment. See John A. Svahn & Mary Ross, Social Security Amendments of 1983: Legislative History and Summary of Provisions, 46 Soc. Security Bull. 3, 7–48 (1983). The 1983 amendments provide that, beginning in 2003, the normal retirement age at which full benefits can be obtained will climb one month per year until it reaches age 67 in 2027. Furthermore, the benefit reduction that retirees must accept for taking the Social Security system's early retirement option at age 62 will be increased from 20% to 30% by 2027. Social Security Amendments of 1983, Pub. L. No. 98-21, 97 Stat. 65 (1983).

Inasmuch as the tendency of Americans to retire earlier seems as much influenced by increases in the subsidization of early retirement through defined benefit plans as by the Social Security system, it is not clear that Congress can encourage later retirement without greater regulation of private pension plans. See Richard A. Ippolito, Toward Explaining Earlier Retirement After 1970, 43 Indus. & Lab. Rel. Rev. 556 (1990); William J. Wiatrowski, Supplementing Retirement Until Social Security Begins, Monthly Lab. Rev., Feb. 1990, at 25, 26. This may explain in part the 1986 congressional passage of a requirement that all pension plans continue contributions and accruals without regard to an employee's age. See Omnibus Budget Reconciliation Act of 1986, Pub. L. No. 99-509, 100 Stat. 1874 (1986). Plans can, however, continue to cap defined benefit levels and "the number of years . . . which are taken into account for purposes of determining benefit accrual." 29 U.S.C. § 623(i)(2).

6. These examples represent the typical structure of early retirement incentives. The Hewitt Associates study, for instance, found that 64% of exit incentive programs augmented the pension benefit (sometimes by eliminating the normal early retirement reduction), 23% liberalized the requirements for pension eligibility, 51% provided for some cash payment, and 16% gave enhanced medical insurance coverage. See Hewitt Associates, [Plan Design and Experience in Early Retirement Windows and in Other Voluntary Separation Plans 1 (1986)]. Bridge subsidies that would continue until social security eligibility have also been common. For a description of particular plans from major employers such as Exxon and Dupont, see Meier, [Elizabeth L. Meier, American Ass'n of Retired Persons, Early Retirement Incentive Programs—Trends and Implications 1 (1986) (unpublished manuscript, on file with the Virginia Law Review Association).]

Employers are somewhat restricted by the Employee Retirement Income Security Act ("ERISA") in structuring the form of their offered benefits. Because any plan designed to provide retirement benefits is a pension plan under ERISA, employers must meet this Act's requirements, including those prohibiting discrimination in favor of highly compensated employees. See Larry I. Stein, Through the Looking Glass: An Analysis of Window Plans, 42 Lab. L.J. 665, 670–73 (1991).

7. Open windows for a majority of conditional exit incentive plans last for one to three months. See Bureau of Nat'l Aff., Older Americans in the Workforce: Challenges & Solutions 65 (1987).

8. Expressed algebraically, where preferences for employment = E, preferences for retirement = R, preferences for retirement with increased benefits = RIB, perceived chance of continued employment = C, and perceived chance of termination without enhanced benefits = $(1.00 - C)E > RIB$, but $RIB > C(E) + (1.00 - C)R$.

9. If the incentive offers were not conditional, or if any forced retirement would also come with incentives, the two preferences would be contradictory. See supra note 8. If $R = RIB$, then $R > C(E) + (1.00 - C)R$ and $R > C(E) + R - C(R)$ and $0 > C(E) - C(R)$ and $R > E$. But $E > RIB$ and if $R = RIB$, then $E > R$.

10. The retirement of 75% of the older workers enabled the employer to achieve the retirement of 37.5% of the targeted workforce. The displacement of 12.5% more of the original workforce would be necessary for the employer to achieve its 50% goal. If older workers were as likely to be displaced as younger workers at this point, one fifth of the residual 12.5%, or 2.5%, would come from older workers. This would mean that 80% of the younger workers would not be displaced and only 20% would be, while 80% of the older workers would be displaced and only 20% would not be.

11. The assumptions made in this hypothetical are not unrealistic. The Hewitt Associates

study of exit incentive programs found that almost one fourth of the programs studied had acceptance rates of over 75%. See Hewitt Assocs., [Plan Design and Experience in Early Retirement Windows and in Other Voluntary Separation Plans 1 (1986)]. Another study found that the work performance of employees who accepted exit incentive offers was similar to that of employees who declined such offers. See Larry Reibstein, AT&T Study Shows Early Retirees Share a Range of Character Traits, Wall St. J., Sept. 4, 1987, at 17.

Furthermore, recent surveys of retired workers demonstrate that a substantial number are willing and able to continue to work, including many who retired because of special benefit incentives. See Employment Benefit Research Inst., Issue Brief: Economic Incentives for Retirement in the Public and Private Sectors 5 (1986) (discussing 1981 survey by Louis Harris and Associates); William McNaught, Michael C. Barth & Peter H. Henderson, The Human Resource Potential of Americans Over 50, 28 Hum. Resources Mgmt. 455, 464–65 (1989) (analyzing 1989 survey of retired workers by Louis Harris and Associates). Moreover, the threat of layoff after declining a retirement incentive offer has proven to be a very real one. Employers such as Combustion Engineering and Exxon have fired hundreds of employees after exit incentive programs failed to reach their targets. See Bruce Nussbaum, Kathleen Failla, Christopher S. Eklund, Alex Beam, James R. Norman & Kathleen Deveny, The End of Corporate Loyalty?, Bus. Wk., Aug. 4, 1986, at 42–49.

12. It is clear that by magnifying the threat of increased layoffs an employer can boost the number of acceptances of conditional exit incentives from employees who would prefer continued work. Consider again the formula $RIB > C(E) + (1.00 - C)R$. See supra note 8. This formula can be transformed into $RIB > C(E) + R - C(R)$, then $RIB - R > C(E - R)$, then $RIB - R/E - R > C$. The lower the value of C, the more relative values of RIB and E, for cases where employees prefer continued employment to enhanced retirement ($E > RIB$), will satisfy this equation. The perceived chance of continued employment for those who decline exist incentives (C) is in the control of any employer.

The value of RIB can also be controlled by employers. By increasing the value of the exit incentives to a level that is still below the value of continued work for many employees, the employer can reduce the threat necessary to achieve the retirement of many who would continue to work. Through their control of these two variables, employers can balance several different objectives: maximizing the retirement of those they could not legally discharge, minimizing their outlay of funds, and insuring their threat of discharge is not so blatant as to be illegal.

13. Cf. Cass R. Sunstein, Legal Interference with Private Preferences, 53 U. Chi. L. Rev. 1129, 1152–53 (1986) (arguing that a democratic majority may decide that certain preferences, such as those for discrimination, "should not be gratified—not only because of harm to others or to the actor involved, but also because those preferences are . . . not . . . defensible on grounds other than self-interest").

14. Nevertheless, some age-based discrimination by younger management may be the unconscious product of unresolved child-parent conflicts, rather than a failure to empathize with older workers. See Martin L. Levine, Age Discrimination and the Mandatory Retirement Controversy 133–45 (1988).

15. See Wirtz Report, supra note 3. It is interesting that 20% of the employers in the Hewitt Associates study stated that one of the reasons for offering their plans was to give "career opportunities" to "younger employees." See Hewitt Assocs., [Plan Design and Experience in Early Retirement Windows and in Other Voluntary Separation Plans 1 (1986)].

Historians have correlated the spread of age-based thinking in the last century with the rationalization of modern society and the need for new organizing principles for social control as traditional family and community structures have eroded. See, e.g., Howard P. Chudacoff, How Old Are You? Age Consciousness in American Culture 184–85 (1989); Levine, supra note 14, at 75–94.

16. For some jobs, however, even generalizations about age-related productivity decline may be inaccurate. For instance, some recent studies suggest that discriminating in *favor* of older workers in some jobs may be efficient because of lower turnover, absenteeism, and pilferage. See ICF Inc., Study for The Commonwealth Fund's Americans Over 55 At Work Program 6 (1991); see also Levine, supra note 14, at 108 (summarizing research and concluding that it has "failed to show a great overall decline in job performance at about typical retirement age"); Note, The Cost of Growing Old: Business Necessity and the Age Discrimination in Employment Act, 88 Yale L.J. 565, 576 (1979) (citing studies showing "an absence of meaningful connection between advancing age and declining levels of job performance" in most industries); Daniel Goleman, The Aging Mind Proves Capable of Lifelong Growth, N.Y. Times, Feb. 21, 1984, at C1.

17. See Kenneth J. Arrow, Models of Job Discrimination, Some Mathematical Models of Race in the Labor Market, *in* Racial Discrimination in Economic Life 83, 187 (Anthony H. Pascal ed., 1973); Edmund S. Phelps, The Statistical Theory of Racism and Sexism, 62 Am. Econ. Rev. 659 (1972). For an application of statistical arguments to age discrimination, see Robert Hutchens, Delayed Payment Contracts and a Firm's Propensity to Hire Older Workers, 4 J. Lab. Econ. 439 (1986).

18. See, e.g., EEOC v. County of Los Angeles, 706 F.2d 1039, 1042 (9th Cir. 1983); Smallwood v. United Air Lines, Inc., 661 F.2d 303, 307 (4th Cir. 1981), cert. denied, 456 U.S. 1007 (1982); Hahn v. City of Buffalo, 596 F. Supp. 939, 953 (W.D.N.Y.), aff'd, 770 F.2d 12 (2d Cir. 1985) (all holding that economic justifications for age discrimination are not acceptable under ADEA). [The primary exception to the general rule against discrimination both in the ADEA and in Title VII is the bona fide occupational qualification ("BFOQ"). Congress, however, intended this exception to be interpreted narrowly not to allow even cost-based defenses to disparate treatment in employment. *Johnson Controls,* 111 S. Ct. at 1209. The *Johnson Controls* Court held that the Title VII BFOQ defense should be applied "as narrowly" as the BFOQ provision in the ADEA was applied in *Western Airlines v. Criswell,* 472 U.S. 400 (1985). *Johnson Controls,* 111 S. Ct. at 1204. An employer claiming a BFOQ must be able to establish that it "had reasonable cause to believe . . . that all or substantially all [persons over the age qualifications] would be unable to perform safely and efficiently the duties of the job involved," or the "employer could establish that age was a legitimate proxy for the safety-related job qualifications by proving that it is 'impossible or highly impractical' to deal with the older employees on an individualized basis." *Criswell,* 472 U.S. at 414 (quoting *Weeks v. Southern Bell Tel. & Tel. Co.,* 408 F.2d 228, 235 & n. 5 (5th Cir. 1969)). This defense therefore would only help to insulate from challenge an age-based exit incentive program where the employer could establish either that all or substantially all the older offerees could no longer perform their job, or that it was highly impractical to determine which of the offerees were exceptions to such a generalization.] But cf. Laugesen v. Anaconda Co., 510 F.2d 307, 312 n.4 (6th Cir. 1975) (noting that a committee report on the ADEA suggests that the Act should not be read to "prevent an employer from achieving a reasonable age balance in his employment structure") (quoting H.R. Rep. No. 805, 90th Cong., 1st Sess. 7 (1967), *reprinted in* 1967 U.S.C.C.A.N. 2213, 2219), cert. denied, 422 U.S. 1045 (1975).

19. There is now an extensive theoretical literature based on the assumed importance of implied delayed payment contracts. See, e.g., Robert M. Hutchens, A Test of Lazear's Theory of Delayed Payment Contracts, 5 J. Lab. Econ. S153 (1987); Edward P. Lazear, Agency, Earnings Profiles, Productivity, and Hours Restrictions, 71 Am. Econ. Rev. 606 (1981); James L. Medoff & Katharine G. Abraham, Are Those Paid More Really More Productive? The Case of Experience, 16 J. Hum. Resources 186 (1981); Michael L. Wachter & George M. Cohen, The Law and Economics of Collective Bargaining: An Introduction and Application to the Problems of Subcontracting, Partial Closure, and Relocation, 136 U. Pa. L. Rev. 1349, 1360–64 (1988).

20. See Robert M. Hutchens, Do Job Opportunities Decline with Age?, 42 Indus. & Lab. Rel. Rev. 89, 90 (1988).

21. However, similar express commitments to unionized employees, as embodied in collective bargaining agreements through wage scales, competitive seniority provisions governing layoffs in reductions in force, and protections from discharge without just cause, have been enforceable. See generally Wachter & Cohen, [Michael L. Wachter & George M. Cohen, The Law and Economics of Collective Bargaining: An Introduction and Application to the Problems of Subcontracting, Partial Closure, and Relocation, 136 U. Pa. L. Rev. 1349, 1360–64 (1988)] (describing a variety of collective bargaining agreements enforced by the courts).

In addition, some recent state law protecting nonunion employees from bad faith discharge can be viewed as achieving the enforcement of implied long-term employment contracts. See, e.g., Mont. Code Ann. §§ 39-2-901 to 39-2-914 (1992); Foley v. Interactive Data Corp., 765 P.2d 373 (1988).

22. Cf. Gray v. New England Tel. & Tel. Co., 792 F.2d 251, 254 (1st Cir. 1986) ("'[T]he company took steps to ease people out on retirement, which to me involved age. We didn't want to spend the money to retrain them and go on.'") (quoting testimony of management supervisor in ADEA litigation).

23. EEOC Guidelines provide that a "differentiation based on the average cost of employing older employees as a group is unlawful." 29 C.F.R. § 1625.7(f) (1992).

24. Some lower courts have interpreted the ADEA to prohibit the disparate impact resulting from the refusal of continued employment to those who are paid more because of longer service. See, e.g., Geller v. Markham, 635 F.2d 1027 (2d Cir. 1980), cert. denied, 451 U.S. 945 (1981); Leftwich v. Harris-Stowe State College, 702 F.2d 686 (8th Cir. 1983); see also Note, supra note 16 (discussing disparate impact analysis in this situation).

These decisions, which do not permit a cost reduction defense, seem to expand disparate impact theory to condemn generalizations based on status closely associated with age, such as seniority, when individual consideration would be feasible. See Alfred W. Blumrosen, Interpreting the ADEA: Intent of Impact, *in* Age Discrimination in Employment Act: A Compliance and Litigation Manual for Lawyers and Personnel Practitioners 68, 106–07, 111–15 (Monte B. Lake ed., 1982); Steven J. Kaminshine, The Cost of Older Workers, Disparate Impact, and the Age Discrimination in Employment Act, 42 Fla. L. Rev. 229 (1990); Mark A. Player, Title VII Impact Analysis Applied to the Age Discrimination in Employment Act: Is a Transplant Appropriate?, 14 U. Tol. L. Rev. 1261 (1983).

A Seventh Circuit decision seems to take the further step of condemning the discharge of an older worker after individualized consideration of whether his present contributions to the firm justifies his high salary. See Metz v. Transit Mix, 828 F.2d 1202 (7th Cir. 1987). In Hazen Paper Co. v. Biggins, 61 U.S.L.W. 4323 (Apr. 20, 1993), however, the Supreme Court rejected the *Metz* decision by holding that an employer's discharge of an employee because of a factor that is highly correlated with age, such as seniority, does not constitute actionable disparate treatment under the ADEA. Furthermore, the *Hazen* majority expressly reserved judgment on whether the ADEA encompasses any disparate impact claims. Justice Kennedy, in a dissenting opinion, noted that "there are substantial arguments that it is improper to carry over disparate impact from Title VII to the ADEA." Id. at 4325, 4327 (Kennedy, J., dissenting); see also Geller v. Markham, 451 U.S. 945, 948 (1981) (Rehnquist, J., dissenting from denial of certiorari) (stating that "[t]his Court has never held that proof of discriminatory impact can establish a violation of the ADEA").

CHAPTER 9

Pensions

Adequate retirement income is essential for workers to voluntarily retire. Retirement income is said to rest on a three-legged stool made up of savings, Social Security, and pensions. Although not universal, pensions are a major reason many retirees enjoy a relatively prosperous lifestyle. In the following article, Ms. Reno examines the prevalence and importance of pensions as a source of retirement income.

Virginia P. Reno

The Role of Pensions in Retirement Income: Trends and Questions

* * *

Pensions from public or private plans are an important and increasingly common supplement to Social Security benefits for the elderly. By 1990, pension income was reported by 44 percent of all elderly units—57 percent of couples and 34 percent of unmarried persons (see Table 1).

Social Security is the most evenly distributed source of income of the elderly, and it is the major share of income of those in the lowest three income quintiles and is the largest single source of income for all but those persons in the highest income quintile (see Chart 1). Among the elderly, receipt of pensions, asset income, and earnings rises with income. The vast majority of pension, asset, and earnings income is received by those in the middle and upper income quintiles. Among the middle and upper income elderly, pensions are more evenly distributed than are earnings or asset income, according to data from the Current Population Survey (CPS).

56 *Social Security Bulletin* 29 (Spring 1993).

TABLE 1. Percent of Couples and Unmarried Persons Aged 65 or Older Receiving Various Sources of Income, 1990

			Unmarried persons		
Source of income	*Total*	*Couples*	*Total*	*Men*	*Women*
Social Security	92	93	91	89	92
Pensions, total[1]	44	57	34	41	32
Public	17	22	13	13	14
Private	30	41	22	29	20
Earnings	22	34	13	16	12
Asset income	69	79	63	61	63
Public assistance	7	3	9	8	10

[1] Includes some who receive both public and private pensions.

Source: Susan Grad, *Income of the Population 55 or Older, 1990*. Office of Research and Statistics, Social Security Administration, April 1992.

Among active workers, the proportion covered by a private pension plan grew rapidly in the 1940s and 1950s and more slowly in the 1960s and 1970s. The coverage rate declined slightly between 1979 and 1988. The decline in private plan coverage affected men more than women, thereby narrowing the gender gap in the private pension coverage rate. Among full-time workers, the decline was greater for young men (under age thirty-five) and among both men and women with less than a high school education.

Participation in defined contribution plans is growing, both as a source of primary pension coverage and as supplemental coverage to a primary defined benefit or defined contribution plan. The expansion in private plan coverage has been in multiple plan coverage—that is, workers with any private pension coverage are increasingly likely to be included in more than one plan. Often the supplements are 401(k) plans, which are more often offered to and used by higher-earning workers. The shift toward defined contribution private plans, and the lump-sum distributions they typically pay, pose problems in assessing the total role of private pensions in the retirement income system.

Pension receipt among the elderly is expected to continue to grow over the next 20 or 30 years because of past growth in coverage and vesting.

* * *

Sources of Income, 1990

Of the total population of married couples and nonmarried persons aged 65 or older in 1990, 44 percent reported some income from a public or private pension. They include 30 percent with a private pension and 17 percent with a public pension, and 3 percent who received both public and private pensions (Table 1). A couple is counted as receiving a pension if either the husband or wife has a pension. Nearly 6

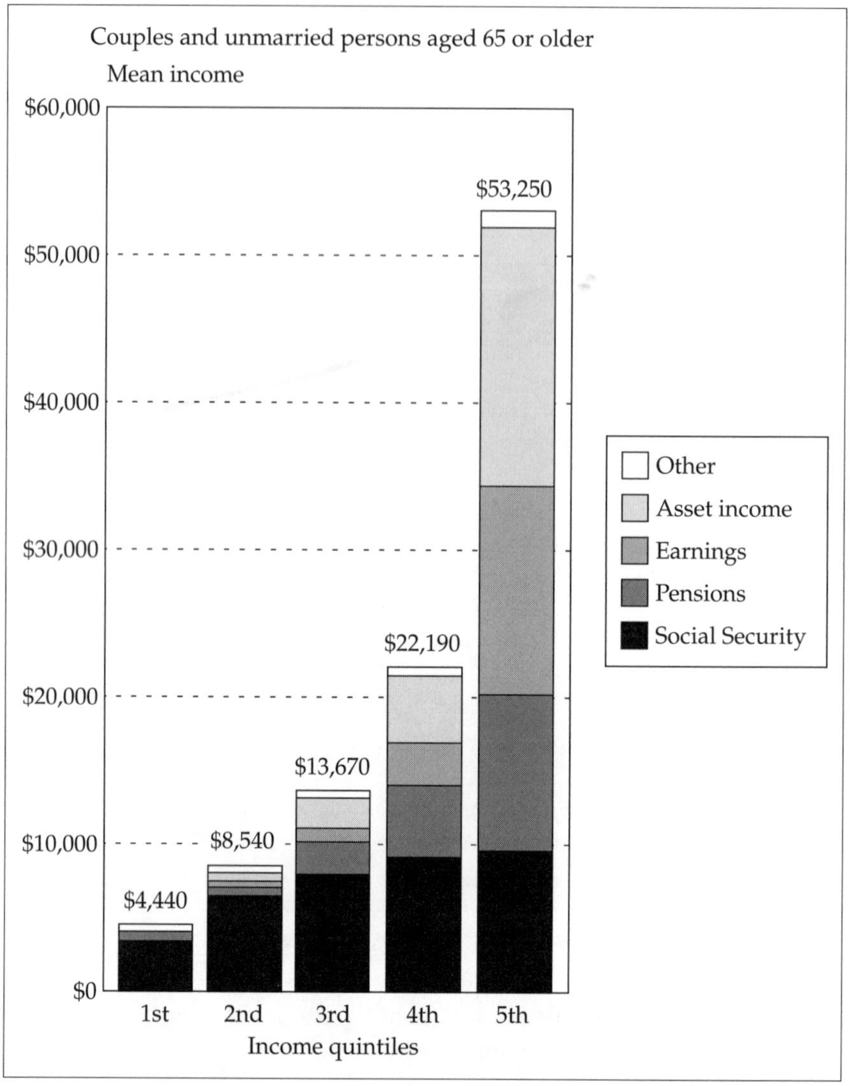

CHART 1 Composition of mean income by total income quintiles, 1990

in 10 elderly couples (57 percent) had pensions, while among the unmarried, 41 percent of the men and 32 percent of the women received a pension.

Social Security is the most commonly received source of retirement income, with about 9 in 10 elderly couples and unmarried persons receiving benefits. Public and private pensions differ somewhat in the roles they have filled relative to Social Security. Because nearly all private sector jobs have been covered by Social Security for several decades, nearly all private pensions are designed to supplement Social Security benefits. In 1988, the median annual private pension income received by elderly individuals was $3,590. Because private pensions are designed to supplement Social Security, such pensions rarely are the major source of income for the elderly. In 1990,

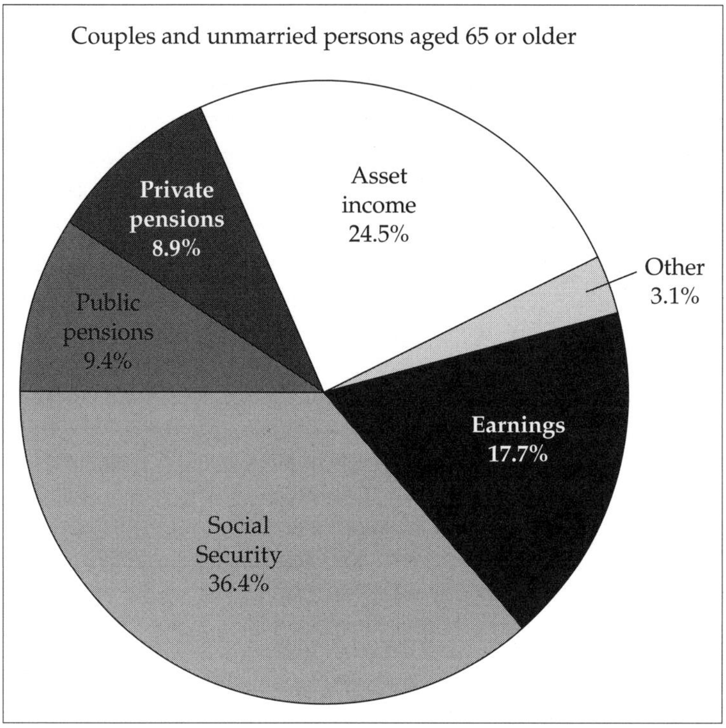

CHART 2 Shares of aggregate income from major sources, 1990

for example, private pensions accounted for 50 percent or more of total income for just 8 percent of the elderly units who received such pensions (or 2 percent of all the elderly).

* * *

Income from public and private pensions combined accounted for about 18 percent of the reported aggregate income of the elderly in 1990 (see Chart 2). Because public pension amounts are larger, they are a slightly larger share of aggregate income than private pensions—despite the fact that private pensions are nearly twice as likely to be received.

* * *

Why do employers pay pensions? Well, not out of the goodness of their hearts or because they want their retirees to live a good life. Pensions are not gifts. They are something the employees earn. In essence, pensions represent deferred wages. They are part of the compensation earned by employees during their working years.

Employer-provided pensions enjoy special federal income tax advantages that have greatly contributed to their adoption. By granting tax advantages to pensions, Congress hoped that more employers would adopt them. More pensions meant less poverty among retirees and would encourage retirement and so create more jobs for younger workers. Moreover, the exis-

tence of private pensions would lessen the burden on Social Security by ensuring that it would not be the sole source of retirement income.

Employer-provided pensions that meet strict and complex statutory requirements are known as "qualified pension plans." The employer must fund the pensions as they are earned by creating a pension trust, which is operated either by directors appointed by the employer or by the union representing the workers. Each year the employer funds the trust with the actuarial estimate of the pension obligations that the employer has incurred to its employees. The money placed in the trust by the employer may be deducted from the income of the employer for federal income tax purposes. This means that the employer saves the taxes it would otherwise have to pay. However, the funds paid to the pension trust are not subject to income tax, because the trust is a tax exempt entity and pays no income taxes. Nor are the employees taxed, even though it is their efforts that the trust payments reward. The trust invests the proceeds paid to it by the employer. The earnings on these investments—in mortgages, stocks, bonds, and the like—are not taxed since the trust is a tax exempt entity. When the employee retires, the trust will pay to the retiree whatever is called for under the pension plan. These payments are then finally taxed to the employee.

In general, the favorable tax treatment granted to pension plans has not been seriously questioned. Employees favor it, of course, and even employers like it, as pension plans tend to encourage employee loyalty and so reduce employee turnover. However, the favorable tax treatment of pensions is not without its critics. In his article, Professor Halperin asks whether the tax benefits are necessary. That is, would employers offer comparable pension plans without the tax breaks they now enjoy? (Note: When he refers to the "Code," he means the Internal Revenue Code.)

Daniel I. Halperin

Special Tax Treatment for Employer-Based Retirement Programs: Is It "Still" Viable as a Means of Increasing Retirement Income? Should It Continue?

I. Introduction

The Code traditionally has granted preferential treatment for compensation in a form that provides for the security of employees upon retirement and for protection in the

Tax Law Review, Vol. 49, 1–51 (1993). Reprinted by permission.

case of illness or untimely death.[1] In particular, funds set aside for retirement under employer-sponsored "qualified" plans[2]—plans that provide for employees at all income levels and do not discriminate in favor of highly compensated employees[3]—are effectively not subject to tax on investment income.[4] Since these nondiscrimination rules[5] require some level of benefits to be provided to lower income workers,[6] it appears that the requirements of the tax law serve to spread at least some retirement protection to low and moderate income employees who otherwise might not be included in the employer plan.

There are, however, a number of reasons, apart from tax savings, why both employers and employees would prefer that a portion of wages be set aside by the employer to become available to employees only upon retirement; thus, it is unclear to what extent the widespread existence of employer-sponsored retirement plans depends upon the special tax treatment as opposed to being responsive to the desires of both employers and employees independent of tax savings.

In any event, the generous benefits for employer-sponsored plans,[7] as compared to the more limited tax deduction for contributions, at the employee's option, to individual retirement accounts (IRAs)[8] or 401(k) plans[9] suggest a belief that left to their own devices, low and moderate earners will not save enough for retirement. Their savings must be forced by making it a condition to tax benefits for the high earners. Such "paternalism" is perhaps justified because of the perceived inability of individuals to anticipate and accommodate their future needs and because of the failure of Social Security to adequately replace pre-retirement income.[10]

Despite these incentives for coverage, at present employer-sponsored plans fall well short of universal coverage. At any given time over the past several decades, no more than 50 percent of the private workforce participated in employer-sponsored pension or retirement plans.[11] In 1990, 44 percent of persons aged sixty-five and over reported income from a public or private employer plan—57 percent of couples, 41 percent of unmarried men, and 32 percent of unmarried women.[12] It is expected that even twenty or so years from now, only about 70 percent of the retiring workforce will be entitled to a pension,[13] and many fewer will receive an adequate amount.[14] Moreover, those lacking coverage come disproportionately from those who arguably need it the most, the lower paid.[15]

Thus, recent legislation has attempted to require employers who have established plans to cover a greater proportion of their workforce.[16] But there may be limits to how far one can push a voluntary program.[17] No employer is required to have a pension plan. Tax benefits may encourage adoption of a plan that otherwise would not exist, but if the availability of tax benefits depends upon satisfying significant requirements, there may not be enough takers. It may be that the harder we push to ensure that the tax benefits achieve the goal of greater coverage, the less likely it will be that plans will be adopted.

* * *

To summarize, tax incentives traditionally have been provided to encourage employers to offer retirement protection for rank and file employees. These incentives were never fully effective and are likely to have become even less so since rates were reduced. At the same time, as discussed in Section II, nontax reasons supply a strong incentive for employment-based retirement savings.

* * *

II. Why an Employer-Based Retirement Program

Both employers and employees may prefer some set-aside for retirement without regard to any tax advantage. Thus, it is not surprising to find employer-based retirement programs. In fact, because of this preference, employees may be willing to accept an overall pay cut if part of their compensation is deferred, while employers might be willing to pay more. The size of the wedge thereby created may be an important factor in the continued viability of qualified plans.

Employers may hope that the establishment of a pension plan will attract workers with a long-term perspective and both discourage turnover[18] and facilitate retirement of less productive workers. To the extent benefits are not vested,[19] employees will lose out by changing jobs. More significantly, retirement plans of the defined benefit type[20] are "backloaded," in the sense that older employees earn greater amounts. Thus, retirement income is generally a percentage of earnings at the time of retirement or other separation from service (for example, average of the highest three years) multiplied by years of service. If an employee changes jobs, benefits from the first employer will be based upon earnings at the time of separation unadjusted for future real increases in wages or even for inflation.[21] Therefore, even if two employees have identical earnings histories and a fully vested pension for all periods of service, one who has worked thirty years for a single employer will earn a higher pension than one who has changed jobs during the course of her career. Obviously, the establishment of a defined benefit plan discourages job changes.[22]

While employers sometimes seek to reduce turnover, they typically want the less productive workers to retire. Since mandatory retirement generally is prohibited,[23] efforts must be made to ensure voluntary retirement at the appropriate time. Employees are more likely to retire voluntarily when retirement income is "adequate." In addition, employees may earn less than full pay by continuing to work past certain points, because, when they do so, they lose out on retirement benefits. For example, since benefits under a defined benefit plan generally are not actuarially increased to reflect later retirement and a shorter expected payout period, employees who work past normal retirement age, in effect, earn only the amount that their wages exceed the pension they otherwise would receive.[24] A similar reduction in the real wages earned by continuing to work occurs when employers "subsidize" early retirement by reducing the benefits by a lesser amount than would be required to reflect the longer expected payout period. Since continuing to work reduces the value of the pension, an employee who does so earns less than the normal wage rate.

As to employees, there would seem to be at least three advantages to deferred compensation. First, those who fear they lack the discipline to forego excess consumption might prefer forced savings.[25] Second, employer-sponsored plans may earn a higher rate of return from investments due to additional opportunities and to the advantages of professional management and greater ability or willingness to take risks.[26] Since the higher rate of return would enable the employee to reach a targeted level of retirement savings even if a lesser amount were set aside, the employee might have the same amount available for current needs even if overall compensation were reduced.

In a defined contribution plan,[27] where the employer makes a certain contribution and the benefits depend upon the value of the accumulated assets, a higher rate of return directly increases the employee's benefit. In defined benefit plans, the employer would seem to be the beneficiary of a higher rate of return since the contributions required to fund the promised benefit would be reduced. Nevertheless, to the extent the higher rate of return is anticipated in determining the level of contributions and the impact on wages, employees gain in that the portion of their earnings that must be set aside to provide adequate retirement income is reduced.[28]

Finally, an employer plan may provide access to an annuity at group rates. A direct purchase of an annuity would be more expensive because of loading charges and the insurer's expectation of adverse selection.[29] In addition, under a defined benefit plan, the annuity ordinarily would be based on earnings at retirement[30] and thus give the employee assurance of replacement of pre-retirement earnings, which while a likely concern, is very difficult to plan for.[31]

For these reasons, employer-based retirement programs, perhaps, in particular, defined plans, are to be expected without regard to tax advantages.

* * *

Notes

1. Tax-free treatment is given to employer-provided health benefits, IRC §§ 105, 106, and to a limited extent, life insurance, IRC § 79 (exempting from tax the cost of $50,000 of group term life insurance). Although the analysis of this Article in many ways can be applied to health insurance, the two subjects are better considered separately, given the number of recent proposals to expand health coverage. See, e.g., The White House Domestic Policy, Health Security: The President's Report to the American People (1993) (President Clinton's proposal for mandatory coverage); Health Security Act, H.R. 3600, 103d Cong., 1st Sess. (1993); S. 1757, 103d Cong., 1st Sess. (1993); S. 1779, 103d Cong., 1st Sess. (1993).

2. IRC § 401 et seq. For a more detailed discussion of my views on the goals of the special tax treatment of retirement savings, see Daniel Halperin, Tax Reform Act of 1986 and the Equity of the Nation's Retirement System, in 1987 Proceedings of the 80th Ann. Conf. on Tax'n, Nat'l Tax Ass'n 93 [hereinafter Tax Reform Act]; Daniel I. Halperin, Tax Policy and Retirement Income: A Rational Model for the 21st Century, in Search for a National Retirement Income Policy 159 (Jack L. VanDerhei ed., 1987) [hereinafter Tax Policy]; Daniel I. Halperin, Retirement Security and Tax Equity: An Evaluation of ERISA, 17 B.C. Indus. & Com. L. Rev. 739 (1976); Halperin on Tax and Pension Policy, 10 Tax Notes 803 (June 2, 1980) (interview). Among the issues discussed in these articles, which, while still of critical importance, are not discussed herein, is the concern over the potential decline in defined benefit plans and the dissipation of

pension benefits prior to retirement. As to the latter, see Paul Yakoboski, Retirement Program Lump-Sum Distributions: Hundreds of Billions in Hidden Pension Income (Employee Benefit Research Institute Issue Brief No. 146, Feb. 1994).

3. IRC § 401(a)(4). A plan is not qualified unless the percentage of non-highly compensated employees covered is at least 70% of the percentage of highly compensated employees covered, or an average benefit percentage test is satisfied (generally requiring that the average benefit for the non-highly compensated from all employer plans be at least 70% as great as the average benefit for the highly compensated). IRC § 410(b). There are extensive regulations under §§ 401(a)(4) and 410(b) applying the nondiscrimination test. The term "highly compensated employee" is defined in § 414(q). See also Temp. Reg. § 1.414(q)-1T. It includes 5% owners, employees earning in excess of $75,000, the top paid 20% if earning in excess of $50,000 and certain officers earning in excess of $45,000. The $75,000 and $50,000 are inflation adjusted to $99,000 and $66,000, respectively, for 1994. IRS News Release IR 94-3 (Jan. 13, 1994).

4. The advantage of qualified plans sometimes is described in terms of the ability of the employer to claim a deduction at the time of contribution while the employee is not taxed until distribution. I have demonstrated, however, that in terms of present value, the deferred tax on the amount distributed is, assuming no change in marginal rates, equal to the tax that would be imposed if the employee were taxed on the contribution. Again, assuming no change in tax rates, the real advantage is the tax exemption for investment income or the ability to earn a pretax as opposed to a post-tax rate of return. See Daniel I. Halperin, Interest in Disguise: Taxing the "Time Value of Money," 95 Yale L.J. 506, 520–24 (1986) [hereinafter Time Value]. [In the most simple of instances, assume a tax rate of 40% and a pretax rate of return of 10%. If an individual were to pay taxes on $100 when received in Year 1, she would pay $40. If instead she were able to defer the payment of tax for one year, the value of the compensation at the end of Year 2 would be $110. If she were forced to pay taxes on this amount in Year 2, her tax would be $44, or the future value of the original tax payment that would have been made if not for the availability of deferral. For a more detailed discussion, see Halperin, Time Value, at 521–22.]

Some support the favorable tax treatment of retirement plans, which, as noted, amounts to a tax exemption for investment income, because of their belief that an income tax, by lowering the rate of return from investment, discriminates against savings in favor of consumption. For this group, qualified plans receive correct consumption tax treatment and it is the taxation of other investment income that needs to be explained. See, e.g., Richard A. Ippolito, Pensions, Economics and Public Policy 208–09 (1986). I do not find this a satisfactory explanation for a subsidy focused on savings for retirement. If the goal is to increase overall savings, there has to be a better way. The special treatment of employer-sponsored plans should be defended, if at all, on the basis of its contribution to retirement security, not the overall savings level.

5. In recent years, the nondiscrimination test, which has long been applied to retirement plans, Revenue Act of 1942, Pub. L. No. 77-753, § 162, 56 Stat. 798, 862, has been extended to other tax-favored benefits. See IRC § 79(d) (group term life insurance), originally added by Pub. L. No. 97-248, § 244(a), 96 Stat. 324, 523 (1982); IRC § 105(h) (self-insured medical reimbursement plans), originally added by Pub. L. No. 95-600, § 366, 92 Stat. 2763, 2855 (1978); IRC § 120(c)(1) (prepaid legal expenses) (the income exclusion has since expired, IRC § 120(e)), as originally enacted by Pub. L. No. 94-455, § 2134(a), 90 Stat. 1520, 1926 (1976); IRC § 129(d)(2) (dependent care), as originally enacted by Pub. L. No. 97-34, § 124(f)(1), 95 Stat. 172, 198 (1981). Otherwise, it is feared that these benefits would be provided primarily for higher-income employees.

In 1986, Congress attempted to extend the nondiscrimination test to the last remaining holdout, health insurance, and to provide uniform rules for other than retirement benefits, under § 89. Tax Reform Act of 1986, Pub. L. No. 99-514, § 1151, 100 Stat. 2085, 2494. This attempt ended in failure when § 89 was repealed. Pub. L. No. 101–140, § 202, 103 Stat. 830, 830 (1989). That act also restored the previous nondiscrimination tests under §§ 79(d) and 105(h). Id. at 831.

6. Employers might take steps to minimize benefits for lower income employees. For example, in recent years, it has become more common to allocate contributions to defined contribution plans on the basis of age or service as well as compensation, thus benefitting higher income employees, who are bound to be older and have more years of service. The Clinton administration proposes to ban this practice. Retirement Protection Act, H.R. 3396, 103d Cong., 1st Sess. (1993); S. 1780, 103d Cong., 1st Sess. (1993); see also Meegan M. Reilly, PBGC Hopes for Action on Reform Bill in Early 1994, 61 Tax Notes 1487 (Dec. 20, 1993). Benefits also would be lost if the employee leaves before vesting occurs. See note 19.

7. Annual contributions of up to $30,000 per year may be made under defined contribution plans. IRC § 415(c)(1). In the alternative, defined benefit plans may provide for a joint and survivor annuity for employee and spouse, beginning at age 65, of up to $90,000 annually adjusted for inflation ($118,800 in 1994, IRS News Release IR 94-3 (Jan. 13, 1994)). IRC § 415(b)(1)(A), (d)(1)(A). The defined benefit type plan could require much higher contributions for older employees.

8. IRC §§ 219, 408. The maximum contribution is $2,000 per year. IRC § 408(a)(1).

9. Under § 401(k), employees may be given a choice between current compensation and a contribution on their behalf to a deferred compensation arrangement. The maximum contribution on behalf of any employee is now $9,240 for taxable years beginning in 1994. IRS News Release IR 94-3 (Jan. 13, 1994). For a discussion of the rationale behind § 401(k), see Daniel I. Halperin, Cash or Deferred Profit-Sharing Plans & Cafeteria Plans, 41 Inst. on Fed. Tax'n 39 (1983).

10. Social security is most adequate for the lowest paid. For example, it replaces nearly 70% of preretirement income for workers earning one-half of average wages. Henry J. Aaron, Barry P. Bosworth & Gary T. Burtless, Can America Afford to Grow Old? Paying for Social Security 28 (1989).

As to paternalism, some disagree, arguing that people ought to be left alone to make their own mistakes, if indeed they are mistakes. See, e.g., Milton Friedman, Capitalism and Freedom 187–89 (1962). They assert that paternalism cannot be completely successful since those who do not wish to save may be less likely to take jobs that force savings or may use other means, such as expensive borrowing, to maintain a desired pattern of lifetime consumption. See John H. Langbein & Bruce A. Wolk, Pension and Employee Benefits Law 38 (1990). If this view prevails, it suggests to me the elimination of the tax preference, although its supporters presumably would prefer expansion of IRAs. A case for paternalism *and* the expansion of IRAs is found in Deborah M. Weiss, Paternalistic Pension Policy: Psychological Evidence and Economic Theory, 58 U. Chi. L. Rev. 1275 (1991).

11. Estimates of pension coverage differ depending upon the data source and the definition used. For a collection of studies, see U.S. Dep't of Labor, Pension and Welfare Benefits Administration, Pension Coverage Issues for the '90s (Richard P. Hinz, John A. Turner & Phyllis A. Fernandez eds., 1994) [hereinafter Pension Coverage Issues]. One source of data is John R. Woods, Pensions Coverage Among Private Wage and Salary Workers: Preliminary Findings from 1988 Survey of Employee Benefits, Soc. Security Bull., Oct. 1989, at 18. It finds that of the

full-time private wage and salary workers aged 16 and over, the percentage participating in employer plans was 48% in 1972, 50% in 1979, 48% in 1983 and 46% in 1988. Id. tbl. 12; see also Virginia P. Reno, The Role of Pensions in Retirement Income, in Pensions in a Changing Economy 19, 23 (Richard V. Burkhauser & Dallas L. Salisbury eds., 1993) (tbl. 2.8). In 1991, the number was 43.4% of the nonfarm wage and salary workforce. Dallas L. Salisbury, Pensions Tax Expenditures: Are They Worth the Cost? Employee Benefit Research Institute, Issue Brief No. 134, Feb. 1993 at 15, tbl. 8 [hereinafter Expenditures]. The latest data based on the April 1993 Current Population Survey show that 47.1% of all civilian nonfarm wage and salary workers participated in an employer-sponsored plan suggesting that the downward trend in participation may have bottomed out. Paul Yakoboski, Employment-Based Retirement Income Benefits: Analysis of the April 1993 Current Population Survey, Employee Benefit Research Institute, Special Report SR-25 and Issue Brief No. 153, Sept. 1984 at 8, tbl. 2. Pension participation among all workers, including part-time employees, was 46.4% in 1979, 44.2% in 1983 and 43.6% in 1988. Reno, supra, at 23, tbl 2.8.

As a general matter, the participation numbers for those aged under 25 are significantly lower than for other age groups. See Woods, supra, at 10, tbl. 5, 18, tbl. 12; compare id., tbl. 5 (giving figures for workers aged 16 and over) with Paul Yakoboski & Sarah Boyce, Pension Coverage and Participation Growth: A New Look at Primary and Supplemental Plans, Employee Benefit Research Institute, Issue Brief No. 144, Dec. 1993 at 5, tbl. 2 (giving figures for workers aged 25 and over).

12. Reno, note 11, at 19, 20, tbl. 2.1.

13. Of those aged 25–34 in 1979, the estimated percentage of families who will receive benefits at age 65 is 71% for all families, 75% for married couples and 65% for single persons. See Dallas L. Salisbury, What Impact Has ERISA Had on Different Types of Pension Plans? in Senate Special Comm. on Aging, 98th Cong., 2d Sess., Employee Retirement Income Security Act of 1974: The First Decade 107, 122, tbl. 12 (Comm. Print 1984). See also Sylvester J. Schieber & Gordon P. Goodfellow, U.S. Dep't of Labor, Pension Coverage in America: A Glass Two-Thirds Full or One-Third Empty?, in Pension Coverage Issues, note 11, at 125, 135–36 (finding that if the people who had not worked in the previous year and were not already receiving a pension are not counted, among those individuals between 45 and 59 years of age, 70.1% were receiving some form of benefit from the tax preferences favoring pensions in 1990). With respect to married persons, Schieber and Goodfellow maintain that, given the structure of our income tax system, the tax benefits that accrue to one spouse because of pension coverage generally accrue to the other as well. One estimate would place about 67% of couples in 2010 as receiving a pension, in contrast to the 57% for 1990, as noted above. Reno, note 11, at 28–29. Some simulation models suggest higher numbers. Projections for year 2010 show that of those aged 65 and over, 86% of couples, 70% of unmarried men and 50% of unmarried women will receive any pension. The respective numbers for year 2018 are 88%, 73% and 67%; for year 2030, 93%, 85% and 73%. Id. at 29, tbl. 2.15. Such forecasting, however, is complex and uncertain. See id. at 32.

14. According to the Department of Labor, in 1988, the median pension income for single women was $2,153, for single men $3,820, for married women $1,848 and for married men $4,285. Donald L. Bartlett & James B. Steele, The Vanishing Pensions—Will Money Be There When You Retire?, The Seattle Times, Nov. 5, 1991, at A4. For 1990, the average annual pension for a retired federal worker was $12,966, for a retired local or state worker $9,068 and for a private sector worker $6,512. Id.

15. Emily S. Andrews, Pension Policy and Small Employers: At What Price Coverage? 73 (1989) [hereinafter Pension Policy].

16. Halperin, Tax Reform Act, note 2, at 96.

17. While there may be special circumstances that can explain the heated opposition to § 89 (which extended nondiscrimination requirements to health insurance), certain of the events surrounding the legislative battle raise significant doubts concerning the ability of tax incentives to achieve the stated goal of widespread, perhaps close to universal, coverage for low and moderate income employees. See Rosina B. Barker, Lessons from a Legislative Disaster, 47 Tax Notes 843 (May 14, 1990). During the debate, opponents repeatedly stated that if the nondiscrimination requirements had been allowed to continue, many firms, particularly small business, would have made no attempt to prove compliance. Neal Lipshitz, Sec. 89 is Repealed, Nat'l L.J., Dec. 4, 1989, at 5. See also Andrews, Pension Policy, note 15, at 65–87 (discussing establishment of retirement plans by small employers). Rather than increasing coverage of the lower paid, employers would bear the consequences of "discrimination," namely, taxation of the highly compensated employees on the value of health insurance in excess of the maximum permitted benefit. See IRC § 89(a)(1), (b) (before repeal in 1989). Opponents argued it would be cheaper for employers to reimburse highly paid employees for the consequences of such taxation than it would be to bear the cost of compliance. Harry Conaway & Carolyn E. Smith, Policy Background: Section 89 Nondiscrimination Rules, 42 Tax Notes 121, 123 (Jan. 2, 1989); Roy Cordato, The Unhealthy Consequences of Section 89, 42 Tax Notes 119, 120 (Jan. 2, 1989). It may have been implied that by "costs," employers meant the administrative burden of gathering data and establishing conformity with one of the alternative tests of § 89. But costs also included the cost of coverage of employees who previously had opted out of a contributory plan by electing not to make contributions.

18. This is not a concern with unskilled labor. Andrews, Pension Policy, note 15, at 82, 89–92.

19. Tax qualified plans are required to provide fully vested benefits after no longer than seven years of service. IRC § 411(a)(2)(B). Most often plans provide no vesting for five years and full vesting after that. IRC § 411(a)(2)(A). So-called "top-heavy plans" (plans most of whose benefits accrue to "key employees" as defined under § 416(i)(1), see IRC § 416(g)), are subject to slightly more stringent rules. IRC § 416(b). Similar rules apply to nonqualified plans under the Employee Retirement Security Act of 1974, Pub. L. No. 93-406, 88 Stat. 829 ("ERISA"), but there is an exception for *unfunded* plans primarily for a select group of management or highly compensated employees. See ERISA § 201(2) ("top hat plans").

20. Retirement plans fit into two principal categories:

(1) defined contribution plans, under which an employer sets aside a certain percentage of pay and the benefit explicitly depends upon investment performance, ERISA § 3(34); and

(2) defined benefit plans, under which an employer promises a specific benefit, for example, 1% of pay per year of service, and makes whatever contributions are necessary to fund the benefit, ERISA § 3(35).

21. See Zvi Bodie, Pensions as Retirement Income Insurance, XXVIII J. Econ. Lit. 28, 31–33 (1990); Halperin, Tax Policy, note 2, at 185–86.

22. Andrews suggests that employees in these circumstances have much to lose if fired and therefore are less likely to shirk responsibilities. Small firms who are able to monitor workers more closely may not gain as much from this situation. Andrews, Pension Policy, note 15, at 54. It seems at least theoretically possible to accomplish the same result by structuring the

pattern of wages to provide significantly higher pay to long-term employees. Employers apparently find this less acceptable. Could it be because employees do not fully appreciate the potential cost of an early separation when it is encompassed in a defined benefit plan?

23. Age Discrimination in Employment Act, 29 U.S.C. §§ 623, 631 (Supp. III 1987) (prohibition of age discrimination applicable to individuals 40 and older). Older workers may be more expensive to retain because of the additional cost of medical insurance.

24. "Current wages" would include any additional pension earned by the increased period of service. Payment of pension benefits, however, must begin by about age 70½ regardless of retirement. IRC § 401(a)(9).

25. Olivia S. Mitchell, The Effects of Mandating Benefits Packages 2–3 (National Bureau of Economic Research Working Paper No. 3260, 1990).

26. Andrews, Pension Policy, note 15, at 84. The increasing trend in defined contribution plans to give employees control over investments has apparently led to excessive caution and low rates of return. Leslie Wayne, Pension Changes Raising Concerns, N.Y. Times, Aug. 29, 1994, at A1, D3.

27. [This is not a concern with unskilled labor. Andrews, Pension Policy, note 15, at 82, 89–92.]

28. Bodie suggests that employers do not attempt to maximize the investment return from a defined benefit plan. He postulates that rather than considering these funds as equivalent to corporate assets, they view defined benefit plans as essentially participating annuities with a guaranteed minimum rate of return. Whether or not the minimum is achieved, promised benefits will be paid. If the minimum is exceeded, benefits will be improved. This suggests that a relatively conservative rate of return will be assumed and that since the employer has no upside potential, it will invest so as to protect against its downside risk. [See Zvi Bodie, Pensions as Retirement Income Insurance, XXVIII J. Econ. Lit. 28, 31–33 (1990).]

On the other hand, during the debate over the right to assets when, upon plan termination, assets exceed the amount necessary to provide for accrued benefits, employers have asserted that they bear the investment risk and therefore should be entitled to all investment gains. Norman P. Stein, Reversions from Pension Plans: History, Policies and Prospects, 44 Tax L. Rev. 259, 316 (1989). It would seem this is not the case if the rate of return implicit in the salary adjustment is less than the expected rate of return (which is true if Bodie is correct about the nature of the arrangement as a participating annuity).

29. Andrews, Pension Policy, note 15, at 83; [Zvi Bodie, Pensions as Retirement Income Insurance, XXVIII J. Econ. Lit. 28, 31–33 (1990)]. If a plan allows employees to elect to receive a lump sum in lieu of an annuity, particularly if the employer purchases annuity contracts on an individual basis, it may not be able to purchase them at a cheaper rate.

30. The most common practice is to base the pension on the average over the five years that the employee's earnings are the highest. [See Zvi Bodie, *Pensions as Retirement Income Insurance,* XXVIII J. Econ. Lit. 28, 31–33 (1990).] A sensible practice under a defined contribution plan would be to base the contribution on the amount necessary to achieve a given level of income replacement under reasonable assumptions as to salary changes and plan earnings. Employers perhaps should be required to inform employees as to the target and provide updates as to the extent the assumptions have been realized.

31. See id. at 33. This seems particularly true since the difficulty of predicting future inflation would make it hard for an employee to determine what she would view as an adequate retirement income. One reason for employees' preference for defined contribution plans may be that among a given cohort of employees who start at the same level but progress unevenly,

under a defined contribution plan, retirement income would be closer together than under a defined benefit plan where it would fully reflect final pay. Thus, the employee diversifies her risk by making the pension "investment" less closely tied to achievement of expected salary increases. See Zvi Bodie, Alan J. Marcus & Robert C. Merton, Defined Benefit Versus Defined Contribution Pension Plans: What are the Real Tradeoffs? 12–13 (National Bureau of Economic Research Working Paper No. 1719, 1985). I am not persuaded this is a reasonable description of human behavior, but, in any event, it ignores the employer's ability to take account of the type of retirement plan in setting wage levels.

CHAPTER 10

Social Security

For many, old age is synonymous with the federal Social Security program. Created in 1935 during the Great Depression, Social Security—officially titled Old Age, Survivors and Disability Insurance—has been the single most popular and successful governmental aid program. The following material from the Social Security Bulletin describes its history.

Social Security Bulletin 1991

Section I: Social Insurance Programs

By the mid-1920s, both the states and the federal government had begun to recognize that certain risks in an increasingly industrialized nation could best be met through the application of social insurance principles. In social insurance programs, certain risks—injury, disability, unemployment, old age, and death—are pooled; premiums, or contributions, are paid by employees and employers; and benefits are paid as an earned right, without regard to a beneficiary's resources other than his or her earnings. In the United States, as in most industrialized countries throughout the world, social insurance began with workers' compensation (or industrial accident insurance). A federal law covering the federal government's civilian employees engaged in hazardous jobs was enacted in 1908, and the first state compensation law to be held constitutional was enacted in 1911. By 1929, workers' compensation laws were in effect in all but four states. These laws made industry responsible for the costs of compensating workers or their survivors when the worker was injured or killed in connection with his or her job.

54 *Social Security Bulletin* 5 (September 1991).

The severe depression of the 1930s dramatized the fact that many American workers were now almost totally dependent on factors beyond individual control for their economic security. Previous methods used to meet the economic risks of unemployment, old age, death, and disability no longer provided adequate or guaranteed security in the face of nationwide economic disaster.

Federal action became a necessity, as neither the states, local communities, nor privately organized charities had the financial resources to cope with the growing needs of citizens. Beginning in 1932, the federal government instituted programs of direct relief and work relief. In January 1935, President Franklin D. Roosevelt proposed to Congress long-range economic security recommendations embodied in the report of a specially created, cabinet-level Committee on Economic Security. The introduction of identical legislation in the House and Senate was followed by passage of the Social Security Act, which was signed into law on August 14, 1935.

The 1935 law established two social insurance programs on a national scale to help meet the risks of old age and unemployment: A federal system of old-age benefits for retired workers who had been employed in commerce or industry and a federal-state system of unemployment insurance. The choice of old age and unemployment as the risks to be covered by social insurance was a natural development, resulting from the Great Depression that had wiped out much of the lifetime savings of the aged and had reduced the opportunities for gainful employment.

Title II of the Social Security Act created an Old Age Reserve Account and authorized payments of old-age benefits from this account to eligible individuals upon attainment of age sixty-five or on January 1, 1942, whichever was later. The monthly benefit was to be determined by the total amount of wages earned in covered employment after 1936 and before age sixty-five. The initial benefit formula was designed to give greater weight to the earnings of lower-paid workers and persons already middle-aged or older. The minimum monthly benefit was $10 and the maximum was $85.

Benefits were to be financed by payroll taxes imposed on covered employers and employees in equal shares under Title VIII of the act. The first $3,000 of annual salary from one employer was taxable and considered as counting toward the total of annual wages on which benefits would be computed. While this amount covered the total earnings of 97 percent of those in the labor force, only 56 percent were actually covered by the new program. Although all wage and salary workers in commerce and industry were covered, many individuals—such as self-employed persons, agricultural and domestic service workers, casual laborers, and employees of nonprofit organizations—were not. Railroad workers were excluded from Title II coverage by the Railroad Retirement Act of 1935.

As discussed in detail below, the Social Security Act of 1935 was significantly amended in 1939. Among the revisions enacted that year was the extension of protection to a worker's dependents and survivors. In 1956, the scope of the program was broadened through the addition of the Disability Insurance program. Initially, benefits were provided for severely disabled workers aged fifty to sixty-four and for adults disabled before the age of eighteen who were children of deceased or retired workers.

* * *

Origins and Development of OASDI

Background. The Social Security program has been shaped by both long-standing traditions and changing economic and social conditions. It was enacted in 1935, at the height of the Great Depression. Because American society had changed from primarily agricultural to primarily industrial and urban, many families were devastated by the loss of cash wages that accompanied the widespread unemployment of that era. For vast numbers of the aged and those nearing old age, the loss of savings brought with it the prospect of living their remaining years in destitution.

During the worst years of the Depression, many old persons were literally penniless. In fact, less than ten percent of the aged left estates large enough to be probated at the time of their death. The "poor houses" and other public and private relief efforts of the time were totally inadequate to respond to the needs of the elderly. Although by 1934 thirty states had enacted laws providing pensions for the needy aged, total expenditures for State programs for some 180,000 needy aged that year amounted to only $31 million. Many needy older persons were not served by such programs, and the waiting lists were long. As the Depression worsened, benefits to individuals were cut to enable states to spread limited funds among as many individuals as possible.

Meanwhile, both the states and the federal government had begun to recognize that in such an increasingly industrialized country, workers and their dependents could be protected effectively from certain economic risks through social insurance.

* * *

Major milestones. Under the 1935 law, workers in commerce and industry would earn retirement benefits through work in jobs covered by the system. Benefits were to be financed by a payroll tax paid by employees and their employers on wage and salary earnings up to $3,000 per year (the wage base). Monthly benefits would be payable at age sixty-five to workers with a specified minimum amount of cumulative wages in covered jobs. The amount of benefits payable also varied with the worker's cumulative earnings in covered jobs. Individuals who continued to work beyond age sixty-five would not be eligible for benefits until their earnings ceased. Lump sum refunds, in amounts somewhat larger than the total taxes paid by the deceased workers, were to be paid to the estates of workers who died before reaching age sixty-five or before receiving benefits. Collection of taxes was scheduled to begin in 1937, but monthly benefits would not be payable until 1942.

Before the old-age insurance program was actually in full operation, important changes were adopted based largely on the recommendations of the first Advisory Council on Social Security. In 1939, Congress significantly expanded the old-age insurance program by extending monthly benefits to workers' dependents and survivors. Also, the basis for computing benefits was changed from cumulative lifetime earnings after 1936 to average monthly earnings in covered work, making it possible to pay reasonably adequate benefits to many workers then approaching retirement age and to their dependents. The 1939 law also established the concept of "quarter of coverage" as the basis for measuring if an individual had sufficient covered employment to qualify for a benefit. Also, individuals who continued to work after age sixty-five could receive full benefits as long as their earnings did not exceed a specified amount. The 1939 amendments made monthly benefits first payable in 1940, instead of 1942 as originally planned.

No major changes were made in the program from 1940 until 1950, when benefit levels were raised substantially, the wage base was increased, and a new schedule of gradually increasing tax rates was provided in the law. Coverage was broadened to include many jobs that previously had been excluded—in some cases because experience was needed to work out procedures for reporting the earnings and collecting the taxes of persons in certain occupational groups. Among the groups covered by the 1950 amendments were regularly employed farm and household employees and self-employed persons other than farmers and professional people. Coverage was made available on a group voluntary basis to employees of state and local governments not under public employee retirement systems and to employees of nonprofit organizations.

In 1950, when coverage under the program was extended, the law was amended to allow a worker's average monthly earnings to be figured on the basis of his or her earnings after 1950. Similar consideration was given to the groups newly covered by the program in 1954 and 1956 (including members of the Armed Forces, most self-employed professional persons, and state and local government employees under a retirement system under certain conditions) by providing that the five years of lowest earnings would be dropped from the computation of average earnings. To assure that persons already covered by the program would not be treated less favorably than the newly covered groups, these special provisions were made available to all persons who worked in covered employment after 1950, regardless of when their jobs were first covered. Similarly, insured status requirements were modified to relate the amount of work required to the time a worker could have been expected to have worked after 1950; further liberalization of the work requirements (on a short-term basis) accompanied the extensions of coverage under the 1954 and 1956 amendments.

* * *

Also during this period, further refinements were made in the benefit and financing provisions of the Old Age and Survivors Insurance program (OASI). The age of first eligibility for retirement benefits was lowered from sixty-five to sixty-two for women in 1956 and for men in 1961—benefits claimed before age sixty-five are reduced to take into account the longer period over which they will be paid. Additional categories of dependent and survivor benefits were added throughout the 1950s and 1960s. Gradually, the conditions for receipt of such benefits were modified so that additional persons were eligible and dependents and survivors of female workers could qualify under more nearly the same circumstances as those of male workers. Also, the earnings test—the provision that limited the amount of benefits payable to persons with substantial earnings—was modified to take into account persons with noncovered earnings or income from self-employment. From time to time throughout this period, general benefit levels were increased to adjust for rising prices, and the tax rates and the applicable wage base were raised.

By 1972, however, concern was expressed that beneficiaries continued to be vulnerable to substantial declines in purchasing power between benefit adjustments. In 1972, Congress enacted a 20 percent benefit increase—which provided a real increase in the purchasing power of benefits—and provided for future annual automatic cost-of-living benefit increases equivalent to the increase in the Consumer Price Index (CPI) whenever the CPI had increased by at least 3 percent. The wage base and the maximum amount a beneficiary could earn before experiencing a reduction in his or her benefits (the earnings test exempt amount) would also be subject to automatic increases based on increases in average wages in the economy. The 1972 amendments also created the delayed retirement credit, under which initial benefit amounts are increased for those who delay their entitlement or continue to have earnings above the amount exempted under the retirement test after they reach normal retirement age (currently age sixty-five).

* * *

In the late 1970s and early 1980s, benefit costs were driven up rapidly by inflation while slow growth in wages and high unemployment held down payroll tax income to the system. The resulting short-term financing crisis, along with growing awareness of a long-run problem caused primarily by declining birth rates and increasing life expectancy, led to the formation of a National Commission on Social Security Reform in late 1981. Based on the recommendations of this bipartisan commission, the 1983 Amendments to the Social Security Act included a number of changes to increase program revenues: The effective dates for scheduled tax rate increases in prior law for employees and employers were advanced, self-employment tax rates were permanently increased, and up to one-half of benefits to certain upper-income beneficiaries were included in taxable income. Resulting revenues are appropriated to the OASI and DI trust funds. In addition, coverage was expanded to include federal civilian employees hired after December 31, 1983, and all employees of nonprofit organizations (on a mandatory basis). To address the long-term outlook of the system, Congress approved a gradual increase in the age of eligibility for full benefits from sixty-five to sixty-six for workers reaching age sixty-two in 2000 to 2005, and from sixty-six to sixty-seven for workers reaching age sixty-two in 2017 to 2022. Actuarially reduced benefits will continue to be available at age sixty-two, but with a greater reduction than under previous law.

* * *

In 1986, Congress eliminated the requirement that the CPI had to rise by at least 3 percent before a cost-of-living benefit increase would take effect. Under the 1986 law, any rise in the CPI in the preceding twelve-month measurement period calls for an equivalent percentage increase in benefits, applicable to persons eligible for benefits.

* * *

Program Principles

Certain basic principles have been adhered to throughout the development of the OASDI program.

Work related. Economic security for the worker and his or her family grows out of the individual's own work history. A worker's entitlement to benefits is based on past employment, and the amount of cash benefits the worker and his or her family will receive is related to earnings in covered work. In general, the higher the worker's average amount of taxable earnings, the greater the protection.

No means test. Benefits are an insured worker's earned right and are paid regardless of income from savings, pensions, private insurance, or other forms of nonwork income. A worker knows beforehand that he or she will not have to prove the existence of need to receive benefits. The absence of a means test, in turn, encourages the building of additional protection for the worker and his or her family on the foundation that Social Security benefits provide.

Contributory. The concept of an earned right is reinforced by the fact that workers pay earmarked Social Security taxes to help finance current benefits. The contributory nature of the program encourages a responsible attitude toward it. Knowing that the financing of the present program and any improvements made in it depend on Social Security taxes that he or she helps to pay, the worker has a vested interest in the soundness of the program.

Universal compulsory coverage. Another important principle is that, with minor exceptions, coverage is universal and compulsory. As in private insurance systems, spreading the insured risks among the broadest possible group helps to stabilize the cost of the protection for each participant by making the probability of random fluctuations in insured risks smaller. In addition, nearly universal coverage is desirable for a social insurance system because it assures virtually everyone in society a base of economic security.

Rights defined in the law. An additional principle is that a person's rights to Social Security benefits—how much he or she gets and under what conditions—are clearly defined in the law and are generally related to facts that can be objectively determined. The area of administrative discretion is thus severely limited. A person who meets the conditions in the law must be paid. If a claimant disagrees with a decision, he or she may appeal to the courts after all administrative appeals have been exhausted.

* * *

Although Social Security is not without its critics, it enjoys broad public support. William Dauster explains that the program's popularity arises out of its alleviation of poverty among the elderly.

William G. Dauster

Protecting Social Security and Medicare

* * *

I. Historical Origins[1]

A. Social Security

When the Great Depression swept America, from 1929 to the beginning of 1933, the nation's economy declined by nearly nine percent per year.[2] In those four years, per capita personal income fell from $705 to $374 (in 1970 dollars).[3] In 1933, one full quarter of the labor force could not find a job.[4] Americans began to look to the federal government to play a greater role in the economy.

At this economic abyss, Franklin Roosevelt became president, promising "a New Deal for the American people."[5] President Roosevelt chose Labor Secretary Frances Perkins to head the Committee on Economic Security, which recommended the creation of the old-age social insurance program that became Social Security.[6] In January 1935, President Roosevelt presented the plan to Congress as part of a larger social welfare measure, and Congress responded with the Social Security Act of 1935.[7]

B. Medicare

In the decade following the enactment of Social Security, liberals called unsuccessfully for national health insurance.[8] President Harry Truman repeatedly advocated national health insurance funded through payroll deductions, but his efforts were unsuccessful.[9] In 1951, planners at the Federal Security Agency, the predecessor of the Department of Health and Human Services, explored the idea of extending health insurance to retired persons, who had particular difficulty obtaining insurance in the private sector, and the idea slowly gained popularity in the 1950s.[10]

Senator John Kennedy raised health care as a campaign issue in the 1960 presidential campaign. Assuming the presidency after President Kennedy's assassination,

Harvard Journal on Legislation, Vol. 33, 461 (1996). Reprinted by permission.

President Lyndon Johnson spoke of moving "not only toward the rich society and the powerful society, but upward to the Great Society."[11] In July 1965, at the height of legislative action on President Johnson's Great Society, Congress enacted Medicare into law in the Health Insurance for the Aged Act.[12] When President Johnson signed the bill in Independence, Missouri, former President Truman told President Johnson, "You have made me a very, very happy man."[13]

C. Social Insurance

Congress created both Social Security and Medicare as social insurance programs.[14] Congress intended that they operate as earned benefits, not as welfare.

* * *

II. Results of Medicare and Social Security

A. Populations Served

Social Security and Medicare serve an enormous number of people. Social Security pays monthly benefits to 43 million persons.[15] Medicare covers about 32 million seniors—virtually everyone age sixty-five or older[16]—and 4 million disabled enrollees for hospital and related care (under the Hospital Insurance program).[17] It covers nearly as many people for doctors' services, outpatient hospital services, and other medical expenses (under the Supplementary Medical Insurance program).[18] Roughly 140 million workers—96 percent of the nation's workforce[19] and 54 percent of all Americans[20]—pay Social Security and Medicare payroll taxes to support the programs and stand to benefit from the programs as they grow older.[21]

B. Poverty

Social Security and Medicare have successfully reduced poverty among seniors. More than one-third of seniors lived in poverty as recently as 1959.[22] After the enactment of Medicare in 1965 and its implementation in 1966, poverty among seniors declined dramatically (see Figure 1).[23] The poverty rate for seniors dropped 4.5 percent in 1968 alone, and since 1984, has remained stable between 11 and 13 percent, a mere third of its 1959 level.

While it is true that poverty in the population as a whole declined in the 1960s and early 1970s, it did not decline nearly as quickly as it did among seniors. In 1982, the poverty rate for seniors fell below that for the population as a whole, and it has remained there. In contrast, the poverty rate for the population as a whole rose by four percentage points between 1973 and 1993. After hitting a low of 11 percent in the 1970s, the rate remained about 13 percent in every year but one since 1980, and it stood at roughly 15 percent in 1992 and 1993.[24]

Despite progress on poverty among seniors, they are by no means an affluent

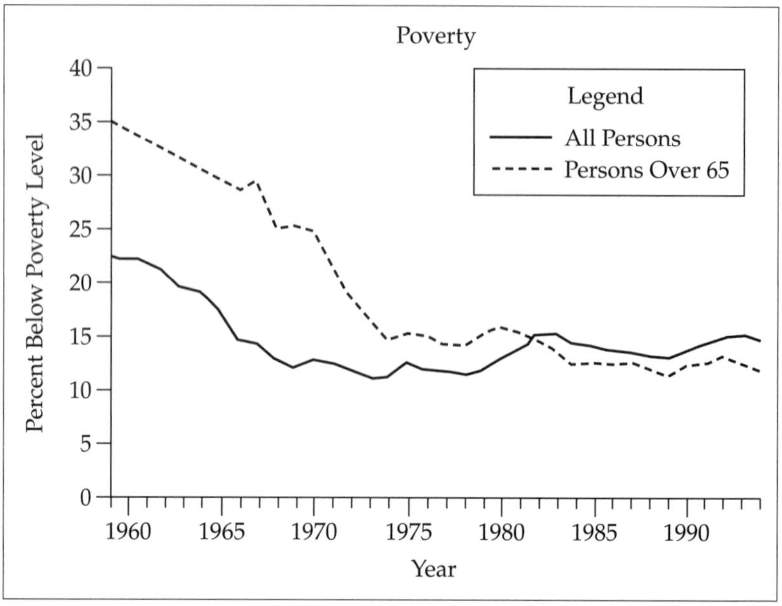

FIGURE 1

group. Nearly six out of ten seniors rely on Social Security for most of their income.[25] Practically one-third of seniors rely on Social Security for 80 percent or more of their income.[26] Most Social Security recipients have incomes from other sources of less than $6,000 per year.[27] Fully two-thirds of all Social Security beneficiaries have non-Social Security incomes below $10,000 per year.[28] Similarly, three-quarters of Medicare beneficiaries have total annual incomes below $25,000.[29] Thus, a vast segment of America's seniors need Social Security and Medicare to remain above the poverty level. Without Social Security, most seniors would fall below the poverty level today.[30]

* * *

IV. Budgetary Realities

A. Share of the Budget

When asked why he robbed banks, the bank robber Willie Sutton replied, "Because that's where the money is."[31] Sutton's Law explains why conversations about reducing the federal budget deficit often turn to Social Security and Medicare.[32] Social Security has become the federal government's largest mandatory spending program, projected to amount to over a third of a trillion dollars today and half a trillion by 2003.[33] Medicare requires roughly $200 billion per year today and at current growth rates will cost more than a third of a trillion dollars in 2002.[34]

Together Social Security and Medicare compose more than one-third of all federal spending and three-fifths of all entitlement spending.[35] Social Security accounts for

22 percent of federal spending and 39 percent of entitlement spending. Medicare constitutes 12 percent of federal spending and 22 percent of entitlement spending.[36]

The Congressional Budget Office (CBO) projects that the federal government's two major health care programs, Medicare and Medicaid (which provides mostly long-term health care to low-income individuals), will grow at a rate of about 10 percent per year over the next ten years.[37] This growth rate is significantly faster than other large components of the federal budget.[38] If these projections hold true, by 2001 Medicare will exceed spending on the military, becoming the second-largest program in the government.[39] By 2002, Medicare will take a larger share of the federal budget than all domestic discretionary programs funded in annual appropriation acts.[40] By 2002, Medicare will surpass net interest expenditures to finance the government debt.[41] And by 2005, Medicare spending will grow to twice its present level.[42]

* * *

Since 1981, Social Security spending has stabilized at a little less than five percent of the economy, and the CBO projects that this spending will grow at roughly the same rate as projected economic growth over the next decade. In contrast, the CBO expects Medicare to grow significantly faster than the economy as a whole.[43] Growth in Medicare and Medicaid essentially explains the projected growth in the size of the federal government over the next decade.

* * *

That the government devotes a greater share of its resources to Medicare and Social Security is not necessarily bad. The United States could rationally choose to devote a greater share of its resources to the health and well-being of its seniors. As discussed above, these programs are both successful and popular. Seniors have contributed to the economy throughout their lives, and have contributed through their payroll taxes to the Social Security and Medicare systems. By and large they are not affluent recipients, and can use the support.[44] On the other hand, the levels of growth projected for Medicare cannot go on forever, and as the economist Herbert Stein notes, if something is unsustainable, it tends to stop.[45]

* * *

C. Social Security

Are Social Security and Medicare part of the deficit problem? One can best understand the relationship of Social Security to the budget deficit by dividing the program's history into three time periods: before the Social Security Amendments of 1983,[46] between the 1983 amendments and 2020, and the long run thereafter. Each period presents a distinct picture of how Social Security contributes to the budget deficit.

1. Prior to the 1983 Amendments Before the Social Security Amendments of 1983, Social Security functioned on a pay-as-you-go basis. Revenues coming into the fund roughly matched expenditures from the fund.[47] The system accumulated relatively few assets in preparation for future retirees. Often through ad hoc legislative changes,

Congress increased benefit levels at roughly the rate necessary to keep pace with the growing income to the system from rising wages.[48]

During this nearly fifty-year period, Social Security never ran an annual surplus greater than $6 billion nor a deficit greater than $8 billion.[49] For its first twenty-five years of operation, through 1961, Social Security ran small annual surpluses averaging about $1 billion per year.[50] Between 1967 and 1975, the system generated slightly larger surpluses, averaging around $3 billion.[51] The Social Security Amendments of 1972[52] liberalized the program and instituted the Nixon administration's proposal to pay automatic cost-of-living adjustments, or "COLAs." Consequently, from 1976 through 1982, Social Security ran deficits averaging a little more than $3.5 billion per year, as price inflation outpaced wage growth.[53] Thus, before the Social Security Amendments of 1983, Social Security had a relatively negligible effect on the total surplus or deficit of the federal government.

2. Between the 1983 Amendments and 2020 The inflation of the late 1970s and early 1980s drew down the assets (or "reserves") of the system, and when the recession of 1981 struck, headlines began to warn of the impending bankruptcy of Social Security.[54] Meeting in 1982 and 1983, the bipartisan National Commission on Social Security Reform made recommendations that Congress enacted into the Social Security Amendments of 1983.[55] These amendments raised the retirement age through 2027, delayed or reduced COLAs, and instituted a program of payroll tax increases, all to help ensure the solvency of the system for the retirement of the baby boom generation. The 1983 amendments fundamentally changed the relationship of the trust fund to the budget. Beginning in 1984, the Social Security Trust Fund ran a surplus. According to projections, the trust fund should run surpluses through 2021[56] (see Figure 2).[57]

The National Commission and the 1983 amendments ensured that the Social Security system would take in substantially more revenue, in the form of payroll taxes, than it needed to expend for benefits.[58] In five of the years since 1983, the annual surpluses in the Social Security Fund have exceeded $50 billion.[59] The fund's trustees predict that these surpluses will reach $164 billion in 2011, and will continue through 2019.[60] These surpluses are valuable because they increase national saving. They decrease the demand for money, lower interest rates, and thus spur growth-producing investment. The desire to protect these surpluses has driven much of the debate over Social Security since the 1983 amendments.

Unfortunately, the effects of large deficits in the rest of the federal budget have overwhelmed the benefits from the Social Security surpluses. For most of the post–World War II era, the federal government conducted its entire budget roughly on a pay-as-you-go basis.[61] Beginning in the mid-1970s and expanding in the Reagan administration, however, the federal government ran substantial budget deficits in the non–Social Security programs.[62] These budget deficits have far outweighed the surpluses generated by the Social Security Trust Fund.[63]

* * *

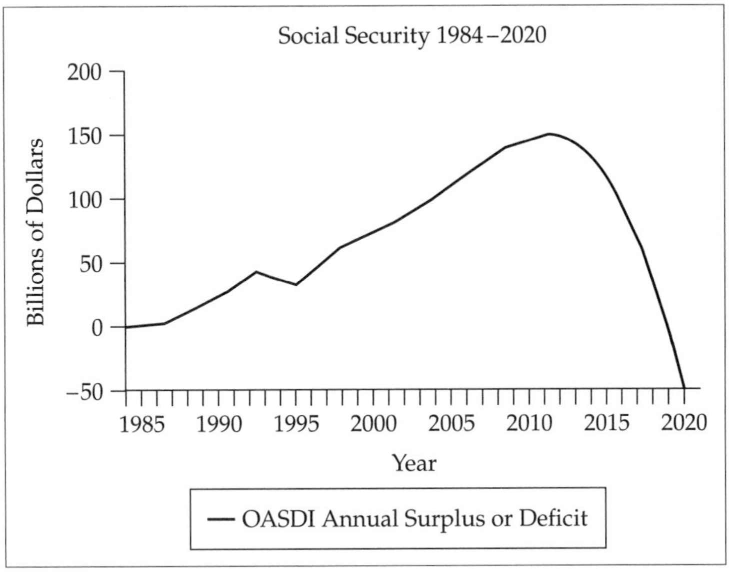

FIGURE 2

The availability of the Social Security surpluses makes the unified budget deficit smaller than it otherwise would be. Thus, some accuse policy makers of using Social Security surpluses to hide the true size of the budget deficit.

The Social Security Trust Fund surpluses must by law be invested in United States government securities.[64] Thus, the Trust Fund loans the United States government money. Some have characterized this borrowing from the Social Security Trust Fund as improper, and some even describe it as "embezzlement."[65] Such characterizations are exaggerations at best, as the reserves of the Social Security Trust Fund are invested in the safest possible investment—United States government securities—and are backed by the full faith and credit of the United States. One would find it hard to imagine how the reserves could be more safely housed.

Investing surpluses in United States Treasury securities also means that the treasury need not borrow as much money from the public to finance the government's unified budget deficit. Running on-budget deficits that far exceed the Social Security surpluses, however, undermines the benefits of national saving sought in the 1983 amendments. Thus, the first step the government must take to protect the Social Security Trust Fund is to reduce on-budget deficits.

3. 2020 and Beyond

* * *

Beginning in 2019, the Social Security Trust Fund will stop running surpluses. Social Security's reserves, its accumulated surpluses, will then begin to decline as the fund begins to pay out more than it brings in, and the trustees project that the assets of the fund will be exhausted in 2031. The trustees state in their 1995 report:

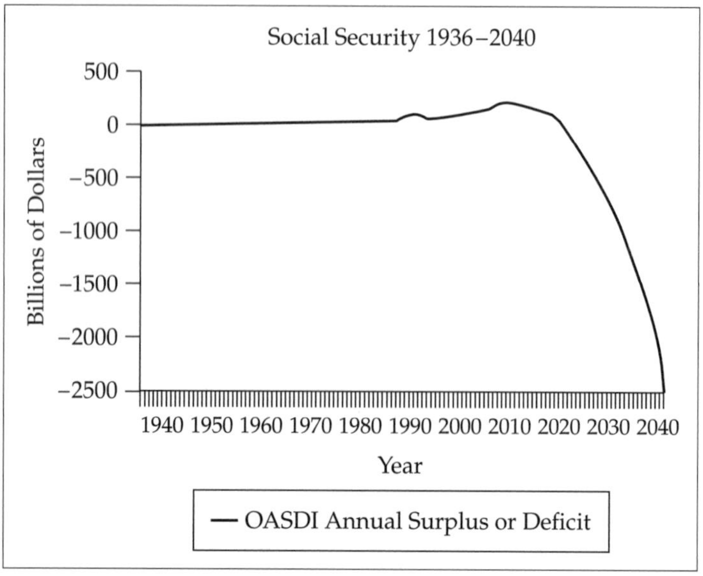

FIGURE 3

> The Federal Old Age and Survivors Insurance (OASI) Trust Fund, which pays retirement benefits, will be able to pay benefits for about thirty-six years. The board believes that the long-range deficit of the OASI Trust Fund should be addressed. The Advisory Council on Social Security is currently studying the financing of the program and is expected to recommend later this year ways to achieve long-range actuarial balance in the OASI fund.[66]

The retirement of the baby boom generation will cause the Social Security Trust Fund to run increasingly large annual deficits. As Figure 3[67] shows, beginning in 2020, the deficits in the trust fund will quickly dwarf the reserves that it will have taken the fund more than thirty-five years to accumulate.

The trustees of the fund predict that these deficits will persist. To remain in actuarial balance, the Social Security Trust Fund requires significant changes in the long run. The good news is that we have time to phase in these changes gradually, if we act now.

* * *

Notes

1. For discussions of the historical origins of Social Security and Medicare, see, e.g., ERIC R. KINGSON & EDWARD D. BERKOWITZ, SOCIAL SECURITY AND MEDICARE: A POLICY PRIMER 27–52 (1993); Ted Marmor & Julie Beglin, *Medicare and How It Grew—To Be Confused and Misjudged*, BOSTON GLOBE, May 7, 1995, at 73.

2. BUREAU OF THE CENSUS, U.S. DEP'T OF COMMERCE, HISTORICAL STATISTICS OF THE UNITED STATES, COLONIAL TIMES TO 1970, pt. 1, 226 (1975) (ser. F 31) (noting 8.6% average annual growth rates in gross national product).

3. *Id.* at 225 (ser. F 17–30).

4. *Id.* at 135 (ser. D 85–86) (reporting that 24.9% of the civilian labor force was unemployed).

5. Franklin D. Roosevelt, Speech Accepting the Democratic Nomination for President in

Chicago (July 2, 1932), *in* SPEECHES OF THE AMERICAN PRESIDENTS, at 481 (Janet Podell & Steven Anzovin eds., 1988).

6. *See* KINGSON & BERKOWITZ, *supra* note 1, at 30, 32–34.

7. Ch. 531, 49 Stat. 620 (1935) (codified as amended at 42 U.S.C. §§ 301–1397e (1994)).

8. *See* Marmor & Beglin, *supra* note 1, at 74.

9. *See* DAVID MCCULLOUGH, TRUMAN 473–74, 476, 532, 586, 628, 915 (1992).

10. *See* KINGSON & BERKOWITZ, *supra* note 1, at 44.

11. Lyndon B. Johnson, Address at the University of Michigan (May 22, 1964), *in* THE PENGUIN BOOK OF TWENTIETH-CENTURY SPEECHES, at 346 (Brian MacArthur ed., 1992).

12. Pub. L. No. 89-97, tit. I, 79 Stat. 290 (1965) (codified as amended in scattered sections of 26, 42, and 45 U.S.C. (1994)).

13. MCCULLOUGH, *supra* note 9, at 984.

14. For a discussion of the social insurance approach, see KINGSON & BERKOWITZ, *supra* note 1, at 13–25.

15. BOARD OF TRUSTEES, FEDERAL OLD-AGE AND SURVIVORS INS. AND DISABILITY INS. TRUST FUNDS, 1995 ANNUAL REPORT OF THE BOARD OF TRUSTEES OF THE FEDERAL OLD-AGE AND SURVIVORS INSURANCE AND DISABILITY INSURANCE TRUST FUNDS, H.R. Doc. No. 57, 104th Cong., 1st Sess. 3 (1995) [hereinafter OASDI TRUSTEES' REPORT] (year-end 1994 data).

16. *See* BUREAU OF THE CENSUS, U.S. DEP'T OF COMMERCE, STATISTICAL ABSTRACT OF THE UNITED STATES: 1994, at 16 (1994) [hereinafter 1994 STATISTICAL ABSTRACT] (table no. 16) (middle series projection of 1994 population over 65 years old of 33,170,000).

17. BOARD OF TRUSTEES, FEDERAL HOSPITAL INS. TRUST FUND, THE 1995 ANNUAL REPORT OF THE BOARD OF TRUSTEES OF THE FEDERAL HOSPITAL INSURANCE TRUST FUND, H.R. Doc. No. 56, 104th Cong., 1st Sess. 1 (1995) [hereinafter HI TRUSTEES' REPORT] (1994 data).

18. BOARD OF TRUSTEES, FEDERAL SUPPLEMENTARY MEDICAL INS. TRUST FUND, THE 1995 ANNUAL REPORT OF THE BOARD OF TRUSTEES OF THE FEDERAL SUPPLEMENTARY MEDICAL INSURANCE TRUST FUND, H.R. Doc. No. 55, 104th Cong., 1st Sess. 1 (1995) [hereinafter SMI TRUSTEES' REPORT] (1994 data).

19. *See* STAFF OF HOUSE COMM. ON WAYS AND MEANS, 103D CONG., 2D SESS., OVERVIEW OF ENTITLEMENT PROGRAMS: 1994 GREEN BOOK 3 (Comm. Print 1994) [hereinafter GREEN BOOK].

20. *See* 1994 STATISTICAL ABSTRACT, *supra* note 16, at 9 (table no. 3) (middle series projection of 1994 U.S. population of 260,711,000).

21. OASDI TRUSTEES' REPORT, *supra* note 15, at 3; HI TRUSTEES' REPORT, *supra* note 17, at 1.

22. *See* BUREAU OF THE CENSUS, U.S. DEP'T OF COMMERCE, CURRENT POPULATION REPORTS, INCOME, POVERTY, AND VALUATION OF NONCASH BENEFITS: 1993, at D-17 (table D-5) (ser. P 60-188) (1993) [hereinafter CURRENT POPULATION REPORTS] (noting that 35.2% of persons 65 and older had incomes below the poverty level in 1959).

23. *See id.* at D-13, D-17 (table D-4 for all persons, table D-5 for persons 65 and older); Daniel H. Weinberg, Chief, Hous. & Household Economic Statistics Div., Bureau of the Census, Press Briefing on 1994 Income and Poverty Estimates (Oct. 5, 1995) (supplemental tables B-5 & B-6) (on file with the author). The Bureau of the Census does not provide annual data for persons 65 and older for years between 1959 and 1966.

24. *See* CURRENT POPULATION REPORTS, *supra* note 22, at D-13, D-17. While Social Security and Medicare have buoyed seniors up out of poverty, increasing numbers of children have fallen below the poverty level. *See id.* at D-17 (percentage of all persons under 18 years below poverty level). The poverty rate for children hit its low in 1969, and has increased to nearly 23%, the highest rate since 1964. Changes in family structure account for much of this change in childhood poverty, but decreasing governmental support has contributed as well. Since

1970, for example, the average state grant under Aid to Families with Dependent Children has fallen by more than $300, after adjusting for inflation. CHILDREN'S DEFENSE FUND, THE STATE OF AMERICA'S CHILDREN Y.B.: 1995, at 22 (1995) (median monthly state AFDC grant for a family of three with no other income).

25. *See* OFFICE OF RESEARCH AND STATISTICS, SOCIAL SECURITY ADMIN., INCOME OF THE POPULATION, 55 YEARS OR OLDER 31 (chart P-11) (1992) (noting that 59% of the elderly rely on Social Security for 50% or more of their income).

26. *See id.*

27. *See* GREEN BOOK, *supra* note 19, at 862 (data for 1992).

28. *See id.*

29. *Concurrent Resolution on the Budget for Fiscal Year 1996, Medicare Solvency: Hearings Before the Senate Comm. on the Budget,* S. HRG. NO. 162, 104th Cong., 1st Sess. 309, 311 (1995) [hereinafter *Medicare Solvency Hearings*] (statement of Karen Davis, President of the Commonwealth Fund).

30. *See* OFFICE OF RESEARCH AND STATISTICS, SOCIAL SECURITY ADMIN., FAST FACTS & FIGURES ABOUT SOCIAL SECURITY 8 (1995) (using 1992 data, Social Security lifts 38% of the aged out of poverty, leaving only 14% below the poverty level).

31. WILLIE SUTTON & EDWARD LINN, WHERE THE MONEY WAS 119–20 (1976); *see also* Lawrence K. Altman, *A Law Named for Willie Sutton Assists Physicians,* N.Y. TIMES, Jan. 3, 1970, at A12.

32. *See, e.g., The Republican Medicare Plan,* WASH. POST, Sept. 28, 1995, at A28; *Cutting Medicare,* WASH. POST, Sept. 12, 1995, at A18; James K. Glassman, *Social Insecurity,* WASH. POST, Sept. 5, 1995, at A17.

33. *See* CONGRESSIONAL BUDGET OFFICE, THE ECONOMIC AND BUDGET OUTLOOK: AN UPDATE 26 (1995) [hereinafter CBO UPDATE] (using fiscal year 1996 baseline projection data for current spending).

34. *See id.* at 26 (using fiscal year 1996 baseline data for current spending).

35. *See id.* at 22, 26 (using fiscal year 1996 baseline projection data, and using all mandatory spending for entitlements, including offsetting receipts and deposit insurance).

36. Other spending is allocated as follows: Defense, 17%; Interest, 15%; Other Discretionary, 17%; Other Entitlements, 16%. *Id.*

37. *See id.* at 27.

38. *See id.*

39. *See id.* at 22, 26.

40. *See id.*

41. *See id.*

42. *See id.* at 27.

43. *See* CBO UPDATE, *supra* note 33, at 27.

44. With regard to military spending, on the other hand, it is not unreasonable to expect that after the fall of America's principal adversary, the Soviet Union, America might devote less funding to defending against the Russian Federation.

One might reasonably be concerned, however, about the declining share of the economy devoted to domestic discretionary spending. This is the fund from which the government makes its investments in the future of the nation's physical and human capital. *See, e.g.,* OFFICE OF MANAGEMENT & BUDGET, BUDGET OF THE U.S. GOVERNMENT: FISCAL YEAR 1996, at 41–45 (1995) (discussing public investment).

45. *See* Peter G. Peterson, *A Summit On the Budget,* N.Y. TIMES, Feb. 3, 1987, at A27.

46. Pub. L. No. 98-21, 97 Stat. 65 (1983) (codified as amended at 12 U.S.C. § 3413, scattered

sections of 26 U.S.C., 38 U.S.C. § 3023 note, scattered sections of 42 U.S.C., and scattered sections of 45 U.S.C. (1994)).

47. *See* [OFFICE OF MANAGEMENT & BUDGET, HISTORICAL TABLES: BUDGET OF THE UNITED STATES GOVERNMENT, FISCAL YEAR 1996, at 98 (1995) (hereinafter HISTORICAL TABLES)], at 220–22, 224 (table 13.1—Cash Income, Outgo, and Balances of the Social Security and Medical Trust Funds: 1936–2000).

48. *See* Robert M. Ball, *Social Security Across the Generations, in* SOCIAL SECURITY AND ECONOMIC WELL-BEING ACROSS GENERATIONS 11, 20 (John R. Gist ed., 1988).

49. *See* [OFFICE OF MANAGEMENT & BUDGET, HISTORICAL TABLES: BUDGET OF THE UNITED STATES GOVERNMENT, FISCAL YEAR 1996, at 98 (1995) (hereinafter HISTORICAL TABLES)], at 220–22, 24 (table 13.1—Cash Income, Outgo, and Balances of the Social Security and Medical Trust Funds: 1930–2000). Note that these figures include interest paid by the federal government to the trust fund.

50. *See id.*

51. *See id.*

52. Pub. L. No. 92-603, 86 Stat. 1329 (1972) (codified as amended at scattered sections of 5, 7, 25, 26, 42, and 45 U.S.C. (1994)).

53. *See* Ball, *supra* note 48, at 23.

54. *See id.*

55. *See generally* 39 CONG. Q. ALMANAC 219–26 (1983) (providing a history of the Social Security "rescue plan").

56. SOCIAL SECURITY ADMIN., OASDI TRUST FUND OPERATIONS (Apr. 3, 1995) [hereinafter OASDI TRUST FUND OPERATIONS] (tables available on file with the *Harvard Journal on Legislation*).

57. *See id.*; [OFFICE OF MANAGEMENT & BUDGET, HISTORICAL TABLES: BUDGET OF THE UNITED STATES GOVERNMENT, FISCAL YEAR 1996, at 98 (1995) (hereinafter HISTORICAL TABLES)], at 224, 226.

58. *See* [OFFICE OF MANAGEMENT & BUDGET, HISTORICAL TABLES: BUDGET OF THE UNITED STATES GOVERNMENT, FISCAL YEAR 1996, at 98 (1995) (hereinafter HISTORICAL TABLES)] at 224, 226; OASDI TRUST FUND OPERATIONS, *supra* note 56.

59. *See* [OFFICE OF MANAGEMENT & BUDGET, HISTORICAL TABLES: BUDGET OF THE UNITED STATES GOVERNMENT, FISCAL YEAR 1996, at 98 (1995) (hereinafter HISTORICAL TABLES)], 78, at 224, 226.

60. *See* OASDI TRUST FUND OPERATIONS, *supra* note 56.

61. *See* [OFFICE OF MANAGEMENT & BUDGET, HISTORICAL TABLES: BUDGET OF THE UNITED STATES GOVERNMENT, FISCAL YEAR 1996, at 98 (1995) (hereinafter HISTORICAL TABLES)], at 13–14.

62. *See id.* at 14.

63. *See id.*

64. Social Security Act § 201(d), 42 U.S.C. § 401(d) (1994); *see also* [SOCIAL SECURITY & MEDICARE BOARD OF TRUSTEES, STATUS OF THE SOCIAL SECURITY AND MEDICARE PROGRAMS: A SUMMARY OF THE 1995 ANNUAL REPORTS 1 (1995) [hereinafter TRUSTEES' SUMMARY REPORT], at 2–3. The Trustees explain:

> In all trust funds, assets that are not needed to pay current benefits or administrative expenses (the only purposes for which trust funds may be used) are invested in special issue U.S. Government securities guaranteed as to both principal and interest and backed by the full faith and credit of the U.S. Government.

Id.

65. *E.g.*, 136 CONG. REC. S15,780 (daily ed. Oct. 18, 1990) (statement of Sen. Moynihan (D-N.Y.)).

66. [SOCIAL SECURITY & MEDICARE BOARD OF TRUSTEES, STATUS OF THE SOCIAL SECURITY AND MEDICARE PROGRAMS: A SUMMARY OF THE 1995 ANNUAL REPORTS 1 (1995) [hereinafter TRUSTEES' SUMMARY REPORT], at i.

67. *See* [OFFICE OF MANAGEMENT & BUDGET, HISTORICAL TABLES: BUDGET OF THE UNITED STATES GOVERNMENT, FISCAL YEAR 1996, at 98 (1995) (hereinafter HISTORICAL TABLES)], at 224, 226; OASDI TRUST FUND OPERATIONS, *supra* note 99.

The Social Security program is often thought to be a major component in retirement patterns. Many believe that its existence has led to the decline in the retirement age. This may not be the case. Michael V. Leonesio has analyzed the effect of Social Security on retirement patterns and concluded that the decision to retire is not greatly affected by the existence of Social Security.

Michael V. Leonesio

Social Security and Older Workers

* * *

OASI and the Decision to Retire

The economic literature on the determinants of individual retirement decisions is both extensive and difficult to summarize. In addition to the problem of evaluating the relative credibility of the various studies, problems are created by the use of different models, different populations (for example, workers aged sixty-two to sixty-five versus workers aged sixty or older), and different definitions of what constitutes retirement. Because there is no universally employed definition of the term, it is possible for different "retirement" studies to arrive at apparently conflicting conclusions about the importance of suspected causes because they are not actually studying the same phenomenon.

In a way, the research results are probably somewhat at odds with what one might expect on the basis of casual observation. After all, Social Security is the largest source of income for the retired population and certainly seems to play a very large role in the economic well-being of the aged. The post–World War II expansion of the Social Security system roughly coincides with the well-documented decline in the average retirement age of men and the sharp decline in the labor-force participation rate of

56 *Social Security Bulletin* 47 (Summer 1993).

men aged sixty and older. Retirement at ages sixty-two and sixty-five—Social Security's early and normal retirement ages—is popular.

* * *

The data show that over the past three decades there has been a gradual, marked increase in the popularity of retirement at age sixty-two. If the benefit reduction rate for retirement before age sixty-five is actuarially fair, which it roughly appears to be (Aaron 1982, pp. 62–63), and if individuals could borrow against future Social Security entitlements, then there should be no observed bunching of retirement at age sixty-two. Individuals wanting to retire before age sixty-two could help finance this choice by establishing a retirement fund through private lenders, using their Social Security entitlements as collateral. That capital markets do not finance such an arrangement results in the peak at age sixty-two in the retirement age profile (Crawford and Lilien, 1981). Most individuals with small amounts of liquid assets cannot afford to retire before age sixty-two, when they first have access to their Social Security wealth.

* * *

In surveys of retirees conducted during the first three decades of the existence of Social Security, respondents usually claimed that they retired either because their employers terminated their jobs, or because of health problems. The pronounced decline in labor-force participation by men aged sixty-two or older during the 1960s and 1970s was associated with an increased incidence of voluntary departures from the labor force (Quinn et al., 1990). Thus, according to Sherman (1985), by the early 1980s, a majority of new male Social Security beneficiaries were indicating that retirement was self-initiated.

* * *

Most economic research now reflects the view that, for the most part, retirement is a choice made by workers who rationally weigh the personal advantages and disadvantages of continued labor-force participation. Although the emphasis in economic models is certainly on the financial aspects of the decision, the research also addresses the coincidental impact of general economic conditions, personal characteristics (particularly age), health status, and individual attitudes toward work. In general, the findings support the view that earlier retirements have been largely voluntary, as workers have been increasingly able to afford to retire.

At the core of much of the economic analysis of retirement behavior is a *life-cycle* view of work, saving, and consumption. That is, individuals are assumed to be well-informed, far-sighted planners whose economic decisions represent integrated, long-term plans expected to generate adequate income to support a desired standard of living. Because the level of work activity that is anticipated in each future year is part of a long-range plan, any factor that ostensibly affects the incentive to work during one period can influence the amount of work planned for other periods as well. For example, a progressive tax on earned income might cause work to be shifted from high-earnings years to low-earnings years in order to lower lifetime tax liability. Viewed from a life-cycle perspective, decisions about leaving a career job, accepting a pension, applying for Social Security benefits, working in a post retirement job, and the like are all interdependent.

Within this life-cycle framework, the effects of Social Security on work are ambiguous; perhaps some persons are induced to retire earlier and others later. To the extent that the system forces people to save for their retirement and that the adjustment in benefit levels for delaying the onset of benefits is less than actuarially fair, *earlier* retirements are more likely to be encouraged. The material that follows summarizes the empirical evidence. In the interest of brevity, specific citations are limited to studies that are representative of the most persuasive scholarship; omission should not be taken to construe rejection or criticism.

Because Social Security benefits represent a substantial portion of retirement income for most Americans, their role in the retirement decision has been closely examined. Monthly benefit amounts influence both the timing of retirement and the choice of post retirement hours of work. Other things being equal, higher benefits are expected to promote earlier retirement, decrease the likelihood of working among retirees, and reduce the hours of work by labor-force participants. Causation runs in the other direction as well, however, with the retirement decision affecting the value of the monthly benefit via three separate channels. First, at any time between the ages of sixty-two and seventy, the actuarial adjustment and delayed retirement credit increase the amount of the monthly benefit when acceptance of benefits is postponed. Second, as long as annual earnings are greater than the smallest value included in the computation years for determining average indexed monthly earnings (AIME), postponing retirement will increase the primary insurance amount upon which the benefit amount is based. Third, for some individuals, a delay in retirement can result in their accumulating the minimum number of quarters of covered employment to qualify for retirement benefits. Therefore, although in all three instances a delay in retirement would lead to increased monthly benefit amounts, higher benefit levels in and of themselves lower the probability of labor-force participation.

* * *

In one of the few studies of women's retirement behavior, Pozzebon and Mitchell (1989) find that the retirement decisions of married women appear to be relatively insensitive to financial incentives such as Social Security, a conclusion that is similarly drawn by McCarty (1990). Working married women value retirement leisure highly, and there appears to be complementarity with their husbands' retirement leisure. In general, family considerations such as the husband's health status and income, as well as the difference between the husband's and wife's ages, appear to be the stronger influences.

Despite the shortcomings that are inherent in most empirical work, the retirement literature has evolved to the point where certain conclusions can be drawn about the role of Social Security. Viewed in total, the evidence indicates that the OASI program has contributed to the decline in the labor-force participation of older men but that the direct financial effects appear to be modest. The Social Security system has contributed to the popularity of retirement at ages sixty-two and sixty-five but appears to be a minor force in the long post–World War II trend to retire at earlier ages.

* * *

References

Aaron, Henry J. 1982. *Economic Effects of Social Security,* Washington, DC: Brookings Institution.

Crawford, Vincent P. and David Lilien. 1981. "Social Security and the Retirement Decision," *Quarterly Journal of Economics,* Vol. 96, No. 3, ppg. 505–529.

McCarty, Therese A. 1190. "The Effect of Social Security on Married Women's Labor Force Participation," *National Tax Journal,* Vol. 43, No. 1, pp. 95–110.

Pozzebon, Silvana and Olivia S. Mitchell. 1989. "Married Women's Retirement Behavior," *Journal of Population Economics,* Vol. 2, No. 1, pp. 39–53.

Quinn, Joseph F.; Richard V. Burkhauser; and Daniel A. Myers. 1990. *Passing the Torch: The Influence of Economic Incentives on Work and Retirement.* Kalamazoo, MI: W.E. Upjohn Institute for Employment Research.

Sherman, Sally R. 1985. "Reported Reasons Retired Workers Left Their Last Job: Findings From the New Beneficiary Survey," *Social Security Bulletin,* Vol. 48, No. 3, pp. 22–30

Because Social Security benefits are predicated upon the retired worker's lifetime earning and projected life expectancy, the program rewards retirees with higher wages and rewards longer post-retirement lifetime with greater benefits. Women, who on average outlive men by six or seven years, thus can expect to receive benefits for more years than men. Offsetting that advantage are the lower earnings of women (estimated to be only 70 percent of males), which depresses benefits paid to women. Similar arguments can be made on behalf of African Americans as Mr. Holtz does in the following article.

Geoffrey T. Holtz

Social Security Discrimination Against African Americans: An Equal Protection Argument

Introduction

The Social Security Act (the Act) was passed in 1935[1] in order to alleviate the problems associated with an expanding elderly population and the difficulties such persons were encountering in trying to take care of themselves financially.[2] As with any insurance program, Social Security was established on the assumption that more participants would pay into the system than were expected to be paid out from the system.[3] This assumption was based on the fact that when the first Social Security checks were mailed in 1940, only 54 percent of the men and 61 percent of the women who paid Social Security taxes could expect to celebrate their sixty-fifth birthdays and start collecting benefits.[4] And even those lucky enough to reach retirement age could only expect to collect benefits for an average of fourteen years before dying.[5]

However, these figures tell only half the story. African Americans, as a group, have never received a proportionate share of the benefits paid out of the Social Security trust fund compared to the taxes they have paid in.[6] While the original Social Security Act of 1935 contained a number of provisions designed explicitly to exclude African Americans,[7] the current discrepancy is due primarily to the fact that African Americans have a significantly lower life expectancy than white Americans.[8] Since all workers pay into Social Security at the same rate,[9] but become eligible for full benefits only upon reaching age sixty-five,[10] the lower life expectancies of African Americans result in the program serving as a wealth transfer from black to white Americans.[11]

* * *

I. The Discriminatory Impact of Social Security on African Americans

A. Life Expectancies of White Americans and African Americans

African Americans have a significantly lower life expectancy than white Americans.[12] The reasons for this discrepancy are uncertain and the proffered explanations are varied—among the possibilities suggested by commentators are that African Americans suffer generally higher poverty rates,[13] are more likely to engage in backbending labor,[14] have comparably higher rates of illness and disability,[15] and are more prone to the effects of street violence.[16]

The actuarial tables illustrate the stark results of these phenomena. A white male infant born in 1990 can expect to live to an age of 72.7 years.[17] His black male counterpart, however, will live, on average, to the age of 64.5.[18] The life expectancies for white and black females born that year are 79.4 and 73.6 years, respectively.[19] This difference in the longevity of African Americans and whites has been fairly consistent throughout the twentieth century, even as the life expectancies of all Americans have steadily increased. In 1935, for example, the year that the Social Security Act was passed,[20] white and black males born that year could expect to live to 61.0 and 51.3, respectively, while white and black females could expect to live to 65.0 and 55.2.[21] Thus, from the moment the Social Security Act was passed until the present, glaring discrepancies have existed in the numbers of whites and African Americans who actually live to retirement age.

B. The Effects of Life Expectancy Differences on Social Security Benefits

Full Social Security benefits are scheduled to be paid upon reaching age sixty-seven for those Americans born after 1960.[22] The effect of the eight-year difference in life expectancies between black and white men is magnified by the fact that an individual must survive to at least retirement age before becoming eligible to collect from the system. Thus, even assuming the longer life expectancies of those born in 1990, the average African American male will die two-and-a-half years before the age at which he can receive full benefits. The average white male, however, will live past retirement age and receive benefits for 5.7 years. In pure dollar terms, the average black male will die before receiving a single dollar in benefits, while the average white male will receive $42,800.[23] The discrepancy for females is similar, with the typical African American woman expected to receive benefits for 6.6 years compared to 12.4 years for whites.

While the courts and Congress have given little attention to this situation,[24] some commentators in the mainstream press have noted the problem. Columnist Walter Williams observes, "The only official racism left in America is Social Security racism. . . . It's a racial rip-off; they know I'm going to croak eight months before eligibility starts and the white guy is going to get at least eight years or so of benefits."[25] The National Caucus on the Black Aged recognized the problem as far back as 1970 and urged Congress to take racial differences in life expectancy into account in amending the Social Security Act.[26] Some generally conservative sources have also proven sympathetic to the problem, with the Orange County (CA) Register editorializing that the current system "is a massive robbery from black taxpayers to white recipients."[27] Even commentator and two-time presidential candidate Pat Buchanan has acknowledged this discrepancy.[28]

Official Social Security acknowledgment of the problem has been scant, however. In a classic glass-is-half-full argument, Robert Myers, the former chief actuary of Social Security, observed that his tables show that 50.1 percent of African American males born today will make it to age sixty-seven, so it's "certainly not a total washout."[29] Others have suggested that, with higher mortality rates, at least African Americans will receive a disproportionate amount of survivor benefits.[30] Survivor benefits are available, however, only to the surviving spouse and minor children of deceased workers, are much smaller than regular benefits, and at any rate are not disproportionately paid out to African Americans.[31] Social Security Commissioner Gwendolyn S. King bravely but inexplicably asserts that "it is precisely because of the African American mortality rates, it is because of the comparably high rates of illness and disability . . . that Social Security is such a critically important program for black Americans."[32]

Social Security is a two-stage program: before retirement age working Americans pay into the program; after retirement, they are then paid from the system. African Americans are affected adversely by this system on both ends. On the pay-in side, Social Security taxes are regressive in that they take a greater percentage of the earnings of low-income taxpayers—a group that includes a disproportionate number of African Americans—than from high-income taxpayers.[33] On the pay-out side, after retirement, Social Security is highly progressive; recipients with lower lifetime incomes receive a greater proportion of their earnings than do those with higher lifetime incomes.[34] Thus, the progressive pay-out side would essentially make up for the regressive pay-in side of Social Security if all Americans lived the same number of years past retirement. But, as seen above in Part IA, this is not the case, and the lower life expectancies of African Americans rob them of this benefit. In short, since African Americans on average do not live as long after retirement as do white Americans, they never reap the benefits of the progressive pay-out system even though they suffer the inequalities on the regressive pay-in side.

C. Congressional Failure To Confront the Life Expectancy Differences

Although life expectancy differences between black and white Americans have been significant since the original enactment of the Social Security Act in 1935,[35] in amending the Act Congress has continued to treat all taxpayers as equally situated.[36] For example, since the 1970s, retirement benefits have included automatic annual cost of living adjustments,[37] which assist those who have reached retirement age, but do nothing for the disproportionate number of African Americans who do not receive any benefits. During the Social Security funding crisis of the early 1980s, the congressional response was to dramatically raise the tax rate, exacerbating the regressive effects of the pay-in side of the program.[38]

Recent changes to the program indicate a continued lack of concern for the black-white discrepancies. For example, the 1983 amendments to the statutes raised the retirement age from sixty-five to sixty-seven,[39] which markedly increased the racial gap in the number of post-retirement years in which one could collect benefits. In addition, Senators Bob Kerrey and John Danforth have proposed further raising the retirement age to seventy, a revision that would only continue to compound this problem.[40] While it may be true that changes in Social Security are necessary to maintain the solvency of the program,[41] future modifications should take into account the effects on African Americans and other minorities.

* * *

A. A Race-Based Congressional Response

The most straightforward response that Congress could take toward remedying the discriminatory effects of Social Security would be to amend the Act using race-specific means. A number of commentators have suggested some possibilities. Columnist Walter Williams proposes that Congress "race-norm" Social Security.[42] Under this proposal, African American males would become eligible for retirement benefits at age fifty-six rather than age sixty-five, so that both white and African American males would average eight years of benefits.[43] Jacquelyne Johnson Jackson has also recommended taking into account the mortality rates and life expectancies of different races in determining Social Security taxes and benefits.[44] Conservative commentator Pat Buchanan has argued that participation in the Social Security program should be voluntary for African Americans given that their shorter life expectancies cheat them of benefits.[45]

* * *

B. Race-Neutral Congressional Remedies

Congress need not respond to the problem of the racially discriminatory effect of the Social Security Act by resorting to a race-based remedy that would invoke strict scrutiny by the federal courts. A number of race-neutral remedies that would effectively eliminate the discrepancy have been proposed.[46]

The most radical yet fairest reform, as far as the problems engendered by racial life-expectancy differences are concerned, would be to privatize Social Security; i.e., to transform the program from a government insurance program to an individual investment plan. For example, the Heritage Foundation has proposed allowing any individuals who wish to do so to opt out of the current Social Security program and to receive from the government a check for their contributions to date.[47] These individuals "would then be obliged to invest that money plus all future contributions that would have otherwise gone into the Social Security trust fund into a mandatory individual retirement account (IRA)."[48] The earnings from these investments would vest in the name of the worker rather than be pooled in the single trust fund that currently manages Social Security revenues. This would allow African Americans, or any other individuals, to collect their fair share upon retirement or disability, or would at least ensure that their heirs received the accrued benefits.[49]

At the other extreme are calls to means-test the program. Under this scheme, Social Security would be transformed into a true insurance program with mandatory contributions by all workers, as under the current system, but with benefits going only to those who need them without regard to an individual's history of payments.[50] This would convert Social Security into a welfare-type safety net with a floor of protection guaranteed for all.[51] Of course, in order to avoid the discrepancies detailed in Part I of this Note, the threshold for means-testing would have to be grounded on some basis other than age, such as disability or other inability to continue working.[52]

Finally, many reformers, including Senators Bob Kerrey and John Danforth, have suggested a two-tier system of Social Security that is a hybrid of the two proposals mentioned above. Under the Kerrey-Danforth plan, the Social Security tax would be cut, with 4.7 percent of a worker's wages being paid into the government trust fund that would be used to provide a floor of support for all retirees or disabled elderly.[53] However, the additional 1.5 percent of wages that are now going into the trust fund would be available to invest in a mandatory IRA in the individual worker's name.[54] This would give all workers, including the 50 percent who are not currently covered under any type of private pension plan, an increased pool of private assets that would help to alleviate the demand for Social Security trust fund benefits.[55]

None of these proposals is without its critics, and any fundamental changes to such an enormous program as Social Security would require a great deal of study to assess the pros and cons. However, given the stark racial discrepancies inherent in the current Social Security program, there is a great need for Congress to enact some type of reform. In considering any amendments to the Act, Congress must take into account its inequitable treatment of African Americans. It can ameliorate these effects by either an explicit race-based response, or by a race-neutral response that eliminates the racial discrepancies, but it must at least consider the effect of any such changes on African Americans with their shorter life expectancies. To fail to do so will simply perpetuate the unconstitutionally discriminatory impact that the program has produced for the last sixty years.

* * *

Notes

1. Social Security Act, Pub. L. No. 74-271, 49 Stat. 620 (1935).

2. See Helvering v. Davis, 301 U.S. 619, 642 (1937) (discussing the purposes of the Social Security Act).

3. See, e.g., Nancy J. Altman, The Reconciliation of Retirement Security and Tax Policies: A Response to Professor Graetz, 136 U. Pa. L. Rev. 1419, 1429–30 (1988).

4. See George J. Church & Richard Lacayo, Social Insecurity, Time, Mar. 20, 1995, at 24, 28.

5. Id. At age 65, men had a life expectancy of 78 years, women 80 years.

6. See infra notes 22–23.

7. [Note deleted.]

8. The life expectancies for white and black male infants born in 1990 are 72.7 years and 64.5 years, respectively. The life expectancies for white and black females born that year are 79.4 and 73.6, respectively. U.S. Nat'l Ctr. for Health Statistics, Vital Statistics of the United States (annual), reported in U.S. Dep't of Com., Statistical Abstract of the United States, tbl. No. 115, at 87 (1994).

9. 42 U.S.C. §§ 1401, 3101, 3111 (1995). Given that there is an earnings cap, however, with wages over that cap not taxed under Social Security, low-income earners actually pay a higher rate than do those with incomes over the cap. 42 U.S.C. § 430 (1995).

10. This retirement age is scheduled to be raised to age 67 for those Americans born after 1960. 42 U.S.C. § 416(l)(1)(E) (1995).

11. See The '80s in Black and White, Orange County Reg., July 28, 1992, at B8. Note that this criticism could be made for any identifiable group who has a lower than average life expectancy, such as smokers or the poor. However, these groups do not receive the same treatment under the Court's equal protection jurisprudence as do those individuals who are members of a "protected class" based on immutable characteristics such as race or gender. See San Antonio Indep. Sch. Dist. v. Rodriguez, 411 U.S. 1, 24 (1973) (noting that the Equal Protection Clause does not require absolute equality between the wealthy and the poor). Furthermore, it is unlikely that a member of such a group could prove the requisite intent for finding an equal protection violation. See supra text accompanying notes 3–9.

12. See actuarial data infra Part IA.

13. See Allen L. Otten, People Patterns, Wall St. J., June 14, 1988, at 37.

14. William E. Gibson, Medicare, Social Security Cuts Collapse, Ft. Lauderdale Sun-Sentinel, Dec. 15, 1994, at 1A.

15. Sarah Pekkanen, SSA Commissioner Takes Aim at "Myths," Politics Behind Rumor of Inadequate Funds, King Says, Balt. Eve. Sun, Mar. 5, 1992, at 1A.

16. Jack Germond & Jules Witcover, Tax-Cut Stampede Kills Serious Budget Reform, Balt. Sun, Dec. 15, 1994, at 2A.

17. U.S. Nat'l Ctr. for Health Statistics, Vital Statistics of the United States (annual), and

Monthly Vital Statistics Reports, reported in U.S. Dep't of Com., Statistical Abstract of the United States, tbl. No. 115, at 87 (1994).

18. Id.

19. Id. This Note uses the life expectancies of African-Americans and whites for comparison primarily because these data are less readily available for other racial and ethnic groups, particularly for prior decades. In addition, while the discriminatory impact of the Social Security Act exists for many ethnic groups which have a lower than average life expectancy rate, the only group which has suffered from intentional discrimination under the Act, a critical element of equal protection jurisprudence, is African-Americans.

20. Social Security Act, Pub. L. No. 74-271, 49 Stat. 620 (1935) (codified as amended at 42 U.S.C. §§ 301–1397(f) (1995)).

21. Dep't of Health, Education, and Welfare, annual reports, and Vital Statistics of the United States (annual), reported in U.S. Dep't of Com., Statistical Abstract of the United States, tbl. No. 62, at 58 (1960).

22. 42 U.S.C. § 416(l)(1)(E) (1995). Reduced benefits are available at age 62. 42 U.S.C. § 402(a)(3)(B) (1995). Full benefits are available at age 65 for those born before 1936, with a sliding scale for those born between 1936 and 1960. 42 U.S.C. § 416(l)(1) (1995).

23. This figure assumes the average 1991 monthly Social Security benefit for retirees of $629. Given that this average figure includes payments to men and women, and that men generally receive higher payments due to their higher lifetime earnings, the black-white discrepancy is actually even greater. See Social Security Bulletin, reported in U.S. Dep't of Com., Statistical Abstract of the United States, tbl. No. 583, at 377 (1994).

24. See infra notes 34–40.

25. Walter Williams, Little Abuses Add Up to Height of Injustice, Cincinnati Enquirer, Nov. 20, 1994, at F3.

26. Jacquelyne Johnson Jackson, Social Security Should Be a True Insurance Program, Durham Herald-Sun, Nov. 29, 1994, at A8.

27. The '80s in Black and White, supra note 11, at B8.

28. See John Hanchette, Sharp Tongue, Quick Wit, Could Come Back To Haunt Buchanan, Gannett News Service, Feb. 26, 1992 (quoting Pat Buchanan).

29. Spencer Rich, Inside: Health and Human Services, Senior Aide May Leave Post He's Held Less than a Year, Wash. Post, July 15, 1985, at A13.

30. See id.; see also David L. Randall, Who's Subsidized?, Chi. Trib., Mar. 16, 1990, at 24.

31. 42 U.S.C. § 402(d), (e), (f); see Katharine Silbaugh, Turning Labor Into Love: Housework and the Law, 91 Nw. U. L. Rev. 1, 68 (1996) (observing that survivor benefits are unavailable to the children of a woman who was never married; she must rely on less generous AFDC benefits). 68.1% of African-American children were born to unmarried mothers in 1992 compared to 22.6% of white children. U.S. Dep't of Com., Statistical Abstract of the United States, tbl. No. 94, at 77 (1995). Thus, it is unlikely that African-American children could receive a disproportionate amount of Social Security survivor benefits, although they may receive a disproportionate share of AFDC.

32. Pekkanen, supra note 15.

33. This is due to three features of the program. First, Social Security taxes are imposed only on wages, and thus exclude unearned investment income which is more likely to be earned by higher-income taxpayers. Second, Social Security is taxed at a flat rate, with no deductions or exemptions as with income taxes. Third, Social Security taxes are only imposed on the first $65,000 of income, resulting in lower-income earners paying a higher total percentage of their

earnings. Jonathan Berry Forman, Promoting Fairness in the Social Security Retirement Program: Partial Integration and a Credit for Dual-Earner Couples, 45 Tax Law. 915, 928 (1992); 42 U.S.C. §§ 415(a)–415(e) (1995). The median family income of African-Americans in 1992 was $21,161, while that of whites was $38,909. U.S. Bureau of the Census, Current Population Reports, P60-184.

34. Forman, supra note 33, at 935; 42 U.S.C. § 415(a) (1995).

35. See supra notes 20–21.

36. [Note deleted.]

37. Social Security Amendments of 1973, Pub. L. No. 93-233, 87 Stat. 947 (1973) (codified as amended at 42 U.S.C. § 415(i) (1973)).

38. The 1983 amendments raised the employee's tax rate from 5.08% for 1980 wages to 6.20% for 1990 wages. Social Security Amendments of 1983, Pub. L. No. 98-21, 97 Stat. 65 (1983). In fact, these higher rates arguably have pushed more lower-income taxpayers into greater poverty, a factor which may contribute to lower life expectancy in the first place. For example, in part because of rising Social Security taxes, the total federal tax burden on a family of four at the poverty line rose from 1.8% of income in 1979 to 10.4% by 1985. The Next Tax Reform, The New Republic, Sep. 15 & 22, 1986, at 5.

This method of increasing revenue will ultimately lead to tax rates that are even more crippling. Once the baby boom generation starts to retire en masse in the near future, if benefits are maintained at today's levels those entering the work force today will have to pay at least 33% of their income into Social Security, according to the CATO Institute. Social Security: Prospects for Real Reform, Nat'l J., Aug. 17, 1985, at 1917.

39. Social Security Amendments of 1983, Pub. L. No. 98-21, 97 Stat. 65 (1983).

40. Robert A. Rosenblatt, Social Security is Target of Plan to Control Deficit, L.A. Times, Dec. 10, 1994, at A1.

41. For more on this issue, see [(115 S. Ct. 2097,) 2136 (1995) (Ginsburg, J., dissenting)].

42. Williams, supra note 25.

43. Id. Williams did not mention the discrepancies as applied to African-American females.

44. Jackson, supra note 26. Dr. Jackson first proposed such a solution in 1968, but no longer supports this remedy. She argues instead for transforming Social Security into a true insurance program that would ensure monetary benefits for the estates of all Americans who do not live long enough to recoup their Social Security taxes. See infra notes 50–52.

45. Hanchette, supra note 28. Note the irony in that the original drafters of the 1935 Social Security Act excluded African-Americans from coverage in order to treat them unfairly. Given the likelihood that today's younger workers will fail to recover anything close to the taxes they are paying, some now want to exclude African-Americans from the program in order to benefit them. See, e.g., Church & Lacayo, supra note 4, at 24.

46. There are a number of other reasons for reforming Social Security that are beyond the scope of this Note, not the least of which is the threatened insolvency of the program. For a summary of these concerns see Dorcas R. Hardy & C. Colburn Hardy, Social Insecurity (1991). For a fuller treatment of the pros and cons of the proposals suggested in this Note, see the sources cited infra in notes 47–54.

47. Church & Lacayo, supra note 4, at 24, 30. See also David Wise, Six Initiatives to Promote Private Saving, Challenge, Nov., 1992, at 13; Forman, supra note 33, at 949.

48. Church & Lacayo, supra note 4, at 24, 30.

49. See, e.g., Eric Kingson & Jill Quadagno, Social Security: Marketing Radical Reform. The

Future of Age-Based Public Policy, American Society on Aging, Generations, Sept. 22, 1995, at 43; Wise, supra note 47, at 20, 26–27.

50. Peter Peterson, former Secretary of Commerce, has offered one such proposal: households with annual incomes of more than $35,000 would have their benefits reduced on a sliding scale starting at 7.5% and going up an additional 5% for every $10,000 of extra income. At incomes of $185,000 or above, households would thus lose 85% of their benefits. Church & Lacayo, supra note 4, at 24, 30–31. See also Kingson & Quadagno, supra note 49. Currently, benefits are pegged to an individual's past earnings. See Forman, supra note 35, at 922.

51. Church & Lacayo, supra note 4, at 24, 31–32. See also Robert Pear, Attacks Begin on Plan to Cut Social Programs, N.Y. Times, Dec. 10, 1994, at 30 (noting the public hostility to welfare programs). In effect, this proposal would greatly expand the current Supplemental Security Insurance (SSI) program. See 42 U.S.C. §§ 1381, 1381a, 1382a–1382j (1995).

52. See Forman, supra note 33, at 949.

53. [Robert A. Rosenblatt, Social Security is Target of Plan to Control Deficit, L.A. Times, Dec. 10, 1994, at A1.]

54. Id. Cf. Wise, supra note 49, at 26–27 (discussing a similar reform plan offered by Senator Moynihan).

55. Wise, supra note 49, at 26–27.

Higher income individuals often accuse Social Security of being a costly pension plan that is not worth its expense. They claim that if they did not have to pay the wage tax for Social Security, they could purchase a private pension plan that would yield better benefits to them. In response, proponents claim that the "value" of Social Security is unappreciated. In his article, Dean R. Leimer attempts to analyze whether workers receive their money's worth from the Social Security program.

Dean R. Leimer

A Guide to Social Security Money's Worth Issues

* * *

The question of whether workers receive their money's worth from Social Security has received a great deal of public attention. Most analysts agree that past retirees have generally received benefits worth well in excess of the taxes that they paid. This result reflects the nature of a pay-as-you-go social insurance program that grants full benefit rights to workers who have contributed to the program for only a short time

58 *Social Security Bulletin* 3 (Summer 1995).

after the program begins.[1] As the program matures, workers contribute over more of their working lives, and the balance between taxes and benefits naturally becomes less favorable.

As this balance becomes less favorable, criticism of alleged inequities under the program is likely to increase. Some analysts have projected, for example, that many young workers can no longer expect to receive their money's worth from Social Security.[2] Others have suggested that the redistribution of lifetime resources under Social Security is excessive or that the program effectively discriminates in possibly inappropriate ways on the basis of gender, race, marital status, or other individual characteristics.[3]

To facilitate the evaluation of such arguments, this article discusses some of the major issues associated with Social Security money's worth questions. An effort is made to keep the discussion as nontechnical as possible and to explain technical terms and concepts where necessary. Various measures that have been used in money's worth analyses are explained and contrasted. Some of the major assumptions and analytical methods used in such analyses are identified, along with indications of how these assumptions and methods affect the conclusions. The results of some of the more important money's worth studies are summarized, and the article closes with a discussion of the limitations and appropriate usage of money's worth analyses.

Frequently Used Money's Worth Measures

Four different measures are frequently used to evaluate the money's worth question. These measures are referred to in this article as the "payback period," the "benefit/tax ratio," the "lifetime transfer," and the "internal rate of return." Although different in concept, all of these measures are concerned with the balance between Social Security taxes and benefits over workers' entire lifetimes.[4]

The payback period is an estimate of the length of time required for a beneficiary or beneficiary couple to recover in benefits the value of the taxes that they paid into the Social Security program while they were working. If the payback period is shorter than their expected remaining lifetimes when they start receiving benefits, then they can expect to receive more than their money's worth from Social Security. Conversely, if the payback period exceeds their life expectancies, then Social Security would be a "bad deal" from their perspective. The payback period measure is often used in articles appearing in publications with broad readership. Unfortunately, some of these articles lack technical competence, and the payback period measure is sometimes misused, as discussed in the following section. The payback period is also referred to as the "break-even period"; a similar measure used in some studies is the "break-even age."

* * *

The benefit/tax ratio compares the total lifetime value of a worker's Social Security benefits with the total lifetime value of his or her Social Security taxes. If the ratio of lifetime benefits to lifetime taxes is greater than one, then workers receive more than their money's worth from Social Security. If the ratio is less than one, then workers fail to get their money's worth. The benefit/tax ratio is sometimes referred to as the "benefit/cost" ratio; the inverse of this ratio, the lifetime "tax/benefit" or "cost/benefit" ratio, is also used in some studies.

The lifetime transfer is a similar measure that compares the difference, rather than the ratio, between the total lifetime value of benefits and the total lifetime value of taxes. If lifetime benefits exceed lifetime taxes, then the lifetime transfer is positive, and workers get more than their money's worth from Social Security. A negative lifetime transfer indicates that workers do not get their money's worth. The lifetime transfer measure is also referred to in some analyses as the "net lifetime transfer" or the "lifetime wealth increment."[5]

Finally, the internal rate of return measures the interest rate that a worker would have to receive on his or her Social Security tax payments in order to generate benefits equal to those received under Social Security. That is, if a worker made savings account deposits equal to (and at the same time as) his or her Social Security tax payments and then made withdrawals from the account equal to (and at the same time as) his or her Social Security benefits, then the internal rate of return is equal to the savings account interest rate that would leave the worker with a zero balance at the end of his or her life. Thus, if the internal rate of return is larger than the interest rate available to workers for their own investments, then they receive more than their money's worth from Social Security—that is, they receive a higher "interest rate," or internal rate of return, from the Social Security program than from their private savings. Conversely, if the internal rate of return is smaller than the interest rate that workers can earn privately, then they do not get their money's worth from Social Security.

* * *

It is also important to recognize that the four money's worth measures discussed above do not always give equivalent indications of whether workers receive their money's worth from the program.[6] More generally, the different measures can produce different rankings of outcomes across workers with different tax and benefit streams.[7] As such, it is important to use the money's worth measure most appropriate for the particular question being asked.

The payback period measure is often used in articles aimed at the general public, because it is relatively easy to explain and understand. Technical deficiencies limit its usefulness in more rigorous analyses, however.[8] Because of these deficiencies, the payback period generally can give only a rough indication of whether or not particular workers can expect to get back their money's worth from Social Security over their remaining lifetimes.

By definition, the lifetime transfer measure is the appropriate indicator of the extent to which the lifetime incomes of participants are affected by the balance between lifetime benefits and taxes, because this extent depends on the difference, rather than the ratio or rate of return relationship, between lifetime benefits and taxes. For many money's worth questions, then, specifically those that aim to identify the effect of lifetime taxes and benefits on the lifetime incomes of program participants, the lifetime transfer is the most appropriate money's worth measure.[9]

For other money's worth questions that focus on the relative attractiveness of the Social Security program as an "investment" alternative, regardless of the size of the tax "investments" that different participants are required or allowed to make, the internal rate of return or benefit/tax ratio measures are more appropriate. The internal rate of return, benefit/tax ratio, or other relative money's worth measure is also generally used to establish whether lifetime redistribution under the program is "progressive" or "regressive" with respect to some lifetime measure of economic well-being—for example, the program might be described as progressive if the internal rate of return or benefit/tax ratio declines as lifetime earnings increase."[10]

Assumptions and Analytical Methods

Unfortunately, money's worth measures are sometimes used or developed incorrectly, with misleading results. The implications of the assumptions or analytical methods used in money's worth studies are not always fully appreciated, leading to incorrect interpretations of the estimates.

This section discusses a number of key assumptions and analytical methods that can lead to incorrect interpretations. As the discussion below indicates, some of the views expressed in this section are not universally held by money's worth analysts.

Tax Incidence

One problem with many money's worth analyses is that they ignore the employer's share of the Social Security payroll tax. Some analysts believe that the employer contribution should not be included in money's worth calculations.[11] One rationale sometimes cited is that the employer's contribution should be considered as pooled for the general benefit of all covered workers or to fund the redistributional component of the program. The view of most economists addressing the money's worth issue is that this type of argument really misses the point. The question is simply one of whether employees are paid less than otherwise because of the employer tax, or whether the tax is shifted to consumers in the form of higher prices or paid by the owners of the business in the form of lower profits. If workers' wages are lower because of the tax on employers, for example, then, in reality, workers actually pay the tax, even though it is collected from the employer.

Obviously, money's worth analyses become much simpler under the assumption that employers shift the tax directly to workers, since this allows the employer share of the tax to be assigned to specific workers or groups of workers. Under other assumptions of who ultimately pays the employer share of the tax, identifying the specific individuals or groups who bear the burden of the tax becomes much more difficult. Because workers are also consumers and shareholders, however, they collectively bear much of the burden of the employer share of the tax under any of the shifting assumptions.

In any event, ignoring the employer share of the tax is clearly inappropriate, because it results in the comparison of benefits with taxes that are insufficient to fund those benefits; as a consequence, Social Security appears to be a much better deal than it actually is when all taxes required to fund the program are considered. While the question of who bears the burden of the Social Security payroll tax is still a matter of debate among economists, the most widely adopted assumption in money's worth analyses is that the tax is shifted over time by employers to workers in the form of lower wages.[12]

Financial Balance

A similar problem arises in some money's worth analyses that make estimates under currently legislated tax and benefit provisions, even when the program is projected to be out of long-run financial balance. If the program is in long-run financial deficit, for example, money's worth estimates for at least some age groups will be more favorable than the outcomes that those groups will actually experience when the tax increases or benefit cuts required to bring the program back into financial balance are enacted. An analogous effect is that money's worth estimates for some groups would be too pessimistic if the program were projected to have a long-run actuarial surplus that will not be maintained. While such estimates are of interest since they indicate program outcomes under current legislation, they are misleading in the sense that they compare taxes and benefits that will have to be changed for at least some groups to bring the program back into financial balance.

Interest Rate

A third problem with many money's worth analyses is that they fail to correctly incorporate the effect of the interest rate or, more generally, fail to rationalize the interest rate used in the study or fail to provide a range of estimates under alternative interest rate assumptions. In some simplistic payback period analyses, for example, workers' tax payments in each year of their working lives are simply added together to compute total lifetime tax payments. Simply adding together taxes over time, of course, is equivalent to trying to compute one's current savings account balance by simply adding together all prior deposits to the account. Obviously, such an approach would underestimate the current balance to the extent of any interest earnings that were posted to the account. If the deposits were made over an extended period of time, these interest earnings could be substantial.

While it is clear that interest must be taken into account, there is disagreement among analysts about the appropriate interest rate to use. In fact, the differences in the conclusions reached by different money's worth studies are often due to differences in the interest rates used in the studies. The issues involved include whether Social Security should be compared to risky or conservative investments, whether different interest rates are appropriate for individuals in different economic circumstances, and whether the interest rate should be net of income taxes.

Some of these issues can be resolved if the money's worth question is carefully stated. A critical factor in the choice of the interest rate is the nature of the alternative to which the Social Security program is being compared. A frequent form of the money's worth question is whether workers could do better than under Social Security if they were required to save privately for their own retirement.[13] For this type of question, a strong argument can be made that the interest rate should reflect the rate at which workers could accumulate funds over time with the same assurance of nondefault and stability of return as under the present Social Security program. Otherwise, the present program would be compared to an inherently different program in terms of the risks faced by participants.[14] In the context of present income tax rules, an after-tax rate of return is appropriate from the perspective of the individual. Together, these criteria suggest that the after-tax rate of return to long-term federal government bonds[15] is an appropriate market comparison for money's worth questions of this type, with some downward adjustment in the rate to account for other risk-reducing characteristics of the Social Security program, such as the automatic inflation-adjustment of benefits.[16]

Of course, other types of money's worth questions can also be posed, requiring the use of other interest rates. For example, one money's worth question that might be raised is given the interest rates that different workers presently face with regard to their borrowing or lending decisions, would they consider Social Security to be a good or bad investment? This latter type of question could lead to the use of widely varying interest rates for different individuals, depending on whether they were net borrowers or lenders, on the types of assets in their investment portfolios, and on their personal income tax rates; much higher interest rates might be appropriate for many individuals, including those who are net borrowers and those preferring to invest in riskier alternatives. An additional factor arguing for the use of a higher interest rate for some individuals in the context of this latter type of money's worth question is the potential uncertainty they may have concerning future legislative changes in the program. One way to incorporate such uncertainty into the analysis is to increase the "risk premium" component of the interest rate used in the comparison.[17]

It should be kept in mind that this individual-specific type of money's worth comparison is incomplete in that it implicitly ignores some of the social costs and gains of leaving decisions about retirement saving, disability insurance, and life insurance entirely up to individual workers. For example, workers benefit from greater freedom of choice in developing their own retirement saving and insurance strategies, but social costs are generated by those workers who fail to adequately provide for these contingencies or whose investments perform poorly.[18] In addition, well-known insurance problems such as adverse selection affect the ability of the private sector to provide "fair" insurance in many cases, implying other potential social advantages of universal public insurance programs that are not reflected in this latter type of money's worth comparison.[19]

In summary, then, the appropriate interest rate to use in a money's worth analysis depends critically on the particular question the estimates are intended to address. In this sense, no single interest rate is "correct" for all money's worth analyses. As such, it is important for money's worth studies to rationalize the particular interest rates used and to indicate the nature of the money's worth questions that the estimates are designed to answer. Providing estimates for a range of interest rate assumptions broadens the range of questions that can be addressed. In most studies, readers are left to sort out these issues on their own or, worse, are misled by authors with particular political biases—the higher the interest rate, for example, the less favorable the Social Security program tends to appear. In general, if the intended comparison is between the present program and some compulsory private alternative program with equivalent assurance of nondefault and stability of return, then a relatively low interest rate somewhat below the rate of return to long-term Federal Government bonds is appropriate. Alternatively, if the intended comparison does not incorporate an alternative compulsory program, then higher interest rates may be appropriate for many individuals.[20] By comparing inherently different alternatives, however, this latter type of money's worth comparison is incomplete in that it ignores some important social costs and gains that differ among the alternatives considered.

Administrative Costs

A deficiency of nearly all money's worth analyses is that they ignore the administrative costs of the alternative to which the Social Security program is being compared. Because past or projected Social Security taxes and benefits appear directly in the money's worth measures, administrative costs of the Social Security program are already implicitly incorporated.[21] That is, the past or projected benefits that can be paid under the program for a given level of tax collections are reduced by the costs of administering the program. The corresponding costs of administering the alternative to which the Social Security program is being compared, however, are not typically represented in the money's worth measures. This omission biases the money's worth measures against the Social Security program. This bias is larger as a percentage of benefits for the Disability Insurance (DI) program than for the Old Age and Survivors Insurance (OASI) program, but important for both.[22] Even if the alternative being compared to OASI, for example, simply consists of requiring workers to save privately by investing in a certain type of government bond, additional administrative costs would be created under the alternative for both the worker and the government. One difficulty of including such alternative administrative costs into the comparison, of course, is that they are difficult to quantify.[23] Nevertheless, it is important to recognize this inherent bias in nearly all money's worth analyses.

* * *

Limitations and Appropriate Usage of Money's Worth Measures

Some of the technical limitations of money's worth measures and methods of analysis have already been mentioned. Two broader issues also merit emphasis. First, money's worth measures provide only one perspective on the performance of the program and ignore some of its political and social value. For example, money's worth measures examine the effect of the program over individual lifetimes, while some analysts believe that the program is more appropriately viewed from the perspective of a current period tax and transfer program.[24] Such analysts might focus on the current period regressivity of the Social Security payroll tax over the top range of the income scale, for instance, and consider whether such a tax is an appropriate vehicle for transferring resources to the elderly population or whether the Social Security benefit structure adequately targets needy recipients in the current period, regardless of their prior tax contributions. The internal rate of return and benefit/tax ratio measures provide little information concerning the adequacy of benefits compared to measures of current need or even relative to prior earnings; the lifetime transfer measure provides only indirect information on the adequacy of benefits relative to current needs and no information on adequacy relative to prior earnings. In short, the relevance of money's worth measures depends in part on one's view of the purpose and goals of the Social Security program. Specifically, money's worth measures are most appropriate for revealing the intercohort and intracohort redistributional effects of the program using lifetime, rather than current period, measures of economic well-being.

The second broader issue is that money's worth measures are potentially narrow or misleading indicators of the true effect of the program on lifetime incomes. Some analysts believe, for example, that many of the transfers effected by the Social Security program simply substitute public transfers for private transfers that would have occurred otherwise.[25] They argue that children or, more generally, the working community would privately support the aged population if Social Security did not. To the extent that Social Security transfers exceed those that would have occurred privately, they argue that much of the excess is privately transferred back to heirs to compensate for the increased unfunded liability of the program (in the form of future benefit promises), which the heirs also inherit as a form of government indebtedness. To the extent that these arguments hold, money's worth measures can be interpreted as an accounting artifice with limited policy relevance; in other words, the "redistribution" implied by the money's worth measures either would have occurred in the absence of the program or is negated by offsetting private transfers.

On the other band, if these arguments do not hold, the redistribution effected by the program and identified by the money's worth measures is likely to have altered the labor supply and saving behavior of the lifetime transfer recipients. Depending on the intensity of such behavioral effects, their economic consequences may be substantial. For example, cohorts receiving positive net lifetime transfers would likely have increased their lifetime consumption to some extent, reducing saving and capital formation, and thereby reducing the rate of economic growth and the lifetime earnings of program participants in subsequent years. From this perspective, then, money's worth measures may give only a narrow and possibly distorted view of the total economic effects of the Social Security program on lifetime incomes.

It is also important to keep in mind the narrower technical issues and limitations of money's worth analyses discussed earlier in this article. Great care must be taken in interpreting the results of money's worth analyses, since many have been developed improperly or qualified insufficiently. Assumptions of particular importance are the interest rate and the incidence of the employer's share of the payroll tax. An important technique to watch for is the use of hypothetical individuals that are not really representative of the corresponding categories of workers.

While all of these cautions should be kept in mind, money's worth analyses that are carefully done can nevertheless provide important information about the lifetime effects of Social Security tax and benefit provisions. Such analyses can help determine if intended differential treatment is effective and whether the program has other, unintended, distributional effects.

Notes

1. The liberalization of benefits for current retirees has the same effect.

2. As examples, see Boskin *et al.* (1983), Boskin *et al.* (1987), Hurd and Shoven (1985), Pellechio and Goodfellow (1983), and Wolff (1993).

3. As examples, see Bennett (1979), Boskin *et al.* (1987), Burkhauser (1979), Holden (1979), and Hurd and Shoven (1985).

4. Another measure that is sometimes mistakenly referred to as a money's worth measure is the "replacement rate." The replacement rate typically compares initial benefit levels with earnings in the period preceding the receipt of benefits; as such, the replacement rate can be used as a measure of the adequacy of benefits relative to the prior earnings that the benefits partially replace. In contrast, money's worth measures reflect the balance between Social Security taxes and benefits over entire lifetimes.

5. Other variants of these money's worth measures have also been used. Several measures related to the benefit/tax ratio and the lifetime transfer compare the current benefit with the actuarially fair annuity that could be purchased with the accumulated value of lifetime taxes,

assuming the availability of such annuities. These measures include the benefit/fair annuity ratio" and the "current transfer" measures, where the current transfer is defined as the difference between the current benefit and the fair annuity. Although not discussed elsewhere in this article, the "benefit/fair annuity ratio" and the "current transfer" measures are simply the current period analogues to the lifetime benefit/tax ratio and the lifetime transfer measures, respectively. A key implicit assumption associated with these current period analogues is the intertemporal pattern of the inflation adjustments (and any other intertemporal adjustments, such as those associated with the earnings test or income taxation of benefits) to the expected annuity stream over the period during which benefits may be received. For a fair comparison of the current benefit to a current annuity value, for example, the inflation adjustments assumed for benefits over the entire benefit period would also have to be assumed for the annuity stream. Contrary to suggestions sometimes encountered in the literature, current period analogues such as the benefit/fair annuity ratio or current transfer do not possess any special advantages over their corresponding lifetime measure analogues in "disentangling" the "earned" and "transfer" components of Social Security benefits. In fact, the current period analogues in some studies are misleading indicators of lifetime redistributional effects, since they fail to incorporate the same (proportional) pattern of intertemporal adjustments in the computation of the annuity stream as are assumed to apply to the benefit stream. If the same pattern is applied to both streams, *relative* current period analogues should have identical values, except in special cases, to their lifetime measure counterparts; as examples, the benefit/fair annuity ratio generally should be identical to the lifetime benefit/tax ratio, and the ratio of the current transfer to the current benefit generally should be identical to the ratio of the lifetime transfer to lifetime benefits. Taken by itself, however, the current transfer is an individual-specific proportion of the lifetime transfer, generally precluding its use as an indicator of lifetime money's worth outcomes across individuals or groups. Examples of other money's worth measures that can be found in the literature include the ratio of the net lifetime transfer to lifetime taxes, the ratio of the net lifetime transfer to lifetime earnings, and the ratio of the current transfer to the fair annuity based on accumulated taxes.

6. If properly computed, the benefit/tax ratio and lifetime transfer measures do give the same indication of whether a given tax and benefit stream is associated with a positive or negative money's worth outcome, since one is the ratio and the other the difference between lifetime benefits and lifetime taxes. For certain kinds of tax and benefit streams, however, the payback period and internal rate of return measures may give different indications than the benefit/tax ratio and life-time transfer measures.

7. This applies even to the benefit/tax ratio and lifetime transfer measures. See Leimer (1994) for further discussion and some examples.

8. The payback period does not actually indicate expected outcomes in the statistical sense, because it simply allows the comparison of an expected remaining lifetime with the payback period. Put another way, the lifetime transfer measure compares the expected value of lifetime taxes and benefits in a statistically correct way, with the potential tax and benefit component at each possible future age weighted by (that is, multiplied by) the probability of its occurrence. In contrast, the payback period measure generally is derived from a projected stream of potential benefits unweighted by the probabilities of their occurrence. As such, the payback period measure can produce different conclusions than the lifetime transfer measure.

9. The lifetime transfer may not be a reliable indicator of the total effects of the program on the economic well-being of program participants, of course, because of other factors such as

borrowing constraints or broader effects of the program on economic growth that affect the lifetime incomes of program participants but are not reflected in their taxes and benefits.

10. Money's worth studies generally have not rationalized their choice of progressivity measures. In the context of *current* period tax or transfer programs, progressivity is often defined in terms of the pattern of taxes or net transfers under the program relative to some *current* measure of "ability to pay" or "economic well-being;" a progressive income tax, for example, might be defined as one where the tax as a proportion of income (the tax rate) rises as income rises. In the *lifetime* context of money's worth analyses, the analogous approach would examine the pattern of *lifetime* net transfers relative to a measure of *lifetime* economic well-being relevant to the program. One reasonable progressivity measure in money's worth analyses, then, would be the ratio of the lifetime transfer to lifetime earnings; a social security program might be defined as progressive if this ratio declines as lifetime earnings increase. The internal rate of return and benefit/tax ratio might be rationalized as progressivity measures because they indicate the relative attractiveness of the social security program as an "investment" alternative or because of their generally close relationship to the lifetime transfer/lifetime earnings ratio; for example, if the social security tax rate were proportional over all earnings and constant over workers' lifetimes, then the lifetime benefit/tax ratio could be derived as a linear transformation of the lifetime transfer/lifetime earnings ratio. In general, however, the internal rate of return and benefit/tax ratio are not direct measures of lifetime transfers relative to a measure of lifetime economic well-being.

Although money's worth analyses generally have used *relative* measures to examine the progressivity or regressivity of lifetime redistribution under Social Security, some have instead defined progressivity to require that the *absolute* lifetime transfer (not the lifetime transfer/ lifetime earnings ratio or other relative measure) must decline as lifetime earnings increase. This absolute definition has some undesirable properties in both current period and lifetime contexts. An analogous standard of progressivity applied to current period income tax analysis, for example, would characterize a flat-rate income tax as progressive, implying a different standard of progressivity than that generally adopted. In a lifetime context, an absolute lifetime transfer standard of progressivity can be inconsistent in its characterization of a pay-as-you-go social security program at different stages of program maturity—this absolute standard may imply that such a program is extremely regressive in its early stages, when all generations are receiving large absolute transfers, even if higher lifetime earners in each generation of participants experience lower lifetime transfer/lifetime earnings ratios than lower lifetime earners; this absolute standard could then imply that the same program is extremely progressive when the program matures to the point that, say, workers break even on average, with high earners receiving negative, and low earners positive, net lifetime transfers.

11. For example, see Myers and Schobel (1992), pp. 48–49.

12. While different studies have reached different conclusions, the assumption that the employer share of the tax is shifted directly or indirectly to workers is supported by a number of theoretical and empirical analyses. Based on a theoretical analysis, for example, Feldstein (1974) concludes that in the long run labor will bear at least 100 percent of the net burden of a tax on labor income. See Dye (1984) for a summary of a number of empirical analyses.

13. This article focuses on money's worth questions that are posed from the standpoint of the options available to individual participants in the program. An alternative type of analysis would evaluate the efficiency of the pay-as-you-go financing of the Social Security program from the standpoint of the options available to society as a whole. Different interest rate con-

siderations are appropriate for such analyses and are not addressed in this article. See Leimer (1991) for a further discussion of these issues.

14. For this type of money's worth question, the risks faced by participants under the Social Security program are appropriately evaluated from the perspective of the policymaker comparing the present program against some alternative private saving program in which workers might be required to participate. For other forms of the money's worth question, these risks may be more appropriately evaluated from the perspective of program participants, as discussed below.

15. A number of money's worth analyses use the (before-tax) rate of return to Social Security trust fund assets. This generally is not an appropriate interest rate for the type of money's worth question discussed in this paragraph, because the return to trust fund assets generally does not reflect the rate at which workers themselves could accumulate funds over time with the same assurance of nondefault and stability of return as under the present Social Security program. The rate of return to trust fund assets may be an appropriate rate, however, to identify lifetime redistribution under Social Security from the perspective of the *program* (rather than from the perspective of individual workers). See Leimer (1994) for further discussion of this distinction as well as estimates of both *money's worth* outcomes and *lifetime redistribution* across successive generations of workers.

16. See Leimer and Richardson (1992) for empirical estimates and a discussion of the theoretical issues associated with the risk-reducing characteristics of the program. Their estimates suggest that an inflation-adjusted interest rate close to zero or even negative may be appropriate from the perspective of individual workers. In this article, the term "inflation-adjusted interest rate" refers to the interest rate after an adjustment for inflation has been made to the observed nominal interest rate. For small rates of inflation, the inflation-adjusted interest rate is approximately equal to the nominal interest rate minus the inflation rate, and is sometimes referred to as the "real" interest rate.

17. This form of risk adjustment is strictly appropriate only if the risk component associated with future taxes and benefits is perceived to grow exponentially over time.

18. In addition to increased public or private spending to assist such workers, these social costs can include the social disutility associated with increased poverty or a less equal distribution of income as well as the social stigma experienced by beneficiaries of means tested programs or private charity.

19. Adverse selection refers to the tendency of those who are "bad" insurance risks to buy insurance, and those who are "good" insurance risks to avoid its purchase, when insurance purchase is voluntary. This problem arises even if insurance coverage is mandatory, but plans with different provisions are marketed by different insurance providers. Consumers with high risks in particular areas will tend to gravitate toward plans offering better coverage of those risks, driving insurance costs above what would be required to cover those risks in the general population. See Thompson (1983), pp. 1440–1442, for additional discussion of other advantages of universal public insurance programs.

20. To provide a feel for potential differences in the rates of return to relatively conservative and risky investments, the average annual inflation-adjusted yield on long-term government bonds over the period 1937–92 was 0.6 percent, while the average annual inflation-adjusted yield on common stocks over the same period was 7.3 percent.

21. These administrative costs exclude some associated costs incurred by employers, the self-employed, and other government agencies in their transactions with the Social Security

program. These associated costs should also be incorporated into the analysis to the extent that they are avoided under the alternative to which the Social Security program is being compared, but obvious difficulties arise, analogous to those discussed above in the tax incidence section, in identifying who ultimately pays these costs.

22. In 1992, for example, net administrative expenses amounted to 2.7 percent of benefits under the DI program but only 0.7 percent of benefits under the OASI program. Administrative costs and operating expenses in the private insurance industry are generally much higher, reflecting marketing costs, adverse selection, and the inability to exploit the economies of scale enjoyed by a compulsory, nearly universal, public program. See Leimer (1991) for additional discussion.

23. Conceptually, one way to incorporate the omitted administrative costs of the alternative into the money's worth measures is to include those costs as a type of Social Security benefit in each period of the analysis, that is, increase Social Security benefits in each period by an appropriate amount to reflect the omitted administrative costs of the alternative in that period. The rationale behind this approach is that those costs are avoided under the present program and can therefore be treated as a benefit of the present program when comparing it to the alternative. Again, there may be difficulties in identifying who ultimately pays these costs, depending on the nature of the alternative.

24. For example, see Pechman, Aaron, and Taussig (1968), especially pp. 74–77.

25. See Lesnoy and Leimer (1985) for a more complete, nontechnical, discussion of these issues.

CHAPTER 11

Social Security Reform

Notwithstanding its success, Social Security is often cited as being in need of reform, if not total elimination. Proponents of reform vary from those who support the concept of Social Security but who believe that the present program treats some workers unfairly, such as women who stay at home and so do not earn credit for retirement benefits, to those who fear for the financial stability of the program and those who object to it on ideological grounds and advocate privatization of public pensions. Unfortunately, much of the demand for reform is predicated on misunderstandings of Social Security. As Professor Kaplan points out in his article, the myths about Social Security interfere with rational discussion and obscure an understanding of both its strengths and its problems.

Richard L. Kaplan

Top Ten Myths of Social Security

* * *

The purpose of this article is to examine the principal myths surrounding the Social Security program as a prelude to understanding budget reform proposals that might emerge affecting this program. As the Kerrey-Danforth Commission Study revealed, Social Security must contribute to the ongoing effort to bring the federal budget deficit under control.[1] How that is accomplished will, in many ways, depend upon the resiliency of what might be described as the "Top Ten Myths of Social Security."

The Elder Law Journal, Vol. 3, No. 2, pp. 191–214 (Fall, 1995). Reprinted by permission.

I. There Is a Trust Fund

There is probably no single, more enduring myth among Americans than the existence of some separately constituted Social Security trust fund. In public opinion surveys and collections of anecdotes, Americans, particularly older Americans, genuinely believe that there is an accumulation of funds in some dedicated account somewhere that consists of genuine financial assets.[2] Such a fund does not exist and was never envisioned even when Social Security was created.[3] Quite to the contrary, Social Security collects revenues from a payroll tax on current workers. That payroll tax is 12.4 percent—split between the employee and the employer—of a worker's earnings, imposed on earnings up to an annually adjusted cap.[4] For 1995, that cap was $61,200.[5] Workers earning above this cap do not pay Social Security taxes. These tax revenues, however, do not get placed into some isolated fund. Instead, the program uses these revenues to pay benefits to current beneficiaries, and that has always been the program's operative design.[6]

At the present time, Social Security brings in revenues in excess of the amounts needed to pay benefits to current recipients.[7] In 1995, for example, Social Security revenues were $390 billion, while benefits were only $332 billion.[8] This $58 billion difference, or "surplus," is used *currently* by the federal government to pay other federal expenditures; e.g., defense, other domestic spending, and interest on the national debt.[9] To be sure, the federal government does not simply take this money without obligating itself to repay it in the future. In fact, the federal government *does* obligate itself to repay those funds to the Social Security program, with interest, at a regular market rate.[10] But no funds accumulate in some Social Security trust account. Rather, it is simply a bookkeeping entry, recording the fact that the federal government has taken the currently generated surplus and has given obligations that are essentially tantamount to government IOUs.[11] In some sense, this government IOU is the fiscal equivalent of a U.S. government bond. Indeed, even if there were a bona fide "trust fund," Social Security's need for absolute safety of principal and predictable convertibility into cash would probably compel it to invest in the world's safest security—namely, U.S. government obligations. But the point remains that there is no single accumulation of marketable government securities, nor is there some wad of money sitting in some Federal Reserve Bank account.[12]

* * *

II. Social Security Does Not Increase the Federal Budget Deficit

A myth related to the preceding Social Security trust fund myth is that Social Security does not "contribute" to or aggravate the federal budget deficit in any manner. In a sense, this assertion is factually correct. *At the present time,* Social Security brings in more money than it pays out.[13] To that extent, therefore, the program produces a net increase in revenues, which operates to reduce what the government's budget deficit would otherwise look like. For example, in the preceding section, it was noted that Social Security brought in revenues in excess of beneficiary payments of some $58 billion in 1995. Were that $58 billion segregated into some sort of separate account—and not available to the federal government generally—the current year's budget deficit would be $58 billion larger than is being currently reported.[14] In other words, the federal government is spending the net revenue intake of the Social Security program on current expenditures, rather than using non-Social Security revenues to fund those needs exclusively. As a result, it is indeed true that if the Social Security program did not exist, the federal budget deficit would actually be *higher* than currently reported.

Nevertheless, the current use of those net revenues is simply a means of borrowing from Peter to pay Paul. That is, in future years when the Social Security program will require more outlays than revenues will provide, the federal government will need to raise funds from other sources to cover all of its commitments. In those later years, it will be obvious to all that the Social Security program is a net drain on the federal budget and does in fact aggravate the budget deficit on a current-year basis.

* * *

III. Retirees Are Only Recovering Their Own Money

One of the myths that makes the Social Security program so politically untouchable is the belief that current retirees are simply recovering their own contributions. If this were true, one would indeed be hard pressed to suggest reducing Social Security benefits. If people do not recover their own investments, after all, Social Security might be seen as just another tax-like government imposition. Social Security, in fact, is partially a program of social insurance[15] and partially a program of ensuring retirement income.[16] Yet many, if not most, retirees seem to believe that its retirement income function is its overwhelmingly predominant, if not sole, characteristic. Accordingly, they view the monthly payments that they receive as a return of the taxes that they paid to the system during their working life.

During much of Social Security's existence, its taxes were imposed at much lower rates and on a much lower wage base than is currently the case. For example, from 1937 through 1949, the Social Security tax rate was only 2 percent rather than the present 12.4 percent, which continues to be split between the employer and employee.[17] Rates were increased after that date, but on an irregular schedule—sometimes once every four years, sometimes every year. But the total tax rate was only half of the current rate as recently as 1962, and did not reach 10 percent until 1978.[18] Similarly, the wage base on which this tax was imposed was only $3,000 through 1950, and was then raised on an irregular schedule until it reached $7,800 in 1968.[19] The wage base was then raised again in 1972 and every year thereafter. Even so, it did not rise above $30,000 until 1982.[20] Due to these low rates and a low wage base during many of the years in which current retirees were working, their maximum Social Security tax—including their employer's portion—was only $60.[21] As recently as 1972, in fact, the maximum amount paid in was only $828.[22] And of course, during those years, persons who did not earn the maximum wage cap paid in even smaller amounts. Consequently, when current retirees relate their payments of Social Security taxes—both their own and their employer's share—to current benefits, a low-wage earner retiring in 1995 at age sixty-five recovers in forty months all of the Social Security taxes paid.[23] Even a maximum-wage earner who paid tax on whatever wage cap was in effect, recovers the cumulative investment in less than seven years.[24] In other words, after four and one-half years of receiving Social Security benefits, an average-wage-earning retiree is collecting welfare.[25] That is, *all* of that worker's money has been repaid, including the employer's portion paid on the worker's behalf. Even if one includes interest earned during that interval, at some point most current retirees are receiving funds in excess of what they had put into the system.[26]

On the other hand, the relationship between payments to and benefits received from Social Security is changing over time. As noted above, the Social Security tax rate has increased dramatically in the past twenty years or so.[27] The wage base on which those Social Security taxes are collected, moreover, has risen dramatically since 1972, and has more than tripled since 1978.[28] As a result, people who retire in the future may not, in fact, recover all of their investments in the form of retirement benefits. Some computations involving unmarried men earning maximum earnings and having average life expectancies indicate that they may not recover all of their Social Security taxes when they retire.[29] Another way of describing this phenomenon is that the number of years needed to recover the much-greater Social Security taxes paid into the system in recent years may exceed the person's anticipated life expectancy upon attaining retirement age.[30] On the other hand, huge categories of beneficiaries will not face this predicament for many years—namely, married men (whose spouses receive additional Social Security benefits and who have longer life expectancies generally), women (who have longer life expectancies generally), and workers who earned less than the wage cap (whose taxes paid into the system were necessarily lower).[31]

To summarize, in the future, some retirees will be simply recovering their own funds. But at the present time, and for many years to come, almost all retirees will have long since recovered their tax payments into the Social Security program, often many times over.

IV. Social Security Will Not Be There When One Retires

A prevailing myth among current *workers,* rather than current retirees, is that the Social Security program is so doomed to insolvency that the program will not be there for them at all. In one widely quoted survey of younger Americans, only 28 percent believed that the Social Security system would pay benefits to them when they retire.[32] In that same survey, fully 46 percent of the respondents said that they believed that unidentified flying objects (UFOs) exist.[33] Young Americans, in other words, have nearly twice as much faith in UFOs as in the continued existence of Social Security.

The idea that Social Security will disappear is a particularly pernicious canard, because it demoralizes younger workers whose current taxes are needed to fund the program. It is also patently untrue. Regardless of whether one can fully recover one's contributions to Social Security, the program will continue to provide retirement benefits for future generations of retirees. Those retirement benefits may not be as generous as those being received by the current generation of retirees, and the qualifying retirement age may be delayed, but Social Security will certainly continue to pay benefits when people retire.

In a sense, the myth of Social Security's impending collapse is related to the myth described earlier that there is a single isolated trust fund. After all, if there is a trust fund, and if that fund is depleted, then presumably no further benefits will be paid. But the obligations of Social Security are not limited to some finite trust fund.[34] Social Security is backed by the full faith and credit of the federal government.[35] It is precisely because there is no single segregated fund that the government's commitment to generations of future retirees continues even when the balance in that "fund" is gone. To put this matter somewhat differently, even if no balance remains in the Social Security fund, and even if benefit expenditures exceed Social Security's revenues, the government remains obligated to make those payments to retirees.[36]

Indeed, one of the most significant differences between Social Security and other pension plans is the absolute solvency, in a cash flow sense, of the Social Security system. No matter what happens, the government cannot go bankrupt, unlike a private company. If worse comes to worst, the federal government will simply raise federal taxes generally, reduce other government spending, or borrow the funds necessary to continue Social Security's commitments. The absolute worst case scenario would have the government inflating the value of its currency by printing up enough money to meet its Social Security commitments. While this prospect is hardly reassuring, the point remains that the federal government is the single most reliable creditor. Accordingly, Social Security will be there when a person retires, and its benefits will be paid on time.

V. Retirement Benefits Are Proportional to One's Lifetime Earnings

Most Americans, both current retirees and workers, seem to believe that there is a mathematically correlative relationship between one's lifetime earnings and one's Social Security retirement benefits. To be sure, the more that one earns while working, the more one will receive in Social Security benefits. But the correlation is not nearly as mathematical as would exist in a true pension plan.

The derivation of Social Security benefits follows an extremely convoluted methodology that is almost never alluded to, let alone explained, in any materials that are available to the general public. This methodology is not exactly secret, for it is explained in treatises that are addressed to professional advisors.[37] But only rarely do these treatises clearly set forth the bottom-weighted calculation of Social Security retirement benefits.

* * *

In contrast, a person's *contributions* into Social Security are proportional to one's earnings. But as the preceding analysis has shown, one's *benefits* are not. Thus, a person making $40,000 a year pays exactly twice the amount of Social Security tax as someone making $20,000 a year. While that first person will get a larger Social Security benefit than will the second person, the first person's benefit will not be twice as large, and therein lies the rub.

A further complicating factor is the fact that only those Social Security earnings that were initially subject to tax—that is, that were under the annually adjusted wage cap—are ever considered in deriving Social Security benefits. Thus, someone with earnings of $100,000 in 1995 would be treated for Social Security's purposes as earning only $61,200—the wage cap for that year. Earnings above the wage cap are completely ignored in deriving the AIME statistic. Consequently, the Social Security benefit for a high-wage earner will be a smaller percentage of that person's lifelong earnings.

* * *

VII. Social Security Favors Long-Lived Marriages

Social Security is often described as a program that rewards the "traditional" marital relationship, sometimes called "Ozzie and Harriet" after a popular 1950s television program, of a working man married his entire adult life to a woman who does not work in the compensated work force.[38] Indeed, the preceding discussion demonstrated that married couples receive greater benefits when only one spouse is employed than when both spouses produce the equivalent earnings. Nevertheless, it is not true that Social Security favors lifelong marital partners.

Social Security provides a derivative benefit not only to the spouse of a worker who has retired, but also to the ex-spouse of a worker, if that ex-spouse was married at least ten years to the worker and has not remarried.[39] In certain circumstances, subsequent remarriages are ignored—namely, when the remarriage occurs after reaching age sixty.[40] But in any case, a person who is a divorced spouse can collect benefits based on the worker's work history without affecting benefits that are paid to that worker, to that worker's current spouse, or to any other recipients (for example, children) who may be, however, collecting derivative benefits from that worker's account.[41] Their marriage, however, must have lasted at least ten years. So if, for example, Hank was married to Alice for eleven years, then to Betty for twelve years, and then to Carol for ten years, all three of his ex-wives could collect benefits equal to one-half of his worker's retirement benefit. Once a person has been married at least ten years, in other words, that person's spouse has become vested in that person's Social Security record, and further years of marriage do not increase the amount of that spouse's Social Security benefit. In effect, Social Security provides no incentive to stay married once a marriage has lasted ten years.

* * *

Thus, Social Security recognizes the increasing prevalence of divorce and does not tilt its benefits in the direction of long-lived marriages once a couple celebrates their tenth wedding anniversary.

VIII. One Could Do Better Investing Directly

Few myths are more violently asserted than the idea that Social Security is a rip-off to workers who could take the taxes that they pay to Social Security and obtain better benefits on their own. At a certain level, this assertion actually is true. Because of the bottom-weighted PIA benefit formula methodology described above, a person's Social Security payments *could* typically provide a larger benefit upon retirement, if those funds were invested privately.[42]

But there are several major caveats to that assertion. First, one must recognize that Social Security payments are collected from the employee automatically, every year, regardless of the person's other financial needs and preferences.[43] The payments do not depend upon the fiscal discipline of the particular person involved. Second, as indicated above, Social Security is guaranteed to make its payments on time.[44] Unlike private pension systems, there is no realistic risk of default. Whether the government will use borrowed or newly printed funds to meet its obligations, the fact remains that private pension plans are not able to "print their way" out of any fiscal difficulties that might arise. Social Security is uniquely dependable in that regard. Third, Social Security is completely portable. With very limited exceptions, virtually every type of employment is covered by Social Security,[45] including self-employment. No other defined benefit plan credits *every* year of a person's work life, regardless of that person's employer, industry, or profession.

But the benefits of Social Security go much beyond the complete portability and guaranteed liquidity of Social Security's retirement benefit program. The entire range of derivative benefits adds to a person's potential benefits far in excess of what private pension plans could ever hope to provide. For example, even in a "traditional" marriage such as Ozzie and Harriet's from the preceding section, Social Security pays the retired worker's spouse half of the worker's benefit.[46] No private pension plan provides *any* spousal benefit while the worker spouse is still alive. Joint-and-survivor annuities and other survivor-oriented benefits are paid only when the worker/retiree has died.[47] Social Security is unique in this regard. Moreover, Social Security provides benefits to a divorced spouse,[48] or as in the case of Hank from the preceding section, to several divorced spouses. Once again, there is simply no private sector counterpart that would try to provide benefits to more than one spouse of a worker based upon that worker's work history.

In addition to these spousal and former spouse benefits, Social Security pays benefits to certain children under age nineteen.[49] These benefits can also be half of the retiree's PIA, but there is a "family maximum" that limits payments to a worker's current spouse and dependent minor children.[50] The family maximum is derived from a four-part formula tied to the worker's PIA,[51] but the point remains that certain children receive derivative benefits while the retiree is still alive—a benefit that is also unmatched by any private sector pension plan.

Moreover, these derivative benefits are all augmented when the retiree dies. A surviving spouse or ex-spouse receives increased benefits, as described previously. A surviving child's benefit is increased to 75 percent of the worker's PIA, although still subject to the family maximum. Even a worker's *parents* may be eligible for Social Security benefits if they received half of their support from the deceased worker.[52] Once again, this package of survivors' benefits simply has no counterpart in private plans.

Perhaps even more significantly, *all* Social Security benefits are adjusted annually, across the board, on the basis of inflation, via the mechanism of a cost-of-living allowance, or COLA.[53] Some version of a cost-of-living allowance may characterize other public pension systems, but few are as comprehensive as Social Security's. Moreover, inflation adjustments are very uncommon in private pension plan payouts.[54] Most private plans utilize annuities and other mechanisms that fix the payment amount when the payments begin. These private plans simply ignore inflation that occurs after payments begin. Social Security, in short, is inflation-protected to a degree that few other pension plans even attempt.

Finally, but by no means insignificantly, Social Security provides benefits beyond retirement benefits, derivative benefits, and survivors' benefits. Social Security's official name is the Old Age, Survivors, and Disability Insurance.[55] The focus of this article has thus far been on the old-age and survivors aspects of Social Security. But the taxes that workers pay into Social Security also provide the person with *disability* coverage.[56] Though most workers simply ignore this feature of Social Security unless and until they are disabled, the coverage remains in effect nevertheless. Under this program, if a person is unable to perform "any substantial gainful activity by reason of any medically determinable physical or mental impairment,"[57] then the person can receive disability payments starting as young as twenty-one years of age. These payments continue until that person reaches full retirement age, at which time the person's Social Security retirement benefit begins. In addition, if a person receives Social Security disability benefits for twenty-four consecutive months, he or she becomes eligible for Medicare,[58] the federal government's health care program, which covers most of the person's medical needs.

* * *

The sum of these features—universal access, complete portability, guaranteed liquidity, derivative benefits, survivors' benefits, inflation adjustments to all benefits paid, and disability coverage—is a comprehensive package that would be impossible to replicate on a private basis, at any price. To be sure, some employees might prefer a less comprehensive package if they had the choice, but the fact remains that Social Security—when analyzed as an entire package—is simply better than what they could otherwise obtain.

IX. Working After Retirement Makes Financial Sense

As noted previously, Social Security benefits are payable as early as age sixty-two. At that age, however, one's Social Security benefit is reduced actuarially to take account of the longer period over which those benefits will be paid.[59] Many such persons can, of course, still earn income as an employee or from self-employment. Accordingly, some retirees consider working part-time while receiving Social Security. The question becomes: does this strategy make financial sense?

Continuing to work past age sixty-two might provide additional years of earnings history and could lead to a recalculation of a person's PIA, especially if that person's earnings average increases due to these additional years of earnings.[60] For example, someone with less than thirty-five years of wages before age sixty-two would benefit by replacing a year of zero or low wages with a year of higher wages after age sixty-two, thereby increasing that person's average. This effect is moderated rather significantly, however, by the bottom-weighted PIA formula. As a result of that formula, increases in average earnings produce relatively small increases in one's Social Security benefits. But the point remains that increased earnings can produce higher Social Security benefits if the impact on one's average earnings is large enough.

On the other hand, Social Security imposes a "retirement earnings" test on recipients who perform compensated work while receiving retirement benefits.[61] Reduced to its essence, this test limits the amount of earnings that a retiree can receive before losing some of his or her Social Security benefits.

The "retirement earnings test" focuses exclusively on income earned from performing personal services. It ignores a person's income from investment sources, such as interest income, dividends, capital gains, rentals, and annuities. Similarly, it ignores pension payments. Only income from wages and self-employment, including director's fees and commissions, is considered,[62] thereby reflecting the test's underlying rationale—namely, that retirement benefits are for persons who have retired from active employment.

* * *

Clearly, if a person wishes to continue working beyond a certain age, that person should consider delaying receipt of Social Security retirement benefits, because those benefits will be reduced in many cases.[63] There are, of course, many sound social and psychological reasons for continuing to work after one retires. But the point remains that if post-retirement earnings would trigger Social Security's retirement earnings test, working after retirement usually does *not* make financial sense, particularly for persons who have not yet reached "full retirement age."

X. Retirement Benefits Are Taxed More Heavily Than Other Pension Payments

In nearly all private pension plans, the entire amount of the benefit payment is taxable when received.[64] Recipients have had, of course, the advantage of deferring tax on this income from when the pension benefit was earned during their working years until the date of its receipt, but when the benefit is finally received, it is taxable *in full*, in most cases.[65]

In contrast, Social Security retirement benefits are generally received tax-free. Until 1983, in fact, Social Security recipients did not pay tax on any Social Security benefits.[66] . . .

* * *

To summarize, three out of four Social Security recipients pay no federal tax at all on their benefits. About one in eight pay tax on between 50 percent and 85 percent of their Social Security benefits. This treatment is far more generous than that accorded to private pension plans, the benefits of which are fully taxable to all recipients, regardless of their income from other sources.

Notes

1. [*See* BIPARTISAN COMM'N ON ENTITLEMENT & TAX REFORM, FINAL REPORT TO THE PRESIDENT 22–24, 216–38 (1995).]

2. *See, e.g.*, George J. Church & Richard Lacayo, *Social Insecurity*, TIME, Mar. 20, 1995, at 24, 29; Michael Kinsley, *The Best Way to Fix Medicare*, TIME, Sept. 4, 1995, at 24.

3. MICHAEL J. BOSKIN, TOO MANY PROMISES: THE UNCERTAIN FUTURE OF SOCIAL SECURITY 7–8, 126 (1986); Kinsley, *supra* note 2, at 24.

4. I.R.C. §§ 3101(a), 3111(a), 3121(a) (1995); 42 U.S.C. § 430 (Supp. 1995).

5. Spencer Rich, *Plan Deepens Cuts for Future Retirees; Separate Social Security Panel Appears Split*, WASH. POST, May 22, 1995, at A21.

6. *Social Security Q&A*, BOSTON GLOBE, June 18, 1995, at 17.

7. David Steinberg, *Don't Tamper with Social Security*, S.F. EXAMINER, July 29, 1995, at C-7.

8. *See* Church & Lacayo, *supra* note 2, at 28.

9. [*See* BIPARTISAN COMM'N ON ENTITLEMENT & TAX REFORM, FINAL REPORT TO THE PRESIDENT 22–24, 216–38 (1995).]

10. Church & Lacayo, *supra* note 2, at 26; *see* BOSKIN, *supra* note 3, at 7–8, 126.

11. Carolyn Lochhead, *Trust Fund Myth Sank Budget Plan—Social Security Is Spent, Not Saved*, S.F. CHRON., Mar. 6, 1995, at A1.

12. BOSKIN, *supra* note 3, at 7–8, 126; Church & Lacayo, *supra* note 2, at 28.

13. [Carolyn Lochhead, *Trust Fund Myth Sank Budget Plan—Social Security Is Spent, Not Saved*, S.F. CHRON., Mar. 6, 1995, at A1.]

14. *See* Church & Lacayo, *supra* note 2, at 27.

15. Kelly W. Schemenave, Adams v. Weinberger *and* Dubinski v. Bowen: Posthumous Illegitimate Children and the Social Security Child Survivorship Provision, 25 Soc. Sec. Rep. Serv. (West) 685, 686 (1989); . . . .

16. [Nancy J. Altman, *The Reconciliation of Retirement Security and Tax Policies: A Response to Professor Graetz,* 136 U. PA. L. REV. 1419, 1426–27 (1988).]

17. *See* COMMERCE CLEARING HOUSE, 1994 SOCIAL SECURITY EXPLAINED 25 (1994) [hereinafter CCH]. Since 1950, Social Security taxes have multiplied 10 times.

18. CCH, *supra* note 17, at 25.

19. *Id.* at 36.

20. *Id.*

21. *See id.* at 25–38 (wage base of $3,000 × 1.0% = $30 paid by both employer and employee, or $60 in total).

22. *See id.* (wage base of $9,000 × 4.6% = $414 paid by both employer and employee, or $828 in total).

23. *See* Church & Lacayo, *supra* note 2, at 29 (20 months × 2 [employer + employee] = 40 months); *see also* BOSKIN, *supra* note 3, at 8. *See generally CRS Finds Falling Social Security Recovery,* Daily Tax Rep. (BNA) No. 11, at H-1 (Jan. 18, 1994).

24. Church & Lacayo, *supra* note 2, at 29.

25. Robert D. Hershey Jr., *Misunderstanding Social Security,* N.Y. TIMES, Aug. 20, 1995, § 4, at 4.

26. *Id.; see also* [BIPARTISAN COMM'N ON ENTITLEMENT & TAX REFORM, Final Report to the President, 22–24, 216–38 (1995).]

27. *See supra* note 17.

28. *See supra* note 19.

29. *Data Show Class of Retirees Already Will Receive Less in Benefits than Taxes Paid,* Daily Tax Rep. (BNA) No. 47, at G-5 (Mar. 12, 1993).

30. *Id.*

31. *Id.*

32. *Boomers, Generation X'ers May Fight over Benefit Scraps,* ARIZ. REPUBLIC, Feb. 4, 1995, at E1.

33. *Id.*

34. BOSKIN, *supra* note 3, at 7–8, 126.

35. *Id.*

36. *Id.*

37. *See, e.g.,* Hans Sprohge & Carl A. Brooks, *Understanding Social Security Retirement Benefits,* 174 J. ACCOUNTANCY 53, 56–57 (1992); [*see* C. Eugene Steuerle & Jon M. Bakija, *Basic Features of the Social Security System,* 62 TAX NOTES 1457, 1458–60 (1994)]; Richard B. Toolson, *Should a Worker Who Continues to Work Beyond Normal Retirement Age Immediately Draw Social Security Benefits?,* 57 TAX NOTES 539, 540 (1992); *see also* LOUIS A. MEZZULLO & MARK WOOLPERT, ADVISING THE ELDERLY CLIENT §§ 15:184 to 15:195 (1992); PETER J. STRAUSS ET AL., AGING AND THE LAW 147–49 (1990).

38. Steve Sakson, *Women Become Losers Under Conditions of Social Security Rules; Retirement: Married Working Women Usually Earn No More in Benefits Than If They Had Never Worked a Day,* L.A. TIMES, Nov. 25, 1990, at A46.

39. 42 U.S.C. § 416(d)(1), (4) (1988).

40. *Id.* § 402(e)(3)(A).

41. *See* CCH, *supra* note 17, ¶ 524.

42. *See, e.g.,* Church & Lacayo, *supra* note 2, at 29 (illustrating how Social Security payments invested in U.S. Treasury Bills or corporate bonds would have yielded a higher monthly payout than Social Security provides).

43. 42 U.S.C. § 430 (Supp. 1995); I.R.C. §§ 3101(a), 3102(a) (1995).

44. *See* Church & Lacayo, *supra* note 2, at 29.

45. Noncovered employment includes the following principal categories: most employees of state and local governments, students who work at the school or college that they attend, children under age 18 who are employed by their parent, and certain religious objectors. *See generally* [LAWRENCE A. FROLIK & RICHARD L. KAPLAN, ELDER LAW IN A NUTSHELL 279–80 (1995).]

46. 42 U.S.C. § 402(b)(2), (c)(2) (1988).

47. *See* 29 U.S.C. § 1055(e) (1988 & Supp. 1993); I.R.C. §§ 401(a)(11), 417 (1995).

48. 42 U.S.C. § 416(d)(1), (4) (1988).

49. 42 U.S.C. § 402(d)(1) (children must generally be under age 18, but children who are 18 years old can qualify if they are still attending elementary or high school).

50. *See* CCH, *supra* note 17, ¶ 538.

51. *Id.* (illustrating the computation of the "family maximum").

52. 42 U.S.C. § 402(h) (1988).

53. *See* CCH, *supra* note 32, ¶ 541.

54. GARY S. FIELDS & OLIVIA S. MITCHELL, RETIREMENT, PENSIONS, AND SOCIAL SECURITY 39 (1984).

55. 42 U.S.C. § 401(a), (b) (1988).

56. *See generally* CCH, *supra* note 17, at 202–23; LAWRENCE A. FROLIK & MELISSA C. BROWN, ADVISING THE ELDERLY OR DISABLED CLIENT 4-19 to 4-33 (1992).

57. 42 U.S.C. § 416(i)(1)(A) (1988).

58. *Id.* § 1395c(2).

59. The benefits are reduced by 5/9 of 1% for every month that benefits commence before the recipient reaches "full retirement age." 42 U.S.C. § 402(q)(1)(A) (1988). Thus, someone who starts receiving benefits at age 62 would receive 80% of what that person would receive at age 65 (3 years early × 12 months = 36 × 5/9 = 20% reduction).

60. 42 U.S.C. § 402(q)(10) (1988).

61. *Id.* § 403(b).

62. *Id.* § 403(f)(5). *See generally* CCH, *supra* note 17, ¶ 555.1.

63. There is a compensating adjustment for persons who lose Social Security benefits due to "excess" earnings. Their age of benefit commencement is increased to take account of the lost benefits, and this adjustment will increase their benefits in the future, although by relatively small amounts. *See* 42 U.S.C. § 402(q)(7) (1988); *see also* Bruce D. Schobel, *Letter to the Editor,* 57 TAX NOTES 1219 (1992).

64. I.R.C. § 61(a)(11) (1995); *see* FROLIK & BROWN, *supra* note 57, at 7–8.

65. *Id. See generally* DIANNE BENNETT ET AL., TAXATION OF DISTRIBUTIONS FROM QUALIFIED PLANS (1991).

66. CCH, *supra* note 17, ¶ 250A.

Although much of the criticism of Social Security is based on misinformation and misunderstanding of the program, there are legitimate concerns about its future viability. The biggest fear, of course, is that in the years to come the program will be unable to pay the benefits promised to today's workers. At present, Social Security wage taxes produce more revenue than is distributed as benefits. This excess of revenues is the intended result of a policy choice.

In addition to providing a source of funds in later years, the Social Security surplus has another significant consequence because it plays an enormous role in determining the apparent size of the deficit. The annual federal deficit is reduced on paper by the amount of the Social Security excess revenues. Other self-financing trust funds have the same effect, but not to the extent of Social Security. In 1989 alone, the inclusion of Social Security reserves offset $55 billion in the general revenue deficit.

The excess Social Security trust funds mean that the federal government borrows less, thereby keeping interest rates lower. Under law, any Social Security reserves are invested in interest-paying treasury securities and the assets are then used to finance other federal programs. In effect, the government is borrowing from itself. Although the revenue surplus was expected to continue until the year 2020, in 1997 estimates moved the date up to 2013.

As the public awareness of the impeding short-fall in Social Security revenues has grown, so have calls for reform. Among those who have written extensively about the problems of Social Security and other governmental entitlement programs, perhaps the most outspoken is Peter G. Peterson, former-Secretary of the United States Treasury. In a series of articles in magazines such as the Atlantic Monthly *and* The New York Review of Books, *Peterson has sounded the alarm of the impending crises caused by what he refers to as our "entitlement ethnic"; that is, the creation of excessive public entitlements for older Americans. Peterson's argument is relatively simple. He claims that because of the future growth in the number of older citizens, it will be impossible to provide them with all the benefits promised to them, and still provide adequately for younger Americans. Peterson urges that we reject the prevailing "entitlement ethic" and return to our former "endowment ethic."*

According to Peterson, unless current benefits are curtailed the combined Social Security and Medicare deficit in the year 2040 will be over $3.2 trillion annually. Trying to meet this deficit by raising taxes would require the Social Security share from workers to rise to over 20 percent of wages. With the inclusion of Medicare, the wage tax rate would be from as little as 35 percent to as much as 55 percent, rates that will be impossible to sustain. According to Peterson, by any sensible accounting system, the Social Security and Medicare balance sheets are "disastrously insolvent" in the sense that promises have been made which far exceed any reasonable expectation of future revenues.

These arguments are not novel to Peterson, but he has added a different twist. He points out that these high demands for entitlements erode savings and investment in education, training, research, infrastructure, and other items that are necessary if we are to increase productivity. Without increasing productivity, we shrink the future national economic pie and so further reduce our ability to pay promised benefits. In short, according to Peterson, we have entered a vicious cycle by overpromising and overspending on today's older persons. Conversely, if we cut back on benefits for the elderly, we can increase the national savings, increase productivity, and eventually increase benefits to older citizens or at least be able to afford a reasonable range of benefits, although Peterson believes even that may not be possible given our current slow growth, low investment cycle.

His solution is to increase productivity, encourage a modest increase in the rate of savings, and to rein in the cost of Medicare. But even these changes will not be sufficient to avoid the coming impending major shortfall of revenue. According to Peterson we need to change our cultural attitudes about old age. First, we need to discourage retirement and encourage con-

tinuation working well past age sixty-five. The longer people work, the more they can contribute to those who are retired, and the fewer years they will need the support from Social Security or their own savings. Peterson argues that our transformation of health care and changing personal aging patterns mean that people after age sixty-five are in much better health and are much more able to continue working.

While extending the work years will help, even more important is that America save more and consume less. Peterson offers a number of steps to move in that direction. First, we need to guarantee a federal budget that is in balance for the long term by the year 2002. Peterson suggests reducing the percent of the gross national product spent by the federal government by 1 or 2 percent, thereby creating a budget surplus between the years 2000 and 2020. Alternatively, the surplus could be spent by investing in research and development, worker training, education, and other programs that are likely to increase productivity.

Peterson then argues that all entitlements must be subject to an "affluence" test: essentially, benchmark entitlements and begin to reduce them for individuals as retirees' incomes exceed the U.S. median household income, then gradually zero them out for higher income retirees. He would also raise the eligibility age for full Social Security benefits, which is currently scheduled to go to age sixty-seven by the year 2027. Peterson would raise it to age seventy by the year 2015. He would allow early retirement before then, but only with reduced benefits. Next, he would severely reduce payments for Medicare by a combination of higher co-payments and larger deductibles, and attempt to reduce the costs of what he calls "defensive medicine." Finally, he would institute a system of mandatory pensions or personal retirement accounts. Peterson has no faith in individuals voluntarily saving sufficiently for retirement and therefore would advocate forced savings through government taxation. Unlike the present Social Security system, however, he would allow individuals to privately manage their individual retirement accounts. This mandatory retirement fund would be a 4 to 6 percent wage tax and would be an addition to the current Social Security wage tax, which will need to continue for some time to pay off currently promised benefits.

According to Peterson, the only way to make the transition from the current system to a more private one is for today's workers to bear the double burden of both paying for the current retirees and also start saving for their own retirement. He argues that such a double burden is not only acceptable but necessary because it would shift the economy from a consumption-based culture to a savings-based culture. Peterson does not discuss how such a damper on consumption would affect our economy.

*Peterson sums up his vision of a reformed Social Security and entitlement culture in the following manner: "A people who have made a tradition of quick gratification must now be asked to focus on the requirements of a society graced with a patina of age, on saving rather than consumption, on prudence rather than desire, on collective restraint rather than individual satisfaction."**

Section 706 of the Social Security Act requires the Secretary of Health and Human Services to appoint an Advisory Council on Social Security every four years for the purpose of reviewing the status of the Social Security trust fund (as well as the state of the Medicare trust fund).

*THE ATLANTIC MONTHLY, vol. 277, p. 55 (1996).

The Council is required to address the financial status of the Social Security program and general issues of fairness. In 1994 Secretary of Health and Human Services Donna Shalala appointed the 1994 Advisory Council on Social Security. As might be expected, the council appointees represented a wide spectrum of interest groups. The result was a deeply divided panel that was unable to agree on a single set of recommendations.

Advisory Council on Social Security Report: Findings, Recommendations and Statements*

* * *

The Council identified four major areas of concern.

Long-Term Balance

Under their intermediate assumptions, the Trustees of the Social Security Funds estimated that income (the sum of the revenue sources plus interest on accumulated funds) will exceed expenses each year until 2020. The trust fund balances will then start to decline as investments are cashed in to meet the payments coming due. The Trustees estimated that although 75 percent of costs would continue to be met from current payroll and income taxes, in the absence of any changes full benefits could not be paid on time beginning in 2030.

The deficit over the traditional 75-year projection period was 2.17 percent of taxable payroll. This means that if payroll tax rates had been increased in 1995 by just over 1 percentage point each on employers and employees—from their present level of 12.4 percent combined rate to 14.57 percent combined rate (excluding Medicare)—the system would be in balance over this 75-year period. In the early decades of the projection period there would be surpluses, followed by deficits later in the projection period, but because of earnings on the trust funds, the 2.17 percent payroll tax increase would eliminate the 75-year deficit.

Little support exists today for increasing payroll tax rates by 2.17 percentage points to provide long-term balance. But there are other ways to address the financing issue, including other ways of increasing income to the system and changes in benefits.

*Located at: http://www.ssa.gov/policy/adcouncil/findings.htm (May 1997)

The program can be brought into long-run balance without departing from its basic principles or undermining the economic well-being of future workers and program beneficiaries.

The council's work, and the work of a task force of experts appointed by the council to review the estimates of the trustees, basically confirm the 1995 trustees' estimates of the finances of the program. Consequently, one of the three major tasks the council set for itself in the area of financing was to make recommendations that would eliminate the 2.17 percent of taxable payroll deficit. All members of the Council agree that this should be done, though there are differences of opinion on how the goal should be met.

Long-Term Balance Beyond the 75-Year Horizon

The second major problem with Social Security financing is the deterioration in the program's long-range balance that occurs solely because of the passage of time. Because of the aging of the U.S. population, whenever the program is brought into 75-year balance under a stable tax rate, it can be reasonably forecast that, without any changes in assumptions or experience, the simple passage of time will put the system into deficit. The reason is that expensive years previously beyond the forecasting horizon, with more beneficiaries getting higher real benefits, are then brought into the forecast period. There is no simple answer to the question of how much higher the long-term actuarial deficit is above the 2.17 percent to bring Social Security into balance beyond the 75-year horizon, but there could be a significant increase. All members of the council agree that it is an unsatisfactory situation to have the passage of time alone put the system into long-run actuarial deficit, though there are again differences on how the problem should be corrected.

Contribution/Benefit Ratios

The third area of concern for the Council arises from the fact that from now on many young workers and workers of future generations under present law will be paying over their working lifetimes employee and employer taxes that add to considerably more than the present value of their anticipated benefits. This is the inevitable result of a pay-as-you-go system such as the United States has had and an aging population. Although the money's worth that workers get from Social Security is only one of many criteria for judging the value of the Social Security system, the council believes that the system should meet a test of providing a reasonable money's worth return on the contributions of younger workers and future generations, while taking account of the redistributive nature of the Social Security system.

The council is breaking new ground by dealing so explicitly with money's worth issues. It does so because of concerns about equity from one generation to another.

The council feels that equity among generations is a serious issue and that it is important to improve the return on retirement savings for young people.

All members of the council favor the objective of improving the money's worth given by Social Security to younger generations. There are again differences on how this objective should be achieved.

Public Confidence

The final issue involves public confidence in the system. Polling data suggest that younger people have unprecedentedly low levels of confidence that Social Security benefits "will be there" for them when they retire. Polling data also suggest some erosion in public confidence in Social Security over time. While some of this skepticism runs well beyond issues the council was dealing with, the council does want to reassure people about the future viability and fairness of Social Security.

* * *

In the past, efforts to deal with Social Security's financial difficulties have generally featured cutting benefits and raising tax rates on a pay-as-you-go basis. All council members agree that the pay-as-you-go approach should be changed. But despite its best efforts, the council was not able to agree on one single plan for dealing with Social Security's financial difficulties. Rather, council members expressed interest in three different approaches to restoring financial solvency and improving money's worth returns. One group of members favors an approach, labeled the Maintenance of Benefits (MB) plan, that involves an increase in income taxes on Social Security benefits, a redirection to the OASDI funds beginning in 2010 of the part of the revenue from taxes on OASDI benefits now going to the Hospital Insurance (HI) Trust Fund, coverage of newly hired state and local government workers not currently covered by Social Security, a payroll tax increase in 2045, and serious consideration of a plan allowing the government to begin investing a portion of trust fund assets directly in common stocks indexed to the broad market. Historically, returns on equities have exceeded those on government bonds (where all Social Security funds are now invested). If this equity premium persists, it would be possible to maintain Social Security benefits for all income groups of workers, greatly improving the money's worth for younger workers, without incurring the risks that could accompany individual investment.

Another group of members supports an approach, labeled the Individual Accounts (IA) plan, that creates individual accounts alongside the Social Security system. This plan involves an increase in the income taxation of benefits (though not the redirection of HI funds); state and local coverage; an acceleration of the already-scheduled increase in the age of eligibility for full benefits up to year 2011 followed by an automatic increase in that age tied to longevity; a reduction in the growth of future Social Security benefits structured to affect middle- and high-wage workers the most; and an increase in employees' mandatory contribution to Social Security of 1.6 percent of covered payroll, which would be allocated to individual defined contribution accounts. These individual accounts would be held by the government but with constrained investment choices available to individuals. If individuals were to devote the same share of their IA funds to equities as they now do for their 401(k) private pension funds, the combination of the annuity income attributable to their individual accounts and their scaled-back Social Security benefits would on average yield essentially the same benefits as promised under the current system for all income groups.

A third group of members favors an approach, labeled the Personal Security Accounts (PSA) plan, that creates even larger, fully-funded individual accounts which would replace a portion of Social Security. Under this plan, workers would direct 5 percentage points of the current payroll tax into a PSA, which would be managed privately and could be invested in a range of financial instruments. The balance of the payroll tax would go to fund a modified retirement program and modified disability and survivor benefits. When fully phased in, the modified retirement program would offer all full-career workers a flat dollar benefit (the equivalent of $410 monthly in 1996, the amount being automatically increased to reflect increases in national average wages prior to retirement) plus the proceeds of their PSAs. This plan also would involve a change in benefit taxation; state and local coverage, an acceleration of the already-scheduled increase from sixty-five to sixty-seven in the age of eligibility for full retirement benefits, with the age increased in future years to reflect increases in longevity; a gradual increase from sixty-two to sixty-five in the age of eligibility for early retirement benefits (although workers could begin withdrawing the proceeds of their PSAs at sixty-two); a reduction in future benefits for disabled workers; a reduction in benefits for women who never worked outside the home; and an increase in benefits for many elderly widows.

If individuals allocated the assets in their PSAs in the same proportion as they do for their 401(k) private pension plans, the combination of the flat benefit payment and the income from their PSAs would, on average, exceed the benefits promised under the current system for all income groups. There would be a cost associated with the transition to this new system equivalent to 1.52 percent of payroll for seventy-two years. This transition cost would be met through a combination of increased tax revenues and additional borrowing from the public.

All of these approaches have in common that they seek to achieve more advance funding of Social Security's long-term obligations. They would also result in a higher level of national saving for retirement, although the impact on the nation's overall retirement saving would differ under the plans. The two individual account plans would raise overall retirement and national saving much more than the MB plan in the early years of the forecast horizon through the mandatory contributions of the IA plan or the transition tax of the PSA plan. These two plans are then likely to generate higher national income in the twenty-first century. While each of the proposals would increase investment in the stock market, one approach invests new Social Security funds directly into equities to realize a higher rate of return; another approach adds additional, mandatory saving on top of a scaled-back version of the existing benefit system; and the third approach moves from the current pay-as-you-go, largely unfunded system to one in which future benefits are more than 50 percent funded through PSAs. Each of these plans has different potential to create real wealth for retirement and provides for different ownership of that wealth. And each involves a very different vision for the future evolution of the U.S. retirement system.

* * *

Not surprisingly, the Advisory Council on Social Security Report brought forth many responses—some supportive, many critical. The council's inability to reach consensus gave its critics three different main targets—and various subtargets, such as a recommended rise in the retirement age—to attack. The following speech by Merton Bernstein, a long-time supporter of Social Security, is typical of many of the critics of the report.

Merton C. Bernstein

Social Security: Prospects and Proposals for Privatization

* * *

Pros and Cons of the Major Proposals

Transfer a Portion of Contributions to Private Investment (MB Proposal)

Prior to 1983, Social Security operated essentially on a pay-as-you-go basis with a relatively small reserve fund to tide over difficult periods. In the early 1980s, higher than expected inflation (which affects benefit payments) and somewhat lower than expected wages (caused in part by the two "oil shocks" of the 1970s) put the Social Security trust fund in precarious shape.

The 1982–1983 National Commission on Social Security reform decided that to restore public faith in the system, financing should be actuarially adequate for the next seventy-five years. To do this with a level payroll-tax rate builds up "reserves" (often called surpluses). The Treasury collects the payroll tax and credits individual contributions to individual wage records and total contributions to the system. After Trea-

Professor of Law, Washington University. Speech delivered February 11, 1997, before the Society of Investment Analysts of Chicago. Reprinted by permission.

sury pays benefits, it credits the trust fund with any amounts left over and issues special obligation bonds for them. By law, Treasury must credit the trust funds with the interest rate paid for other government obligations; that is, essentially, a market bond rate, in practice Treasury issue bonds.

By law, the bonds carry a rate based on a mix of short-term and long-term government notes and bonds, thereby yielding roughly the return private investors obtain from their government note and bond purchases. The risks must be spread over the entire Social Security population. But no one account would vary because mutual funds yield. The historic real difference between government bonds and equities has been 4.7 percent. Assuming such additional earnings for the trust fund improves its income and substantially reduces the shortfall—about 30 percent of the shortfall.

Trust Fund Surplus Operates Like Savings

Some urge the private account approach as a means of augmenting the supply of savings. However, this argument overlooks the effect of the Social Security surplus on investments. To the extent that the trust fund runs a surplus, Treasury does not have to sell bonds to private investors. That tends to lower interest rates for Treasury, which is good for the national debt and the rest of the economy. Also, many investors who would have bought U.S. Treasury bonds must invest their funds elsewhere. So, the trust fund surplus operates as the equivalent of savings and has decidedly positive effects on the economy.

Risks of Government Private Investment

Some object to the MB proposal to consider investing a portion of the surplus in several broad-based mutual funds. The proposal requires "passive" ownership, that is, the administrators would not participate in managerial decisions. The MB group suggests several ways of insulating private companies from influence by the share owners.

* * *

Privatizing Adds Cost But Doesn't Demonstrably Boost Savings

Both privatizing proposals boost FICA tax rates while reducing Social Security benefits. Although both require savings accounts, neither assures any net addition to savings. Many individuals may conclude that the forced contributions will be all the savings they need.

* * *

Some Risks of Privatizing

The risks of private investment are dramatized every day in the financial pages. Take, for example, the spectacular failure of Orange County's investments, the speculative excesses that led to the failure of the oldest private bank in Britain, to say nothing of the S&L investment scandals. Almost daily the media present new and shocking reports of losses and mismanagement of major private companies. For example, on March 24, 1995, *The New York Times* described a stock plunge of 70 percent for Future Healthcare. One of the Big Four accounting firms was dismissed, apparently for bungling financial reports of earlier years. The development warranted a three-column story. (Page C10, cols. 4–5–6.) And who can forget the New Era Foundation fiasco where experienced fund managers lost tens of millions when they took the bait that an anonymous donor would match whatever amount they gave "temporarily" to New Era.

Such developments, involving major companies and philanthropies and a respected accounting firm, show concretely that private investment of Social Security funds, especially by individuals, entails grave risks.

Raising Normal Retirement Age (NRA) Reduces All Benefits

NRA is the age at which full benefits become payable. Current NRA is sixty-five. Retirement benefits can begin at age sixty-two—with an actuarial reduction of 20 percent. Beginning receipt of benefits at ages between sixty-two and sixty-five involves proportional decreases. Those decreases persist throughout retirement.

Raising normal retirement age to sixty-six—as will happen in the first decade of the next century—means that full benefits begin for those retiring at age sixty-six. Hence, the benefit payable to those who start receipt of benefits at age sixty-two will become 75 percent of a full benefit—a reduction of 25 percent rather than 20 percent. Benefits for those retiring after age sixty-six are reduced commensurately. Under present law, NRA reaches sixty-seven in 2022. Thereafter, those first receiving benefits at age sixty-two will obtain 70 percent of NRA with proportional reductions for those retiring at higher ages. The IA and PSA proposals would advance the effective date to 2012—applying it to people now aged forty-six and younger (those born in 1966 and later).

* * *

Trimming the Cost of Living Adjustment (COLA): Pros and Cons

The cost of living adjustment equals the percentage difference in the Consumer Price Index-Workers (CPI-W) during the fall of one year and the same period the prior year. The adjustment is paid starting the following January. CPI-W consists of a "market basket" of goods regarded as typical for working individuals and families, including items like rent, car repairs, a fraction of an overcoat (because it will last for several years), and, quite importantly, food. When the net cost of items in the basket goes up, the difference registers as a higher CPI number.

Currently the grounds for reducing CPI and COLA have shifted to the argument that CPI overstates inflation because it does not take account of the substitution of less costly items, does not reflect stocking up on bargains, does not include the lower prices available in discount stores, and ignores improvements in quality. A panel of economists headed by Michael Boskin, who chaired President Bush's Council of Economic Advisors, estimates that these factors result in CPI overstating inflation by 1.1 percentage points. If COLA were reduced by such a factor, it would reduce benefits and benefit payouts enormously, by the tens of billions, cutting the Social Security shortfall by about two-thirds. Initially that change would reduce benefits almost $100 a year for the average earner. To those of us with current earned income, that may not sound like much. But if you depend on Social Security, and it averages $720 a month for a retiree, the impact is substantial. And the reductions compound so that after ten years the reduction would be about 15 percent.

Some analysts question the validity of the Boskin criticisms, question whether the overstatement is as substantial as the Boskin committee asserts, and argue that even if both hold up, it does not follow that CPI and COLA should be reduced by the amount of the overstatement.

Critics of the Boskin analysis assert that substituting lower-cost goods and services results in a lowered standard of living. Others contend that many buyers already purchase the least expensive items and so cannot substitute. Further, many city dwellers have no choice but to make their purchases at high-cost outlets, such as so-called convenience stores, and do not have access to suburban discount stores. Similarly, many Social Security recipients lack the transportation, storage space, and cash needed to stock up on bargains. And, the Bureau of Labor Statistics asserts that it does adjust for improved quality. (Kenneth Dalton, BLS "The Consumer Price Index," in "Report of the 1994–1995 Advisory Council," Vol II, pp. 388–389.) Moreover, the "market basket" for the employed does not include the higher out-of-pocket costs of the elderly and disabled for medical care and the higher home heating costs they incur because they stay home while working people lower the thermostat when they leave for work.

And some critics point out that whatever the overstatement may prove to be on close analysis, it does not follow that COLAs should be reduced by that percentage because the annual cost of living adjustment does not compensate for price increases that occur between adjustments.

A majority of the Advisory Council urged waiting for the Bureau of Labor Statistics to complete its analysis, which may take some years. The council members assumed that the adjustment would be about one-fifth the size of the Boskin estimate.

* * *

Supporters of the council had no single set of reforms to rally around and so have had difficulty engendering support that focused on particular recommendations. The one common goal for many reformers was privatization: the investing of at least some of the Social Security funds in the private sector, preferably the stock market.

Not all proponents of reform of the Social Security system believe that the council went far enough. Steve Forbes, owner of Forbes Magazine *and erstwhile presidential candidate, wrote an editorial arguing for a more radical reform: complete personal retirement accounts funded by a federal payroll tax. In essence, Forbes picked up the idea, which has long been advocated by conservatives and libertarians, that Social Security should not be an income redistribution scheme, but should only be a form of retirement savings with each individual saving for his or her own retirement years. The savings would be "forced," however, as workers would be taxed on their wages, with tax revenue from each worker going into an account for that individual.*

Under such a plan of total privatization, Social Security would shift from a system of taxes paid by current workers to pay the retirement benefits of older retirees to a system where each individual would set up a retirement account, save the money, and upon retirement draw down whatever might be in that account. Under Forbes' proposal, current retirees would be protected by a transition period under which a tax on wages would pay the current retirees their promised benefits, pay present workers at least some benefits based on their number of years of having paid into the current system, while the new workers who had not yet paid into the current Social Security system would pay only into their individual retirement accounts.

The argument for individual retirement accounts is seductive since it rests on the right of individuals to determine how their money is invested and how rapidly, if at all, to draw it out. Forbes, for example, argues that individuals might well choose to draw little or nothing out from the retirement account and either leave it to charity or to their heirs. He correctly points out that under a private retirement system, there would be no more need to argue about inflationary adjustments for payouts. (Forbes criticize the attempts to reduce the costs of living increases in Social Security benefits as merely tinkering at the edges and not getting at the heart of the problem.) Of course, what Forbes does not point out is that an individual retiree would not be protected against inflation since once he or she ceased putting money into the account, there would be no protection against its loss of value due to inflation.

Forbes claims that the current retirees can be accommodated because of the massive surplus built up in Social Security. To some extent he is correct. The system currently anticipates that the current pay-ins, together with the accumulated surplus, should keep the system solvent until approximately the year 2040. (Although that year is probably going to move up in time.) Of course, this will require the federal government to pay back the enormous sums that it has been borrowing from the Social Security trust fund.

Forbes criticizes those who would dispute the ability of individuals to make intelligent investment choices with their retirement savings account. He points out, for example, that "by that standard we shouldn't be trusted to handle our paychecks, to choose our own leaders, to pick our own careers, spouses, etc." Certainly, limits on what are acceptable investments (no investing in race horses or foreign gold mines) would provide some protection against complete foolishness in investing. This, however, does not solve the problem of individuals who have not a clue as to how to invest. Most people are much too conservative and keep their personal savings in certificates of deposits, savings accounts, and fixed interest bonds. Too many people avoid the stock market for fear of losing their investment. Forbes does not discuss how we can encourage individuals to invest in equities and thereby reap the growth that he believes is likely over the next forty or fifty years.

Total privatization is very appealing to many younger people who resent having their taxes transferred to "greedy geezers," particularly when coupled with a fear that when they retire the system will not be able to support them with the same level of benefits. What they do not comprehend, however, are the ancillary benefits offered by Social Security in the form of disability benefits, death benefits for minor children and spouses, and retirement benefits for spouses. Under the Forbes privatization plan, none of these aspects of the social safety net would exist.

What advocates of privatization do not deal with is why there should be any forced savings. That is, why should the government be able to force individuals to put part of their wages into a retirement account? If Forbes believes that individuals are quite capable of taking care of themselves as responsible adults, why should they be forced to save for retirement?

We could simply terminate Social Security (except for the current retirees) and provide a diminishing scale of benefits for those who retire in the future. The government would announce to its citizens that if they want retirement savings, they should save. Otherwise the government will only provide a very modest monthly benefit comparable to today's supplemental security income to retirees who otherwise would be destitute. In short, if you want to live better than a welfare client, you better save for the future.

Experience, unfortunately, has taught us that most people won't save for the future for any number of reasons. Some argue that for lower income Americans it is impossible to save given their current needs and their low income. This argument is, of course, obviously false on its face since low income workers are already paying a Social Security wage tax. If that tax were repealed, presumably they could save the money rather than send it to the government. But no one doubts that in most cases they would spend rather than save it. The inability to save argument makes even less sense for middle- and upper-income workers. Nothing stops them from saving more. Certainly the current Social Security wage tax cannot be considered so high as to completely discourage savings. It must be that most of us either are unable to empathize with our older selves and therefore fail to provide adequately for our old age, or we are victims of a consumer society in which current consumption is promoted by advertising and life styles, while savings is something that seems grim and better started tomorrow than today.

Some sort of mandatory retirement savings will always be with us. Whether it continues as a transfer system so that the current workers pay for retirees or is converted to some sort of personal savings system remains to be seen. But what we can be sure of is that we are not going to return to a day when the government says to its citizens, "You're on your own, buddy. If you don't save and so have no paddle, you'll just find yourself up the proverbial creek."

* * *

Reform proposals did not begin with the Advisory Council. For many years, many have complained that Social Security disadvantages women. Because women's monthly earnings are lower then men's, women receive lower monthly benefits upon retirement. The lower earnings of women have been attributed to many causes including discrimination in the work force, cultural and social attitudes that discourage women from full participation in the work force, and child care responsibilities that take women out of the work force. Reformers have long advocated that benefit calculations be revised to reflect the disadvantage of women under the current method of calculations. In the following article, Howard Iams and Steven Sandell explain why reforms aimed at curing the so-called "child care earning gap" are not likely to be enacted.

Howard M. Iams and Steven H. Sandell

Changing Social Security Benefits to Reflect Child-Care Years: A Policy Proposal Whose Time Has Passed?

* * *

In 1992, about 16 percent of women aged sixty-five and over were below the poverty line. The problem of poverty focuses attention on women's Social Security benefits, because Social Security benefits are the most important source of income of the aged. It is well known that women's monthly benefits are on average lower than men's. This reflects the lower lifetime earnings of women rather than any variation in treatment of men and women by program regulations. In part, these lower averages result from zero or reduced earnings in years when women take care of young children or disabled relatives. Removing the effect of dropping out of the work force to care for children is worth examining for adequacy reasons, as a possibility for reducing poverty among older women (1979 Advisory Council on Social Security; Kingson and O'Grady-LeShane, 1993; Sandell and Iams, 1994). Moreover, some advocates support this approach for equity reasons, arguing that society should not penalize women who perform unpaid work in the home raising children by giving them lower Social Security benefits [American Association of Retired Persons (AARP), 1991; Older Women's League, 1990].

57 *Social Security Bulletin* 10 (Winter 1994).

Child care proposals would increase retirement benefits for women who had no earnings or very low earnings when they raised young children. Two proposals receiving the most attention are adding a child care dropout-year exclusion to the retired worker benefit formula and a child care credit to the formula for calculating the special minimum benefit (SMB), a more generous Social Security benefit given to long-term workers with low earnings.

We review these proposals and assess their effects using an enhanced version of the 1990 Survey of Income and Program Participation (SIPP) file, which includes each respondent's Social Security Administration record of lifetime earnings. We conclude that both proposals have minimal effects and are not targeted to those women in the most economic need. Furthermore, the effect of full-time caregiving is cohort specific. Because most proposals would be implemented only for future retirees, we estimate the effects of these policies for women born in the 1930s and 1940s. More recent cohorts of working women have fewer years of full-time child care than earlier cohorts, which will diminish the impact of full-time caregiving adjustments in Social Security benefits in the long run.

* * *

Child-Care Proposals

Although several variations have been proposed, excluding, caregiving years from the computation of benefits is one main thrust of the 1979 Advisory Council on Social Security (AARP, 1991). For example, H.R. 865 of the 102nd Congress proposed to disregard up to five years with no paid work "occasioned by a need to provide child care or care to a chronically dependent relative" in addition to the five years of lowest earnings currently excluded from the benefit calculation. By reducing the averaging period, this disregard raises the average lifetime earnings per month and the Social Security benefits based on the average.

Proponents claim their proposals improve equity by removing the penalty for caregiving (that is, the penalty for including years of zero earnings in the benefit formula). The retired worker benefit would be the same for a woman who earned $15,000 a year for thirty-five years as it would be for one who earned $15,000 a year for thirty years while providing five years of full-time care for young children. Implicitly, this values full-time caregiving for Social Security purposes as the average earnings in years where there had been no caregiving. It is designed to improve adequacy by raising benefits of women workers, which often are low, particularly among mothers of many children (Kingson and O'Grady-LeShane, 1993).

The special minimum benefit is awarded only if it is higher than the Social Security benefit calculated in the usual way. Another policy to subsidize child care is to count caregiving years toward the SMB. The SMB is a guarantee based on *years with covered earnings* rather than level of earnings. Consequently, it helps persons with a long history of limited earnings. An individual is credited with a year toward the SMB if in a given year earnings exceed a threshold. The SMB is first payable with eleven credited years and increases with additional credit years up to a maximum of thirty years. In December 1992, the SMB was $24.50 at eleven years of credit and increased $24.50 for each additional credit year. Under the caregiving proposal, a year with no earnings or earnings below the SMB threshold while providing care would be credited. Thus, a year of caregiving could establish eligibility for the SMB or increase the SMB of eligibles by $24.70.

Cohort Changes in Labor Force Participation

Because the impact of child care dropout proposals substantially depends on the extent of full-time caregiving, it is sensitive to secular changes in labor force participation of women.

Women's labor force participation has dramatically increased in the twentieth century (Goldin, 1990; Levine and Mitchell, 1992). Gunderson (1989, p. 46) called women's increased labor force participation "the single most important development in the labor market in the past forty years." The labor force participation rate of adult women increased from 29 percent in 1950 to 59 percent by 1992 (Goldin, 1990; Bureau of the Census, 1993, table 622).

Perhaps the biggest change was the increasing labor force participation of mothers of young children. Oppenheimer (1970, p. 10) concluded from 1940 Census data that "if a woman worked, it usually was before marriage; if she worked after marriage, it was most likely before the advent of children." By the 1950s, mothers of young children still did not often work but many women entered the labor force in their late thirties when their children were school aged (Oppenheimer, 1970; Bowen and Finegan, 1969). Subsequently, labor force participation rates of wives with young children markedly increased from 19 percent in 1960 to 60 percent in 1992 (Bureau of the Census, 1993, table 633). Part of this shift results from a tendency for first-time mothers to work longer into pregnancy and to return to work sooner after childbirth (O'Connell, 1990). Juhn and Murphy (1992) show that the dramatic increase in women's labor force participation rates in the 1980s has been concentrated among women married to men with high earnings.

As a result, more recent birth cohorts of married women have had more years of Social Security covered earnings and higher levels of average indexed earnings (Iams, 1993). Furthermore, in more recent cohorts, the earnings of wives are higher relative to their husbands' earnings (Iams, 1993). Earned benefits will increase among future women retirees.

Dropout estimates must therefore be cohort specific. We cannot estimate future dropout effects based on current beneficiaries because these women were mothers when most mothers did not work. Women born in the 1930s are still of working age but were mothers in the 1950s and 1960s when, again, most mothers of young children did not work. However, women born in the 1940s were mothers in the late 1960s and 1970s when more women with young children worked.

Empirical Results

Again, this analysis is conducted using the 1990 Survey of Income and Program Participation of the Bureau of the Census, with information appended from the respondents' records of annual Social Security covered earnings from 1951 through 1990. These records are the basis for computing Social Security retirement benefits. SIPP Wave II interviews collected marital and fertility histories, which permits identification of the birth year of the youngest and oldest child. Wave VI provides the work history and reason for being out of the labor force for at least six months. The main reasons listed include caring for minor children, caring for elderly relatives, and caring for disabled relatives. Using these SIPP reports, we also construct a variable measuring the period of labor force withdrawal to care for elderly or disabled relatives.

A child care dropout year is defined as a year with no recorded Social Security covered earnings when SIPP histories indicate the presence of a child under age six. A caregiving credit year for the purposes of the special minimum benefit is a year with no earnings or earnings below the required minimum level for a woman with a child under age six.

Women born in the 1930s and the 1940s form the focus of this article; they reach eligibility for early Social Security retirement benefits (age sixty-two) in the years between 1992 and 2001, and between 2002 and 2011, respectively. We analyze child care dropout and credit years between ages twenty-two and forty-one for both retirement cohorts. Our general analysis includes (1) samples of all women, (2) women we estimate to be future retired-worker beneficiaries, and (3) mothers whom we expect to receive benefits based on their own earnings only. The first group of women is used to facilitate comparison with the literature, and the latter two groups are used for policy analysis.

Our estimate of future retired-worker beneficiaries is obviously imperfect. Future retired-worker women beneficiaries are defined as women with at least five years of covered earnings while aged twenty-two to forty-one. The Social Security Act requires forty quarters of coverage, the equivalent of a quarter each year between ages twenty-two and sixty-one, in order to be permanently insured for retired-worker benefits (Social Security Administration, 1993, paragraph 203). In 1992, a quarter of coverage was credited for each $570 of covered earnings to a maximum of four quarters earned for the year. The shortest working career that could yield forty quarters would be ten years. Because ten years of earnings are one-fourth of the Social Security computation period of forty years, five years of earnings are the equivalent of one-fourth of the twenty years being used in our study. Because individual women's labor-force participation patterns may be very different after age forty-one than before, work patterns in the first twenty years cannot precisely estimate retired-worker status at retirement age.

Some women will be dually entitled to retired-worker and wife/widow benefits, and therefore will receive benefit amounts based solely on their husbands' earnings. Whether they will be in dual status partly depends on whether their husbands are still alive and partly on the size of their husbands' lifetime earnings relative to their own earnings. Under present law, a few women who would have received benefits based (de facto) on their husbands' earnings will receive benefits based on their own earnings if caregiving years are dropped from the benefit computation. To estimate which women could be affected by the caregiving policy, we exclude nonmothers, wives with average indexed monthly earnings below 30 percent of their husbands' earnings from the year in which these women were age twenty-two through 1990, and widows in the 1990 SIPP. Women who are not mothers cannot care for their own children by definition. Wives with monthly earnings below 30 percent of their husbands' earnings usually receive spousal benefits at retirement age. Widows are excluded because most of them receive benefits based on their husbands' earnings (see Iams, 1993).

Removing Dropout Years from Benefit Computation

Compensating for child care dropout years increases retirement benefits for women by increasing the average indexed monthly earnings used as the basis for calculating their retirement benefits.

* * *

The impact on benefits would be less dramatic. Earnings do not translate directly into benefits.

* * *

The average lifetime increase in Social Security for women who would benefit from the child care dropout years would be about $4,200.

* * *

Women of higher socioeconomic status would benefit more. This partly reflects their higher number of child care dropout years, and partly reflects their greater earnings level. Thus, socioeconomic bias appears for both policies examined, and when using several different measures of socioeconomic status (for example, the woman's education, the annual family income relative to the poverty level, and the husband's education).

* * *

The policies examined do increase the retirement benefits of some women. However, the increases on average are small, decline with each successive retirement cohort, and disproportionately aid women from more privileged socioeconomic groups more than other women. As a rough estimate, we expect that the average lifetime benefit increase for a woman receiving increased benefits would be about $4,200. The benefit increase is received over an average of fourteen years, until widow benefits begin. Thus, because the benefit is low and will be diminishing in the future, the time that this policy would have been effective has passed. Full-time mothers have been eclipsed by mothers who have combined paid work with their caregiving. From an adequacy perspective, subsidizing child care dropout years in the foreseeable future does not seem to be a well-targeted policy.

* * *

References

Advisory Council on Social Security. 1979. *Social Security Financing and Benefits: Report of the 1979 Advisory Council.* Washington, DC. Transmitted December 1979.

American Association of Retired Persons. 1991. "Women and Social Security: Challenges Facing the American System of Social Insurance." *Issue Brief,* No. 2 (February) 1991.

Bowen, William G. And T. Aldrich Finegan. 1969. *The Economics of Labor Force Participation.* Princeton, NJ: Princeton University Press.

Bureau of the Census. 1993. Statistical Abstract of the United States. Washington, DC: U.S. Government Printing Office.

Goldin, Claudia. 1990. *Understanding the Gender Gap: An Economic History of American Women.* New York: Oxford University Press.

Gunderson, Morley, 1989. "Male-Female Wage Differentials and Policy Responses." *Journal of Economic Literature,* Vol. XXVII (March), pp. 46–72.

Iams, Howard M. 1993. "Earnings of Couples: A Cohort Analysis." *Social Security Bulletin,* Vol. 56, No. 3 (Fall, pp. 22–32.

Kingson, Eric R. And Regina O'Grady-LeShane. 1993. "The Effects of Caregiving on Women's Social Security Benefits." *The Gerontologist,* Vol. 33, No. 2, pp. 230–239.

Levine, Phillip B. And Olivia S. Mitchell. 1992. "Expected Changes in the Workforce and Implications for Labor Markets," in *Demography and Retirement: The 21st Century,* Anna Marie Rappaport and Sylvester Schiefer (eds.). Philadelphia: University of Pennsylvania Press.

O'Connell, Martin. 1990. "Maternity Leave Arrangements: 1961–85." *Current Population Reports.* (Special Studies Series P-23, No. 165). Washington, DC: Bureau of the Census.

Older Women's League. 1990. "Heading for Hardship: Retirement Income for American Women in the Next Century." Washington, DC.

Oppenheimer, Valerie K. 1970. *The Female Labor Force in the United States: DEMOGRAPHIC AND ECONOMIC FACTORS GOVERNING ITS GROWTH AND CHANGING COMPOSITION.* Population Monograph Series, No. 5, Berkeley, CA: University of California.

Sandell, Steven H. And Howard M. Iams. 1994. "Caregiving and Women's Social Security Benefits: A Comment on Kingson and O'Grady-LeShane." *The Gerontologist,* Vol. 34, No. 5 (October), pp. 680–684.

Social Security Administration. 1993. *Social Security Handbook 1993.* 11th Edition. Washington, DC: U.S. Government Printing Office.

In her article, Professor Alstott examines several proposals for reforming Social Security to make it fairer (or more supportive) for women.

Anne Alstott

Tax Policy and Feminism: Competing Goals and Institutional Choices

* * *

Social Security provides cash benefits upon retirement to covered workers and their dependents.[1] Workers become eligible for Social Security coverage by working in covered employment for a minimum period and by paying Social Security payroll (FICA) taxes on wages. Social Security benefits are calculated based on lifetime earnings, but the formula for determining Social Security benefits is progressive, so that Social Security benefits replace a higher proportion of total wages for low earners than for high earners.[2] Social Security also provides an additional "spousal benefit" equal to 50 percent of the benefit the covered worker would receive if single. A spouse who is covered independently under the system through her own FICA contributions does not receive both the 50 percent spousal benefit and her own independent benefit, but instead receives the larger of the two amounts.[3] One consequence of the spousal benefit rules is that a single-earner couple can receive larger total Social Security benefits than a two-earner couple with the same total earnings and payroll tax contributions.[4]

As a group, women receive larger Social Security benefits relative to their payroll tax contributions than do men.[5] Women are the principal recipients of spousal benefits and thus by definition receive benefits that exceed those to which wives would be entitled based on their own contributions. Women also typically live longer than men and so collect benefits longer. In addition, because women tend to earn less than men, they gain more from the progressivity of the benefit formula.[6] At the same time, however, elderly women's average Social Security benefits are smaller than elderly men's,[7] and elderly women remain significantly poorer than elderly men, due to their dependence on husbands' incomes, their longer lives, and their lower lifetime earnings.[8]

a. *Equal Treatment and the Spousal Benefit Rules*—One feminist critique of Social Security is that the system discourages married women's market work.[9] Married women must pay Social Security payroll taxes on their full earnings, but the spousal

This article originally appeared at 96 *Columbia Law Review* 2001 (1996). Reprinted by permission.

benefit rules mean that many working wives receive no additional benefit for the payroll taxes they pay. If a wife's earnings are low enough relative to her husband's, she will in the end collect only the spousal benefit, which she could claim even if she had never worked outside the home.[10]

* * *

The goal of equal treatment suggests repealing the spousal benefit entirely, so that primary and secondary workers would receive an equal benefit from their payroll tax contributions.[11] The revenue saved through repeal of the spousal benefit could be used to reduce payroll taxes or increase benefits across the board. The dilemma, of course, is that equal treatment would help some women but hurt others. By definition, repealing the spousal benefit would reduce Social Security benefits for many wives, particularly full-time caregivers and those with low earnings.[12] Without spousal benefits, a married woman would receive as much as (but no more than) a single woman with the same earnings history.[13] The resulting redistribution of Social Security benefits could reduce benefits for many wives, particularly those with low market earnings or an intermittent or nonexistent work history.

Thus, there is a tension between achieving equal treatment in Social Security and assisting caregivers (if we assume, realistically, that many homemakers are also caregivers and that caregiving work tends to reduce many women's lifetime earnings). This tension may recede a bit with time because younger generations of women tend to have consistently higher rates of labor force participation than older generations had.[14] Even younger generations of women, however, do not duplicate men's patterns of market work: women continue to encounter significant disruptions in their work patterns during childbearing years, and women's lifetime earnings still are lower than men's.[15]

* * *

b. *Assisting Caregivers Through Homemakers' Credits*—A second feminist critique of Social Security is that it does too little to assist caregivers. Although the spousal benefit rules are intended to ensure coverage for women in "traditional" families, critics point out that spousal benefits are derived from husbands' coverage and thus provide limited benefits for divorced or never married women and women married to low earners.[16] Some scholars propose replacing the spousal benefit with a system of "homemakers' credits," which would provide independent Social Security earnings credits for women (or men) primarily engaged in family labor.[17] Homemakers' credits would essentially impute to the caregiver a deemed earnings amount, which would be added to her lifetime Social Security earnings record. Repealing the spousal benefit would ensure that each worker received benefits based on her own earnings record, while the additional homemakers' credits would ensure that caregivers would be protected. Unlike the spousal benefit, homemakers' credits would be fully independent of marital status, and thus equally available to married, divorced, and never married women.[18]

Proposals for homemakers' credits raise a host of serious difficulties, however. First, the proposal only reshapes rather than removes the conflict—created by the spousal benefit—between equal treatment and assisting caregivers. Repeal of the spousal benefit would eliminate the secondary-earner bias that current law creates, so that working wives would no longer pay payroll taxes without receiving additional benefits. Homemakers' credits, however, would recreate an incentive for wives to stay out of the labor force by awarding a new class of benefits that are not paid for (in the financial sense anyway).[19] Second, critics point out that the credits would help only those women who can afford to be full-time housewives and would provide no benefit for women who work in the market while also performing significant family labor.[20] While women who work in the market would pay payroll taxes beginning with the very first dollar of their earnings, housewives would earn Social Security credit without making any contribution at all.[21] Although the current spousal benefit has somewhat the same effect—by definition, it provides "unearned" benefits to wives—the spousal benefit is available both to (low earning) working wives and to homemakers. Third, homemakers' credits create a host of administrative difficulties, including identifying women and men engaged in family labor and valuing family labor for purposes of imputing earnings credits.[22] Finally, it is not clear that homemakers' credits would effect any dramatic improvement in homemakers' retirement security, at least if the change is close to revenue neutral. One empirical simulation found that the distribution of the benefits of homemakers' credits would differ little from that of spousal benefits, unless family labor were valued highly enough to increase the aggregate benefits available to women.[23]

c. *Earnings Sharing: Another Compromise Solution*—Another popular Social Security reform proposal is earnings sharing, which seeks a compromise between the goals of equal treatment and assisting caregivers by removing the worst distortionary effects of spousal benefits while maintaining or improving Social Security coverage for women engaged in family labor.[24] Although earnings sharing proposals differ in important details, in general they would repeal the spousal benefit and provide that a husband and wife would each receive Social Security credit for half of the couple's combined earnings, regardless of the distribution of earnings between spouses.[25] For example, suppose that in 1996 a husband earns $100,000 and his wife is a full-time housewife. For 1996, the Social Security system would record $50,000 of earnings credits for each spouse. If the husband earns $60,000 and the wife earns $40,000, again each spouse would receive $50,000 in earnings credits.

Earnings sharing implements a "partnership" model of marriage, treating each spouse as making an equal economic contribution, whether through market work or family labor.[26] Proponents point to three advantages of this model. First, earnings sharing would improve the situation of two-earner couples. Under earnings sharing, couples with equal aggregate incomes would receive equal total benefits; that change would tend to benefit two-earner couples, who can receive smaller benefits than single-earner couples under current law.[27] Second, earnings sharing would eliminate the secondary-earner bias that the current spousal benefit rules create: both spouses would earn incremental credits for their work, although credits would be shared fifty-fifty with the other spouse.[28] Finally, earnings sharing could help divorced women by creating "portable" earnings credits that could ensure some independent Social Security coverage for divorced women not now entitled to coverage.[29]

Although earnings sharing is an attractive compromise, it is not a panacea. Without a politically difficult increase in aggregate Social Security expenditures, larger benefits for some groups must come at the expense of others. The major tradeoff is that earnings sharing plans that are roughly revenue neutral would reduce benefits for single-earner couples and survivors (usually widows) of such couples or for other couples in which the wife does not have a significant work history.[30] Even if these benefit reductions were seen as acceptable in the long run as the price of change, the question of transition is a difficult one. As always, the tradeoff is between protecting expectations under the old regime and slowing the evolution to a new system, but Social Security changes are particularly sensitive because they can disappoint very long-term expectations (and a sense of entitlement), and have a serious impact on elderly persons' economic security.[31]

* * *

Notes

1. For a description of Social Security, see [House Comm. on Ways and Means, 103d Cong., Overview of Entitlement Programs: 1994 Green Book 324–31 (Comm. Print 1995) (hereinafter 1994 Green Book)].

2. See William H. Simon, Rights and Redistribution in the Welfare System, 38 Stan. L. Rev. 1431, 1460 (1986) (noting that although "payout rates . . . replace relatively large percentages of average earnings for relatively low earners," the benefit structure "tends to give larger benefits to people with larger preretirement incomes, who tend to be relatively wealthy retirees").

3. See [House Comm. on Ways and Means, 103d Cong., Overview of Entitlement Programs: 1994 Green Book 324–31 (Comm. Print 1995) [hereinafter 1994 Green Book], at 15, tbl. 1–6 (spousal benefit 50% of primary insurance amount). Thus, a married couple receives a total retirement benefit equal to the greater of (1) 150% of the higher earning spouse's independent benefit (i.e., the benefit the spouse would receive if single) or (2) the sum of the two spouses' independent benefits. Although men and women are equally eligible for spousal benefits, wives tend to earn less than husbands and so account for the vast majority of spousal benefit recipients. See Social Security Administration Annual Statistical Supplement to the Social Security Bulletin 187–88, tbl. 5A1 (1994) [hereinafter 1994 Annual Statistical Supplement].

4. In other words, 150% of the benefit for a single earner may exceed the greater of (1) two independent benefits for two earners or (2) 150% of the primary insurance amount for the higher earner in the two-earner couple. See Congressional Budget Office, Congress of the United States, Earnings Sharing Options for the Social Security System xiii (1986) [hereinafter CBO]. Consider a simple example. There are two couples, (A) and (B). In couple (A), the husband's average monthly earnings were $1000 and the wife earned $0; in couple (B), the husband's average earnings were $700 and the wife's were $300. Suppose that a simple Social Security system replaces 75% of the first $300 of earnings and 25% thereafter and also has a 50% spousal benefit rule. Under that system, couple (A) receives a total benefit of $600 ($400 for the husband and $200 for the wife), while couple (B) receives a total benefit of $550 ($325 for the husband and $225 for the wife). There are two competing effects here: the single-earner couple

tends to receive a lower proportionate benefit because of the progressive replacement-rate schedule but also receives a spousal benefit.

5. See [Mary E. Becker, Obscuring the Struggle: Sex Discrimination, Social Security, and Stone, Seidman, Sunstein & Tushnet's *Constitutional Law,* 89 Colum. L. Rev. 264, 276–85 (1989)].

6. See W. Andrew Achenbaum, Social Security: Visions and Revisions 133 (1986); Simon, supra note 2, at 1482.

7. See 1994 Annual Statistical Supplement, supra note 3, at 200 tbl.5.A10 (showing that by end of 1993 women comprised 59% of Social Security beneficiaries (20,987 of 35,307) but received only 52% of total benefits); [Mary E. Becker, Obscuring the Struggle: Sex Discrimination, Social Security, and Stone, Seidman, Sunstein & Tushnet's *Constitutional Law,* 89 Colum. L. Rev. 264, 276–85 (1989)] (noting that women receive about 52% of Social Security benefits paid to elderly but represent 60% of elderly Social Security beneficiaries).

8. See CBO, supra note 4, at xiii; see also [David L. Kirp et al., Gender Justice 186–90 (1986)] (pointing out that averaging zero-earnings years into lifetime average also hurts women, whose family labor responsibilities may reduce number of years worked); Marianne A. Ferber, Women's Employment and the Social Security System, Soc. Security Bull., Fall 1993, at 33, 43.

9. See Richard V. Burkhauser, Earnings Sharing: Incremental and Fundamental Reform, *in* A Challenge to Social Security 76–77 (Richard V. Burkhauser & Karen C. Holden eds., 1982); Robert J. Lampman & Maurice MacDonald, Concepts Underlying the Current Controversy About Women's Social Security Benefits, *in* A Challenge to Social Security, supra, at 21, 30.

10. See [Mary E. Becker, Obscuring the Struggle: Sex Discrimination, Social Security, and Stone, Seidman, Sunstein & Tushnet's *Constitutional Law,* 89 Colum. L. Rev. 264, 276–85 (1989)]. The number of wives with "dual entitlement" to benefits as retired workers and as spouses of retired workers has grown dramatically over time. See 1994 Annual Statistical Supplement, supra note 3, at 201 tbl.5.A14 (showing that in 1960, only 4.6% of women beneficiaries age 62 or older were dually entitled, while in 1993, 25.1% were dually entitled).

11. Repeal of the spousal benefit is analogous to the adoption of individual filing in the income tax context: each worker would pay payroll taxes only on her own earnings (as under current law) *and* would also receive benefits based solely on her own contributions. More precisely, the current Social Security rules use individual filing for purposes of calculating payroll taxes but determine benefits on a joint basis. Repeal of the spousal benefit would calculate both taxes and benefits using individual filing.

12. For a description and critique of a 1975 proposal to repeal spousal benefits, see [Grace G. Blumberg, Adult Derivative Benefits in Social Security, 32 Stan. L. Rev. 233 (1980)], at 264–66.

13. Although the repeal of spousal benefits would initially reduce or leave unchanged *every* married woman's benefits (because under current law they receive the higher of their own coverage or the spousal benefit), the revenue saved by repealing the additional benefits could be used to lower payroll taxes or increase benefits for workers.

14. See Ferber, supra note 8, at 34, 36–37.

15. See id. at 41–43.

16. A never married mother cannot receive a spousal benefit even if the father of her children is covered. See 42 U.S.C. §§ 402(b)(1), 416(b) (1994); see also [Mary E. Becker, Obscuring the Struggle: Sex Discrimination, Social Security, and Stone, Seidman, Sunstein & Tushnet's *Constitutional Law,* 89 Colum. L. Rev. 264, 276–85 (1989)] (arguing that the system links "old-age security for women (but not for men) to continuation of the marriage bond until death"). A divorced woman receives a spousal benefit only if she was married to a covered worker for ten years or more. See id. §§ 402(b), 416(d). The spousal benefit system pays greater (absolute)

benefits to women married to high earners than to women married to low earners, even if they perform the same caregiving work (although, once again, the progressivity of the benefit formula generally helps low earners and their dependents). See Lampman & MacDonald, supra note 9, at 30. For an analysis of the distributional effects of spousal benefits, see Karen C. Holden, Supplemental OASI Benefits to Homemakers Through Current Spouse Benefits, a Homemaker Credit, and Child-Care Drop-Out Years, *in* A Challenge to Social Security, supra note 9, at 41, 44–51.

17. The analysis in the text assumes that (1) the homemakers' credits are financed by repeal of the spousal benefit, and (2) the repeal of the spousal benefit raises enough revenue to fund the new benefit. There are other ways to finance such a proposal. See, e.g., [Nancy C. Staudt, Taxing Housework, 84 Geo. L.J. 1571, 1610 n.163 (1996) (noting that white women are more likely to be married than are black women)].

18. See Holden, supra note 16, at 54.

19. The spousal benefit discourages market work for women whose own earned benefits would ultimately be less than the "free" spousal benefits, equal to 50% of their husband's benefits. Homemakers' credits discourage market work for women whose own earned benefits would be less than the benefits created by the "free" homemakers' credits.

20. The homemakers' credit proposal is arguably worse in this respect than the current system of spousal benefits. Although the current system of spousal benefits assists housewives, it also helps wives whose earnings are low relative to their husbands'. In contrast, homemakers' credits help only those women who are full-time housewives.

21. Depending on the valuation of family labor, homemakers could receive a "free" credit that exceeds actual earnings of many low-earning working women. See Holden, supra note 16, at 58–59; see also Simon, supra note 2, at 1485 (arguing that homemakers' credits would benefit wealthy homemakers with or without children, but probably not working mothers). In addition, homemakers' credits would not guarantee a benefit even equal to the spousal benefit, so some women could be worse off. See Achenbaum, supra note 6, at 138.

22. See Achenbaum, supra note 6, at 138; see also [Edith U. Fierst, Discussion, in A Challenge to Social Security 66, 66–67 (Richard V. Burkhauser & Karen C. Holden eds., 1982) (discussing how women's market work decisions often are not affected by possible changes in Social Security benefits]; Holden, supra note 16, at 54–55; [Nancy C. Staudt, Taxing Housework, 84 Geo. L.J. 1571, 1610 n.163 (1996) (noting that white women are more likely to be married than are black women)].

23. See Holden, supra note 164, at 55–58.

24. See [Grace G. Blumberg, Adult Derivative Benefits in Social Security, 32 Stan. L. Rev. 233 (1980)], at 243–44 (arguing that Social Security rules "fail[ ] to take into account the effect of women's dual roles on their participation in the labor force," including women's shorter work lives, interrupted work lives, and lower earnings).

25. For a detailed discussion of several different earnings sharing plans, [See Congressional Budget Office, Congress of the United States, Earnings Sharing Options for the Social Security System (1986) (hereinafter CBO)], at xvi–xviii; [Grace G. Blumberg, Adult Derivative Benefits in Social Security, 32 Stan. L. Rev. 233 (1980)], at 278–90.

26. See CBO, supra note 4, at 17–18.

27. See supra note 4 and accompanying text.

28. See [Mary E. Becker, Obscuring the Struggle: Sex Discrimination, Social Security, and Stone, Seidman, Sunstein & Tushnet's *Constitutional Law*, 89 Colum. L. Rev. 264, 276–85 (1989)].

29. See id. at 284.

30. See [Mary E. Becker, Obscuring the Struggle: Sex Discrimination, Social Security, and Stone, Seidman, Sunstein & Tushnet's *Constitutional Law,* 89 Colum. L. Rev. 264, 276–85 (1989)] at 36–37; Ferber, supra note 8, at 44; see also Achenbaum, supra note 6, at 139–40 (arguing that because earnings sharing would reduce benefits for one-earner couples, guaranteeing survivors' benefits as large as those under current law would require increasing taxes or cutting benefits); Simon, supra note 2, at 1483–84 (arguing that earnings sharing would "substantially redirect benefits away from many of the neediest women" by reducing survivors' benefits for widows, which are well targeted in terms of need).

31. Major earnings sharing proposals have devoted significant attention to issues of transition. See CBO, supra note 4, at 21–24.

Part III

Housing

Traditionally, the two most basic human needs have been food and shelter, at least within the realm of physical needs. Today, we should add a third—medical care. For most older persons basic food and shelter needs are met, and their basic medical needs are usually met, though not always in a satisfactory manner. For those elderly who cannot afford food, our society provides cash grants such as Social Security or Supplemental Security Income, food stamps, and direct provision of food though programs such as meals-on-wheels or free lunches at senior citizen centers. As for shelter, we provide cash (Social Security and Supplemental Security Income), rental assistance in the form of programs such as Section 8 Housing or state rebates of rent or property taxes, and subsidized housing such as subsidized mortgages for elderly housing operated by nonprofit organizations and public housing limited to older residents. As a result of these public efforts, few elderly persons are without housing. However, the quality of housing of the elderly leaves much to be desired, as least according to many older persons. Many older persons live in substandard housing. Yes, they have a roof over their heads, but is it a roof that many of us would call adequate? Others live in dangerous neighborhoods, virtually prisoners in their homes. Some live in relative isolation on farms or in small towns, cut off from services and medical care. Many older persons involuntarily live with their children or other relatives, forced by economics or their health to sacrifice independence and privacy.

Yet, it is not at all clear that mere dissatisfaction of many older persons with their housing constitutes a "need" for better housing that should occasion a societal response. Like our desire for many other consumer goods, most of us would prefer better housing or at least the same housing at less cost. In that sense, we all "need" better housing. Once older persons have a roof over their heads, and assuming that roof includes the basics such as indoor plumbing, it is not at all obvious how to decide whether they have "adequate" housing. For example, should older persons who live in poorly insulated, drafty apartments with high heating bills be considered inadequately housed? If so, how do we classify older persons living in the South who cannot afford air-conditioning? If your response is "open a window," what if they live in a high crime neighborhood and are too afraid to open their windows? And what of the ninety-year-old New York City resident whose rent controlled apartment means a four-story climb? Yes, the apartment is affordable, but can her heart "afford" the daily climb? Or should our sympathy be directed toward the eighty-five-year-old man living on a combination of Social Security and Supplemental Security Income who suffers from mild dementia and so has no choice but to live in a rundown board and care home? In short, it is easy to say that the elderly deserve better housing, but it not so easy to draw a bright-line test that differentiates those truly in need *of better housing and those who merely (and understandably so)* desire *better housing.*

CHAPTER 12

Housing Needs

The following article summarizes many of the housing concerns of the older population.

Lawrence A. Frolik

The Special Housing Needs of Older Persons: An Essay

* * *

Older persons differ physically from their younger counterparts. Though generalizations about the effects of aging may be untrue as to any particular individual, there are certain general physical patterns associated with growing older that, although not true for the individual, are statistically true for the group. All persons inexorably age. Many older persons experience a decline in mental capabilities, primarily because of short-term memory loss. A significant minority of the old will suffer from acute or chronic health conditions that will necessitate a change in their housing. As a result of these physical and mental changes, many elderly persons must reconsider their housing choices with the thought of moving into housing that is more appropriate for their changed circumstances.

A. Physical Changes

A universal aspect of aging is the inevitable physical decline. We all begin to degenerate as the years go by.[1] As we grow older, we experience signs of aging such as

Stetson Law Review, Vol. 26, No. 2, 647 (Winter 1996). Reprinted with permission.

graying of hair, loss of skin tone, and wrinkles;[2] however, these outward signs of aging usually do not affect our choice in housing. It is not until we are much older, normally beyond our sixties, that the more profound effects of aging begin to affect us in ways that impact our choice of housing.

The most important effects of aging are the decline in physical strength, loss of vigor, and increase in frailty.[3] As we age, our bones gradually lose calcium, become weaker, and fracture more easily, and joints become stiff and painful. As a result, walking becomes more difficult.[4] Aging causes a loss of muscle, resulting in less upper body strength. Because stairs may cause shortness of breath and contribute to pain in the knees and hips, many older persons try to avoid houses with two or three stories, even though it may be difficult to negotiate. With declining strength, vigor, and flexibility, housework becomes more of a burden and heavy cleaning almost impossible. A large, older house that requires a good deal of maintenance is increasingly seen as overly burdensome. Failing eyesight interferes with modest home repairs and makes a dark, cluttered house physically dangerous.[5] Hearing loss, common among older persons,[6] may make it difficult to live in a large or sprawling house because the individual is unable to hear what is said or called from another part of the house. Yard work and outside house maintenance also become more difficult as the physical vigor of the homeowner declines. Gardens and lawns cease to be a source of pleasure and instead become a burdensome maintenance duty. Of course, the degree of frailty and the loss of muscle varies greatly from one older individual to the next, but for many older persons, the decline of physical strength and vigor reveals that their current housing situation has become inappropriate.

The loss of vision in an elderly person can precipitate the need for a change in housing. Almost all older individuals suffer some vision loss. Typically, older persons have less ability to see close objects, are more sensitive to glare, suffer a decline of peripheral vision, and have difficulty in adjusting from light to dark.[7] An older person's eyes are particularly weak in dim light, are less able to focus on moving objects, and are less capable of perceiving color. In addition to these generalized losses, many older persons experience more serious vision problems. Some are afflicted by cataracts that cloud their vision. Generally, cataracts are correctable, but not always.[8] Others are victims of macular degeneration, the loss of vision in the central region of the pupil.[9] The effect for victims is a blurred space when they look directly at an object. For example, if they sit across a table from another individual, that person's face will appear blurred and possibly unrecognizable. Most people with macular degeneration cannot read except with the aid of special magnifying devices. While not blind, the affected individual finds it difficult to maintain household records, pay bills, or use the Yellow Pages phone book to locate services. Macular degeneration also interferes with performing household chores such as cooking and cleaning. Because of the difficulty of using even simple tools such as a screwdriver, basic house maintenance becomes a formidable, if not impossible, task. Even simple chores, such as replacing a light bulb, become difficult, and duties that require the ability to read, such as reading the instructions for a new kitchen device, become insurmountable. In addition, glaucoma also affects some elderly and can result in partial or total blindness.[10] Living alone or in a large house with reduced or no vision is obviously very difficult and even unsafe.

Many older persons will also experience a decline in their hearing.[11] Beginning near age fifty, there is often a gradual loss of perception of higher and lower frequencies. This permanent hearing loss, called presbycusis, results in the gradual physical deterioration of the inner ear.[12] Even if corrected with a hearing aid, individuals may still be less perceptive of noises that alert them to problems or dangers in the household. The sense or reality of being less alert may make an older person fearful of living alone in an isolated or insecure house.

B. Mental Changes

A decline in cognition or mental capacity may necessitate a reevaluation of housing. While growing old does not necessarily mean the loss of mental alertness, many older persons find that they are not as sharp as they once were. Sometimes this takes the form of being less comfortable making decisions, perhaps because the loss of physical abilities adds to the stress of decisionmaking. The loss of physical vigor, a decline in vision, and a loss of hearing can make it much more difficult, for example, to deal with home repairs, maintenance personnel, and cleaning personnel. For example, if you cannot see well, you may be at the mercy of the veracity of a roofer who tells you that you need a new roof. If, because of increasing age, you tire easily, you may not have the energy to comparison shop when you need to buy a new window air conditioner.

Mental or cognitive decline also affects many older individuals. Typically, older persons suffer short-term memory loss.[13] This is not to be confused with the onset of dementia, such as Alzheimer's disease.[14] The loss of short-term memory is associated with the natural aging of the brain and does not indicate mental disease or precipitous loss of function. The individual can reason as well as ever but has more difficulty remembering facts, numbers, or other information, such as memorizing a phone number. If a sales person quotes a different price for three models of washing machines, an older customer may find it more difficult to remember the quoted prices. To compensate, many older persons create lists, write down information, ask for it to be repeated, or bring along a companion to assist in remembering what has transpired. Still, the inability to remember causes confusion, impatience, and frustration. It is hard to make good decisions if you cannot remember the facts of the situation. For example, trying to remember and compare the variables in quoted prices given by contractors for painting a house can make it very difficult to choose the best option.

Perhaps the most serious interference with an older person's ability to live independently is the loss of mental acuity due to dementia or other neurological problems. Individuals with mental problems require housing arrangements appropriate to their reduced mental capabilities. The most common form of dementia is Alzheimer's disease, but many elderly suffer from Parkinson's disease or other forms of neurological deterioration.[15] Whatever the source, dementia is irreversible and incurable. It gradually leads to the inability to care for property and eventually even for oneself. Living alone becomes impossible. Even living with a caring spouse can in time become untenable.

Some older persons suffer from mental illness, which makes living alone particularly problematic. Although older persons can be afflicted with any kind of mental illness, depression is prevalent among the elderly.[16] Older women in particular are likely to exhibit symptoms of depression, such as a lack of personal care, increasing isolation, and a failure to eat properly.[17] Such problems call for medical attention and often suggest that new housing arrangements are necessary.

* * *

D. Death of a Spouse

Perhaps the single most significant event in a older person's life who has been married or has had a life partner is the death of that spouse or life partner.[18] The older the individual, the more likely that the spouse will have died, so that for those age eighty-five or older, almost seventy percent are widows or widowers.[19] The death of a spouse has many reverberations for the survivor, all of which affect the housing choices of the survivor.

Certainly one person usually needs less space than two. Many surviving spouses find themselves lonely, rambling around in a large house that might have been somewhat large even for two but certainly is too large for one. Even if the expenses of the house do not seem inordinate, the burden of keeping up a larger house may overwhelm the survivor, particularly as the survivor continues to age and becomes less capable of dealing with the requirements of maintenance and repairs.

The death of a spouse may provide the survivor with the freedom to move. For example, the couple may have stayed in the family house for years even though the surviving spouse may have preferred to move to a warmer climate or to a more stimulating or safer community. Alternatively, a surviving spouse may have longed to move into a condominium or a small apartment rather than continue to maintain a house and yard. When an appropriate interval has passed after the death of the spouse (at least one year), the surviving spouse should be encouraged to analyze whether the living conditions that were appropriate for two remain desirable for one.

The death of a spouse can be an enormous loss and cause deep bereavement for the survivor. Individuals react to that loss in quite different ways. Some find it overwhelmingly depressing to remain in the same house or apartment, so they seek out new housing to avoid the painful memories of the past. Others find the loss of a spouse overwhelming but are comforted by remaining in the same house, which holds warm memories of the deceased. In many cases, however, the financial and practical considerations overwhelm the emotional decision and new housing is, in fact, required.

* * *

E. Family and Locational Considerations

Family considerations, such as children, often dictate where older persons want to live and the kind of housing in which they wish to live. A majority of older persons live within fifty miles of their children,[20] while many other older persons live near a sibling or other relative. In any case, before moving to be near a child or relative, the older person should consider the possibility that the child or relative might leave the area because of a new job or a personal reason, such as the breakup of a marriage. Still, for older persons who are willing to take the chance that they may have to move yet again, living near a child or a relative can be very desirable, providing, as it does, a source of support both emotional and more tangible, such as help with household chores or running errands.

Some housing arrangements selected by older persons are influenced by expected visits from children or grandchildren. Many older persons keep a larger house than they need because they hope to encourage visits by the children and grandchildren. Others will continue to own vacation houses because it encourages family get-togethers. In either case, the financial burden on the older homeowner can be significant. Rather than owning a house large enough to house relatives or owning a vacation house, older persons should consider renting, on a short term, housing for their children or grandchildren. By relying on rental property or using motels, the older person can free up capital and live in more appropriate housing that is smaller, less costly, and less maintenance-intensive. Financially, it may be much cheaper for the parents to pay the costs of a motel for a week rather than own a house that has enough extra bedrooms to accommodate the relatives. Many condominiums and age-restricted residences also have guest rooms that can be rented for a period of time. A cruise ship is another alternative that allows the grandparents to bear the costs without the burdens of ownership.

Older persons who are considering relocating often do so because they want warmer weather that will allow them to enjoy golf or swimming, or because they want to live somewhere that offers social and recreational opportunities. Moving in search of recreational and social opportunities presents two alternatives. The first is to seek out a housing arrangement that directly provides recreational and social opportunities. For example, people who move to retirement cities such as Sun City in Arizona can expect a wealth of social organizational opportunities and recreation right within the city.[21] Even individuals who move into a condominium for older citizens can expect to find a library, a game room, or even a workshop within the building. The residents of age-restricted condominiums or apartments often organize numerous clubs that reflect the interests of the residents.

The alternative is to move into housing not designed specifically for the older person, but that is located in an area that offers the desired recreational and social facilities. For example, millions of older persons who have moved to Florida live in regular communities with the knowledge that there will be golf and tennis available within the community, even though such communities are not necessarily designed for older persons. Increasingly, older persons are moving to university communities, even places such as State College in Pennsylvania or Cambridge, Massachusetts, which are not known for the weather.[22] They do so because the college atmosphere offers stimulation in terms of classes, lectures, musical presentations, and the like. Because college towns are thought to be desirable places to live as a retiree, privately-built housing designed for older residents is increasingly being created in these towns.[23]

II. Planning for Housing Needs

Individuals should begin to plan for their later-life housing needs long before retirement, preferably while they are still in their fifties. After their children are grown, many individuals decide that they need to reorient their housing to something more appropriate, less family-oriented, and more adapted to the needs of an older couple or older individual. If considering either buying a new house or finding a new apartment or condominium, individuals in their fifties should consider whether they will want to relocate again after retirement, or whether the housing pattern they select at this age will be appropriate for their retirement years. What is appropriate housing at age sixty-five may not be appropriate housing at age eighty. The question is whether the older person is willing to relocate years after he or she has entered "old age." For most people the answer is yes. They realize that a house appropriate at age sixty-five (perhaps the house with room for gardening) may not prove so desirable at age eighty when they no longer want the burden of a lawn and garden. Because it is difficult at age sixty-five to select housing that will meet all of one's needs for the next twenty-five or thirty years, older individuals must realize that their initial retirement housing may not be appropriate for their later years. Some persons are perfectly happy to move frequently, and therefore would not be dismayed with the thought that the pattern they select at age fifty-five might be inappropriate after they retire at age sixty-five. Others would prefer to make a choice when they are age fifty-five that will continue to be appropriate when they turn age sixty-five and retire.

The most significant impact on pre-retirement and post-retirement housing is the individual's financial circumstances. Individuals who relocate in their mid-fifties are often at the peak of their earnings. Those who relocate after retirement often face reduced financial circumstances. Individuals who relocate in their fifties may be doing so based upon a recent inheritance, lifetime savings not likely to be replaced, and the expectation of relatively high earnings. In short, they are at their financial peak. They should consider that, although their capital will remain intact upon retirement, their consumable income will decline. They probably will be unable to replace or add to their savings (capital) after retirement and should ask whether they will be able to continue to afford the kind of housing they are considering in their mid-fifties. Of course, as long as they are willing to relocate after retirement, they may choose to purchase or rent housing that might not be appropriate for their post-retirement years.

However, even if finances do not require new housing after retirement, the inevitable path of aging may dictate new housing arrangements. Younger individuals often look upon retirement as a homogenous age period; that is, everyone over the age of sixty-five is about the same. This is inaccurate. Gerontologists like to classify old age into three periods: the period from age sixty-five to seventy-five sometimes called the "young old"; the period from age seventy-five to eighty-five sometimes called the "old"; and the period post age eighty-five, sometimes referred to as the "old old."[24] The division of old age into three periods highlights the reality that old age can conceivably extend for thirty years, from age sixty-five to ninety-five. Over that potential thirty-year plus span, the wants and needs of the elderly will change. More specifically, their housing needs will change.

Individuals age sixty-five to seventy-five are sometimes referred to as the young old. Attaching the term "young" helps emphasize that although they are old, many of the problems that are associated with old age, such as chronic illness, frailty, and the loss of mental capacity, generally do not apply to most individuals in this age group. Many of these individuals are recently retired and in good health, and they often have fairly reasonable retirement incomes because their source of income has not yet been eroded by inflation. These are the individuals who are often portrayed as examples of why older persons are over-endowed with income and government benefits, the so-called "greedy geezer."[25] Certainly, when seen on the street, in shopping malls, or at restaurants, they seem to be doing fine. They look healthy, are in good spirits, and appear to have plenty of disposable income. In fact, older persons age sixty-five to seventy-five are generally in good health and are better off financially than persons age seventy-five or older.[26]

Of course, there are individuals age sixty-five to seventy-five who are in bad health. Members of minority groups are more likely to experience poor health at a younger age than the white majority.[27] But it must be recalled that the average life expectancy of someone who reaches age sixty-five is fifteen years or so for males and almost twenty years for females.[28] To put it another way, half of the individuals who reach age sixty-five will still be alive fifteen to twenty years later. To achieve that kind of life expectancy means that most persons reach age seventy-five in reasonably good health.

The housing needs of this age group primarily depend upon their personal choices rather than health or physical concerns. Many in this age group do not change their housing.[29] They find that whatever was desirable prior to retirement is just as appropriate thereafter. Others do relocate upon retirement, not because of necessity but by choice. They may, for example, choose to move to a warmer climate, or they may choose to divide their time between a summer and a winter home. Others move from a large house to a smaller house or even to a condominium because they do not want the burden of maintenance, because they choose to travel, or because they simply have other things with which they would prefer to occupy their time. Some move to live closer to children or grandchildren.

Individuals past age seventy-five often find that their housing no longer meets their needs. The possibility or actuality of poor health and increasing frailty and the concern about physical safety grow significantly after age seventy-five. Individuals want a smaller housing unit, one without stairs, with good security, and with low maintenance. Their financial situation may also be eroding if inflation has reduced the value of their pension plan and medical expenses have reduced their disposable income. They may also face increasing medical or long-term care costs and so have fewer dollars to spend on housing. Individuals in this age group may find themselves reducing the cost of their housing in order to meet other expenses or to ensure for themselves a safe and physically comfortable environment. As physical strength wanes, and eyesight and hearing diminish, individuals become more concerned for their personal safety. They worry more about being assaulted either on the street or in the home, and they worry more about accidents in the home. The retirement home in exurbia, which once seemed so private, may be seen as isolated and vulnerable. The city condominium that was selected because it was near culture and entertainment may be seen as a target for criminals that gives rise to daily exposure to possible street crime. The small apartment that once permitted the older couple the financial wherewithal to constantly travel may become cramped as physical infirmity makes traveling a chore rather than a delight.

Beyond age eighty-five almost everyone has to be concerned with the physical ability to live independently and the appropriateness of their housing for an older, frailer person. Those past age eighty-five tend to be single, less often part of a couple.[30] Given their longer life expectancy, women comprise the majority of those age eighty-five or older, and most are single or widowed.[31] For these women, safety and a sense of community is often paramount. They often relocate into apartments or condominiums that offer a secure environment with companionship, while also freeing them from burdens of house maintenance and repair. Perhaps the most salient issue for those eighty-five and over is whether they will need assistance in their daily life activities such as housecleaning and cooking, or even to the extent of needing assistance in dressing or bathing. Those of advanced years must consider whether they ought to move into housing that offers personal care assistance either daily or on an as-needed basis. Even those who are in good health over age eighty-five must consider the possibility of someday needing assistance and must plan accordingly. As a result of these special needs for the very old, many who purchase a "retirement" house when they are in their late sixties find that in their eighties they need to move again, this time into congregate housing or an assisted living facility.

Although those over age eighty-five are more likely to have health concerns, at any age an individual can become frail, either because of a general decline in health, an acute medical problem, or a chronic medical condition. For these individuals, housing decisions are a critical component of the quality of life. Older persons who have special medical needs will have to decide whether those needs can best be met in their current home or whether they ought to move to an assisted-living facility or a nursing home. In short, health concerns define housing needs, but they do not dictate the solution. There are many ways of providing assistance to a frail or ailing older person. The individual must consider the range of possibilities to decide which makes the most sense in light of physical and mental capabilities, financial resources, and personal taste.

* * *

Notes

1. *See* DAVID EVERAL & JULIE WHELAN, RESEARCH AND THE AGING POPULATION 5 (1988).

2. *See* CARY S. KART ET AL., AGING AND HEALTH: BIOLOGICAL AND SOCIAL PERSPECTIVES 32 (1978).

3. *See* CAROLE BERNSTEIN LEWIS, AGING: THE HEALTH CARE CHALLENGE 62 (2d ed. 1990).

4. *See* A.N. EXTON-SMITH & P.W. OVERSTALL, GERIATRICS 282–84 (1979).

5. "[F]ocal length of the lens becomes impaired (with age) as a result of degenerative changes in the muscles of accommodation and of loss of elasticity of the lens." *Id.* at 19.

6. One-third of adults between 65 and 74 experience hearing loss and one-half between 75 and 79 experience it. *See* THE MERCK MANUAL OF GERIATRICS 1315 (William B. Abrams et al. eds., 1995).

7. *See* LEWIS R. AIKEN, AGING: AN INTRODUCTION TO GERONTOLOGY 43 (1988).

8. *See id.*

9. *See* DONALD H. KAUSLER & BARRY C. KAUSLER, THE GRAYING OF AMERICA 325 (1996).

10. *See* AIKEN, *supra* note 7, at 43–44; *see also* NANCY R. HOOYMAN & H. ASUMAN KIYAK, SOCIAL GERONTOLOGY: A MULTIDISCIPLINARY PERSPECTIVE 108 (3d ed. 1993).

11. The percentage of hearing loss in those over 65 was 43% in 1980 and is projected to be 46% in 2000 and 54% in 2020. *See* LEWIS, *supra* note 3, at 76.

12. *See* MERCK MANUAL OF GERIATRICS, *supra* note 6, at 1315–16.

13. *See* DANIEL L. SCHACHTER, SEARCHING FOR MEMORY 290–91 (1996).

14. *See* KAUSLER & KAUSLER, *supra* note 9, at 23.

15. *See* JAMES A. THORSON, AGING IN A CHANGING SOCIETY 209 (1995).

16. *See* AIKEN, *supra* note 7, at 157.

17. *See* GENDER & AGING: GENERATIONS AND AGING SERIES 34 (Lou Glasse & Jon Hendricks eds., 1992).

18. For purposes of this discussion, the individual will be called a spouse with recognition that in many cases the individual may not be married either because they have not chosen to be married or because they are prohibited from marrying because it is a same-sex relationship. Nevertheless, the term spouse will be used as a generic term for a life partner.

19. [*See* STATISTICAL HANDBOOK ON AGING OF AMERICANS 15 (Frank L. Schick & Renee Schick eds., 1994) (hereinafter STATISTICAL HANDBOOK).]

20. In 1984, 66% of older people lived within 30 minutes of one of their children. *See* THORSON, *supra* note 15, at 86.

21. *See* AIKEN, *supra* note 7, at 317–18.

22. *See* Tom Gibb, *State College-Retirement Mecca Transplanted Retirees Up 42% in 1980–90, Tend to Be Well-Heeled, Well-Educated,* PITTSBURGH POST-GAZETTE, July 7, 1996, at B1.

23. *See id.*

24. "There are significant differences among the 'young old' (ages 65 to 74), the 'old-old' (ages 75 to 84) and the 'oldest old' (over 85)." HOOYMAN & KIYAK, *supra* note 10, at 5.

25. *See generally* Peter G. Peterson, *Will America Grow Up Before It Grows Old?*, Atlantic Monthly, May 1, 1996, at 55.

26. *See* CHRISTINE R. VICTOR, OLD AGE IN MODERN SOCIETY: A TEXTBOOK OF SOCIAL GERONTOLOGY 48 (2d ed. 1994).

27. *See* THORSON, *supra* note 15, at 311.

28. The average life expectancy for a male who reaches 65 is an additional 15.2 years and for a female, it is an additional 19.0 years. [*See* STATISTICAL HANDBOOK ON AGING OF AMERICANS 15 (Frank L. Schick & Renee Schick eds., 1994) (hereinafter STATISTICAL HANDBOOK).]

29. For those between 65–69, 570 out of 10,123 moved in 1990–91, and for those between 70–74, 348 out of 8114 moved in 1990–91. *See id.* at 35.

30. *See supra* note 18 and accompanying text; *supra* note 21, at 56.

31. Of those 85 and older, there are 39 men per 100 women, and 90% of women over 85 are either single or widowed. [*See* STATISTICAL HANDBOOK ON AGING OF AMERICANS 15 (Frank L. Schick & Renee Schick eds., 1994) (hereinafter STATISTICAL HANDBOOK).]

While on the surface transportation seems quite different than housing, the two are closely related. Most Americans assume transportation is easily solved by driving, and therefore where they live is only a question of how far they have to drive and are willing to drive for services. While this may be true for younger Americans, as individuals age they must consider the possibility that driving will become burdensome, dangerous, or impossible. Problems with vision, mental capacity and reflexes all make driving more problematic as individuals grow older, so it is important to select housing that minimizes the dependency upon driving, particularly for individuals who are beyond age eighty. Here again, the solution may be to admit that what is appropriate housing between ages sixty-five and eighty may not be appropriate thereafter.

Unfortunately, much American housing is predicated upon the homeowner being able to drive. Suburbs are notorious for being car-dependent; woe unto the homeowner who cannot drive. What seemed a comfortable, friendly neighborhood turns into an isolated environment bereft of goods and services, hostile to elderly pedestrians. Rural America is also unkind to the nondriver and can create real hardships for isolated elderly homeowners. In a city, there may be buses or other public transportation, and the delivery of goods such as groceries and laundry is possible. In rural settings, however, it is very difficult, if not impossible, to have necessary support brought to the door, and there may be no public transportation. Certainly, the problems that arise for a nondriver play a major role in forcing older persons to move into more urban settings that provide services either on-site or at least within easy walking distance.

CHAPTER 13

Appropriate Housing

Housing opportunities for older persons stretch across a continuum from housing for healthy, vibrant older persons whose housing needs differ little if any from younger persons to housing such as a nursing home designed specifically for frail, chronically ill older persons. Between these extremes are a myriad of possible housing choices, including single-family housing, condominiums, apartments, age-restricted communities or buildings, continuing care communities, assisted living arrangements, board and care homes, living with relatives, and nursing homes. For an older person considering housing options, however, the type of housing selected is only part of the solution. The older person must also decide whether to live in age-segregated housing.

Many older persons choose to live in housing that is age restricted. Such housing can be an apartment, a retirement hotel, a condominium, a mobile home park, or even a small community or city that limits its residents to persons over a certain age, typically age fifty-five or older. Many older persons prefer age-segregated housing because it offers a safe and secure environment that caters to their interests and needs. The exclusion of children means a quieter, more peaceful community. All the neighbors are experiencing the challenges (and advantages) of aging and retirement. Social and recreational activities can be planned that reflect the abilities of the older presidents. Many age restricted communities feature a wide variety of clubs, study groups, charitable or religious activities, and even travel groups. Within the age segregated group, the older resident feels more at ease, and rather than being a burden, he or she becomes a valued member of the group.

Despite its advantages, many older persons reject age-restricted housing as being sterile and cut off from the larger community. They prefer a heterogeneous community complete with both young and old. They like being the wise older person who can still benefit by learning from the young. Many critics of age-restricted housing agree and argue that the old should not be warehoused in isolated elderly apartment houses. Yet, many older persons disagree and prefer to live exclusively among the old. The only response seems to be to create housing for older persons that gives them a choice. Some will choose age-restricted housing; others will not.

Given the federal, state and local laws against discrimination in housing, how is it possible to exclude potential owners or renters merely because of their age? Until 1988, federal law (but almost no state or local law) prevented housing from excluding persons on account of age. It was possible, for example, to refuse to sell or rent to families with minor children or to limit prospective owners or renters to persons over age fifty-five. In 1988, however, Congress enacted the federal Fair Housing Amendments Act to prohibit discrimination in housing against families with minor children. In her article, Ms. Panjwani explains how the Act bars discrimination in housing against families with minor children and yet permits housing that is reserved for older residents.

Andrea D. Panjwani

Beyond the Beltway: Housing for Older Persons Act of 1995

Throughout the 1980s, Congress received a substantial amount of evidence suggesting that housing providers discriminate against families with minor children on a widespread basis and that this discrimination affects minority families on a disproportionate basis.[1] Congress sought to remedy this form of discrimination by enacting the Fair Housing Amendments Act of 1988, which amended the Fair Housing Act. The Amendment's purpose was to prohibit discrimination on the basis of family status (and disability).[2]

In essence, the Fair Housing Amendments Act made it unlawful for housing providers to deny housing to families with minor children and thereby invalidated the "adults only" policy prevalent in housing complexes throughout the country. The Fair Housing Amendments Act did, however, create a senior's housing exemption to this prohibition. The Fair Housing Act, as amended, did not apply to (1) housing provided under state or federal programs specifically designed to assist the elderly, (2) housing intended for and solely occupied by persons sixty-two years of age or older, and (3) housing intended for occupancy by at least one person fifty-five years of age or older per unit. In determining whether housing qualified for exemption as housing for older persons, the secretary of HUD was directed to develop regulations that would require at a minimum (1) the existence of significant facilities and services specifically designed to meet the physical or social needs of older persons; (2) that at least 80 percent of the units are occupied by at least one person fifty-five years of age or older per unit; and (3) the publication of, and adherence to, policies and proce-

Journal of Affordable Housing & Community Development Law, Vol. 5, No. 1, 197 (Fall 1995).

dures that demonstrate an intent by the owner or manager to provide housing for persons fifty-five years of age or older.[3]

Since 1988 there has been a great amount of debate as to the meaning of "significant facilities and services," in addition to the widespread claim that the "significant facilities and services" requirement has the impact of discriminating against low income senior citizens. Many seniors complain that the "significant facilities and services" requirement raises the cost of their housing and tells them how to live.[4]

Many perceive this requirement as objectionable for four primary reasons. First, it is viewed as a violation of the constitutional right to freedom of association. Second, it is considered an insult because many seniors are independent, capable people who do not believe that they need special facilities or services and resent the fact that they are required to pay for such facilities and services against their will. Third, the cost of providing facilities and services has a "devastating effect on keeping a community's costs down, particularly in the mobile home communities."[5] The increase in cost causes greater harm to low income senior communities and has the effect of reducing the availability of affordable senior housing. Many development companies are reluctant to build senior communities because they believe the Fair Housing Act hinders demand for these communities.[6]

Finally, senior communities have been subjected to costly administrative and legal challenges to their exempt status under the Fair Housing Act. Senior communities rarely prevail in these actions. According to Bill Williams, president of the Federation of Mobile Home Owners of Florida, HUD received twenty thousand fair housing complaints alleging discrimination on the basis of familial status by October 1992. Of these twenty thousand complaints, seventeen thousand were resolved by 1992, resulting in $7 million penalties.[7] The belief has been expressed that the "significant facilities and services" requirement poses two fundamental problems to housing providers. First, there are no guidelines or officials available for consultation when a housing provider is in doubt as to whether it meets the "significant facilities and services" requirement. Second, when a complaint is filed, a housing provider has the choice of defending against the complaint or pursuing conciliation, and both options are very costly.[8] Parenthetically, some have made the argument that the costs incurred by HUD and the Department of Justice have increased as a result of this type of fair housing litigation.[9]

* * *

It is this history that led Congress to enact the Housing for Older Persons Act of 1995. This legislation serves two primary purposes. First, it eliminates the "significant facilities and services" requirement and replaces it with a four-prong, fact-based bright-line test to be employed when making a determination of whether a housing complex is legitimately exempt from the Fair Housing Act under the "housing for older persons" (or senior) exemption. This bright-line test is designed to make it easier for housing providers to determine whether they qualify for this exemption.

The four-prong test provides a specific definition of housing for older persons. The test requires that (1) the housing is intended and operated for older persons; (2) of the occupied units, 80 percent actually are occupied by at least one person fifty-five years of age or older; (3) the housing provider has policies and procedures that demonstrate the housing is intended for older persons; and (4) the housing provider complies with HUD rules.[10]

The first two prongs give the housing provider the opportunity to demonstrate its intent to provide housing for persons fifty-five years or older. The housing provider can allow persons under age fifty-five to occupy dwelling units, as long as the housing complex maintains the 80 percent occupancy threshold. The third prong requires the housing provider to publish and adhere to "polices and procedures" that demonstrate an intent to provide housing for older persons in at least 80 percent of its dwelling units. The Housing for Older Persons Act, however, does not require that these policies and procedures be set forth in the housing provider's governing documents. The fourth prong, which requires the housing provider to comply with HUD regulations relating to the verification of the 80 percent occupancy threshold requirement, allows the housing provider to submit relevant surveys and affidavits that establish compliance. In addition, the Act specifically deems these surveys and affidavits admissible in administrative and judicial proceedings for the sole purpose of verifying compliance with the 80 percent occupancy threshold requirement.

In addition, the Housing for Older Persons Act creates a good-faith defense for the person who can establish that (1) he or she had no actual knowledge that the complex was not eligible for the housing for older persons exemption, and (2) the complex has formally stated in writing that it complies with the exemption.[11] In short, a person who wishes to establish good faith reliance has to make a showing of no actual knowledge that the complex is not eligible for the exemption and that the complex has certified in writing that it complies with the requirements of the exemption. Although the writing does not need to be notarized or witnessed, it must contain indicia of authenticity. For example, it should be written on stationery that contains the housing provider's or operator's letterhead and must be signed by an officer, employee, or agent of the complex.

The purpose of this amendment to the Fair Housing Act is to shield individuals from personal liability for money damages when they rely, in good faith, on the existence of the senior housing exemption and later discover that the exemption did not apply. The amendment, however, does not protect the individual from injunctive relief. Congress considers the good faith defense necessary because the senior housing exemption contemplates a fact-intensive showing that the complex meets the age and occupancy requirements and does not expect someone who inherits or acquires a home or dwelling unit to conduct this inquiry. Similarly, Congress believes that real estate agents should not be required to perform a census of a housing complex every time they list a home or dwelling unit for sale. Nevertheless, if, after inquiring of the community manager, a person seeking this good faith reliance defense has actual knowledge that the complex is not eligible for the exemption, the good faith defense will not apply.[12]

* * *

In the end, the bright-line test embodied in the Housing for Older Persons Act trades the "significant facilities and services" requirement for the requirement that at least one person age fifty-five or older live in at least 80 percent of the complex's units. If a complex contains one hundred units, all of which are occupied by two people, and 80 percent of the units are occupied by someone age fifty-five or older, as few as eighty of the two hundred tenants are necessarily fifty-five years of age or older.[13] In essence, the amended exemption creates a situation where a complex can qualify for the senior housing exemption even though over half of its tenants are not senior citizens. This fact can lead to the conclusion that the Housing for Older Persons Act may permit housing providers to discriminate legally against families with children and therefore may signal a return to the prevalent "adults only" housing complexes that Congress sought to invalidate in 1988.

Notes

1. S. Rep. No. 72, 104th Cong., 1st Sess., at 12 (1995).
2. Fair Housing Amendments Act of 1988, Pub. L. No. 100-430, 102 Stat. 1619 (1988).
3. 42 U.S.C. § 3607(b)(2)(C).
4. S. Rep. No. 172 at 9.
5. *Id.*
6. *Id.* at 10.
7. *Id.* at 5.
8. *Id.*
9. The Congressional Budget Office does not believe that the Housing for Older Persons Act will have an effect on the costs incurred by the Department of Justice or HUD. *Id.* at 7.
10. 42 U.S.C. § 3607(b)(2)(C).
11. 42 U.S.C. § 3607(b)(5)(A) and (B).
12. S. Rep. No. 172 at 4.
13. *Id.*

CHAPTER 14

Continuing Care Communities

Older individuals who either need assistance with their daily lives or fear that they might need such assistance in the future are increasingly turning to continuing care communities. The following material describes these communities.

Christine A. Semanson

The Continuing Care Community: Will It Meet Your Client's Changing Needs?

Introduction

* * *

The traditional living arrangements for the elderly in America have been rather limited. Either they moved in with family or into a nursing home when they became unable to live alone. This picture is changing. Today's Americans are a mobile group, and often there is no close family on which the elderly can rely. Modernly, nursing home placement is generally reserved for those who are totally dependent on the care of others. However, long term health care costs and nursing home costs are astronomical and can devastate a person or couple who has spent a lifetime saving for the

Detroit College Law Review 771 (1990). Reprinted by permission.

golden years.[1] A growing number of persons are looking for viable alternatives to the traditional housing and health care choices for their later years.

The continuing care community is one of the alternatives that has been enjoying a certain amount of popularity in the last one or two decades.[2] These communities provide living arrangements on a progressive needs basis. Their goal is to attract healthy older residents who can live independently in either an apartment or house within the community. However, there often is an intermediate care facility for those who are unable to live in total independence, but who do not need the level of care provided in a nursing home. There may also be total care provisions at the facility for those whose health has deteriorated to the point that they are unable to care for themselves and/or need nursing/medical services on a regular basis.[3]

This comment will discuss the life care community concept and the problems associated with these communities. It will identify Michigan's regulatory approach to minimize problems in this state, and then offer a practical approach to the practitioner whose client expresses an interest in this type of living arrangement and wants to avoid pitfalls.

I. Origins of Community Care Concept

The sixty-five-and-older population is actually comprised of subgroups, each having different needs. The youngest of the groups are the newly retired who are still physically and socially active, are independent, and have relatively few medical problems.[4] The middle group, those in their mid-seventies to mid-eighties, are comparatively less active and may need more assistance with the activities of daily living than their younger counterparts.[5] The oldest of the subgroups, those eighty-five and older, are generally the least active, have the greatest health care problems, and, thus, are those least likely to be able to live in total independence.[6]

Independence, however, is a strongly held value that does not wane with age.[7] Increases in the incomes of the older population have enabled more elderly to continue to live independently in recent years.[8] Fewer elderly are now living with other family members.[9]

Understandably, long term care is a major concern among the elderly.[10] Traditionally, aged persons moved in with relatives or friends when they became unable to live independently.[11] Some were placed in nursing homes.[12] However, private insurers and Medicare do not provide significant coverage for nursing home care, and these costs can be catastrophic.[13]

The traditional choices are not ideal in our modern society. The trend is moving away from nursing home placement unless a person is totally dependent on the care of others.[14] However, with the increase of women in the work force, and the increase in single adult households, often there is no one at home to care for an aging parent or other relative. Furthermore, as longevity increases, many older Americans are finding themselves in a position where they are in the sixty-five-and-older population themselves and have elderly parents who are still alive and need assistance. Consequently, older Americans are looking for viable alternative living and health care arrangements that will more appropriately meet their changing needs.

The continuing care community, sometimes called life care community or continuing care retirement community (CCRC), is a concept that was developed as a nongovernmental approach to meet these changing needs.[15] It is a relatively new concept, most communities being developed in the mid to late 1970s.[16] One half to two thirds of these communities are nonprofit, but the for-profit sector is gaining an interest in them.[17]

The goal of a life care community is to provide an environment where elderly residents can maintain their highest level of independence while ensuring progressive care as the need arises.[18] It provides a pooling of monies that are then used for health care of its residents. As with insurance plans, direct benefits are received only by those who ultimately require the use of the specific services. These services are utilized at different rates by the residents because of differences in life spans and differing health care needs in general. Investment in a life care arrangement, therefore, is essentially a nursing home insurance aimed at protecting the elderly who can afford it against catastrophic long term care expenses.[19]

Life care communities typically provide housing, recreational facilities, social activities, congregate meals, and progressive health care for residents.[20] The resident receives a lifetime guarantee of these and other specific contract benefits in exchange for an entrance fee (sometimes called an endowment fee) and a promise to pay monthly fees.[21] The housing can consist of apartments or individual houses located on the community campus. There is a wide range of services offered by the different communities that can include housekeeping, transportation, etc. The typical community has a nursing home facility either on the campus or associated with the community for use by the residents when the need arises. There may also be an intermediate facility available for those residents who are unable to live in independent housing but do not need the level of care provided by the nursing home.

The Special Committee on Aging reported an endowment fee range of $40,000 to more than $150,000 in January of 1987.[22] It reported a monthly fee range of $500 to $2,000.[23] Monthly fees are usually subject to increases.[24] Typically, both fees are higher for double occupancy.[25] The cost of this type of living arrangement makes it prohibitive for all but those who are in the middle and upper income levels.[26]

* * *

II. Inherent Problems

A. Financial Forecasting

The success of a life care community in achieving its goals and promises to its residents lies primarily in the financial stability of the organization.[27] This financial stability is dependent on accurate financial predictions and sound management. Clearly, it is these areas that are highly susceptible to fraud and mismanagement, increasing the risk to the elderly who rely on the community for secure living.[28] Unfortunately, bankruptcy is not uncommon in the life care arena.[29]

The Federal Trade Commission (FTC) was inundated with complaints from life care residents who claimed that they were induced to invest in a life care community by means of misrepresentation of services that were to be provided.[30] A full investigation, performed between 1978 and 1983, revealed problems more complex than the complaints had indicated.[31] In addition to misrepresentations, many of the problems discovered were the result of poor financial planning.[32]

Continuing Care Retirement Communities (CCRCs) are financially dependent on revenues from residents unless the facilities are receiving some support from charitable organizations.[33] Ideally, the endowment fees are put in reserve for future services for residents.[34] The monthly fees are then used, similarly to rental fees. Problems arise where monies are used inappropriately to manage the organization through fraud or miscalculation of future expenditures.[35]

Initial operating costs of a CCRC are relatively low because of the requirement that residents be healthy when they enter the community.[36] Thus, utilization of the long term facility is at its lowest in a new community.

As noted previously, it is long term care that is so costly. Financial maturity is not reached until after approximately ten to fifteen years of operation.[37] The increasing age and deteriorating health of the initial residents increases utilization of the long term facilities and, consequently, the institution's costs. This situation is more reflective of actual operating costs.

When the reserve is inadequate, or nonexistent, as in some cases, the resident is at risk of receiving less than the bargained-for services.[38] This is a devastating situation for those who have sold a home to raise the amount required for the entrance fee. The residents may have had a large amount of equity in their homes, but have no equity or ownership rights in the living unit of the CCRC.[39] Research indicates that this is a common scenario.[40] Consequently, if the organization fails, the typical resident has decreased resources to get set up in another dwelling and obtain health care security. Instead of being independent with secure health care, this person is at risk of dependence on family or society and an inability to afford health care when needed. In fact, because of the expenditure of personal reserves, this person is more likely to be in a worse position than if he/she had not made the decision to provide future security through the life care contract in the first place.

As previously mentioned, endowment fees are intended to be used for future services for residents. Resident turnover is relied upon to boost depleted reserves.[41] As demonstrated by the Pacific Homes fiasco,[42] undercalculations of the resident turnover rate leads to inadequate reserves, and can have a significant impact on the financial picture of the community.[43] To avoid these problems it is necessary for communities to conduct a financial analysis that projects into the future for a signifinumber of years. A study of CCRCs conducted by the Wharton School of the

University nsylvania concluded that such a projection should reach twenty or more years into the future.[44]

Contracts generally provide that monthly rates can be increased over time to meet rising costs of expenses.[45] This is believed to be a sounder practice than fixed rates because it does not lock the facility into a rate that becomes impractical over time.[46] Consider the resident who moves into a facility at age sixty-five or seventy and lives fifteen, twenty, or more years. Consider also the fixed income status of many elderly, and the prospect of being able to afford twenty years of monthly fee increases is unsettling.

* * *

B. The Cost of Health Care

* * *

This is the major draw for CCRCs. A resident who pays the endowment fee essentially has purchased an insurance policy for long term care. In exchange for paying the fee, the organization promises to provide intermediate and long term care for the life of the resident. The premise is similar to an insurance policy in that the cost of the care is spread out over the number of residents in the community. Each resident will have the security of knowing the care is available when needed, but not all will require the same level of care.

C. Dissatisfied Residents

Of the top ten frauds found by a national survey conducted by the Special Committee on Aging, nursing home frauds (which included life care communities) ranked seventh.[47] A broad range of complaints were received in response to questionnaires sent to persons in the law enforcement and consumer protection fields.

The following is a partial list of complaints and problems identified by the committee:

1. Lack of resident control over operations;[48]
2. Cancellation of contract provisions after the resident signed;[49]
3. Monthly fees escalating to a level above residents' ability to pay;[50]
4. Insufficient (or no) refunds from homes after residents' died only a few months after taking occupancy;[51]
5. Inadequate disclosure of organization's financial stature and residents' financial risk;[52]
6. Misrepresentation of services offered;[53]
7. Lack of legal standing for residents once bankruptcy is declared;[54]
8. Misrepresentation of religious affiliation.[55]

Although it is unlikely that any living/health care arrangement is going to be complaint free, it is clear from the range of complaints associated with certain life care communities that the potential for significant problems does exist. Even in the best of circumstances, all problems will not be eliminated.

* * *

Notes

1. *Long Term Care and Personal Impoverishment: Seven in Ten Elderly Living Alone at Risk: Hearing Before the Select Comm. on Aging, H.R.*, 100th Cong., 1st Sess. 644 (1988) [hereinafter *Long Term Care*].

2. *Life Care Communities: Promises and Problems: Hearing Before the Spec. Comm. on Aging, U.S. Sen.*, 98th Cong., 1st Sess. 276 (1983) (statement of Patricia P. Bailey, Commissioner, F.T.C.).

3. *Id.* at 69. The Continuing Care Accreditation Committee (CCAC) of the American Association of Homes for the Aged (AAHA), defines a Continuing Care Retirement Community (CCRC) as "a community offering a contract based on an entrance fee. In the contract, the CCRC agrees to provide facilities for independent living and various healthcare services to an individual who is eligible to remain in the CCRC for the balance of his or her life." Continuing Care Accreditation Com'n, *Handbook*, Nov. 1989, at 9.

4. [Riche, *Retirement's Life Style Pioneers*, AM. DEMOGRAPHICS, Jan. 1986, at 42 (hereinafter Riche).] The author designates the three groups as "young-old," aged 65–74; "old," aged 75–84; and the "very old," aged 85 and up. *Id.*

5. *Id.*

6. *Id.* In its 1994 supplement, the National Health Interview Survey showed 15% of 65–69 year olds reported difficultly performing some level of personal care. This figure rose to 49% for the 85-and-older group. [S. REP. NO. 80, 100th Cong., 2nd Sess. 1 (1988), Table 2 at 5 (hereinafter S. REP. NO. 80); *see also* CONG. Q. INC., AGING IN AMERICA: THE FEDERAL GOVERNMENT'S ROLE 1 (1989) (hereinafter CONG. Q.)]. *But cf.* Russell, *Ed's Note*, AM. DEMOGRAPHICS, March 1989 at 2. The average elderly person suffers from some disability or illness for almost 80% of the years gained by increased life expectancy. The editor cited a Canadian study which reported chronic ailments in 4 out of 5 noninstitutionalized persons in the 65-and-over population. *Id.* citing *Am's Elderly.*

7. CONG. Q. INC., AGING IN AMERICA: THE FEDERAL GOVERNMENT'S ROLE (1989), at 4 [hereinafter AGING].

8. *Id.*

9. A Congressional Budget Office (CBO) study reported a 7% decrease in married elderly who also live with other family between 1960 and 1984. *Id.*

10. *Id.* A public opinion survey reports that 82% of all Americans could not afford the cost of long term illness. Even 61% of those with incomes of over $50,000 report that they would not be able to afford such costs. *Need for Long-Term Care: A Survey of Public Opinion: Hearing Before the Subcom. on Health and Long-Term Care of the Select Comm. on Aging, H.R.*, 100th Cong., 2nd Sess. 659 (1988).

11. [S. REP. NO. 80, 100th Cong., 2nd Sess. 1 (1988), Table 2 at 5 (hereinafter S. REP. NO. 80).] Currently, 79% and 84% of caregivers for older females and males respectively fall into this category. *Id.*

12. *Id.* A 1985 National Nursing Home Survey reported that only approximately 5% of the older population are in nursing homes at any given time. The heaviest users are those 85 years and older. *Id.*

13. AGING, *supra* note 7, at 5. The average cost of nursing home care in 1988 was $23,000 per year. *Id.* Medicaid assistance is not available for long term care until one's own resources are exhausted. *Id. See also Long Term Care, supra* note 1, for discussion on effects of long term care on financial status of the elderly.

14. AGING, *supra* note 7, at 5.

15. *Life Care Communities: Promises and Problems: Hearing Before the Spec. Comm. on Aging, U.S. Sen.*, 98th Cong., 1st Sess. 276 (1983) [hereinafter *Promises*] (statement of Patricia P. Bailey, Commissioner, F.T.C.); AGING, *supra* note 7, at 93.

16. *Id.*

17. *Id.* at 70. In 1987, there were a reported 680 CCRC's in existence, serving approximately 170,000 people. AGING, *supra* note 7, at 6. Taninexz, *Hotel Companies Test Market for Long-Term Care of Elderly*, HOTEL & MOTEL MGMT., April 18, 1988 at 1.

18. Comment, *Continuing-Care Communities for the Elderly: Potential Pitfalls & Proposed Reg.*, 128 U. PA. L. REV. 883, 917 (1980), [hereinafter Comment].

19. S. REP. No. 80, 100th Cong., 2nd Sess. 1 (1988), at 322 [hereinafter S. REP. No. 80]; Paulson, *Sizing Up Life Care*, CHANGING TIMES, May 1987, at 66 [hereinafter Paulson].

20. Hospitalization is not typically a benefit of a CCRC contract. S. REP. No. 80, *supra* note 19, at 69. Medicare continues to cover some of the cost when residents need nursing home care. *Id.* at 56.

21. *Promises, supra* note 15, at 55.

22. S. REP. No. 80, *supra* note 19, at 322. The American Association of Retired Persons (AARP) reported a fee range of $40,000 to $200,000. Coleman, *Growing Pains: Life Care Pacts Create Woes for Some People*, AARP News Bull., Apr. 1988, at 1, col. 1 [hereinafter Coleman].

23. S. REP. No. 80, *supra* note 19, at 322. Coleman, *supra* note 22, reported a range of $400 to $1,500.

24. *Promises, supra* note 15, at 69. These increases are intended to reflect cost-of-living increases. *Id.*

25. For instance, the entrance fee is increased by $4,000 and the monthly fee by $425 for a second person residing in a unit at Freedom Plaza, a life care facility in Peoria, Arizona. This is added to fees ranging from $42,000–$117,500 and $775–$1,235 respectively at this facility. Freedom Plaza Pricing Plan, 1989, (copy on file with DET. C. L. REV. office).

26. *Planning for an Aging America: The Void in Reliable Data: Hearing Before the Select Comm. on Aging, H. Rep.*, 100th Cong., 1st Sess. 645 (1988). The median family income of persons 65 years and older was reported as $19,922 in 1986. Although the poverty rate for that age group dropped 15.7% between 1966 and 1986, it still included 12.8% of that population. Furthermore, our elder Americans were more likely than their younger counterparts to be in the "near poor" range, defined as "between the poverty level and one and one half times the poverty level"—15.5% as compared with 8.4% of those under 65 years. S. REP. No. 80, *supra* note 19, at 6. As a guide, note that the 1987 poverty levels for elderly were: $5,393 and $6,802 per year for singles and couples respectively. *Id.* at 284.

27. *Life Care Communities: Promises and Problems: Hearing Before the Spec. Comm. on Aging, U.S. Sen.*, 98th Cong., 1st Sess. 276 (1983) [hereinafter *Promises*] at 55. *See also* Comment, *supra* note 18, at 899, 901.

28. The reader is directed to Comment, *supra* note 18, for a comprehensive look at financial difficulties in the CCRC industry.

29. *See* Barr v. Methodist Church, 90 Cal. App. 3d 259, 153 Cal. Rptr. 322 (1979), documenting the Pacific Homes Bankruptcy, to date, the largest financial collapse in the CCRC industry. This involved a chain of communities which were sponsored by the Methodist Church which operated under a typical "Ponzi" scheme. Instead of reserving residents' money for future services, the funds were diverted for use to pay current debt obligations. When it filed under Chapter X of the Bankruptcy Code in 1977, almost 2,000 elderly residents were affected. In the

early 1980's, the FTC reported that one third of CCRC's in Michigan were reportedly bankruptcy. *Promise, supra* note 15, at 78.

30. *Promises, supra* note 15, at 55.

31. *Id.* This investigation focused on for-profit organizations managed by Christian Services International, Inc. (CSI). The Commission found that the homes managed by CSI were apparently underfunded from the start and were unlikely to be able to deliver life care services as promised. *Id.*

32. *Promises, supra* note 15, at 56.

33. *Id.* Although many communities suggest an affiliation with a church or religious organization, few actually receive financial support from these organizations. *Id.*

34. *Promises, supra* note 15, at 57. Michigan has mandated that life care facilities file for registration, and one requirement is disclosure of the "proposed application of the proceeds of the entrance fee by the facility." MICH. COMP. LAWS ANN. § 554.808 (West Supp. 1987). Furthermore, the corporations and securities bureau has the authority to require the facility to escrow a "reasonable" amount if it finds the facility is financially unstable. *Id.* at § 554.816.

35. Comment, *Continuing-Care Communities for the Elderly: Potential Pitfalls & Proposed Reg.*, 128 U. PA. L. REV. 883, 917 (1980) at 900 for discussion of the Pacific Homes Bankruptcy; the classic example of miscalculation and fraud in connection with a life care community. Undercalculations in the inflation rate, deteriorating health of residents, and death rate resulted in a situation where operating costs were greater than revenues. The organization succumbed to the temptation to expand, thereby collecting new endowment fees, to generate additional revenue. Ultimately bankruptcy was declared, but not before a more than 2,000 elderly persons were taken in by this scam. *See also* Barr v. Methodist Church, 90 Cal. App. 3d 259, 153 Cal. Rptr. 322 (1979).

36. *Promises, supra* note 15, at 57.

37. *Id.* at 103. Maturity is defined by such variables as relative stability of average residents' age, turnover rates, numbers of residents permanently residing in the long term facility, etc. *Id.* at 104.

38. *Id.* at 57. Because the monthly fee is equivalent to rental of a comparable apartment, the right to occupy the dwelling does not constitute value for the endowment fee. *Id.*

39. *Id.*

40. *Id.*

41. *Id.* at 56; Comment, *supra* note 32, at 893.

42. *See supra* note 29 and accompanying text for a brief discussion of circumstances surrounding the Pacific Homes bankruptcy.

43. Promises, *supra* note 15, at 103.

44. *Id.* The author of the study, Howard E. Winklevoss, reported that, of the CCRC's studied, such feasibility projections were limited to five to seven years. *Id.* It is interesting to note that Winklevoss found the life expectancy of CCRC residents in seven communities studied (representing 25,000 persons) to be 20% higher than in the general population. This was found to be roughly equivalent to life expectancies among purchasers of annuities from insurance companies. Several factors were suggested to play in this finding: good health of the individual when entering the contract, social aspect of the CCRC, ready access to health care, etc. The researchers suggested that further study was needed in this area. *Id.* at 101–02.

45. *Healthcare Fin. Mgmt. Assoc. Prin. & Prac. Bd. Stmt. No. 9: Acct. & Rep. Issues Related to CCRC's*, HEALTHCARE FIN. MGMT., Nov. 1986, at 88 [hereinafter *Acct. Issues*].

46. *Life Care Communities: Promises and Problems: Hearing Before the Spec. Comm. on Aging, U.S. Sen.,* 98th Cong., 1st Sess. 276 (1983), at 58.

47. *Life Care Communities: Promises and Problems: Hearing Before the Spec. Comm. on Aging, U.S. Sen.,* 98th Cong., 1st Sess. 276 (1983) [hereinafter *Promises*] at 83. The survey was released in Feb., 1983. *Id.*

48. *Id.* This complaint involved an Alabama community run by Dr. Kenneth Berg. Dr. Berg has been involved in approximately 200 life care homes spread over 25 states, and has greatly influenced the growth of the CCRC industry. *Id.* at 87. He was the CEO of Christian Service International (CSI), a for-profit organization which was the focus of the FTC investigation reported to the Special Committee on Aging. *Id.* at 55. *See also* Bennett v. Berg, 685 F.2d 1053 (8th Cir. 1982), where Dr. Berg was charged with violation of the RICO Act.

49. *Promises, supra* note 47. . . .

50. *Promises, supra* note 47, at 73. The ability to increase monthly fees allows a CCRC to adjust to changes in operating costs. These adjustments should reflect cost of living changes. A community that contracts for fixed monthly fees is likely to be unable to maintain its level of services as costs increase. *Id.* at 58. However, prospective residents should be informed of the potential amounts of increases in the monthly fees so that they may make an informed decision regarding their ability to make future monthly fee payments. *Id.*

51. *Id.* at 75.

52. *Id.* at 75, 77.

53. *Id.*

54. *Id.*

55. *Id.* at 78. Often the "affiliated" religious organization has no financial liability for the CCRC. The FTC also found that "affiliation" with a religious group tended to lull potential residents into a false sense of security. *Id.* at 58.

CHAPTER 15

Board and Care Homes

Continuing care communities are costly. Most residents pay the entry fee by using the proceeds from the sale of their houses. But less affluent elderly, who have no way of paying for a costly continuing care community, may also need daily assistance. These individuals often turn to family and move in with children, siblings or even grandchildren. If there is no option of living with a family member, lower income elderly who cannot live alone may turn to board and care homes. Alternatively called personal care homes, rest homes or even boarding homes, these lower-cost institutions fill the need for housing that fits between independent living, whether in a house or apartment, and publicly subsidized nursing home care. Unfortunately, conditions in these homes are often substandard as detailed in the following congressional hearings.

Board and Care: A Failure in Public Policy

Thursday, March 9, 1989

U.S. Senate, Special Committee on Aging, Joint With Subcommittee on Health And Long-term Care And The Subcommittee on Housing And Consumer Interests, Select Committee on Aging, U.S. House of Representatives,

Washington, D.C.

* * *

Opening Statement
Senator David Pryor
Chairman, Senate Special Committee on Aging
March 9, 1989 hearing
Board and Care: A Failure in Public Policy

Good morning. On behalf of my colleagues on the Special Committee on Aging, I would like to welcome everyone to this morning's joint hearing on board and care homes. We are pleased to be joined today by our colleagues from the House Select Committee on Aging's Subcommittee on Health and Long-Term Care and the Subcommittee on Housing and Consumer Interests. This is also the committee's first hearing of the 101st Congress; I hope it is one of many hearings that this committee will convene to examine the vital concerns and interests of older Americans.

We are gathered here today to discuss a critical, but often overlooked, component of this nation's long-term care system—the board and care home. They have a vital place on the long-term care continuum in that they can provide elderly and disabled persons with a degree of protective oversight that enables them to maintain a level of independence and autonomy they would not find in a more restrictive and more costly institutional setting, such as a nursing home. The hearing is being held to investigate the problems as well as the attributes of the board and care system, and to explore ways to solve these problems while preserving the good qualities that board and care has to offer.

What exactly is board and care? "Board and care" is a catch-all term used to describe a wide variety of nonmedical residential facilities. These include group homes, foster homes, personal care homes, and rest homes. There is a great deal of variance among board and care with regard to size, type of resident, the range of services offered, and the ownership. They usually provide room, meals, and assistance with activities—such as bathing, dressing, and the taking of medication—and can house anywhere from one to one hundred residents. Although traditionally dominated by small "mom and pop" operations and larger establishments sponsored by nonprofit charitable groups, the board and care industry has recently seen the emergence of "assisted living facilities" built by for-profit housing developers. Residents of board and care include the elderly, the physically disabled, the deinstitutionalized mentally ill, and the developmentally disabled.

The General Accounting Office (GAO) report on board and care in six states, which is being released today, found that board and care homes serving the elderly are usually located in cities, have an average of twenty-three beds, and are privately operated. Residents of board and care homes typically have physical limitations requiring some oversight, limited incomes (and are frequently Supplemental Security Income, or SSI, recipients), and have often lived in an institution because of a mental disability. They are also unlikely to have friends or relatives visit them on a regular basis, and are therefore often isolated from the community and without an advocate to look out for them and protect their rights.

Board and care homes present unique quality problems. They provide care for poor, often mentally ill, disabled individuals who frequently have no place else to go. One of the major problems with operating board and care is that the providers, who are often poor themselves, do not receive enough money from their SSI residents to cover the cost of their care. Individual SSI recipients receive $368 per month, and couples receive $553 per month. Although several states supplement SSI, the average supplement being about $200 per month, it is nonetheless a very small amount of money with which to provide room, meals, supervision, etc. The task of providing adequate care is complicated further by the fact that many of the residents have illnesses or disabilities that demand more care than the board and care operator can afford or is trained to provide.

In 1976, in response to concern about problems in board and care homes, Congress enacted the Keys Amendment to the Social Security Act. It required states to certify to the Department of Health and Human Services (HHS) that all facilities with a large number of SSI recipients as residents met appropriate standards. A 1987 survey of licensed facilities identified about 41,000 licensed homes, with about 563,000 beds serving the elderly, mentally ill and mentally retarded. Of this amount, about 264,000 beds were identified as serving the elderly only. Unfortunately, there are no data available on the number of unlicensed homes. However, it is generally acknowledged that a greater number of homes are unlicensed than licensed. In 1981, HHS estimated that there were anywhere from 500,000 to 1,500,000 residents of board and care facilities. The date and wide range of that estimate illustrate how little we know about board and care.

Problems exist in licensed and unlicensed homes alike; in other words, licensing does not ensure quality care. Licensing requirements vary widely from state to state, and even the very definition of what constitutes a board and care facility differs, so that what may be considered a board and care home in one state (and hence subject to the licensing requirements) is not in another. Further, most inspections focus on the physical plant, with little or no emphasis on the residents and their quality of life. Because states do not aggregate the data gleaned from the inspection reports, the GAO report was limited in its ability to determine the magnitude and type of violations or the kinds of homes in which the violations frequently occur. However, GAO did find that homes with predominately low-income residents (i.e., SSI recipients) had about twice as many violations on the average as homes with predominately private-pay residents.

A related problem is the lack of strong, efficient enforcement mechanisms for the licensing requirements. The six states that GAO surveyed had the authority to close or revoke the license of a home that was threatening the residents' safety or well-being; in three of the states, this was the only sanction against substandard homes. Although closing a facility is sometimes the only way to handle a chronically substandard home, this all or nothing sanction is usually not invoked—not only is it a time consuming and difficult process, but there are many instances in which it would do more harm than good. In a situation in which the problems could be remedied, or the residents have no place else to go, closing the facility is no solution. Some states have intermediate sanctions, such as fines or receiverships; GAO reports that the states of California and Florida have had limited success with these sanctions, as they are difficult to both invoke and collect.

The Department of Health and Human Services has played a circumscribed role in overseeing board and care facilities. While the Keys Amendment requires states to establish and enforce board and care standards, it only requires HHS to receive the states' annual certifications concerning compliance. HHS currently allocates only one-eighth of one person's time to checking that the states have sent in their certifications. This amounts to about one hour per day, or five hours per week. Under this policy of very limited follow-up and oversight, a state can report its compliance with Keys even though it may have done little or nothing with respect to monitoring or licensing board and care homes. Furthermore, Keys requires states to report substandard board and care homes to the Social Security Administration so that it can reduce the SSI benefits of any recipient living in such homes. Because this penalizes the residents and not the homes, it acts as a disincentive for states to report deficiencies.

As we will hear today, far too many homes are providing grossly substandard care that endangers the health and well-being of their residents, who are among the most vulnerable and isolated of our citizens. There are a myriad of reasons for why this occurs—a lack of state and federal involvement in oversight and regulation; the need for training and education among care providers; and an absence of knowledge in most communities that these facilities, much less the problems, even exist.

* * *

Statement of Representative Claude Pepper, Chairman, Subcommittee on Health and Long-Term Care

MR. PEPPER. Thank you, Mr. Chairman.

We found that board and care residents, largely elderly, female and dependent, typically turn over the entirety of their SSI check, which averages about $500 excluding their personal needs of $35, to the home. Now we know, Mr. Chairman, that the minimum SSI benefit is about $360 a month, but the state supplements that somewhat. So generally the amount that the patients turn over to their board and care homes is around $500, less $35. More than half of the residents of these homes come from mental institutions. The rest come from hospitals, nursing homes, and the streets. We found that most homes were not equipped with fire safety equipment, were unsanitary and ill-kept, and were roach- and pest-infested.

We observed at least one incident of fraud, waste, and abuse in literally every state that we visited.

In New York, we found Medicaid cards illegally sold to providers who then billed Medicaid for services never rendered. We also found about six hundred residents in three facilities warehoused and, in the words of one home owner, "drugged three times a day whether they need it or not." Incidentally, Mr. Chairman and members, we did not find any staff to speak of any one of these ten state board and care homes that we visited. They relied primarily on drugging these people to keep them quiet in the absence of staff people to look after them.

In New Mexico, ten Alzheimer's patients were found bound to their wheelchairs in spite of a law requiring residents to be able to leave the home on their own accord in emergency situations. We also found drugs improperly stored, creating life-threatening situations.

In California, and we are going to hear from one of the people who survived it, we investigated the murder of seven residents by an ex-felon manager who continued to cash their Social Security checks long after they died. By the way, Mr. Chairman, one of the things that we recommend is that the Social Security Administration follow up more carefully when authority is given to anybody to cash a Social Security check. We have to make sure that proper use is made of that Social Security money—whether it is appropriately expended or not. We will hear today from the one resident who lived because he did not turn over his checks to that woman in Sacramento who allegedly killed her boarders. In another state, we found a ninety-five-year-old woman who had been beaten and dragged across the floor by her manager, and we have a picture of that pitiful lady.

In Maryland, an owner continued to house eleven residents in her burned-out home that lacked fire safety equipment. One resident was robbed of all his possessions.

In the District of Columbia, a bed-bound elderly woman was found by subcommittee staff lying in her own urine begging for food in her roach-infested, three-story, walk-up room. That was in our city of Washington, D.C., the capital of the United States of America.

In Illinois, we found two hundred residents of a home forced to turn over their small personal income allowance to the home operator. We also were told of home owners recruiting and signing up the homeless in order to cash their checks, which would be sent to their board and care home. Yet no effort was made to assure the shelter they purchased.

In Florida, we investigated the deaths of two residents. One died of a drug overdose, and the other died bed-bound, tied down, with multiple decubitus ulcers. In another home, we found out how profitable board and care can be. While the owner skimped on the quality of care provided for his patients, outside the home—and we have the picture—were parked a Cadillac, a speed boat, a van, and two motorcycles. In other words, the proprietor was doing very well, but the patients on the inside were doing very poorly.

In Louisiana, city officials closed down a pest-infested, unlicensed board and care home following the subcommittee's unannounced inspection unveiling deplorable and life-threatening conditions. One elderly woman we found lying in her own urine died, and others were hospitalized within hours of the subcommittee visit. I could not help but think as I looked at the picture of this lady lying there pitifully in her bed with urine all over it that at one time this was a beautiful lady. You can tell that she was at one time a lovely person. Imagine that she had to come to that kind of miserable end to her life.

In Alabama, a home cited for numerous violations by the subcommittee—including floors covered with human waste and inoperative unsanitary toilets—burned down, injuring two of the homes' frail elderly residents. This occurred several days after the subcommittee's visit.

In Virginia, we found eleven former mental patients, two of whom required skilled nursing care, warehoused in an old row house. Numerous other violations were recorded by the subcommittee in photographs, which fill over two hundred pages of our report.

Unfortunately, the states confirm that the incidence of abuse, ranging from neglect to death, are increasing and are not likely to abate.

* * *

Statement of David Lazarus, Director of Litigation, Community Health Law Project, East Orange, New Jersey

MR. LAZARUS. My name is David Lazarus, and I have been the Director of Litigation for the Community Health Law Project for the last twelve years. The Law Project is New Jersey's largest nongovernment public interest law firm employing about thirty attorneys and thirty advocates in our four offices around the state. We were initially sponsored in 1977 by the State of New Jersey, the American Bar Association, and the New Jersey State Bar Association to provide legal and advocacy services to the mentally ill and elderly.

Today, we represent about thirty-five hundred other elderly and disabled persons per year, most of whom are poor. Many of our clients live in board and care facilities, and over the years we have had a great deal of contact both positive and negative with the owners and operators, state officials, and other community service providers. I have written portions of New Jersey's laws regulating the board and care industry and for the last ten years have been one of the few nongovernmental members of the state's interdepartmental committee responsible for suggesting regulations and coordinating governmental and industry efforts.

Our attorneys and advocates have represented many clients in board and care facilities in disputes with the operators. Cases have included theft of Social Security's or other clients' funds, unconscionable rent increases, illegal evictions, work for pay lower than minimum wages, and incidents of abuse and exploitation. In one case we represented an eighty-six-year-old woman who paid her entire life savings of $32,000 and her monthly Social Security check to the operator of a board and care facility in exchange for a life tenancy. Two years later she was evicted. We found in the course of representing her that the operator had several felony convictions, and although state authorities were informed, he still operates that facility today. Our staff has witnessed assaults on residents and reported them to the proper authorities. But after investigation, these incidents were dismissed as unsubstantiated without the investigator even interviewing our staff.

I could go on describing a litany of horror stories and incidents of abuse and exploitation in board and care facilities, but I am sure you will hear that from others. I would prefer to focus on New Jersey's laws, who the residents are that live in these facilities, why it is impossible to provide appropriate standards of care and rehabilitation, and why board and care facilities have become bargain basement warehouses for the mentally ill and disabled elderly. I would also like to provide you with some recommendations, but please remember that even if you forget all else: We spend less for the board and care of a disabled adult or senior citizen than for the board and care of a dog in a kennel.

New Jersey's laws governing board and care facilities on paper are probably the strongest in the nation. They provide for licensing of all facilities and their operators, standards of care appropriate to residents' needs, inspection by state officials, mandated reporting of incidents of abuse and exploitation and investigation, the power to fine and place facilities in receivership, and mandated social and health services. But unfortunately for many residents, what exists on paper in New Jersey's laws and what exists in reality are miles apart.

In New Jersey the board and care industry includes both boarding homes, rooming houses and what we call residential health care facilities. According to regulation, the boarding home and residential health care facility provides virtually the same services and meals to residents. Rooming houses provide only shelter but no meals or services. Of the ten thousand residential health care facility residents, 50 percent are over age seventy-five, 25 percent are over eighty-five, one-half of the residents have a history of state or county psychiatric hospitalization, are chronically mentally ill and frequently require powerful psychotropic medication, and one-half of the residents' sole source of income is Supplemental Security Income because they are disabled or elderly. There are about thirty-two hundred people living in boarding homes and the residential profile is much the same, except they tend to be younger and the incidence of chronic mental illness is even greater. There are seventeen thousand people living in rooming houses, which includes YW/MCAs and shelters. Little is known about who they are, their medical condition and impairments, and their need for services, although nationally as many as one-third of the shelter population are thought to be mentally ill. They are the least inspected facilities.

In New Jersey a residential health care facility is supposed to provide a room, meals, personal services including laundry, 24-hour supervision, assistance with bathing and dressing, twelve minutes of nursing care per resident per week, medication monitoring, some transportation, referral to community agencies, maintenance of records, and budgeting and safekeeping of residents' funds; all for $15 per day for the five thousand or so Supplemental Security Income recipients. Of that $15, $11 comes from the federal government and $4 from the state.

Boarding homes are supposed to provide the same room, meals, and services to residents except for the limited on-site nursing care, starting at $11 per day for the sixteen hundred residents receiving Supplemental Security Income and Social Security. Of that $11 per day, $10 comes from the federal government and $1 from the state. Residents of residential health care facilities and boarding homes receiving Supplemental Security Income are expected to take care of all of their personal needs, including the purchase of clothing, on $55 per month. The state share of Supplemental Security Income has not been increased in more than ten years.

In New Jersey community service providers are suppose to identify resident needs and provide services, but the funding to do so is always inadequate at best or nonexistent. In fact, the system conspires against the delivery of many essential on-site services. The system's problems include restrictions on Medicaid and Medicare funds. If, for example, a community mental health center or clinic wanted to provide mental health services to a Medicaid recipient at the boarding home or residential health care facility, the center or clinic would not be reimbursed for the service. Neither would home health aides nor programs aimed at rehabilitation. Disabled persons who have a work history and receive Social Security disability are not even eligible for Medicare benefits for two years after they become disabled. People with work history are therefore treated as second class citizens and are entitled to less in medical benefits than if they had not worked at all.

The persons that own and manage these facilities are a mixed group. Some are conscientious, caring, and excellent operators and run homes that I would live in myself; many are not. At present only a forty-hour training course is mandated in order to operate a facility that may have as few as two residents or more than two hundred. No testing is required. No professional or educational background is required. The quality of care ranges from excellent to poor and is usually proportionate to what you can afford to pay. Even the most conscientious well-intentioned operator, and there are many, can only do so much on the $11 or $15 per day per resident allowed for room, meals, laundry, and a variety of other essential services. It is no wonder that many operators most qualified to provide for these elderly and disabled residents would not go near the board and care industry.

* * *

Statement of Pam Hinckley, Owner/operator, Board and Care Home, Cleveland, Ohio

Ms. Hinckley. Hello. I do feel targeted in a way because I'm listening here and everything is going on bad in these homes and I feel—oh, no.

Chairman. Well, let's hear the other side.

Ms. Hinckley. I do run an adult family home in Cleveland, Ohio, with my husband. I have been working with the elderly in group homes and private homes over the past eleven years. We are approved by the county department of human services, and I do attend the care providers support group meetings.

We can accommodate up to five residents as far as our zoning is concerned. We did have problems with this at one time. Each resident is provided with a furnished room—private or shared—three well-balanced meals and snacks, laundry, and supervised medications, and we help with the guidance for daily living activities. We also do provide in-home foot care by a regular podiatrist on a regular basis, and we can provide access to medical services and a local senior citizen activity center.

We have a nurse we have been working with now for the past year who comes in every six to eight weeks. She goes over the general health of all of our residents. If she sees any problems or if the residents have any questions, she's really good as far as providing information on such things as diets, medications, or even, for that matter, physical or social changes in the home.

All of my residents are over sixty-five. Most were placed there by their relatives, and they were placed just because they needed to be with somebody because they weren't eating right or they weren't taking their medication on time. Most of my residents are pretty well up and about. I have nobody in bed. I have nobody who needs any skilled nursing care.

We also offer the resident a sense of belonging, and I pride myself on our family-oriented atmosphere. I have two kids myself. I have a three-year-old boy and an eight-year-old girl. We have a dog and birds. We live in a old-fashioned type farm house. It is kept up-to-date. It isn't as horrifying as some of the stories I've heard here about homes. We try hard. We have a good interaction with our residents and a good rapport with the residents and their families.

Most of my residents have been with me for at least a year or more. Some of them were even with me at the time when I had my three-year-old. They do stay with us, I would say, until death do us part. When we do see signs of weight loss or gain, or incontinence, or if they would be in need of skilled nursing care—I do not diagnose this either, so don't take my word on this—we do work closely with the family doctors. Anyway, when we do see them going down hill, we do attend to their needs. We do make sure that they are watched by a physician or the nurse. When the time comes to say good-bye, we do let them go. Only once have I had to have a resident placed in a nursing home. Most of the people have stayed with me until death.

As it stands in Ohio today, we do have a house bill that is currently pending before the House of Representatives. I think it is great. I wish it would pass now. We've been waiting for years for some type of regulations or standards to help us get our homes organized. We know that we're not perfect at what we're doing. I know that I'm not perfect. I do try as far as diets and medications to keep up with things as much as I can. I don't want to harm my residents in any way. I want them to enjoy living with me, and I want them to stay with me until death. I enjoy doing this for a living.

I know that you are fully aware that there is a lot of abuse in these homes, and I am fully aware of it, too. I have worked for a few of these homes that you could say are abusing or neglecting the elderly. That is one of the reasons why I started my own. I could give you all kinds of examples of abuse in these homes, and I just don't think it's necessary now. You have heard and seen quite a bit already.

One thing I would like to say is that it is very easy for care providers to go into hiding at these homes. It is very easy. We can place ads in papers. We can go to social service departments. We can contact the friends or relatives of the people that we have taken care of to get access to residents to move into our homes. It's quite easy to fill up a home.

It was brought up earlier about Social Security checks. It's easy to cash a Social Security check. Have a resident sign it, take your resident to the bank, and they will turn all the funds over to you. It is that simple. I won't handle finances at all for any of my residents. I just refuse. I have all of the residents in their home—their families pay me directly. They write a check direct to me. I do deposit and I even pay tax on it. We keep up pretty well with records, and it works out well.

Most of the abuse and neglect that you have heard about in these homes are taking place in homes that I would say are in hiding. These are the homes that aren't approved or licensed or regulated by any type of agency. They don't have any type of help or organization coming in to check on these residents. These are the homes that you have to go after. It's the ones that are trying to tell you what we do for a living and are trying to get help—why would I be here today if I was abusing my residents? I wouldn't subject myself to you. Most care providers who operate these kinds of homes, you would know right off the bat. You could talk to a few of them and just by talking to them and by looking at their own personal appearances, you could tell just by their attitudes whether they should take care of residents or not. It's that easy to differentiate the different types of care providers.

CHAPTER 16

Assisted Living

Board and care homes are, in effect, a form of "assisted living," and in existence long before that term came into popular use. While some board and care homes provide inadequate care, many live up to their name and adequately house and care for low-income elderly persons. The promise of assisted living for low-income older persons in the form of board and care homes is explored in the following article.

David Abromowitz and Rebecca Plaut

Assisted Living for Low-Income Seniors

* * *

What Is Assisted Living?

Assisted living is a model of housing for the elderly that blends residential and personal services. For a standard monthly payment, assisted living residences usually provide basic residential services, such as laundry, light housekeeping, and one meal a day. Additionally, maintenance of a resident's living quarters is provided. Residents choose and pay for additional services they need, ranging from help with dressing, bathing, medication, and errands to transportation services, private companions, guest meals, physical therapy, and medical services.

Assisted living currently does not have a precise definition, partly because of the

Journal of Affordable Housing & Community Development Law, Vol. 5, No. 1, 63–72 (Fall 1995).

variety of the residents' needs and the services provided. Also, there is no single legal definition that is widely accepted. The following legal definitions vary in their approaches and in the level of detail.

* * *

In Massachusetts the statutory definition includes the provision of room and board and assistance with activities of daily living; it specifically excludes facilities that are regulated as nursing homes, hospices, or continuing care communities.[1] All assisted living residences in Massachusetts must provide "only single or double living units with lockable doors on the entry door of each unit," at least a private half bathroom for each living unit, at least one bathing facility for every three residents, and access to cooking capacity for all living units.[2] If newly constructed, an assisted living residence in Massachusetts must provide a private bathroom for each living unit, equipped with one lavatory, one toilet, and one bathtub or shower stall.[3]

By contrast, assisted living in Alaska includes any residential facility that provides food service and offers to provide or obtain personal assistance for three or more adults who are not related to the owner of the facility by blood or marriage.[4] In Ohio, an assisted living facility has multiple residential units and "provides or arranges for skilled nursing care for one or more individuals who reside in the facility and are not related to the owner or operator."[5]

Why Is Assisted Living Becoming Popular?

Several factors have contributed to the growth of assisted living in recent years. One factor is the well-documented aging of the U.S. population. The number of Americans over sixty-five has increased from 19.9 million in 1970 to 31.5 million in 1990. According to the Census Bureau, that population will double to 65.6 million by 2030. The population of people over eighty-five is expected to increase even more dramatically, from 2.2 million in 1980 to 15 million in 2050.[6] As Americans live longer, the years in which senior citizens need assistance with activities of daily living are prolonged.

A second factor is that public policy approaches to the elderly population have changed. With the 1965 adoption of Medicare and Medicaid, the profitability and, therefore, the number of nursing homes increased dramatically.[7] Many nursing home residents did not require the level of medical care that nursing homes provided,[8] but found that residence in a nursing home provided the level of assistance they needed with ADLs and reduced their personal expenses. [Editor's Note: ADLs are "Activities of Daily Living," a term used by gerontologists to assess the degree of independence of older persons. ADLs include bathing, toileting, eating, dressing, and ambulating (ability to get out of bed or a chair).] For this reason, the federal-state Medicaid program, perhaps unintentionally, provided an incentive for older people who needed some assistance with ADLs to move into nursing homes.[9] Elderly people without assets could live in nursing homes to receive housing and assistance with ADLs, and

Medicaid would pay the bill. As a result of this and other developments in the health economy, Medicaid costs have skyrocketed.

In recent years, federal budgetary concerns have focused attention on the need for more cost-effective ways to provide housing and appropriate care for low-income elderly. For example, a 1987 study calculated that annual Medicaid nursing home bills averaged $100 a day, or at least $3,000 a month. In contrast, assisted living facilities can provide room, board, and light housekeeping services for $35 to $45 per day, for monthly payments of $1,200, or $14,400 annually.[10] The potential savings, approximately $20,000 a year per resident, provide a significant incentive to public officials to encourage the development of assisted living facilities for low-income seniors.

In addition to this increase in financial pressures for change in the provision of care for the frail elderly, personal priorities also have contributed to the rise of assisted living. Increasingly, seniors, their families, and their caretakers perceive the provision of social and health care services in a residential setting as an attractive, dignified living option.

Growth of Regulation

In response to the recent growth in assisted living facilities, legislators and public health officials have started to regulate assisted living. The facilities are regulated under a variety of names. In California, Illinois, and Nebraska, regulatory rules refer to "residential care facilities for the elderly," while in Maine and Wyoming similar operations are called "boarding homes."[11]

A wide range of regulatory approaches has developed. At one end of the spectrum, as in New Jersey, a proposed assisted living facility is subject to a restrictive "certificate of need" process much like that typically applied to a proposed new nursing home. To avoid costly duplication of facilities, the state regulators require the proponent to demonstrate why such a facility is needed, given the existing sources of care in the proposed service area. In other states, regulation is limited to a set of prescribed operating rules, but there is no approval process. Responsibility for a state regulatory scheme may rest with the state social services office, public health department, or office charged with responsibility for the aging.

The Massachusetts statute governing assisted living residences places responsibility for administration with the Executive Office of Elder Affairs (EOEA). Massachusetts requires certification by EOEA prior to advertising or operating an assisted living residence.[12] The certification process is functionally equivalent to a licensure process. It requires the applicant to file an operating plan that includes a description of mandatory services, optional services, training standards for management and staff, residency agreements, and the fee structure. Developers and managers of assisted living residences must reveal the identities of interested parties, including prior involvement in the housing industry or in elder care or the provision of health care services. In addition, EOEA inspectors are required to visit each facility at least once every two years.[13]

* * *

Many states impose limitations on the amount of nursing care for residents of assisted living facilities. For example, in Ohio an assisted living residence may not admit individuals who require twenty-four-hour skilled nursing care and may not provide such care "for a period longer than reasonably necessary to complete an appropriate transfer of the person."[14] In Alaska, residents may not receive more than forty-five days of twenty-four-hour skilled nursing care.[15] In contrast, under the Massachusetts statute, assisted living residences may not admit individuals who require twenty-four-hour skilled nursing care and may provide such skilled care only for a period of under ninety days, for short-term illnesses, and if provided by staff unaffiliated with the residence.[16]

Although some entrepreneurs regard the regulatory efforts of the various states as constricting, others welcome them for providing a level of certainty and credibility. In some regions, lenders have been wary of entering a market in which regulation is anticipated, but unknown. The uncertainty makes it difficult to quantify cost and evaluate the sufficiency of proposed project designs and management schemes. Although regulation may impose more costs, it also sets a standard of quality and regularizes practices in the industry, thereby reducing further the obstacles to obtaining financing.

* * *

An Untapped Market: Low-Income Elders

To date, most assisted living facilities have targeted a population that can pay for both the rent and the personal care services provided. However, the need for assisted living facilities is not limited to senior citizens who can afford market-rate elder care. Low-income seniors represent a large segment of the elderly, and the assisted living community has yet to address their needs.

The low-income housing tax credit may make it possible for developers of assisted living facilities for low-income elderly residents to attract excellent potential sources of equity. The low-income housing credit provides tax credits to residential rental properties that meet the complex requirements of section 42 of the Internal Revenue Code. Generally these properties are owned by limited partnerships in which a sponsor controls the property by owning a 1 percent general partner interest and a corporate investor makes a substantial equity contribution in exchange for a 99 percent limited partner interest. The limited partner interest entitles the investor to 99 percent of the partnership's tax losses and tax credits, which reduce dollar for dollar the investor's federal tax liability on income derived from other sources.

Assisted living facilities that meet the requirements of section 42 may be eligible for low-income housing tax credits. One important requirement of section 42 is that at least 20 percent of the living units must be rented to persons whose income is 50 percent or less than area median income (or 40 percent of the units must be rented to persons whose income is less than 60 percent of area median income). In addition, these units must be "rent-restricted," which means rents cannot be more than 30 percent of 50 percent of area median income (or 30 percent of 60 percent of median income, if the 60 percent test is used).[17] Also, the amount of tax credit is dependent on the percentage of rent-restricted low-income living units in the facility above the 20 percent or 40 percent minimum level described above. The larger the percentage of low-income units in the facility, the greater the amount of credits that can be claimed by the owners.

Assisted living facilities present some special issues under the tax credit rules because of the combination of housing and services offered. For example, tax credits are only available for residential rental projects. The credit is not available for any residential unit that is part of a hospital, nursing home, sanitarium, life care facility, trailer park, or intermediate care facility for the medically or physically handicapped.[18] Accordingly, it is important that the level of services provided does not transform the project so greatly that it can no longer be defined as residential real estate. For example, residents should be required to secure their own medical providers. Also, each living unit should have a lockable door and be separate and distinct from the other living units, and leases should be for a minimum of six months.

As noted above, the low-income housing tax credit requires that "rents" be restricted. The rules under section 42 provide that "rent" includes charges for services that are "not optional" and that the cost of services that are "required as a condition of occupancy" must be included in the gross rent calculation.[19] Therefore, if a facility requires residents to pay for services and rent in a combined mandatory package, and if the cost exceeds the rent limitation in section 42 (as would almost certainly be the case), the facility would not be eligible for tax credits. Consequently, residents must have the option to reject services provided by the facility and to purchase the same services from one or more alternative service providers. Whether a service is considered optional is a fact-specific determination that depends on factors such as a facility's day-to-day operation and its fee structure. The analysis may differ for all services and facilities. The scope of this analysis is illustrated when one questions whether charges for meals should be included in gross rent or billed separately. The regulations state that meals provided in a common dining facility are considered optional only if payment for the meals is not a condition of occupancy and a practical alternative exists for tenants to obtain meals.[20] The determination of whether meals are truly optional, therefore, could vary for two facilities similarly organized, based perhaps on the design of cooking space in the units, accessibility to supermarkets, and other project-specific factors.

The tax credit rules also exclude certain subsidies for supportive services from the gross rent calculation. To qualify for this exclusion, the subsidy must be paid to the owner of the project and must be from a governmental program of assistance (or a tax-exempt organization) for a supportive service that is designed to enable the resident to remain independent and avoid placement in a nursing home or hospital. The subsidy for supportive services also must not be "separable" from the amount of assistance provided for rent.[21] Many services provided at assisted living facilities are likely to fit this definition.

One issue that arises under the above exclusion is whether Supplemental Security Income (SSI) payments, which are paid directly to individual elderly recipients, qualify for this exclusion. The SSI program for assisted living is an optional program under the federal Social Security Act. In a state that offers the SSI program, individuals who meet certain financial eligibility criteria as well as clinical eligibility criteria receive payments that raise their income sufficiently to enable them to pay for room and board. In some states, the SSI program is supplemented by additional payments. For example, the group adult foster care program in Massachusetts enables an individual to pay for personal services and administrative services in an assisted living facility.[22] The Internal Revenue Service has recently issued a private letter ruling to the effect that SSI payments under one state program may be excluded from rent.[23] Although this letter ruling is a helpful indication of the IRS approach in this area, in general there is still very little guidance, and many issues must be resolved as tax credits are more widely used for assisted living.

Conclusion

The development of affordable assisted living is likely to accelerate, propelled by the same forces at work in the national debates on the budget crisis and health care reform. Assisted living for low-income senior citizens is seen as an alternative extended care option that can reduce the need for hospital and nursing home beds and slow the growth of Medicaid expenses in both federal and state budgets. But developing sound, financially attractive, and affordable projects is difficult in light of the multidisciplinary nature of assisted living and the many new regulatory, financing, and operational issues and questions still being identified and addressed.

Assisted living facilities deliver more than residential services; they provide a range of assistance and facilitate access to a spectrum of more intensive services as the needs of residents change from time to time. Record keeping and staff development and retention are very important in an assisted living facility. Also, relationships with nursing homes, home health care providers, and other health care resources must be viable if the assisted living facility is to be successful in the marketplace. In many respects, assisted living facilities operate in a unique market and regulatory context. Responsible property management and financial analysis alone do not ensure the success of an assisted living facility.

Notes

1. Mass. Gen. L., ch. 19D, § 3 (1995).
2. *Id.* § 16.

3. *Id.*

4. ALASKA STAT. § 47.33.010 (1994). As in Massachusetts, certain specific types of residential facilities are excluded from the definition. *Id.*

5. OHIO REV. CODE ANN. § 3726.01 (Page's 1995). Again, certain specific types of residential facilities are excluded from the definition. *Id.*

6. PAUL A. GORDON, DEVELOPING RETIREMENT COMMUNITIES 6–7 (1993) (citing U.S. SENATE SPECIAL COMMITTEE ON AGING, AGING IN AMERICA: TRENDS AND PROJECTIONS (1991)).

7. MARY ADELAIDE MENDELSON, TENDER LOVING GREED 36 (1974).

8. GORDON, *supra* note 6, at 21 (citing M. BALTAY, CONGRESSIONAL BUDGET OFFICE, LONG-TERM CARE FOR THE ELDERLY AND DISABLED (1977)).

9. MENDELSON, *supra* note 7, at 41.

10. GORDON, *supra* note 6, at 40 (citing D. Seip, *Specializing in Assisted Living Facilities, Contemporary Long Term Care,* 34 ASSISTED LIVING TODAY, 18–19 (Winter 1994)).

11. Seip, *supra* note 10, at 18–19.

12. MASS. GEN. L., ch. 19D, §§ 1 and 3 (1995).

13. *Id.* § 5.

14. OHIO REV. CODE ANN. § 3726.03 (Page's 1995).

15. ALASKA STAT. §§ 47.33.020(d) and (g) (1994).

16. MASS. GEN. L., ch. 19D, § 11 (1995).

17. I.R.C. § 42(g)(2)(A) (1988 and Supp. V 1993).

18. Treas. Reg. § 1.42-9(b) (1994).

19. *Id.* § 1.42-11(b)(3).

20. *Id.* § 1.42-11(a).

21. I.R.C. § 42(g)(2)(A)(iii).

22. MASS. GEN. L., ch. 19D, § 6 (1995).

23. Priv. Ltr. Rul. 95-26-009 (Apr. 14, 1995).

Part IV

Mental Capacity Issues

The image of an aged person with diminished mental capacity—with reduced memory, poor judgment, and even dementia—is often the common image of the old. Though older persons do often suffer from diminished mental capacity, being old should not be equated with senility. Yes, many older persons do suffer a loss of short-term memory. For example, as we grow older it becomes more difficult to memorize a phone number or commit a short grocery list to memory. But dementia, severe loss of memory, and other mental dysfunctions are not the result of normal aging. Rather, they are the result of a pathology—perhaps a virus, a genetic defect triggered by environmental factors, or hormonal imbalances. A loss of mental capacity can even result from a series of mini-strokes that cut off blood to parts of the brain. Still, while the loss of mental capacity is "abnormal," it is unfortunately not unusual. It is estimated, for example, that over half of those who live past age eighty-five will suffer from dementia.

CHAPTER 17

Evaluating Mental Capacity

Because of the frequency in loss of mental capacity among the elderly, the law has responded with a number of ways to assist individuals who can no longer make rational decisions. Of course, before invoking any of those legal solutions, the first question concerns how to determine that the older person suffers from a loss of mental capacity. For example, the state can declare someone incapacitated and appoint a guardian to act on his or her behalf, but before doing so the state is almost certain to seek a medical determination of the individual in an attempt to ascertain whether the individual is mentally disabled or merely voluntarily acting in an eccentric or apparently irrational manner. After all, there is no requirement that older persons act in ways that promote their best interests, as measured by the dictates of others. In the following material, Dr. Roca discusses how physicians approach the question of diagnosing mental disorders.

Robert P. Roca

Determining Decisional Capacity: A Medical Perspective

* * *

I. The Diagnosis Of Mental Disorders

Clinical syndromes are clusters of symptoms, signs, and impairments that tend to occur together and have a distinct natural history. They may be attributable to one or more causes or pathogenic mechanisms. Fever, shortness of breath, and cough, for example, are components of the clinical syndrome termed "pneumonia." This syndrome is often caused by bacteria (e.g., *streptococcus pneumoniae*), but other infectious agents (e.g., viruses) may be implicated. The symptoms subside in most cases when appropriate antibiotic therapy is instituted. Recognizing the clinical syndrome is thus the first step in the process of clinical management, and this rule applies throughout general medicine.

Recognizing clinical syndromes is even more important in psychiatry because this is the principal—and in some cases the *only*—means of validating the presence of a condition; there is no biopsy, blood test, or X-ray to do the job. Psychiatric diagnosis has an historic reputation for being unreliable; however, the ability of psychiatrists to recognize and describe psychiatric syndromes has improved recently as a result of the growth of empirical research in psychiatry and the concerted effort of the American Psychiatric Association to standardize the use of diagnostic terms through the development of the Diagnostic and Statistical Manual of Mental Disorders (DSM).[1] This document demystifies psychiatric diagnosis, establishing explicit criteria for the assignment of diagnostic labels and improving the reliability of psychiatric classification, i.e., improving the odds that different examiners will agree about the diagnosis in a given case.

The clinical syndromes described in DSM are heterogeneous in many respects—including the nature of their causes and the degree to which these causes are understood. Some of these syndromes are associated with demonstrable disturbances in brain anatomy or physiology (e.g., dementia, delirium). Others are believed, but not yet proven, to be associated with brain abnormalities (e.g., schizophrenia, bipolar affective disorder). Still others are believed to be entirely psychological in their origins and have no basis whatsoever in bodily malfunction. As this article will demonstrate, the disorders that often compromise capacity in the elderly are known or

Fordham Law Review, Vol. 62, 1177–1196 (1994). Reprinted by permission.

believed to be associated with disturbances of brain function and are therefore conditions about which physicians might be expected to speak with special authority. Before the conditions themselves are discussed, the clinical methods by which physicians arrive at diagnostic decisions and assess the degree of disability imposed by these conditions will be considered.

II. The Psychiatric History And Mental Status Examination

The purpose of the psychiatric history and mental status examination is to obtain information relevant to decisions about diagnosis and functional capacity. The psychiatric history is a biography, gathered from as many informants as possible, focusing on details relevant to these decisions. The most important components of the history are those bearing most directly on these details. In the case of dementia, for example, critical history includes information regarding the onset of forgetfulness, the rate of decline in cognitive functioning, and the specific impairments that have developed. But other kinds of history are relevant as well. Because dementia, like many psychiatric disorders, runs in families, it is important to ascertain whether any family members, particularly first-degree relatives, have experienced similar symptoms. In addition, because dementia, like many psychiatric disorders, precipitates functional decline in many domains, it is important to know the patient's maximal level of educational and occupational attainment to help determine whether deterioration has occurred.

The mental status examination is the formal process by which physicians discover the presence of signs and symptoms of specific psychiatric disorders. It is a brief sampling of the contents of consciousness, focusing on features that are diagnostically discriminating. The physician watches for abnormalities in motor behavior, listens for disruptions in the coherence of speech, and asks specific questions designed to reveal disturbances in mood, belief (i.e., delusions), perception (hallucinations and/or illusions), and cognition.[2]

* * *

III. Psychiatric Disorders That May Compromise Capacity

A. Dementia

Dementia is a clinical syndrome characterized by generalized cognitive impairment and a normal level of consciousness (i.e., normal level of attention and wakefulness). . . . About five percent of persons over sixty-five and twenty percent of persons over eighty are affected severely. The primary deficits occur in the realms of orientation, memory, and reasoning; however, hallucinations, delusions, major depression, and a host of behavioral symptoms (e.g., wandering, yelling, banging, combativeness, "agitation") also may occur.

The single most common cause of dementia is Alzheimer's disease, a progressive degenerative disorder of multiple neuronal systems in the brain. Forgetfulness is usually the first symptom, followed by difficulty with language (aphasia) and difficulty carrying out complex motor behaviors such as dressing and eating with utensils (apraxia). Hallucinations, aggressiveness, agitation, and other behavioral symptoms often emerge as cognitive impairment worsens.

The cause of Alzheimer's disease is unknown, although recent evidence supports the primacy of genetic factors. There is no cure. The one drug approved for use in Alzheimer's disease helps only a minority of patients and even then is only modestly effective.

Dementia may also be a product of multiple strokes (i.e., multi-infarct dementia), other neurologic conditions (e.g., multiple sclerosis, Huntington's disease), various systemic medical disorders (e.g., hypothyroidism, vitamin B12 deficiency), and drug toxicity. Severe depression may also cause a dementia syndrome.

The prognosis of dementia depends on the cause. Because most dementing conditions are not reversible, most demented patients do not recover lost cognitive abilities. But there are important exceptions. Persons with dementia due to drug toxicity, depression, or treatable medical conditions, such as hypothyroidism, may recover completely. Furthermore, even persons with irreversible dementing conditions may improve somewhat in response to treatment of a superimposed medical condition (e.g., pneumonia, urinary tract infection).

B. Dementia and Incapacity

Because of the variability of the prognosis of dementia depending upon the cause, it is critical to know the cause of the dementia before making any pronouncement about incapacity, particularly about its likely duration. This generally means that the patient should have seen a physician for a complete medical history, a thorough physical examination, and laboratory testing, including measurement of blood chemistries, thyroid hormone concentration, and blood counts. Blood testing for syphilis, an electrocardiogram, a chest x-ray, and urinalysis should be obtained. Many authorities would recommend some form of neuroimaging study (e.g., computed tomography or magnetic resonance imaging of the brain), although these tests often yield little of diagnostic or therapeutic importance, particularly when dementia has been chronic and slowly progressive. A mental status examination[3] also should be performed. When this work-up does not yield a specific treatable dementing condition, the odds are very high that the person has a progressive degenerative brain disease, usually Alzheimer's disease.

Demented persons with treatable conditions temporarily may lack decisional capacity but generally improve with treatment and may regain fully their ability to decide for themselves. Persons with progressive degenerative dementing diseases lose their decision-making capacity at some point in the course of their illness and do not recover. Early in their illness, however, they are able to make many kinds of decisions, and the clinician is faced with the difficult task of determining how long and for what purposes their decision-making capacity remains intact.

Persons with dementia, by definition, have experienced a global decline from a higher level of functioning, but this does not imply global incapacity at any particular point in the course of their illness, particularly among persons of superior intellect. The higher their premorbid baseline, the greater their residual cognitive capacity is likely to be at any point in time. It is not unusual for very intelligent persons to score in the "normal" range on tests of cognitive functioning early in the course of a dementing illness. This does not mean that they are not demented; after all, they have deteriorated in terms of their baseline functioning. But their remaining intellect may be sufficient to allow them to make competent decisions about many matters. So a diagnosis of Alzheimer's disease, even if fully justified, is not in itself the last word on decisional capacity.

Standardized tests are often used to help measure the severity of impairment and assist the clinician in judgments about the adequacy of cognitive functioning for decision-making. The most widely used brief "bedside" test of cognitive functioning is the MMSE.[4] It tests orientation, memory, attention, and concentration as well as language use, aptitude for serial subtraction, and the ability to copy a complex figure. Perfect performance earns 30 points. Scores below 24 are the rule in persons with dementia, and few demented persons score 24 or above. Persons with scores of 24 or above rarely are judged to have inadequate cognitive function for decision-making purposes. But many persons with scores below 24 are neither demented nor seriously impaired in their decision-making capacity. This is because dementia is not the only factor affecting scores on the MMSE. The greatest number of "false positives" occurs in persons who have limited formal education, particularly those whose schooling ended at or before the eighth grade.[5] Overreliance on the usual "cut-off point" for the MMSE thus can lead to overestimation of the prevalence of dementia and of the severity of disability. In fact, no cut-off point perfectly distinguishes persons with and without decisional capacity.[6] For this reason, the results of standardized tests are best regarded as simply one source of information about capacity. The final judgment must integrate data from many sources.

C. Delirium

Delirium is a clinical syndrome of confusion in association with fluctuating levels of consciousness and attention. Its most distinctive feature—and the feature that distinguishes delirium from dementia—is a reduced ability to focus attention on external stimuli and to shift attention to new stimuli, usually accompanied by drowsiness or distractibility. Additional features include disorganized speech, visual and/or auditory hallucinations, paranoid delusions, disorientation, and memory impairment. These signs and symptoms generally develop over a period of hours or days and wax and wane over time; periods of profound confusion and agitation typically alternate with lucid intervals.

* * *

While delirium often accompanies terminal illness and carries a poor prognosis, many delirious patients have treatable underlying medical conditions and recover fully. The challenge to the clinician is uncovering the cause of delirium and treating it promptly. Delirium generally clears as the underlying condition is treated, although full resolution of symptoms and signs may lag days or weeks behind the initiation of effective treatment for the etiologic illness. In the meantime, it may be necessary to use symptomatic treatments to help ameliorate the most dangerous symptoms of delirium (e.g., antipsychotic drugs to treat delusions and extreme agitation).

D. Delirium and Incapacity

Like dementia, delirium is characterized by significant impairment in cognitive functioning and therefore often compromises decision-making capacity. Unlike most dementia syndromes, delirium is usually transient and reversible, and therefore delirium-related decisional incapacity is often temporary. For this reason, distinguishing delirium from dementia is very important in decisions about the likely duration of incapacity. An additional complication is that dementia and delirium may coexist because demented patients are particularly vulnerable to delirium in the face of superimposed medical illness or drug toxicity. The evaluating clinician who recognizes the presence of delirium may be justifiably reluctant to make a simultaneous diagnosis of dementia and may insist on waiting until the delirium clears before making a judgment about the degree of irreversible cognitive impairment and the likely duration of incapacity.

E. Major Affective Disorders

1. Major Depression Sadness is a normal part of our emotional repertoire. It usually occurs in response to loss or disappointment and gradually subsides as we regain what was lost or adjust to its absence. In contrast, clinical (or "major") depression is a clinical syndrome of which sadness is just one component. It may be precipitated by loss or disappointment but ultimately takes on a "life of its own," compromising the ability to experience pleasure, feel hopeful, and believe in one's personal value and goodness. Without treatment, it may persist for months or years and lead to serious functional incapacity and even premature death.

* * *

As devastating and disabling as major depression can be, the prognosis is excellent with appropriate treatment. Properly prescribed antidepressant medications are effective in the vast majority of cases within one or two months, and often much sooner. Complete recovery is the rule.

2. *Bipolar Affective Disorder* Persons with bipolar affective disorder, or manic-depressive illness, experience episodes of mania as well as depression. In mania, as in depression, the most characteristic symptoms are in the dimensions of mood, vitality, and self-esteem, but the deviations are in the opposite direction—manic persons are elated, boundlessly energetic, grandiose in their self-appraisal, and unfailingly optimistic. Talk is rapid, pressured, and abundant. Sex interest is amplified, and multiple sexual partners may be engaged in a short period of time. Money is spent impulsively. Grandiose delusions of personal beauty, genius, or identity (e.g., "I'm the mother of God.") may occur. Without treatment, mania generally persists for months. In response to mood stabilizing medications such as lithium carbonate, manic symptoms generally abate within two or three weeks. Lithium is also prescribed to preserve mood stability in bipolar persons who are in remission.

3. *Mood Disorders and Incapacity* In persons with major affective disorders, the clinical dimensions most relevant to decision-making capacity are hopefulness and self-esteem. Irrational hopelessness, a depressive symptom, and hopeless optimism, a manic symptom, both can disable reasonable decision-making. Feelings of worthlessness, a depressive symptom, and excessive confidence, a manic symptom, both can undercut the ability to make best-interest decisions. Furthermore, delusions and hallucinations, whatever the tone (e.g., self-aggrandizing or self-deprecating), can undermine the ability to assess realistically what one needs, desires, deserves, and can do.

Decisions about incapacity are relatively easy when psychotic symptoms (e.g., hallucinations and delusions) are present. When such symptoms are absent, these decisions are much more difficult and are subject to the influence of ageism—often disguised as empathy. The capacity of nondemented but severely depressed older persons to refuse potentially life-saving treatment may go unquestioned if the examiner believes it is normal and understandable for elderly people to feel depressed and wish to die; in contrast, similar decisions by younger depressed persons are usually challenged.

The best protection against ageism in the determination of decisional capacity is to adhere strictly to explicit diagnostic rules and to link judgments about capacity directly to demonstrations that clear-cut depressive symptoms are exerting irrational influences on the decision-making process. Sometimes it is necessary to treat depressive disorders before making confident judgments about capacity.

4. *Schizophrenia* Schizophrenia is a chronic mental disorder characterized by particular kinds of hallucinations and delusions, disorganized thinking, and impairments in occupational and interpersonal functioning. . . . Although often regarded as an illness of the young, schizophrenia also occurs in elderly persons, most of whom have grown old with early-onset illnesses; however, a distinct minority develop their first symptoms in mid- or late-life. It was in recognition of this fact that the current edition of DSM does not include age of onset as a diagnostic criterion. Elderly schizo-

phrenics are commonly encountered in public housing for indigent elderly or in nursing homes, where they may be misdiagnosed as demented.

5. *Schizophrenia and Incapacity* Persons with schizophrenia may have delusions that specifically interfere with particular decisions, and in such cases judgments about incapacity are not difficult. In other cases, however, the delusions have no relationship to the decisions under consideration, and patients show a fair understanding of the issues at stake. The diagnosis of schizophrenia does not in itself imply global decisional incapacity.

IV. Role of Diagnosis in Considerations of Capacity

No diagnosis, in and of itself, invariably implies incompetency. Patients with dementia, delirium, schizophrenia, bipolar affective disorder, and other psychiatric conditions *may* be capable of making responsible decisions. Establishing that a patient lacks decisional capacity requires more than making a psychiatric diagnosis; it also requires demonstrating that the specific symptoms of that disorder interfere with making or communicating responsible decisions about the matter at hand. Because it is this practical, functional issue that is most critical, it might be argued that diagnosis is, at best, irrelevant to judgments about capacity and, at worst, seriously misleading in that diagnosis might be taken as grounds for incompetence in the absence of evidence of impaired decision-making capacity.

But the fact that diagnosis can be misused or overemphasized in judgments about competency does not imply that diagnosis should be discarded as a consideration. It is a critical anchor and validator in competency judgments.

* * *

The requirement for the demonstration of a recognized diagnosis made by explicit criteria has another important role in considerations of capacity: it helps preserve the freedom of the individual to make unpopular and even unwise choices. Consider an elderly man who refuses to stop smoking despite severe progressive obstructive pulmonary disease. His physicians inform him that he is hastening his demise by continuing to smoke. He retorts that he does not believe smoking is harming him and that in fact he relaxes and breathes more comfortably when he smokes. His choice is unwise, unreasonable, and at odds with general knowledge about the relationship between smoking and pulmonary disease. A psychiatric evaluation is requested and reveals no evidence of dementia, major depression, or any other capacity-compromising psychiatric syndrome. His refusal to accept commonly-held beliefs about the relationship between smoking and lung disease might lead ardent anti-smokers to question his "competency," and this challenge might be sustained if there were no requirement for the demonstration of a disabling psychiatric disorder. The existence of such a requirement protects the patient against such a challenge and in effect preserves his right to make an unpopular choice.

V. Uncertainty, Dangerousness, and Incapacity

So diagnosis is an essential consideration in decisions about capacity. But it is not the only one. It is also necessary to show that the symptoms of the disorder specifically compromise the ability of the patient to make the decision at hand. This is generally a more difficult decision than determining whether a psychiatric disorder is present. The judgment about the extent to which the symptoms interfere with decision-making is made with degrees of confidence or certainty ranging from a little bit to a great deal.

* * *

In practice, the examiner cannot resist taking into account the consequences of the decision the patient is making. If the patient's decision has little potential for causing harm, then a moderate degree of uncertainty regarding capacity is tolerable. On the other hand, if the patient is likely to be seriously harmed or to lose out on substantial benefit by virtue of her decision, then the examiner will tolerate much less uncertainty regarding decisional capacity. The physician will want to be as certain as possible that the patient knows what she is doing before rendering the opinion that the patient has the capacity to make the dangerous choice. The consequences of the patient's choice thus enter into the process of determining decisional capacity as modulating factors, influencing the level of confidence that the examiner requires in order to judge the person capable of making the decision at hand.

* * *

Conclusion: An Approach to Determining Capacity

The special role of physicians in determining decisional capacity lies in judging whether the symptoms of a mental disorder compromise the ability of a person to make a particular decision. Psychiatric diagnosis plays a major role in this judgment; it serves as an anchor and validator, helping protect persons against ageism and other inappropriate influences on capacity judgments. But psychiatric diagnosis is not sufficient. There must also be direct evidence that psychiatric symptoms are specifically interfering with decision-making. Thus the process of assessing decisional capacity has two principal components: (1) the psychiatric history and mental status examination—to determine whether a diagnosable psychiatric disorder is present—and (2) specific inquiry into the patient's understanding of and reasoning about the decision at hand—to determine whether psychiatric symptoms are disabling decision-making. When this process reveals that the symptoms of a psychiatric disorder are determining the patient's choice, a judgment of incapacity is clearly justified. But persons with psychiatric disorders, including dementia, may be quite capable of making particular decisions, and persons without psychiatric disorders may make unwise, unpopular, or eccentric—but nonetheless competent—choices. Neither psychiatric disorders nor foolish choices by themselves signal incapacity.

The physician does not always arrive at conclusions about capacity with complete confidence. In particular, it is sometimes difficult to be certain that psychiatric symptoms are interfering with choice. In such cases, it may be helpful to obtain other data (e.g., information about earlier choices about similar matters). However, sometimes other data are unavailable or unilluminating, and a judgment must still be made. In such cases, the dangerousness of the patient's decision enters into consideration: the more dangerous the decision, the more inclined the physician to lean toward safety and find the patient incapacitated.

The principle guiding this approach is respect for the autonomy of the person. As long as the capacity for autonomous choice is intact, the patient is the unchallenged decision-maker. But when the capacity for autonomous choice is compromised by serious psychiatric symptoms, others must enter into the decision-making process to promote the patient's good and/or to prevent harm. The approach described is systematic and practical but is not fail-safe. It is contingent on many factors: the skill of the examiner, the willingness of the patient to cooperate, the current medical status of the patient, the availability of history from other informants, and other variables. Even the best effort may require revision after an additional interview with the patient or a critical informant. For this reason it is best to view decisions about capacity as "best possible" judgments—well-reasoned opinions that are based on careful assessments but are subject to review and repair in the future if conditions change or new data become available. This is a modest stance—one born of respect for the difficulty of judgments about capacity in marginal cases and the important implications of such judgments in all cases. But it is also a bold stance, asserting that physicians are specially qualified to make judgments about the impact of sickness on decisional capacity and that these judgments can be made by explicit criteria. The protection of the sick—their autonomy and welfare—requires that their doctors be both modest and bold.

Notes

1. *See* American Psychiatric Ass'n, Diagnostic and Statistical Manual of Mental Disorders (3d ed. rev. 1987) (4th ed. forthcoming) [hereinafter Diagnostic Manual].

2. *See* Robert P. Roca, *Psychosocial Aspects of Surgical Care for the Elderly, in* Surgical Clinics of North America (forthcoming 1994).

3. *See supra* part II.

4. [*See* Marshal F. Folstein et al., *"Mini-Mental State": A Practical Method for Grading the Cognitive State of Patients for the Clinician,* 12 J. Psychiatric Res. 189 (1975).]

5. *See* James C. Anthony et al., *Limits of the 'Mini-Mental State' as a Screening Test for Dementia and Delirium Among Hospital Patients,* 12 Psychol. Med. 397 (1982).

6. *See* Jeffrey S. Janofsky et al., *The Hopkins Competency Assessment Test: A Brief Method for Evaluating Patients' Capacity to Give Informed Consent,* 43 Hosp. & Community Psychiatry 132 (1992); L. Jaime Fitten et al., *Assessing Treatment Decision-Making Capacity in Elderly Nursing Home Residents,* 38 J. Am. Geriatrics Soc'y 1097 (1990).

Mental capacity is always situational. Whether individuals are considered incapacitated depends on the type, consequences, and complexity of the decision they are asked to make. Dr. Lo explains how physicians should approach assessments of capacity.

Bernard Lo

Assessing Decision-Making Capacity

Physicians frequently are asked to assess whether a patient has the capacity to make informed decisions about his or her medical care. Such assessments may be difficult and controversial. There are few explicit legal standards for judging competency to make medical decisions. Furthermore, clinical practices for evaluating decision-making capacity are problematic.

* * *

The Significance of Competence and Capacity

Strictly speaking, competence is a legal category.[1] Adults are presumed to be competent unless a court determines that they are incompetent. However, in clinical practice, courts and legally appointed guardians are rarely involved in making decisions about medical care. Instead, health care professionals identify persons whose competency to make medical decisions is questionable and decide whether further evaluation of competency is warranted.[2] Furthermore, physicians often make *de facto* determinations that a patient is incompetent and arrange for decisions to be made by surrogates.[3] For instance, if a person is unconscious or severely demented, she clearly lacks the capacity to make decisions. When physicians determine that patients are incapacitated, standard medical practice is to ask the family members to act as surrogates. This clinical approach has been defended because routine judicial intervention would entail unacceptable delays and superficial reviews. In addition, in most cases family members are appropriate surrogates because they know the patient best and act in her best interests. The term *incapacity* is used to refer to assessments by physicians that patients lack the ability to make informed decisions about their health care.[4] In this paper, we shall focus on such clinical assessments of decision-making capacity as distinguished from determinations of competency by the courts.

Law Medicine & Health Care, 18, 193–201 (1990). Reprinted by permission.

Determining that a person is incapacitated is significant because her decision-making power may be taken away. The rationale for this practice is that patients who lack the capacity to make informed decisions should be protected from serious harm that might result from their decisions.[5] Physicians have an ethical obligation to use their expertise for the benefit of patients.[6] Such an obligation makes sense because physicians have special knowledge about harms which might result to such patients and are in a position to prevent such harms.

The obligation of physicians to protect patients from harm conflicts with their obligation to respect the autonomy of persons to make decisions that others might regard as foolish, unwise, or harmful.[7] These two obligations can be reconciled when a patient lacks the capacity to make informed decisions. In this situation, it makes little sense to talk about patient autonomy. Interventions to protect such incapacitated patients thus do not violate the duty to respect patient autonomy.

In assessing decision-making capacity, physicians must balance protecting patients from harm with respecting their autonomy. A sliding scale has been suggested for such assessments: the more probable or serious the risk posed by the patient's decision, the more stringent the standard of capacity that should be required.[8] Such a sliding scale can be justified because it affords more protection to patients of questionable capacity when the potential harm resulting from their decisions is greater. Thus, it is appropriate to apply a more rigorous standard of capacity when Mrs. C. refuses treatment for symptomatic, life-threatening cardiac disease than when she refuses a screening test or treatment for risk factors.

But there are potential problems with such a sliding scale. Determinations of incapacity may be made inconsistently on different patients or by different physicians. A sliding scale might give too much weight to the views of physicians regarding the harms and benefits of medical treatment, rather than the views of patients. It might allow physicians to exercise control over patients who disagree with them.[9]

* * *

Legal Standards for Competence

Even though competence is decided by the courts, there are no clear legal standards for determining whether a person is competent to make medical decisions.[10] A recent comprehensive legal treatise about life-sustaining treatment concludes that "the meanings of competence and incompetence are usually taken for granted or dealt with only in a cursory way by courts."[11] Often the ruling merely concludes or states that the patient is incompetent. There are several reasons for this lack of clear legal standards. In most landmark cases about life-sustaining treatment, the patient was unconscious or severely demented and thus clearly incompetent. Because findings of incompetence depend heavily on the facts of the particular case, it is difficult to formulate general standards. Furthermore, usually the crucial issue before the court is whether treatment should be given, not whether the patient is competent.

* * *

Assessing Capacity to Make Decisions

Physicians can do a great deal to enhance the decision-making capacity of elderly patients. Almost all elderly persons have some impairment in hearing, which may make it difficult to understand information presented by the physician. Because elderly patients may have difficulty with rapid speech, loud sounds, and background noises, it is helpful to speak slowly and distinctly and not to raise one's voice. The speaker should face the patient directly to provide visual clues. Furthermore, because some slowing of mental function is normal in the elderly, they may need more time to think about issues and to make a decision. If a patient is overwhelmed by too much information or pressured to make a decision quickly, she may become more confused.

Physicians should appreciate that decision-making capacity may change over time. As an illness progresses, patients may lose the capacity to make decisions. More importantly, the illness may have a fluctuating course. Impairments in decision-making capacity may be temporary or reversible. Patients with dementia typically worsen when they are hospitalized, particularly at night.[12] Such deterioration may be caused by any concurrent medical illness, such as infection, dehydration, or electrolyte abnormalities. If possible, decisions should be deferred until such reversible conditions can be treated. Even after the acute medical problems are treated, the additional impairment of mental functioning may persist. Iatrogenesis is also common in elderly hospitalized patients. Medications given to treat anxiety, insomnia, pain, or hypertension commonly impair mental functioning.[13] Elderly patients are more susceptible to side effects of drugs because they often receive many drugs which interact with each other and because drugs have a longer duration of half life in the elderly. If there is concern that a particular medicine might be impairing the patient's capacity to make decisions, the interview should be repeated after the drug has been discontinued and its effect has worn off. Social factors, such as loneliness, depression, or unfamiliar hospital surroundings may also temporarily worsen dementia. It is helpful to bring in familiar items from home and have the hospital staff orient the patient repeatedly.

Physicians can also enhance patients' decision-making capacity by addressing their reluctance to discuss treatment. Some elderly patients may find it difficult to trust strangers and discuss life-sustaining treatment with them. Arranging for continuity of care by hospital personnel and for involvement of primary care physicians, family members, and friends in decision-making can be helpful.

Patients must express their choices and decision-making process in order for physicians to assess their decision-making capacity. Communication may be difficult for patients who cannot speak or write, as after a severe stroke. In such cases, caregivers may need to devise imaginative ways to communicate, such as asking questions that can be answered by nodding the head or spelling out words with an alphabet board. While such communication may be painstakingly slow, these patients would otherwise be excluded from decision-making.

People vary in their capacity to make decisions, and there is no natural cut point for how much capacity to make a medical decision is sufficient. Reasonable people may disagree over what operational criteria for decision-making capacity should be, how well a patient should be required to perform, and how certain observers should be that the patient meets the standards. Our impression is that standards required for performance and certainty may vary, depending on the risks associated with the patient's decision. There are sound reasons for adopting a sliding scale, with stricter requirements when the stakes for the patient are greater. It may be valuable, however, to define the requirements more explicitly.

* * *

The Role of Mental Status Testing and Psychiatric Evaluation

Clinicians often use mental status tests to assess whether a patient has the capacity to make medical decisions. Such tests assess a variety of mental functions.[14] The level of consciousness, orientation of the subject to person, place, and time, attention span, immediate recall, short-term and long-term memory, and ability to perform simple calculations are tested with questions like those reported in the case description of Mrs. C. Language skills are tested by asking the patient to name objects like a watch and pen, to follow commands, and to repeat a sentence. Judgment and problem-solving abilities are assessed by asking the patient how to carry out a task such as getting a taxicab. The examiner also notes whether the subject appears depressed or has bizarre thoughts or delusions. More sophisticated neuropsychiatric tests assess abstract reasoning, disturbances of higher cognitive function, and spatial relationship.[15]

The mental status test is useful to identify patients whose attention span and short-term memory are so impaired that they cannot keep in mind basic information about the proposed treatment. Such patients clearly cannot give informed consent and therefore lack the capacity to make informed decisions. But there are several problems with using mental status tests to assess decision-making capacity. There are no naturally defined "passing scores." Standards for scoring are statistically determined by comparing scores of persons judged for other reasons to have severely impaired mental status with scores of persons who are judged to be normal. In addition, scores on mental status tests may not be related to ability to make medical decisions.

* * *

Disagreements Between Physicians and Patients

Patients may refuse treatments even though physicians believe the benefits far outweigh the risks. When this occurs, physicians should keep in mind their duty of beneficence, to act in the best interests of their patients. Further efforts are appropriate to assess whether the patient is truly informed and has the capacity to make decisions. The amount of effort by physicians should be proportional to the likely consequences of the patient's refusal. The greater the potential harm to the patient resulting from the refusal, the greater the duty on physicians to probe for misunderstandings or lack of capacity. But physicians should do more than consider whether there is something wrong with the patient. They also should ask what might be wrong with doctor-patient communication or with the doctor-patient relationship.

When a patient refuses recommended treatments, health care workers should consider whether sufficient options are being offered to the patient.

* * *

Even if the patient's capacity to make decisions is questionable, it may be useful to negotiate a mutually acceptable plan of care with the patient. It is impractical as well as morally uncomfortable to impose treatment on an unwilling patient. Patients may balk at blood draws or x-rays. In addition, patients may shout or scream their refusal. Even if such a patient were declared incompetent by the courts, it would still be difficult to carry out treatment. It is preferable if the patient assents to treatment, even if she cannot give truly informed consent. Persuasion, education, and asking family members and friends to talk to the patient would be acceptable to try to gain the patient's assent and cooperation. Often a patient will agree to treatment after caregivers have listened to her feelings and objections, modified the treatment plans, or changed the hospital routine.

* * *

Notes

1. P. S. Appelbaum, C. W. Lidz, A. Meisel. *Informed Consent: Legal Theory and Clinical Practice.* New York, Oxford University Press, 1987; A. Meisel, *The Right to Die.* New York, John Wiley & Sons, 1989; A. E. Buchanan, D. W. Brock, *Deciding for Others.* Cambridge, Cambridge University Press, 1989.

2. *Id.* Buchanan; President's Commission for the Study of Ethical Problems in Medicine and Biomedical and Behavioral Research, *Making Health Care Decisions.* Washington, U.S. Government Printing Office, 1982; President's Commission for the Study of Ethical Problems in Medicine and Biomedical and Behavioral Research, *Deciding to Forego Life-Sustaining Treatment.* Washington, U.S. Government Printing Office, 1983.

3. *Id.*, Buchanan; *Id.*, Meisel; *Id.*, President's Commission, *Making Health Care Decisions.*

4. President's Commission, note 2 *supra, Making Health Care Decisions, Deciding to Forego Life-Sustaining Treatment.*

5. A. Buchanan, D. W. Brock, "Deciding for others," *Milbank Memorial Quarterly* 1986, 64 (supp. 2): 17–94.

6. E. D. Pelegrino, D. G. Thomasma, *For the Patient's Good: The Restoration of Beneficence in Health Care.* New York, Oxford University Press, 1988.

7. Appelbaum, et al., *supra note 1.*

8. J. F. Drane, "Competency to give an informed consent," *JAMA* 1984, 252:925–927; Buchanan, *supra* note 1.

9. S. M. Wolf, "Conflict between doctor and patient," *Law, Medicine & Health Care* 1988, 16: 197–203.

10. Appelbaum, *supra* note 2; Meisel, *supra* note 2.

11. Meisel, *supra* note 2.

12. Z. J. Lipowski, "Delirium in the elderly patient," *N. Engl. J. Med.* 1989, 320:578–582; R. Katzman, "Alzheimer's disease," *N. Eng. . J. Med.* 1986, 314:964–973.

13. E. B. Larson, W. A. Kukull, D. Buchner, B. V. Reifler, "Adverse drug reactions associated with global cognitive impairment in elderly persons," *Ann. Intern. Med.* 1987, 107:169–173.

14. R. L. Kane, J. G. Ouslander, I. B. Ibrass, *Essentials of Clinical Geriatrics* (2nd ed.). New York, McGraw-Hill, 1989.

15. *Ibid.*

CHAPTER 18

Legal Standards of Mental Incapacity

The determination of whether a person is legally incapacitated and in need of a guardian is a legal question, not a medical determination. After the medical testimony has been given, the court will usually accept lay testimony about the condition of the alleged incapacitated person. A legal finding of incapacity results in the appointment of a guardian, something that may not be desired by the proposed ward. In the following article Professor Barnes describes why guardianship, though often needed, results in a severe loss of autonomy, self-determination and independence for the ward.

Alison P. Barnes

Florida Guardianship and the Elderly: The Paradoxical Right to Unwanted Assistance

I. Introduction

Involuntary guardianship of the person and/or property is a device by which a court substitutes the judgment of a more capable person for the judgment of an impaired individual. A guardian is one to whom the law entrusts the custody and control of an impaired person, the management of that person's property, or both.

Univ. of Florida L. Rev. 40, 949 (1988). Reprinted by permission.

Guardians of the property are called curators or conservators; the impaired person is a ward or conservatee. The appointment of a guardian follows an adjudication of incompetency.

The purpose of a guardianship is to appoint a surrogate decision-maker, with authority to control the ward's decisions or to make decisions the ward cannot make. A guardianship of the person, and perhaps of the estate as well, is usually established to allow the guardian to authorize medical treatment for which the patient is unwilling or unable to give consent, or to change the ward's residence to one where more or different assistance can be provided.[1] A court is likely to appoint a guardian of the property when an incompetent individual fails to use available resources to meet personal needs or needs of dependents, when he or she appears likely to be victimized by others, or when it appears the individual's use of the assets will in some other way dissipate the estate.[2] Relatives of the incompetent individual or the state file nearly all guardianship petitions.[3]

* * *

The law and practice of guardianship are significant to older persons and their advocates because over 500,000 elderly persons are wards of the court, and the number will increase.[4] The population of individuals age eighty-five and older, who are most likely of all adults to need guardian assistance, has a growth rate of 25 percent, compared to 5 percent for the under-sixty population.[5]

* * *

The appointment of a substitute decision-maker for an individual impaired by old age is a particularly grievous loss to that individual, and should be imposed with care. Elderly wards typically have led active, autonomous adult lives in which they contributed to society and accrued wealth for their own use and enjoyment. In this respect, they differ from children and developmentally disabled persons, who comprise most of the balance of disabled persons in the population.[6] Depriving an elderly person of independent choice by appointing a surrogate decision-maker curtails long-held rights and expectations.

* * *

II. Identifying The Ward

Definitions of incompetency typically require two findings: a diagnosis of mental disorder or impairment and descriptive proof of behavior or manifestations of that mental status.[7] A diagnosis of mental illness alone fails as a basis for a declaration of incompetency because, without resulting behavior that requires compensation or control, the guardianship serves no purpose.[8] Neither can behavior, without mental disorder, support a finding of incompetence.[9] Every adult in possession of a sound mind has the right to engage in foolish, risky, or harmful behavior, whether or not that person fully appreciates the risk involved.[10] The law does not restrict such behavior unless it is negligent or criminal.

There has been some confusion in practice as to the two aspects of proof of incompetency. Under traditional statutes, courts conducting guardianship proceedings emphasize the diagnosis of mental disorder. The court receives evidence regarding the respondent's ability to manage tasks necessary for daily living only incidentally; this evidence consists of behavioral descriptions offered to support the diagnosis of mental disorder.[11] As a result, the court determines competency solely on the status of mental illness. Such a determination ignores the requirements for proof of incompetency in typical traditional statutes relying entirely upon the controversial art of psychiatric prediction.[12]

The court's reliance on diagnosis of mental disorder is the inevitable result of the composition of traditional examining committees, which provide the principal evidence on the issue of competency. In Florida's typical traditional statute, the examining committee includes two physicians and one layman,[13] but no professional with training in functional assessment.[14] Social, mental health, and community health workers routinely conduct such assessments, which are inventories of daily activities, that can provide the court with objective information about the respondent's ability to manage independently or with voluntary assistance. To provide the court with evidence on both aspects of competency, examining committees should include an individual with professional training in functional evaluation to examine every prospective ward.

In contrast with the emphasis on diagnosis found in traditional statutes, reform statutes emphasize functional impairment over mental disorder.[15]

* * *

The definition of the appropriate incompetent or incapacitated[16] ward requires both legs—mental impairment and behavioral limitations—on which to stand. Proving this definition requires a functional assessment, without which diagnosis of mental disorder is too uncertain and too tenuous to link mental impairment and behavioral limitations to harmful results. This link is necessary to justify curtailment of individual autonomy. The individual's functional impairment must result from mental disorder, because behavioral assessment alone may result in loss of autonomy for an individual who rationally chooses socially disfavored behavior.

* * *

Notes

1. Frolik, *Plenary Guardianship: An Analysis, a Critique and a Proposal for Reform,* 23 Ariz. L. Rev. 599, 625 (1981).

2. *Id.*

3. See Friedman & Savage, *Taking Care: The Law of Conservatorship in California,* 61 S. Cal. L. Rev. 273, 280 (1988) (citing a study of guardianship actions in San Mateo County, Cal., during 1982, 1984, and 1986). Demographic data on guardianship participants is scarce, but practitioners' impressions suggest the San Mateo findings are typical of demographics in many jurisdictions.

4. Pepper, *Abuses in Guardianship of the Elderly and Infirm: A National Disgrace,* Sept. 25, 1987 (Claude Pepper, Chairman, Sub-Committee on Health and Long-Term Care, House Select Committee on Aging) [hereinafter *Abuses in Guardianship*]. The number of guardianship cases in Florida is unknown.

5. Fowles, *The Numbers Game,* AGING MAG., 1987, at 44. In 1986, there were 29.2 million Americans, 12.1% of the population, age 65 or older. *Id.* On the need for guardians in Florida, see Schmidt & Rogers, *Legal Incompetents' Need for Guardians in Florida,* 15 BULL. AM. ACAD. PSYCHIATRY LAW 67 (1987).

6. A number of states have created separate provisions governing the legal incompetency of minors. *See, e.g.,* CAL. PROB. CODE §§ 1501–1502 (West 1981) (California procedures for incompetency of minors). On distinctions between legal incompetency of children and disabled adults, see Katz, *Elder Abuse,* 18 J. FAM. L. 695, 716–20 (1979–80).

7. *See, e.g.,* FLA. STAT. § 744.102(5) (1987) ("An 'incompetent' is a person who, because of minority, mental illness, mental retardation, senility, excessive use of drugs or alcohol, or other physical or mental incapacity, is incapable of either managing his property or caring for himself, or both."); *see also* Note, *The Disguised Oppression of Involuntary Guardianship: Have the Elderly Freedom to Spend?,* 73 YALE L.J. 676, 679 (1964) (proposing the following synthesis of state statutory definitions: A mental incompetent is one "who, by reason of mental illness, mental deficiency, mental infirmities of old age, or any other cause, is unable to manage his own affairs or property or is likely to become the victim of designing persons.").

8. *See* Green, *Proof of Mental Incompetency and the Unexpressed Major Premise,* 53 YALE L.J. 271, 276–78 (1944) (observation of symptomatic conduct of an alleged incompetent is the only way to prove mental disorder requiring supervision).

For civil commitments, courts require behavior with specific characteristics in addition to diagnosis of mental status. *See* Donaldson v. O'Connor, 422 U.S. 563, 574–76 (1975) (initial diagnosis of mental illness alone, without further rendering of treatment, found insufficient for adjudication of incompetency in civil commitment, when patient is not dangerous and is capable of surviving alone or with the help of friends or family); Lake v. Cameron, 364 F.2d 657, 658, 661 (D.C. Cir. 1966) (patient prone to wandering away and being exposed at night, but not dangerous to self or others, is not a proper subject for indeterminate commitment), *In re* Beverly, 342 So. 2d 481, 490 (Fla. 1977) (though evidence was sufficient to show patient was mentally ill, behavior consisting of two violent occasions, quitting a job because of religious beliefs, and having delusions of power from identification with God and Jesus Christ, was insufficient to show civil commitment was necessary). Distinctions between civil commitment and guardianship actions fail to suggest mental status should be sufficient for guardianships only.

9. *See* 1 W. BLACKSTONE, COMMENTARIES 228 (Chitty ed. 1913) ("When a man on an inquest of idiocy hath been returned an *unthrift* and not an *idiot* . . . , no farther proceedings have been had.").

10. *See* Frolik, *supra* note 1, at 627.

11. *See* Statement of Recommended Judicial Practices, adopted by the Nat'l Conf. on the Judiciary on Guardianship Proceedings for the Elderly, June 1986, at 23–24 [hereinafter Recommended Judicial Practices].

Definitions of incompetency for which medical evidence alone may seem to be dispositive consist of lists of specific disorders and far less specific resulting behaviors. *See, e.g.,* FLA. STAT. § 744.102(6) (1987) (definition of incapacitated person); WASH. REV. CODE § 11.88.010(2) (1967

& Supp. 1988) (an incapacitated person is one who "by reason of mental illness, developmental disability, senility, habitual drunkenness, excessive use of drugs, or other mental incapacity [is incapable of] either managing his property or caring for himself or both"), WYO. STAT. §§ 3-1-101(a)(vii, viii) (Michie 1977 & Supp. 1988) (an incompetent is one who is "unable unassisted to properly manage and take care of himself or his property as a result of the infirmities of advanced age, physical disability, disease, the use of alcohol or controlled substances . . . mental illness, mental deficiency or mental retardation.").

12. [Mental disorder and behavior or symptoms are inevitably bound together in some circular reasoning. That is, erratic or unacceptable behavior indicates some mental illness, diagnosis of which serves as a tool for interpretation of other instances of questionable behavior. *See supra* note 7, at 687 (property mismanagement tends to reinforce and itself becomes evidence of mental weakness).]

13. FLA. STAT. § 744.331(5) (1987).

14. For a discussion of functional assessments, see Casananto, Saunders & Simon, *Individual Functional Assessment: A Guide to Determining the Need for Guardianship Under New Hampshire Law*, 28 N.H. B.J., Fall 1986, at 13.

15. *See* Mitchell, *The Objects of Our Wisdom and Our Coercion: Involuntary Guardianship for Incompetents*, 52 S. CAL. L. REV. 1405, 1431 (1979).

16. Traditional statutes use the term "incompetent" to describe the ward's legal status. Reform statutes, in keeping with the concept of limited guardianship, use the term "incapacitated." *See, e.g.*, FLA. STAT. § 744 (1987).

CHAPTER 19

Guardianship Procedures

Although as Professor Barnes points out guardianship results in the deprivation of individual liberty, it is a necessary component of a society that requires a minimum level of competency for an individual to participate in the legal culture. Because guardianship is so intrusive, however, many observers have expressed their concerns as to how it operates. Concern covers, but is not limited to, the definition of guardianship, court procedures, selection of the guardian, and the need for court monitoring of the guardianship. The following articles examine these and other issues.

Phillip B. Tor and Bruce D. Sales

A Social Science Perspective on the Law of Guardianship: Directions for Improving the Process and Practice

I. Introduction

* * *

The ramifications of imposing a guardianship can be far-reaching. It can result in the loss of liberty and many legal and civil rights; rights that were once taken for granted may no longer exist for the ward. Through the court's action, for example, a guardian may have the final word on whether the ward can marry or whether the

Law and Psychology Review, Vol. 18, No. 1 (1994). Reprinted by permission.

ward may enter into a contract.[1] Because guardianship can have such a profound impact on an individual's life, many legal and mental health professionals have been concerned about the absence of legal safeguards in the guardianship system.[2] In some guardianship cases, critics have argued, the state's power to protect the interests of incompetents under the doctrine of *parens patriae* drifts into an exercise of the state's police power intended to control persons who pose a danger to others.[3] Unless state guardianship statutes have built-in safeguards to protect the rights of proposed wards, these individuals may become the victims of a system that does less to help them than to control them.

Over the past decade, research has revealed a number of weaknesses in the guardianship laws and practices of many states. Deficiencies in state guardianship are evidenced by vague and overly broad standards for determining incompetency, inadequate due process protection, infrequent use of less restrictive alternatives to plenary (total) guardianship, inadequate monitoring of guardianships, and a lack of training programs for guardians.[4] As a result, many states have initiated efforts to reform their guardianship laws to protect an individual's right to counsel or representation, ensure his or her presence at the hearing, provide objective standards for determining incapacity, limit the powers of the guardian, and require regular and periodic reviews of the ward's condition.[5]

* * *

II. Statutory Guardianship Standards and Incompetency Definitions

The chief purpose of a guardianship hearing is to make a legal determination about a subject's competency. Since determination of incompetency is a legal conclusion, each state spells out in its guardianship statute the legal requirements for making such a finding. The statutory standards can be categorized into three groups: the causal link approach, the Uniform Probate Code (UPC) approach, and the functional approach.[6]

A. Causal Link Approach

The causal link approach refers to the traditional standards of incompetency where mental or physical conditions are linked to a generalized incapacity for self care.[7] Under these statutes, the court could declare a person incompetent on the basis of a diagnostic label, such as aged or mentally retarded, if there is testimony that the subject is inadequately caring for himself or herself or his or her property.[8]

* * *

Because causal link statutes offer only vague standards for incompetency, they give the judge wide discretion in deciding what evidence is admissible. In turn, broad judicial discretion gives rise to the likelihood of different outcomes of incompetency determinations for persons with similar disabilities who are adjudicated in the same jurisdiction.

* * *

B. Uniform Probate Code Approach

In an effort to escape the stigmatic labels of the traditional causal link statutes, the Uniform Probate Code (UPC) approach defines "incapacity" as an impairment of cognitive and communicative abilities resulting from one of a number of mental or physical conditions.[9] The operative wording for incapacity in UPC statutes is the lack of "sufficient understanding or capacity to make or communicate responsible decisions concerning his person."[10] Most state legislatures have made changes to their guardianship statutes by incorporating this language.

* * *

This legislative desire to measure incompetency by the impairment of cognitive processes does not alleviate many of the problems with the causal link approach. UPC statutes perpetuate the use of causal categories and give the court too much discretion because the key cognitive processes upon which they focus (i.e., understanding or capacity to make or communicate responsible decisions) remain vague. In addition, although the UPC emphasizes the defendant's ability to make decisions, it allows the court to discount that ability if the decisions are not deemed responsible.[11] This standard of incompetency fails to distinguish the capacity to make a decision, albeit a foolish one, from the capacity to make a socially or morally responsible decision.

* * *

C. Functional Approach

The functional approach represents the most recent innovation in guardianship standards.[12] It requires that the court look at objective behavioral evidence of functional limitations in the person's daily activities when determining an individual's need for assistance.[13] These statutes list specific activities, such as securing food, clothing, and health care for oneself.[14] Courts will thereby have useful guidelines for determining when and how much assistance is needed to protect the individual from that person's incapacity, without imposing unnecessary restrictions on the individual's autonomy.

The functional approach is familiar and useful to mental health professionals because it focuses on behavioral objectives in the care and treatment of people with mental and physical disabilities.[15] Nolan has argued that the functional approach can aid judicial decision-making by referring to the very same objective criteria used by geriatric nurses, social workers, psychologists, physicians, and related health workers to evaluate patients with mental, physical, and social disabilities.[16] This information is expected to help the court in deciding when and to what degree intervention is called for.

* * *

III. Due Process in Guardianship Proceedings

Due process may be defined roughly as using the legal system to protect a person's rights.[17] It should be noted, however, that there is less due process protection in a civil lawsuit than in a criminal prosecution. For example, a criminal defendant is presumed innocent until proven guilty. To overcome this presumption, the prosecution must establish, beyond a reasonable doubt, that the defendant is guilty of the crime charged.[18] On the other hand, most civil cases require less exacting proof, a preponderance of the evidence, in order to render a defendant liable.[19] In general, due process requirements in a civil action are more uncertain than in a criminal action[20] and are subject to competing individual, societal, and sovereign interests at issue in the particular controversy.[21]

Because guardianship results in a restriction of the ward's right to make decisions for himself or herself, most states require clear and convincing evidence of the proposed ward's incompetence or incapacity. This is a higher standard of proof than a preponderance of the evidence, but lower than beyond a reasonable doubt.

* * *

The importance of due process rights cannot be over-emphasized in guardianship proceedings because proposed wards are even more susceptible to abuses or violations of their civil rights than defendants in other kinds of civil actions. Perhaps because courts place so much confidence in a physician's undocumented opinions, most proposed wards, particularly the elderly,[22] are perceived to be incompetent even before the guardianship hearing begins.[23] This perception leads to a relaxation of important procedural rights, including the right to notice; an indigent's right to appointed legal counsel; and the right to be present at one's hearing to confront the allegations of incompetency. How pervasive this perception of prehearing incompetency is and how courts respond to it at the hearing should be explored. Some critics note a paternalistic attitude among courts toward guardianship subjects.[24] Instead of conducting an impartial hearing, courts may tend to look for what they believe to serve the best interests of the proposed ward.

* * *

It is possible that courts grant guardianships because attorneys do not zealously defend clients who are the subject of guardianship petitions. This result can occur because of ignorance and misperceptions about his or her client's condition. Judges, like attorneys, may also suffer from ignorance and misperceptions about incompetency or incapacity and may rely too heavily on medical opinion.[25] Research assessing legal professionals' knowledge about, and attitudes toward, the mental, physical, and behavioral status of proposed wards will provide a foundation for educational programs directed at training persons involved in the implementation of guardianship programs. A better informed bar and judiciary may result in more expedient disposal of specious guardianship petitions.

Finally, research is needed to address how experts' pretrial reports regarding proposed wards influence the court's ultimate determination. The substantive content of affidavits from physicians and mental health professionals in support of a particular guardianship, the frequency with which defenses are asserted in the pleadings, and the relative importance that courts place on the pleadings and affidavits should also be studied.

Once a petition is filed, due process requires that notice be served upon a party in any civil action.[26] Its purpose is to inform the party that an action involving that party's interests has been taken. Adequate notice provides the party with sufficient information about the action and affords the proposed ward a reasonable opportunity to prepare and present an adequate defense.[27] If a proposed ward is not apprised of this information and the meaning of the proposed guardianship, the ward may not be motivated to seek legal and other expert assistance.

Studies reveal that notice to a prospective ward may often be deficient.[28] Although most prospective wards are given some form of notice about an impending hearing,[29] several problems with notification exist. One is that in many jurisdictions the language of the notice is too legalistic. Ordinary citizens consequently have difficulty understanding the court notices.[30] In addition, the notice is often served by mail or by deputies without further explanation to the individual about his or her rights as a potential ward. Finally, the particular basis for, or implications of, the hearing are often not set forth in the notice.[31]

At the time of the Associated Press study,[32] only fourteen states required that notification of an impending guardianship proceeding include information about the proposed wards' rights to oppose the petition and the rights they stand to lose.[33] Furthermore, the study reported instances where the ward discovered after the fact that a guardian had been appointed to make decisions on the ward's behalf.[34] Individuals who became wards were sometimes not even aware that a hearing had taken place.[35]

Another notice problem arises when a prospective ward does not have much time to prepare for a hearing. In one study, the proposed ward was notified one week or less before a scheduled hearing in 29 percent of the cases.[36] Considering the seriousness of the rights and liberty interest at stake, it is doubtful that one week is a reasonable amount of time for a defendant to prepare an adequate defense to challenge the guardianship petition.

* * *

At least thirty-five states have adopted legislation providing for the right to an attorney to represent the defendant or the right to a guardian ad litem[37] to act as advocate for the best interests of the defendant.[38] By statute or court practice, the function of the court-appointed attorney or guardian ad litem may be to investigate for the court the proposed ward's condition and need for a guardian[39] rather than to carry out or advocate the proposed ward's desires. Whether the person who is supposed to represent the interests of the proposed ward should do so as advocate or as court investigator is subject to dispute.[40] In addition, some court functionaries reportedly doubt that attorneys have a useful role in guardianship proceedings.[41]

* * *

A proposed ward's attendance at the hearing depends on some factors that are beyond the court's control. For instance, the individual may be comatose or too disabled to attend. But in other cases, the individual may not attend because he or she has not received notice or is not encouraged or required to do so by the court.[42]

Notes

1. Bruce D. Sales et al., DISABLED PERSONS AND THE LAW 459 (1982).

2. *See, e.g.,* Anne K. Pecora, *The Constitutional Right to Court-Appointed Adversary Counsel for Defendants in Guardianship Proceedings,* 43 ARK. L. REV. 345 (1990) (right to counsel); Jan E. Rein, *Preserving Dignity and Self-Determination of the Elderly in the Face of Competing Interests and Grim Alternatives: A Proposal for Statutory Refocus and Reform,* 60 GEO. WASH. L. REV. 1818 (1992) (arguing that statutes should be reformulated to allow state intervention of elderly decision making only when the court has factual support that the proposed ward will realize some real benefit); Windsor C. Schmidt et al., *A Descriptive Analysis of Professional and Volunteer Programs for the Delivery of Public Guardianship Services,* 8 PROB. L.J. 125 (1988) (public guardians); John W. Parry & Sally Balch Hurme, *Guardianship Monitoring and Enforcement Nationwide,* 15 MENTAL & PHYSICAL DISABILITIES L. REP. 304 (1991) (guardianship monitoring); Melvin T. Axilbund, EXERCISING JUDGEMENT FOR THE DISABLED: REPORT OF AN INQUIRY INTO LIMITED GUARDIANSHIP, PUBLIC GUARDIANSHIP AND PROTECTIVE SERVICES IN SIX STATES, (ABA Commission on the Mentally Disabled ed., 1979) (limited guardianship); Anita Radcliffe, *Guardianship of Incapacitated Adults in Utah,* 427 UTAH L. REV. (1982) (vague guardianship statutes); and Annina Mitchell, *The Objects of Our Wisdom and Our Coercion: Involuntary Guardianship for Incompetents,* 52 SO. CAL. L. REV. 1405 (1979) (due process deficiencies in guardianship practices).

3. SALES ET AL., *supra* note 1, at 6; Annina M. Mitchell, *Objects of Our Wisdom and Our Coercion: Involuntary Guardianship for Competents,* 52 SO. CAL. L. REV. 1405 (1979) ("A determination of incompetency is often the first step in the forced displacement of the disadvantaged into undesirable custodial facilities"). *Id.* at 1408.

4. Associated Press Special Report, *Guardians of the Elderly: An Ailing System* (1987) [hereinafter *AP*]. Many AP reporters investigated guardianship records and cases across the United States in a series of reports published in over 300 newspapers. The Associated Press articles used as source material for this paper were captured on LEXIS from the L.A. TIMES, Sept. 27, 1987.

5. Judith McCue, *The States Are Acting to Reform Their Guardianship Statutes,* TR. & EST., 32 July (1992).

6. Bobbe S. Nolan, *Functional Evaluation of the Elderly in Guardianship Proceedings,* 12 L., MED. & HEALTH CARE 210, 212–214 (1984).

7. *Id.* at 212.

8. *Id.*

9. UNIFORM PROBATE CODE § 5-103 (Supp. 1993).

10. UNIFORM PROBATE CODE § 5-103(7) (Supp. 1993).

11. That standard [capacity to make or communicate responsible decisions concerning his person], standing alone, would allow a guardian to be appointed for a person who makes decisions regarded by some as irresponsible, even though he has sufficient capacity to make personal management decisions which allow him to function in a manner acceptable to himself and without any threat of injury to himself. *In re* Boyer, 636 P.2d 1085, 1088 (Utah 1981).

12. Nolan, *supra* note 6, at 213.

13. Nolan, *supra* note 6, at 213.

14. *See, e.g.*, [N.H. REV. STAT. ANN. § 464-1:2 (VII) & (XI) (1992).]

15. *See* Nolan, *supra* note 6, at 211.

16. *See* Nolan, *supra* note 6, at 211.

17. More formally stated, due process of law is "[a] course of legal proceedings according to those rules and principles which have been established in our systems of jurisprudence for the enforcement and protection of private rights." BLACK'S LAW DICTIONARY 500 (6th ed. 1990).

18. *See, e.g., In re* Winship, 397 U.S. 358 (1970).

19. *See, e.g.*, Ziegler v. Hustisford Farmers Mutual Ins. Co., 298 N.W. 610 (Wis. 1941).

20. Morrissey v. Brewer, 408 U.S. 471 (1972).

21. Mathews v. Eldridge, 424 U.S. 319 (1976).

22. *See* AP, *supra* note 4.

23. *See generally* Bruce D. Sales & L.R. Kahle, *Law and Attitudes Toward the Mentally Ill*, 3 INT'L J. L. & PSYCHIATRY 391 (1980).

24. *See generally* [Daniel B. Griffith, *The Best Interests Standard: A Comparison of the State's Parens Patriae Authority and Judicial Oversight in Best Interests Determinations for Children and Incompetent Patients*, 7 ISSUES IN LAW & MEDICINE 283, 287 (1991) (quoting 1 W. Blackstone, Commentaries *462)]; Mitchell, *supra* note 3.

25. [*See* THOMAS GRISSO, EVALUATING COMPETENCIES: FORENSIC ASSESSMENTS AND INSTRUMENTS (1986) for a discussion of issues surrounding the use of psychological evidence in evaluating a number of competencies, and for a review of several efforts to standardize assessments for guardianship purposes.]

26. *See* FED. R. CIV. PROC. rules 4 and 5. The United States Supreme Court has consistently considered notice fundamental to due process of law: "Parties whose rights are to be affected are entitled to be heard; and in order that they may enjoy that right they must first be notified." Baldwin v. Hale, 68 U.S. 223, 233 (1864). "An elementary and fundamental requirement of due process in any proceeding which is to be accorded finality is notice reasonably calculated, under all the circumstances, to apprise interested parties of the pendency of the action and afford them an opportunity to present their objections." Mulane v. Central Hanover Bank & Trust Co., 339 U.S. 306, 314 (1950).

27. *See supra* note 29.

28. AP, *supra* note 4; [Roger Peters et al., *Guardianship of the Elderly in Tallahassee, Florida*, 25 THE GERONTOLOGIST 532, 535 (1985).]

29. AP, *supra* note 4 (reporting that some 87% of the wards were given some notice about an impending guardianship).

30. AP, *supra* note 4.

31. AP, *supra* note 4. One story recited the wording of notices to elderly people facing guardianship in Texas:

> (A)t or before 10 a.m. of the Monday morning next after the expiration of 10 days after the date of service of this citation by filing a written answer to the application of (petitioner) filed in said court on the (date) alleging said ward has no guardian and praying for the

appointment of the person and estate of said ward. At said above mentioned time and place, said ward and all other persons may contest said application if they do so desire.

These notices were delivered without any further explanation about the allegations. Reported in Fred Bayles and Scott McCartney, *Guardianship: "If You're Old, You Can't Be Foolish"*, AP, Sept. 27, 1987.

32. AP, *supra* note 4.

33. AP, *supra* note 4.

34. AP, *supra* note 4.

35. AP, *supra* note 4.

36. [Roger Peters et al., *Guardianship of the Elderly in Tallahassee, Florida*, 25 THE GERONTOLOGIST 532, 535 (1985).]

37. In general, a guardian ad litem is a person, not necessarily an attorney, appointed by the court to act on behalf of the proposed ward.

38. McCue, *supra* note 5, at 35.

39. Madelyn A. Iris, *Guardianship and the Elderly: A Multi-Perspective View of the Decision-making Process*, 28 THE GERONTOLOGIST 39, 43 (1988).

40. *See* John Parry, *Selected Recommendations from the National Guardianship Symposium at Wingspread*, 12 MENTAL & PHYSICAL DISABILITY L. REP. 390, 400 (1988).

41. [Lawrence Friedman & Mark Savage, *Taking Care: The Law of Conservatorship in California*, 61 S. CAL. L. REV. 273, 283 (1988).]

42. *See supra* the accompanying text to notes 31–32.

Paula L. Hannaford and Thomas L. Hafemeister

The National Probate Court Standards: The Role of the Courts in Guardianship and Conservatorship Proceedings

I. Guardianship and Conservatorship: An Overview

Guardianship refers to a legal arrangement in which a person (the guardian) is given legal responsibility for another person (the ward) who is unable to take care of his or her affairs due to minority or incompetency.[1] In its most common interpretation, guardianship refers to the guardian's legal responsibility for the health and welfare of the person adjudged incompetent by a court.[2] In some jurisdictions, however, a guardian also may be responsible for an incompetent person's property. Other jurisdictions appoint two separate individuals—one to look after the ward's health and welfare and one (often called a conservator) to look after the ward's property. In spite of differences in terminology, the substantive law governing these arrangements is

The Elder Law Journal 2:147 (1994).

similar or identical in most U.S. jurisdictions.[3] For the purposes of this article, guardianship will refer to both arrangements unless otherwise indicated.

* * *

Despite its widespread availability, the use of guardianship as a means to serve the elderly has been tarnished over the past two decades. Some commentators bemoan the failure of the legislatures to establish and the courts to make use of modified or "limited" guardianships.[4] For elderly individuals requiring only partial assistance with their affairs, full guardianship is an unnecessary and inappropriate restriction on their liberty and autonomy.[5] However, failure to order a full guardianship on the grounds that it is unwarranted, without recourse to a less restrictive alternative, may result in elderly individuals being denied any assistance.[6]

Other commentators appear more concerned that the courts lack sufficient means and determination to oversee and enforce existing guardianships. Pointing to instances of wards left alone and impoverished after dishonest guardians had stripped the assets from their estates,[7] these commentators charge that a lack of judicial monitoring results in substantial risk of abuse and neglect to the wards of these proceedings.[8] Complicating their concerns is the fact that very little information has been available with which to define the nature and scope of guardianships in the United States.[9]

* * *

V. Limited Guardianships and Alternatives to Guardianships

Other major problems that the Associated Press reported were the extensive and unwarranted restrictions placed on the rights of persons under guardianship protection and the difficulty wards encountered while trying to overturn or modify guardianship provisions. In one case, a Florida woman was placed under guardianship protection after a traffic accident left her in a coma.[10] Although she recovered her mental capabilities within two months of the accident, an additional eight months elapsed before she was able to overturn the guardianship and regain her full rights.[11] In another case, a Kansas woman placed under guardianship protection following a stroke wanted to return home after her full recovery.[12] Instead, her guardian had her sedated and placed in a nursing home.[13] In both cases, appropriate monitoring and restrictions on the duration of the guardianship and the authority of the guardians over their wards might have prevented these abuses.

The *Standards* address these issues in their discussions of temporary guardianship and less intrusive alternatives to guardianship.[14] The *Standards* specifically recognize that the imposition of a temporary guardianship—even when warranted under emergency circumstances—has "the potential to produce significant or irreparable harm to the interests of the respondent."[15] To prevent abuse, they recommend that probate courts award temporary guardianships only under very specific circumstances and that the duration and scope of the guardianship extend only as far as necessary to meet the requirements of the emergency.[16] In particular, the court should only consider an ex parte petition for an emergency or temporary guardianship if it is accompanied by a petition for a permanent guardianship.[17] They also specify that only under the most extraordinary circumstances should a temporary guardianship extend for more than thirty days.[18]

In addition to limiting the duration of a temporary guardianship order, the court should consider whether an alternative to guardianship is more appropriate under the circumstances.[19] For example, in a medical emergency, the court may issue a protective order permitting appropriate medical care but deferring a decision about imposing a guardianship for future proceedings.[20]

Another alternative that the court may consider is limiting the guardian's powers over a ward to specifically delineated duties and responsibilities.[21] By restricting the authority of the guardian to the minimum required for the situation, the respondent's self-reliance, autonomy, and independence will be promoted, perhaps contributing to the respondent's ability to reestablish his or her functional capacity.[22] In addition, specifically enumerating the duties and powers of the guardian provides a guide for the court and others in evaluating and monitoring the performance of the guardian, as well as a road map for the guardian to use in determining what the guardian can or cannot do in carrying out assigned responsibilities.[23]

In determining the appropriate scope of a proposed guardianship, the court also should consider the preferences of the ward[24] and the availability of social service agencies to support limited guardianships or alternatives to guardianship.[25] The *Standards* recommend that courts defer to any appropriate alternatives previously established or proposed by the ward (e.g., in a durable health care power of attorney).[26] Furthermore, the *Standards* add that "[e]ven if the respondent [to a guardianship proceeding] lacks current capacity to make decisions regarding his or her personal care, the court should solicit the respondent's opinions and preferences and should give these appropriate consideration where they are not unreasonable."[27]

Finally, the *Standards* suggest that courts make greater use of court visitors,[28] thus promoting two goals: better protection of the proposed ward[29] and better conservation of judicial resources.[30] With respect to the first goal, the court visitor typically is responsible for explaining to the proposed ward the nature and purpose of the guardianship, as well as his or her legal rights during the proceedings. Such information will help ensure that the respondent's procedural rights are not violated. In addition, the *Standards* encourage the court visitor to conduct independent interviews with the respondent, the petitioner, and the proposed guardian, as well as with any professionals who have conducted evaluations of the respondent.[31] As a result, the court visitor is strategically placed to learn much about a given case. The court visitor's findings and recommendations can assist the court in determining whether a need for a guardianship exists and, if so, the appropriate scope of the guardianship and the proposed guardian's authority.[32]

Such independent evaluations will not only protect the proposed ward against inappropriate intrusions on his or her autonomy, they will also help the court conserve its own resources. Using the court visitor's evaluation and recommendations during a preliminary screening process, for example, can help divert inappropriate guardianship cases toward those services and treatment alternatives most likely to yield desirable results for the proposed ward, thus preventing unnecessary expenditures of judicial time and resources.[33]

VI. Court Procedures to Monitor Guardians' Activities

In addition to concerns about the inappropriate imposition of guardianships, some commentators have argued that courts should engage in greater scrutiny of guardians' qualifications, training, and ongoing activities.[34] Of particular concern are public agencies and, more recently, entrepreneurial ventures that offer guardianship services.[35] To address these concerns, the *Standards* recommend that courts carefully review the qualifications of proposed guardians[36] and provide appropriate training and orientation to newly appointed guardians to ensure that these individuals fully understand and are capable of carrying out their responsibilities.[37] In addition to ensuring that guardians are competent to meet the existing needs of their wards, the *Standards* exhort courts to ensure that appointed guardians are capable of handling responsibilities that may arise in the future.[38]

Among the duties frequently required of guardians is the filing of periodic reports with the court about the ward's condition.[39] The *Standards* recommend that these reports include a comprehensive description of the ward's physical condition, the services and care provided to the ward, significant actions taken by the guardian on behalf of the ward, expenses incurred in providing these services, and any major anticipated changes in the ward's treatment and care.[40] This information would keep the court fully apprised of the ward's condition. In addition, the *Standards* encourage courts to require guardians to file an initial guardianship plan to inform the court of how the guardian intends to carry out the assigned duties and responsibilities.[41] This initial plan also would encourage guardians to effectively plan how to meet the needs of the wards and to delineate the steps they should undertake to carry out their plans from the beginning.[42]

As important as the requirement that guardians file reports with the courts is the need for courts to promptly review these reports. As one commentator observed, "[i]f an annual guardian report is merely going to be placed in a file, unread or at most given a cursory review, it is nothing but a palliative that squanders the guardian's time and energy."[43] Consequently, the *Standards* recommend "[p]rompt review of the guardian's report [to] enable the court to take early action to correct abuses made apparent by the reports [and] to take early action in issuing a show cause order if the guardian has violated a provision of the original order."[44] Additionally, the court's reporting procedures should include a mechanism for alerting the court when reporting deadlines occur and for providing prompt notice to guardians who fail to meet these deadlines.[45]

Finally, commentators have suggested that courts periodically reevaluate the necessity for continuing a guardianship.[46] Although most jurisdictions permit the ward or other interested persons to petition for a termination or change in the status of a guardianship, the *Standards* also encourage courts to establish procedures for sua sponte examinations of the need to continue the guardianship.[47] In addition to the guardian's annual report, the court may employ a court visitor to periodically investigate the ward's circumstances to determine if either a less intrusive alternative or termination of the guardianship might be more appropriate.[48] Moreover, the *Standards* note that "the court's review of the continuing need for a guardianship should not be limited by its established review date" but may be initiated "at any other time at [the court's] own discretion."[49]

* * *

Notes

1. BLACK'S LAW DICTIONARY 706 (6th ed. 1990).

2. Guardianship (and conservatorship) proceedings are available when an individual is incompetent or is a minor. Some issues and requirements of protective proceedings for minors are unique, *see* UNIF. GUARDIANSHIP AND PROTECTIVE PROC. ACT §§ 2-101 to 2-112 (Guardians of Minors), 2-301 to 3-335 (Protection of Property of Persons Under Disability and Minors), 8A U.L.A. 467–82, 499–542 (1982 & Supp. 1993); however, the prescribed proceedings for incompetents and minors are relatively similar. Like the *National Probate Court Standards,* the focus of this article will be on guardianship (and conservatorship) proceedings for adults who lack decision-making capacity and are found incompetent by a court.

3. Provisions of the Uniform Probate Code (Article V, the Uniform Guardianship and Protective Proceedings Act), drafted by the National Conference of Commissioners on Uniform State Laws, serve as a widely emulated model. UNIF. PROB. CODE §§ 5-501 to 5-505, 8 U.L.A. 429–518 (1983 & Supp. 1993).

4. *See, e.g.,* Jan E. Rein, *Preserving Dignity and Self-Determination of the Elderly in the Face of Competing Interests and Grim Alternatives: A Proposal for Statutory Refocus and Reform,* 60 GEO. WASH. L. REV. 1818 (1992).

5. Rein frames the issue in contemporary guardianship law as a fundamental tension between freedom and safety. *Id.* at 1864–67. Some senior citizens, she asserts, "would prefer to give up safety if safety were to require them to relinquish control over their own lives." *Id.* at 1864.

6. Alison P. Barnes, *Florida Guardianship and the Elderly: The Paradoxical Right to Unwanted Assistance,* 40 U. FLA. L. REV. 949, 970 (1988) (discussing traditional "all-or-nothing" guardianship arrangements).

7. For example, a Missoula, Montana, court "had no record of what happened to the $131,000 estate of a 92-year-old man found ill and alone in a cabin in 1985 after a couple described as 'friends' became his guardians." Fred Bayles & Scott McCartney, *Declared 'Legally Dead' by a Troubled System, in* FRED BAYLES & SCOTT MCCARTNEY, GUARDIANSHIP OF THE ELDERLY: AN AILING SYSTEM 1 (Associated Press Special Report, Sept. 1987).

8. The Associated Press report described a "dangerously burdened and troubled system that regularly puts the lives of the elderly in the hands of others with little or no evidence of

necessity, and then fails to guard against abuse, theft and neglect." *Id.* at 1. Specifically identified were a lack of resources to adequately monitor the activities of guardians and the financial and personal status of their wards, guardians with little or no training, a lack of awareness about alternatives to guardianships, and a general lack of due process protections for individuals for whom guardianships were proposed. *Id.* at 7–8, 11–12, 14–17, 23; *see also* Lawrence A. Frolik, *Abusive Guardians and the Need for Judicial Supervision,* TR. & EST., July 1991, at 41.

9. Even the most basic nationwide data on guardianships has been lacking. For example, the Associated Press report estimated that 300,000 to 400,000 persons were under guardianship in 1987 based on a random sampling of state court files. Bayles & McCartney, *supra* note 7, at 1. However, no state or federal agency has attempted an independent account of national guardianship statistics. As part of its State Court Statistics Project, the National Center for State Courts compiles data about the quantity and types of civil cases filed in state courts, including guardianship and conservatorship filings. The accuracy of the data, however, depends entirely upon the ability and willingness of the state courts to disclose reliable information. By extrapolating the data provided to the National Center for State Courts, project staff from the *National Probate Court Standards* estimated that in excess of 300,000 guardianship cases are filed each year in the United States.

10. Dan Erwell, *Woman Fights Back from Coma, Then Against Guardianship System, in* BAYLES & MCCARTNEY, *supra* note 7, at 10.

11. *Id.* During the period that she was under protection, her guardian put her house up for sale and sold most of her furniture. In addition, she lost her job, her driver's license, and her right to vote. She even had difficulty drawing her money from bank accounts after she recovered. *Id.*

12. Fred Bayles & Scott McCartney, *Lack of Safeguards Leaves Elderly at Risk, in* BAYLES & MCCARTNEY, *supra* note 7, at 11–12.

13. *Id.*

14. [COMMISSION ON NAT'L PROBATE COURT STANDARDS, NATIONAL COLLEGE OF PROBATE JUDGES & NATIONAL CTR. FOR STATE COURTS, NATIONAL PROBATE COURTS STANDARDS (1993)], at 61–63, 67–68.

15. *Id.* at 61.

16. *Id.* at 61–63.

17. *Id.* at 61. Specifically, the *Standards* state:

> By requiring the showing of an emergency and the simultaneous filing of a petition for a permanent guardianship, the court will confirm the necessity for the temporary guardianship and ensure that it will not extend indefinitely. When the temporary guardianship is established, the date for the hearing on the proposed permanent guardianship should be scheduled. The order establishing the temporary guardianship should provide that it will lapse automatically upon that hearing date.

Id. at 62.

18. *Id.*

19. *Id.*

20. *Id.* The *Standards* explain that "[t]he use of a protective order may be particularly appropriate in the case of a respondent who has suffered a physical injury that leaves him or her unable to make decisions for a short period of time, but who is expected to soon regain full decision-making capacity." *Id.*

21. *Id.* at 67–68, 70–71. Even absent statutory authority to do so, the court may create a

limited guardianship through its inherent or equity powers. *Id.* at 67; *see also* UNIF. PROB. CODE § 5-306(c), 8 U.L.A. 468 (1991) ("The Court . . . may limit the powers of a guardian . . . and thereby create a limited guardianship.").

22. [COMMISSION ON NAT'L PROBATE COURT STANDARDS, NATIONAL COLLEGE OF PROBATE JUDGES & NATIONAL CTR. FOR STATE COURTS, NATIONAL PROBATE COURTS STANDARDS (1993)], at 67.

23. *Id.* at 70.

24. *Id.* at 67.

25. *Id.* at 56.

26. *Id.* at 56, 67.

27. *Id.* at 67.

28. The *Standards* describe the court visitor as one who "serves as the eyes and ears of the court, making an independent assessment of the need for a guardianship." *Id.* at 59; *see also* UNIF. PROB. CODE § 5-103(21), 8 U.L.A. 438 (1983) ("'Visitor' means a person appointed in a guardianship or protective proceeding who is trained in law, nursing, or social work, is an officer, employee, or special appointee of the Court, and has no personal interest in the proceeding.").

29. [COMMISSION ON NAT'L PROBATE COURT STANDARDS, NATIONAL COLLEGE OF PROBATE JUDGES & NATIONAL CTR. FOR STATE COURTS, NATIONAL PROBATE COURTS STANDARDS (1993)], at 58–59. The specific duties of the court visitor may vary according to the jurisdiction, particularly regarding the court visitor's responsibility for representing or speaking on behalf of the proposed ward. *Id.* at 58 & n.68.

30. Where available, the *Standards* also encourage the use of volunteer court visitors, such as specially trained Association for Retarded Citizens and American Association of Retired Persons volunteers to reduce the costs associated with independent judicial investigations. *Id.* at 59.

31. *Id.*

32. *Id.*

33. *Id.* at 55–56.

34. *See* Frolik, *supra* note 8, at 42–44.

35. *See* Fred Bayles & Scott McCartney, *Guardianship Entrepreneurs Entering the Field, in* BAYLES & MCCARTNEY, *supra* note 7, at 19; Fred Bayles & Scott McCartney, *Public Guardians Struggle to Keep Pace, in* BAYLES & MCCARTNEY, *supra* note 7, at 14; Sharon Cohen, *Public Guardian Patrick Murphy: Scourge of the Bureaucrats, in* BAYLES & MCCARTNEY, *supra* note 7, at 17; George Esper, *Veterans Administration Watches over 124,000 Wards, in* BAYLES & MCCARTNEY, *supra* note 7, at 16.

36. In evaluating the ability of a proposed guardian to care for a ward, the *Standards* urge the court to consider "the training, education, and experience [including] such factors as familiarity with health care decision making, residential placements, and social services benefits." [COMMISSION ON NAT'L PROBATE COURT STANDARDS, NATIONAL COLLEGE OF PROBATE JUDGES & NATIONAL CTR. FOR STATE COURTS, NATIONAL PROBATE COURTS STANDARDS (1993).]

37. *Id.* at 71–72.

38. *Id.* at 68. The National Guardianship Association and a number of state courts have developed training materials to inform newly appointed guardians of their duties toward the ward. *See, e.g.,* NATIONAL GUARDIANSHIP ASS'N, ETHICS AND STANDARDS FOR GUARDIANS (1991); SERVING AS GUARDIAN AND CONSERVATOR (Lang Telecommunications 1989) (train-

ing video produced for the Michigan Judicial Council); VIDEO IMAGINATION TELEVISION, INSTRUCTIONS FOR GUARDIANS AND CONSERVATORS (1990) (training video produced for the Pima County (Arizona) Superior Court).

39. The time frame permitted for filing these reports may vary according to the jurisdiction. *See* [COMMISSION ON NAT'L PROBATE COURT STANDARDS, NATIONAL COLLEGE OF PROBATE JUDGES & NATIONAL CTR. FOR STATE COURTS, NATIONAL PROBATE COURTS STANDARDS (1993)], at 72. The *Standards* recommend that an initial report be filed with the court within 60 days of the imposition of the guardianship and that annual reports be required thereafter for the duration of the guardianship. *Id.* The required content of these reports varies somewhat for conservatorships. *Id.* at 96–98.

40. *Id.* at 72–73.

41. *Id.* at 73.

42. *Id.*

43. Frolik, *supra* note 8, at 44.

44. [COMMISSION ON NAT'L PROBATE COURT STANDARDS, NATIONAL COLLEGE OF PROBATE JUDGES & NATIONAL CTR. FOR STATE COURTS, NATIONAL PROBATE COURTS STANDARDS (1993)], at 72–73.

45. *Id.* The failure of a Virginia court to demand timely explanations for guardians' reporting delinquencies was cited as one of the contributing factors to that state's failure to prevent an attorney from embezzling nearly $42 million from his clients' accounts. DALE EVANS & KENNETH ARMSTRONG, SEE NO EVIL, DAILY PRESS (Newport News, Va.), Nov. 15–19, 1992, Special Report.

46. Frolik, *supra* note 8, at 42–44.

47. [COMMISSION ON NAT'L PROBATE COURT STANDARDS, NATIONAL COLLEGE OF PROBATE JUDGES & NATIONAL CTR. FOR STATE COURTS, NATIONAL PROBATE COURTS STANDARDS (1993)], at 74–75.

48. *Id.*

49. *Id.*

CHAPTER 20

Guardianship Reform

Jan Ellen Rein

Preserving Dignity and Self-Determination of the Elderly in the Face of Competing Interests and Grim Alternatives: A Proposal for Statutory Refocus and Reform

* * *

V. Freedom Versus Safety: The Right to Be Left Alone

Social workers, court investigators, probate judges, and others engaged in the guardianship process frequently see the fundamental issue as one of freedom versus safety.[1] My surmise is that many tend to opt on the side of safety. This choice may be appropriate in many cases, although, as noted earlier, the premise that intervention poses fewer risks than nonintervention and that institutional settings are safer than an individual's home have been persuasively challenged by mounting evidence to the contrary. Even assuming the soundness of the premise of safety, however, some elders—perhaps a minority, perhaps not—would prefer to give up safety if safety were to require them to relinquish control over their own lives, especially if that means living out their remaining days in a nursing home. For such individuals, guardianship as we know it is not an adequate answer.

Although the analogy is not perfect, a similar kind of tension inheres in *Cruzan v.*

George Washington Law Review, 60:1818 (1992). Reprinted by permission.

Director, Missouri Department of Public Health[2] and the other right-to-die cases that have perplexed our courts.[3] These cases recognize an individual's privacy right to refuse or demand withdrawal of life-prolonging treatment, but founder on perplexing issues such as who should be the decision-maker when the patient is comatose or marginally cognitive, what criteria should be applied, and what quantum of proof should be required when a comatose patient's previously expressed wishes become an issue.[4]

Increasingly, Americans are expressing a desire to be allowed to refuse medical treatment that merely prolongs life without improving its quality. This concern has been manifested in rather dramatic fashion by the growing number of right-to-die cases breaking out in courts across the land,[5] in the increasing suicide rate for elder Americans, and in the stampede to make living wills and durable powers of attorney for health care decisions[6] that followed in the wake of *Cruzan*.[7] The phenomenon that prompts this concern received judicial recognition by Justice Brennan, who, dissenting in *Cruzan*, observed:

> "Medical technology has effectively created a twilight zone of suspended animation where death commences while life, in some form, continues. Some patients, however, want no part of a life sustained only by medical technology. Instead, they prefer a plan of medical treatment that allows nature to take its course and permits them to die with dignity."[8]

By rough analogy to the issue that triggered *Cruzan* and the other right-to-die cases, if an individual should be allowed to refuse acute medical care when the quality of life is gone, shouldn't she also be allowed to refuse interference or long-term maintenance care under the auspices of a guardian or institution when such care will only prolong life without in any way improving its quality? Suppose, for example, X, who has a tendency to fall, would prefer to remain at home unattended—even though that would entail the risk of a harmful or fatal accident—rather than to have her freedom and independence curtailed by solicitous intervention.[9] Such a decision to encounter risk is often interpreted as evidence of incompetency or incapacity.[10]

* * *

Consider also the case of an individual who has lost short-term memory and cannot retain a grasp of the situation beyond the immediate moment, but who is capable of remembering her lifelong values and preferences,[11] puttering around the house, preparing meals, and reliving her past in familiar surroundings. At age eighty something, does it really matter whether she knows what day or time it is or whether the friendly face of a relative is a daughter or a niece? By commonly accepted standards, she may be incompetent or incapacitated, but does she really belong under a guardianship or in an institution?[12] Wouldn't an assistant bill-payer and a simple housekeeper with whom she feels comfortable suffice for her level of actual need?

In light of the foregoing discussions, I believe it is permissible to infer that many older Americans, particularly those who opt for suicide, would prefer risk and freedom to the so-called safety of guardianship and institutionalization. In short, many such individuals would prefer to be left alone to manage their own affairs, however badly, rather than to submit to the kinds of interventions presently available. It also seems reasonable to assume that even those individuals who truly consent to guardianship or institutionalization would like more opportunities to retain control and would prefer interventions that offer more by way of therapy and encouragement to become active and involved than do so many of today's standard interventions.

Although blame for the predicament that our elders face cannot be laid entirely or even primarily at the feet of the law, it is nevertheless important for lawyers and lawmakers to ask whether our statutory and judicial criteria for intervention sufficiently address our senior citizens' needs, not the least of which is the need to retain individuality, choice, and dignity until death.

VI. The Statutes

A. A Proposal for Statutory Change

Our statutes should be designed to ensure that the judiciary will vigilantly insist, in law and in practice, that: (1) the privacy and autonomy of those who wish to be left alone receive the utmost respect; (2) those who want or need help actually get the kind of help that will bestow a real benefit and enhance their remaining powers rather than produce atrophy of such powers through discouragement and want of use; and (3) the justification of a benefit to the ward that is traditionally used to sanction unwanted, reluctantly received, or passively received interventions is supported by fact, not just theory.

To carry out these goals, statutory provisions setting forth the substantive grounds for appointment of a guardian of the person or conservator of the estate should carefully distinguish between inability to make decisions and inability to execute decisions without help. Only the former should justify removal of decision-making control via guardianship or conservatorship.[13] Indeed, state-sanctioned interventions that override the decisions of those who can make decisions, but are precluded by mere physical incapacity from executing them, may be unconstitutional.[14]

The statutes should categorically forbid the imposition of guardianship or conservatorship when the impairment or dysfunction is purely or primarily physical. Instead, the statutes should authorize the court to appoint a competent and trustworthy assistant to act as the handicapped person's agent. The order should make it clear that the assistant's role is to carry out the handicapped person's decisions—as in a principal-agent relationship—and that the assistant-agent has no decision-making power except with regard to purely ministerial matters.

A statutory scheme that is serious about implementing the policy of preserving autonomy and self-determination should also require the court and its investigators to insist upon a careful and competent determination regarding the causes of the proposed ward's decisional dysfunction or impairment before allowing anyone to jump to the conclusion that guardianship or conservatorship is warranted. Although some state statutes require that the proposed ward be examined by a physician or other professional,[15] many are vague or silent on this point.[16] Even statutes that address the matter provide no guidelines to ensure that the physicians and investigators employ evaluation methods that reliably determine decisional inability, or even that the physicians and investigators are qualified to make such assessments.[17] In fact, evaluation reports, if required at all, tend to be extremely conclusory, often merely restating the state's statutory definition of incompetence or incapacity.[18] Instances of misdiagnosis are commonplace.[19] As one researcher reported: "Examinations reportedly have been performed by plastic surgeons, urologists, gynecologists, and the petitioner, if performed at all. The testimony that is offered has been called conclusory by numerous commentators. In spite of these deficiencies, medical evaluations usually are dispositive: Courts are unlikely to depart from the assessments of physicians."[20] If decisional dysfunction or impairment is found, the statute should require the court to determine whether the deficiency is irreversible, reversible, or correctable by compensatory measures. Many deficiencies that appear cognitive are actually caused by overmedication, inappropriate medication, poor diet, depression, environmental deficiency, sensory deprivation, poor eyesight, or impaired hearing.[21] Deficiencies produced by such causes can often be reversed or corrected by adjustments in diet, medication, and environment or by personal attention, mental and physical therapy, or prostheses and other corrective devices.[22]

Statutes should require that the possibility of reversible or correctable causes be specifically explored and eliminated by clear and convincing evidence before the court proceeds to remove decision-making power via guardianship or conservatorship. If it appears that reversible or correctable causes are substantially responsible for the ward's dysfunction or deficiency, the statute should require the court to deny the petition for guardianship or conservatorship and to make a temporary, self-limiting order permitting a qualified person to render only such assistance—e.g., provision of a hearing aid, adjustment of medication, treatment of depression or correction of environmental deficiencies—as may be needed on a temporary basis to restore the proposed ward to competency.

"The court should consider the full range of legal, mental health and social service options available."[23] This need not invariably involve an overriding of the proposed ward's decision-making powers even in the limited areas affected,[24] but if it does, the order should state that it automatically expires on a certain date. Only if competently executed good faith measures to correct or reverse the mental dysfunction or deficit fail should the court be authorized to conclude that the ward's mental condition is irreversible or irremediable.

As indicated, the protected person's well-being is the sole modern justification of the state's power as *parens patriae* to appoint a guardian or conservator of that person.[25] There may occasionally be extremely vital, legitimate interests of third parties, society at large, or the state that justify overriding the individual's free-will and liberty interests. In such cases, however, it is not the *parens patriae* power that justifies the unwanted or reluctantly received intervention. Our legal system should recognize frankly that whenever a court imposes guardianship or conservatorship over a proposed ward's objection or reluctance for the convenience, mental well-being, or financial interests of family members or other third parties, the court is going beyond the confines of the *parens patriae* concept to interfere with fundamental liberty interests, potentially including freedom from involuntary physical confinement. Before a court interferes with such fundamental interests over the proposed ward's objections, the petitioner should be required by statute to prove by clear and convincing evidence that such a drastic step is absolutely necessary to protect third-party or societal interests of the highest magnitude—i.e., the life and physical safety (not just the convenience, emotional reassurance, or financial hopes)[26] of others—from an imminent threat of serious harm posed by the proposed ward's behavior.

* * *

Notes

1. [Mary J. Quinn, Remarks at a Seminar on Guardianship and Conservatorship: Uses and Abuses (July 12, 1991).] For a discussion of the tension between autonomy and protection, see Lawrence A. Frolik & Alison P. Barnes, *An Aging Population: A Challenge to the Law*, 42 HASTINGS L.J. 683, 703–06 (1991). The authors conclude that the task of the legal profession is to rebut the myth of elder incompetence and to strike a better balance than currently exists between those two societal values. *Id.* at 718.

2. 110 S. Ct. 2841 (1990).

3. *See, e.g., In re* Peter, 529 A.2d 419 (N.J. 1987); *In re* Farrell, 529 A.2d 404 (N.J. 1987); *In re* Conroy, 486 A.2d 1209 (N.J. 1985); *In re* Quinlan, 355 A.2d 647 (N.J.), *cert. denied,* 429 U.S. 922 (1976).

4. *See* cases cited *supra* notes 3–4.

5. *See, e.g.,* cases cited *supra* notes 3–4.

6. [Marshall B. Kapp, *Medical Empowerment of the Elderly,* HASTINGS CENTER REP., July–Aug. 1989, at 5, 5–7 (arguing that the decision to defer to a doctor's decision is respectable)]; *cf.* Bruce Vignery, *Legislative Trends in Nonjudicial Surrogate Health Care Decision Making,* 23 CLEARINGHOUSE REV. 422, 422–25 (1989) (discussing recent legislative enactments in this area).

7. 110 S. Ct. 2841 (1990) (recognizing a state's power to require clear and convincing evidence of a comatose patient's previously expressed desire for termination of measures that maintain bodily functions when there is no hope of recovery).

8. *Id.* at 2863 (Brennan, J., dissenting) (quoting Rasmussen v. Fleming, 741 P.2d 674, 678 (Ariz. 1987) (en banc)).

9. *Cf.* [Marshall B. Kapp, *Medical Empowerment of the Elderly,* HASTINGS CENTER REP., July–Aug. 1989, at 5, 5–7 (arguing that the decision to defer to a doctor's decision is respectable)], (discussing the empowerment of older individuals through informed consent and the tension that this empowerment has created in the health care profession). Doctor Kapp cautions that empowerment can only occur when adequate information is received and *understood* prior to the elderly patient making a voluntary choice between meaningful alternatives. *Id.*

This is not to ignore that empowerment can provide a convenient excuse for negligence and neglect, as Dr. Kapp also notes. The point, however, is that the proposed ward's expressed wishes should be paramount or at least should receive greater weight than they are given today. Respect for the individual should ensure that decisional opportunities are always accompanied by appropriate offers of assistance, with the proposed ward's informed rejection of such help being final.

10. [Bart J. Collopy, *Autonomy in Long Term Care: Some Crucial Distinctions,* 28 GERONTOLOGIST 10, 10 (Supp.1988) (citations omitted); *see, e.g., Cummings v. Stanford,* 388 S.E.2d 729 (Ga.Ct.App.1989) (court appointed daughter as guardian of her mother's property because the 65 year-old widow spent $35,000 on a third home, took a vacation with two adult sons while leaving petitioner-daughter at home, and spent money freely). In another guardianship case, the court declared Mr. S. incompetent and placed him under the guardianship of his stepson because Mr. S. insisted on leaving his estate to friends instead of family. Mr. S.'s decision was cited as the primary evidence of incompetency in a report that stated: It is evident that Mr. S. does have a great deal of understanding of what is going on around him. However, he does clearly suffer from a lack of judgment. As the head nurse, Mrs. J., indicated, he doesn't see why he shouldn't be allowed to give away all his money since it is his.] [Kris Bulcroft et al., *Elderly Wards and Their Legal Guardians: Analysis of County Probate Records in Ohio and Washington,* 31 GERONTOLOGIST (1991) at 160. In a similar case, a guardian ad litem report on Mrs. F., a 76 year-old woman, inferred a lack of competency from Mrs. F.'s choice of a companion. The report sanctimoniously stated: Unfortunately, Mrs. F. has not always used good judgment in handling her affairs and in making decisions as is attested to by the fact that during the past couple of years, she has kept company with Max M., a man with an allegedly dubious character and an alcoholic. *Id.* at 162; *see also* THOMAS S. SZASZ, LAW, LIBERTY, AND PSYCHIATRY 11–17 (1963) (discussing the various meanings associated with the value-laden term "mental illness") (additional references deleted).]

11. *See* Nancy N. Dubler, *Some Legal and Moral Issues Surrounding Informed Consent for Treatment and Research Involving the Cognitively Impaired Elderly, in* LEGAL AND ETHICAL ASPECTS OF HEALTH CARE FOR THE ELDERLY 250–51 (Marshall B. Kapp et al. eds., 1985) (suggesting that lifelong preferences may survive newly developed cognitive deficiencies).

12. Although an adjudication of incompetency is not the equivalent of institutionalization, the two frequently are treated together because the former so greatly increases the risk of the latter.

13. As one court recognized,

> The capability to manage one's person does not resolve itself upon the question of whether the individual can accomplish tasks without assistance but rather whether that individual has the capability to take care and intelligently direct that all his needs are met through whatever device is reasonably available under the circumstances.

In re Estate of McPeak, 368 N.E.2d 957, 960 (Ill. 1977); *see* [Bart J. Collopy, *Autonomy in Long Term Care: Some Crucial Distinctions,* 28 GERONTOLOGIST 10, 10 (Supp.1988) (citations omitted)], at 11. Doctor Collopy, who arrived at a conclusion similar to this author's, provides an insightful discussion of how aging and advanced frailty can decrease executional ability, even though the decisionmaking ability remains intact. *Id.* Doctor Collopy goes on to note that elder autonomy can be preserved in decisionmaking even when execution becomes dependent on others. *Id.*

14. In Schafer v. Haller, 140 N.E. 517 (Ohio 1923), a statute making physical disability a ground for placing a mentally competent individual under guardianship was held to be violative of Ohio's constitution as an unjustified abridgment of the proposed ward's liberty. *Id.* Al-

though other state statutes have withstood similar challenges, in each case the proposed ward had deficiencies which affected her mental or communicative abilities. *See* Loss v. Loss, 185 N.E.2d 228 (Ill. 1962); Macdonald v. LaSalle Nat'l Bank, 142 N.E.2d 58 (Ill. 1957); *In re* Guardianship of Schmidt, 352 P.2d 152 (Or. 1960).

Of course, if one's physical impairment is so total as to remove utterly all ability to communicate thought, it may as a practical matter be necessary to appoint someone else to communicate decisions for her. Because this surrogate communication necessarily involves guesswork, all possible means of eliciting communication should be exhausted first.

15. *See, e.g.*, FLA. STAT. § 744.331(3)(a) (1991) (specifying the qualifications of three-member examining committee); N.M. STAT. ANN. § 27-7-22B(3) (Michie Supp.1992) ("The evaluation shall include at a minimum . . . an evaluation of the adult's present physical, mental and social conditions including, as necessary, a medical, psychological, psychiatric or social evaluation and review. . . ."); UNIF. PROB. CODE § 5-303(b) (1992) (stating that a "person alleged to be incapacitated must be examined by a physician or other qualified person appointed by the court").

16. *See, e.g.*, CAL. PROB. CODE §§ 1801–1849.5 (Deering 1991).

17. *See generally* [STEPHEN J. ANDERER, DETERMINING COMPETENCY IN GUARDIANSHIP PROCEEDINGS 3 (1990)], at 16–18 (providing an overview of the statutory requirements for evaluation of proposed wards).

18. Bobbe S. Nolan, *Functional Evaluation of the Elderly in Guardianship Proceedings, in* LEGAL AND ETHICAL ASPECTS OF HEALTH CARE FOR THE ELDERLY, *supra* note 13, at 212, 213–14. Professors Rosoff and Gottlieb have also commented on this evaluation process:

> Turning to the specifics of the court's evaluation, while statutes require documentation of functional disability, courts rarely insist upon such evidence. Far too often, they are satisfied with only a perfunctory assessment of the alleged incompetent's mental capacity. A complete psychiatric evaluation and formal mental status exam are rarely included. Inasmuch as the physician is rarely present in court, the judge must accept this letter as the only evidence of disability. Consequently, the individual is usually found incompetent, and it is estimated that a guardian is appointed in approximately 95 percent of all cases.

[Arnold J. Rosoff & Gary L. Gottlieb, *Preserving Personal Autonomy for the Elderly: Competency, Guardianship, and Alzheimer's Disease,* 8 J. LEGAL MED. 1, 15 (1987) (citations omitted) (emphasis added).]

19. [*See generally* PAUL S. APPELBAUM & THOMAS G. GUTHEIL, CLINICAL HANDBOOK OF PSYCHIATRY AND THE LAW 218–24 (2d ed. 1991) (discussing legal efforts to define competency in the context of guardianships and the resulting reliance on vague and overbroad descriptions); Alan Meisel, *The "Exceptions" to the Informed Consent Doctrine: Striking a Balance Between Competing Values in Medical Decisionmaking,* 1979 WIS. L. REV. 413, 439–53 (discussing the incompetency exception to the requirement of informed consent for medical treatment). On the subject of misdiagnosis, *see generally* Gerald K. Good enough, *The Lack of Objectivity of Physician Evaluations in Geriatric Guardianship Cases,* 14 J. CONTEMP. L. 53 (1988) (discussing the unfairness that results from the absence of objective measures of mental capacity for determining competency of elderly subjects). Misdiagnoses of incompetence are commonplace.] [CHAIRMAN OF SUBCOMM. ON HEALTH AND LONG-TERM CARE OF THE HOUSE SELECT COMM. ON AGING, 100TH CONG., 1ST SESS., ABUSES IN GUARDIANSHIP OF THE ELDERLY AND INFIRM: A NATIONAL DISGRACE 1 (Comm. Print 1987) (hereinafter ABUSES) at 59, 67. For example, a treatable condition

or disease can mimic the symptoms of Alzheimer's disease or senile dementia. Only an autopsy can conclusively confirm Alzheimer's disease, but alternative tests can provide clues. For a discussion of this and other problems, see Joan M. Krauskopf, *New Developments in Defending Commitment of the Elderly,* 10 N.Y.U. Rev. L. & Soc. Change 367 (1980) (additional references deleted).]

20. [Stephen J. Anderer, Determining Competency in Guardianship Proceedings 3 (1990); Arnold J. Rosoff & Gary L. Gottlieb, *Preserving Personal Autonomy for the Elderly: Competency, Guardianship, and Alzheimer's Disease,* 8 J. Legal Med. 1, 15 (1987) (citations omitted) (emphasis added) (additional references deleted)]; Nolan, *supra* note 20, at 213 (discussing the conclusory nature of guardianship proceedings).

21. *See* [Gerald K. Good enough, *The Lack of Objectivity of Physician Evaluations in Geriatric Guardianship Cases,* 14 J. Contemp. L. 53 (1988) (discussing the unfairness that results from the absence of objective measures of mental capacity for determining competency of elderly subjects); Cheryl Simon, *Age-Proofing the Home,* Psychol. Today, Dec. 1987, at 52, 52. The failure of society to view life from the elder's perspective is illustrated clearly in the context of environmental failures: [S]urroundings can have a tremendous effect, good or bad, on the mobility, self-reliance and mental state of the elderly. "Part of what has happened is that we've approached older people as we approach other disability groups," says environmental psychologist and gerontologist Lorraine Hiatt. Their needs, however, are distinct. Often, there is no overriding disability . . . , but "little bits of losses" in vision, hearing and mobility. None is necessarily disabling in itself, but combined, they reduce an older person's overall ability to function. . . .

Some environments, by exaggerating an older person's feelings of disability and dependency, may actually speed the aging process. A younger person, for example, reads, unlocks a door and rises from a chair without thinking, but these actions may demand an elderly person's complete attention. Out of habit, sentiment or deference to people who may visit occasionally, an older person may keep lighting levels, physical layout and furnishings the same over the years. As a result, the living quarters may present so many obstacles that simply getting to the kitchen consumes attention and energy, and the original purpose is forgotten.

Such lapses, a matter of environment rather than ability, are often interpreted as a sign of mental deterioration. "A lot of so-called first-level memory impairment may really be related to sensory dysfunction." . . . An older person who is distracted by the glare of the building's hallway and confused by the noise of traffic and construction may simply stay home, withdrawing from the world. Concerned family members may consider moving the older person to new living quarters. This solution, however, may aggravate the problem. "Lots of people don't understand the attachment that older people have to their home." . . . In addition to the emotional distress a move can cause, the sudden absence of familiar views, sounds and textures that aided memory can magnify problems that were lessened in known surroundings. In a nursing home, for instance, the crisp interiors and sleek wall coverings may create distracting echoes, and the shiny floors may glare. Such conditions may make an older person appear and feel frail and confused. Conversely, the old, richly textured draperies, high-backed chairs and "clutter" that bother well-meaning adult sons and daughters may stimulate the inhabitant's recall, as well as baffle background noise and screen out blinding outdoor light. *Id.*]

22. [*See generally* Paul S. Appelbaum & Thomas G. Gutheil, Clinical Handbook of Psychiatry and the Law 218–24 (2d ed. 1991) (discussing legal efforts to define competency in

the context of guardianships and the resulting reliance on vague and overbroad descriptions); Alan Meisel, *The "Exceptions" to the Informed Consent Doctrine: Striking a Balance Between Competing Values in Medical Decisionmaking*, 1979 WIS. L. REV. 413, 439–53 (discussing the incompetency exception to the requirement of informed consent for medical treatment). On the subject of misdiagnosis, *see generally* Gerald K. Good enough, *The Lack of Objectivity of Physician Evaluations in Geriatric Guardianship Cases*, 14 J. CONTEMP. L. 53 (1988) (discussing the unfairness that results from the absence of objective measures of mental capacity for determining competency of elderly subjects). Misdiagnoses of incompetence are commonplace.] [CHAIRMAN OF SUBCOMM. ON HEALTH AND LONG-TERM CARE OF THE HOUSE SELECT COMM. ON AGING, 100TH CONG., 1ST SESS., ABUSES IN GUARDIANSHIP OF THE ELDERLY AND INFIRM: A NATIONAL DISGRACE 1 (Comm. Print 1987) (hereinafter ABUSES]) at 59, 67. For example, a treatable condition or disease can mimic the symptoms of Alzheimer's disease or senile dementia. Only an autopsy can conclusively confirm Alzheimer's disease, but alternative tests can provide clues. For a discussion of this and other problems, see Joan M. Krauskopf, *New Developments in Defending Commitment of the Elderly*, 10 N.Y.U. REV. L. & SOC. CHANGE 367 (1980) (additional references deleted).]

23. [STEPHEN J. ANDERER, DETERMINING COMPETENCY IN GUARDIANSHIP PROCEEDINGS 3 (1990).]

24. For example, voluntary acceptance of social services such as homemaker/home health aides, transportation, shopping, friendly visiting, congregate and home delivered meals, senior centers, case management, day care facilities, sheltered housing, board and care homes, and programs for financial management may allow the respondent to care for self and property and thus relieve the need for an incapacity determination.

Id. at 47 n.133.

25. See [Peter M. Horstman, *Protective Services for the Elderly: The Limits of Parens Patriae*, 40 MO. L. REV. (1975) at 221. Although the two overlap at times, the state's police power should be distinguished from its power, as parens patriae, to protect the well-being of individual citizens unable to care for themselves. While the police power may be exercised to the detriment of the individual if a substantial public benefit is to be achieved thereby, the individual's well-being is the sole justification for the exercise of the state's authority as parens patriae. *Id.* (footnote omitted); *see also* 1 MICHAEL L. PERLIN, MENTAL DISABILITY LAW (1989) § 2.17, at 139 (noting that power arising from the parens patriae doctrine—as opposed to the state's police power—is based on the person's inability to protect herself).]

26. Whether third-party economic considerations should ever justify overriding a proposed ward's objections is a difficult question to answer in the abstract because of situational variables and the near-impossibility of separating the decisionmaker's value system from the decision. My own weighing of the competing interests would lead me to say that if the only threat is to third-party expectations of inheritance or tax savings, the court should not override the proposed ward's objections. On the other hand, if the proposed ward's decisions threaten to impoverish a person or force that person to expend substantial amounts of his or her own funds for the proposed ward's support, some compromise may be warranted. What should be clear, however, is that when a court places another person's economic interests above a ward's autonomy interests, it is not necessarily exercising its *parens patriae* power. A goal of the approach suggested in this Article is to encourage a reallocation of resources from institutional to home and community care so that such hard choices will arise less frequently.

Lawrence A. Frolik

Plenary Guardianship: An Analysis, a Critique and a Proposal for Reform

* * *

III. Reforms

Although there is no dearth of guardianship reform proposals, there is a lack of critical examination of the efficacy of such proposals.[1] Moreover, because the reforms emanate from a variety of sources[2] who formulate their proposals under the influence of quite differing assumptions, it is not surprising that the reform efforts differ in both their means and ends.[3] One exception is the almost universal call for the right of an alleged incompetent to have counsel represent him at the initial hearing of incompetency.[4]

A. Right to Counsel

If we accept the premise that guardianship is desirable for an incompetent, then the value of having counsel represent the alleged incompetent would seem to be that the presence of counsel might prevent a competent individual from being found to be incompetent. In short, counsel might assist in reducing the number of findings of false positives at incompetency hearings. The cost of having counsel present at such hearings, however, is the likelihood that the number of incompetent persons who need a guardian, but who are wrongly judged to be competent, will increase.[5] In short, more false negatives will occur. There is no way of determining whether the presence of counsel is more likely to reduce false positives or increase false negatives.

In fact, we are presented with five possibilities:

1. Presence of counsel increases false negatives *and* increases false positives, *i.e.*, more incompetents are falsely found to be competent, and more competent individuals are falsely found to be incompetent;
2. Presence of counsel results in fewer false positives and fewer false negatives, *i.e.*, incompetency hearings become more accurate;
3. Presence of counsel results in fewer false negatives and more false positives, *i.e.*, determinations of incompetency increase;
4. Presence of counsel has no effect upon the outcomes (in gross if not in particular cases);

Arizona Law Review, Vol. 23, 599 (1981). Reprinted by permission.

5. Presence of counsel results in more false negatives and fewer false positives, *i.e.*, determinations of incompetency decrease.

Possibility number one, that presence of counsel results both in more false positive and more false negative decisions, seems highly improbable. Counsel are unlikely to be random contributors to judicial inaccuracy. Possibility number two, that presence of counsel results in greater accuracy in the determination of incompetency, would be a most desirable development. If true, it would present a compelling argument for mandating counsel's presence. Possibility number three, that presence of counsel results in more guardians, seems highly unlikely. Assuming almost any level of skill, it would seem either that counsel would have no effect or that their presence would result in a decrease in the number of determinations of incompetency.[6] If possibility number four, that counsel have no effect, is correct, then there seems little reason to have them present. Surely, the cost in time, money and other resources might be better spent elsewhere. If the system is already fair, or if it cannot be affected by the presence of counsel, then they seem unnecessary unless the presence of counsel is thought to be important merely to legitimize the proceeding by lending an appearance of procedural fairness. Possibility number five, that presence of counsel results in fewer findings of incompetency, seems the most likely outcome. Although, in some instances, counsel might prevent the unlawful appointment of a guardian (a false positive), in other instances counsel's efforts might prevent the appointment of a guardian for an incompetent (a false negative). Would this result be desirable?

(1) Benefits Versus Burdens Let us postulate that the presence of counsel would result in more petitions for guardians being denied, either because of more false negatives or because of fewer false positives. If the latter were the case, then counsel would be serving a valuable service by preventing the appointment of unneeded or, at least, unlawful guardians. This would advance the public interest in two ways: (1) it would cut costs; and (2) the reduced possibility of success in borderline or bad faith cases would diminish the number of guardianship hearings.[7] But are there other, more significant, savings? To be sure, there is the John Donne "No man is an island" gain; we are all served when any one of us is more justly treated. But in a more concrete manner, we are all better off if we live in a society that minimizes the denial of liberty of its members. Certainly, few competent individuals would voluntarily relinquish their adult rights and liberties to a guardian. Therefore, we must be concerned that the system that appoints guardians operates in a manner designed to minimize the appointment of guardians for adults who ought not to have one. But there must also be a consideration of the cost of the failure to appoint a guardian when one is needed. How should we measure the cost if the presence of counsel increases the number of false negatives? It might be a poor trade indeed if we were to save one competent man from a guardian at the expense of denying ten incompetents the benefit of a guardian.

Here again, however, the possibility that counsel might result in the denial of needed and beneficial guardians assumes that all individuals can truly be categorized as competent or incompetent. But what if this were not so? Suppose that instead of conceiving of the world as consisting of two groups, competent and incompetent, we were to think of it as a continuum stretching from the rational, careful individual who never or only rarely makes decisions not in his interest to the incompetent individual who is incapable of understanding or making decisions in his own interest. Somewhere in the middle of that continuum people begin to lack the ability to care for themselves. In the case of the young, we distinguish the competent from the incompetent by an arbitrary age classification.[8] As for adults, we have tried to distinguish the merely foolish or weak-willed from the incompetent. This we have done through the concept of capacity. So long as one has capacity, one is competent regardless of the wisdom of the decisions or of the choice of lifestyle. We have essentially used a medical model to winnow out the sick from the foolish or eccentric.[9] But the medical model assumes that there is a state—health—that can be distinguished from another state—illness. This may well be so in the case of physical illness. For example, one either is or is not suffering from measles. But is the same true of mental illness or mental retardation, senility, drug addiction, or alcoholism? While it might be true for senility, drug addiction, or alcoholism, there exist grave doubts as to whether there is any "bright-line" that distinguishes the mentally ill[10] or mentally retarded.[11] Of course, to say that it is difficult to define precisely the line between the sane and the insane and the nonretarded and the retarded is not the same as saying that mental illness or mental retardation do not exist. Still, the lack of convincing definitions may well mean that there is no bright-line or litmus test of capacity. If capacity cannot be identified with any true degree of certainty (the degree of uncertainty itself being unclear), then there exists a group "in the middle" or "on the border-line" as to whom we can make no certain judgments. If we turn to behavior to identify the incapacitated, we face the problem that there is no unanimity of opinion as to what kind of behavior is rational or in one's best interest. We compound our problem if we venture to ask what is the measure of one's best interest. Whose values are to rule? Clearly, we are dealing with extraordinarily difficult decisions.

To raise the specter, then, that the presence of counsel might result in the denial of needed guardians is to flail against a strawman. At most, the presence of counsel will reduce the number of guardians appointed in the gray or shadow area where no judgment is certain or where conflicting values bar agreement as to the "correct" outcome.

(2) Role of Counsel

* * *

The issue of the proper role of counsel at a guardianship healing is similar to the debate over the proper role of counsel at a civil commitment hearing. Commentators have, in general, concluded that counsel should act as an adversarial advocate rather than as a promotor of the best interests of the client.[12] Several reasons compel adoption of the adversarial role. First, if counsel has already concluded that his client needs "help" and that a guardian might be an effective source of that "help" (albeit, not the only possible source), then counsel is less likely to challenge expert testimony, either by effective cross-examination or by introducing experts with opposing points of view.[13]

Second, counsel acting for the "best interest" of his client has no standard by which to judge the quality of his efforts. In any particular case, it would be difficult for anyone (including the counsel) to judge whether the strategy employed by counsel was, in fact, in the best interest of the client. In the extreme instance, it would be almost impossible to claim an attorney was guilty of ineffective assistance of counsel. As one commentator put it: "[C]ourts will experience great difficulty separating out those lawyers who have acted in a manner they considered consistent with the best interests of the client from those who have acquiesced in commitment simply as a means of avoiding work."[14]

Third, the best interest test can too easily lead to counsel providing only procedural formality to legitimize the routine approval of guardianship petitions.[15] Presence of counsel does not necessarily mean that the petition for incompetency will be vigorously resisted. True adversarial counsel will result only if the lawyer takes seriously his obligation to "zealously" defend his client.[16]

Finally, and perhaps most fundamentally, to allow counsel to act in the "best interest" of the client would allow attorneys to make decisions concerning the mental capacity and well-being of their clients: decisions that attorneys are totally unqualified to decide. Attorneys are presumed to know the law and the legal procedures for marshaling evidence, but they are not equipped to independently determine the physical and psychological needs of their clients. It is for the court, not counsel, to decide what *lawful* course of action will serve the best interests of the client. The appointment of a guardian for a person who is not legally incompetent is not a lawful course of action, no matter how "beneficial" it might seem to counsel. A paternalistic counsel who allows the appointment of a guardian which might have been avoided by a vigorous defense has not acted in the best interests of his client.

If the client claims to be competent and wishes to avoid becoming a ward, then it seems clear that the client's counsel should attempt to defeat a showing of incompetency. Less clear, however, are those cases when the client is uncooperative and expresses no opinion or when counsel sincerely believes that the client does not know where his interests lie. The ABA Model Statute provides that when the client either can neither form nor communicate decisions or is unable to determine his own interest without assistance, then a guardian ad litem should be appointed to assist the client in reaching a decision (which would then be acted upon by counsel). The Model Statute goes on to provide, "If an individual is wholly incapable of determining his or her own interests, the guardian ad litem shall make that determination and advise counsel accordingly."[17] Granting that degree of power to the guardian ad litem would seem to undercut the "zealous" advocacy role of counsel, for the guardian ad litem would be duty bound to promote the best interests of the client, even if that meant acquiescing in the determination of incompetency. If the Model Statute were to be adopted, it would mean the triumph of the "best interest" role, and the right to counsel would be only a shadow protection.

There is little need or excuse for allowing counsel to forswear from promoting a vigorous defense of the competency of his client. Only four possible circumstances present themselves: (1) a competent client instructs counsel to resist the guardianship, (2) a competent client expresses no opinion or desires that a guardian be appointed, (3) an incompetent client instructs counsel to resist the guardianship, or (4) an incompetent client expresses no opinion or expresses a desire that a guardian be appointed.

The proper role of counsel in situation (1) is obvious: to defend his client from an unlawful guardian. In situation (2), the role of counsel is also clear: defend the client from an unlawful guardian. As an officer of the court, it would be unethical for counsel to cooperate in the appointment of a guardian for a competent person. Moreover, whatever benefits were sought by the client through the appointment of the guardian could be reached by other avenues—principally, a general power of attorney and the voluntary entrance into a full-care facility, *e.g.*, a nursing home, or by the employment of a personal caretaker, *e.g.*, a practical nurse.

In situation (3), when an incompetent client desires to resist guardianship, counsel is cast into a role not unlike that of a criminal defense attorney who serves society best by an active, adversarial defense of his client. The analogy is an apt one for, although being declared an incompetent is not the same as being convicted of a crime, it nevertheless results in a serious loss of personal autonomy, freedom, and self-esteem. Certainly, the cost to the unwilling ward is sufficient to warrant requiring society to prove its case in the face of a determined, opposing counsel.[18]

Similarly, in situation (4) when the incompetent client expresses no opinion or desires a guardian, the role of counsel must be that of advocate. Counsel is not empowered either by training or law to decide that his client is incompetent or that society is best served by the appointment of the guardian.

* * *

Notes

1. The most elaborate guardianship reform proposal, including detailed commentary, is the ABA MODEL STATUTE, [Guardianship and Conservatorship: Statutory Survey, ABA COMMISSION ON MENTALLY DISABLED, MODEL STATUTE (1979) (hereinafter ABA MODEL STATUTE)]. The Uniform Probate Code, while not directed specifically at guardianship reform, also presents a complete (but more modest than the ABA MODEL STATUTE) statutory scheme. *See* UPC Art. V. A reform proposal not in the form of a statute but presented rather as a prose discussion and critique is THE NATIONAL CENTER FOR LAW AND THE HANDICAPPED, GUARDIANSHIP OF THE MENTALLY IMPAIRED: A CRITICAL ANALYSIS (1977). A model pubic guardianship act may be found in SPECIAL COMMITTEE ON AGING, UNITED STATES SENATE, *Protective Services for the Elderly*, at 111 (1977).

2. *See* [CONN. GEN. STAT. ANN § 45-70a (West Supp. 1981); PA. STAT. ANN. tit. 20 § 5501 (Purdon 1975)].

3. *Compare,* for example, [Horstman, *Protective Services for the Elderly: The Limits of Parens Patriae,* 40 Mo. L. Rev. 215 (1979)]; who attacks paternalistic protective service guardianship *with* [Regan, *Protective Services for the Elderly: Commitment, Guardianship and Alternatives,* 13 Wm. & Mary L. Rev. 569 (1972)], who strongly supports guardianship in the context of the delivery of protective services.

4. [Guardianship and Conservatorship: Statutory Survey, ABA Commission on Mentally Disabled, Model Statute (1979) (hereinafter ABA Model Statute)] at 136; [National Center for Law and the Handicapped, Guardianship of the Mentally Impaired: A Critical Analysis (May, 1977) (hereinafter National Center for Law and the Handicapped)], at 34; *cf.* UPC § 5-303(b) (providing that if the alleged incompetent lacks counsel of his own choice, the court shall appoint an appropriate official or attorney to act as his guardian ad litem). *Contra* Rud v. Dahl, 578 F.2d 674 (7th Cir. 1978), where the court held that the state is not constitutionally compelled to provide counsel for the alleged incompetent. The court felt that the "intrusion on liberty interests . . . was far less severe than the intrusion from other types of proceedings in which the presence of counsel has been mandated." *Id.* at 679. The court continued, "Moreover the technical skills of an attorney are less important as the procedural and evidentiary rules of an incompetency proceeding are considerably less strict than those applicable in other types of civil and criminal proceedings." *Id.* at 678. This is a rather amazing admission as to the laxity that is permitted at guardianship hearings. The court failed to address the question of why such informality is permissible.

5. This assumes counsel acts in an adversarial role rather than independently determining what outcome is "best" for the client and acting accordingly. For a discussion of why lawyers in analogous civil commitment hearings should always perform an adversarial role, rather than in the "best interest" of the client, see [Morris, *Conservatorship for the "Gravely Disabled": California's Nondeclaration of Nonindependence,* 15 San Diego L. Rev. 201 (1978)], at 234; Note, *The Role of Counsel in the Civil Commitment Process: A Theoretical Framework,* 84 Yale L.J. 1540, 1553–59 (1975). Some commentators advocate a "best interest" role for counsel rather than the more narrow adversarial one. *E.g.,* Janopaul, *Problems in Hospitalizing the Mentally Ill,* 13–14 (American Bar Foundation Research Memorandum Series No. 31, 1962); Brofman, *Civil Commitment of the Mentally Ill in the Denver Probate Court,* 46 Den. L. Rev. 469, 566 (1969).

6. The quality of counsel in civil commitment hearings is often very poor, however. *See* [Elkins, *Legal Representation of the Mentally Ill,* 82 W. Va. L. Rev. 157, 159–162 (1979) (containing an exhaustive bibliography)].

7. "The adversary system apparently does not provoke a generally more vigorous search for facts, but does instigate significantly more thorough investigation by an advocate initially confronted with plainly unfavorable evidence." Linda, Thibaut, & Walker, *Discovery and Presentation of Evidence in Adversary and Nonadversary Proceedings,* 71 Mich. L. Rev. 1129, 1143 (1973).

8. Even with juveniles, the "bight-line" age test of competency is not always used. For example, a juvenile has the right, independent of her guardian, to elect an abortion. *See* Planned Parenthood v. Danforth, 428 U.S. 639 (1976).

9. [It is *not* necessary that anyone be able to explain why the disability occurred. Thus, it is irrelevant why someone is retarded; it is enough that the court can be apprised of the existence of the retardation. Similarly, once we have identified someone as suffering from mental illness, it is not necessary that we understand the cause of the illness.]

10. [Morse, *Conservatorship for the "Gravely Disabled": California's Nondeclaration of Nonindependence,* 15 San Diego L. Rev. 201 (1978)], at 554–60.

11. The most widely accepted definition is the one adopted by the American Association on Mental Deficiency: "Mental Retardation refers to subaverage general intellectual functioning which originated during the developmental period and is associated with impairment of adaptive behavior." *Quoted in* [R. WOODY, LEGAL ASPECTS OF MENTAL RETARDATION: A SEARCH FOR RELIABILITY 3 (1974)], at 13. Admittedly, at some point the I.Q. is so low that any observer would agree that the individual is mentally retarded. But at the borderline, the term is loose and little more than a behavior description of ill-adapted behavior. The validity of the legal classifications of mental retardation is sharply challenged in *Sorgen, The Classification Process and Its Consequence,* 215, 229–32, in THE MENTALLY RETARDED CITIZEN AND THE LAW (1976).

12. *See* [Elkins, *Legal Representation of the Mentally Ill,* 82 W. VA. L. REV. 157, 159–162 (1979) (containing an exhaustive bibliography)], at 240; [*Developments in the Law—Civil Commitment of the Mentally Ill,* 87 HARV. L. REV. 1190 (1974) (hereinafter *Developments*)], at 1289; Note, *supra* note 6, at 1561.

13. The importance of challenging psychiatric testimony is discussed in [Elkins, *Legal Representation of the Mentally Ill,* 82 W. VA. L. REV. 157, 159–162 (1979) (containing an exhaustive bibliography)], at 188–93.

14. Note, *supra* note 6, at 1561.

15. Andalman & Chambers, *Effective Counsel for Persons Facing Civil Commitment: A Survey, A Polemic, and a Proposal,* 45 MISS. L.J. 43, 72 (1974).

16. CODE OF PROFESSIONAL RESPONSIBILITY, EC7-1, EC7-7, & EC7-12 (1979).

17. ABA MODEL STATUTE, [Guardianship and Conservatorship: Statutory Survey, ABA COMMISSION ON MENTALLY DISABLED, MODEL STATUTE (1979) (hereinafter ABA MODEL STATUTE)], § 34(7).

18. The societal value of a vigorous defense for the guilty criminal client is discussed at Bress, *Professional Ethics in Criminal Trials: A View of Defense Counsel's Responsibility,* 64 MICH. L. REV. 1493 (1966); Freedman, *Professional Responsibility of the Criminal Defense Lawyer: The Three Hardest Questions,* 64 MICH. L. REV. 1469 (1966); Orkin, *Defense of One Known To Be Guilty,* 1 CRIM. L.Q. 170 (1958).

In the 1980s many commentators recommended procedural reforms as a means of assuring that guardianship operates in the best interest of the incapacitated person. In response, most states reformed their guardianship statutes and adopted many of the proposed reforms. Unfortunately, procedural reforms have not proven to be a panacea and problems remain, as described in the following article.

Lawrence M. Friedman and June O. Starr

Losing It in California: Conservatorship and the Social Organization of Aging

* * *

The trends of an age of reform were felt in this area of law as they were elsewhere. The laws changed, in state after state, to give the ward more rights, to cut the discretion of the conservator down to size, and to give judges power to craft a more flexible, less limiting form of conservatorship.[1] There was also a feeling that souls placed in tutelage were not getting the proper attention. The National Senior Citizens' Center had done a study of 1,010 conservatorships in Los Angeles County.[2] In 93 percent of the adult cases, the wards never appeared at their own hearing; 97 percent had no counsel or other representation.[3] The whole system seemed to smell of rot, or neglect, and a thorough revamping followed in California and other states.[4] In California, a central feature of the reform was the invention of a new actor in the drama, an impartial third party, responsible to the court and nobody else, who would advise wards of their rights and look after their interests. This, of course, was the Court Investigator.

Over the last generation or so, then, the law has been traveling away from darkness to light—toward empowerment. The various waves of reform were meant to set up a fair, loose, minimal system. The ward was to keep as many rights as possible and suffer as few restrictions as possible. The petition to the court requesting a conservatorship must address "[a]lternatives to conservatorship considered by the petitioner and reasons why those alternatives are not available."[5] The legislature, according to the words of the statute, meant to "set goals for increasing the conservatee's functional abilities to whatever extent possible" and to use "community-based services," if one could, so as "to allow the conservatee to remain as independent . . . as possible" and to carry on, as much as possible, in the "least restrictive setting."[6]

California is considered an extremely progressive state in matters of conservatorship. The laws are carefully drafted, and the Court Investigator has no precise equivalent elsewhere. But it is one thing to be progressive on paper, quite another to make sure reality matches the words. After all, rights can be ignored; they can be *waived;*[7] and sometimes they can turn into a caricature of themselves. Whether the rights have any muscle is an empirical question. Finding the answer is one of the goals of this study. Obviously, a study at this stage, mainly examining the paper record, cannot be really definitive. But one gets a lot closer by looking into files than by just reading the statutes, their legislative history, and the handful of decided cases.

Washington University Law Quarterly, 73:1501 (1995). Reprinted by permission.

II. Assessing Conservatorship: The Santa Clara Files

The sixty-one files from the Santa Clara study provide us with a good deal of information. We learn, for example, *who* becomes a ward. Most are women. In the sample of sixty-one, women made up 61 percent of the group. In a larger sample drawn from San Francisco, 71 percent of the wards were women. The wards were, not surprisingly, elderly: 82 percent were sixty years old or over. The average age for men was seventy-one; for women, seventy-seven. The San Francisco sample was significantly older: the average age for men was seventy-seven, for women, eighty-three; and 95.2 percent of the sample was over sixty.

The age discrepancy between men and women, of course, is not surprising. Men do not, on the whole, last as long as women do. Wives outlive their husbands and often care for them during their decline. Most of the women in the sample were widows, facing their last years alone; the sample included twenty-five widows and only four widowers.

* * *

A. What Triggers a Conservatorship in Santa Clara County?

The Santa Clara sample was fairly affluent. More than two-thirds of the estates for which there was information available were worth more than $100,000, and one-fifth were worth more than $500,000.[8]

* * *

The most common reason for establishing a conservatorship was "a slow decline in ability to cope with everyday life." This accounts for 36.2 percent of our sample—over one-third of the case files examined. Still, 15.9 percent of the conservatorships in our sample were triggered by some single, precipitous event. The ward might be arrested after a drunken spree; might be found wandering around the streets in a dazed condition; or might have fallen or been in an accident, hospitalized, and then assessed by the nurses as someone not capable of caring for herself.

In another 14.5 percent of the files examined, the conservatorship was triggered by the need to move a proposed ward to a locked facility, a hospital, or a nursing home against her wishes. The law allows someone to be moved against her wishes when a Lanterman-Petris-Short (LPS) conservatorship has been set up, which allows the conservator to arrange placement and mental health treatment for people who are unable to provide for their food, clothing, or shelter as a result of a mental disorder or chronic alcoholism.[9] This type of conservatorship is only used when the person needs mental health treatment but cannot or will not accept it voluntarily. This situation often occurs together with a general slow decline in abilities, and both categories of triggering event might apply.

Perhaps the most interesting of all precipitating events is alleged "undue influence." This is a familiar term in the law of wills; a will can be invalidated (in whole or in part) if it is the product of "undue influence."[10] This rather bizarre concept is defined to mean a degree of psychological pressure that goes so far as to mesmerize or overpower the unfortunate soul who is the object of the influence.[11] The concept also crops up in these petitions. There were eleven cases (15.9 percent) in our sample with this allegation. In seven of them, the claim was that some family member exerted the undue influence; in four cases, it was an outsider. When a relative alleges "undue influence" by another relative, this suggests a potential or actual family feud, and such a feud may indeed trigger a conservatorship. Someone may be hovering in the background, looking with a protective eye at the way the proposed ward is spending her money, or with a jealous or greedy eye. A sister may think mother is giving more money to brother than she ought to. Or children may be resentful that an elderly father has taken a new girlfriend, who wraps him around her finger.

It can also be alleged that some elderly person has fallen under the spell or become subject to the "will power" of a stranger. A *Los Angeles Times* study of conservatorships in Southern California reported that smooth-talking salesmen often target retirement homes for their fraudulent schemes.[12] To combat this, some retirement communities like Leisure World "run seminars, distribute flyers, and counsel people on how to avoid being swindled."[13] It is hard to tell how widespread the problem is, but there is at least an echo of similar problems in the case files.

B. How Effectively Does the Probate Judge Decide Among Quarreling Families

Family quarrels or disputes form the basis of many conservatorships, but this fact is not always apparent from the files. There were eleven cases in which such quarrels seemed obvious from the record; in each of them, the proposed ward had assets worth fighting about. Families do not need a financial excuse to start battling, but the money helps.

In one case, a daughter petitioned the court to be named conservator for her decrepit mother. She was afraid that her sister had plans to take the mother out of her (intermediate care) facility in Santa Clara County and move her to Los Angeles. This was presumably for the nefarious purpose of gaining control over assets parked in a revocable trust.[14] In another case, a daughter claimed that the proposed ward was unable to "resist undue influence." The proposed ward had let another relative collect veteran's disability payments; the relative (it was said) kept the money for herself and never turned it over to its rightful owner. To get this money back and to make sure future payments went where they belonged, the petitioner demanded to be named conservator. In this case, there was also a need for a temporary restraining order—a relative was (allegedly) harassing the proposed ward through phone calls and visits.[15]

* * *

In fifty of the petitions, the petitioner requested specific powers. Forty of these petitions asked for the power to consent to medical treatment for the proposed ward. Twenty-six asked for various economic or financial powers or the power to decide the ward's residence and change it, if need be. The court granted the requests unconditionally in thirty-eight cases, but imposed conditions in five cases. In the remaining cases, the petitions were dropped.[16]

The theory of the modern law, as we saw, is to cut the conservatorship to the particular needs of the ward and to take away only so much power and right as is absolutely necessary.[17] In fact, the typical course of action in the typical conservatorship goes in the opposite direction. Decision-making power is taken away from the ward, and the power of the conservator is increased.

C. How Many Proposed Wards Objected to Being Conserved and How Did the Judge Decide This Issue?

With few exceptions, California does not provide the right to a jury trial in conservatorship hearings.[18] It is thus generally up to the judge to take into consideration any objections that the proposed ward might have about the proceeding. In twenty-eight of the sixty-one files examined, the proposed wards objected to some aspect of the conservatorship. They either did not want to have a conservator of their person or their estate, or they had some kind of objection to the particular person who wanted to be or was proposed as conservator. In nine out of sixty-one cases, there was a formal motion made, objecting to some aspect of the proceedings. In seven of these nine cases, the judge overruled the proposed ward and granted a conservatorship. In one case the conservatorship was not granted,[19] and in one other case the petition was dropped.[20]

In six of nine cases when a proposed ward objected to the particular conservator, that conservator was appointed nonetheless. In only one case was the ward successful in preventing the person she objected to from becoming conservator;[21] in two other instances the petition was dropped. Therefore, it seems that, on the whole, the system is tilted in favor of the petitioner and against the ward. Most of the time, the judge ignores or overrules the wishes, complaints, and objections of the ward. This is especially the case when the ward is elderly. Here again, the Investigator's report and her presence at the hearing plays a decisive role.

D. Should the Court Pay More Attention to the Ward?

Of course elderly people (like people in general) can be difficult at times: needlessly cranky and irrational. They may feel neglected and accuse their relatives of ignoring them or of trying to move them to a nursing home against their own wishes (no one *wants* to move to a nursing home). There were echoes of such complaints in the dossiers. It is also true that some older people lose the capacity to judge how much they have declined in memory or management capacity. Some of these elderly people are unaware that others may be using them, misleading them, defrauding them, or manipulating them. They may be unaware of how neglectful they had become in keeping body and soul together. There were wards who had not had a hot meal in months.

For such people, conservatorship can be a real protection. Does the opposite situation occur—situations where the conservatorship itself is a kind of fraud or manipulation, or simply misguided? In one case, a fifty-five-year-old woman had suffered a stroke and felt that she was at risk: "I realize that my medical condition may at times affect my mental condition and may make me vulnerable to persons who wish to take advantage of me." Once (she claimed) she was "defrauded of several thousand dollars." Her sister was appointed conservator, but less than two years later, the ward came to court, complaining (through a lawyer) about the sister's behavior. The sister—it was alleged—was milking the estate, using it as an excuse to buy herself vacations in California. The Court Investigator found no need for a conservator because the ward was able to "manage her full life." She was, in fact, taking courses at a community college, and, despite her disability, had "a social life," and "active membership at a local church." The court terminated the conservatorship.[22]

The Court Investigator rarely disagreed with the petitioner; the Investigator almost invariably felt that a conservatorship *should be* established. In fact, the Court Investigator recommended conservatorships in all but one of the fifty-eight Santa Clara cases for which information was available—in seventeen of these, as we have seen, with conditions.

* * *

E. When the Court Investigator Recommended a Conservatorship, Did the Court Grant It?

The Court Investigator recommended forty conservatorships unconditionally and recommended seventeen others with conditions. In only one case did the judge deny a conservatorship that the Investigator had recommended. This case involved a thirty-eight-year-old man who was a chronic alcoholic living at home. His parents thought they could control him better if they were appointed conservators. The Investigator apparently agreed, but the judge had constitutional objections.[23]

Of the seventeen cases in which a conservatorship was conditionally recommended, fifteen were granted and two cases were dropped. The Investigator's opinion seems to be of critical importance to the judge's determination whether to grant the petition. In the Chief Investigator's words, investigators are the "eyes and ears of the court," and the court seems to agree.

III. Some Reflections on Conservatorship

In some jurisdictions, there are reports of corruption and incompetent management in the courts which handle conservatorships. Not so in the North District of Santa Clara County, or, for that matter, in San Francisco. The office of the Court Investigator seems to work fairly well, institutionally speaking. The investigators themselves were able, hard-working individuals—people who sincerely wanted the process to be humane and who aimed to protect the rights of elderly wards.

In our total data set of sixty-one cases, there were revealed fifty-three instances where the Investigator made a review visit to the ward after a year or so and filed a "review report." In not one of these instances did the conservator feel the ward had improved enough to terminate the conservatorship completely. In one case, the Investigator felt the elderly ward had sufficiently recovered from a coma to have voting rights restored. In seven cases, the Investigator recommended some change, often comparatively small—suggesting, for example, that the ward might need more sweaters or socks. In twenty-three instances no change whatsoever was recommended.

This suggests a certain amount of complacency. Nonetheless, it is reassuring that the Investigators did manage to revisit their wards (sometimes much sooner than the required visit at one year after the commencement of the conservatorship). Although the Investigators' busy work schedules sometimes work against their making the review visit at the required twelve-month interval, all Investigators did make a return visit within a sixteen-month interval. Also, if circumstances drastically changed (for example, when a conservator resigned and a new one was appointed), the Investigator made the required visit within the stipulated six-week time period to notify the ward of the change and determine his attitudes concerning it.[24]

The Investigators' responsibilities seem to be increasing. The legal culture has been changing, and the law has been evolving; as a result, their duties have become deeper and broader.[25] Investigators attend planning meetings that consider the program, its future, and possible expansion. Some helped write the *Handbook for Court Investigators.*[26] Others have been working on training films for new conservators—there have been six or seven of these. Still others, like the Chief Investigator, attend meetings with judges and work with a commission charged with the duty of developing ethical standards for professional conservators. The commission is also developing guidelines for a training program for professional conservators, who may come to occupy a role in conservatorships in the county.[27] To us, the Investigators' work day seemed long, arduous, and at times stressful. The stories of the lives of wards had few happy endings. But Investigators find their work exciting—on the cutting edge of humane social change. Some of them value the job because it works toward humane treatment, human contact, comfort, and companionship for those near the end of life. It was our impression that, for the most part, the Investigators knew their job and did it well.

* * *

But do abuses occur mostly in places which have poor or retrograde procedures? We would not want to say that there is *no* relationship between process and justice. This would mean that the reform work of the legislature was essentially useless. But good laws and good procedures, quite obviously, are not nearly enough. Discretion is inevitable and unavoidable all over the legal system, but this area is unusually open-ended and free of restraints. It depends very much on the good will, intelligence, and authority of judges and other court workers—not to mention the conservators themselves. The reader might find this last sentence startling. Is it not true that the system is much tighter than before? That the processes have been reformed, safeguards instituted, and so on? Does this not limit excessive discretion? Indeed it does:

on paper. The reality is otherwise. The reality is waivers of this and waivers of that, and a great deal of power lodged in the court and its staff.

The California system has much to recommend it, to be sure, and the Investigator is definitely an important feature. Nevertheless, there are nagging questions remaining that have to be asked. To begin with, in many real-life situations, there is a definite conflict of interest between petitioner and ward. The typical petitioner—a daughter, a son, a friend—probably does have the interests of the old man or woman at heart, or at least thinks she does. But there is the ugly fact of the money. If somebody spends the money during mother's declining years, there will be nothing left to inherit. The children cannot help but be aware of this mournful fact.

* * *

There is also the inherent difficulty of trying to reduce to a legal formula a very variable and complex human problem: What constitutes competence? In our times, legal doctrine has retreated from the situation when it made sharp, brittle, black-and-white distinctions between competence and incompetence in issues of civil commitment, conservatorship, and the like.[28] California law now recognizes that you cannot simply label people one way or another. The two end-states merge gently into each other (perhaps for all of us).

Yet judges still have to decide, and do decide, whether men and women can manage their money for themselves; or even whether they know if they can do so. Psychologists have struggled to devise tests of decision-making capacity, but few of them would claim that the problem is anywhere near a solution.[29] It is not even clear that we know what *the* problem is. In any event, when people start sliding downhill, they often slide slowly, almost imperceptibly. They have good days and bad days. They can manage some things and not others.

The solution, such as it is, in the Probate Code, does avoid and supersede the older legalisms and slides away from hard-and-fast judgments. But the Code nonetheless embodies a kind of new legalism. What results is a paper system which is at the same time highly formalized and highly discretionary. In any event, it is strongly procedural. There are elaborate processes, safeguards, steps to be taken, occasions of review, and so on. All this, of course, has its costs. The more rights and procedures, the harder it is for ordinary people—members of the family, friends, neighbors—to handle matters by themselves and to run the conservatorship once it gets established. The process has become much more legalized. It almost demands that a conservator work with a lawyer. And, indeed, the presence of lawyers was felt in file after file.[30] This, of course, adds to the costs of conservatorship[31]—a cost borne by the individual estates for the most part.[32]

* * *

Yet, as we said, even though the process has been legalized, it also remains highly discretionary. The statute sets out a flock of procedural steps, forms, and requirements that must be met (or waived). But the heart, the guts of the conservatorship, remains a matter of discretion. Whose discretion? A combination of the conservator and the court. The one proposes; the other disposes. The legalization, in other words, is procedural—you must follow the rules, you must get permission for your acts, and especially, you must file petitions. Courts, however, are allowed to grant permission under the vaguest of standards.

* * *

Of course, social attitudes are not static, and attitudes toward the elderly in this society are no exception. In some ways, the elderly are better off than in past generations. Economically, this seems to be generally true. They live longer, and that is not *always* a curse. The changes in the California law on conservatorship, whether effective or not, are symptoms of changes for the better in attitudes. They reflect, among other things, the emergence of the elderly as a powerful lobby. There are other symptoms, too: the passage of age discrimination laws[33] and the abolition of mandatory retirement among others. The changes also run parallel to other changes in law—reforms in the law of civil commitment, for example.

California's attempt to reform the law of conservatorship marks another step in the due process revolution. But in the case of those among the elderly who are fading, it may be that law reform—at least procedural reform—is not enough. There must be a further change in the way the elderly are perceived and received and conceived. This, of course, is a tall order. Still, to be a humane society, we need to work harder on the issues that underlie conservatorship and related institutions. Procedure is only a start. What is needed are institutions that work, that are supportive, and that deal justly and adequately with the frailty and infirmity of an increasing number of older Americans.

Notes

1. One of the first signals of this change in attitude towards the elderly can be seen in the UNIF. PROB. CODE § 5-409 (1969). The Uniform Probate Code was first adopted (with some changes) in Arizona in 1973. The Arizona formulation granted judges broad powers to provide less drastic alternatives to conservatorship appointments: If it was established that a conservator could be appointed, the court might *instead*

> authorize, direct or ratify any transaction necessary or desirable to achieve any security, service or care arrangement meeting the foreseeable needs of the protected person. Protective arrangements include, but are not limited to, payment, delivery, deposit or retention of funds or property, sale, mortgage, lease or other transfer of property, entry into an annuity contract, a contract for life care, a deposit contract, a contract for training and education, or addition to or establishment of a suitable trust.
>
> ARIZ. REV. STAT. ANN. § 14-5409 (1995).

2. CAL. ASS'N SUPER. CT. INVESTIGATORS, COURT INVESTIGATOR HANDBOOK (1991).

3. *Id.* at 1.1. It was not until 1977 that judges were allowed to appoint attorneys for prospective wards, and that automatic review of conservatorship by Court Investigators was instituted. CAL. PROB. CODE §§ 1461, 1500 (West 1977).

4. On the history of reform in New York, see Allen Federman, *Conservatorship: A Viable Alternative to Incompetence,* 14 FORDHAM URB. L.J. 815 (1985–86). On Oklahoma, see Teresa Collett,

Keeping my Brother's Keeper: An Introduction to Article III of the Oklahoma Guardianship Act, 42 OKLA. L. REV. 243 (1989).

5. CAL. PROB. CODE § 1821(a)(3) (West 1991).

6. CAL. PROB. CODE § 1800(b), (d) (West 1991). Note the lack of these requirements in the 1957 CALIFORNIA PROBATE CODE §§ 1751, 1752, or 1754.

7. *See, e.g.,* Conservatorship of Mary K., 285 Cal. Rptr. 618 (Cal. Ct. App. 1991). The ward's lawyer orally waived the right to jury trial, and certain other statutory requirements. *Id.* at 620. The ward, who was resisting conservatorship, probably expected the judge to take her side; when he instead ordered a conservatorship, she appealed, trying to undo the waiver; but the appeal court turned her down. *Id.* at 622.

8. Large estates seem to be highly correlated with home ownership in our study. Home ownership constitutes the primary (if not sole) substantial asset for many wards. Given that in Los Altos, approximately 95% of homes are valued at over half a million dollars, it is a small wonder that we found a great number of large estates. [U.S. Census Database, Section 18 (1990), available in LEXIS (RN 49 90 06 001625).]

9. Technically, the LPS conservatorship is identical to the conservatorship outlined in §§ 1400–2808 of the California Probate Code except that: 1) the LPS conservatorship can be for a youth; 2) the priorities of conservatorship may be waived upon the Court Investigator's recommendation, CAL. PROB. CODE § 1812 (West 1991); and 3) the LPS conservatorship proceeding guarantees a right to a jury trial on the issue of impairment. CAL. WELF. & INST. CODE § 5350 (West 1991 & Supp. 1995). Note that under CALIFORNIA PROBATE CODE § 1452, there is not a right to a jury trial for ordinary conservatorships. CAL. PROB. CODE § 1452 (West 1991). Thus, the mentally disturbed have, potentially, a major procedural advantage over the elderly in contesting a conservatorship proceeding.

10. CAL. PROB. CODE § 6104 (West 1991). For recent scholarship on undue influence, see John E. Fennelly, *Up From* Carpenter: *Undue Influence in Will Contests,* 16 NOVA L. REV. 515 (1991), and Joseph W. deFuria, Jr., *Testamentary Gifts Resulting from Meretricious Relationships: Undue Influence or Natural Beneficence?,* 64 NOTRE DAME L. REV. 200 (1989).

11. *See, e.g.,* Haynes v. First Nat'l Bank of New Jersey, 432 A.2d 890 (1981).

12. Davan Maharaj, *Retirement Centers Are Swindlers' Paradise,* L.A. TIMES, Nov. 3, 1991, at A1.

13. *Id.*

14. Doc. No. 3 (on file with authors).

15. Doc. No. 4 (on file with authors).

16. We found an extreme example of a request for additional powers in a case where the nephew-petitioner was a partner in a local law firm. The list of additional powers requested was an entire page long and included: the right to perform and enter contracts, grant and take options, sell real or personal property, borrow money, purchase real property, lease property, lend money, exchange property, exercise stock options, participate in voting trusts, pay and collect debts and claims, and employ an attorney. All of these powers were granted by the court. Part of the court's compliance in this case may have derived from the fact that the total estate was valued at less than $43,000, and that the ward was on her deathbed (in fact, dying within a month of the court order instituting the conservatorship). However, it is worth noting the rather large bill paid by the estate to the petitioner's law firm (almost $3400) for a completely uncontested conservatorship.

17. [For a discussion of the development of the notion of incompetence and its practical consequences, *see* Margaret K. Krasik, *The Lights of Science and Experience: Historical Perspectives on Legal Attitudes Toward the Role of Medical Expertise in Guardianship of the Elderly,* 33 AM. J.

LEGAL HIST. 201 (1989). For example, California's 1957 conservatorship statutes not only made no provision for limited conservatorships, but granted "every conservator" the same broad powers allowed to guardians of "incompetents." CAL. PROB. CODE § 1852 (West 1957); Arizona has taken this so far as to give any court faced with sufficient grounds to appoint a full conservatorship the alternative of authorizing any necessary or desirable arrangement, including the establishment of a trust. ARIZ. REV. STAT. ANN. § 14-5409.A (1995).]

18. CAL. PROB. CODE § 1452 (West 1991).

19. Doc. No. 7 (on file with authors).

20. Doc. No. 8 (on file with authors).

21. Doc. No. 9 (on file with authors).

22. Doc. No. 10 (on file with authors).

23. Doc. No. 11 (on file with authors).

24. We did find one instance in which the ward herself, after two years in conservatorship, complained and got the conservatorship terminated. *See supra* text accompanying note 22.

25. In the last three years, for whatever reason, conservatorship caseloads of the Investigators have gradually declined. It seems likely that this decline is only temporary. In any event, the decline has not meant less work for Investigators; they have been given the added job of investigating guardianships for minors. CAL. FAM. CODE § 3111 (West 1994). Since no additional staff was assigned, Investigators have had to make many more visitations than previously.

26. HANDBOOK FOR COURT INVESTIGATORS.

27. Santa Clara County, as we noted, now has 23 professional conservators. Telephone Interview with the Santa Clara County Clerk's office (Aug. 15, 1994).

28. *See* RICHARD W. FOX, SO FAR DISORDERED IN MIND: INSANITY IN CALIFORNIA, 1870–1930 (1978).

29. *See generally* Marshall B. Kapp, *Evaluating Decisionmaking Capacity in the Elderly: A Review of Recent Literature,* 2 J. ELDER ABUSE & NEGLECT 15 (1990).

30. By 1979, in situations where the ward might be confused or otherwise need a lawyer, the court could refer cases to a list of private attorneys on a panel of conservatorship lawyers. CAL. PROB. CODE § 1470 (West 1991 & Supp. 1995).

31. An attorney who renders service to a conservatorship is entitled to "reasonable" compensation, which can be charged to the estate. CAL. PROB. CODE § 2640(c) (West 1991 & Supp. 1995); CAL. PROB. CODE § 2642 (West 1991).

32. On the whole, in our judgment, the lawyers' fees listed in the files did not seem excessive, although there did seem to be occasional examples where lawyers charged what seemed to be a good deal of money for relatively straightforward services. *See supra* note 16.

33. *See* LAWRENCE M. FRIEDMAN, YOUR TIME WILL COME: THE LAW OF AGE DISCRIMINATION AND MANDATORY RETIREMENT (1984).

CHAPTER 21

Personal Autonomy and Families

Mental incapacity is not the only source of erosion of personal autonomy. Older persons may either permit or merely endure the involvement of family members in very personal decisions, often medical care decisions.

Marshall B. Kapp

Who's the Parent Here? The Family's Impact on the Autonomy of Older Persons

I. Introduction

* * *

Professionals in gerontology, law, and ethics during the past two decades have studied several facets of the relationship formed between older persons and their families.[1] Very little of the scholarly activity thus far, however, has addressed the impact of family dynamics on the personal autonomy of the older person who still retains cognitive capacity to participate meaningfully in decision-making concerning financial, medical, housing, and other personal matters.

* * *

With regard to the relationship between health care professionals and patients, the prevailing contemporary legal and ethical opinions tilt strongly in favor of patient

Emory Law Journal, Vol. 41, No. 3, 773 (1992). Reprinted by permission.

self-determination, including the right to make bad decisions or to take foolish risks (i.e., the civil liberties model). In addition, current opinions oppose paternalism, however well-meaning and firmly predicated on professional expertise and experience, as a justification for uninvited intervention into the patient's life (i.e., the medical model).[2] In the realm of family participation, though, where a very different type of history, affectional bond, and exposure to direct consequences exists between the parties than in the case of paid professionals entering the scene,[3] there are no clearly articulated consensus guidelines for balancing the self-determination and the paternalistic models of decision-making and behavior. An equilibrium is especially elusive when the individual has fluctuating decisional capacity.[4]

Family members may act, on their own or in cooperation with each other and/or professional caregivers, to preserve and enhance the older person's autonomy or to override it. Family intervention ranges along the spectrum from assistance and support to persuasion and coercion.[5]

Several arguments support the idea of family participation as an enhancer of, and contributor to, the older person's autonomy.[6] First, people live their lives embedded within various relationships, among which the family for most of us is paramount. Since these relationships tend to grow stronger over time, they take on added significance for most older persons. These relationships have an empowering quality, contributing to the older person's potential for positive, affirmative autonomy to think and act, as opposed to the simple, negative autonomy to be left alone.[7] In this view, power is not a zero-sum game in which there is a finite amount that has to be divided among the participants and one party's gain or domination is another party's corresponding loss or disenfranchisement. Instead, sharing power multiplies it through a collaborative, supportive exercise in which the parties and their sense of control grow individually and collectively.

Another point underlying shared decision-making for older persons is the growing body of data suggesting that many individuals of advanced years possess less desire for information about, and control over, health care decision-making than do their younger counterparts.[8] Many older persons welcome the opportunity to share what they perceive as the burden, not just the right, of decision-making. Contrary to the pure autonomy model, some persons may not want to be empowered exclusively.[9]

* * *

Another reason an older person may be willing to share authority with family members is to minimize family burden. By sharing decisions, the individual may intend to reduce feelings of tension or guilt that otherwise might bother a family which believes it must override the patient's wishes on a specific issue. The family's involvement may instill the individual's choice with special meaning, as an opportunity for the individual to do something unselfishly positive for others by taking into account the impact of the decision on the family.[10]

Even where the older person is decisionally capable, he or she may still have serious communication problems with formal caregivers for reasons ranging from linguistic or ethnic differences to sensory impairments. In such circumstances, involving family members in the participatory loop facilitates the requisite communication or translation of information and questions between formal caregiver and older person, and thereby enhances the latter's autonomy.

* * *

In actual practice, however, family members may exercise the medical model of paternalistic decision-making even where the older person maintains a high degree of decisional capacity, as long as the individual does not protest too loudly.[11] The family may adopt as its chief concern the maintenance of a high degree of control over the older family member's environment,[12] resulting in the restriction of the older person's freedom in order to eliminate or reduce risks while maximizing protection and safety.[13] Family members who seek to reach filial domination, in which the older person is hectored into doing what the family member wants done, ordinarily are motivated by a conviction that they really know what is in the best interests of their relative, although less noble reasons, such as the opportunity for exercising dominion in a family that has a long history of rivalry for preeminence, are possible.[14] In an illustration of the conflicting and confusing factual data underlying ethical and legal discussion in this area, at least one study suggests that families may be more concerned about autonomy than are the elderly themselves. Often, the elderly are more worried about their own health and safety than in preserving the principle of self-determination.[15]

* * *

Notes

1. Throughout this essay, the term "family" will be used in an expansive sense, while recognizing that it is usually spouses and adult children who are involved in decision-making with and for older persons. See Amy L. Brown, *Broadening Anachronistic Notions of "Family" in Proxy Decision-Making for Unmarried Adults,* 41 HASTINGS L.J. 1029 (1990).

2. For a discussion of the tension between the medical and civil liberties models in the context of services to the aged, see Arthur Schafer, *Civil Liberties and the Elderly Patient, in* ETHICS AND AGING: THE RIGHT TO LIVE, THE RIGHT TO DIE 208–09 (James E. Thornton & Earl R. Winkler eds., 1988).

3. *See* [Amy Horowitz et al., *A Conceptual and Empirical Exploration of Personal Autonomy Issues Within Family Caregiving Relationships,* 31 GERONTOLOGIST 23, 30 (1991)]; Steven H. Miles, *Paternalism, Family Duties, and My Aunt Maude,* 259 JAMA 2582 (1988).

4. Clara C. Pratt et al., *Ethical Concerns of Family Caregivers to Dementia Patients,* 27 GERONTOLOGIST 632, 636 (1987).

5. Sara T. Frye, *Health Care and Decision-Making, in* ETHICS AND AGING 171, 174–76 (Nancy S. Jecker ed., 1991).

6. Marshall B. Kapp, *Health Care Decision-Making by the Elderly: I Get By with a Little Help from My Family,* 31 GERONTOLOGIST 619 (1991).

7. Phillip G. Clark, *Individual Autonomy, Cooperative Empowerment, and Planning for Long-Term Care Decision-Making,* 1 J. AGING STUD. 65 (1987).

8. Roberta A. Smith et al., *Health Care Implications of Desire and Expectancy for Control in Elderly Adults,* 43 J. GERONTOLOGY: PSYCHOL. SCI. 1 (1988).

9. [See Marshall B. Kapp, *Medical Empowerment of the Elderly,* 19 HASTINGS CENTER REP. 5 (July/Aug. 1989).]

10. [See Dallas M. High, *A New Myth About Families of Older People?*, 31 GERONTOLOGIST 611 (1991)], at 613; Braulio Montalvo, *The Patient Chose to Die: Why?*, 31 GERONTOLOGIST 700, 701 (1991).

11. *See* Miles, *supra* note 3.

12. *See* Gregory C. Smith et al., *Problems Identified by Family Caregivers in Counseling*, 31 GERONTOLOGIST 15 (1991).

13. *See* Rosalie A. Kane & James R. Reinardy, *Family Caregiving in Home Care, in* HOME HEALTH CARE OPTIONS: A GUIDE FOR OLDER PERSONS AND CONCERNED FAMILIES 89, 102–03, 111–12 (Connie Zuckerman et al. eds., 1990).

14. *See* Herbert S. Donow, *Am I My Father's Keeper? Sons as Caregivers*, 31 GERONTOLOGIST 709 (1991). Donow reviews TOM KOCH, MIRRORED LIVES (1990) and PHILIP ROTH, PATRIMONY (1991); the author states that if he could add a subtitle to these books, it might be "How I Achieved Dominion Over My Dad."

15. [See Amy Horowitz et al., *A Conceptual and Empirical Exploration of Personal Autonomy Issues Within Family Caregiving Relationships*, 31 GERONTOLOGIST 23, 30 (1991)], at 25–26.

In a very personal essay, Professor Watson argues that the family has a very important role to play in the lives of the elderly. In his view, the "party at interest" is not the older person, nor the younger family member, but rather the family as an entity.

Sidney D. Watson

When Parents Die: A Response to *Before Guardianship: Abuse of Patient Rights Behind Closed Doors*

I.

* * *

While acknowledging that intrafamily disputes may arise, . . . I begin with a slightly different premise, for I think it is inaccurate to assume at the outset that the interests of the patient and family compete.

* * *

With good reason, I reject the concept of radical individualism in the context of home and institutional health care decisions for the elderly. First, autonomy and dig-

Emory Law Journal, Vol. 41, No. 3, 863 (1992). Reprinted by permission.

nity premises frequently make little sense where death and dying loom great. Second, on still broader terms, unless the family is truly dysfunctional. . . . It denies who we are. When this denial is imposed upon clients by the way in which they are represented, the problem they bring to us is distorted and, as others have argued, this is done to fit what is thought of as our expertise.[1]

The crux of my position is that any process or form of representation must take account of both the individual and his or her ongoing relationships within a family and a community. Rather than just announcing this truth of who we are in these decisions, as I have done so far, and rather than offering my analysis of why this is so, I want instead to try to display this truth and to do so, as Tom Shaffer tells us, in the way truths are best displayed, by telling a story.[2] The story I want to tell is mine. It is the story of my parents' death. It is a story from which I neither claim nor want analytical distance.[3] It comes to you with all the emotions our clients bring to us when they ask for our assistance in the decision to place a parent in a nursing home or to care for a parent in one's own home. At their core these are emotional issues—at times overpoweringly so. Watching a parent or other loved one die forces us to confront all our fears and loneliness. It forces us to confront our own mortality more forcefully perhaps than any other experience. It is only through telling my own story that I am able to share with you the enormity of the emotion and make plain why it is that liberal theory marginalizes the emotional connections within these decisions to nonexistence. It is the emotion that makes this law different, and that demands representational sensibilities to which traditional models are often oblivious. Liberalism has a hard time with the search for the love that should provide the foundations for and disclose the common interests that underlie these decisions.

II.

In February 1990, my father, Bob,[4] was diagnosed with terminal, inoperable lung cancer. Bob was an energetic, robust man. He was always outside: fixing things, planting vegetables, mowing the grass, manicuring the hedges, catching fish (or trying), or simply visiting. Suddenly, however, the doctors gave him six months to a year to live. He lay in bed without the strength to do the things he enjoyed.

My parents were stricken. My mother had suffered from chronic leukemia for three years, and Bob had lovingly cared for her. As a couple, my mother and father had struggled to face my mother's certain death from leukemia, but neither of them ever contemplated that my father would be the first to die. Bob felt that by getting cancer and dying he was abandoning my mother. My mother was devastated that her husband and lover of twenty years was going to die and she would be left alone.

As the initial shock wore off, or settled in, we began to think about the next few months—the months that would inevitably lead to Bob's death. Our immediate, strong instincts were to bring Bob home to die. My mother's shock and grief was compounded by her almost pathological fear of hospitals and nursing homes. The hospital made her nervous and edgy; she did not want Bob to be there. In Bob's pain and weakness, he lost the joy for life that was his core. My brother and I thought Bob would be happier at home where he could be around the land and water he loved, and around Amos, his black labrador.

Getting Bob home was not easy. We needed equipment, services, people, and, of course, funds to pay for such things. My brother, a trained social worker, made things happen. He spent days phoning and visiting people. Finally, he found the right social service agencies, health care providers, and financially responsible parties. He located the necessary equipment, services, and personnel. He also took more than a month's leave from work so that he could be available, at least at the beginning, to provide additional care for Bob and emotional support for my mother.

As my brother marshaled the available resources, reality intruded—new fears. My mother was torn. She loved Bob deeply and wanted to do what she thought was the "right" thing: to take Bob home. At the same time, though, the reality was that her chronic illness left her ill, tired, and afraid. Three years of battling leukemia had taken its toll. Each daily three-hour round-trip drive to the hospital made her weaker and more tired. She was afraid of the hospital, but she was also fearful that no matter what help was provided, she would not be able to care for Bob. She was scared to watch her husband, lover, and best friend die.

My mother, Bob in his brief moments of apparent lucidity, and all four children began to discuss this fear. The conversations were hard. They were full of pain and doubt and searching. Sometimes they were angry. Often they were full of loss. A nurse trained in hospice care sat with us—sometimes with one of us alone, sometimes in conversation with all or portions of the family. Somehow during these conversations we were able to grab hold of our commonality, our common concerns and desires, which was the love and caring we shared for Bob. We came to a decision. It was not a perfect decision, but it affirmed Bob and Mom and encompassed all of our needs and pain.

Bob stayed in the hospital hospice unit to die. Bob's wish that he get no further treatment was honored. Mom had a bed to sleep in so she did not have to drive to the hospital every day. We children could be with Bob and Mom both day and night.

The professionals helped Mom see that Bob's death was drawing near. One afternoon, the children and grandchildren filled Bob's hospital room and gathered around him.

That night, Bob died. Mom lay in her bed near Bob; his son and grandson held his hands.

III.

Not long after Bob died, Mom left her Virginia home to live near me in Macon, Georgia. Although she had close friends and neighbors in her rural community, she knew her death was probably no more than two years away. She wanted to be with family.

My mother was an independent, self-reliant woman reluctant to ask anyone for help. I learned my independence and self-reliance from her. I revel in living alone and find strength and solace in solitude. I gladly moved away from home as soon as I graduated from high school. Now my mother was moving to town!

Even when my mother moved to Macon, she maintained her independence. She had sworn for as long as I knew her that she would never be dependent on or live with one of her children. So when she moved, it was into her own apartment.

As Mom's leukemia progressed, however, she became weaker and more frail. She soon became too weak to fix meals; later she was even too frail to get a drink of water. Nevertheless, Mom's independence and self-reliance never waned: she did not want to live with her daughter! She did not want to depend on anyone else, especially her children.

I was worried. Mom was not getting enough to eat. She became dehydrated from lack of water. She did not have the energy to leave her apartment or even to talk on the phone. She was often alone and even more often lonely. I was scared for her to live alone. I was even more scared of what it would be like for us to live together. As Mom's condition continued to deteriorate, the choices lessened. Finally, reluctantly, I decided there was no other choice. Mom needed to live with me.

With trepidation, I tried to convince Mom that the sensible thing was for her to come live with me. When that failed, I played on her guilt. I spent evenings sleeping on her couch fully dressed so she would see me tired and rumpled. When none of these strategies worked, I simply announced that I was moving her. I terminated her apartment lease, called the movers, packed her possessions, and moved my mother into my home. Mom was too sick to fight. She resigned herself to my decision, but anticipated the worst.

For both of us, living together was at once a source of great joy and great frustration. We relived the fights we had when I was fifteen years old—my hair was wrong, my clothes were wrong, and my bedroom was still a mess. But even as we fought, we grew closer. We lay together in Mom's bed and talked as we had never talked before. We spoke of my childhood, of Mom's childhood, of love and pain, of flowers and cats, and of death. And as we sat together Mom turned to me, smiled, and said, "You know, this is where I belong—this is good—why didn't we do this sooner?"

As my mother weakened, I cared for her and mothered her. Yet even within hours of her death, in some of her last words to me, Mom was still mothering and caring for me, saying, "Hey, squirt, what do you think you're doing!"

My mother and I lived together for six months. She died on October 15, 1991. She was in her own bed, in what had become her bedroom. I was holding her hand and my brother was stroking her shoulder.

IV.

* * *

The problem with using rights theory to analyze long-term health care decisions for the terminally ill is that it ignores the ongoing relationships, the connectedness, and the dependence within which we know ourselves. Rights theory is not premised on a search for the commonality and abundance that endures in loving relationships. Yes, my mother wanted to be independent and live independently. Yes, she valued her autonomy and independence. But her relationships with her children were also a primary concern—so primary that it would be wrong to think of her as having a self apart from the self that was mother. She valued her autonomy and independence, but she did so because she thought it strengthened her family. It strengthened what she brought to us and it strengthened the "us." When her autonomy and independence ceased to strengthen us, it was—rightly and justly—subordinated to that relationship.

Bob did not need an advocate to argue his autonomy interests against those of my mother and the children. In both dying experiences, what was needed were professionals sensitive to our family: lawyers and others who could develop solutions that took into account our past as a family, who strengthened and supported the individuals within these relationships, and who strove to bring to the surface the love at the center.

Thus, the question is not "Who represents Bob?" or "Who represents Mom?" It is "Who represents—who understands—this family, its history, its web of connections, and its love?"

We need to begin thinking of lawyers and other professionals who are called upon to counsel families with terminally ill members as working for the family. The lawyer to the family practices a deeper form of representation than is provided by the intermediator proposed by the Model Rules of Professional Conduct, who withdraws if conflict develops among the individual members of the group.[5] The lawyer to the family must recognize that conflicts are inherent in ongoing relationships and seek to mediate and to resolve those conflicts by strengthening—or at least not undermining—the healthy aspects of the ongoing relationship. He or she should seek to uncover common ground. Thus, the lawyer serves as a problem-solver and facilitator for the group with the problem defined, not based upon the liberal individualistic assumptions that suit the lawyer's presumed expertise, but upon relationships as they exist in our complex world.

* * *

Notes

1. Donald A. Schon, The Reflective Practitioner 39–42 (1983).
2. *See generally* Thomas L. Shaffer, Faith and the Professions (1987).
3. However, I do claim the creative paradox of detachment.
4. Technically, it is my stepfather, Harry R. Bell, of whom I speak. However, Webster's Dictionary defines father as a male parent or one deserving the respect and love given to a father. The endearment "father" more accurately describes my relationship with Bob.
5. *See* Model Rules of Professional Conduct Rule 2.2 (1983).

CHAPTER 22

Alternatives to Guardianship

While guardianship is one formal legal response to mental incapacity, it is not the only solution. Individuals can largely obviate the need for guardianship if they plan for the possibility of incapacity. Signing an advance health care directive or appointing a surrogate health care decision maker eliminates one of the most common reasons for seeking a personal guardian. Property management can be dealt with by joint property arrangements, revocable trusts, or by signing a durable power of attorney. The following article describes several of these options.

Ramona C. Rains

Planning Tools Available to the Elderly Client

* * *

II. Conservatorship and Durable Power of Attorney

* * *

Sometimes called the "foundation of estate planning for disability,"[1] the durable power of attorney for financial management ("durable power of attorney") is a valuable tool in planning for the possibility of future incompetence or disability. It is especially appropriate for clients with modest assets who may not want or need more

American Journal of Trial Advocacy, Vol. 19, No. 3, 599 (1996). Reprinted by permission.

complicated trust arrangements.[2] If well drafted, the durable power of attorney will enable the client to avoid the costly, time-consuming, and sometimes embarrassing process of court-appointed guardianship or conservatorship[3] should he become unable to manage his own affairs.

The durable power of attorney allows the principal to grant a third party the power to act in his stead in a variety of situations. The durable power of attorney can be very broad, allowing the agent to perform all but a few nondelegable acts, or more limited, restricting the agent to activities relating to only specifically designated accounts or acts. To execute a durable power of attorney, the principal must have sufficient mental capacity to understand that he is appointing someone else to handle his financial affairs.[4] It is not necessary that the principal understand how the appointee will manage the assets.[5] Moreover, unlike the common law power of attorney, which expired when the principal became incompetent, the durable power of attorney survives the incapacity of the principal.[6]

To qualify as a durable power of attorney, the document creating this duty must be in writing and must contain words sufficient to demonstrate that the principal intended to create a durable power of attorney.[7] The Uniform Probate Code defines a durable power of attorney as

> a power of attorney by which a principal designates another his attorney in fact in writing and the writing contains the words "This power of attorney shall not be affected by subsequent disability or incapacity of the principal, or lapse of time," or "This power of attorney shall become effective upon the disability or incapacity of the principal," or similar words showing the intent of the principal that the authority conferred shall be exercisable notwithstanding the principal's subsequent disability or incapacity.[8]

The code thus provides for two different types of durable power of attorney—immediate and "springing." The first type is intended to take effect immediately upon execution of the durable power of attorney. The latter is intended to spring into effect at the occurrence of some event, such as the disability of the principal.

The appropriate type of durable power of attorney will depend on the goals and circumstances of the client. If the client is in relatively good health, he may be reluctant to give another person the power to act for him. The springing durable power of attorney may offer the protection the client needs in the event of incapacity, without any feeling that he has currently sacrificed control. There are, however, weaknesses in the springing durable power of attorney. Individuals, institutions and companies may be reluctant to honor a power of attorney that does not become effective until the occurrence of a particular event.[9] One possible solution to this problem is to include an indemnification clause in the document that would absolve the party honoring the document in good faith from any liability.[10] Another problem associated with the springing durable power of attorney is the difficulty inherent in determining when a person has become incapacitated.[11] If it becomes necessary to have a court determine the mental capacity of the principal, part of the benefit of the durable power of attorney over conservatorship proceedings will be defeated. Some commentators suggest designating an attorney or relative to decide whether the individual has become incapacitated, thus triggering the springing durable power of attorney.[12] Another technique is to state in the durable power of attorney that the agent's affidavit will serve as conclusive proof that the springing durable power of attorney has been triggered.[13] If the client is concerned that the agent will abuse the durable power of attorney, the attorney may want to advise his client to choose another agent. Not all states recognize the springing durable power of attorney; thus, the attorney should be aware of the current law in the jurisdiction in which he practices.[14]

A durable power of attorney can be terminated at will by the competent principal.[15] However, once the principal becomes incompetent or incapacitated, he will be unable to revoke a previously executed durable power of attorney.[16]

* * *

It should be noted that the existence of a durable power of attorney does not prevent an interested party from requesting that a court appoint a conservator, thus potentially defeating the intentions of the principal.[17] This is most likely to happen when conflicts arise between family members and the attorney-in-fact.

* * *

While a durable power of attorney can be very powerful and broad, certain powers are nevertheless nondelegable. These nondelegable powers include: the power to make, amend, or revoke a will; the power to change insurance beneficiaries; the power to contract a marriage; the power to take an oath; the power to vote; and the power to perform a personal service contract.[18]

* * *

III. Living Wills

A common desire of many elderly people is to remain autonomous and self-sufficient until death. They do not want to burden their children, friends, or extended family.[19] Advancements in medical technology have resulted in an increasing number of elderly patients being kept alive for extended periods in a "persistent vegetative state"[20] or even in a state of "brain death."[21] In 1991, approximately ten thousand people in irreversible comas were being kept alive by artificial means.[22] Relatives of the patient may petition hospitals or the courts to remove the life sustaining measures,[23] but courts are reluctant to make such decisions at the demand of someone other than the patient because of the state's interest in the preservation of life.[24] In addition, family members may find themselves unable to make the decision to remove life support, despite the knowledge that the patient will never recover.[25] A living will, sometimes called an antidysthansia contract,[26] an advanced directive,[27] or an advance health care directive,[28] is one solution available to the elderly client who wishes to maintain as much control as possible over his own terminal care.

A living will can be defined as "an informed medical consent statement authorizing the refusal or discontinuance of further medical treatment by artificial means or devices."[29] The living will "documents a person's treatment preferences when, after certain triggering conditions have occurred, that person is unable to communicate these preferences."[30] The living will protects physicians against liability when complying with the patient's wishes, and assures the patient's family that those wishes are being carried out.[31]

* * *

To execute a living will, the maker must be a competent adult who is capable of understanding the meaning and consequences of the document that he is executing.[32] Most statutes require that the patient be "terminally" ill before the living will can be triggered.[33] This presents a problem in that most states do not define what constitutes a terminal illness.[34] Some scholars say that a terminal illness is an "incurable or irreversible condition that, without the administration of life-sustaining treatment, will, in the opinion of the attending physician, result in death within a relatively short time."[35] Others have said that "life itself is a terminal condition, and old age more obviously so."[36]

Because the majority of jurisdictions with living will statutes require the attending physician to certify that the condition is terminal,[37] the job of defining terminal usually falls to the physician. Because of the ambiguity inherent in the language of living will statutes, physicians may be hesitant to follow the terms of the document prior to exhausting virtually all known treatments in an attempt to reverse the patient's condition.[38] One method employed by drafters to assist physicians in interpreting the term "terminally ill" is to include a list of specific conditions or circumstances and the treatments that the patient wishes to receive or forego in those circumstances.

* * *

Formalities required for the execution of a living will vary from state to state. Some states honor an oral living will.[39] A number of state statutes prohibit persons such as those with an interest in the estate, persons with responsibility for the declarant's medical expenses, or the attending physician from acting as a witness.[40] A number of states require that the living will be notarized.[41] A few states with living will statutes require that the form provided be substantially or exactly followed.[42] Typically, living wills are silent as to duration, but the drafter should check his own state's statute regularly to be aware of any changes to existing legislation.[43]

The majority of states having living will statutes do not hold the physician liable for failure to comply with the terms of the will.[44] Thirty-nine states require a physician who refuses to comply to transfer the patient to a physician who will follow the terms of the will.[45] Twelve states, and the District of Columbia, penalize physicians who do not comply with the terms of a valid living will.[46]

Following are suggestions for drafting an effective living will:

- Discuss the terms of the living will with a physician. If the physician does not seem to understand the client's wishes, or does not seem willing to comply, the client may consider changing physicians.
- Include a copy of the living will in the client's medical file.

- Use specific and detailed language to describe treatment the client does or does not want to receive.
- Sign and date the document. The client should initial and redate the will every five years so it is clear that the wishes of the client have not changed since the original drafting of the will.
- Use two witnesses who are not relatives of the client nor beneficiaries of his estate.
- Keep the original of the document in a safe, accessible place. Do not keep the original in a safe deposit box.[47]

The drafting of a living will must be done carefully and with an eye toward clarity to ensure that the client's wishes will be given effect. The drafter must be sure to consult statutes and case law in his jurisdiction. This is important not only to comply with the state's requirements, but also to avoid pitfalls and mistakes suffered by parties to earlier litigation.

IV. Durable Health Care Power of Attorney

An alternative to the living will, a durable health care power of attorney allows the client to delegate authority to a third party to make a variety of health care decisions.[48] In many ways, the durable health care power of attorney may be a stronger, more useful instrument than the traditional living will. Living wills may not be uniformly honored by the patient's physician, hospital, or state.[49] The durable health care power of attorney, in contrast, places the power to make the decision to terminate life support in the control of an agent appointed by the patient.[50] Any questions of liability on the part of the physician are eliminated, and the physician can be required to follow the patient's wishes as they are expressed through his agent.[51]

As discussed above, the living will, in most jurisdictions, is triggered only when the patient is found by the attending physician to be in a terminal condition or in a persistent vegetative state.[52] Thus, the living will may never be triggered in a case where the patient has a degenerative disease such as Alzheimer's that is not deemed to satisfy the terminal condition or persistent vegetative state requirements. The durable health care power of attorney, in contrast, is a springing power of attorney and springs into effect when the principal becomes incompetent.[53]

Where living wills primarily apply to decisions relating to suspending or continuing life sustaining treatments, the durable health care power of attorney grants the agent a broader variety of powers. For example, the holder of a durable health care power of attorney is authorized to make decisions relating to medication, home health care services, consent to surgery, and similar day-to-day decisions in addition to decisions relating to life-sustaining treatment.[54] In addition, the durable health care power of attorney may delegate related powers necessary to give effect to the patient's wishes such as access to medical records, power to access funds to pay for health care, and the power to hire and terminate home health care personnel.[55]

The durable health care power of attorney may be especially useful in a case where the client does not want to leave the responsibility of making health care decisions, in particular those relating to termination of life support, to members of his family. The principal may feel that the decision would be too difficult, or in some cases, too easy, for close family members to make. The durable health care power of appointment allows the client to select the person who will, upon his incompetence, have the power to make medical decisions.

Finally, the durable health care power of attorney may more likely ensure that the true wishes of the patient will be honored. The agent acting under a durable health care power of attorney will presumably be someone who knows the patient well and has had occasion to discuss a variety of possible decisions with the patient. Thus, the agent will likely be more capable of predicting what the patient would want than would a physician acting from the "laundry list" of instructions contained in a living will. The durable health care power of attorney is also less likely to be overlooked or lost in the patient's medical file because the agent will be present and acting as an advocate for the patient.[56]

Despite the discussion above, the living will may still be a better choice than the durable health care power of attorney for some clients. Some hospitals may be reluctant to end life-support procedures without express authorization.[57] Thus, it may be advisable to draft both a living will and a durable health care power of attorney.[58] Moreover, the living will may be a better choice than the durable health care power of attorney in situations where the client is already in the final stages of a terminal illness, making it likely that the conditions triggering a living will may soon be met.[59] Also, some clients may have difficulty selecting an agent for a durable health care power of attorney.[60] For these clients, the burden of choosing the agent may outweigh the risks associated with the living will.

Ultimately, the choice between a living will and a durable health care power of attorney, or a combination of the two, depends on the individual circumstances and wishes of the client, coupled with the legislative environment of the state in which the client lives. It is the job of the attorney to be fully aware of both options in order to properly advise the client.

* * *

Notes

1. Susan F. Buchanan & James W. Buchanan III, *Strategies for Clients Residing in Nursing Homes,* 20 EST. PLAN. 27 (1993).

2. Paul A. Sturgul, *Financial Durable Powers of Attorney,* 41 PRAC. LAW., July 1995, at 21, 22.

3. Often, the terms conservator and guardian are used interchangeably. Because some states use the term guardian to describe a person appointed for a minor and conservator to describe a person appointed for someone other than a minor, the term "conservator" is used in this Note.

4. F. Douglas Lofton, *Determining Legal Mental Capacity,* NAT'L B. ASS'N MAG., May–June 1995, at 14.

5. *Id.* at 15.

6. *See* Sturgul, *supra* note 2, at 22.

7. [Michael N. Schmitt & Steven A. Hatfield, *The Durable Power of Attorney: Applications and Limitations,* 132 MIL. L. REV. 203, 204 (1991).]

8. UNIF. PROB. CODE § 5-501, 8 U.L.A. 341 (1990).

9. *See* Sturgul, *supra* note 2, at 23.

10. *Id.* at 24.

11. *Id.* at 25.

12. *Id.* at 26.

13. [Linda S. Whitton, *Durable Powers as a Hedge Against Guardianship: Should the Attorney-at-Law Accept Appointment as Attorney-in-Fact?,* 2 ELDER L.J. 39, 48 (1994)], at 58–59.

14. *E.g.,* S.C. CODE ANN. § 62-5-501(A) (Law. Co-op. Supp. 1995) (recognizing immediate and continuing powers of attorney).

15. [Michael N. Schmitt & Steven A. Hatfield, *The Durable Power of Attorney: Applications and Limitations,* 132 MIL. L. REV. 203, 204 (1991)], at 207.

16. *Id.*

17. Sturgul, *supra* note 2, at 35.

18. *See* Schmitt & Hatfield, *supra* note 7, at 210; Sturgul, *supra* note 2, at 29–30. This list is not exhaustive, nor may all of the powers listed be prohibited in every state. The attorney should check the statutes in his state for an applicable list of non-delegable powers in his jurisdiction.

19. *See* Alfred F. Conard, *Elder Choice,* 19 AM. J.L. & MED. 233, 256 (1993).

20. Shelley Shepherd, Note, *Living Wills: Why a Patient's Last Wishes are not Always Respected,* 34 HOW. L.J. 229 (1991). This is a state of being "awake, yet not totally aware." *Id.* at 230. The condition is characterized by an inability to eat, speak or recognize others. *Id.*

21. Susan J. Steinle, Note, *Living Wills in the United States and Canada: A Comparative Analysis,* 24 CASE W. RES. J. INT'L L. 435 (1992).

22. Shepherd, *supra* note 20, at 229.

23. *Id.* at 230.

24. *Id.; see* Cruzan v. Director, Missouri Dep't of Health, 497 U.S. 261, 110 S. Ct. 2841, 111 L. Ed. 2d 224 (1990).

25. Conard, *supra* note 19, at 242.

26. Shepherd, *supra* note 20, at 231.

27. Susan J. Nanovic, Comment, *The Living Will: Preservation of the Right-to-Die Demands Clarity and Consistency,* 95 DICK. L. REV. 209, 210 (1990).

28. Conard, *supra* note 19, at 237.

29. Shepherd, *supra* note 20, at 231.

30. Nanovic, *supra* note 27, at 210.

31. Steinle, *supra* note 21, at 436.

32. Steinle, *supra* note 21, at 442–43.

33. *See, e.g.,* FLA. STAT. ANN. § 765.303 (West Supp. 1996). *But see* CONN. GEN. STAT. ANN. § 19a-571(a)(2) (West Supp. 1996); MD. CODE ANN., HEALTH-GEN. § 5-602(e)(1) (Supp. 1995); N.J. STAT. ANN. § 26:2H-53.3 (West Supp. 1995); OKLA. STAT. ANN. tit. 63, S 3101.5.A.2 (West

Supp. 1996); TENN. CODE ANN. § 32-11-107 (Supp. 1995); TEX. HEALTH & SAFETY CODE ANN. § 672.008 (West 1992).

34. *See* Steinle, *supra* note 21, at 443 & n.46.

35. Nanovic, *supra* note 27, at 217 (quoting prefatory note to UNIF. RIGHTS OF THE TERMINALLY ILL ACT 9B U.L.A. 609 (1989)).

36. Conard, *supra* note 19, at 246.

37. Steinle, *supra* note 21, at 443–44.

38. *See* Shepherd, *supra* note 26, at 239.

39. *See* CONN. GEN. STAT. ANN. § 19a-578(b) (West Supp. 1996); FLA. STAT. ANN. § 765.101(1) (West Supp. 1996); LA. REV. STAT. ANN. § 40:1299.58.2(2) (West 1992); MD. CODE ANN., HEALTH-GEN. § 5-602(d) (Supp. 1995); TEX. HEALTH & SAFETY CODE ANN. § 672.005 (West 1992); VA. CODE ANN. § 54.1-2983 (Michie 1994).

40. See Steinle, *supra* note 21, at 447.

41. *See id.* at 448.

42. Steinle, *supra* note 21, at 448 & n.74. The attorney should consult the applicable statute in his state to determine language requirements.

43. Conard, *supra* note 19, at 251.

44. Steinle, *supra* note 21, at 450.

45. *Id.* at 450–51.

46. *Id.* at 451.

47. Shepherd, *supra* note 20, at 240. Regarding specificity, Shepherd suggests saying "Should I ever have a terminal illness, with irreversible brain damage that makes me unable to recognize people or to swallow, I would (or would not) want to be connected to a respirator, cardiopulmonary resuscitation, or a feeding tube," as opposed to only saying, "I do not wish to receive heroic measures." *Id.*

48. Sally M. Wagley, *After* Cruzan: *The Changing Art of Drafting Living Wills and Durable Powers of Attorney*, 7 ME. B.J. 160, 161 (1992).

49. Cynthia M. Garraty, *Durable Power of Attorney for Health Care: A Better Choice*, 7 CONN. PROB. L.J. 115, 129 (1992). Other weaknesses include the failure of some jurisdictions to relieve physicians and hospitals from criminal liability if life-support is withdrawn, the failure to require that the physician recognize a living will, and the failure of most states to require a physician who refuses to honor the living will to transfer to another physician. *Id.*

50. Garraty, *supra* note 49, at 131.

51. *Id.*

52. *See supra* note 33 and accompanying text.

53. Garraty, *supra* note 49, at 131. While the durable health care power of attorney is generally not required to be springing, it is difficult to imagine an occasion when a third party would need to make a health care decision for a competent person.

54. Wagley, *supra* note 48, at 161.

55. *Id.*

56. *Id.*

57. *Id.*

58. *Id.* In some cases, it is not advisable to draft both a living will and a durable health care power of attorney. In Illinois, for example, the living will statute limits a person's right to direct withdrawal of feeding and hydration. *See* Howard B. Eisenberg, *Durable Power of Attorney v. Living Will: Counseling Older Clients*, 79 ILL. B.J. 384, 386 (1991). That power is not limited under

a durable health care power of attorney. *Id.* Thus, the existence of both documents could cause conflict if the patient is being kept alive by such measures and the attorney-in-fact decided that these measures should be withdrawn. *Id.* at 387. The attorney should consult the living will statute in his state to avoid a similar conflict when advising that both documents should be prepared.

59. Eisenberg, *supra* note 58, at 387.

60. *Id.*

Another planning device to deal with mental incapacity is the revocable trust, or as it is commonly called, the "living trust." A revocable living trust is a trust established by the individual, known as the settlor, under which the settlor retains the right to the income and principal, and the right to alter, amend, or revoke the trust at any time. The settlor transfers into the trust all or some portion of his assets. However, because the trust is revocable, the trust is ignored for federal income tax purposes, and all the trust income is considered to be taxable income of the settlor. Thus, the trust yields no income tax advantages. The settlor usually acts as the sole trustee of the trust. At the death of the settlor, the trust becomes irrevocable, and the assets are distributed according to the provisions of the trust. For example, the trust might terminate and the assets distributed to the settlor's spouse or children. Or the trust could continue, with its income paid to the settlor's children, and then terminate at the death of the last surviving child, with the principal distributed to the settlor's grandchildren. Even though the settlor's assets were in the trust, because the trust was revocable and could benefit the settlor, the value of those assets is nevertheless included in the settlor's estate for federal estate tax purposes. Therefore, the living trust does not reduce the possibility of federal estate taxes.

Because a living trust offers no federal income tax or estate tax advantages, its attraction is the avoidance of probate and the planning for incapacity. The trust assets are not included in probate (the legal term for property passing by a "will" or "intestacy") because technically the property was not owned by the settlor at the time of death. Rather, the trust, in the representative of the trustee, owned the property. Thus, after the death of the settlor, the property continues to be owned by the trust (represented by the successor trustee to the settlor), and the property is distributed according to the provisions of the trust, not the will. Many lay persons believe that avoiding probate will save court costs, fees, and lawyer charges and permit more rapid distribution of assets. Most lawyers disagree. Probate fees in most states are very minor, and the cost for an attorney is not affected because one still must be hired to assist in filing state death and federal estate tax returns. Moreover, the settlor is likely have some assets, such as personal property, not included in the trust that will require the estate (although not the assets in the trust) to go through probate. The trust may be able to distribute assets more quickly than a probated estate, but not if the estate is liable for federal estate or state death taxes. In those instances, since the trustee is personally liable for unpaid taxes, the trustee will prudently delay distributions until the federal estate taxes and state death taxes are paid.

If the avoidance of probate is not a compelling reason for a living trust, planning for the possible incapacity of the settlor may well be a reason to create one. Because it is fundamental trust law that an incapacitated person cannot act as a trustee, the living trust will specifically provide that if the settlor/trustee should become incapacitated, a named successor trustee will take over administration of the trust. Often the successor trustee is the settlor's spouse or a child, though it may also be a corporate trustee, such as a bank. The standard that the successor trustee takes over in the event of the settlor's incapacity means that the settlor cannot revoke the trust or name a new trustee, since incapacity renders a settlor incapable of altering, amending, or revoking a trust. A demented, incapacitated settlor, for example, cannot attempt to terminate the trust and regain control of its assets. With the assets safely guarded within the trust, the settlor has the comfort of knowing that the assets will be properly managed without the need for guardianship in the event that he or she becomes incapacitated.

Of course, in theory, a well drawn durable power of attorney should be able to grant an agent sufficient authority to manage the assets of an incapacitated settlor. But in practice, durable powers of attorney are not always honored by third parties. (Trustees rarely have that difficulty.) Financial institutions are often more accepting of a trust arrangement. Moreover, even if an incapacitated person has a durable power of attorney, a third party may still file for guardianship by claiming that the agent is not acting in the incapacitated person's best interest. A trust and the trustees are much less susceptible to court interference as long as the trustees abide by the instructions in the trust document. A durable power of attorney terminates upon the death of the principal, but a trust can be drafted so that it continues to operate after the death of the settlor.

Part V

Health Care Decision Making

As we grow older we grow sicker. The effects of acute sickness or injury—such as the flu or a broken bone—become more severe, and chronic illness—such as heart conditions or arthritis—become commonplace. The increased need for medical care among the old raises intense concern over how to pay for it (discussed in Part VII). Indeed, paying for health care and for long-term care might well be the most worrisome aspects of old age. Even if the older person has the wherewithal to pay for health care, another problem plagues older patients: how to make health care decisions in the face of declining mental capacity. As discussed in the previous chapter, many older persons—though certainly not all—suffer a decline in mental capacity. For some, that decline is severe enough to interfere with their ability to make rational decisions about their health care, a complex and confusing enough subject even for the clear of mind and even more difficult if it involves end-of-life decisions. If, because of mental incapacity, patients are unable to participate in their health care decisions, who is authorized to make those decisions? That question is the subject of this chapter.

CHAPTER 23

The Doctrine of Informed Consent

The need for a mentally competent patient who is capable of rationally participating in health care decisions arises from the doctrine of informed consent, which is described and analyzed in the following material.

William M. Altman, Patricia A. Parmelee, and Michael A. Smyer

Autonomy, Competence, and Informed Consent in Long-Term Care: Legal and Psychological Perspectives

* * *

II. The Legal Doctrine of Informed Consent

A. Introduction

Despite the broad principles of autonomy enunciated in recent legislation, the informed consent doctrine has been criticized as an unattainable legal and ethical ideal.[1] This section provides an overview of the legal informed consent doctrine, considers its limitations as applied to the elderly, and suggests ways in which inte-

Villanova Law Review, Vol. 37, 1671–1170, (1992). Reprinted by permission.

gration of psychological perspectives into the legal doctrine can facilitate autonomous decision-making among elderly nursing home residents.

With certain exceptions,[2] the law of informed consent requires health care providers to disclose sufficient information for patients to make informed decisions about medical care. Informed consent encompasses the gamut of treatment decisions: "do not resuscitate" orders, execution of living wills, refusal of treatment, or even termination of treatment (commonly referred to as the "right to die"). Failure to provide sufficient information or to obtain consent prior to treatment has historically subjected providers to liability for assault and battery[3] and, more recently, for negligence.[4]

The legal doctrine of informed consent, as gleaned from a patchwork of state judicial opinions and statutes, contains three essential elements: patients with *decision-making capacity* must be provided *sufficient information* to make an informed decision *voluntarily*, or free of undue influence or duress.[5] Stating the legal elements so tersely perhaps raises more questions than answers. How much and what type of information must providers disclose? Should providers be obligated to ensure that patients understand the information? When is consent truly voluntary, especially in an institutional environment and with a dependent, often acquiescent group, such as the frail elderly? Perhaps most difficult, how does the doctrine apply to those with transient or waning competence? Are providers obligated to facilitate competence through therapy or environmental manipulation? The complexity of these and similar issues will be highlighted as we turn to an analysis of the three elements of informed consent.

B. Analysis of Informed Consent Elements

1. Decision-making Capacity Consent can be informed only if exercised by a patient of "sound mind" or, in more contemporary parlance, with "decision-making capacity."[6] Hence, decision-making capacity is a precondition to informed consent.[7] Given the complexity of the determination, it is not surprising that no standard legal definition of capacity has emerged. Instead, each state develops its own definition through limited judicial precedent and, in some instances, by statute.[8] Courts have spoken in vague generalities that make consistent application difficult at best. Some commentators have suggested that judicial decisions on the issue can be broken into three standards: (1) capacity to reach a decision based on rational reasons; (2) capacity to reach a reasonable result through a decision; and (3) capacity to make a decision at all.[9] Because of their generality, these categories offer little guidance in evaluating individuals' capacity to make health care decisions.

Despite lack of uniformity and specificity, several important legal trends are noteworthy. First, it is generally recognized that informed consent law requires a determination about specific capacity to make a particular health care decision, rather than an evaluation of overall competency.[10] Thus, courts have recognized that although a patient may be declared legally incompetent to handle her affairs—for example, in a guardianship proceeding—she may nevertheless retain cognitive capacity to decide whether to have her leg amputated.[11]

Second, the law increasingly recognizes that competency is not an all-or-nothing phenomenon. Instead, decisional capacity is viewed along a continuum as a matter of degree. One court recently noted that "there are degrees of incompetency; some individuals are more incompetent than others."[12] Some state statutes define decision-making capacity in terms of patients who, while lacking complete capacity, nevertheless are able to understand and appreciate the consequences of proposed medical treatment and communicate a choice about their preferences.[13]

Third, courts and legal commentators increasingly require assessment of patients' "functional capacity" to make decisions, rather than an evaluation of the reasonableness of their decisions or an assessment of status (such as old age or medical diagnosis) that is purported to interfere with decisional capacity.[14] Thus, an "unreasonable" decision such as refusing medications may nevertheless be implemented if the patient has the functional capacity to make such a decision. As one commentator noted: "The most important task for the legal standard of competency is to distinguish effectively between foolish, socially deviant, risky, or simply 'crazy' choices made competently, and comparable choices made incompetently. Although incompetent behavior may be restrained, identical competent behavior may not."[15]

In articulating such standards, the law has borrowed from the burgeoning ethical, medical, and psychological literature on decision-making capacity.[16] Though no widely accepted standard has emerged, some commentators have identified factors that should be accounted for under such an assessment: "(1) evidencing a choice, (2) 'reasonable' outcome of choice, (3) choice based on 'rational' reasons, (4) ability to understand [the implications of the choice], and (5) actual understanding [of the implications of the choice]."[17] Others question measures that include "rationality" of the decision and instead suggest that capacity depends on an individual's ability to understand the nature of the treatment choice presented, appreciate the implications of the various alternatives, and make and communicate a reasoned choice.[18] Finally, several commentators have suggested a risk-benefit analysis, where the amount of capacity required should depend in part on the gravity of the decision at hand; the more serious or life-threatening the decision, the greater the capacity courts should require of the decision-maker.[19]

While there is no shortage of literature identifying standards for decisional capacity, several problems in application persist. First, little progress has been made in identifying specific psychological, environmental, social, or other factors that mediate between mental status and decision-making capacity. The law's focus on the individual's decisional capacity gives short shrift to the array of external factors that could facilitate or inhibit exercise of such capacity.[20]

Second, despite near universal recognition that specific decisional capacity be assessed, some persist in deferring to general competency evaluations to determine specific capacity.

* * *

Third, legal precedent rarely views decisional capacity as a dynamic process involving the interplay of a variety of variables that constantly change over time. The element of time is crucial to the extent that external events—for example, moving into a nursing home—might cause temporary incapacity that could be restored over time.[21]

* * *

Finally, and perhaps most importantly, current legal informed consent applications do not recognize the interrelationships among all of the elements of the doctrine. Instead, the law typically requires an initial evaluation of whether a patient possesses decisional capacity pursuant to the factors described above, and then separate assessments of whether adequate information was provided and whether the decision was made voluntarily. More contextual psychological perspectives view the elements as interrelated such that a patient's decisional capacity could be facilitated (or inhibited) by the manner in which the information was conveyed or by the circumstances under which the information was presented. Thus, contextual psychological perspectives suggest that informed consent doctrine should view decision-making as an ongoing process and should recognize the importance of individual characteristics of patients, the relevance of environmental influence, and the reversibility of apparent defects in the decision-making process.

2. *Informed* The second element of informed consent requires that patients be provided with adequate information to enable them to make an informed decision. Courts and legislatures have developed three standards to determine whether a decision is "informed"; each reflects the law's primary concern with guaranteeing that relevant information is disclosed, rather than that it is understood and assimilated by the patient.[22]

The traditional standard requires disclosure of information that "reasonable" health care providers would disclose in similar circumstances.[23] This provider-centered approach has been rejected in numerous jurisdictions. Instead, these jurisdictions adopt a patient-centered standard, requiring that providers disclose information that "reasonable" patients in similar circumstances would want to know in order to make informed decisions.[24] While this enhances individual autonomy to a degree, some courts have gone further and adopted a purely "subjective" test that requires providers to disclose information the individual patient at issue would want to know.[25] It generally is recognized that legal informed consent requires, at a minimum, disclosure of information "about the nature and purpose of the proposed treatment, its risks and benefits, and any available alternatives."[26]

More recent commentators argue that informed consent also should require that the patient demonstrate actual understanding of the information presented.[27] However, this suggestion has been slow to infiltrate legal or clinical practice. The law continues to be preoccupied with the quantity and quality of information disclosed rather than with the format of the disclosure or the comprehension and assimilation of information by the patient.[28] In clinical practice, information is often disclosed via written consent forms, especially when advice has been sought from legal counsel.[29] Simply providing information may be ineffective in securing meaningful consent with nursing home residents whose comprehension is impaired by a variety of physical, emotional, and psychological factors.[30]

As noted earlier, the information disclosure element typically is analyzed separately from the other elements of informed consent. This overlooks the fact that, especially for elderly people, the manner in which information is disclosed can dramatically affect the patient's capacity to make decisions. As we shall argue at length in a later section, viewing the capacity and informed elements as interrelated encourages consideration of intervention techniques to help even cognitively impaired residents understand the relative risks and benefits of various decisions facing them. In this way, autonomous decision-making can be facilitated.

3. *Voluntary* Informed consent also requires that competent patients making health care decisions do so voluntarily. From the law's perspective, any element of force, coercion, fraud, or duress may render a decision void.[31] Voluntariness should be viewed as a matter of degree; it can be compromised by overt force or more subtly by coercion or manipulation.[32] Nursing home residents may be particularly susceptible to subtle influences, in part because of the psychological effects of institutional living. However, the "voluntariness" requirement may be difficult to enforce, because health care decisions are ordinarily questioned only when residents disagree with proposed treatments.[33]

* * *

Notes

1. *See* JAY KATZ, THE SILENT WORLD OF DOCTOR AND PATIENT 1–4 (1984) (discussing inconsistency between theory of having patients share decisionmaking and medical practices); Jay Katz, *Disclosure and Consent: In Search of Their Roots, in* GENETICS AND THE LAW II 121, 128 (Aubrey Milunsky & George J. Annas eds., 1980) (arguing that implementing doctrine of informed consent in context of genetic counseling will require many changes in existing practice).

2. *See* Alan Meisel, *The "Exceptions" to the Informed Consent Doctrine: Striking a Balance Between Competing Values in Medical Decisionmaking,* 1979 WIS. L. REV. 413, 431–33 (discussing various situations where there are exceptions to general rule requiring disclosure). Many states have enacted statutory exceptions to the requirement of informed consent, some of which are framed in terms of "defenses" to an informed consent action. *See* Theodore R. LeBlang, *Informed Consent: Common Law and Statutory Considerations,* 1–18 (ABA National Institute on Medical Malpractice 1991) (reviewing state statutes and case law on informed consent); *see also* Theodore R. LeBlang & Jane L. King, *Tort Liability for Nondisclosure: The Physician's Legal Obligations to Disclose Patient Illness and Injury,* 89 DICK. L. REV. 1, 45 (1984) (specifically discussing limits on duty to disclose).

Possible exceptions to the duty to disclose include the following: (1) where an emergency situation exists that precludes the ability of a patient to give consent, or the opportunity for a provider to secure consent, *see* ARTHUR F. SOUTHWICK, THE LAW OF HOSPITAL AND HEALTH CARE ADMINISTRATION 355-57 (2d ed. 1988) (discussing emergency exception to informed consent); (2) where the patient does not desire to be informed or would have wanted medical care despite the known risks, *e.g.,* ALASKA STAT. § 09.55.556(a)–(b)(2) (1983); (3) where the risks are known by the patient, are commonly known, or are too remote or insubstantial, *e.g.,* N. Y. PUB. HEALTH LAW § 2805-d.4(a) (McKinney 1985 & Supp. 1992); and (4) where there is a "therapeutic privilege" such that a provider may use reasonable discretion in deciding to refrain from a full disclosure in order to avoid negatively affecting the patient's condition, *e.g.*, ALASKA STAT. § 09.55.556(b)(4) (1983). In addition, a signed consent form may create a presumption that information was disclosed. *See, e.g.*, GA. CODE ANN. § 31-9-6.1(b)(2) (Michie 1991).

3. *See, e.g.*, Pratt v. Davis, 79 N.E. 562, 563 (Ill. 1906) (operating without consent gives rise to "an action for trespass to the person"); Schloendorff v. Society of New York Hosp., 105 N.E. 92, 93 (N.Y. 1914) (Cardozo, J.) ("[A] surgeon who performs an operation without his patient's consent commits an assault. . . ."), *overruled by* Bing v. Thwnig, 143 N.E.2d 3 (N.Y. 1957); Rolater v. Strain, 137 P. 96, 99 (Okla. 1913) (stating that physicians will be liable for damages if during surgery they go beyond that to which patient consented).

4. *See, e.g.*, Salgo v. Leland Stanford Univ. Bd. of Trustees, 317 P.2d 170, 181 (Cal. Ct. App. 1957) (stating in medical malpractice suit based in negligence that "[a] physician violates his duty to his patient . . . if he withholds any facts which are necessary to form the basis of an intelligent consent by the patient to the proposed treatment"). *But cf.* Moure v. Raeuchele, 604 A.2d 1003, 1008 n.8 (Pa. 1992) (stating that in Pennsylvania, lack of informed consent gives rise to action for intentional tort of battery, not action for negligence).

5. *See* MARSHALL B. KAPP & ARTHUR BIGOT, GERIATRICS AND THE LAW: PATIENT RIGHTS AND PROFESSIONAL RESPONSIBILITIES 23–32 (1985) (outlining elements of valid consent); *see also* [TOM L. BEAUCHAMP & JAMES F. CHILDRESS, PRINCIPLES OF BIOMEDICAL ETHICS 79 (3d ed. 1989) ("Competence to consent . . . might be . . . described as a presupposition of the practice of obtaining informed consent. . . .")], at 78 (listing elements of informed consent).

6. *See* PRESIDENT'S COMMISSION FOR THE STUDY OF ETHICAL PROBLEMS IN MEDICINE AND BIOMEDICAL AND BEHAVIORAL RESEARCH I, MAKING HEALTH CARE DECISIONS: THE ETHICAL AND LEGAL IMPLICATIONS OF INFORMED CONSENT IN THE PATIENT-PRACTITIONER RELATIONSHIP 15, 55 [hereinafter PRESIDENT'S COMMISSION] (Washington, D.C.: U.S. Government Printing Office, 1982).

7. [TOM L. BEAUCHAMP & JAMES F. CHILDRESS, PRINCIPLES OF BIOMEDICAL ETHICS 79 (3d ed. 1989) ("Competence to consent . . . might be . . . described as a presupposition of the practice of obtaining informed consent. . . . ")], at 79.

8. For a 50 state review of competency standards used in guardianship proceedings, see STEPHEN J. ANDERER, DETERMINING COMPETENCY IN GUARDIANSHIP PROCEEDINGS 3–15 (American Bar Association, 1990).

9. [TOM L. BEAUCHAMP & JAMES F. CHILDRESS, PRINCIPLES OF BIOMEDICAL ETHICS 79 (3d ed. 1989) ("Competence to consent . . . might be . . . described as a presupposition of the practice of obtaining informed consent. . . . ")], at 83.

10. PRESIDENT'S COMMISSION, *supra* note 6, at 3, 55; *see also* ANDERER, *supra* note 8, at 13–14 (discussing trend in guardianship law toward evaluation of specific decisionmaking capacities).

11. Lane v. Candura, 376 N.E.2d 1232, 1233–34 (Mass. App. Ct. 1978).

12. *In re* Guardianship of Ingram, 689 P.2d 1363, 1371 (Wash. 1984).

13. *See, e.g.*, IDAHO CODE § 39-4302 (1985) ("Any person of ordinary intelligence and awareness sufficient for him or her generally to comprehend the need for, the nature of and the significant risks . . . is competent to consent . . . .").

14. *See* ANDERER, *supra* note 8, at 8–10 (discussing trend in guardianship law toward functional definitions of incompetency or incapacity).

15. Paul R. Tremblay, *On Persuasion and Paternalism: Lawyer Decisionmaking and the Questionably Competent Client*, 1987 UTAH L. REV. 515, 537–38. As former United States Supreme Court

Chief Justice Warren Burger noted, the right to self-determination is so important that it protects even "a great many foolish, unreasonable and even absurd ideas which do not conform, such as refusing medical treatment even at great risk." *In re* President & Directors of Georgetown College, 331 F.2d 1000, 1017 (D.C. Cir.) (Burger, J., dissenting from denial of rehearing *en banc*), *cert. denied*, 377 U.S. 978 (1964).

16. For a critical review of recent medical, psychological and legal literature on defining and assessing decisionmaking capacity, see Marshall B. Kapp, *Evaluating Decisionmaking Capacity in the Elderly: A Review of Recent Literature*, *in* PROTECTING JUDGMENT-IMPARIED ADULTS: ISSUES, INTERVENTIONS AND POLICIES (Edmund F. Dejowski ed., 1990).

17. Loren H. Roth et al., *Tests of Competency to Consent to Treatment*, 134 AM. PSYCHIATRY 279, 280 (1977); *see also*, Paul S. Appelbaum & Thomas Grisso, *Assessing Patients' Capacities to Consent to Treatment*, 319 NEW ENG. J. MED., 1635, 1635–37 (1988) (offering standards similar to Roth's for functional assessment of decisional capacity).

18. PRESIDENT'S COMMISSION, *supra* note 6, at 57–59.

19. *See, e.g.*, James F. Drane, *The Many Faces of Competency*, 15 HASTINGS CENTER REP., Apr. 1985, at 17–21 (recommending use of sliding scale to determine competency whereby required level of competency increases as risks of treatment increase); Robert Weinstock, *Informed Consent and Competence Issues in the Elderly*, *in* GERIATRIC PSYCHIATRY AND THE LAW, 49, 61–64 (Richard Rosner & Harold Schwartz eds., 1987).

20. In particular, the law has not attempted in any significant way to assess the relationship between the environment and the person's capacity to make decisions, a relationship that psychologists view as paramount in assessing decisional capacity. [Remainder of note omitted.]

21. *See* L. Jaime Fitten & Martha S. Waite, *Impact of Medical Hospitalization on Treatment Decision-Making Capacity in the Elderly*, 150 ARCHIVES INTERNAL MED. 1717, 1719–20 (1990) (reporting study suggesting that presumably competent elderly persons may be at risk for developing decisional impairments during hospitalization for acute illness).

22. *See* KAPP & BIGOT, *supra* note 5, at 25–27 (discussing standards for disclosure).

23. *See, e.g.*, Fain v. Smith, 479 So. 2d 1150, 1152 (Ala. 1985) (stating that in deciding whether disclosure of risks was adequate, objective standard used is whether physician disclosed all risks that reasonable physician in same or similar circumstances would have disclosed); Doctors Memorial Hosp. v. Evans, 543 So. 2d 809, 811–12 (Fla. Dist. Ct. App. 1989) (stating that expert witness required to establish standard of care of similar prudent health care provider that radiologist should have met in disclosing risks); Leiker v. Gafford, 778 P.2d 823, 830 (Kan. 1989) (standard is what "a reasonable medical practitioner would [disclose] under the same or similar circumstances"); Foard v. Jarman, 387 S.E.2d 162, 164–66 (N.C. 1990) (holding that physician who acted in accord with community standard of disclosure made sufficient showing of informed consent).

24. *See, e.g.*, Hartke v. McKelway, 707 F.2d 1544, 1548 (D.C. Cir.), *cert. denied*, 464 U.S. 983 (1983) (stating that physician should focus on "patient's position" in determining what information to disclose); Canterbury v. Spence, 464 F.2d 772, 786 (D.C. Cir.), *cert. denied*, 409 U.S. 1064 (1972) (risk must be revealed if material to patient's decision); Cobbs v. Grant, 502 P.2d 1, 11 (Cal. 1972) ("In sum, the patient's right of self-decision is the measure of the physician's duty to reveal.").

25. *See, e.g.*, Scott v. Bradford, 606 P.2d 554, 558 (Okla. 1979) (requiring disclosure of risks "likely to affect patient's decision"); *see also* [TOM L. BEAUCHAMP & JAMES F. CHILDRESS, PRINCIPLES OF BIOMEDICAL ETHICS 79 (3d ed. 1989) ("Competence to consent . . . might be . . .

described as a presupposition of the practice of obtaining informed consent . . . .")], at 90–91 (discussing advantages and disadvantages of subjective standard). *But cf.* Barclay v. Campbell, 704 S.W.2d 8, 10 (Tex. 1986) (using "reasonable person" standard).

26. [*See also* Paul S. Appelbaum et al., Informed Consent: Legal Theory and Clinical Practice 35–36 (1987) ("Law's concern for the bodily integrity of the individual . . . can be traced to . . . [civil] assault and battery and to the criminal law proscription of homicide, battery and mayhem.")], at 49 (detailing the elements of disclosure).

27. *See* [Tom L. Beauchamp & James F. Childress, Principles of Biomedical Ethics 79 (3d ed. 1989) ("Competence to consent . . . might be . . . described as a presupposition of the practice of obtaining informed consent. . . .")], at 99 ("[U]nderstanding is a more important element than disclosure and may be the most important element in . . . obtaining an informed consent.").

28. *See* Lori B. Andrews, *Informed Consent Statutes and the Decisionmaking Process,* 5 J. Legal Med. 163 (1984) ("Judicial opinions . . . focus on the standards of disclosure and causation rather than the content or format of the communication. . . .").

29. *See, e.g.,* Southwick, *supra* note 2, at 299 (recommending use of written consent forms).

30. [*See* Tamra J. Lair & Dons C. Lefkowitz, *Mental Health and Functional Status of Residents of Nursing and Personal Care Homes,* DHHS Publication No. (PHS)90-3470, at 6 (Washington, D.C. 1990) (estimating prevalence of mental disorders, problem behaviors and self-care deficits among nursing home residents).]

31. *See* [Tom L. Beauchamp & James F. Childress, Principles of Biomedical Ethics 79 (3d ed. 1989) ("Competence to consent . . . might be . . . described as a presupposition of the practice of obtaining informed consent. . . .")], at 106. Voluntariness of consent requires "absence of psychological compulsion, and the absence of external constraints." *Id.*

32. *See* Kapp & Bigot, *supra* note 5, at 23–24 (discussing interferences with voluntariness of patients' decisionmaking).

33. *See* Thomas Grisso, Evaluating Competencies: Forensic Assessments and Instruments 315–16 (1986) (stating that "the question of competency simply might not be raised if the patient does not refuse the proposed treatment"); Gary B. Melton et al., Psychological Evaluations for the Courts: A Handbook for Mental Health Professionals and Lawyers 251 (1987) (suggesting that where patient assents to treatment, competency is likely to be questioned only when physician is concerned about potential tort liability).

Of course, the doctrine of informed consent can only function if the treating authorities are willing to share all relevant information with the patient. Indeed, the unstated assumption of the doctrine is that patients want full disclosure. But suppose that a patient would prefer not to "know the bad news." Some patients idiosyncratically would choose the bliss of ignorance over the gloom of reality. They prefer to let their physician make the necessary choices, serene in the knowledge that the "doctor knows best." Other patients do not expect to fully participate in treatment decisions because such involvement would be contrary to their cultural upbringing and beliefs. How to deal with patients who might prefer to leave the difficult decisions to the professional, or who would prefer to permit family members to make decisions on their account, is the subject of Ms. Michel's brief article.

Vicki Michel

Factoring Ethnic and Racial Differences into Bioethics Decision Making

Among the stories that health care professionals tell are tales of the frustration they experience when members of a patient's family block access to the patient and in particular make it impossible to engage the patient in the conversation about diagnosis, prognosis, and treatment that American bioethics and American law demand take place. In the last thirty years we have adopted the view that respect for patient autonomy requires that patients be told everything about their condition and that each patient him- or herself is the only legitimate decision maker about treatment or nontreatment. The vision of human existence that underlies such requirements is an impoverished and noncontextual one that sees people as isolated beings whom the law protects from the interference of others, rather than as beings embedded in relationships.

What is becoming more and more apparent, as those of us in bioethics familiarize ourselves with the work of medical anthropologists and other social scientists, is that the norm in many cultures—perhaps in most cultures—is for patients *not* to be told their diagnosis and prognosis when the prospects for recovery or survival are poor. Instead family members are given information, and family members make decisions. When the family insists on shielding the patient from information, we are forced to confront a tension in our concept of patient autonomy. Does the value of individual autonomous informed decision-making transcend cultural norms that accord it less importance than "the family's moral imperative-filial duty" (Orona et al., 1994)? Can we be certain that our insistence that the patient be informed is truly respectful of who the patient is and of the patient's real preferences?

We have tended to see our movement from medical paternalism to patient autonomy as progress, and rightly so, to the extent that the physician as sole decision maker has ignored the possibility that physicians and patients might not share the same values and/or goals. Medical paternalism does not acknowledge the context in which the patient is located, but it may be that our emphasis on patient autonomy also disregards the patient's context.

The basic issue is how we are to deal with difference. Are we to tell the family of any elderly Chinese/Mexican/Korean/Italian cancer patient that they are in the United States now and our law requires informed consent from the patient, so therefore the patient must be given all information about her condition? Or should we

Generations, Vol. 18, No. 23 (Winter 1994). Reprinted with permission from *Generations*, 833 Market St., Suite 511, Copyright 1994, American Society on Aging.

look for ways to accommodate cultural differences on the understanding that being respectful involves recognizing patients for who they are—including in cultural context?

Mary Catherine Bateson puts it this way: "The question for everyone, living in a world of constant contact between cultural groups, is how to become routinely sensitive to patterns, even with minimal cues, suspending judgment and looking for how they fit together" (Bateson, 1994). This comment, it seems to me, alludes to the complexity of situations that may seem simple at first glance. How do we understand what is going on when no adult children in a family will explicitly acknowledge that a parent is dying, and yet it also seems clear that everyone knows and is implicitly preparing for the death? Is this behavior dishonest, hypocritical? Or is this family acting out cultural rituals that make the experience of death coherent for them. Mary Catherine Bateson is again helpful: "Living in unfamiliar cultures, learning to feel and express culturally appropriate emotions, I have been nagged by the issue of sincerity, yet this is a singularly American concern, which only arises in the context of a belief in some autonomous inner self, separate from interactions with others" (Bateson, 1994).

Given that we cannot all be experts concerning the myriad cultural differences we are likely to encounter, our problem is to determine what we can do, in a practical sense, to facilitate care-giving relationships in health care settings. The first step is to recognize difference and be curious rather than judgmental in response to it. A psychiatrist at a bioethics meeting questioned the need for education about cultural differences because in his view a health care professional should always get to know the patient as an individual and that process of "getting to know" will inevitably include awareness of cultural difference. But encounters between professionals and patients or families seem rarely to include the luxury of time to truly "get to know" each other.

* * *

Differences may also exist concerning time orientation, privacy, expression of pain, willingness to engage in dialogue, the meaning of gifts, the roles of family members, and many other things that can affect relationships among caregivers, patients, and family members (Galanti, 1991).

There are pitfalls in acting with sensitivity toward cultural difference, however, especially if the sensitivity is based on knowledge that is general and superficial. . . . In fact, all cultures are heterogeneous; individuals vary according to education, religion, socioeconomic status, and, in this country, degree of acculturation. And then an individual's behavior may be idiosyncratic—a product of his or her particular personality, which can be in rebellion against cultural norms as well as in conformity with them.

Another pitfall lies in defining a "culture" too broadly. In referring to Asians, Hispanics, or Africans, we are not talking about specific cultures—Chinese is not the same as Japanese, Vietnamese, Cambodian, Korean, and so on. We should avoid lumping together groups that have clear identities of their own.

We also should be careful not to confuse cultural attitudes with differences in perspective that occur between health care professionals and virtually all lay persons. For example, the inability or unwillingness to accept "brain death" has death as been ascribed to cultural difference, but in reality very few people find it easy to accept that a body with lungs and heart functioning—albeit only because of technological intervention—is truly dead. Actually, even many health care professionals have trouble with this.

In short, in attempting to recognize cultural differences care must be taken not to ascribe every controversy to culture. Good judgment and common sense should govern here as in other aspects of caregiving.

An additional issue related to culture that can be an obstacle to communication is language. Both new immigrants and long-time residents in the United States may not speak English well enough to have a conversation about medical decisions.

* * *

A most difficult problem occurs when family members want to keep a poor prognosis from the patient and the patient does not speak English. If a family member serves as interpreter, it is certain that the patient will not be told the truth, and more serious, that caregivers will have no way of knowing whether the patient wants truthful information about his or her condition. We cannot assume that because the patient comes from a culture where patients generally are not told the truth and the patient's family does not want the truth told, this particular patient does not want to know. Cultural norms, after all, may not be entirely controlling when it comes to patients' desires to know the truth about their own condition.

* * *

This ambiguity makes it hard for American caregivers to know what approach to take. How do we express our respect for people and their cultural contexts and also meet the demands not only of the American value system but also of the legal system—to obtain informed consent, for example, when family members do not want the patient to be told the truth.

* * *

The point of informed consent is that the patient has a right to the information he or she needs to make a decision about treatment. It is not that every patient has a duty to hear everything, whether they want to or not.

I take this position while very much aware of a compelling argument made by Jay Katz (1984) that patients do indeed have a duty to reflect and to converse with their physicians that cannot be waived. He says, "The right to self-determination about ultimate choices cannot be properly exercised without first attending to the processes of self-reflection and reflection with others." And he notes, "The imposition of an obligation to converse is disrespectful of the right to have one's initial choice, including the right not to converse, honored." But he goes on to say that the principle of privacy (keeping one's thoughts and feelings to oneself) must yield to "psychological autonomy."

Although Katz was not addressing the issue of cultural difference in medical decision making, his reasoning can be used as a strong argument for insisting that the patient always be the decision maker. Yet it seems to me profoundly disrespectful to force a patient into any style of decision making. In fact, to do so would be to contradict the very principle that is at stake in all this: respect for persons—persons seen as not the isolated beings mentioned early in this article but rather as situated in relationships that are themselves constitutive of individual identity.

In conclusion, medical decision-making is just one of the many contexts in which awareness of cultural differences can open doors for learning. It is unlikely that we can "get it right" with every patient or family we encounter, but we can be guided by the perspective expressed by Mary Catherine Bateson: "Because it is not possible to stand aside from participation until we know what we are doing, it is essential to find styles of acting that accept ambiguity and allow for learning along the way. Perception, attention, grace, all of these, varied or sustained, provide materials for constructing both self and world, and patterns for joining in the dance" (Bateson, 1994).

References

Bateson, M. C. 1994. *Peripheral Visions.* New York: HarperCollins.

Galanti, G. 1991. *Caring for Patients from Different Cultures.* Philadelphia: University of Pennsylvania Press.

Katz, J. 1984. *The Silent World of Doctor and Patient.* New York: The Free Press.

Orona, C. J., et al. 1994. "Cultural Aspects of Nondisclosure." *Cambridge Quarterly of Healthcare Ethics* 3: 338-46.

As stated, incapacitated adults have the right to control their health care decisions by instructions, whether oral or by documents (such as a living will) created before the onset of the incapacity. The effectiveness of such instructions or documents is very problematical, as discussed in the following research report.

A Controlled Trial to Improve Care for Seriously Ill Hospitalized Patients:

- The Study to Understand Prognoses and Preferences for Outcomes and Risks of Treatment (SUPPORT)
- The SUPPORT Principal Investigators

* * *

Physicians and ethicists have debated when to use cardiac resuscitation and other aggressive treatments for patients with advanced illnesses. Many worry about the economic and human cost of providing life-sustaining treatment near the end of life.

In response, professional organizations, the judiciary, consumer organizations, and a president's commission have all advocated more emphasis on realistically forecasting outcomes of life-sustaining treatment and on improved communication between physician and patient. Statutes requiring informed consent and communication, like the Patient Self-determination Act, have been passed. Advance care planning and effective ongoing communication among clinicians, patients, and families are essential to achieve these goals. Previous studies indicate, however, that communication is often absent or occurs only during a crisis. Physicians today often perceive death as failure, they tend to be too pessimistic regarding prognoses, and they provide more extensive treatment to seriously ill patients than they would choose for themselves.

* * *

Comment

Findings from phase I of SUPPORT documented many shortcomings of care. The SUPPORT patients were all seriously ill, and their dying proved to be predictable, yet discussions and decisions substantially in advance of death were uncommon. Nearly half of all DNR orders were written in the last two days of life. The final hospitalization for half of patients included more than eight days in generally undesirable states: in an ICU, receiving mechanical ventilation, or comatose. Families reported that half of the patients who were able to communicate in their last few days spent most of the time in moderate or severe pain. Based on a study in a defined population at our Wisconsin site, we estimate that patients meeting SUPPORT criteria account for approximately 400,000 admissions per year in the United States and that another

925,000 people are similarly ill but would not meet SUPPORT entry requirements of being hospitalized or in intensive care. Patients with SUPPORT illnesses and severity account for about 40% of persons dying in the defined population.

Building on the findings in phase I, observations of others, the opinions of physicians at the five sites, and the marked variation in their baseline practices, the phase II intervention aimed to make it easier to achieve better decision-making for these seriously ill patients. The intervention gave physicians reliable prognostic information and timely reports of patient and surrogate perceptions, the two most important factors cited recently by physicians when considering life-support decisions for critically ill patients. The intervention nurse also undertook time-consuming discussions, arranged meetings, provided information, supplied forms, and did anything else to encourage the patient and family to engage in an informed and collaborative decision-making process with a well-informed physician.

The intervention was limited by its application to a diverse group of physicians and patients, all of whom had to comply voluntarily. The intervention had to be perceived as helpful, polite, and appropriate. As an initial attempt to change outcomes for seriously ill patients, we did not seek authority to be coercive or more than minimally disruptive. As designed, however, the intervention was vigorously applied. The SUPPORT nurses were committed, energetic, and highly trained. They engaged in the care of virtually all our patients, and nearly everyone had printed reports delivered promptly.

Because we thought that changes in the decision-making processes that were not reflected in improved patient outcomes would not be worth much expense, we specified five outcomes, each indicating an important improvement in patient experience, as the main targets of the intervention.

The intervention had no impact on any of these designated targets. Furthermore, even though the targeted outcomes are objectives of much ethical and legal writing and of some explicit social policy (such as informed consent statutes, the Patient Self-determination Act, and guidelines on pain), there were no secular trends toward improvement for intervention or control patients during the five years of SUPPORT data collection.

These results raise fundamental questions about the intent and design of this trial. Do patients and physicians see the documented shortcomings as troubling? Can enhanced decision-making improve the experience of seriously ill and dying patients? Were the inevitable limitations of this project too great to draw strong conclusions?

Because there was no movement toward what would seem to be better practices, one could conclude that physicians, patients, and families are fairly comfortable with the current situation. Certainly, most patients and families indicated they were satisfied, no matter what happened to them. Physicians have their established patterns of care, and while they were willing to have the SUPPORT nurse present and carrying on conversations, physician behavior appeared unchanged. Perhaps physicians and patients in this study acknowledged problems with the care of seriously ill patients as a group. However, when involved with their own situation or engaged in the care of their individual patients, they felt they were doing the best they could, were satisfied they were doing well, and did not wish to directly confront problems or face choices.

The study certainly casts a pall over any claim that, if the health care system is given additional resources for collaborative decision-making in the form of skilled professional time, improvements will occur. In phase II of SUPPORT, improved information, enhanced conversation, and an explicit effort to encourage use of outcome data and preferences in decision-making were completely ineffectual, despite the fact that the study had enough power to detect small effects.

It is possible that the intervention would have been more effective if implemented in different settings, earlier in the course of illness, or with physician leaders rather than nurses as implementers. Perhaps it would have been effective if continued for more time or tested at later end points. However, the overall results of this study are not encouraging. No pattern emerged that implied that the intervention was successful for some set of patients or physicians or that its impact increased over time. The five hospitals had been chosen for their diversity and their willingness to undertake a substantial and controversial challenge. Yet none showed a tendency toward improvement in these outcomes.

* * *

In conclusion, we are left with a troubling situation. The picture we describe of the care of seriously ill or dying persons is not attractive. One would certainly prefer to envision that, when confronted with life-threatening illness, the patient and family would be included in discussions, realistic estimates of outcome would be valued, pain would be treated, and dying would not be prolonged. That is still a worthy vision. However, it is not likely to be achieved through an intervention such as that implemented by SUPPORT. Success will require reexamination of our individual and collective commitment to these goals, more creative efforts at shaping the treatment process, and, perhaps, more proactive and forceful attempts at change.

* * *

CHAPTER 24

The Right to Die of Competent Older Adults

Competent adults have the right to refuse life-sustaining medical treatment, as illustrated in the following case.

Pocono Medical Center v. Harley, 11 Fiduc. Rptr. 2d 128 (1990) (Penna. Monroe County)

* * *

In the Court of Common Pleas of Monroe County. Pocono Medical Center and John G. Kauderer, M.D. v. Richard J. Harley. Petition for declaratory judgment. No. 3467 Civil of 1990.

* * *

Opinion by O'Brien, J., December 14, 1990:

I. Findings of Fact

1. Yolanda B. Black (hereinafter patient) is a widow who was born on February 19, 1937. She has no children.

2. On November 30, 1990, the patient arrived at the Pocono Medical Center by ambulance with complaints of weakness and rectal bleeding. The patient personally signed admitting documents including an authorization for blood transfusions. The patient advised the admitting physician that she had been treated for rectal cancer

for an extended period of time but had discontinued chemotherapy in December, 1989. The admitting physician upon examination determined the patient to have stage IV rectal carcinoma.

* * *

4. On November 30, 1990, Dr. Kauderer undertook treatment of the patient and met with her to discuss the course of her treatment. They discussed the serious stage of her rectal cancer and the imminent prospect of kidney failure which would require dialysis. The patient advised the doctor that she did not wish any extraordinary means to be utilized in her treatment and specifically rejected any resuscitation, dialysis, or use of a ventilator. The conversation between the doctor and the patient was in the presence of a registered nurse.

5. On the day of the patient's admission, defendant Richard J. Harley appeared at the hospital and presented an "Unlimited Power of Attorney," which he asserted authorized him to control treatment of the patient. He advised the attending physician that all means, including extraordinary means, should be taken to prolong the life of the patient.

6. On Friday, November 30th, Dr. Kauderer requested James A. Taylor, M.D., Chief of Neuropsychiatry of Pocono Medical Center to meet with the patient. . . .

7. Dr. Taylor found the patient to be alert, coherent, oriented in all spheres and fully cognizant of the terminal nature of her illness and the alternative treatments available. The patient advised Dr. Taylor that she did not want any extraordinary treatment and specifically rejected the prospect of tubes or breathing machines. The patient acknowledged that her refusal of these extraordinary means could result in death.

8. On December 1, 1990, Dr. Kauderer again met with the patient and advised her of the instructions he had received from Mr. Harley. The patient again reiterated her desires that no extraordinary means be used in her treatment and advised the doctor that she would "make Mr. Harley understand her wishes." This conversation between the doctor and the patient also took place in the presence of a registered nurse.

9. On December 3, 1990, the patient lapsed into a coma and is presently unable to communicate in any fashion with anyone. She does groan or moan on occasion.

II. Discussion

The timing of death, once a matter of fate, has become in many cases a matter of human choice. Eighty percent of the approximately two million people who die each year in the United States die in hospitals or long-term care institutions.[1] It is estimated that as many as 70 percent of deaths occur after a decision to forego life-sustaining treatment has been made.[2] A majority of deaths each year in the United States involve a decision whether to undertake some medical procedure that could prolong the process of dying. Such decisions are difficult and personal. They must be made on the basis of individual values, informed by medical realities, yet within a framework governed by law. The role of the courts must be to provide some order to this decision making process which has heretofore been characterized by chaos.

* * *

The procedural posture of the case at bar is akin to that followed in the Court of Common Pleas of Philadelphia County in *Newman Medical Center, Inc. v. Popowich, D.O.*, No. 5663 January Term 1990. In that proceeding, the Newman Medical Center filed a petition for declaratory relief and expedited hearing seeking to discontinue the life support systems maintaining a terminal patient. Since the patient in that case was conscious and apparently capable of communicating by way of blinking her eyes, the trial judge and counsel met with the patient personally to determine her wishes with respect to life support systems. Following that in-hospital proceeding, Judge Nicholas M. D'Alessandro authorized the Medical Center to comply with the patient's wishes. While the procedural posture of the case at bar is akin to the aforementioned, the intervention of a friend holding a power of attorney adds a further dimension to our inquiry.

* * *

[W]e conclude that a hospital or treating physician has a duty to comply with the express wishes of a competent adult with respect to the use of extraordinary means to sustain life. Further we conclude that with respect to a comatose patient, a hospital or treating physician has a duty to follow the wishes of a person holding a power of attorney only if the power of attorney contains both of the following provisions:

1. "to authorize my admission to a medical, nursing, residential or similar facility and to enter into agreements for my care; to authorize medical and surgical procedures." [20 Pa. C.S.A. 5602(8,9)]
2. "this power of attorney shall become effective upon my disability or incapacity." [20 Pa. C.S.A. 5604]

Since the power of attorney in the case at bar fails to meet the above requirements, the plaintiffs are entitled to the declaratory judgment requested. However at hearing, counsel for defendant made an oral motion requesting this court to appoint the defendant or her sister as a legal guardian to authorize treatment for the patient. . . . Should this court allow the patient's wishes to be overruled by another? Would the guardian share the prolonged suffering provoked by the tubes and machines? Could it be that the author's words dwell in the heat of this patient? "Death is not the enemy, doctor, inhumanity is."

Resolving this dilemma first requires a credibility determination as to which witness has accurately represented the patient's wishes. We find the testimony of the patient's sister, translated from French by her son, to be most illuminating. She testified that the patient knew that her condition was terminal but had terminated chemotherapy and refused surgery. The patient recently observed to a relative "we all have to die sometime." The sister also testified that the patient does not like to complain but appears to be "suffering for nothing." The sister's testimony conflicted in many respects with that of the defendant. While Richard J. Harley seems anxious to force his agenda, we do not find his testimony credible. Although he challenged the professional judgment of the treating physician, he presented no expert medical testimony.

On the other hand we find the positive and certain testimony of Dr. Kauderer very believable. His professional credentials are impeccable and we discern no motivation to misrepresent the patient's desires. The easy course for Dr. Kauderer would be to acquiesce in the defendant's demands. However, he apparently takes seriously the Hippocratic Oath which provides in part:

> "The regimen I adopt shall be for the benefit of my patients according to my ability and judgment and not for their hurt or for any wrong. I will give no deadly drug to any, though it be asked of me. . . ."

The physician who acts to protect the right of his patient to die with dignity is true to his oath and persuasive to the conscience of this court.

III. Conclusions of Law

* * *

4. The Pocono Medical Center and John G. Kauderer, M.D. have presented clear and convincing evidence that the patient was fully cognizant of her medical condition, the alternative treatments available and the risk of death involved in foregoing extraordinary medical procedures to sustain her life, at the time she gave treatment instructions to her treating physician.

5. The Pocono Medical Center and John G. Kauderer, M.D. have presented clear and convincing evidence that the patient's decision to forego extraordinary treatment to preserve her life was a rational and intelligent decision by a competent adult.

6. The United States Constitution and the Pennsylvania Constitution guarantee the right of a mature, competent adult to refuse to accept medical treatment that may prolong one's life and a right to die with dignity.

Notes

1. See President's Commission for the Study of Ethical Problems in Medicine and Biomedical and Behavioral Research, Deciding to Forego Life Sustaining Treatment 15, n. 1 and 17–18 (1983).

2. See Lipton, Do-Not-Resuscitate Decisions in a Community Hospital: Incidence, Implications and Outcomes, 256 JAMA 1164, 1168 (1986).

CHAPTER 25

Competent Older Adults

Cases like Pocono Medical Center v. Harley *have been criticized by some commentators who claim that the courts, when deciding whether the patient had sufficient capacity to refuse medical treatment, have paid insufficient attention to psychological factors. Because the courts focus on whether the patient has capacity, they miss—according to some commentators—the more subtle motives or pressures that may be affecting the decision-making of the so-called competent adult. In a Nevada case, a nonterminal but respirator-dependent patient asked to be taken off the respirator and permitted to die. He was about to suffer the death of his only living relative, who was both his parent and sole caregiver. While the court felt that his competency was affirmed by the fact that he was able to understand the health care options available to him, perhaps the court should have considered whether his reason for refusing life-sustaining care arose from his loss of a caregiver, which left him emotionally vulnerable. As a result, he may have been incapable of making a rational decision.*

Some commentators are also concerned that a decision to reject further treatment may result from the patient believing he has been rejected or that the continuation of his life is unimportant. Though the patient asks not to be treated, what he is really asking is whether his life is worth continuing. The concurrence of caregivers that the patient need not continue life-sustaining treatment may re-enforce his deepest fear that his life is worthless. If caregivers had objected and insisted upon the patient receiving treatment, he might have felt wanted enough and believed that his life was sufficiently valued, and thus agreed to continuation of life-sustaining treatment.

Depression is the other issue lurking in these cases. Many commentators contend that most requests for termination of treatment are a result of mental depression. If the underlying depression were treated, the person would have a more positive attitude toward a continuation of treatment. Of course, others argue that depression is often a realistic response to the patient's condition. Persons who are dying or severely ill are naturally likely to feel less than optimistic about life. The refusal to continue treatment may be a rational response to a depressing situation, not the irrational response of a depressed mind.

The difficulty for commentators who challenge the decisions of an allegedly competent patient is that in essence they are claiming that the patient is not competent, that depression or personal pressures in their lives have left these patients unable to make considered decisions about their care. If accepted, this claim would significantly expand the number of persons who can be considered incapacitated by law. For example, factors such as mild depression are usually considered insufficient to justify the imposition of a guardianship. Of course, there is no requirement that the level of capacity to make health care decision-making be as low as the capacity necessary to have a guardian appointed. But it would be odd indeed that persons could have sufficient capacity to make all their other legal decisions, but not be considered competent to determine whether they should terminate their health care.

Though life-sustaining treatment can be refused and though many of us while healthy may make bold claims about our willingness to refuse health care treatment if we are very sick, many older patients, for whom the issue is not a classroom hypothetical but something real, choose life-sustaining treatment as described in the following article.

Linda O'Brien, Jeane Ann Grisso, Greg Maislin, Karin LaPann, Karol P. Krotki, Peter J. Greco, Elisabeth A. Siegert, Lois K. Evans

Nursing Home Residents' Preferences for Life-Sustaining Treatments

* * *

Comment

These results indicate that a majority of decisionally capable nursing home residents prefer life-sustaining treatments and that the types of life-sustaining treatments nursing home residents prefer vary considerably. Similar to other nursing home studies,[2,3] our subjects preferred hospitalization most frequently (89 percent) followed by CPR (60 percent) and tube feedings (33 percent). That most study participants reported a preference to be hospitalized in the event of a serious illness is important because the pivotal decision to hospitalize often begins the chain of events leading to decisions regarding the use of life-sustaining treatments.

A majority of study subjects reported preferring CPR be performed in the event of sudden cardiac arrest. In previous studies, the percentage of residents who preferred to have CPR in their current state of health ranged from 47 percent to 67 percent.[2,3,4]

274 *Journal of American Medical Association* 1775 (December 13, 1995).

We expected that CPR preference rates would, in fact, be lower in this study because subjects were required to evidence comprehension of CPR procedures. Of interest, poorer self-perceived measures of health and physical mobility appeared to be more associated with not wishing to receive CPR than the number of chronic illnesses or staff evaluations of functional disability.

While we have no substantive explanations regarding the emergence of the factors of ethnicity and marital status on preferences for CPR, we can only speculate that African Americans may feel disenfranchised from the health care system and, therefore, prefer to err on the side of overtreatment rather than undertreatment. Future studies need to examine further how ethnicity, marital status, and social support systems affect life-sustaining treatment preferences.

Caution should be taken regarding the finding that those classified by nursing home staff on the MDS [Minimum Data Set] as having moderate-to-severe impairment in daily decision-making skills were, in fact, more likely to prefer CPR. Concern exists that these individuals could potentially be excluded from advance care planning discussions because of global rather than decision-specific assessments of cognitive capacity. Future studies are needed to examine how MDS assessments are made and the basis for classification.

An additional study objective was to determine whether CPR preferences were influenced by the provision of additional information regarding CPR procedures. Information regarding specific components of CPR (electrical defibrillation and mechanical ventilation) altered 14 percent of the study participants' preferences. Why this information did not have more of an impact on treatment preferences remains unclear. While our treatment descriptions may have been overly hygienic, our goal was to provide standardized information about the technical aspects of treatment. Schonwetter et al.[5] also demonstrated that CPR preferences in a group of older veterans who desired CPR (75 percent) did not dramatically change following receipt of additional information about CPR procedures. However, other studies[4,6] have demonstrated that additional information can affect responses. Murphy et al.[6] found that preferences for CPR decreased substantially following the provision of outcome information to older outpatients. That study, however, was based on less standardized discussions with known health care providers in an outpatient setting in which physicians were allowed to use their clinical skills to clarify concepts and to explore inconsistencies in responses. Our interviewers were required to strictly adhere to the questionnaire and to remain neutral throughout the interview process. While arguments can be made for both methods of inquiry, we believe the method used in this study had less chance of introducing caregiver bias.

We also found it interesting that a substantial percentage of patients would prefer tube feedings if no longer able to eat. One explanation for this finding may be that residents of nursing homes frequently witness patients receiving tube feedings and may believe that this is the expected course of treatment.

Despite having specific life-sustaining treatment preferences, relatively few residents reported having discussed their preferences with care providers at the nursing home or with family members. This finding is similar to that of other investigators among various patient populations[1,7] and particularly among nursing home patients who often are excluded from advance planning discussions. It is also interesting that despite having specific treatment preferences, the majority (69 percent) believe that doctors should make most important treatment decisions. Care should be taken in interpreting this finding, however, because many nursing home residents come to believe that their status as a nursing home resident requires them to relinquish decision-making powers.[8] Furthermore, we did not obtain sufficient information regarding actual advance directives, in part because of the nonuniform nature of those documents in the institutions. Whether the individuals' advance directives reflect their stated preferences is not known.

This study was limited to individuals who have decision-making capacity. Nevertheless, our study participants suffered from a median number of five chronic illnesses, and in a 24-month period, 24 percent of the residents died. Thus, while our study population was more cognitively intact than the general nursing home population, they were also physically frail at the time of interview.

* * *

Notes

1. Lo B, McLeod GA, Saika G. Patient attitudes to discussing life-sustaining treatment. *Arch Intern Med.* 1986; 146:1613–1615.

2. Danis M. Southerland LI, Garrett JM, et al. A prospective study of advance directives for life-sustaining care. *N Engl J Med.* 1991; 324:882–888.

3. Gerety MB, Chiodo LK, Kanten DN, Tuley MR, Cornell JE. Medical treatment preferences of nursing home residents: relationship to function and concordance with surrogate decision-makers. *J Am Geriatr Soc.* 1993; 41:953–960.

4. Shadlen F, Shadlen M, Tornabene J, Drank S, Habib S, Brock D. Preferences for life support measures among nursing home residents. *J Am Geriatr Soc.* 1990; 38:A55.

5. Schonwetter RS, Teasdale TA, Taffet G, Robinson BE, Luchi RJ. Educating the elderly: cardiopulmonary resuscitation decisions before and after intervention. *J Am Geriatr Soc.* 1991; 39:372–377.

6. Murphy DJ, Burrows D, Santilli S, et al. The influence of the probability of survival on patients' preferences regarding cardiopulmonary resuscitation. *N Engl J Med.* 1994; 330:545–549.

7. Singer PA, Siegler M. Advancing the cause of advance directives. *Arch Intern Med.* 1992; 152:22–24.

8. Collopy B, Boyle P, Jennings B. New directions in nursing home ethics. *Hastings Cent Rep.* March–April 1991; 21 (suppl 2): 1–16.

CHAPTER 26

Structural Responses to Competency and Informed Consent Controversies

Treatment decisions can be a source of significant tension between doctor and patient and between patient and family. Any decision involving life and death issues is likely to be controversial, but when made in a strange, forbidding environment such as a hospital, and when a decision about a highly technical topic has to be made under the pressure of time, it is almost certain that disagreements or even arguments can erupt. Fortunately, almost all hospitals have mechanisms in place to defuse hostility, mistrust, and disagreements arising over health care decision making.

Erica Wood and Naomi Karp

"Fitting the Forum to the Fuss" in Acute and Long-Term Care Facilities

* * *

II. Options for Dispute Resolution

A. Doctor-Patient Communications

The cornerstone of the doctor-patient relationship is the legal notion of informed consent—"the very basic and simple premise that you [the patient] have the right to choose what will be done from a range of suggested options and you will be given enough information to decide which is the most appropriate for you."[1] Informed consent should rest on ongoing communications regarding the benefits, burdens, and risks of medical treatments. Through this process, and through healthy airing of issues and emotions, disputes can often be prevented or addressed at an early point. Talk among doctors, patients/residents, and often families is the most basic "dispute resolution forum," on which all the others stand.

Making informed consent work, however, is not an easy task. It "is a constant struggle for professionals and patients alike."[2] Many factors can block communications and escalate misunderstandings. Patients/residents and families may be intimidated and fail to ask questions or to voice their hopes and expectations. They may not understand medical terminology or concepts. ("The doctor speaks doctor, and the nurse speaks nurse and nobody speaks patient.")[3] They may bring their own personal history to the process and create barriers unknown to the health care provider. Different physicians may have very different ideas about how to discern that a patient understands. Health care providers may be under time constraints and may be on rotating shifts. A crisis mode may inhibit full exchange of information. Cultural differences can make for starkly different assumptions about health care and the decision-making process. A patient's uncertain or fluctuating capacity can engender dilemmas about family participation, identifying the appropriate surrogate, maintaining the patient/resident's values, and enhancing the patient/resident's involvement. Recognizing these factors at play can be a first step toward animating the doctor-patient relationship and moving toward resolution of problems.

Clearinghouse Review, Vol. 29, No. 6, 621–628 (October 1995). Reprinted by permission.

B. Interdisciplinary Care Team

Many providers use a care-team approach to decision making. This informal process generally means that the providers involved in an individual's care "sit in a room and thrash out the dilemma," with the goal of moving toward consensus.[4] Physicians may like this approach because it diffuses responsibility for the decision. But it can exclude patients and family members and may lack a consistent focus on informed consent. Some facilities do conduct care conferences that include patients and family members as well as physicians, nurses, social workers, and other providers. Family members may be heard more effectively in this setting than in communications with the physician alone because they may find these professionals less intimidating than physicians. On the other hand, sometimes physicians dominate care conferences, and large numbers of staff attendees may overwhelm patients and families.[5]

C. Patient Representatives

In 1983, the President's Commission for the Study of Ethical Problems in Medicine recommended that, in implementing the informed consent doctrine, health care institutions should designate a liaison between health care professionals and patients.[6] "Patient representatives" fill this role in many hospitals. They must be "skilled at seeking consensus, clarifying values, promoting dialogue, and translating medical terminology and issues into everyday language."[7] They help patients navigate the system and crystallize patients' thoughts for presentation to the health care team. They "typically are tuned in to the 'unit culture'" and thus are able to aid patients and their advocates in charting an immediate course of action to address emergent disputes.[8] Patient representatives convey the stories and expectations of patients and families to physicians and other care givers and seek to encourage a patient-focused ethic. One patient representative described herself as "the stitch-in-time lady," urging doctors to take the time with patients now to save time and prevent difficulties later.[9]

Patient representatives may serve a triage function—helping patients to access physicians, the ethics committee, the risk manager, the hospital counsel, or the chaplain. They may provide support for patients and families in ethics committee meetings by clarifying the patient's perspective. They also play a role in identifying patterns of patient care and patient complaints, thereby prompting the institution to be proactive in solving problems and improving the quality of care. Finally, patient representatives often are responsible for educating staff on patient's rights and interpersonal problem-solving skills.

Patient representatives are employed by the hospital and thus are in a conflicted position. Moreover, they sometimes lack the necessary clout with the hospital hierarchy to effect needed action. But they can offer a welcome avenue for families with a "fuss" in the maelstrom of acute care.

D. Bioethics Consultants

> In the late 1970s and early 1980s, major teaching hospitals started bringing in formal ethics consultants to serve a dual role as clinicians and teachers. These consultants are available to doctors, nurses, social workers, medical students, and other staff to help deal with difficult patient care situations; they use "a step-by-step calculus to sort out facts, options and principles raised by each case."[10] Bioethics consultants need to command broad substantive knowledge: "[I]n bioethics, one must, at a minimum, know something about medicine, nursing, health law, health care financing, societal resources for health care professionals and patients, cultural and religious values, and ethics or ethical analysis."[11]

In addition to being a source of substantive expertise, some believe that the primary role of the bioethicist is to facilitate the decision-making process. Thus, the bioethics consultant may play a critical role in managing conflict and mediating between the players.[12] Although the bioethics consultant may be employed by the hospital, she is not allied with a particular department, unit, or profession and therefore can provide "neutral turf" for the resolution of patient care disputes.[13]

E. Ethics Committees

Difficult treatment decisions, particularly those involving termination of life support, spurred many hospitals to establish ethics committees. There are now more than 3,500 hospital ethics committees. In addition, many long-term care facilities—and now some home care and other community-based agencies—also have established ethics committees.[14] This trend has been accelerated by the mandate of the Joint Commission on the Accreditation of Healthcare Organizations that hospitals have a mechanism to identify and analyze bioethical problems and that the mechanism should be made known and available to patients and families.[15]

Ethics committees are multidisciplinary, typically including physicians, nurses, social workers, clergy, and sometimes ethicists, lawyers, and community representatives. These committees can serve three institutional functions. First, they are educational, providing information to staff on ethical issues. Second, they may be policy-making bodies, drawing up institutional policies on such issues as Do Not Resuscitate orders, termination of life-sustaining medical treatment, and treatment for newborns. Finally, they may serve as consultants when difficult patient care decisions must be made. They may be sought out when there is true dispute over a treatment decision, such as a conflict between a treating physician who believes continued life support is futile and family members who want all possible interventions sustained. Alternatively, those seeking the committee's assistance, particularly treating physicians, may simply want assurance that they are "doing the right thing."[16]

As a mechanism for case consultation and dispute resolution, ethics committees have been criticized on several grounds. They have been accused of institutional protectionism and professional bias, particularly when stacked with institutional players such as hospital lawyers and administrators.[17] Committee members may lack expertise in bioethics, legal norms, and other critical issues. In a survey of over three hundred hospital ethics committees, half had no formal ethics training.[18] Committee proceedings may lack due process, and patients and families may not even know that the committee is deliberating about their situation.

Despite these potential weaknesses, ethics committees can serve as an effective dispute-resolution forum for patients and family members who request an ethics committee consultation. Many committees now use a triage-team approach to treatment dilemmas, involving a smaller subcommittee that is on call for consultation on an immediate basis. For example, a committee chair may perform some initial investigating by telephone and by reviewing the patient's chart. Then a subgroup of five to seven ethics committee members may be convened within 24 hours. The group interviews everyone concerned and may bring them together for a meeting before providing an advisory opinion.[19]

In most cases, ethics committee members deliberate among themselves and arrive at a recommendation.[20] But some committees view their role more broadly and may see their function as "helping the persons involved actually reach consensus on how to proceed."[21]

F. Risk Managers and Hospital Counsel

Both risk managers and hospital counsel represent the health care institution. It is the job of hospital counsel to advise on legal issues, to protect the institution against possible liability, and to act in the best interest of the hospital as client. It is the job of the risk manager to control and minimize loss to protect the facility. Both may respond to patient or family complaints or claims and facilitate settlement at an early stage.

Hospital counsel, risk managers, and patient representatives may work together in solving problems. Structural arrangements differ among acute care facilities, with variation in the responsibilities assigned to each of these staff members. They may be a risk management committee involving the risk manager, the patient representative, and the legal counsel, and they may work closely with the physicians' peer review committee, the ethics committee, and/or the quality assurance division.

Risk managers and hospital counsel may exacerbate the "legal paranoia" that exists in many acute care settings, and that can in some cases impede attention to patient values and the principled resolution of bioethical disputes, especially in end-of-life decision making. They may tend to frame a dispute in legal terms too soon, rather than allowing an informal process of communications to pay out. In particular, outside legal counsel for small hospitals may have little grounding in bioethics, patients' rights, and health care decision making. However, many risk managers and hospital counsel taking an enlightened view recognize the significance of patient autonomy, informed consent, and the involvement of patients/families in treatment and care choices. Advocates can help educate these critical players.

* * *

Notes

1. NANCY NEVELOFF DUBLER & DAVID NIMMONS, ETHICS ON CALL 93 (1992).

2. *Id.* at 101

3. NANCY NEVELOFF DUBLER & LEONARD MARCUS, MEDIATING BIOMEDICAL DISPUTES 40 (1994) (quoting Dr. Leonard J. Marcus).

4. Interview with Thomas L. Hafemeister, director, National Center for State Courts' project on end-of-life decision making in health care facilities, Williamsburg, Va (Mar. 27, 1995).

5. *Id.*

6. PRESIDENT'S COMM'N FOR THE STUDY OF ETHICAL PROBLEMS IN MEDICINE & BIOMEDICAL & BEHAVIORAL RESEARCH, DECIDING TO FORGO LIFE-SUSTAINING TREATMENT (1983).

7. L. PHILLIPS, NATIONAL SOC'Y FOR PATIENT REPRESENTATION & CONSUMER AFFAIRS, AMERICAN HOSP. ASS'N, IN THE NAME OF THE PATIENT: CONSUMER ADVOCACY IN HEALTH CARE 10-1 (1994).

8. *Id.* at 10-2.

9. Interview with Melanie Wilson Silver, director of patient relations, Shore Memorial Hospital, New Jersey (Mar. 1995).

10. DUBLER & NIMMONS, *supra* note 1, at 42.

11. JUDITH WILSON ROSS ET AL., HEALTH CARE ETHICS COMMITTEES: THE NEXT GENERATION (1993).

12. DUBLER & MARCUS, *supra* note 3, at 8–9.

13. *Id.* at ix.

14. DUBLER & NIMMONS, *supra* note 1, at 49.

15. JOINT COMM'N ON ACCREDITATION OF HEALTHCARE ORGANIZATIONS, ACCREDITATION MANUAL FOR HOSPITALS (1995). The commission recently extended a similar mandate to long-term care facilities and home care agencies.

16. Diane Hoffman, *Mediating Life and Death Decisions,* 36 ARIZONA L. REV. 821, 823, 843 (1994).

17. *Id.* at 846; DUBLER & NIMMONS, *supra* note 1, at 50–51.

18. Interview with Myra Christopher, Mid-West Bioethics Center, Kansas City, Mo. (Mar. 24, 1995).

19. Interview with Catherine Emmett, ethics committee cochair, Sarasota Memorial Hospital (Mar. 20, 1995). *See also* Hoffmann, *supra* note 16, at 843–44; Mary Beth West et al., *Facilitating Medical Ethics Case Review: What Ethics Committees Can Learn from Mediation and Facilitation Techniques,* 1 CAMBRIDGE Q. OF HEALTHCARE ETHICS 63, 68 (1992).

20. Hoffmann, *supra* note 16, at 845.

21. West, *supra* note 19, at 68.

CHAPTER 27

Mentally Incapacitated Older Patients

A. What is Mental Capacity?

Under the doctrine of informed consent, patients with sufficient mental capacity can determine their health care, which raises the question of what level of mental competency is required. The following Note discusses how to determine whether a patient has the requisite mental competency to make health care decisions.

Kevin R. Wolff

Determining Patient Competency in Treatment Refusal Cases

* * *

B. Medical Tests for Competency

Competency in the medical field does not refer to a judicial determination but, rather, to a medical evaluation of a patient's mental capabilities.[1] Clinicians also refer to this concept as "capacity."[2] Clinicians have identified five traditional approaches to

This Article was originally published at 24 *Georgia Law Review* 733 (1990) and is reprinted with permission.

evaluating capacity in the informed consent context:[3] (1) evidencing a choice, (2) reasonable outcome of choice, (3) rational reasons for choice, (4) ability to understand, and (5) actual understanding.[4] Each approach balances patient autonomy against social goals in a different way. Although judges inherently use a specific competency test, their opinions rarely document which test was used, or what factors about the patient led to the patient's passing or failing the test.[5]

1. *Evidencing a Choice.* The first and least stringent test is "evidencing a choice."[6] If a patient can make a choice—any choice—that decision serves to prove sufficiently his competency.[7] This test values highly the patient's autonomy in the decision-making process[8] and is, therefore, the least paternalistic: only the presence of a decision of some sort by the patient is required, without any evaluation by others of the quality of that decision.[9] By focusing on purely behavioral evidence, the test is also very reliable.[10]

"Evidencing a choice" does not, however, function well for screening competency in refusal of medical treatment cases. All consents or refusals constitute a choice; therefore, under this rationale only nondecisions are incompetent choices.[11]

2. *Reasonable Outcome of Choice.* The "reasonable outcome of choice" test requires that an evaluator agree the patient has made the "right" or "responsible" decision.[12] This test emphasizes social goals by favoring the state interests in the preservation of life and the integrity of the medical profession.[13]

"Reasonable outcome of choice" does not highly value patient autonomy, though, because the opinion of the outside observer unconditionally trumps the patient's decision if the parties merely disagree about the outcome of that decision.[14] Given the medical profession's predisposition for sustaining life,[15] the patient is likely to be adjudged incompetent whenever he chooses to refuse treatment. This result occurred in *United States v. Charters,* where a psychiatric patient's refusal of antipsychotic drugs, which were prescribed to make him competent to stand trial, was a basis of his adjudged incompetency to refuse the medication.[16]

3. *Rational Reasons for Choice.* This third test does not look at the outcome of the decision; instead, this test evaluates the quality of the decision-making.[17] It asks whether the choice was based on rational reasons.[18] Psychiatrists are most comfortable with this "rational" test because of their expertise in assessing irrationality.[19] The traditional irrationality test is an evaluation of the patient's ability to manipulate data and reach a conclusion based on hypothetical situations.[20]

Despite psychiatric expertise in this area, an obvious problem with this test is distinguishing between a rational and an irrational decision.[21] This test necessarily includes a subjective evaluation by the evaluating psychiatrist; however, this subjectivity only impinges on patient autonomy if the psychiatrist does not allow for the possibility that idiosyncratic responses might still result from rational decision-making.[22] One commentator suggests calling this the "recognizable reasons test" to account for reasons that support the patient's decision but with which the evaluator disagrees.[23]

A second problem with this test is proving a causal link between the irrational decision and the patient's incompetence.[24] The irrational decision can result from phobia, panic or depression,[25] but these conditions do not necessarily indicate incompetence.[26] The causation problem should not eliminate this test, however, because it still identifies incompetent decisions although the reason for the incompetence might remain obscured. One proposed solution is to limit the responses that constitute failures under this test to those premised on known falsities or nonsequiturs.[27]

4. *Ability to Understand.* This test requires an evaluation of the patient's ability to understand the risks, benefits, and alternatives of treatment.[28] The traditional method of testing begins when patients are given information necessary to make an informed decision.[29] They are later asked for their decision and the information they considered relevant in making their decision.[30] This test is consistent with standards of informed consent that allow the patient to make treatment decisions only when those decisions are informed, voluntary and competent.[31]

A limitation of this test is that the patient may understand the risks but not the benefits.[32] Furthermore, the test does not specify how sophisticated the understanding must be, a value decision in and of itself.[33] Also, the test's reliability is questionable because the test does not rely on observable behavioral elements but rather on inferential mental processes.[34] Finally, one can criticize the test as placing too much influence on the patient's ability to memorize and recall the information given to him, a factor which may obscure the later impact this information may have.[35]

5. *Actual Understanding.* The fifth test requires that the patient actually understand the costs, benefits, and alternatives of treatment and be able to apply these to his current situation.[36] This shares with the "ability to understand" test the practical problems of determining the nature of understanding.[37] The subjectivity problem is more pronounced, however, because the emphasis is not on the patient's *ability* to understand but on whether the patient *actually* understands.[38] This requirement theoretically makes validation more difficult.[39]

* * *

Notes

1. [R. Meyer, E. Landis & J. Hays, Law for the Psychotherapist 89 (1988).]

2. T. Gutheil & P. Appelbaum, Clinical Handbook of Psychiatry and the Law 215 (1982). This use of the word "capacity" should not be confused with the legal definition of the word. *See* 12A C.J.S. *Capacity* (1980) (distinguishing legal capacities, *e.g.*, to contract, to sue or be sued, and to make a will, from mental capacity or competence).

3. [*See Superintendent of Belchertown State School v. Saikewicz*, 373 Mass. 728, 370 N.E.2d 417 (1977); In re *Conroy*, 98 N.J. 321, 486 A.2d 1209 (1985); 1 F. Harper, F. James & O. Gray, The Law of Torts § 3.10, at 301 & n.20 (2d ed. 1986). The doctrine of informed consent begins with the general principle that a physician or surgeon must obtain the patient's consent, if the patient is a competent adult, or the consent of one legally authorized to give such consent, if the patient is incompetent or a minor. For the consent to be valid, it must be voluntary and informed, i.e., the doctor must explain the details of the treatment including the risks and the benefits involved, and the decision must be made free of outside influences. *Id. See* R. Faden &

T. BEAUCHAMP, A HISTORY AND THEORY OF INFORMED CONSENT 53–150 (1986) (giving historical background and developing case law).]

4. The framework for this discussion comes from Roth, Meisel & Lidz, [Roth, Meisel & Lidz, *Tests of Competency to Consent to Treatment,* 134 AM. J. PSYCHIATRY 279, 280 (1977)]. Other tests have been proposed, but this analysis is the easiest to understand and apply to the refusal of medical treatment context.

5. [Roth, Meisel & Lidz, *Tests of Competency to Consent to Treatment,* 134 AM. J. PSYCHIATRY 279, 280 (1977).]

6. *Id.*

7. *Id.*

8. *Id.* The authors cite Wyatt v. Aderholt, 368 F. Supp. 1383 (M.D. Ala. 1974), for a related application of this test. That case held that mentally retarded inmates of state institutions cannot be sterilized without giving their informed consent. *Id.* at 1384. If the inmate has been judged legally incompetent to give that consent, the Review Committee established to monitor the sterilizations should still attempt to determine "whether the resident has formed, without coercion, a genuine desire to be sterilized." *Id.* at 1385.

9. [Roth, Meisel & Lidz, *Tests of Competency to Consent to Treatment,* 134 AM. J. PSYCHIATRY 279, 280 (1977).]

10. *Id.*

11. [Freedman, *Competence, Marginal and Otherwise,* 4 INT'L J.L. & PSYCHIATRY 53, 58–61 (1981) (explaining that competency attempts to achieve balance between freedom and protection and that this balance is proper inquiry for choice of competency standards).]

12. [Roth, Meisel & Lidz, *Tests of Competency to Consent to Treatment,* 134 AM. J. PSYCHIATRY 279, 280 (1977).]

13. *Id.* at 281. [Remainder of note omitted.]

14. *See* [Freedman, *Competence, Marginal and Otherwise,* 4 INT'L J.L. & PSYCHIATRY 53, 58–61 (1981) (explaining that competency attempts to achieve balance between freedom and protection and that this balance is proper inquiry for choice of competency standards).]

15. [In such cases, the courts must decide whether to allow someone other than the patient to make the crucial decision to terminate treatment or to rely on the patient's advance directives. This situation raises the issue of surrogate decisionmaking, which is beyond the scope of this Note. A summary of the issue is in PRESIDENT'S COMM'N FOR THE STUDY OF ETHICS PROBS. IN MED. AND BIOMEDICAL AND BEHAVIORAL RESEARCH, DECIDING TO FOREGO LIFE-SUSTAINING TREATMENT 126–36 (1983) (hereinafter DECIDING TO FOREGO).]

16. 863 F.2d 302 (4th Cir. 1988) (en banc), *cert. denied,* 110 S. Ct. 1317 (1990). The case history also provides an illustration of judicial disagreement regarding the probative value of this test. Charters was indicted for threatening the President of the United States. Pursuant to federal law, the district court had committed Charters to a medical center and, later, to the Federal Correctional Institution at Butner, North Carolina, for psychiatric evaluation and treatment. The district court adjudged Charters incompetent to stand trial and dangerous to society on five separate occasions. 829 F.2d 479, 482 (4th Cir. 1987), *vacated on reh'g,* 863 F.2d 302 (1988). Each time the court recommitted Charters to Butner; and, each time, the court denied the government's motion to treat Charters with antipsychotic medication against his wishes. The district court eventually granted the government's motion to forcibly medicate Charters in May 1986, but stayed the order pending an expedited appeal to the Fourth Circuit. *Id.* at 482.

The district court's decision allowing forced medication of Charters was based on testimony by the director of Forensic Services and Clinical Research at Butner, Dr. Sally Johnson. Johnson concluded that Charters was incompetent—both incompetent to stand trial and incompetent to make decisions about medical treatment. Johnson's evaluation of Charter's competency was based on Charter's disagreement with Johnson regarding what treatment was in his best interest. *Id.* at 482–84. The district court had endorsed this use of the reasonable outcome of choice test. *Id.* at 496. A panel of the Fourth Circuit reversed the district court and remanded with directions to (1) evaluate Charter's competency to make medical decisions independent of his competency to stand trial and (2) apply a rational reasons for choice test. *Id.* For an explanation of the rational reasons of choice test, see *infra* text accompanying notes 16–26.

On rehearing, the Fourth Circuit sitting en banc vacated the panel opinion. 863 F.2d at 304. Interestingly, Chief Judge Winter, a member of the panel, reversed his position on rehearing. *Id.* at 314 (Winter, C.J., concurring). The majority's rationale for vacating had three main arguments which highlight the disagreement among the judges about the different competency tests. First, the court held that initially separate hearings on competency to refuse treatment and procedures to be followed if the treating psychiatrist considers the patient incompetent are unnecessary because the psychiatrist's competency evaluation inherently considers the patient's best interests. *Id.* at 309. Second, a single competency evaluation can adequately determine both competency to stand trial and competency to refuse treatment because the distinction between these competencies exists "in theory" and is "one of such subtlety and complexity as to tax perception by the most skilled medical or psychiatric professionals." *Id.* at 310. Finally, a two-step procedure would yield, in the court's view, an undesirable result: district judges making the initial decision on treatment, a "purely medical and psychiatric question," based on adverse expert testimony. *Id.* at 309. The court's principal concern with this scenario is that too many patients would be judged competent to decide their own medical treatment, thus preventing the penal institution from medicating inmates against their will. *Id.* at 309 & n.5.

17. [Roth, Meisel & Lidz, *Tests of Competency to Consent to Treatment,* 134 AM. J. PSYCHIATRY 279, 280 (1977).]

18. *Id.*

19. T. GUTHEIL & P. APPELBAUM, *supra* note 2, at 218.

20. *Id.*

21. [Roth, Meisel & Lidz, *Tests of Competency to Consent to Treatment,* 134 AM. J. PSYCHIATRY 279, 280 (1977).]

22. [Freedman, *Competence, Marginal and Otherwise,* 4 INT'L J.L. & PSYCHIATRY 53, 58–61 (1981) (explaining that competency attempts to achieve balance between freedom and protection and that this balance is proper inquiry for choice of competency standards)]; Tancredi, *Competency for Informed Consent: Conceptual Limits of Empirical Data,* 5 INT'L J.L. & PSYCHIATRY 51, 54 (1982). An example is a patient who wants to discontinue life-sustaining treatment because of the financial burden such treatment places on her family. While the psychiatrist might disagree with the patient as to the validity of this reason, he could not dispute its rational support for the patient's decision.

23. [Freedman, *Competence, Marginal and Otherwise,* 4 INT'L J.L. & PSYCHIATRY 53, 58–61 (1981) (explaining that competency attempts to achieve balance between freedom and protection and that this balance is proper inquiry for choice of competency standards).]

24. [Roth, Meisel & Lidz, *Tests of Competency to Consent to Treatment,* 134 AM. J. PSYCHIATRY 279, 280 (1977).]

25. Stromberg & Stone, *A Model State Law on Civil Commitment of the Mentally Ill,* 20 HARV. J.

ON LEGIS. 275, 302 (1983). For a study of the impact of these conditions on competency, see Gutheil & Bursztajn, *Clinicians' Guidelines for Assessing and Presenting Subtle Forms of Patient Incompetence in Legal Settings,* 143 AM. J. PSYCHIATRY 1020 (1986). Judges often conceptualize competency as consisting solely of cognitive, or intellectual capacity. For an explanation of cognitive capacity, see Carroll, *Cognitive Abilities,* in 1 ENCYCLOPEDIA OF PSYCHOLOGY 228 (1984). In doing so, they ignore the impact of subtle psychotic states or affective disturbances. Such judges may be fooled by a patient capable of giving coherent, articulate reasons for his decision, when, in fact, the patient underlying decision-making capabilities are impaired through illness.

26. [Roth, Meisel & Lidz, *Tests of Competency to Consent to Treatment,* 134 AM. J. PSYCHIATRY 279, 280 (1977).]

27. *See* [Freedman, *Competence, Marginal and Otherwise,* 4 INT'L J.L. & PSYCHIATRY 53, 58–61 (1981) (explaining that competency attempts to achieve balance between freedom and protection and that this balance is proper inquiry for choice of competency standards).] An example of the first is the patient who refuses surgery because she thinks a similar surgery caused her aunt's death. In fact, her aunt died of a heart attack a year after the surgery. *Id.* at 62. An example of the second is basing the decision on true facts which weigh heavily on the decision but which are totally unrelated to it. Thus, refusing surgery because it is scheduled for a Tuesday would be a nonsequitur response. *Id.* at 64.

28. T. GUTHEIL & P. APPELBAUM, *supra* note 2, at 219; Roth, Meisel, & Lidz, *supra* note 11, at 281.

29. Roth, Lidz, Meisel, Soloff, Kaufman, Spiker & Foster, *Competency to Decide About Treatment or Research: An Overview of Some Empirical Data,* 5 INT'L J.L. & PSYCHIATRY 29, 31 (1982) [hereinafter Roth & Foster, *Competency*].

30. *Id.*

31. Schloendorff v. Society of N.Y. Hosp., 211 N.Y. 125, 129, 105 N.E. 92, 93 (1914) (removing tumor pursuant to patient's limited consent for exploratory surgery is assault), *overruled on other grounds,* Bing v. Thunig, 2 N.Y.2d 656, 143 N.E.2d, 163 N.Y.S.2d 3 (1957). For the view that understanding tests of competency are practically the same as the "informed" and "voluntary" requirements of informed consent, thereby eliminating the independent nature of the competency requirement, see [Freedman, *Competence, Marginal and Otherwise,* 4 INT'L J.L. & PSYCHIATRY 53, 58–61 (1981) (explaining that competency attempts to achieve balance between freedom and protection and that this balance is proper inquiry for choice of competency standards]. One should note that the authorities conflict on whether this test encompasses a rational reasons test or remains independent of it. Freedman, [idem]; *see also* Stromberg & Stone, *supra* note 25, at 302 (arguing that understanding requires fundamental appreciation of aspects of proposed treatment that reasonable person would find significant in decision-making); [Roth, Meisel & Lidz, *Tests of Competency to Consent to Treatment,* 134 AM. J. PSYCHIATRY 279, 280 (1977).]

32. *Id.* at 282. An example would be a "49-year-old woman whose understanding of treatment was otherwise intact, when informed that there was a 1 in 3,000 chance of dying from ECT [electroconvulsive therapy, also known as electric shock therapy], replied, 'I hope I am the one.'" *Id.*

33. *Id.*

34. *Id. But see* Roth, & Foster, *Competency, supra* note 29, at 42 (confirming utility of understanding approach to measure competency to consent to treatment).

35. Tancredi, *supra* note 22, at 54.

36. [Roth, Meisel & Lidz, *Tests of Competency to Consent to Treatment*, 134 AM. J. PSYCHIATRY 279, 280 (1977)]; Tancredi, *supra* note 22, at 54.

37. *See supra* text accompanying notes 28–35.

38. Tancredi, *supra* note 22, at 54. But see Roth & Foster, *Competency, supra* note 29, at 42.

39. Tancredi, *supra* note 22, at 54. Note that the distinction between the two "understanding" tests may be artificial as at least one court has used language which melds the two tests together. *In re* Farrell, 108 N.J. 335, 354 n.7, 529 A.2d 404, 413 n.7 (1987) ("A competent patient has a clear understanding of the nature of his or her illness and prognosis, and of the risks and benefits of the proposed treatment, and has the capacity to reason and make judgments about that information.").

Mental capacity must be assessed with reference to the patient's ability to understand and process information without regard to the "correctness" of the patient's choice. That is, patients must be allowed to make "irrational" decisions. This is sometimes referred to as the right to be wrong or the right to be eccentric. The following case demonstrates the difficulty for courts in determining mental capacity of a patient who holds highly individualistic views.

In re MILTON
Cite as 505 N.E.2d 255 (Ohio 1987)
Supreme Court of Ohio.
Feb. 20, 1987.

This case arises from an application filed with the Court of Common Pleas of Franklin County, Probate Division, requesting authorization to perform medical treatment on appellant, Nancy Milton. The application, which was filed pursuant to R.C. 5122.271[1] by Dr. Lewis A. Lindner, the Chief Medical Officer of the Central Ohio Psychiatric Hospital (hereinafter "hospital"), alleged that appellant was unable to give informed, intelligent, and knowing consent for surgery. Dr. Lindner petitioned for an order requiring appellant to submit to radiation treatments, transfusions and possible surgery, stating that without these treatments, the patient would suffer an early death.[2]

A hearing on the application was conducted in the probate court. The hospital called two witnesses at this hearing, Dr. Lewis Lindner and Dr. Eugene Green, a psychiatrist. Dr. Green testified that appellant was alert, responsive, did not appear confused, and could function in many areas of everyday life. Dr. Lindner stated that she was of normal intelligence.

Appellant, a fifty-three-year-old patient of the hospital, refused to consent to this medical treatment primarily because it conflicted with her belief in faith healing.[3] Dr. Lindner claimed that appellant's stated reasons for refusing consent constituted a psychotic delusion and that she was unable to understand and appreciate the information necessary to either provide informed consent or to refuse such consent. Dr. Lindner asserted that appellant's entire belief system was delusional because she had a fixed long-standing delusion that she was the spouse of Rev. LeRoy Jenkins, a faith healer and evangelist who is well known in the central Ohio area.

Dr. Lindner conceded that appellant has never been adjudicated incompetent and that the hospital had accepted, without question as to her competency, her informed consent for all prior treatments at the hospital, including the biopsy through which the malignant tumor was diagnosed.

The trial court found that appellant had the mental capability to understand the nature of her illness and the contemplated treatment, but held that since appellant was not receiving spiritual treatment from Rev. Jenkins, the court could intervene. Therefore, the trial court authorized the requested medical treatment. The court of appeals affirmed, holding that appellant's beliefs in faith healing ". . . by all rational evaluation, constitute a delusion."

This cause is now before this court pursuant to the allowance of a motion to certify the record.

* * *

WRIGHT, Justice.

This is a case of first impression in Ohio. Several difficult and delicate questions are before us, including whether a state acting through its courts may compel an individual to submit to medical treatment which is arguably life-extending in derogation of that individual's religious beliefs. We must also decide whether the court below infringed upon appellant's constitutional right of religious freedom in citing the essence of her belief in faith healing as evidence of her lack of capacity to provide informed consent to medical treatment. We believe these questions should be resolved in favor of appellant and, thus, we reverse the holding of the appellate court.

At the outset, we emphasize that at no time has any court found appellant to be incompetent under state law. Appellant is a voluntary patient of the hospital. However, even if she were to be involuntarily committed, that commitment would not be tantamount to a finding of incompetency. Commitments to a mental institution and adjudications of incompetency are distinct legal proceedings which determine separate issues and often lead to different results. Commitment proceedings focus on proof of dangerousness as the primary determinant of the need for commitment, while incompetency adjudications evaluate a person's cognitive ability to make decisions. "[A] finding of 'mental illness' . . . and commitment to a hospital, does [*sic*] not raise even a presumption that the patient is 'incompetent' or unable adequately to manage his own affairs." *Winters v. Miller* (C.A.2, 1971), 446 F.2d 65, 68. Thus, a person who is not in a mental institution may be found to be incompetent, and a person properly committed to a mental institution may be legally competent.

* * *

[1] The fact that appellant has a long-standing delusion that she is Rev. Jenkins' wife and that he will perchance heal her infirmities simply does not strip appellant of her constitutional rights to freely select and adhere to the religion of her choice. The testimony of Dr. Green, the hospital's own witness, supports a conclusion that appellant's belief in spiritual healing stands on its own, without regard to her delusion. Dr. Green explained that appellant's psychosis was "pretty much limited to delusional imaginations" and that "[c]ertain other parts of her seem pretty much intact."

[2] The First Amendment to the United States Constitution and Section 7, Article I of the Ohio Constitution safeguard an individual's freedom to both choose and employ religious beliefs and practices.

* * *

[3][4] While religiously inspired *acts* do not receive absolute protection, ". . . [o]nly the gravest abuses, endangering paramount interests, give occasion for permissible limitation."

* * *

Appellee does not suggest any state interest sufficient to justify interfering with appellant's religiously inspired refusal to consent to medical treatment. Appellee argues that appellant's delusion that she was Rev. Jenkins' spouse negated her religious views and made her entire belief in faith healing a delusion. The court of appeals looked to the content of appellant's religious beliefs and found that her belief in faith healing constituted a delusion. We do not accept this contention.

There is a dichotomy between modern medicine which is scientific and based upon provable theories and religion which is *inherently* mystical, intangible, and a matter of individual faith. Yet, the Ohio and United States Constitutions mandate that when the dictates of modern medicine and religious beliefs collide, the conflict be resolved by leaving the medical treatment decision to the individual. As the court stated in *United States v. Ballard* (1944), 322 U.S. 78, 86, 64 S.Ct. 882, 886, 88 L.Ed. 1148, freedom of religion "embraces the right to maintain theories of life and of death and of the hereafter which are rank heresy to followers of the orthodox faiths. . . . Men may believe what they cannot prove. They may not be put to the proof of their religious doctrines or beliefs. Religious experiences which are as real as life to some may be incomprehensible to others."

While there may be a variety of opinions as to the efficacy of spiritual healing through faith, the courts below acknowledged that it is a form of religious belief and practice. We recognize that extending constitutional protection to a belief in spiritual healing and other religiously motivated refusals to accept medical treatment can be very troubling to those who do not share these beliefs, since, in cases such as this one, the patient may die as a result of refusing the recommended treatment. ". . . But freedom to differ is not limited to things that do not matter much. That would be a mere shadow of freedom. The test of its substance is the right to differ as to things that touch the heart of the existing order. If there is any fixed star in our constitutional constellation, it is that no official, high or petty, can prescribe what shall be orthodox in . . . religion . . . or force citizens to confess by word or act their faith therein." *West Virginia Bd. of Edn. v. Barnette, supra,* 319 U.S. at 642, 63 S.Ct. at 1187.

* * *

[5] Appellant has expressed a long-standing belief in spiritual healing, and great weight must be given to her statement of her personal beliefs. We cannot evaluate the "correctness" or propriety of appellant's belief. Absent the most exigent circumstances, courts should never be a party to branding a citizen's religious views as baseless on the grounds that they are non-traditional, unorthodox or at war with what the state or others perceive as reality.

The testimony of Dr. Green supports our conclusion that appellant's belief in spiritual healing stands on its own, without regard to any delusion. We can probe no further. Appellant's religious freedom to believe and act according to the dictates of her belief in spiritual healing prevents a court from ordering treatment against her will that would violate her religious beliefs. Thus, we hold that the state may not compel a legally competent adult to submit to medical treatment which would violate that individual's religious beliefs even though the treatment is arguably life-extending. Therefore, the probate court's determination was erroneous and the judgment of the court of appeals upholding it is reversed.

Judgment reversed.

MOYER, C.J., and SWEENEY, DOUGLAS and HERBERT R. BROWN, JJ., concur.

LOCHER and HOLMES, JJ., dissent.

* * *

HOLMES, Justice, dissenting.

I am in agreement that the state may not compel the medical treatment of a person who is capable of making the determination of granting or denying the consent for a surgical activity where such determination is based upon a religious belief, even though such belief is strange or incomprehensible to others. However, where the facts show that an individual is so confused in the thinking process that such belief is not rationally formulated and is an outworking of a psychosis, as held by the trial court and the court of appeals here, then the question is not one of a religious infringement but is instead one of the degree of mental instability.

* * *

Here the probate court and trial court reasonably found that Nancy Milton was unable because of her confused mental condition to give an informed, intelligent and knowing consent for her surgery. Such a finding should be appealed to this court without the esoteric, constitutional free-exercise-of-religion discussion. Appellant has expressed quite enough to demonstrate to the lower courts, and certainly to this court, that she is *incapable* of making her own medical determination. She has asserted that she is married to LeRoy Jenkins, and that this member of the T.V. and now radio clergy would heal her maladies. However, Jenkins has, by way of press announcement in the *Columbus Dispatch,* publicly removed himself from this appellant and stated that she needs help from others.

It is my view that Nancy Milton does need help from others, and that the probate court and the court of appeals properly recognized that such help should be forthcoming from the medical profession as appropriately prescribed. Accordingly, I would affirm the probate court and the court of appeals.

Notes

1. R.C. 5122.271, which is applicable to mental hospital patients, provides as follows:

"(A) Except as provided in divisions (C), (D), (E), and (F) of this section, the chief medical officer or, in a nonpublic hospital, the attending physician responsible for a patient's care shall provide all information, including expected physical and medical consequences, necessary to enable any patient of a hospital for the mentally ill to give a fully informed, intelligent, and knowing consent, the opportunity to consult with independent specialists and counsel, and the right to refuse consent for any of the following:

"(1) Surgery;
"(2) Convulsive therapy;
"(3) Major aversive interventions;
"(4) Sterilization;
"(5) Any unusually hazardous treatment procedures;
"(6) Psycho-surgery.

2. Dr. Lindner testified that appellant had cancer of the uterus which was in "a relatively advanced stage," and that there was a possibility she might be cured by medical treatment. Nevertheless, he estimated that even if she did receive the prescribed medical treatment, there was less than a fifty percent chance that she would be free of cancer for five years or more. At a minimum, he believed the treatment would arrest the tumor and considerably prolong appellant's life. Dr. Lindner further testified that appellant's death from the cancer was almost inevitable if she did not receive this medical treatment.

3. Dr. Green testified that appellant had stated that her primary reason for refusing medical treatment was her belief in spiritual healing, but she also indicated to him that a secondary reason for her refusal was that she had a background in nursing and desired to avoid the adverse side effects which she knew to be attendant to radiation treatments. He concluded, "I had the feeling again and again that in her hierarchy of beliefs, number one was [the] omnipotence of faith healing. This was her business. * * * This was God's business and we shouldn't tamper with it. We should believe and be healed."

* * *

B. Proxy Decision Making

There are three possible ways of handing health care decisions for a mentally incapacitated individual. First, the individual may have left instructions in the form of a living will. In such cases, the individual controls the nature of future health care by virtue of a decision made prior to the onset of the incapacity. Second, the individual may appoint a surrogate decision-maker, who will be empowered to make the decisions for the incapacitated person. The surrogate may or may not have been given detailed enough instructions to permit the surrogate to act in a manner that the surrogate is fairly certain is consistent with how the incapacitated person would decide. Finally, the incapacitated person may have neither left instructions nor named a surrogate. In such cases, a proxy decision-maker will have to be appointed, either by a guardianship or a health care agent appointed under state law. In her article, Professor Fentiman analyzes the legal response to health care decision-making for incapacitated adults.

Linda C. Fentiman

Privacy and Personhood Revisited: A New Framework for Substitute Decision-making for the Incompetent, Incurably Ill Adult

Introduction

* * *

B. Consequences of the Autonomy Model

Reflecting the high priority our society places upon respect for individual autonomy and self-determination, in the last dozen years, courts and legislatures that have grappled with the problem of decision-making for the incompetent incurably ill have developed a variety of substitute decision-making alternatives that seek to effectuate the right of personal choice. These include two vehicles by which a competent adult can elect in advance the desired treatment approach should she become incurably ill and incompetent—the living will and the designated treatment agent—as well as several forms of judicial and less formal decision-making that provide for a substitute

George Washington Law Review, Vol. 57, No. 4, 801–847 (1989). Reprinted by permission.

decision-maker to act on the patient's behalf if he becomes incompetent. Each of these alternatives will be explored below.

1. Living Wills By far the most well known of the advance directives for substitute decision-making are "living wills." Originally proposed by Dr. Louis Kutner in the late 1960s,[1] and popularized by such groups as the Society for the Right to Die and Concern for Dying, a living will provides a mechanism by which a competent adult can designate in a legally binding manner the particular treatment or non-treatment that he wishes to receive should he become terminally ill and incompetent. . . . These statutes build on the constitutional and common law right to privacy and individual autonomy, often declaring in a formal preamble that each individual has a right to choose for himself the appropriate form of treatment or nontreatment,[2] and that a directive made in advance by a competent adult shall be binding on her physician and family if she later becomes incompetent.

Under a typical living will statute, a competent, non-pregnant[3] adult may execute a written document, witnessed by two disinterested persons, which states that should the declarant later become terminally ill and incompetent, sustained only by "artificial" life support systems, he wishes not to receive further medical treatment. The declarant may indicate a particular form or forms of treatment which he chooses not to receive, or he may make a more general statement that he wishes no medical treatment whatsoever. The statutes in many jurisdictions provide a form for the living will, but jurisdictions differ as to whether this form is mandatory or suggested. Some statutes specifically exclude nutrition and hydration or medication, or both, from the definition of life-sustaining treatment;[4] others are silent on this point.[5]

* * *

Living wills have been widely criticized as inadequate to achieve their laudable goal of promoting individual autonomy and permitting hopelessly ill patients to free themselves from a prolonged and painful dying. Many patients are unable to take advantage of a living will statute, either because they do not know about it or because its provisions do not encompass their situation.

Significantly, many physicians are uncomfortable about discussing death, and may even be reluctant to tell a patient that he is terminally ill. Thus, numerous patients are unlikely to recognize the need to make a living will, or to have the time to execute it before they lapse into unconsciousness.[6] This is obviously so with accident victims, but it is also so with many people whose chronic degenerative disease takes a sudden turn for the worse.

Further, even if a patient desires to execute an advance treatment directive, few physicians have living will forms available. Nor do many physicians either know, or understand, the requirements of the living will act in their jurisdiction.[7] Consequently, they are unable to advise their patients appropriately.

In addition, a number of incurably ill patients are not terminally ill.[8] These include those in a persistent vegetative state, those suffering from a chronic degenerative disease, and those suffering from a condition that is hopeless but not expected to produce death in the near future.[9] Further, because of the pervasive use in the living will statutes of vague and sometimes circular definitions of such crucial terms as "terminally ill," "imminent death," "'artificial' life sustaining treatment," many physicians lack guidance about whether a particular living will is effective.[10] Thus, they may be disinclined to honor it, or honor it only at the eleventh hour.[11] In a leading survey of physician practices in California, researchers found that many physicians defined "imminent death" to mean death within the relatively short time periods of forty-eight hours, one week or one month. Although such a definition may be appropriate clinically, reflecting the need for certainty in prognosis, it may make the beneficial effects of a natural death act illusory to all but a few terminally ill patients.[12]

But perhaps the key drawback of the living will is its inherent inflexibility. The essence of a living will is the function it serves as an *advance* directive for medical treatment decisions. Yet, it is difficult, if not virtually impossible, for any adult to indicate with specificity the types of medical treatment she might wish to forego should she become incurably ill or incompetent. This is so both because what seems like a grave imposition on the quality of life to a thirty-year-old might appear to be an entirely reasonable restriction at the age of seventy,[13] and also because it is difficult to foresee precisely the type of incompetency and incurable illness that might occur.[14]

* * *

2. *Designing a Medical Treatment Agent* Acknowledging that living wills are in many ways inadequate, thirteen states have enacted laws that authorize a competent adult to designate someone to make treatment decisions on her behalf should she become incompetent[15] and, in some cases, terminally ill.[16]

* * *

State statutes permitting the advance designation of a medical treatment agent grow out of the same desire to protect the patient's right to autonomy and personal choice in the making of medical treatment that underlies the living will, but they achieve their goal much more effectively. Utah explicitly recognizes this principle of self-determination, providing that the competent patient will select a treatment agent "with confidence in the belief that this person's familiarity with my desires, beliefs, and attitudes will result in directions to attending physicians and providers of medical services which would probably be the same as I would give if able to do so."[17] Similarly, the Florida and Iowa statutes expressly state that in making their decision, the treatment agent and physician are to be "guided by the express or implied intentions of the patient."[18] Indeed, the very fact of designating a treatment agent enhances the patient's rights of self-determination and privacy in decision-making. Because the competent adult can nominate in advance a person whom he trusts, and who knows him well, he is given the peace of mind that comes from knowing that the ultimate treatment decision will be one that is both consonant with his moral and religious beliefs, and as close as possible to the one that he would have made himself, because it will be based upon accurate, up-to-date medical information.[19]

The designation of a treatment agent is a significant advance over the living will, because it provides for intelligent and informed discussion between the treatment agent and the patient's physician. Because the treatment agent can both provide the attending physician with important background information concerning the patient's health and life habits, increasing the accuracy of the diagnosis and prognosis made, and can also consider the medical information conveyed by the physician in light of the totality of the patient's life, values, and beliefs, she can carefully tailor a treatment decision to be consistent with the patient's medical *and* moral needs. The designation of a medical treatment agent eliminates the risk that the physician will either refuse to comply with an advance treatment directive that he believes to be too sweeping in scope, or that he *will* honor it, no matter what the circumstances.

The designation of a treatment agent is thus an alternative that promotes conversation, compassion, and caring.[20] The attending physician is not bound to follow reflexively the advance directive of a living will, but must consult with the patient's designated treatment agent so that the agent may determine a course that is both medically appropriate and consistent with the patient's values and desires.

* * *

In addition to the judicially developed models for substitute decision-making, ten states have, by statute, authorized informal substitute decision-making for incompetent, terminally ill adults[21] as part of their "living will" or "natural death" acts. Recognizing that competent adults have the right to "a peaceful and natural death,"[22] and "to control the decisions relating to their own medical care, including the decision to have life-sustaining procedures withheld or withdrawn in instances where such persons are diagnosed as having a terminal and irreversible condition,"[23] these statutes permit a substitute medical treatment decision to be made even if the patient has not executed a living will or designated a medical treatment agent. Each of the statutes provides that the patient's attending physician and at least one other person, usually chosen from a statutory list in order of priority, shall make the decision to end treatment.

* * *

Notes

1. Martyn & Jacobs, *Legislating Advance Directives for the Terminally Ill: The Living Will and Durable Power of Attorney*, 63 NEB. L. REV. 779, 787 (1984); see Kutner, *Due Process of Euthanasia: The Living Will, A Proposal*, 44 IND. L.J. 539, 550–54 (1969), *cited in* Garrard, *Right to Forego Medical Treatment*, 30 RES GESTAE 113 (1986).

2. A number of living will statutes emphasize that the statute itself does not create this right to privacy and self-determination, but merely recognizes its existence and makes it easier to be effectuated. ALA. CODE § 22-8A-2 (1984); ARIZ. REV. STAT. ANN. §§ 49-701 to -704 (Supp. 1988); CAL. HEALTH & SAFETY CODE § 7186 (Deering Supp. 1987); COLO. REV. STAT. § 15-18-102(a) (1987); DEL. CODE ANN. tit. 16, § 2502 (1983); FLA. STAT. ANN. § 765.02 (West 1986); GA. CODE ANN. § 31-32-1(d) (1985); HAW. REV. STAT. § 327D-1 (Supp. 1987); IDAHO CODE § 39-4502 (Supp. 1988); IND. CODE ANN. § 16-8-11-1 (West Supp. 1988); IOWA CODE ANN. § 144A.1 (West Supp. 1988); LA. REV. STAT. ANN. § 40:1299.58.1(A)(1) (West Supp. 1988); N.H. REV. STAT. ANN.

§ 137-H:1 (Supp. 1988); N.C. GEN. STAT. § 90-320(a) (1985); S.C. CODE ANN. 44-77-10 (Law Co-op. Supp. 1988); UTAH CODE ANN. § 75-2-1102(2) (Supp. 1988); VT. STAT. ANN. tit. 18, § 5251 (1987); WASH. REV. CODE ANN. § 70.122.010 (Supp. 1989).

3. The question of the extent to which the state may properly place limitations upon a pregnant woman's right to control her own body in order to protect the health of the fetus is a complex and controversial one that is receiving increasing judicial scrutiny today. See Jefferson v. Griffin Spaulding County Hosp. Auth., 247 Ga. 86, 86-90, 274 S.E.2d 457, 458-62 (1981).

4. *See, e.g.*, UTAH CODE ANN. § 75-2-1103(6)(b) (Supp. 1988) (expressly excluding medication, sustenance or any procedure that provides comfort or alleviates pain from the definition of life-sustaining procedure, unless the declarant indicates otherwise); see also [COUNCIL ON ETHICAL AND JUDICIAL AFFAIRS, AMA, CURRENT OPINIONS § 2.18 (1986) (hereinafter AMA COUNCIL)] (defining life prolonging medical treatment to include the provision of food and hydration).

5. *See, e.g.*, N.M. STAT. ANN. § 24-7-2(C) (1978) (defining "maintenance medical treatment" as "medical treatment designed solely to sustain the life processes" without further explanation).

6. Note, *The California Natural Death Act: An Empirical Study of Physicians' Practices*, 31 STAN. L. REV. 913, 928, 938 (1979). Only the District of Columbia requires a physician to inform a patient of his terminal illness, and then only if the patient is alert and communicative. D.C. CODE ANN. § 6-2425(b) (Supp. 1983); Martyn & Jacobs, *supra* note 1, at 790.

7. Note, *supra* note 6, at 930–33.

8. At least one commentator has noted the irony that those who fall within the typical living will statute are the least in need of its benefits. Referring to the California Natural Death Act, Alexander Capron writes:

> [T]he only patients covered by this statute are those who are on the edge of death *despite the doctors' efforts.* The very people for whom the greatest concern is expressed about a prolonged and undignified dying process are unaffected by the statute because their deaths are not imminent.

Capron, *The Development of Law on Human Death*, 315 ANNALS N.Y. ACAD. SCI. 45, 55 (1978), *cited in* [PRESIDENT'S COMM'N FOR THE STUDY OF ETHICAL PROBLEMS IN MEDICINE & BIOMEDICAL & BEHAVIORAL RESEARCH, DECIDING TO FOREGO LIFE-SUSTAINING TREATMENT 17–18 (1983) (hereinafter COMM'N REPORT)].

9. This group includes those whose prognosis is hopeless but who will not die soon unless mechanically supplied food and hydration or antibiotics are withdrawn. It is thus critical to have a clear definition of "artificial" medical treatment.

10. Note, *supra* note 6, at 920–21.

11. *Id.* at 920 n.31.

12. *Id.* at 921 n.38, 932.

13. *In re* Conroy, 98 N.J. 321, 362–63, 486 A.2d 1209, 1230 (1985); *see also* [Hilfiker, *Allowing the Debilitated to Die*, 308 NEW ENG. J. MED. 716, 717 (1983)] (comparing different views of what constitutes a reasonable physical limitation on life activities of a person at different life stages).

14. *In re* Westchester County Medical Center, 72, N.Y.2d 517, 524, 531 N.E.2d 607, 625, 534 N.Y.S.2d 886, 904 (1988) (Simons, J., dissenting).

15. ALASKA STAT. §§ 13.26.332–.332 (Supp. 1988); CAL. CIV. CODE § 2410–43 (Deering 1986); DEL. CODE ANN. tit. 16, § 2502 (1983); FLA. STAT. ANN. §§ 765.02, 765.05(2) (West 1986); IOWA CODE ANN. § 144A.7 (West Supp. 1988); LA. REV. STAT. ANN. § 40:1299.58.1(A)(3)(a) (West Supp. 1988); NEV. REV. STAT. ANN. §§ 449.800–.860 (Michie Supp. 1987); R.I. GEN. LAWS §§ 23.4.10-1 to -2 (Supp. 1988); TEX. REV. CIV. STAT. ANN. art. 4509h (Vernon Supp. 1989);

UTAH CODE ANN. § 75-2-1106 (Supp. 1988); VA. CODE § 54.1-2984 (1988); VT. STAT. ANN. tit. 14, §§ 3451–3467 (Supp. 1988); and WYO. STAT. ANN. § 35-22-102(d) (1988).

16. The Florida, Iowa, Louisiana, Texas, Virginia, and Wyoming statutes provide that the designation of a medical treatment agent is effective only when the declarant becomes "terminally ill." To the extent that this excludes patients who are incurably, but not terminally ill (see *supra* notes 6–12, and accompanying text), the advance designation of a treatment agent suffers from the same weakness as a living will.

17. ALASKA STAT. §§ 13.26.332–.356 (Supp. 1988); CAL. CIV. CODE § 2410-43 (Deering 1986); DEL. CODE ANN. tit. 16, § 2502 (1983); FLA. STAT. ANN. §§ 765.02, 765.05(2) (West 1986); IOWA CODE ANN. § 144A.7 (West Supp. 1988); LA. REV. STAT. ANN. § 40:1299.58.1(a)(3)(a) (West Supp. 1988); NEV. REV. STAT. ANN. §§ 449.800-.860 (Michie Supp. 1987); R.I. GEN. LAWS §§ 23.4.10-1 to -2 (Supp. 1988); TEX. REV. CIV. STAT. ANN. art. 4509h (Vernon Spp. 1989); UTAH CODE ANN. § 75-2-116 (Supp. 1988); VA. CODE § 54.1-2984 (1988); VT. STAT. ANN. tit. 14, §§ 3451–3467 (Supp. 1988); and WYO. STAT. ANN. § 35-22-102(d) (1988).

18. FLA. STAT. ANN. § 765-07(1) (West 1986); IOWA CODE ANN. § 144A.7(1) (West Supp. 1988).

19. See [Cantor, Conroy, *Best Interests, and the Handling of Dying Patients,* 37 RUTGERS L. REV. 543, 556 (1985)], at 547–48, 555–56. Yet even then the decision that is made can only be an approximation, a "best guess" as to what the person whose death is near would choose if he were now competent. See [Beschle, *Autonomous Decisionmaking and Social Choice: Examining the "Right to Die"*, 77 KY. L.J. 319, 354–58 (1988–89).]

20. See *infra* discussion in Section III of text.

21. ARK. CODE. ANN. § 20-17-214 (Supp. 1987); CONN. GEN. STAT. ANN. § 19a-571 (West Supp. 1988); FLA. STAT. ANN. § 765.07 (West 1986); IOWA CODE ANN. § 144A.7 (West Supp. 1988); LA. REV. STAT. ANN. § 40:1299.58.5(A) (West Supp. 1988); N.M. STAT. ANN. § 24-7-8.1 (1986); N.C. GEN. STAT. § 90-322 (1985); TEX. REV. CIV. STAT. ANN. art. 4590h § 4C (Vernon Supp. 1989); UTAH CODE ANN. § 75-2-1105 (Supp. 1988); VA. CODE ANN. § 54.1-2986 (1988). Of these, both Arkansas and New Mexico provide that a substitute decision to forego treatment may be made on behalf of a patient who is either terminally ill or in an "irreversible coma," N.M. STAT. ANN. § 24-7-2(B) (1986), or "permanently unconscious," ARK. STAT. ANN. § 20-17-201(ii) (Supp. 1987).

22. N.C. GEN. STAT. § 90-320(a) (1985).

23. LA. REV. STAT. ANN. § 40:1299.58.1(A)(1) (West Supp. 1988).

Merely having *a right to name a surrogate health care decision-maker by signing an advance directive is meaningless unless the older individual takes advantage of that right. The reasons older individuals often do not name a surrogate health care decision-maker vary, but ethnicity plays an important role. An individual's attitude about advance health care directives is in part a reflection of that person's ethnic background. White, middle class, highly educated persons are the strongest proponents of advance directives. African Americans are less persuaded that their interests are well served by signing an advance directive. Other ethnically identified populations such as Mexican Americans and Korean Americans also have much lower rates of executing an advance directive. Some commentators claim that non-white America will have a more positive attitude towards advance directives as they gain more understanding about them. Others maintain that the lack of enthusiasm for advance directives reflects deeper, more imbedded cultural attitudes.*

For whatever reason, the great majority of Americans have not signed an advance directive. As a result there have been scores of court cases in which the issue arises as to whether a third party, usually a relative or spouse, can terminate life-sustaining treatment for a mentally incapacitated patient. The following case, decided by the Pennsylvania Supreme Court, is representative of the reasoning in many of these cases.

---

673 A.2d 905
In re Daniel Joseph FIORI, an adjudged incompetent.
Appeal of COMMONWEALTH of Pennsylvania, Attorney General.
Supreme Court of Pennsylvania, Eastern District
Argued April 25, 1995.
Decided April 2, 1996.

CAPPY, Justice:

This is an appeal by allowance from the opinion and order of the Superior Court affirming the judgment entered by the Court of Common Pleas of Bucks County, Orphans Court Division. We granted allowance of appeal to decide whether a close relative, with the consent of two physicians but without court involvement, may remove life sustaining treatment from an adult relative who is in a persistent vegetative state where that adult has left no advance directives. For the following reasons, we affirm.

As with all cases where this issue is presented, the facts here are tragic. Daniel Joseph Fiori, the nominal subject of this appeal, suffered severe head injuries in 1972 when he was approximately twenty years old. He regained consciousness after this injury, but his cognitive abilities were severely limited. In 1976, Fiori suffered a second head injury while being treated at a Veterans Administration (VA) hospital. Fiori never regained consciousness after this second injury, and he was diagnosed as being in a persistent vegetative state (PVS). The term "vegetative state" describes:

> a body which is functioning entirely in terms of its internal controls. It maintains temperature. It maintains heart beat and pulmonary ventilation. It maintains digestive activity. It maintains reflex activity of muscles and nerves for low level conditioned responses. But there is no behavioral evidence of either self-awareness or awareness of the surroundings in a learned manner.

Cruzan v. Director, Missouri Dept. of Health, 497 U.S. 261, 267, n. 1, 110 S.Ct. 2841, 2846, n. 1, 111 L.Ed.2d 224 (1990) (citing *In re Jobes,* 108 N.J. 394, 403, 529 A.2d 434, 438 (1987)).[1] This state has been described as a "twilight zone of suspended animation where death commences while life, in some form, continues." *Rasmussen by Mitchell v. Fleming,* 154 Ariz. 207, 211, 741 P.2d 674, 678 (1987).

In this condition, all Fiori's cognitive brain functions were inoperative. He felt no pain or pleasure, and he was unable to communicate with others. Since Fiori had no capacity for voluntary muscular movements, his life functions were maintained by the provision of medications, fluids, and nutrition through a gastrostomy tube, a tube which is surgically inserted in the stomach.[2] There was no hope of Fiori ever recovering.

After Fiori's second accident, his mother, Rosemarie Sherman, was appointed guardian of his person by court order entered in 1980. In February of 1992, Sherman requested that the Mayo Nursing Center, which was the nursing home caring for Fiori, remove his gastrostomy tube. The nursing home refused to comply with her request without a court order;[3] Sherman thus filed a petition in the Court of Common Pleas for Bucks County requesting an order directing the nursing home to terminate treatment. The Attorney General appeared in the proceedings and, pursuant to his request, an independent medical expert was appointed.

The opinions of two neurologists, one retained by Sherman and the other the court appointed independent expert, were entered into evidence. Both agreed that within a reasonable degree of medical certainty, Fiori's condition would not improve and he would remain in a PVS as he had done for the last seventeen years. They also stated that existing medical technology could continue to support Fiori's life functions so that his life span could extend for another ten to twenty years.

Sherman testified that her son had never spoken to her about his wishes should he ever lapse into a PVS. Nevertheless, based on her son's "love of life," Sherman was of the opinion that her son would wish the gastrostomy tube to be removed.

The trial court granted Sherman's motion, and the Attorney General appealed.

The Superior Court, sitting *en banc,* affirmed. The court determined that the decision to remove life sustaining treatment from an adult in a PVS who did not leave directions as to the maintenance of life support may be made by a close family member and two qualified physicians without court approval.

The Attorney General filed a petition for allowance of appeal on January 23, 1995. Prior to the granting of allowance of appeal, Fiori died of pneumonia.[4]

In this appeal, we must determine the procedures and guidelines for removal of life sustaining treatment from a PVS patient where the patient, prior to his incompetency, failed to express his desires on such treatment. Specifically, we must determine who may make the decision for the PVS patient, what standard the decision-maker should employ, and whether the court must approve that decision.

The starting point for our analysis is an examination of the right we are to protect—the right to self-determination in regard to the acceptance or rejection of life sustaining medical treatment. Although some courts have noted constitutional bases for such a right, we choose to follow the example set by the courts which have relied solely on the common-law basis for the right to self-determination, and have eschewed an analysis based upon constitutional principles.

* * *

The right to refuse medical treatment has deep roots in our common law. More than a century ago, the United States Supreme Court recognized that "[n]o right is held more sacred, or is more carefully guarded, by the common law, than the right of every individual to the possession and control of his own person. . . ." *Union Pacific Railway Co. v. Botsford,* 141 U.S. 250, 251, 11 S.Ct. 1000, 1001, 35 L.Ed. 734 (1891).

From this right to be free from bodily invasion developed the doctrine of informed consent. *See Schloendorff v. Society of New York Hospital,* 211 N.Y. 125, 129–130, 105 N.E. 92, 93 (1914) (Cardozo, J.) The doctrine of informed consent declares that absent an emergency situation, medical treatment may not be imposed without the patient's informed consent. *Moure v. Raeuchle,* 529 Pa. 394, 404, 604 A.2d 1003, 1008 (1992). A logical corollary to this doctrine is the patient's right, in general, "to refuse treatment and to withdraw consent to treatment once begun." *Mack,* 329 Md. at 210, 618 A.2d at 755. Courts have unanimously concluded that this right to self-determination does not cease upon the incapacitation of the individual. *See, e.g., In re Colyer,* 99 Wash.2d 114, 660 P.2d 738 (1983); *Mack, supra; In re Quinlan,* 70 N.J. 10, 355 A.2d 647 (1976).

This right, however, is not absolute. The right of the patient to abstain from medical treatment must be balanced against interests of the state. The four state interests most commonly recognized by the courts are: (1) protection of third parties, (2) prevention of suicide, (3) protection of the ethical integrity of the medical community, and (4) preservation of life. *Superintendent of Belchertown State School v. Saikewicz,* 373 Mass. 728, 740–741, 370 N.E.2d 417, 425 (1977); *see also In re Conroy,* 98 N.J. 321, 348–349, 486 A.2d 1209, 1223 (1985).

In examining the state's interest in protecting third parties, the primary focus is on whether the patient has dependents who would be left emotionally and financially bereft were the patient to refuse medical treatment. *See, e.g., In re Farrell,* 108 N.J. 335, 529 A.2d 404 (1987); *Saikewicz, supra.* In Fiori's situation, there was no need to protect third party interests as he did not have any dependents. Thus, this state interest is not applicable here.

Furthermore, the prevention of suicide was not a consideration here. In removing life sustaining measures, the natural death process is allowed to continue; death would not have been the result of a self-inflicted injury, as is the case with suicide. *See Conroy,* 98 N.J. at 351, 486 A.2d at 1224.

Also, the ethical integrity of the medical community would not have been compromised had Sherman's request been honored. As noted by the Superior Court below, *amicus curiae,* the Pennsylvania Medical Society, had stated that the withdrawal of life-support from Fiori would not compromise medical ethical principles. *Amicus* asserted that the medical community supports the withdrawal of life sustaining treatment, including the provision of nutrition and fluid, when there is no hope of recovery and where that decision is made by a surrogate decision-maker who is attempting to effectuate the wishes of the patient. Brief of the Pennsylvania Medical Society to the Superior Court at p. 16.

Lastly, we focus on the state's interest in preserving life. Of these four interests, this one is the most significant. *Rasmussen,* 154 Ariz. at 216, 741 P.2d at 683. It encompasses the separate, but related, concerns of preserving the life of the particular individual and also safeguarding the sanctity of all life. *Conroy,* 98 N.J. at 348, 486 A.2d at 1223. The state's interest in preserving life is certainly applicable in situations such as Fiori's. Yet, this interest does not outweigh the PVS patient's interest in self-determination. The state's interest in maintaining the PVS individual in an endless twilight state between life and death is so weak that it cannot overcome the individual's right to self-determination. *Rasmussen,* 154 Ariz. at 217, 741 P.2d at 683; *see also Colyer,* 99 Wash.2d at 122, 660 P.2d at 743. We thus hold that the state's interest in preserving life does not outweigh the right of the PVS patient to refuse medical treatment.

Having determined that a PVS patient's right to self-determination outweighs any interests the state may have in maintaining life sustaining treatment for the patient, we must examine how that right may be exercised. Where a PVS patient created advance written directives prior to incapacitation, we have statutory provisions which provide for the implementation of the patient's wishes. *See* Advance Directive for Health Care Act, 20 Pa.C.S. § 5401 *et seq.* ("Act"). Yet, the Act does not address the situation where no advance directives were left as to treatment.

Where a statute does not exist on the subject, there are various legal theories on which authorization to terminate life support may be predicated. The approach taken by many of our sister states, and by the Superior Court below, is to allow a close family member to exercise "substituted judgment" on behalf of the patient. . . . The substituted judgment approach "is intended to ensure that the surrogate decision-maker effectuates as much as possible the decision that the incompetent patient would make if he or she were competent." *Id.* at 414, 529 A.2d at 444. Even where the individual has not expressed thoughts concerning life-sustaining treatment, the patient's preferences can still be ascertained by referring to all of the aspects of his or her personality. *See Estate of Longeway,* 133 Ill.2d at 49–50, 139 Ill.Dec. at 787–788, 549 N.E.2d at 299–300.

The minority of states requires that there be "clear and convincing" evidence of the patient's intent to withdraw life support.[5] This is the most stringent approach.

* * *

The Attorney General argues that the clear and convincing evidence standard should be used. To support this argument, he notes that the guardianship statutes employ the clear and convincing evidence standard for the resolution of certain issues; thus, since this standard is applicable to some determinations via the guardianship statute, then it perforce applies to this decision. We disagree. The guardianship statutes simply do not address a situation such as we have before us, and thus we do not find that the clear and convincing evidence standard is mandated here.

Furthermore, we find the clear and convincing evidence test to be overly restrictive, one which would thwart the PVS patient's right to determine the medical care to be received. Were this test to be applied, all of those patients who did not have the prescience or the sophistication to express clearly and unmistakably their wishes on this precise matter would not be able to have life support removed. For those individuals, the choice concerning medical treatment would not be an extrapolation based upon their individual beliefs. Rather, the "choice" would be dependent simply upon how far the frontiers of medical science had advanced: if the life-sustaining procedures were available, they would be automatically administered. This we cannot tolerate.

Thus, we agree with the Superior Court below that the substituted judgment standard is the proper approach. We believe that where a PVS patient has not left instructions as to the maintenance of life-sustaining treatment, the only practical way to prevent the destruction of the PVS patient's right to refuse medical treatment is to allow a substitute decision-maker to determine what measures the PVS patient would have desired in light of the patient's prognosis.

* * *

We also hold that a close family member is well suited to the role of substitute decision-maker. . . . Close family members are usually the most knowledgeable about the patient's preferences, goals, and values; they have an understanding of the nuances of our personality that set us apart as individuals. . . . In addition to the greater knowledge of the PVS patient's personal views, close family members have a special bond with the PVS patient. "Our experience informs us that family members are generally most concerned with the welfare of a patient."

* * *

Furthermore, concomitant with the substitute decision-maker's exercise of the PVS patient's right to refuse treatment, the surrogate must also obtain written statements of two doctors qualified to evaluate the patient's condition. These statements must certify that the patient has been diagnosed as being in a permanent vegetative state. If the patient has an attending physician, that physician shall also prepare a statement.

* * *

In the case at bar, the two neurologists whose opinions on Fiori were presented at the trial court concurred that Fiori's PVS was irreversible. Drawing on her knowledge of her son when he was competent, Sherman testified that based on her son's love of life and his personal ethics, her son would no longer wish to be kept alive in his present condition. The Superior Court held that the medical evidence and Sherman's testimony were sufficient to support her decision to terminate life sustaining measures for her son; we find no fault with the lower court's determination.

The final question for our review is what role the judiciary will play when situations such as Fiori's arise. We believe that where the physicians and the close family member are in agreement, and there is no dispute between "interested parties," there is no need for court involvement.

* * *

The Attorney General argues that approval of the decision to terminate life-support is a uniquely judicial function, and that we would be abandoning our role as a court. We disagree. As Judge Beck stated in her opinion below, the judiciary has no role to play:

> where there is a loving family, willing and able to assess what the patient would have decided as to his or her treatment, all necessary medical confirmations are in hand, and no one rightfully interested in the patient's treatment disputes the family decision. (Citations omitted.) Those who disagree with this view and who favor court intervention in every case often cite the need for the court to protect the patient. Underlying this rationale is the philosophy that only courts can provide the necessary safeguards to assure protection of life. This is a narrow and unhealthy view. It violates the essential and traditional respect for family. It is yet another expansion of the idea that courts in our society are the repository of wisdom and the only institution available to protect human life and dignity.
>
> *Fiori*, 438 Pa.Super. at 627, 652 A.2d at 1358.

At the close of this opinion, we stress that the matter *sub judice* addresses only a very narrow issue: whether life support may be terminated for a PVS patient who was once competent, but did not express desires as to medical treatment, and who may make that choice. It would be unwise for us to speak to alternate scenarios that are not now before us. Thus, we explicitly note that our holding today applies only to situations where the individual in question was once a competent adult, but is now in a permanent vegetative state, and while competent that individual left no advance directives pertaining to life sustaining measures. We think it wise that "in deciding a question of such magnitude and importance . . . it is the [better] part of wisdom not to attempt, by any general statement, to cover every possible phase of the subject." *Cruzan*, 497 U.S. at 277–278, 110 S.Ct. at 2850–2851 (citations omitted).

For the reasons stated herein, we affirm the decision of the Superior Court.

* * *

Notes

1. A recent article published in *The New England Journal of Medicine* introduced a distinction between persistent and *permanent* vegetative states. The article stated that "[a] wakeful unconscious state that lasts longer than a few weeks is referred to as a *persistent* vegetative state. . . . A *permanent* vegetative state, on the other hand, means an *irreversible* state. . . ." Multi-Society Task Force on PVS, *Medical Aspects of the Persistent Vegetative State* (Pts. 1 & 2), 330 New Eng.J.Med. 1499, 1501 (1994) (emphasis supplied). Based on review of prior PVS cases, the article concluded that where a persistent vegetative state was brought on by traumatic injury, the state can be judged permanent twelve months after the occurrence of the injury; the article

noted that recovery after twelve months is exceedingly rare. *Id.* at 1575. For a discussion of one such emergence from a permanent vegetative state, *see* Nancy L. Childs, M.D. & Walt N. Mercer, *Brief Report; Late Improvement in Consciousness After Post-Traumatic Vegetative State,* 334 New Eng.J.Med. 24 (1996).

The diagnosis of Fiori's condition predated this article, and thus the diagnosis of "permanent vegetative state" was not available to the attending physicians. We realize that Fiori, who had been in a vegetative state for approximately nineteen years prior to his death, would probably now be diagnosed as having been in a *permanent* vegetative state; be that as it may, we find that it would be highly improper for a court to "re-diagnose" Fiori. Thus, we will continue to refer to Fiori's condition as having been a *persistent* vegetative state.

2. Artificial hydration and nutrition are viewed as treatment by the medical community and by courts of other jurisdictions. *See, e.g., In re Conroy,* 98 N.J. 321, 372–373, 486 A.2d 1209, 1236 (1985); *In re Grant,* 109 Wash.2d 545, 559–562, 747 P.2d 445, 452–454 (1987).

3. The nursing home did not oppose the discontinuation of life support for Fiori. It expressed no opinion as to the ultimate determination, but rather merely indicated a desire to obtain court approval of any action. *See* Mayo Nursing Center Letter, February 18, 1992. R. at 9a.

4. With the death of Fiori, this appeal is technically moot. Nonetheless, because this case raises an issue of important public interest, an issue which is capable of repetition yet is apt to elude review, we have decided to hear this appeal. *See Jersey Shore School Dist. v. Jersey Shore Educ. Ass'n,* 519 Pa. 398, 548 A.2d 1202 (1988).

5. We note that the term "clear and convincing evidence" in this context refers to the requirement that the individual in question must have stated in an explicit fashion the exact treatment desired were the patient to lapse into various medical conditions. The term "clear and convincing evidence" is used more commonly, however, as a burden of proof. In that context, the standard refers to that quantum of evidence necessary for a party to establish a point. For further illumination on the distinction *see generally* Comment, *The Right to Die,* 96 Dick.L.Rev. 649, 651 and 665-669.

C. Legislative Responses

Because of the need for a means of effectuating health care decision-making for individuals suffering from mental incapacity, every state has enacted a statute that creates either an advance health care directive (often referred to as a living will) or power of attorney for health care. These state laws vary in the authority that can be granted a surrogate decision maker, what kind of decisions can be controlled by the document, when the document takes effect, the signing formalities necessary to make the document effective, and the manner in which the document can be revoked. As a result, the statutory law of advance health care decision-making is a hodgepodge of requirements and legal possibilities. In an attempt to bring order and uniformity, the Uniform Law Commissioners approved the Uniform Health Care Decisions Act. The Commissioners, unfortunately, have no power to enact their model act. Whether states will adopt the Uniform Act or even be influenced by it remains to be seen.

In the following article, Professors English and Meisel explain the Uniform Act.

David M. English and Alan Meisel

Uniform Health Care Decisions Act Gives New Guidance

Every state now has legislation authorizing the use of some form of advance health care directive—a power of attorney, a living will, or, in most cases, both.[1] In addition, more than thirty states have "surrogate decision-making" statutes, allowing family members and, in some instances, others to make health care decisions for individuals who lack decision-making capacity and who have not executed an advance directive.

The premise of both the case law and these statutes is that competent persons have a common-law and possibly constitutional right of self-determination and the right to be free from unwanted interferences with their bodily integrity. In the health care setting, this translates into a right to make decisions about their care, including the right to decline treatment even when that decision would probably or even certainly lead to death. This right ordinarily is implemented through informed consent or refusal. Although decision-making for competent patients presents few legal difficulties, the same cannot be said for patients who have lost capacity since they no longer can make a decision, informed or otherwise.

This existing legislation, however, has developed in fits and starts, resulting in an often fragmented, incomplete, and sometimes inconsistent set of rules. Statutes enacted within a single state sometimes conflict with each other, and conflicts between statutes of different states are common. In an increasingly mobile society where an advance health care directive made in one state must frequently be implemented in another, there is a need for greater consistency.

Much of the present state legislation also inappropriately inhibits, rather than facilitates, the use of advance health care directives. The execution requirements, for example, often go well beyond what is required even for the execution of a will. Furthermore, many of the statutes unnecessarily limit the circumstances when life-

Estate Planning, Vol. 21, 355–362 (November/December 1994). Reprinted by permission.

sustaining treatment may be withheld or withdrawn to situations in which a person is either "terminally ill" or "permanently unconscious." There is a need for simplicity and greater flexibility.

The Uniform Health Care Decisions Act (the Act), which was approved by the Uniform Law Commissioners in August 1993, was drafted with these problems very much in mind. Unlike most current state statutes dealing with medical decision-making for patients who no longer possess the capacity to do so personally, the Act is comprehensive and will enable an enacting jurisdiction to replace its existing legislation on the subject with a single statute. Moreover, the overriding objective of the new Act is to facilitate the use of advance health care directives. It is likely that the Act will serve as an influential model for many years to come. This Act is not the Commissioners' first foray into the field of health care decision-making, but it is the most comprehensive. The 1982 Model Health Care Consent Act[2] addressed primarily the authority of the family to make health care decisions. The Uniform Rights of the Terminally Ill Act, in both its 1985[3] and 1989[4] versions, focused exclusively on the withdrawal or withholding of *life-sustaining* treatment. A state enacting the Health Care Decisions Act should simultaneously repeal any of these other acts that are in force or any other advance directive or surrogate decision-making legislation.

* * *

Overview of the Act

The Health Care Decisions Act consists of 19 sections, but Sections 15 to 19 are boilerplate common to all uniform acts. The heart of the Act is found in Sections 1 to 14. Following a series of definitions (§ 1), the Act contains provisions on making and revoking advance health care directives (§§ 2 and 3). An optional statutory form for making a directive is provided as well (§ 4).

The Act encourages and facilitates the use of advance health care directives, but it also recognizes that many individuals fail to plan. Consequently, two back-up provisions are included. One is Section 5, which specifies when individuals other than a patient's agent or guardian may act as "surrogate" and make health care decisions for the patient. The other is Section 6, addressing health care decision-making by guardians.

To assure the effectuation of a patient's right of self-determination, the Act requires providers to honor a patient's instructions about health care and to comply with a reasonable interpretation of the instruction and with a health care decision made by the patient's agent, guardian, or surrogate (§ 7(d)(1)). The only exceptions are for "reasons of conscience" by health care professionals or as expressed in the policy of the health care institution (§ 7(e)), or that treatment requested by an instruction or an agent is "medically ineffective" (§ 7(f)). In either of these cases, a health care provider need not comply but must assist in the patient's transfer to another health care provider or facility where compliance is assured (§ 7(g)).

Informed decision-making requires access to health care information. For this reason, Section 8 of the Act provides that a patient's agent, guardian, or surrogate has the same rights as the patient to request, receive, examine, copy, and consent to the disclosure of medical or any other health care information.

To induce compliance with the Act, Section 9 provides certain immunities. An individual's agent or surrogate is typically a noncompensated volunteer. Consequently, it is inappropriate to hold an agent or surrogate to the onerous standards of general fiduciary law. Under the Act, an individual acting as a patient's agent or surrogate is not subject to civil or criminal liability for health care decisions made in good faith. The Act also protects providers from liability for (1) complying with a health care decision of a person apparently having authority to make such a decision for a patient; (2) declining to comply with the decision of a person based on a belief that the person lacks authority; and (3) assuming, when complying with an advance health care directive, that the directive was valid when made and has not been revoked or terminated.

* * *

Health Care Directives

Under the Act, an "advance health care directive" refers to either a "power of attorney for health care" or an "individual instruction" (§ 1(1)). The latter term is used instead of "living will," a term that the Act avoids based on the assumption that it does more to confuse than to help. It is possible, though, that "living will" is a phrase so deeply ingrained that this or any effort to halt its usage will not succeed.

Triggering conditions: type of medical condition. Most existing advance directive legislation becomes effective only if a patient is in a "terminal condition" or is "permanently unconscious." Such restrictions have severely limited the usefulness of many state statutes and, indeed, have rendered them virtual nullities. The Act does not attempt to prescribe the circumstances when life-sustaining treatment may be withheld or withdrawn. An individual instruction may be given as to any prospective health care decision, and the authority that may be granted to an agent is similarly broad. The importance of this change cannot be overstated. What many people wish to avoid is not merely futile medical treatment when they are terminally ill or permanently unconscious, but also prolongation of their lives when their quality of life, as they would assess it themselves, is unacceptable (as is often seen in cases of serious dementia resulting from Alzheimer's disease, stroke, or other causes).

Triggering conditions: loss of decision-making capacity. Most people who want to engage in advance planning for future health care decisions probably wish to do so only for situations in which their own decision-making capacity is temporarily or permanently lost. Thus, under a majority of existing statutes authorizing health care powers of attorney, only springing powers are allowed. That is, the agent's authority becomes effective only upon a determination that the principal lacks capacity to make his own health care decisions. Section 2(c) of the Act recognizes, however, that this wish may not be universal and therefore permits a principal to provide in the power of attorney that the agent's authority becomes effective either immediately or upon some event other than the loss of capacity. But if nothing is said in the power, the agent's authority is springing. It is the function of an individual's "primary physician" (defined in § 1(13)) to determine whether the individual has capacity to make his own health care decisions (§ 2(d)). A judicial determination of incompetency is not required and is inconsistent with the Act's overall purpose of avoiding recourse to the courts for making decisions about life-sustaining treatment (§ 14 (comment)).

Who may execute a directive. A power of attorney for health care or individual instruction may be given by any adult or emancipated minor (§ 2(a)). The Act does not address the question of whether unemancipated but "mature minors" may make advance directives.[5]

Execution requirements. The Act keeps execution requirements to a minimum. This bias is based on two assumptions: (1) that the elaborate execution requirements found in many existing statutes make advance directives more difficult to execute and unnecessarily inhibit their use, thereby defeating the intent of advance directive legislation; and (2) that such requirements do little, if anything, to prevent fraud or enhance reliability.

A health care power of attorney must be in writing and signed by the principal but need not be witnessed or acknowledged (§ 2(b)). An individual instruction may be either oral or written (§ 2(a)). Because of the presumed special vulnerability of individuals in long-term care settings, the Act disqualifies an unrelated owner, operator, or employee of a long-term health care institution at which the principal is receiving care from acting as the principal's agent (§ 2(b)).

Standard for decision-making by agents. One of the most debated issues in decision-making about life-sustaining treatment for patients who have lost capacity is the proper substantive standard (subjective, substituted judgment, best interests) for making this decision. The Act (§ 2(e)) follows the general trend of the case law by providing that the agent must comply with the principal's individual instructions if given, and any other of the principal's oral or written wishes of which the agent is aware.[6] Frequently, however, the principal's wishes are unknown. The Act then follows the dominant (though not quite as uniform)[7] trend in the case law, requiring that the agent act in the principal's best interest, as determined in light of the principal's personal values to the extent they are known.

Scope of authority. Persons empowered to make decisions under the Act for a patient who lacks capacity—whether an "agent," "surrogate," or "guardian"—are given broad authority. Decision makers may select and discharge health care providers and institutions; approve or disapprove diagnostic tests, surgical procedures, programs of medication, and orders not to resuscitate; and give directions to provide, withhold, or withdraw artificial nutrition and hydration and all other forms of health care (§ 1(6)). Nevertheless, certain decisions are beyond the Act's scope. For instance, state statutes prohibiting assisted suicide or mercy killing are not overridden (§ 13(c)). Moreover, there are restrictions on the authority of an agent or surrogate to consent to the admission of the principal or patient to a mental health institution (§ 13(e)).

Revocation. Just as a higher standard is imposed for the execution of a power of attorney for health care than for an individual instruction, so is a higher standard imposed for revocation of an agent's designation. A principal may revoke the designation of an agent only by a signed writing or by personally informing the supervising health care provider (§ 3(a)). A spouse's designation as agent is also revoked by a decree of annulment, divorce, dissolution of marriage, or legal separation (§ 3(d)). An individual instruction, however, may be revoked in any manner that communicates an intent to revoke (§ 3(b)). There is no requirement of a writing or personal communication to the health care provider.

* * *

Surrogates

The term "surrogate" is generally used to refer to one who has the authority to make a medical decision for another. There are several different kinds of surrogates. One is patient-designated and often referred to as a "proxy," though under the Act (and some existing statutes) this person is called an "agent." A "guardian" is a judicially appointed surrogate. An individual who is appointed by neither the patient nor a court, but who acts pursuant to custom, common law, or a "surrogate decision-making" statute is generally referred to simply as a "surrogate."

The reality is that a substantial majority of Americans fail to execute directives (as they fail to execute wills or purchase life insurance) because of their general unwillingness to plan for death. Furthermore, there is no reason to believe that this situation will change significantly even if the Act is widely enacted. Health care decision-making for individuals who fail to plan is therefore an important concern, and the Act (§ 5) provides for the designation of a decision-maker in the absence of the written appointment of an agent or judicial appointment of a guardian, or if an agent or guardian has been appointed but is not "reasonably available." Following the common-law terminology, the Act refers to this decision-maker as a "surrogate." The term "surrogate" applies as well to an agent who is orally appointed by the patient.

Common-law status of decision-making by families. For incapacitated individuals who have failed to execute an advance directive and for whom no guardian has been appointed, health care providers have traditionally turned to the family for a decision. Although this reliance on families is based primarily on medical custom, it has received judicial approval—and thus acquired the status of law—in almost all jurisdictions that have considered the issue.[8] Nonetheless, roughly half the states have no judicial decision on this point, and in those that do, there is sometimes uncertainty about its details. Furthermore, few of the cases address the issue of which family member has definitive authority, relying instead on the notion that there should be a consensus among available and interested family members. If consensus cannot be obtained, recourse to the courts may be the only alternative.

As a result of these uncertainties, a growing number of jurisdictions are enacting statutes validating a role for the family. Over thirty states currently have such "surrogate decision-making" (sometimes referred to as "family decision-making") statutes on the books. Most, however, tend to be limited in scope; some focus on only withdrawal or withholding of life-sustaining treatment, and some are specifically intended *not* to apply to life-sustaining treatment.[9] The surrogacy provision of the Act is intended to be comprehensive and to address these problems. A surrogate is empowered to make all "health care decisions" (expansively defined in § 1(6)) for the affected individual.

Triggering conditions. The right of a surrogate to act is triggered by a determination that the patient lacks capacity to make his own health care decisions. Not all patients are covered, however. A surrogate may make a health care decision only for an adult or emancipated minor for whom no agent or guardian has been appointed or whose agent or guardian is not reasonably available (§ 5(a)). Unemancipated minors are excluded on the assumption that health care decision-making for them is best handled by separate legislation.

Priority list. The Act prescribes a priority list of those who may act as surrogate. The drafters concluded that a priority list based on closeness of family relationship—as most existing legislation provides—does not necessarily reflect reality. Unmarried individuals in cohabiting relationships, for example, might be much more likely to prefer that their companions act on their behalf than their parents, siblings, or even their children.

For this reason, appearing first on the priority list is a new type of decision-maker, the orally designated surrogate. This is to be distinguished from an agent, who can be appointed only by a writing signed by the principal, but the function is largely the same. Because of the risk of miscommunication of an individual's oral statement, however, some reliability of proof is required.[10] An individual may orally designate a surrogate only by personally informing the supervising health care provider (§ 5(b)). The health care provider is then in turn obligated to record the designation in the individual's health care record (§ 7(b)).

If an individual has not designated a surrogate, or if the designee is not reasonably available, a rather standard family tree is followed: the spouse, followed by an adult child, a parent, and last an adult brother or sister (§ 5(b)). Should all classes of family members decline to act or otherwise not be reasonably available, a health care decision may be made by another relative or friend who has exhibited special care and concern for the patient and who is familiar with the patient's personal values (§ 5(c)).

The surrogacy provision follows the overall preference for the effectuation of the Act without litigation, and therefore a health care decision made by a surrogate is effective without judicial approval (§ 5(g)). This is consistent with the case law in the overwhelming majority of jurisdictions that have addressed this issue.[11] The Act imposes a requirement that upon assumption of authority, a surrogate must communicate that fact to the members of the patient's family who might otherwise be eligible to act as surrogate (§ 5(d)). Notice to the family is intended to enable them to monitor the course of treatment for their now incapacitated relative and to alert them to take appropriate action, such as seeking judicial review, should the need arise.

Standard for decision-making by surrogates. Like a patient-appointed agent, a surrogate is required by the Act, as he would be by case law, to make decisions for the patient in accordance with that patient's wishes. If the patient has made an advance directive that contains "individual instructions" (but has not designated an agent), the surrogate is bound to follow those instructions and "other wishes to the extent known to the surrogate" (§ 5(f)). If the patient's wishes are not known, the surrogate is bound to make decisions based on the patient's best interests, "considering the patient's personal values to the extent known to the surrogate." This is again consistent with case law and the obligation imposed on agents by the Act.

* * *

Notes

1. See Meisel, *The Right to Die* (1994 Supp.) (Tables 10A-1 and 11-1) [hereinafter "Meisel"]. To obtain a copy of the Uniform Health-Care Decisions Act, contact the National Conference of Commissioners on Uniform State Laws, 676 North St. Clair St., Ste. 1700, Chicago, IL 60611. Phone: 312-915-0195. The Act is also published at 9 U.L.A. (Pt. I) 93 (1994 Supp.).
2. 9 U.L.A. (Pt. I) 453 (1988).
3. 9B U.L.A. 609 (1987).
4. 9B U.L.A. 109 (1993 Supp.).
5. In re E.G., 133 Ill. 2d 98, 139 Ill. Dec. 810, 549 N.E.2d 322 (1989); *In re* Swan, 569 A.2d 1202 (Me. 1990); In re Rosebush; 195 Mich. App. 675, 491 N.W.2d 633 (1992); In re Crum, 61 Ohio Misc. 2d 596, 580 N.E.2d 876 (Probate Ct. Franklin County, 1991); Belcher v. Charleston Area Medical Center, 422 S.E.2d 827 (W. Va, 1992). See generally Meisel, *supra* note 1, § 13.3 (1994 Supp.).
6. See generally Meisel, *supra* note 1, §§ 9.9–9.13, 9.14A (1989 and 1994 Supp.).
7. See generally Meisel, *supra* note 1, §§ 9.7–9.8 (1989 and 1994 Supp.).
8. See generally Meisel, *supra* note 1, ch. 8 (1989 and 1994 Supp.).
9. See generally Meisel, *supra* note 1, § 8.17 (1994 Supp.).
10. In re Browning, 568 So. 2d 4 (Fla., 1990).
11. See generally Meisel, *supra* note 1, ch. 8 (1989) and 1994 Supp.)

CHAPTER 28

Assisted Suicide

While society is approaching a consensus on when it is appropriate to permit the termination of life-sustaining treatment for incapacitated persons, a fierce controversy has erupted over the legality and morality of assisted suicide. The nature of the debate is well presented in the following articles.

T. Howard Stone and William J. Winslade

Physician-Assisted Suicide and Euthanasia in the United States: Legal and Ethical Observations

* * *

I. Physician-Assisted Suicide and Euthanasia Defined

Physician-assisted suicide occurs when a physician provides the means or information necessary for a patient to perform the act of ending the patient's life.[1] This may include, for example, the physician who "provides sleeping pills and information about the lethal dose aware that the patient may commit suicide."[2] Euthanasia takes place when the physician actually performs the act that ends the patient's life.[3] The American Medical Association's Council on Ethical and Judicial Affairs defines euthanasia to mean the "administration of a lethal agent in order to relieve a patient's intolerable and untreatable suffering."[4]

From *The Journal of Legal Medicine,* Vol. 16, p. 481, T. Howard Stone & William J. Winslade, Taylor & Francis, Inc., Washington, D.C. Reproduced with permission.

The distinction between physician-assisted suicide and euthanasia has important legal implications.[5] A physician who commits euthanasia may be criminally charged with the patient's homicide in virtually any state because the physician has purposely and directly caused the patient's death.[6] In contrast, a physician who does not perform the life-ending act, but who assists with a patient's suicide by providing the means or information necessary, can be criminally charged under laws specifically proscribing assisted suicide.[7] Such laws typically provide that persons who deliberately or intentionally advise, promote, aid, or encourage others to commit suicide are guilty of a felony less serious than homicide.[8]

II. History and Current Laws Regarding Assisted Suicide and Euthanasia

The English common law had long considered suicide a felony, but this law was abolished in 1961.[9] American law has rarely considered suicide a crime and generally does not now consider attempted suicide a crime.[10] The basis for not criminalizing suicide or attempted suicide is that there is no criminal punishment acceptable for a completed suicide, nor would punishment effectively deter attempted suicide.[11] In addition, suicide has often been considered an "expression of mental illness,"[12] or an act of a mentally ill, sick, or depressed individual who needs "medical treatment not punishment, compassion not culpability."[13]

Assisted suicide has been treated altogether differently from suicide or attempted suicide. At common law, persons who aided or abetted suicide were guilty of murder.[14] Currently, only seven states construe assisted suicide as murder or manslaughter.[15] Other states that criminalize assisted suicide characterize it as a separately graded felony.[16] The Model Penal Code also criminalizes assisted suicide, but differentiates between that which is purposely caused by "force, duress or deception"[17] and that which results from the purposeful aid or solicitation of another. The former may result in a homicide conviction; the latter may result in a conviction for a felony in the second degree.[18] In both instances, the Model Penal Code commentators are careful to note that the victim's consent or request is no limitation or defense to liability for causing, aiding, or assisting suicide.[19]

* * *

III. Prosecutions for Physician-Assisted Suicide and Euthanasia

A. Physician-Assisted Suicide

Physicians who assist their patients with suicide are not likely to face criminal sanctions for their conduct.[20] First, many states do not even criminalize assisted suicide.[21] Second, even in states that proscribe assisted suicide, prosecutions of physicians for assisted suicide are almost unknown. Furthermore, there are no reported convictions of physicians for the assisted suicide of their patients.[22] This does not mean, however, that prosecutions for physician-assisted suicide have not been attempted. In New York, Dr. Timothy Quill was charged under that state's assisted suicide laws for the death of his patient, Patricia Diane Trumbull, but a grand jury later failed to indict Dr. Quill.[23] And in 1994, Dr. Jack Kevorkian was charged with two counts of assisted suicide under Michigan's new assisted suicide law, the constitutionality of which was recently upheld by the Michigan Supreme Court.[24] Since then, Dr. Kevorkian attended four more suicides; no charges have been filed in these cases. Some prosecutors concede that convicting him would be difficult while others assert that Dr. Kevorkian should be charged with murder.[25]

However, the lack of more prosecutions or of any convictions for physician-assisted suicide—despite the fact that such suicides regularly occur[26]—suggests that convictions will be difficult to obtain given public support of physician-assisted suicide,[27] the lack of laws criminalizing assisted suicide in some states,[28] and the difficulty in obtaining sufficient evidence.[29] The lack of prosecutions for physician-assisted suicide also prevents analysis of possible defenses or mitigating circumstances that could be raised by a physician charged with an offense.

B. Euthanasia

Unlike physician-assisted suicide, prosecutions and convictions of physicians for homicide arising from performing euthanasia have occurred, though such prosecutions are still rare. Since 1950, when the first case arose, there have been six reported cases of physicians prosecuted for homicide following euthanasia.[30] In 1950, Dr. Herman Sander was charged with and acquitted of murder after injecting 40cc of air into a vein of a terminally ill cancer patient at the request of the patient's husband.[31] In 1974, Dr. Vincent Montemarano was acquitted of murder for injecting potassium chloride into a comatose throat cancer patient who had two or fewer days left to live.[32] In 1985, Dr. John Kraii was charged with the murder of a friend who was also a patient, but Dr. Kraii himself committed suicide shortly after his arrest.[33] In 1986, Dr. Joseph Hassman was charged with manslaughter after injecting his mother-in-law with the painkiller Demerol.[34] Dr. Hassman pled guilty and was sentenced to two years probation.[35] Also in 1986, Dr. Peter Rosier was acquitted in the death of his wife, whom he had injected with morphine.[36] And in 1988, Dr. Donald Caraccio was charged with murder after injecting a patient with potassium chloride.[37] Dr. Caraccio pled guilty and was sentenced to five years' probation.[38]

These six euthanasia cases are instructive because they demonstrate that no jury has yet convicted a physician for homicide arising from performing euthanasia.

* * *

Notes

1. American Medical Association Council on Ethical and Judicial Affairs, *Decisions Near the End of Life,* 267 J.A.M.A. 2229, 2229 (1992).

2. *Id.*

3. *Id.* For purposes of this article, euthanasia will not include passive euthanasia, now considered the accepted norm. Risley, *Voluntary Active Euthanasia: The Next Frontier,* 8 ISSUES L. & MED. 361, 362 (1992). Passive euthanasia encompasses the withdrawing or withholding of medical treatment, including artificial hydration and nutrition. *Id.* The United States Supreme Court has essentially conceded that persons have a right to refuse life-saving hydration and nutrition under the fourteenth amendment. Cruzan v. Director, Missouri Dep't of Health, 497 U.S. 261, 279 (1990).

4. AMA Council, *supra* note 1, at 2231. However, at least one critic believes that the distinction between physician-assisted suicide and euthanasia is virtually meaningless because euthanasia is only one step removed from assisted suicide, and because determining whether a physician's conduct comprises assisted suicide or euthanasia may be legislatively unworkable. *See* Potts, *Looking for the Exit Door: Killing and Caring in Modern Medicine,* 25 HOUS. L. REV. 493, 511 (1988). As a practical matter and from a psychological perspective, physician-assisted suicide and euthanasia seem clearly distinguishable. *See* Weir, *The Morality of Assisted Suicide,* 20 LAW, MED. & HEALTH CARE 116, 117–18 (1992). From a moral point of view, however, it is sometimes argued that no substantial difference exists between them. *See* Brock, *Voluntary Active Euthanasia,* 22 HASTINGS CENTER REP. 10 (Mar./Apr. 1992).

5. *See infra* notes 6–8 and accompanying text.

6. CeloCruz, *Aid-In-Dying: Should We Decriminalize Physician-Assisted Suicide and Physician-Committed Euthanasia?,* 18 AM. J.L. & MED. 369, 380–82 (1992). *See also* MODEL PENAL CODE § 210.5(1) (Official Draft and Revised Comments 1980).

7. *See* Bjorck, *Physician-Assisted Suicide: Whose Life Is It Anyway?,* 47 S.M.U.L. REV. 371, 379 (1994) (stating that 25 states have statutes expressly criminalizing assisted suicide, and that the other states do not legislatively provide for such conduct); CeloCruz, *supra* note 6, at 377 (observing that other jurisdictions criminalize assisted suicide under case law). *See also* MODEL PENAL CODE § 210.5(2) (which states: "[A] person who purposely aids or solicits another to commit suicide is guilty of a felony of the second degree if his conduct causes such suicide or attempted suicide, and otherwise of a misdemeanor.").

8. *See, e.g.,* CAL. PENAL CODE § 401 (West 1994); TEX. PENAL CODE ANN. § 22.08(b) (West 1994); N.Y. PENAL LAW § 120.30 (McKinney 1994); FLA. STAT. ANN. § 782.08 (West 1994).

9. *See* Suicide Act, 1961, 9 & 10 Eliz. 2, ch. 60, § 1 (Eng.) (providing that "[t]he rule of law whereby it is a crime for a person to commit suicide is hereby abrogated"). For more extensive historical treatment, see CeloCruz, *supra* note 6, at 373–77.

10. MODEL PENAL CODE § 210.5 comment 2 & N. 10 (stating that all state recodifications pertaining to suicide and attempted suicide follow the Model Penal Code); Note, *The Punishment of Suicide: A Need for Change,* 14 VILL. L. REV. 463, 465 (1969).

11. Note, *supra* note 10, at 470.

12. *In re* Joseph G., 667 P.2d 1176, 1178 (Cal. 1983).

13. CeloCruz, *supra* note 6, at 375 & n.43.

14. *Id.* at 374 (footnote omitted); MODEL PENAL CODE § 210.5 comment 1 & n.7.

15. Bjorck, *supra* note 7, at 378 & nn.73–74. These states are Alaska, Arizona, Arkansas, Colorado, Connecticut, Oregon, and Michigan. *Id.*

16. *Id.* at 379 & n.77 (listing statutes); *Joseph G.,* 667 P.2d at 1179.

17. MODEL PENAL CODE § 210.5(1). The Code's drafters limited the actor's criminal liability under section 210.5(1) for homicide to purposeful conduct on the ground that merely creating

a risk that another would commit suicide "would cast the net of liability too wide." MODEL PENAL CODE § 210.5 comment 4. Under section 210.5(1), the actor's conduct is the cause of another's suicide when the actor's conduct is "an antecedent but for which the [suicide] . . . would not have occurred." *Id.* For the same reason, criminal liability is limited to situations in which the actor induces the suicide of another by the use of "force, duress or deception." *Id.* The Code commentators did not indicate what conduct would comprise force, duress, or deception, but did observe that in a test case where a distraught lover threatened to kill himself if abandoned, a party to the romance who perceived this risk or may even intend such a result would not warrant conviction of homicide if the suicide occurred. *Id.*

18. MODEL PENAL CODE § 210.5(2).

19. *Id.* § 210.5 comments 5 & 7.

20. Bjorck, *supra* note 7, at 372. See also MODEL PENAL CODE § 210.5(2) (1980). *But see* People v. Roberts, 178 N.W. 690 (Mich. 1920) (upholding murder conviction of defendant-husband for mixing poison and placing poison within reach of wife, who later drank poison); People v. Kevorkian, 517 N.W.2d 293, 297 (Mich. App.) (stating that Roberts is still the law in Michigan), *vacated,* Hobbins v. Attorney General, 527 N.W.2d 714 (Mich. 1994), *cert. denied,* 115 S. Ct. 1795 (1995).

21. *See* Bjorck, *supra* note 7, at 379.

22. CeloCruz, *supra* note 6, at 378 & n.67.

23. *Id.* at 379 & n.77. *See* Quill, *Death and Dignity: A Case of Individual Decision Making,* 324 NEW ENG. J. MED. 691 (1991) (providing an account and background of Ms. Trumbull's decision to forego cancer treatment and hasten her death with an overdose of prescribed barbiturates).

24. *Hobbins,* 527 N.W.2d at 714 (holding that Michigan law imposing criminal penalties for assisted suicide was not prohibited by the United States Constitution, and rejecting a lower court decision holding that Michigan's assisted suicide law was unconstitutional for technical reasons).

Dr. Kevorkian remains charged with murder involving the same two deaths. *Kevorkian,* 517 N.W.2d at 298. The deceased are Marjorie Wantz and Sherry Miller. *Id.* at 294. Ms. Wantz died after receiving a lethal intravenous dose of barbiturates delivered through Dr. Kevorkian's "suicide machine," to which Dr. Kevorkian had connected Ms. Wantz. Ms. Miller died from carbon monoxide poisoning, delivered through a mask assembly attached to Ms. Miller's face by Dr. Kevorkian. Both Ms. Wantz and Ms. Miller were severely debilitated and had sought out Dr. Kevorkian in order to end their lives.

25. *After Latest Assisted Suicide, Body Is Left Near a Hospital,* N.Y. Times, Aug. 21, 1995, at A9. *See also Dismissal of Kevorkian Case Sought,* Hous. Chron., Aug. 30, 1995, at 14A.

26. AMA Council, *supra* note 1, at 2233; Wanzer, Federman, Adelstein, Cassel, Cassem, Cranford, Hook, Lo, Moertel, Safar, Stone, & van Eys, *The Physician's Responsibility Toward Hopelessly Ill Patients: A Second Look,* 320 NEW ENG. J. MED. 844, 848 (1989).

27. [Blendon, Szalay, & Knox, *Should Physicians Aid Their Patients in Dying?,* 267 J.A.M.A. 2658, 2659–61 (1992) (finding as the result of over 21 surveys—some conducted over a period of almost 40 years—that of those persons surveyed, 63% said euthanasia and physician aid-in-dying should be legalized, 76% supported allowing withdrawal of life support or life-sustaining treatment, almost 40% would ask their physicians to administer or prescribe lethal drugs, and 11% would ask family or friends to help end their lives, if they had an illness with no hope of recovery and were suffering great pain). *See also* Margolick, *Jury Acquits Dr. Kevorkian of Illegally Aiding a Suicide,* N.Y. TIMES, May 3, 1994, at A1 (reporting juror comments that

"I don't feel it's our obligation to choose for someone else how much pain and suffering they can go through;" "Dr. Kevorkian should continue his work;" and "three-quarters of [my] fellow jurors would agree"); Cohen, Doukas, Lichtenstein, & Alcser, *Attitudes Toward Assisted Suicide and Euthanasia Among Physicians in Washington State*, 331 NEW ENG. J. MED. 89, 91 (1994) (disclosing that a slight majority of physicians surveyed favor legalizing physician-assisted suicide and euthanasia in some circumstances).]

28. *See* Bjorck, *supra* note 7, at 379.

29. *See, e.g.*, Quill, *supra* note 23, at 694 (disclosing that when asked by a medical examiner the cause of death of Diane Trumbull, the patient for whom he had prescribed a lethal dose of barbiturates, Dr. Quill answered "acute leukemia." Dr. Quill admits to providing this "cause" of death to "protect all of us" from criminal prosecution and to "protect Diane from an invasion into her past and her body").

30. Persels, *Forcing the Issue of Physician-Assisted Suicide: Impact of the Kevorkian Case on the Euthanasia Debate*, 14 J. LEGAL MED. 93, 111–12 (1993).

31. CeloCruz, *supra* note 6, at 382 & n.99.

32. Persels, *supra* note 30, at 111.

33. *Id.* at 111–12.

34. CeloCruz, *supra* note 6, at 382 & n.102.

35. *Id.*

36. *Id.* at 382 & n.101.

37. Persels, *supra* note 30, at 112.

38. *Id.*

In the following article, Professor Beauchamp explains why he supports physician assisted suicide.

Tom L. Beauchamp

The Justification of Physician-Assisted Deaths

Introduction

* * *

Euthanasia occurs if and only if: (1) The death of a person is intended by at least one other person who is either the cause of death or a causally relevant factor in bringing about the death; (2) the person killed is terminally ill, acutely suffering, or

Indiana Law Review, Vol. 29, No. 4, 1173–1200 (1996). Reprinted by permission.

irreversibly comatose, which alone is the primary reason for intending the person's death; and (3) the means chosen to produce the death are as painless as possible, or there is a sufficient moral justification for choosing a more painful method.[1]

If a person capable of voluntary action requests the termination of his or her life under these three conditions, the action is *voluntary* euthanasia. If the person is not mentally competent to make an informed request, the action is *nonvoluntary* euthanasia. Both are distinguished from *involuntary* euthanasia, a designation restricted to a person capable of informed choice, but who has not requested euthanasia. Involuntary euthanasia is universally condemned and plays no role in current moral and legal controversies, but the first two forms are actively under discussion.

Active and *passive* euthanasia were distinguished once the intentional omission of life-sustaining treatment came to be categorized as euthanasia. When this distinction is combined with the voluntary-nonvoluntary distinction, four general categories of euthanasia emerge, of which the second and third types have been the focus of discussion.

1. Voluntary passive euthanasia
2. Nonvoluntary passive euthanasia
3. Voluntary active euthanasia
4. Nonvoluntary active euthanasia

"Physician-assisted suicide" is often treated as a form of voluntary active euthanasia[2] on grounds that the voluntary choice of the patient makes the death a suicide and the physician-assistance is active rather than passive. However, the concepts of voluntary active euthanasia and physician-assisted suicide should be kept distinct. "Euthanasia" does not require a *physician* to bring about the death, and "physician-assisted suicide" does not require that the person who dies be acutely suffering or that the person's condition forms the reason for the suicide or for assisting in suicide. There is also no conceptual requirement in physician-assisted suicide that the means chosen must be as painless as possible.[3]

* * *

Assisted suicide and voluntary active euthanasia both involve assistance in bringing about another's death, but "assisted suicide," as this term will be used here, also requires that the person whose death is brought about be the ultimate cause of his or her own death (the final relevant link in a causal chain leading to death), whereas "voluntary active euthanasia" requires that the ultimate cause of one person's death be another person's action. As we will see, when physicians assist in or administer death to their patients, the physicians' *intentions* and the *causes* of death involved can make a decisive difference to both the classification and the evaluation of their acts. However, we need first to consider how the often invoked distinction between *killing* and *letting die* plays a role in these controversies.

* * *

Consider what justifies a physician's act of foregoing treatment. The physician's foregoing is warranted by an *authoritative refusal of treatment* by a patient or authorized surrogate. It would be both immoral and illegal for the physician not to forego treatment in the face of a competent, authoritative refusal. The presence of a competent, authoritative refusal of treatment is what places the physician's act into the category of letting die, rather than killing, and makes the same act by a nonphysician one of killing rather than letting die (a competent, authoritative refusal of treatment is typically absent when nonphysicians perform the same action). "Ceasing useless treatment" is neither conceptually nor morally the proper way to state the situation; "validly refused treatment" is the heart of the conceptual matter and the moral matter.

A similar claim about refusal of treatment has been defended by James L. Bernat, Bernard Gert, and R. Peter Mogielnicki.[4] They suggest that the type of action—killing or letting die—depends on whether a valid refusal warrants the foregoing of treatment, rather than the validity of the foregoing depending on whether it is an act of letting die. This suggestion is illuminating. Traditionally the distinction between killing and letting die was thought to be the first question to be decided, and it was thought that the distinction should be accounted for either in terms of *intention* (whether a person intends someone's death) or *causation* (whether a person causes someone's death).[5] The patient-refusal hypothesis provides a third way. It demotes causation and intention in importance and ascribes a pivotal role to *valid refusal.*

A refusal is valid if a patient or authorized decision-maker autonomously refuses a proposed treatment. This account of a valid refusal is part of a larger account of the limits of the physician's authority, duties, and moral responsibilities. The physician has a duty to follow an appropriate refusal. This duty allows us to say that the physician's action of withholding or withdrawing does not cause death in the legal framework of proximate causation. The close connection between causation, duty, and causal responsibility is again apparent. Those who have looked to some of the nonlegal accounts of causation . . . to determine whether physicians cause death have been looking in the wrong place if the point is to distinguish between killing and letting die; and physicians who have been worried about killing their patients have been thinking about causation in the wrong way. Although the physician's withdrawal of a treatment is a necessary part of a sufficient condition of the death as it occurs, the physician does not cause death in the relevant sense of "cause." The physician does not cause death because there is no duty to treat in the face of a valid refusal, and therefore the patient's preexisting condition becomes the proximate cause of death.

This theory gives meaning to the pivotal terms "killing" and "letting die" in a way that potentially protects the conventional moral thesis in law and medicine that it is justifiable to allow a patient to die and unjustifiable to kill a patient. Valid refusals warrant letting die, and foregoing treatment or active intervention to bring about death in the absence of a valid refusal exposes the physician to a charge of unjustified killing. Still to be considered is whether this thesis begs the central moral question by assuming, without argument, that only letting die is justified. An alternative, and my preference, is to frame acts of killing so that they can be justified on grounds that are strikingly similar to the justification of acts of letting die.

* * *

VI. Valid Requests as the Justificatory Basis of Killing

If the justification of the physician's actions is determined by a valid authorization, must the notion of a valid authorization be confined to a valid *refusal?* Can a valid *request* be as authoritative as a valid *refusal?*

The primary justification advanced in both law and morals for requirements that competent informed refusals be honored is the right of self-determination. The principle of self-determination in recent legal literature is the functional equivalent of the moral principle of respect for autonomy.[6] A major concern of the law is to prescribe the precise duties that devolve upon physicians in order that rights of autonomy be protected. In the last two decades it has become clear that a valid refusal of treatment obligates the physician to forego treatment, even if it is a refusal of hydration and nutrition or a life-support system that will result in death.[7] Whenever valid refusals occur, it is never a moral offense to comply with the refusal, and how the death occurs from the refusal is irrelevant.[8]

By not categorizing the withholding or the withdrawing of a validly refused medical treatment as "killing," we have signaled our acceptance of the physician's non-treatment even when treatment is medically indicated. Had we judged withholding and withdrawing treatment morally unacceptable when competent persons refuse treatment, we would have categorized such conduct by physicians as killing (perhaps mercy killing, but still killing). Similarly, had we found moral grounds not to accept refusals by competent persons, we might have chosen not to categorize such conduct as foregoing life-sustaining treatment, and instead have categorized it as suicide.

* * *

In some cases, patients in a close relationship with a physician *both* decline a possible treatment *and* request an accelerated death in order to lessen pain or suffering. In these cases, the refusal and the request are combined as parts of a single plan. If the physician agrees with the plan, assisted suicide or active euthanasia grows out of the close patient-physician relationship established by the two parties. In the context of such a relationship it would not be surprising if some physicians preferred active euthanasia to the form of physician-assisted suicide envisaged in Oregon, which allows prescribing drugs for suicide, but does not allow providing aid to patients at the point when they most need the care, comfort, and reassurance that a good physician can provide. How society is to judge the quality of such relationships (and whether it should judge them at all) is an unsettled matter, but it is beyond reasonable doubt that at least some patients and physicians have established this type of relationship.

When patients make reasonable requests for assistance in dying, physicians cannot escape responsibility for their decisions by refraining from helping their patients die.

No physician can say, "I am not responsible for the result of my decision when I choose not to act on a patient's request." There has long been a vague sense in the medical and legal communities that if only the physician lets nature take its course, then the physician is not responsible for the resulting death. This account is misleading. A physician is always responsible for the decision taken and for the consequences of any action or inaction. The physician who complies with a patient's request is responsible in the same way a physician who refuses to comply with a request is responsible for his or her decisions.

Physicians who reject requests by patients cannot magically relocate responsibility by transferring it to the patient's disease. The only relevant matter is whether the physician has an adequate justification for the chosen course of action. Physicians have a responsibility to act in the best interests of their patients, and they cannot, without adequate justification, avoid what a patient believes to be in his or her best interests. It is undisputed, physicians often reject courses of action requested by patients and have good reasons for doing so. The question is whether the physician, who conscientiously believes that the patient's request for assistance in dying is justified and assumes responsibility for assistance, acts in a morally justifiable manner in complying with the request even when it is not legally justifiable.

* * *

VIII. The Rightness in Causing or Assisting in Death

These conclusions can now be linked to the earlier conclusions about valid refusals and valid requests. If passive allowance of death based on valid refusals does not harm or wrong persons or violate their rights, how can assisted suicide and voluntary active euthanasia harm or wrong the person who dies? In both voluntary active euthanasia and passive letting die, persons refuse to go on and seek the best means to the end of quitting life. Their judgment is that continuing life is, on balance, worse than not continuing it. The person who attempts suicide, the person who seeks active euthanasia, and the person who forgoes life-sustaining treatment to end life are identically situated except that they may select different means to end their lives.[9] Therefore, those who believe it is morally acceptable to let people die when they refuse treatment, but not acceptable to take active steps to help them die when they request assistance, must give a different account of the wrongfulness of killing and letting die than I have offered.

* * *

Medicine and law now seem to say to many patients, "If you were on life-sustaining treatment, you could withdraw the treatment and we could let you die. Because you are not, we can only give you palliative care until you die a natural death." This position condemns the patient to live out a life he or she does not want—a form of cruelty that violates the patient's rights and prevents discretionary discharge of the fiduciary duties of the physician. This is not to claim that physicians face large numbers of desperately ill patients. Pain management has made circumstances at least bearable for many of today's patients,[10] reducing the need for physician-assisted suicide and euthanasia and increasing the need for adequate facilities, training, and hospice programs.[11] Nonetheless, the available medical literature indicates that some patients cannot be satisfactorily relieved,[12] and, even if they could, questions would remain about the autonomy rights of patients to pursue their own plans in life[13] and about the fact that many patients are more concerned about suffering and indignity than about pain.[14]

* * *

Notes

1. This account is elaborated in Tom L. Beauchamp & Arnold Davidson, *The Definition of Euthanasia,* 4 J. MED. & PHIL. 294 (1979). Contra Michael Wreen, *The Definition of Euthanasia,* 48 PHIL. & PHENOMENOLOGICAL RES. 637 (1988).

2. *See* AMA Council on Ethical and Judicial Affairs, *Decisions Near the End of Life,* 267 JAMA 2229 (1992). This pronouncement seems to treat both as straightforward cases of prohibited killing.

3. For different approaches and a few contrasting analyses, see Glenn C. Graber & Jennifer Chassman, *Assisted Suicide is Not Voluntary Active Euthanasia, but It's Awfully Close,* 41 J. AM. GERIATRICS SOC'Y 88 (1993); James C. Maher et al., *VAE versus Assisted Suicide [Letters to the Editor],* 41 J. AM. GERIATRICS SOC'Y 583 (1993); Franklin G. Miller et al., *Regulating Physician-Assisted Death,* 331 NEW ENG. J. MED. 119 (1994); David T. Watts & Timothy Howell, *Assisted Suicide is Not Voluntary Active Euthanasia,* 40 J. AM. GERIATRICS SOC'Y 1043 (1992); [*see* Robert F. Weir, *The Morality of Physician-Assisted Suicide,* 20 LAW MED. & HEALTHCARE 116 (1992).]

4. *In re* Conroy, 464 A.2d 303 (N.J. Super. Ct. App. Div. 1983).

5. *In re* Conroy, 485 A.2d 1209, 1224–25 (N.J. 1985).

6. The classic origins of this principle for medical contexts is Schloendorff v. Society of New York Hospitals, 105 N.E. 92, 93 (N.Y. 1914) ("Every human being of adult years and sound mind has a right to determine what shall be done with his own body; and a surgeon who performs an operation without his patient's consent commits an assault."). Despite such strong rights language, all courts passing on the issue have ruled that a patient's right to self-determination, as protected by the legal doctrine of informed refusal and informed consent, is not absolute in the sense of always validly overriding every competing claim. Several legally justified exceptions are recognized. In general, legal duties and rights, like moral duties and rights, have no more than prima facie value. A prima facie legal duty such as the duty to obtain informed consent is therefore not always an *actual* duty. Valid exceptions are admitted in both law and ethics if promotion of the best interests of society or of the individual demands them, but many proposed exceptions and justifications are highly controversial.

7. [Recent legal history and legal complexities are thoroughly treated in ALAN MEISEL, THE RIGHT TO DIE (1993). *See also* Alan Meisel, *The Legal Consensus about Forgoing Life-Sustaining Treatment: Its Status and Its Prospects,* 2 KENNEDY INST. ETHICS J. 309 (1992); Robert F. Weir & Larry Gostin, *Decisions to Abate Life-Sustaining Treatment for Nonautonomous Patients,* 264 JAMA 1846 (1990).]

8. For a compelling case of death by seizure after refusal of seizure-preventing medication, see Stephanie Cate, *Death by Choice,* 91 AM. J. NURSING 32 (1991).

9. For the extension to suicide, see Dan W. Brock, *Death and Dying, in* MEDICAL ETHICS 329, 345 (Robert M. Veatch ed., 1989); [Sanford H. Kadish, *Letting Patients Die: Legal and Moral Reflections,* 80 CAL. L. REV. 857 (1992)].

10. [K. M. Foley, *The Relationship of Pain and Symptom Management to Patient Requests for Physician-assisted Suicide,* 6 J. PAIN & SYMPTOM MGMT. 289 (1991)]; D. E. Weissman, *Physician Assisted Suicide,* BIOETHICS BULL., 1991, at 3–4.

11. Greg A. Sachs et al., *Good Care of Dying Patients: The Alternative to Physician-Assisted Suicide and Euthanasia,* 43 J. AM. GERIATRICS SOC'Y 554 (1995); Joan Teno & Joanne Lynn, *Voluntary Active Euthanasia: The Individual Case and Public Policy,* 39 J. AM. GERIATRICS SOC'Y 827 (1991). For a different slant on these issues, see [Ronald E. Cranford, The Physician's Role in Killing and the Intentional Withdrawal of Treatment, in INTENDING DEATH 160 (Tom L. Beauchamp ed., 1996).]

12. *See* Gregg A. Kasting, *The Nonnecessity of Euthanasia, in* PHYSICIAN-ASSISTED DEATH 25–45 (James M. Humber et al. eds., 1994); Timothy E. Quill et al., *Care of the Hopelessly Ill: Proposed Clinical Criteria for Physician-assisted Suicide,* 327 NEW ENG. J. MED. 1380 (1992).

13. Helga Kuhse, *Active and Passive Euthanasia—Ten Years into the Debate, in* THE EUTHANASIA REVIEW 108, 117 (1986); [Malcolm Parker, *Moral Intuition, Good Deaths and Ordinary Medical Practitioners,* 16 JAMA 28 (1990)].

14. [*See* Robert F. Weir, *The Morality of Physician-Assisted Suicide,* 20 LAW MED. & HEALTHCARE 116 (1992).]

Many persons strongly object to the legalization of assisted suicide. Professor Kamisar presents the case against the practice in his response to Professor Robert A. Sedler's "Are Absolute Bans on Assisted Suicide Constitutional? I Say No" (72 U. Det. Mercy L. Rev. 725, 1995).

Yale Kamisar

Against Assisted Suicide—Even a Very Limited Form

* * *

Professor Sedler does not want us to think about the impact on our society of establishing a right or liberty to physician-assisted suicide, however limited (at first). He does not want us to think about other situations where the case for assisted suicide may be equally strong. He only wants us to focus on a very narrowly circumscribed set of circumstances.

University of Detroit Mercy Law Review, Vol. 72, No. 4, 735 (Summer 1995). Reprinted by permission.

Why is that? I think it is because, as Sedler and his colleagues are well aware, a severely circumscribed right to assisted suicide would cause less alarm and command more support than a less restricted one. Most of us balk at the notion of actively intervening to promote or to bring about the death of innocent persons. But if only the terminally ill and, still more narrowly, only those in the final stage of their terminal illness, are afforded a right to assisted suicide, we can still manage to reassure ourselves that such a development constitutes only a very, very slight deviation from our social norms.

Thus, a proposal for a rigorously circumscribed right to assisted suicide or a claim that the Constitution protects a very limited right to assisted suicide is quite inviting; one might even say, seductive. And, if I may quote Justice Frankfurter again, "[t]he function of an advocate is . . . to . . . seduce . . . ."[1]

* * *

I do not deny that one may imagine situations, or recall actual ones, that constitute very dramatic, very compelling cases for assisted suicide (or active voluntary euthanasia for that matter). But I do not believe that a narrow exception to the current prohibition against assisted suicide would or could remain a narrow exception for very long. As I shall try to show, I do not believe there is any principled way to limit the right to physician-assisted suicide to the terminally ill even to those suffering unbearable or great physical pain.

* * *

If a "Right" or "Liberty" to Physician-Assisted Suicide Were Established, Would (Could) it be Limited to the "Terminally Ill"?

As I understand it, the basic argument for assisted suicide is "personal autonomy" or "self-determination" or, as Professor Sedler puts it, paraphrasing the language in *Planned Parenthood v. Casey*,[2] "the right to define one's own concept of existence and to make the most basic decisions about bodily integrity."[3] But if one believes that respect for "self-determination" and "personal autonomy" entitles a person to decide for herself whether, when, and how she wishes to end her life, I do not see any principled way in which this right or liberty can be limited to the "terminally ill," let alone persons in the end stage of a terminal illness.

* * *

If personal autonomy and the termination of suffering are supposed to be the touchstones for physician-assisted suicide, why exclude those with nonterminal illnesses or disabilities who might have to endure greater pain and suffering *for much longer periods of time* than those who are expected to die in the next few weeks or months? If the terminally ill do have a right to assisted suicide, doesn't someone who must continue to live what *she considers* an intolerable or unacceptable existence *for many years* have an equal—or even greater—right to assisted suicide?

If a *competent* person comes to the unhappy but firm conclusion that her existence is unbearable and freely, clearly, and repeatedly requests assisted suicide, and there *is* a constitutional right to some form of assisted suicide, why should she be prevented from obtaining the assistance of another to end her life just because she does not "qualify" under somebody else's standards? Isn't *this* an arbitrary limitation of self-determination and personal autonomy? As Daniel Callahan has observed: "How can self-determination have any limits? [Assuming a person is competent and determined to commit suicide with the assistance of another,] [w]hy are not the person's desires or motives, whatever they may be, sufficient?"[4]

There is another reason I very much doubt that if a right to assisted suicide were established for the terminally ill, it could and would remain limited to the terminally ill for very long. As I understand the position of Sedler and other proponents of a right to assisted suicide, one should have the same right to enlist the aid of others to commit suicide as one presently has to refuse or to withdraw life-sustaining medical treatment. Professor Sedler puts it quite strongly. He sees no "principled difference, *in terms of constitutional doctrine and precedent*," between the alleged right to assisted suicide and the established right to terminate life support.[5] (Nor did Barbara Rothstein, Chief Judge of the United States District Court in Seattle, who recently became the first federal judge to strike down, as violative of the Fourteenth Amendment, a state law prohibiting all assisted suicide.)[6]

But if, as proponents of assisted suicide maintain, there is no significant difference between the right to assisted suicide and the right to reject unwanted life-saving treatment, it is fairly clear that, once established, the right to assisted suicide would not be limited to the terminally ill. For the right of a person to reject life-sustaining medical treatment *has not been so limited.*

* * *

Will the Fine Line between Assisted Suicide and Active Voluntary Euthanasia Endure for Very Long?

How does active voluntary euthanasia differ from assisted suicide? Active voluntary euthanasia occurs when someone other than the person who is to die performs the last act—the one that actually brings about death. Assisted suicide takes place when another person provides assistance (for example, provides the physical means to commit suicide), but the person whose life is to be ended performs the last, death-causing act herself. "Recent [court] decisions draw a distinction between active participation in a suicide [murder] and involvement in the events leading up to the suicide, such as providing the means [assisted suicide]."[7]

Because assisted suicide is less widely condemned by the criminal law and the fact that the final act is in the patient's hands is seen as offering more protection against potential abuse,[8] assisted suicide causes less alarm then active euthanasia and generally commands more support. But I think the two practices are much more alike than they are different—both involve the active intervention of another to promote or to bring about death.

* * *

While the distinction is hard to maintain in practice[9] it is even harder to defend as a matter of principle. If a person who resolves to end her life, but is unable to do so without another's help, is entitled under certain circumstances to the assistance of another in bringing about her own death, what about the person who is similarly determined to end her life but *unable* to perform the last, death-causing act herself? Whey should she be denied the assistance of another in carrying out the final act; i.e., denied active euthanasia?

If the claim that one has, or ought to have, a right to control the time and manner of one's death is well founded—if one who is terminally ill has, or ought to have, the right to make the choice whether or not to go on living until death comes naturally—how can this right be denied to someone simply because she cannot swallow the barbiturates that will bring about death?

Physician-assisted suicide may be less alarming than physician-administered active euthanasia and may be regarded as a lesser deviation from our social norms, but once we cross the line between the rejection of life-sustaining medical treatment and the active intervention of another to promote or to bring about death, I do not see how we could (or why we would) stop short of active voluntary euthanasia.

* * *

Liberals, Conservatives and "Slippery Slope" Arguments

Professor Sedler wants us, and wants the courts, to focus on a specific and narrow question: Do terminally ill patients have a right to physician-assisted suicide? He does not want us, or the courts, to consider the impact, if any, of an affirmative answer on "our views about death and dying or the sanctity of life."[10] He assures us that "we need not worry about any 'slippery slope.'"[11]

Professor Sedler has made the point before. Indeed, he has gone so far as to say that the kind of "slippery slope" arguments I have made in the course of defending the absolute prohibition against assisted suicide have "no place" in constitutional litigation and cannot be utilized "to avoid" grappling with the specific and narrow question he and his colleagues have framed.[12]

I must disagree. I do not believe a court can *responsibly* resolve the constitutional issue Sedler and others have presented *without* considering the general implications of the asserted right. Surely a judge should not put on blinders and forge straight ahead without thinking about the impact of her holding (however "narrow" and "specific" it may seem at first glance). Surely she should not "buy" an advocate's argument without thinking hard about what it is she is really "buying."

I share the view that a court should rest its judgment on a principle of general significance that produces like results in like cases.[13] If so, how can a judge avoid considering what *other* fact situations not presently before the court are (or are not) like cases?

Suppose a right to physician-assisted suicide for the terminally ill *were* established. Is there any doubt that lawyers would soon appear in court arguing that (a) the new right could not be limited to the terminally ill, but had to apply as well to others who would experience unacceptable suffering for many years; and that (b) the new right could not be limited to assisted suicide, but had to include active euthanasia, at least for those severely ill patients who were unable to perform the "final act" themselves? If it is appropriate to transcend the "narrow" and "specific" issue presented in a case *once* it is decided, and to start building immediately on its implications, why is it improper to *anticipate* the implications of a *soon-to-be-decided* case and call the court's attention to them?

I am well aware that a court must decide the case before it and not some other one. But as Justice Felix Frankfurter has observed—

> that does not mean that a case is dissociated from the past and unrelated to the future. We must decide this case with due regard for what went before and no less regard for what may come after.[14]

It is plain that proponents of assisted suicide (and active voluntary euthanasia) consider themselves the "liberals" or "civil libertarians" in this debate. In light of this, I find their disdain for the "slippery slope" argument somewhat unbecoming. For in other settings, "liberals" have been quick to make similar "slippery slope" arguments.

As the author of the leading law review article on "slippery slopes" has pointed out, such arguments appear frequently in discussions about freedom of speech and the rights of those suspected of crime.[15] I have little doubt, for example, that Professor Sedler and many other "liberals" defended the Nazis' right to march to Skokie largely because they feared that denying them First Amendment protection might start us down a slippery slope—that "if the swastika and burning crosses are banned today on good grounds, relatively innocuous symbols may be banned tomorrow on not so good grounds."[16]

The *Skokie* case may be viewed as a controversy between "act utilitarians," who wanted to focus on the particular facts of the case, and "rule utilitarians," who preferred to dwell on the long-range implications for the First Amendment of denying the Nazis the right to march. But this time it was clear that the "liberals" were the rule utilitarians.

Only a day before this symposium was held, the *New York Times* reported that a series of killings by terrorists had prompted the Israeli government to authorize harsher interrogation of suspected Muslim militants and that this decision had aroused the ire of various human rights groups.[17] The Israeli government supported its position by pointing to dramatic individual cases. It made what has been called the "ticking bomb" argument—underscoring the need to resort to torture to extract information that could prevent imminent killings.[18] But a goodly number of Israeli "liberals" were unpersuaded that a very few dramatic cases justified an exception to the absolute ban against torture. They feared that once a crack appeared in the flat prohibition against torture, the crack would gradually widen. Most interrogation situations, they emphasized, were "a far cry" from the "ticking bomb" case.[19] This controversy, too, may be viewed as one between "act utilitarians" and "rule utilitarians." And once again the "rule utilitarians"—those making the slippery slope argument—were the "liberals."[20]

I am well aware that, as Sissela Bok observed a quarter-century ago, "slippery slope" or, as they are often called, "thin edge of the wedge" arguments have been "used so often and for such dubious purposes that they tend to be brushed aside as merely rhetorical."[21] But, added Professor Bok, if these arguments are seen as "expressions of caution in the face of unknown future changes, there must be times when the caution has turned out to be justified."[22] The overuse or misuse of the slippery slope or wedge argument on some occasions does not justify its dismissal in other settings. Whenever such arguments are deployed, "it will be necessary to test the reasonableness of such a use within the context of the specific conflict."[23]

I submit that the experience in the Netherlands suggests that the use of the "slippery slope" argument is reasonable in the context of assisted suicide and active euthanasia.

A survey commissioned by the Dutch government revealed that in 1990 (the year covered by the survey) there were one thousand cases of active, intentional termination of life without an explicit request from the patient (nonvoluntary euthanasia).[24] As would be the case in the United States if current proposals were put into effect, the Dutch guidelines for assisted suicide and active euthanasia "are dependent upon the willingness of doctors to report what they do."[25] But "it is evident that most do not, and certainly not those substantial numbers who engage in nonvoluntary euthanasia."[26]

Recently, in the Assen case (a case referred to by the name of the city where it was tried), the Dutch Supreme Court extended the nation's toleration for assisted suicide and euthanasia to patients who are suffering psychological distress, but not physical (let alone terminal) illness.[27] As Professor Herbert Hendin, the Executive Director of the American Suicide Foundation and a close observer of the Dutch scene, has recently pointed out:

> [T]he Assen case seemed to justify the concerns here as in the Netherlands of a "slippery slope" that moves society inexorably from assisted suicide to euthanasia, from euthanasia for the terminally ill to patients who are chronically ill, from physical suffering to mental suffering, from voluntary requests for euthanasia to killing at the discretion of the physician.[28]

When it comes to assisted suicide (and active euthanasia) the United States is a considerable distance behind (or should one say, ahead of) the Dutch.

* * *

Suicide and Assisted Suicide vs. "Letting Die"

Professor Sedler has challenged those of us who are opposed to any relaxation of the ban against assisted suicide to defend, "*in terms of constitutional doctrine and precedent*," the distinction between the right to die by refusing life-sustaining medical treatment and the right to die by enlisting the aid of another in committing suicide.[29] In response, I should like to make several points.

First of all, "the major Anglo American medical associations vigorously maintain this distinction today" [30] and most courts have had little difficulty grasping its legal significance.[31] "As these courts have recognized, the fact that the refusal of treatment and assisted suicide may both lead to death does not mean that they implicate identical constitutional concerns." [32]

* * *

A recent statement by the Coordinating Council on Life-Sustaining Medical Treatment Decision-Making by the Courts typifies the way many courts and commentators have defended the line between "letting die" and actively intervening to promote or to bring about death:

> There are significant moral and legal distinctions between letting die (including the use of medications to relieve suffering during the dying process) and killing (assisted suicide/euthanasia). In letting die, the cause of death is seen as the underlying disease process or trauma. In assisted suicide/euthanasia, the cause of death is seen as the inherently lethal action itself.[33]

* * *

A society which *prohibited the refusal* of life-sustaining treatment and enforced such a prohibition with any regularity would not be a pleasant place in which to die (or live). Vast numbers of patients would be "at the mercy of every technological advance." [34] If people could decline possibly lifesaving treatment but not discontinue it once initiated, many would probably not seek such treatment in the first place. In short, as one commentator recently put it, "the only way we can offer patients and doctors the chance to prolong life—use life-sustaining treatment—is by also allowing them to decide when to cease such efforts. . . ." [35]

* * *

I realize that many do not consider the arguments made in defense of the distinction between suicide/assisted suicide and the refusal of life-saving treatment completely satisfying. But the distinction between active killing or active intervention to bring about death and "letting die" has more to commend it than mere logic.

For one thing, the distinction represents an historical and pragmatic compromise between the desire to let seriously ill people carry out their wishes to end it all and the felt need to protect the weak and the vulnerable. As Dean (now Judge) Guido Calabresi has observed, when we must make tragic choices—choices that confront us when fundamental beliefs clash—we seek solutions that "permit us to assert that we are cleaving to both beliefs in conflict." [36] As good an example as any of what

Judge Calabresi had described is the way we have dealt with the law and ethics of death and dying.

On the one hand, we want to respect patients' wishes, relieve suffering, and put an end to seemingly futile medical treatment. Hence we allow patients to refuse life-sustaining treatment. On the other hand, we want to affirm the supreme value of life and to maintain the salutary principle that the law protects all human life, no matter how poor its quality. Hence the ban against assisted suicide and active voluntary euthanasia.

I venture to say that one of the purposes of the distinction between the termination of life support and assisted suicide (or active voluntary euthanasia)—or at least one of its principal effects—is to have it both ways. The two sets of values are in conflict, or at least in great tension. Nevertheless, until now at any rate, we have tried to *honor both* sets.

I realize that drawing a line between assisted suicide (or active voluntary euthanasia) and "letting die" will not please every logician or philosopher. But what line will?

This brings us to another factor at work in this area—a factor that I think accounts for a good deal of the support for maintaining the "historic divide" between "active killing" and "letting die."[37] Unless we carry the principle of "self-determination" or "personal autonomy" or "control of one's own destiny" to its ultimate logic—assisted suicide (and active euthanasia) by any competent individual who firmly requests it for any reason *the individual* deems appropriate—we have to draw a line *somewhere* along the way. But *where?* I submit that *no* intermediate line, certainly not the one Sedler and his colleagues suggest, would be any more defensible than the one we have now. So why cross the line we have now?

* * *

Notes

1. FELIX FRANKFURTER, FELIX FRANKFURTER ON THE SUPREME COURT 509, 511 (Philip B. Kurland ed. 1970).

2. 505 U.S. 833, 851 (1992). [Remainder of note omitted.]

3. [*See* Robert A. Sedler, *Are Absolute Bans on Assisted Suicide Constitutional? I Say No,* 72 U. DET. MERCY L. REV. 725 (1995) (in this issue, preceding this article).]

4. DANIEL CALLAHAN, THE TROUBLED DREAM OF LIFE 107–08 (1993).

5. [*See* Robert A. Sedler, *Are Absolute Bans on Assisted Suicide Constitutional? I Say No,* 72 U. DET. MERCY L. REV. 725 (1995) (in this issue, preceding this article).]

6. Compassion in Dying v. Washington, 850 F. Supp. 1454 (W.D. Wash. 1994). Several months after I gave my talk, Judge Rothstein's decision was reversed. *See Compassion in Dying,* 49 F.3d 586 (9th Cir. 1995). At one point in his opinion reversing Judge Rothstein, Judge Noonan, who wrote for a 2–1 majority, observed: "At the heart of the district court's decision appears to be its refusal to distinguish between actions taking life and actions by which life is not supported or ceases to be supported." *Id.* at 593. As this article went to press, the Ninth Circuit announced that the Chief Judge and ten other members of the Court would rehear the case *en banc.* 62 F.3d 299 (1995).

7. People v. Kevorkian, 527 N.W.2d 714, 736 (Mich. 1994), *cert. denied,* 115 S. Ct. 714 (1995). The *Kevorkian* majority discusses, and seems to agree with, two cases from other jurisdictions where the courts found the defendant guilty of murder (which is how American criminal circles currently view active voluntary euthanasia) not assisted suicide: People v. Cleaves, 280 Cal. Rptr. 146 (Cal. Ct. App. 1991) (defendant held decedent down to keep him from falling off bed while decedent completed an act of self-strangulation); States v. Sexson, 869 P.2d 301 (N.M. Ct. App. 1994) (defendant held rifle in position while wife pulled trigger of rifle that killed her).

8. *See* Herbert Hendin, *Selling Death and Dignity,* 25 HASTINGS CENTER REP., May–June 1995, at 19.

9. Consider the following: A competent patient who has resolved to die by suicide and made her wish clear accomplishes her purpose by swallowing a lethal dose of medication which her physician has placed (a) on the night stand next to her bed, (b) in her hand, (c) in her mouth. Has the physician committed murder (which is how active voluntary euthanasia is currently regarded) or has she assisted in a patient's suicide? *Compare* Lawrence O. Gostin, *Drawing a Line Between Killing and Letting Die: The Law, and Law Reform, on Medically Assisted Dying,* 21 J.L. MED. & ETHICS 94, 96 (1993) *with* Kamisar, *Physician-Assisted Suicide: The Last Bridge to Active Voluntary Euthanasia, supra* note 48, at 230–31.

It may be argued that when a physician puts a lethal dose of medication in a patient's hand he is actively participating in an act that directly causes death. On the other hand, it may be argued that when a physician puts the means of committing suicide in a patient's hand, the lethal process has not yet become irreversible; the patient can still change her mind and put the medication on her night stand or throw it away instead of placing it in her mouth. However it comes out, the line between (a) putting a lethal dose of medication in a patient's hand and (b) putting it on top of her pillow or on her night table seems excruciatingly thin.

I think placing a lethal dose of medication in a person's mouth at her request would strike many people as a clear case of active voluntary euthanasia. But suppose a physician tells her patient: "I am going to place some lethal medication in your mouth, but don't be in a hurry to swallow it. You still have a choice. It's your life. I'm going to leave the room. If you decide that when all is said and done you do not want to die by suicide, that is your right. Simply remove the substance from your mouth or, if you prefer, spit it out." Suppose further that, after the physician leaves the room, the patient swallows the medication. It is not at all clear to me that this is active voluntary euthanasia rather than assisted suicide.

10. [*See* Robert A. Sedler, *Are Absolute Bans on Assisted Suicide Constitutional? I Say No,* 72 U. DET. MERCY L. REV. 725 (1995) (in this issue, preceding this article).]

11. *Id.* at 727.

12. *See* [Robert A. Sedler, The Constitution and Hastening Inevitable Death, 23 Hastings Center Rep., Sept.–Oct. 1993, at 20, 24.]

13. *See generally* Herbert Wechsler, *Toward Neutral Principles of Constitutional Law,* 73 HARV. L. REV. 1 (1959).

14. West Virginia State Bd. v. Barnette, 319 U.S. 624, 660–61 (1943) (Frankfurter, J., dissenting).

15. *See* Frederick Schauer, *Slippery Slopes,* 99 HARV. L. REV. 361 (1985).

16. JOEL FEINBERG, OFFENSE TO OTHERS 92–93 (1985); *see also* Schauer, *supra* note 15, at 363.

17. Joel Greenberg, *Israel Permits Harsher Interrogation of Militants,* N.Y. TIMES, Nov. 17, 1994, at A6.

18. *See id.*

19. *See id.*

20. One might argue that if a "ticking bomb" case actually arose, the legal system would somehow allow torture through the use of some subterfuge. Even so, it does not follow that the "absolute prohibition" against torture should be repealed. It is much easier to justify torture if one approaches the problem generally by balancing the "interest" in banning torture against the "interest" in peace and order. On the other hand, by refusing to acknowledge that we should balance the costs and benefits of torture as a general matter, we strengthen the presumption against torture and increase the likelihood that it will only be resorted to in the rarest and most compelling situations. See the discussion in GUIDO CALABRESI, IDEALS, BELIEFS, ATTITUDES, AND THE LAW 167 n.240 (1985) and Charles L. Black, Jr., *Mr. Justice Black, the Supreme Court, and the Bill of Rights,* HARPER'S MAG., Feb. 1961, at 63, 67–68. Both commentators discuss how we should go about deciding whether the police may torture a prisoner to get him to reveal the location of a nuclear bomb when the police knew he has hidden the bomb somewhere in a major city and the bomb is due to explode in a very short time.

21. Sissela Bok, *The Leading Edge of the Wedge,* HASTINGS CENTER REP., Dec. 1971, at 9.

22. *Id.*

23. *Id.*

24. *See* [Daniel Callahan & Margot White, *The Legalization of Physician-Assisted Suicide: Creating a Regulatory Potemkin Village,* U. RICH. L. REV. (forthcoming 1995)]; Herbert Hendin, *Seduced by Death: Doctors, Patients, and the Dutch Cure,* 10 ISSUES IN L. & MED. 123, 155 (1994); John Keown, *Euthanasia in the Netherlands: Sliding Down the Slippery Slope, in* EUTHANASIA EXAMINED 261, 269, 275–76 (John Keown ed., 1995). *See generally* CARLOS F. GOMEZ, REGULATING DEATH: EUTHANASIA AND THE CASE OF THE NETHERLANDS (1991).

25. [Callahan & White, *Id.*]

26. *Id.*

27. *See* Hendin, *supra* note 24, at 123.

28. *Id.* at 124.

29. [*See* Robert A. Sedler, *Are Absolute Bans on Assisted Suicide Constitutional? I Say No,* 72 U. DET. MERCY L. REV. 725 (1995) (in this issue, preceding this article).]

30. Edward J. Larson, *Seeking Compassion in Dying: The Washington State Law Against Assisted Suicide,* 18 SEATTLE U. L. REV. 509, 517 (1995) and medical groups cited therein. *See also* Seth F. Kreimer, *Does Pro-Choice Mean Pro-Kevorkian? An Essay on* Roe, Casey, *and the Right to Die,* 44 AM. U. L. REV. 803, 837–38 (1995).

31. *See* NEW YORK STATE TASK FORCE REPORT, *supra* note 8, and cases collected therein.

32. *Id.* at 71.

33. GUIDELINES FOR STATE COURT DECISION MAKING IN LIFE-SUSTAINING MEDICAL TREATMENT CASES 145 (rev. 2d ed. 1993).

34. [THE NEW YORK STATE TASK FORCE ON LIFE AND THE LAW, WHEN DEATH IS SOUGHT: ASSISTED SUICIDE AND EUTHANASIA IN THE MEDICAL CONTEXT 102 (1994) (hereinafter NEW YORK STATE TASK FORCE REPORT).] As the Task Force observed:

> [I]t is estimated that approximately 70 percent of all hospital and nursing home deaths follow the refusal of some form of medical intervention. A prohibition on the refusal of treatment would therefore require the widespread of restraint of patients unwilling to submit to invasive procedures at the end of their lives.

Id. at 74–75 (footnote omitted).

35. Giles R. Scofield, *Exposing Some Myths About Physician-Assisted Suicide,* 18 SEATTLE U. L. REV. 473, 481 (1995).

36. Calabresi, *supra* note 20, at 88; *cf. id.* at 87–91. *See also* GUIDO CALABRESI, A COMMON LAW FOR THE AGE OF STATUTES 172–77 (1982).

37. *Cf.* Albert W. Alschuler, *Reflection*, *in* ACTIVE EUTHANASIA, RELIGION, AND THE PUBLIC DEBATE 105, 108 (Martin Marty & Ron Hamel eds., 1991) (a publication of The Park Ridge Center).

One of the fears of those who oppose physician-assisted suicide is that if it is made legal, patients will be encouraged to end their lives as a means of foregoing costly medical treatment. Patients, it is alleged, will be made to feel guilty if they insist on life-sustaining treatment in the face of a terminal illness. The following article addresses that concern and other objections to what the author calls "aid-in-dying."

Leonard M. Fleck

Just Caring: Assisted Suicide and Health Care Rationing

* * *

III. Social Kindness or Social Hypocrisy: Aid-in-Dying and Rationing

I now want to turn to a second sort of scenario and some moral issues that seem to emerge from it. As background for this scenario I need to make, for the sake of argument, a strong assumption, namely, that there is nothing inherently morally objectionable to voluntary active euthanasia or physician-assisted suicide. It seems to me that considerations of autonomy and beneficence provide substantial moral grounding for this assumption.[1] I also believe that appropriate social controls can be put in place to prevent or minimize the most feared abuses that might be associated with this practice.[2] In particular, my working assumption is that voluntary aid-in-dying would be a last resort, embraced only because no other options were viable for a given individual. Still, the argument might be made that there would be spillover consequences of the practice that would be strongly morally objectionable, consequences not of the practice itself but of the practice plus some range of social facts that conjointly generated the objectionable consequences. Here we return to a world in which there is some range of rationing practices, just and unjust and morally ambiguous.

University of Detroit Mercy Law Review, Vol. 72, No. 4, 873 (Summer 1995). Reprinted by permission.

A. The Challenge of Unjust Rationing and Voluntary Aid-in-Dying

Consider what seems to be our own societal circumstances. If we have a society in which there is no national health insurance, in which there are 43 million individuals without health insurance, and hence, without assured access to needed health care, in which there are all manner of arbitrary and unjust rationings of access to health care, including rationing that occurs in government-sponsored programs such as Medicare and Medicaid, and if we have a permissible practice of voluntary aid-in-dying, then a likely consequence of these conjoined facts is that poor or uninsured or otherwise vulnerable individuals (such as those who are catastrophically ill but not terminally ill in a strict sense) who are denied access to needed life-sustaining or quality-of-life-preserving health care in order to control the social costs of health care will elect "voluntary" aid-in-dying rather than endure a prolonged process of suffering and/or dying. Prima facie, there is something morally unseemly about this outcome.

There are at least two sources of moral unseemliness in the "voluntary" aid-in-dying described above. First, some individuals are being unjustly denied access to needed health care, and, as a consequence of that are faced with two unpalatable (prima facie morally problematic) choices: unnecessary prolonged suffering and/or dying, or active aid-in-dying (when that individual would have preferred to go on living with their medical problems ameliorated). The result is social hypocrisy wherein society treats "kindly" by means of aid-in-dying an individual who does not want kind treatment to replace the just treatment to which he had a strong moral right. The second source of moral unseemliness is a form of social self-deception, namely, fostering the illusion that individuals who choose aid-in-dying under these circumstances have done so voluntarily. They have not. What we really have here is more properly described as nonvoluntary euthanasia, though clearly the visible social practices will make it appear to all as voluntary aid-in-dying.

The conclusion of this line of argument is that if an inherently morally permissible social practice, such as voluntary aid-in-dying, can be used so easily to mask widespread serious social injustices, and indeed alleviate pressure for remedying those social injustices, then that in itself becomes a powerful moral consideration against permitting that practice in the first place. In short, a society that offers its poorer and more vulnerable citizens the kindness of voluntary aid-in-dying in place of just access to needed health care is neither just nor kind nor honest.

In responding to the above line of argument we need to distinguish between a moral assessment of the "hard choices" that individuals face as a result of rationing practices that are in place and a moral assessment of the larger social policies that may create or modify "hard choices" for individuals.[3] All "hard choices" are by definition difficult because all the options available are unpalatable for various reasons. Individuals faced with hard choices that must be made may make those choices reluctantly and anxiously, especially if either choice requires the sacrifice of a substantial good or the tolerance of a significant bad. But an individual in such circumstances may not be able to claim justifiably that his rights were violated or that an unjustified moral harm was inflicted upon him because he was confronted by this hard choice. Further, in being compelled by circumstance to make a choice, he may not be able to claim justifiably that he acted nonvoluntarily. That is, he may not be able to claim that he was coerced or manipulated into making a choice, and therefore, that his rights of self-determination were unjustifiably violated. For the sake of clarity, let us consider the following examples.

Consider the circumstances of women who are in advanced stages of breast cancer, who have failed all conventional therapies. The only intervention that offers them any chance at all of some extended period of life is an autologous bone marrow transplant (ABMT), to which costs are attached of $100,000 to $150,000 for a 10 percent chance of three-year survival.[4] In general, insurance companies and HMOs will deny women access to this therapy.[5] As a consequence of this denial these women will die. How should we think of these deaths from a moral point of view? Our consciences will be soothed if we can convince ourselves that the cause of their death is their cancer. Such deaths are tragic and regrettable, but they are not morally culpable. But this is obviously not the whole story. The fact is that these women will have died when they did and as they did, in part, because of a rationing decision. It needs to be emphasized that ABMT is not an absolutely scarce medical intervention, as are heart transplants. Rather, it is a matter of fiscal scarcity. Someone made the judgment that these lives are not worth saving in this way at this cost. These are women who desperately wanted to live, but they were denied the only medical option that offered them that opportunity.

To carry this discussion a step further, I want to imagine that some number of these women choose voluntary aid-in-dying to end their lives instead of dying in any number of modes as a result of metastasized cancer. I also want to imagine the following background rationing scenarios to see if any of these ought to affect our judgment about the overall moral permissibility of voluntary aid-in-dying. Scenario One involves a large firm that employs a thousand women. They offer a generous health insurance package, but there are limits. After much discussion one of the trade-offs that these women agreed to was that yearly screening mammograms would be paid for by the plan for women over age fifty in exchange for foregoing access to ABMT for breast cancer. What these women found most compelling was that screening mammograms would reduce the death rate in this group from breast cancer from 36 per 1000 to 29 per 1000, whereas investing in ABMT instead would reduce the death rate to 35 per 1000.[6] (The cost of achieving either of these objectives is roughly the same.) Prima facie, this looks like a just instance of health care rationing.

Now Angie, forty-five years old, is found to have advanced breast cancer. In accord with company policy she is denied ABMT. She now has a hard choice. She can impoverish her family and choose ABMT, or she can accept her terminal status and choose aid-in-dying when the suffering becomes unbearable. Obviously, she can also endure the terminal suffering until she dies if those extra months of life are exceptionally important to her. The point to note, however, is that the hard choices she is faced with are not worsened by having aid-in-dying as an option. There is no obvious sense in which she is (morally) harmed by having this choice. Nor could we justifiably claim that a choice of aid-in-dying would be coerced. On the contrary, a good case can be made for saying that she has more choices in this scenario than would otherwise be the case; and, in addition, she is better off than she would have been if she had been compelled by circumstance to endure an agonizing death because the option of aid-in-dying was not available.

In Scenario Two, Betty is forty-five years old and a member of Maxi-Profit HMO. She is denied ABMT for her advanced breast cancer on the grounds that it is experimental therapy not covered by the plan. But, unbeknownst to her, two other women had ABMT paid for by the HMO, essentially for no better reason than that they were well connected to two Board members. Clearly Betty has been treated unjustly. She is now faced with the same hard choices as Angie. Does the fact that Betty is in her predicament because of an initial injustice alter in any way the judgment we ought to make about the moral justifiability of her having aid-in-dying as an option? As nearly as I can judge, we should offer the same moral analysis for Betty as for Angie. That is, the option of aid-in-dying does not worsen her situation, morally speaking, nor does it represent any diminishing of the voluntary character of her choice. On the contrary, it seems she is better off having aid-in-dying as an option. While obviously the initial injustice ought to be remediated if it is remediable, the improbability of that happening changes nothing with respect to the permissibility of aid-in-dying in this case. That is, society as a whole could not appropriately be judged as being "hypocritically kind" for allowing aid-in-dying as a legitimate social practice when we could anticipate that circumstances like this might arise. However, if that HMO deliberately paid for aid-in-dying in order to deliberately manipulate patients into choosing that option who had unjustly been denied access to life-prolonging medical therapies, then that HMO would be justifiably criticized as being both unjust and hypocritical, though that should still not alter society's judgment to permit aid-in-dying.

B. Social Manipulation and Aid-in-Dying

There is a third scenario that we next need to consider, which I shall refer to as the "Social Manipulation Argument," in which there are larger societal changes that alter background conditions associated with hard choices. I want to begin by recalling that in the debates about age-based health care rationing former Governor Lamm is often cited as the author of the remark that the elderly have a "duty to die."[7] The arguments about aid-in-dying are often couched in the language of individuals having a "right to die." But, the argument in this case maintains, what started out as a liberty right could become a social duty as pressures for health care cost containment mount. We do not have to imagine some draconian social policy being put in place. Instead the more likely, and more insidious scenario, is one sketched by Mayo and Gunderson[8] in which there is a gradual change in social attitudes toward the seriously chronically ill and terminally ill occasioned by the legalization of aid-in-dying. As things are now, such tragically situated individuals naturally elicit our compassion, at both the family and societal levels, because they have no legal options but to endure their suffering and a prolonged process of dying. If aid-in-dying is legalized, however, then these individuals have an option, and then they may be viewed less sympathetically—"especially if they are seen as stubborn when they are thought of as plausible candidates for physician-assisted death, but opt instead to remain alive and continue to require our care."[9] After all, these individuals now are commanding substantial sacrifices from caregivers which are not really necessary; and caregivers may convey in subtle and not-so-subtle ways their feeling of being unnecessarily burdened. Similarly, at the societal level there will be intense public argument about a broad range of social needs that are unmet or underfunded because too many health care dollars are being used to sustain for weeks and months the lives of elderly individuals who are doomed to die, who have had more than their fair share of life, and who now are so selfish that they would deny these social goods to younger members of society.[10] With that kind of social pressure it is easy to imagine many older individuals who want to be thought well of after death coming to the conclusion that they have a duty to die. Morally speaking, however, this looks like manipulated consent.[11]

There is another version of this argument we need to consider with respect to the larger social consequences of legalized aid-in-dying, and I shall refer to this as the "Social Disinvestment Argument." Dougherty points out that over the past twenty years we have struggled mightily as a society to make dying more humane and dignified through the development of hospice programs, through large investments in research and education regarding pain control for the terminally ill, through improved approaches to long-term care, and through massive public education about the value of advance directives.[12] However, the critical question he raises at the end of this list is: "Why take the more difficult road to make the dying process more humane when there is a social shortcut that terminates the dying process itself?"[13] Hospice care is clearly less expensive than aggressive ICU care for the terminally ill; but hospice care is still relatively expensive—relative to voluntary aid-in-dying. As Dougherty points out, virtually all health policy analysts agree that cost pressures "will force future adoption of practice protocols based on patient condition, likely outcome, and the cost of alternative treatments."[14] If aid-in-dying is among our options, then he concludes we will see "reimbursement restrictions, or cost-sharing arrangements that provide de facto incentives for the active killing of terminally ill patients."[15] Those incentives, of course, can be structured in such a way (50/50, for example) that they become effectively compulsory with respect to a certain choice that is socially desired, especially for those individuals and families who are financially less well-off in our society. Or, worse still, there is the argument that Doerflinger makes, namely, that if aid-in-dying is a socially approved option, that effectively demotes "all other options to the status of strictly private choices by the individual."[16] The election of hospice care then comes under an individual's right of privacy, and that fact might undermine public financing for the practice. Again, if that were to happen we would have to question seriously the moral reality of the voluntary part of aid-in-dying. No one doubts that the voluntariness of the practice is an absolutely integral part of the moral justification of the practice as a whole.

In summary, the conclusion of this line of argument is that even if the practice of voluntary aid-in-dying is in itself morally permissible, still, there are social facts about our world (enormous pressures for health care cost containment through rationing) which, taken in conjunction with the practice of aid-in-dying, yield morally intolerable results, including an erosion of the voluntariness of the practice itself in many cases, and therefore, an erosion of the moral legitimacy of the practice. We need to emphasize that the morally intolerable results we have in mind include more than a relatively small number of individuals whose rights might be violated or who may otherwise be treated unjustly. Rather, there are potentially large cohorts of the seriously ill or terminally ill elderly or disabled whose rights and welfare would be threatened by the social changes occasioned by voluntary aid-in-dying. Therefore, the ultimate conclusion of the argument is that when we make an "all things considered" moral judgment regarding aid-in-dying, we will have to reject the practice.

Notes

1. Dan Brock offers what to my mind is a concise and compelling account of the moral argument in support of voluntary aid-in-dying, including responses to the most common moral arguments against the practice. *See* Dan W. Brock, *Voluntary Active Euthanasia,* HASTINGS CENTER REP., Mar.–Apr., 1992, at 10.

2. For a discussion of what such a regulated practice might look like see Howard Brody, *Assisted Death—A Compassionate Response to a Medical Failure,* 327 NEW ENG. J. MED. 1384 (1992). *See also* Franklin Miller, Timothy Quill, et al., *Regulating Physician-Assisted Death,* 331 NEW ENG. J. MED. 119 (1994).

3. The "hard choices" problem I am discussing here was first introduced into the literature by David Mayo and Martin Gunderson. *See* David Mayo & Martin Gunderson, *Physician Assisted Death and Hard Choices,* 18 J. MED. & PHIL. 329 (1993).

4. For a discussion of the moral and policy issues raised by this sort of intervention see David Eddy, *The Individual vs. Society: Is There a Conflict?*, 265 JAMA 1446, 1449–50 (1991); *The Individual vs. Society: Resolving the Conflict,* 265 JAMA 2399, 2399–2401, 2405–06 (1991).

5. *See generally* W. D. Peters and M. C. Rogers, *Variation in Approval by Insurance Companies of Coverage for Autologous Bone Marrow Transplant for Breast Cancer,* 330 NEW ENG. J. MED. 473 (1994).

6. Eddy, *supra* note 4, at 1450.

7. This is a remark that has been erroneously attributed to Governor Lamm. Governor Lamm has been an outspoken proponent of the idea that the need for health care rationing is inescapable, and that the cohort that can reasonably be expected to bear the burden of health care rationing are the elderly. Two reasons for this are that the elderly have become elderly because they have been the disproportional beneficiaries of expensive life-prolonging medical technologies, and they have not borne a proportional share of the social costs incurred. Lamm is therefore correctly described as an advocate of age-based health care rationing. This is essentially the view that the elderly do not have an unlimited right of access to needed health care, that society can justly limit their access in order to meet the morally more compelling claims for needed health care of younger, less well off individuals. What it is important to note is that having such a limited right of access is not morally or logically equivalent to having a duty to die. Lamm's own explanation of his position in response to the "duty to die" accusation may be found in *The New Republic* (Aug. 27, 1984).

8. Mayo & Gunderson, *supra* note 3, at 334.
9. *Id.*
10. There is now a very large literature that discusses the issue of age-based rationing and the disproportionate claims that the elderly make on health care resources. For two books that are at the headwaters of this debate, see DANIEL CALLAHAN, SETTING LIMITS: MEDICAL GOALS IN AN AGING SOCIETY (Simon and Schuster, 1987); NORMAN DANIELS, AM I MY PARENTS' KEEPER? AN ESSAY ON JUSTICE BETWEEN THE YOUNG AND THE OLD (Oxford University Press, 1988). Both of these writers defend in different ways the moral justifiability of age-based rationing. For a more recent collection of essays on this issue is see HEALTH CARE FOR AN AGING POPULATION (Chris Hackler ed., State University of New York Press, 1994). This collection is a mix of essays that extend the arguments of Callahan and Daniels and other essays that are critical of their arguments.
11. For an extended moral discussion of manipulated consent in relation to suicide see Margaret Pabst Battin's essay *Manipulated Suicide reprinted in* MARGARET PABST BATTIN, THE LEAST WORST DEATH: ESSAYS IN BIOETHICS ON THE END OF LIFE 195–204 (Oxford University Press, 1994).
12. [Charles J. Dougherty, *The Common Good, Terminal Illness, and Euthanasia,* 9 ISSUES IN L. & MED. 151, 151–66 (1993).]
13. *Id.*
14. *Id.* at 160.
15. *Id.*
16. [Richard Doerflinger, *Assisted Suicide: Pro-Choice or Anti-Life?*, HASTINGS CENTER REP., Jan.–Feb., 1989, at 16 (special supplement).]

The fear that legalized assisted suicide may lead to a climate of encouraging voluntary euthanasia is particularly compelling in the context of older patients.

Marshall B. Kapp

Old Folks on the Slippery Slope: Elderly Patients and Physician-Assisted Suicide

The current controversy in the United States over the morality and constitutionality of state statutes that prohibit physicians from assisting patients to commit suicide entails a variety of difficult ethical[1] and legal[2] issues. In policy terms, the debate has tended to focus on whether legislatures can erect sufficiently stringent yet workable

Duquesne Law Review, Vol. 35, 443 (1996). Reprinted by permission.

safeguards within state statutes authorizing physician-assisted suicide to protect against serious ethical abuses of this patient/physician prerogative. Proponents of decriminalizing physician-assisted suicide take the affirmative position on this question.[3] Skeptics, on the other hand, suggest that opening the door to physician-assisted suicide, however cautiously and conservatively, would inevitably lead (as it apparently has in the current Netherlands experiment with non-prosecution of physicians for participating in physician-assisted suicide)[4] to a movement in principle and practice down a moral slippery slope toward unintended consequences[5] that almost everyone would condemn.

Most of the arguments on both sides of this discussion have been crafted in generic terms. While a persuasive case against recognition of a constitutional right to physician-assisted suicide generally can be mounted, as analyzed in the particular context of elderly individuals, the anxieties of the slippery-slope skeptics appear especially compelling. These are anxieties evidently shared by a substantial portion of the elderly population, since public opinion polls consistently show lower support for legalization of physician-assisted suicide among older citizens than among younger citizens.[6] The primary reasons for these well-founded worries are briefly outlined below.

I. Particular Risks for the Elderly

A. Decision Making Capacity[7]

In health care decision-making generally,[8] legally and ethically valid choices depend on (besides adequate information and voluntariness)[9] the presence of a cognitively and emotionally capable decision-maker. Although defining and evaluating a patient's decision-making capacity is an extremely complex and uncertain endeavor,[10] in essence an individual capable of making decisions has the functional ability to make and express authentic choices, give reasons for those choices indicating deliberation, comprehend and manipulate information material to those choices, and understand the potential personal consequences of the choices.[11]

As even proponents of physician-assisted suicide have acknowledged,[12] a capable decision-maker is an especially indispensable prerequisite in a physician-assisted suicide situation, as the costs of error are so great and irremediable. Notably, there are at least a couple of grounds for suspecting that a suicidal individual's capacity may be particularly problematic in cases of purported requests for physician-assisted suicide by older persons.

First, the prevalence of dementia increases dramatically in older patients.[13] While the presence of dementia (a diagnostic category) by itself, particularly in its early stages, does not necessarily equate with decisional incapacity (a functional concept),[14] in its more severe stages dementia ordinarily does substantially interfere with an individual's ability to engage in a rational decision-making process with respect to important and complicated matters. Physician-assisted suicide certainly qualifies as such a matter.

Much has been made in contemporary ethical and legal discourse of the possibilities for competent patients to guide their future medical care in the event of subsequent decisional incapacity through the execution of various forms of advance directives.[15] Proposals set forth thus far for physician-assisted suicide would all limit this option to patients with sufficient present decisional capacity to request physician-assisted suicide very shortly before its implementation.[16] It is questionable whether such a restriction, if embodied in a statute, could withstand Equal Protection scrutiny, especially if a right to physician-assisted suicide were not only recognized by the courts but held to be fundamental in kind. Perhaps more pertinent from a practical perspective is the fact that most people want to stay alive as long as they remain mentally intact; indeed, it is only at the point of severe mental deterioration, including decisional incapacity, when some persons would anticipate such a gruesome quality of life that they might ever contemplate an assisted (or an unassisted) suicide option. As G. Kevin Donovan stated:

> After all, if assisted suicide is a benefit, why should it be denied to those who waited too late to ask, aren't yet sick enough to merit it, or will never be competent enough. . . . If the guidelines are meant to protect the most vulnerable members of society, how do we justify at the same time depriving them of this benefit? The conflict is both inherent and inevitable.[17]

At the same time, allowing physician-assisted suicide for patients incapable of making decisions through previously executed advance directives, with all of the ambiguities and uncertainties already attending the rise of advance directives in other contexts,[18] would open the door to precisely the types of abuse that proposals to limit physician-assisted suicide to presently capable patients are intended to prevent. On the other hand, legalizing physician-assisted suicide while restricting its availability to individuals with contemporaneous decisional capacity creates a significant risk that individuals diagnosed with early stage dementias would panic and request physician-assisted suicide preemptively and prematurely out of fear of waiting too long.[19] It is likely, too, that unassisted suicides by early stage dementia patients would become more common in this scenario out of the patients' feeling of necessity to act decisively within an accelerated time frame.[20] The rapid scientific refinement and public availability of genetic testing techniques that may be useful in making more definitive differential diagnoses of early Alzheimer's disease[21] can only complicate this scenario.

A second and closely related decisional capacity problem is the prevalence of depression among older, and especially seriously ill, patients.[22] As with dementia, the simple bestowal of a diagnostic label on older patients should not inevitably lead to an assumption of the global inability of these patients to make medical choices. Nonetheless, an impressive body of evidence indicating a clear connection between severe depression in elderly individuals (not infrequently exacerbated by excessive use of alcohol)[23] and difficulties in complex medical decision-making processes,[24] as well as a connection between treatable depression and a desire for death in critically ill patients,[25] should heighten the discomfort about potential abuses of physician-assisted suicide with the older population.

Further, the notion that physicians are able to distinguish ethically and with any socially acceptable degree of confidence and precision between individuals who are capable of making decisions and older individuals who are not is suspect.[26] Even if psychiatric consultation is sought in difficult cases (and most situations of physician-assisted suicide requests ought to be placed in this category), as suggested by Timothy Quill and colleagues,[27] there is no assurance either that the psychiatrist would have any special training and expertise in evaluating the decisional capacity of older persons for physician-assisted suicide purposes,[28] or that insurers would routinely pay for such consultations.

B. Voluntariness

In health care decision-making generally, and certainly in the context of physician-assisted suicide, only voluntary patient requests made without duress, undue influence, or coercion have any plausible claim to legal and ethical legitimacy.[29] Several factors may significantly and perhaps inherently impinge on the voluntariness of purported requests for physician-assisted suicide made by elderly patients.

First, the United States is currently a fundamentally ageist society in which older individuals are often made to feel that they are of little or vastly reduced worth.[30] Despite the tremendous (arguably even disproportionate)[31] public financial resources devoted to the health care and income support of the elderly mainly for political reasons,[32] the continual social message to which the elderly are exposed is a theme that glorifies youth and vitality while devaluing the present contributions of the aged. The upshot of this psychological atmosphere is a potential endangerment of older individuals' freedom of choice. As Nancy Osgood noted:

> Older people, living in a suicide-permissive society characterized by ageism, may come to see themselves as a burden on their families or on society and feel it is incumbent on them to take their own lives. . . . The right to die then becomes not a right at all but rather an obligation. . . . In a society that devalues old age and old people, in which older adults are seen as "expendable" and as an economic burden on younger members, older people may come to feel it is their social duty to kill themselves.[33]

Put somewhat differently:

> The problem . . . involves the voluntariness of the decision. If choosing death becomes a socially accepted alternative, then patients needing much care may begin to consider themselves selfish merely for choosing to live. The pressure on the elderly . . . would be particularly great if death came to be seen as a "solution" to . . . old age.[34]

Notably, the impact of an ageist society is evidenced already in the disproportionately high rate of suicide attempts and completions among the elderly in the United States.[35] By contrast, the suicide rate of the elderly in societies which hold and communicate more respect for the aged is a much rarer event.[36]

A second ground for suspicion about the voluntariness of an older individual's purported request for physician-assisted suicide arises from the role of an individual's family in this decision. While normally families of older patients are an integral, positive force in supporting and assisting the effectuation of the patient's autonomous decision-making, this is not always the case.[37] The psychological, physical, and financial burdens on family members of very sick and frail individuals, especially those with chronic conditions requiring extensive, ongoing provision of care in the home, are great and can affect the patient's exercise of autonomy in many different ways.[38] With respect to the present analysis, even the most sincere and well-intentioned families[39] in such circumstances may end up, consciously or not, subtly or more directly pressuring the older patient to relieve the family's burden by selecting the physician-assisted suicide option.[40] The stress on the family, regardless of its palpability and magnitude, can never be a morally or legally acceptable justification for unduly influencing a vulnerable older person to agree to premature active death hastening.[41] Nevertheless, when combined with an older person's own sense of guilt about imposing a burden on the family because of continuing life and thus continuing the individual's provision of care,[42] any pressure brought by the family can exert a powerful psychological force on the dependent patient's choices and actions.[43]

C. Ageism in the Health Care System

As noted above, the voluntary nature of an older person's purported request for physician-assisted suicide is threatened both by general ageism in American society and by caregiver burden and other forces acting on the patient's family. Voluntariness, as well as the "informed" component of an older patient's physician-assisted suicide decision, may also be jeopardized by ageist attitudes and practices that directly pervade the present health care delivery system.

From the earliest part of their training, physicians and other health professionals are taught to devalue the lives of older patients.[44] One important way in which this attitude becomes manifested in practice is demonstrated by the overwhelming evidence that chronological age, by itself (that is, not used as a proxy for or indicator of some other, more clinically and ethically defensible consideration such as likely prognosis), frequently is a large risk factor for specific older patients being offered less aggressive medical treatment than normally would be offered to a younger, otherwise identical patient.[45] Thus, as verified most recently in the major national Study to Understand Prognoses and Preferences for Outcomes and Risks of Treatment (SUPPORT),[46] old age per se is used consciously or subconsciously by many physicians as the basis for: (a) slanting the information and options provided to the patient (or surrogate decision-maker, in the case of patients incapable of making decisions), thus diminishing the "informed" part of informed consent; and for (b) applying gentle or more firm pressure on the patient to accept less aggressive care than might otherwise be advised, thus jeopardizing the voluntariness of the patient's decision. This specter of age discrimination in medical practice bodes poorly for any reasonable expectation of just, fair administration of a legalized physician-assisted suicide option for older patients.

The elderly as a group based solely on chronological age are also targeted for proposed discrimination on the macro, or social policy, level as well as at the individual bedside. As American society continues to struggle with the challenge of health care cost containment,[47] a number of serious proposals have been put forward which would, through various strategies, categorically ration health care according to the age of the patient.[48] Although vigorous ethical, legal, economic, and social objections to these proposals have been mounted,[49] the enthusiasm with which age-based rationing proposals have been received if not embraced by key decision-makers ought to shake confidence in our ability, and indeed even our desire, to effectively implement legalized physician-assisted suicide in a non-age discriminatory fashion.

II. Alternatives to Physician-Assisted Suicide

The emotional and intellectual appeal of physician-assisted suicide appears to derive from fears patients harbor about suffering unremitting physical pain,[50] psychological indignity, loss of control and independence,[51] and abandonment during a time of critical illness that for most individuals is likely to occur near the end of life. While end-of-life concerns may be relevant to persons of all ages, the elderly correctly feel that they are particularly vulnerable to the risks of poor and insensitive care in this context.

The track record of health care professionals in humanely and respectfully caring for patients near the end of their lives surely leaves much to be desired.[52] Trying to avoid dealing with deficiencies in current end of life care, however, by allowing and thereby encouraging older persons and others to opt out of the health care delivery system near what elderly persons perceive is the end of their life, and to preempt objectionable care by allowing physician-assisted suicide, is not the answer.

Instead, a more ethically and legally viable alternative is to confront current deficiencies directly and improve the ethical as well as clinical quality and process of end-of-life medical care.[53] The Ethics Committee of the American Geriatrics Society has endorsed enhanced pain control through active palliation efforts.[54] Improved professional and public support of nonprofessional caregivers would help assure older patients that they will not be left to die alone and impersonally, thereby reducing a primary incentive for individuals to seek physician-assisted suicide as a preemptive measure.[55]

Unlike actively intervening for the purpose, intention, and expectation of hastening older patients' deaths by complying with questionably valid physician-assisted suicide requests, physicians who work at improving the quality and process of end-of-life care to make it more responsive to and respectful of the authentic values and preferences of older patients are performing a noble and life-affirming service. To accomplish this objective, initiative is demanded at three distinct but interrelated levels: clinical practice, institutional change, and political action.[56] Legalizing physician-assisted suicide, particularly through judicial fiat, would probably destroy health care professionals' incentive to take these needed initiatives and expose vulnerable, fearful elders to the serious and unnecessary risk of being prematurely deprived of the fullness of their days.

Notes

1. See, e.g., Task Force on Physician-Assisted Suicide of the Society for Health and Human Values, Physician-Assisted Suicide: Toward a Comprehensive Understanding, 70 ACAD. MED. 583 (1995); Peter B. Terry, Euthanasia and Assisted Suicide: Ethics and Politics, 103 CHEST 4 (1993).

2. See Lee v. State of Oregon, No. 96-6467-HO (D.Or. 1996) (invalidating results of state voter initiative legalizing physician assisted suicide); Compassion in Dying v. Washington, 850 F.Supp. 1454 (W.D. Wash. 1994), rev'd, 49 F.3d 586 (9th Cir. 1995), rev'd, 79 F.3d 790 (9th Cir. 1996) en banc, reh'g denied, 85 F.3d 1440 (9th Cir. 1996) en banc (invalidating Washington statute prohibiting physician assisted suicide on 14th Amendment due process right to liberty grounds) *cert. granted sub nom,* Washington v. Glucksburg, 65 U.S.L.W. 3085 (U.S. Oct. 1, 1996) (vNo. 96-110); Quill v. Koppell, 870 F.Supp. 78 (S.D.N.Y. 1994), rev'd in part and aff'd in part, sub nom., Dennis v. Vacco, 80 F.3d 716 (2nd Cir. 1996), cert. granted sub nom, 64 U.S.L.W. 3795 (U.S. Oct. 1, 1996) (No. 95-1858) (invalidating New York statute prohibiting physician-assisted suicide on 14th Amendment equal protection grounds): See generally T. Howard Stone & William J. Winslade, Physician-Assisted Suicide and Euthanasia in the United States: Legal and Ethical Observations, 16 J. LEGAL MED. 481 (1995).

3. See, e.g., Charles H. Baron, et al., A Model State Act to Authorize and Regulate Physician-Assisted Suicide, 33 HARV J. LEGIS. 1 (1996); Paul Cotton, Rational Suicide: No Longer 'Crazy'? 270 JAMA 797 (1993) (noting that "a shift is under way in societal thinking on the issue, the zeitgeist is changing. . . . The question is will we shift wisely and with adequate safeguards?")

4. Nancy S. Jecker, Physician-Assisted Death in the Netherlands and the United States: Ethical and Cultural Aspects of Health Policy Development, 42 J. AM. GERIATRICS SOC'Y 672 (1994); M.T. Muller et al., Voluntary Active Euthanasia and Physician-Assisted Suicide in Dutch Nursing Homes: Are the Requirements for Prudent Practice Properly Met? 42 J. AM. GERIATRICS SOC'Y 624 (1994) (noting that physician-assisted suicide in Dutch nursing homes, which have a primarily elderly patient population, more often than not deviates in practice from the safeguards to which Dutch prosecutors have agreed); CARLOS F. GOMEZ, REGULATING DEATH: EUTHANASIA AND THE CASE OF THE NETHERLANDS (1991). For other international comparisons, see RONALD DWORKIN, LIFE'S DOMINION: AN ARGUMENT ABOUT ABORTION, EUTHANASIA, AND INDIVIDUAL FREEDOM 254 n.3 (1993) (discussing laws against assisted suicide in England, France, Germany, Italy, Switzerland, Denmark, Norway and Poland).

5. Daniel Callahan & Margot White, The Legalization of Physician-Assisted Suicide: Creating a Regulatory Potemkin Village, 20 U. RICHMOND L. REV. 1 (1996); Glenn C. Graber & Jennifer Chassman, Assisted Suicide Is Not Voluntary Active Euthanasia, But It's Awfully Close, 41 J. AM GERIATRICS SOC'Y 88 (1993); Yale Kamisar, Physician-Assisted Suicide: The Last Bridge

to Active Voluntary Euthanasia, EUTHANASIA EXAMINED: ETHICAL, CLINICAL AND LEGAL PERSPECTIVES 225 (John Keown, ed., 1995). See Edmund P. Pellegrino, Compassion Needs Reason Too, 270 JAMA 874 (1993) (stating that " . . . euthanasia and assisted suicide are socially disastrous. They are not containable by placing legal limits on their practice. Arguments to the contrary, the 'slippery slope' is an inescapable logical, psychological, historical and empirical reality").

6. Robert J. Blendon et al., Should Physicians Aid Their Patients in Dying? The Public Perspective, 267 JAMA 2658, 2659 (1992).

7. In this article, the term "decision making capacity," which is a working, clinical concept, is used instead of "competence," which implies a formal legal declaration of the individual's status by a court usually in the context of a guardianship proceeding. See MARSHALL B. KAPP, KEY WORDS IN ETHICS, LAW, & AGING: A GUIDE TO CONTEMPORARY USAGE 15–16 (1995).

8. For background on informed consent generally, see, e.g., PRESIDENT'S COMMISSION FOR THE STUDY OF ETHICAL PROBJEMS IN MEDICINE AND BIOMEDICAL AND BEHAVIORAL RESEARCH, MAKING HEALTH CARE DECISIONS (1982); PAUL S. APPELBAUM ET AL., INFORMED CONSENT: LEGAL THEORY AND CLINICAL PRACTICE (1987).

9. See discussion infra nn.29–43 and accompanying text.

10. Marshall B. Kapp & Douglas Mossman, Measuring Decisional Capacity: Cautions on the Construction of a 'Capacimeter', 2 PSYCHOL. PUB. POL'Y, & L. 73 (1996).

11. See Marshall B. Kapp, Assessment of Competence to Make Medical Decisions, PRACTICAL HANDBOOK OF CLINICAL GERONTOLOGY 174, 179–181 (Laura L. Carstensen et al., eds., 1996); Marshall B. Kapp, Evaluating Decisionmaking Capacity in the Elderly: A Review of Recent Literature, 2 J. ELDER ABUSE & NEGLECT 15 (Fall/Winter 1990).

12. See, e.g., Howard Brody, Assisted Death—A Compassionate Response to a Medical Failure, 327 NEW ENG. J. MED. 1384, 1386 (1992); Timothy E. Quill et al., Care of the Hopelessly Ill: Proposed Clinical Criteria for Physician-Assisted Suicide, 327 NEW ENG. J. MED. 1380, 1382 (1992).

13. David S. Geldmacher & Peter J. Whitehouse, Current Concepts: Evaluation of Dementia, 335 NEW ENG. J. MED. 330 (1996); William E. Reichman & Jeffrey L. Cummings, Dementia, PRACTICE OF GERIATRICS 295–96 (Evan Calkins et al., eds., 2nd ed. 1992); Jeffrey L. Cummings & Lissy F. Jarvik, Dementia, in GERIATRIC MEDICINE 428 (Christine K. Cassel et al., eds., 2nd ed. 1990).

14. Panagiota V. Caralis, Ethical and Legal Issues in the Care of Alzheimer's Patients, 78 MED. CLINICS N. AM. 877, 878 (1994).

15. See NANCY M.P. KING, MAKING SENSE OF ADVANCE DIRECTIVES (rev. ed. 1996).

16. See, e.g., TIMOTHY E. QUILL, DEATH AND DIGNITY: MAKING CHOICES AND TAKING CHARGE 161–62 (1993).

17. G. Kevin Donovan, Letter: Physician-Assisted Suicide, 274 JAMA 1911 (1995).

18. For a discussion of these ambiguities and uncertainties, see Joan M. Teno et al., eds., Advance Care Planning: Priorities for Ethical and Empirical Research, 24 HASTINGS CENTER REPORT S1–S36 (Special Supp. Nov.–Dec. 1994).

19. See Stephen G. Post, Alzheimer's Disease: Ethics and the Progression of Dementia, 10 CLINICS GERIATRIC MED. 379, 385–86 (1994).

20. Kirsten Rohde et al., Suicide in Two Patients With Alzheimer's Disease, 43 J. AM. GERIATRICS SOC'Y 187 (1995).

21. National Institute on Aging/Alzheimer's Association Working Group, Apolipoprotein E Genotyping in Alzheimer's Disease, 347 LANCET 1091 (1996).

22. Agency for Health Care Policy and Research, U.S. Dep't of Health and Human Services, AHCPR Pub. No. 93-0550, Depression in Primary Care, 1 DETECTION AND DIAGNOSIS 40–41 (1993).

23. See Nancy J. Osgood, Assisted Suicide and Older People—A Deadly Combination: Ethical Problems in Permitting Assisted Suicide, 10 ISSUES L. & MED. 415, 427–28 (1995).

24. Linda Ganzini et al., The Effect of Depression Treatment on Elderly Patients' Preferences for Life-Sustaining Medical Treatment, 151 AM. J. PSYCHIATRY 1631 (1994); Melinda A. Lee & Linda Ganzini, The Effect of Recovery From Depression on Preferences for Life-Sustaining Therapy in Older Patients, 49 J. GERONT.: MED. SCI. M15 (1994) (noting that depressed patients exhibit less consistency in their preferences over time than nondepressed persons); Herbert Hendin & Gerald Klerman, Physician-Assisted Suicide: The Dangers of Legalization, 150 AM. J. PSYCHIATRY 143 (1993); Melinda A. Lee & Linda Ganzini, Depression in the Elderly: Effect on Patient Attitudes Toward Life-Sustaining Therapy, 40 J. AM. GERIATRICS SOC'Y 983 (1992). But see Erich H. Loewy, Of Depression, Anecdote, and Prejudice: A Confession, 40 J. AM. GERIATRICS SOC'Y 1068 (1992) (interpreting certain research as casting doubt on the connection between depression and impaired decision-making ability).

25. Harvey Max Chochinov et al., Desire for Death in the Terminally Ill, 152 AM. J. PSYCHIATRY 1185 (1995).

26. See Yeates Conwell & Eric D. Caine, Rational Suicide and the Right to Die, 325 NEW ENG. J. MED. 1100 (1991).

27. Quill et al., supra note 12, at 1382.

28. Cf. Marshall B. Kapp, Implications of the Patient Self-Determination Act for Psychiatric Practice, 45 HOSP. & COMM. PSYCHIATRY 355 (1994).

29. ALAN MEISEL, THE RIGHT TO DIE 98–99 (2nd ed. 1995).

30. See, e.g., ROBERT N. BUTLER, WHY SURVIVE? GROWING OLD IN AMERICA (1968).

31. See, e.g., PHILLIP LONGMAN, THE RETURN OF THRIFT: HOW THE COLLAPSE OF THE MIDDLE CLASS WELFARE STATE WILL REAWAKEN VALUES IN AMERICA 73–86 (discussing Social Security), 93–4 (Medicare), 127–39 (veterans' benefits), 140–56 (military retirement benefits), 157–68 (government retiree benefits) (1996).

32. See, e.g., ROBERT J. SAMUELSON, THE GOOD LIFE AND ITS DISCONTENTS: THE AMERICAN DREAM IN THE AGE OF ENTITLEMENT 143 (1995).

33. Osgood, supra note 23, at 418.

34. JOHN F. KILNER, LIFE ON THE LINE: ETHICS, AGING, ENDING PATIENTS' LIFES, AND ALLOCATING VITAL RESOURCES 114 (1992).

35. Robert L. Frierson, Suicide Attempts by the Old and the Very Old, 151 ARCH. INTERN. MED. 141 (1991); Yeates Conwell et al., Completed Suicide at Age 50 and Over, 38 J. AM. GERIATRICS SOC'Y 640 (1990).

36. Jennifer A. Zima, Student Note, Assisted Suicide: Society's Response to a Plea for Relief or a Simple Solution to the Cries of the Needy?, 23 RUTGERS L. REV. 387, 398 (1992).

37. Carin E. Reust and Susan Mattingly, Family Involvement in Medical Decision Making, 28 FAM. MED. 39 (1996); Marshall B. Kapp, Health Care Decision Making by the Elderly: I Get By With a Little Help From My Family, 31 GERONTOLOGIST 619 (1991).

38. Cf. Marshall B. Kapp, Who's the Parent Here? The Family's Impact on the Autonomy of Older Persons, 41 EMORY L.J. 773 (1992).

39. Not all families meet this ideal. See, e.g., Osgood, supra note 24, at 431–32.

40. See Hendin & Klerman, supra note 24, at 144.

41. James S. Goodwin, Mercy Killing: Mercy for Whom?, 265 JAMA 326 (1991).

42. Concerns about being a burden on one's family are a major reason that Americans cite for considering alternatives to end their lives. Blendon et al., supra note 6, at 2660.

43. Rohde, supra note 20, at 188; Jecker, supra note 4, at 676.

44. See, e.g., Jecker, supra note 4, at 676.

45. Terri R. Fried et al., The Association Between Age of Hospitalized Patients and the Delivery of Advanced Cardiac Life Support, 11 J. GEN. INTERN. MED. 257 (1996); Teri A. Manolio & Curt D. Furberg, Age As a Predictor of Outcome: What Role Does It Play?, 92 AM. J. MED. 1 (1992); Charles L. Bennett et al., Patterns of Care Related to Age of Men With Prostate Cancer, 67 CANCER 2633 (1991); Robert J. Mayer & W. Bradford Patterson, How Is Cancer Treatment Chosen?, 318 NEW ENG. J. MED. 636 (1988) (criticizing this practice and arguing for more individualization of the way physicians shape treatment decisions among elderly patients); Terrie Wetle, Age As a Risk Factor for Inadequate Treatment, 258 JAMA 516 (1987); Steven Neu & Carl M. Kjellstrand, Stopping Long-Term Dialysis: An Empirical Study of Withdrawal of Life-Supporting Treatment, 314 NEW ENG. J. MED. 14 (1986); Norman K. Brown & Donovan J. Thompson, Nontreatment of Fever in Extended-Care Facilities, 300 NEW ENG. J. MED. 1246 (1979). See also, Editorial: Do Doctors Short-Change Old People?, 342 LANCET 1 (1993) (stating that age bias affecting medical care is not a strictly American phenomenon). See also Jeremiah A. Barondess et al., Clinical Decision-Making in Catastrophic Situations: The Relevance of Age, 36 J. AM. GERIATRICS SOC'Y 919 (1988).

46. Rosemarie B. Hakim et al., Factors Associated With Do-Not-Resuscitate Orders: Patients' Preferences, Prognoses, and Physicians' Judgments, 125 ANNALS INTERN. MED. 284, 288, 291 (1996) (Do-Not-Resuscitate orders were written earlier for patients older than seventy-five years of age, regardless of prognosis for survival).

47. For a discussion of the impediments posed by managed care and cost control to the operation of the sorts of effective, collaborative, and committed physician/patient relationships that physician-assisted suicide proponents recognize as essential to assuring that patient choices are voluntarily, knowingly, and capably made, see Eric D. Caine & Yeates C. Conwell, Self-Determined Death, the Physician, and Medical Priorities: Is There Time to Talk?, 270 JAMA 875, 876 (1993).

48. The seminal and best statement of the argument in favor of categorical, age-based health care rationing is found in DANIEL CALLAHAN, SETTING LIMTIS (1987). See also Daniel Callahan, Old Age and New Policy, 261 JAMA 905 (1989); NORMAN DANIELS, JUST HEALTH CARE (1985); NORMAN DANIELS, AM I MY PARENTS' KEOER?: AN ESSAY ON JUSTICE BETWEEN THE YOUNG AND THE OLD (1988); Margaret P. Battin, Age Rationing and the Just Distribution of Health Care: Is There a Duty to Die?, 97 ETHICS 317 (1987). In Great Britain, physicians have made rationing decisions based on the patient's age for years under the charade of "clinical indications." See J.E.C. Dickerson & M.J. Brown, Influence of Age on General Practitioners' Definition and Treatment of Hypertension, 310 BRIT. MED. J. 574 (1995); Tony Hope et al., 'Not Clinically Indicated': Patients' Interests or Resource Allocation?, 306 BRIT. MED. J. 379 (1993).

49. Michael M. Rivlin, Protecting Elderly People: Flaws in Ageist Arguments, 310 Brit. Med. J. 1179 (1995); Too Old For Health Care?: Controversies in Medicine, Law, Economics, and Ethics (Robert H. Binstock & Stephen Post, eds., 1991); Nancy S. Jecker, Age-Based Rationing and Women, 266 J. Am. Geriatrics Soc'y 3012 (1991); Nancy S. Jecker & Robert A. Pearlman, Ethical Constraints on Rationing Medical Care by Age, 37 J. Am. Geriatrics Soc'y 1067 (1989); Marshall B. Kapp, Rationing Health Care: Will It Be Necessary? Can It Be Done Without Age or Disability Discrimination?, 5 Issues L. & Med. 337 (1989); Edward L. Schneider, Options to Control the Rising Health Care Costs of Older Americans, 261 JAMA 907 (1989); David C.

Thomasma, Moving the Aged into the House of the Dead: A Critique of Ageist Social Policy, 37 J. Am. Geriatrics Soc'y 169 (1989); Larry R. Churchill, Should We Ration Health Care by Age?, 36 J. Am. Geriatrics Soc'y 614 (1988); Nancy S. Jecker, Disenfranchising the Elderly From Life-Extending Medical Care, 2 Pub. Aff. Q. 51 (1988).

50. Blendon, supra note 6, at 2660; Kathleen Foley, The Relationship of Pain and Symptom Management to Patient Requests for Physician-Assisted Suicide, 6 J. PAIN & SYMPTOM MGMT. 290 (1991); Zima, supra note 36, at 399. But see Ezekiel J. Emanuel et al., Euthanasia and Physician-Assisted Suicide: Attitudes and Experiences of Oncology Patients, Oncologists, and the Public, 347 LANCET 1805 (1996) (finding that oncology patients experiencing pain are unlikely to seek physician-assisted suicide unless they are also suffering from clinical depression).

51. See Anthony L. Back et al., Physician-Assisted Suicide and Euthanasia in Washington State: Patient Requests and Physician Responses, 275 JAMA 919 (1996).

52. The SUPPORT Principal Investigators, A Controlled Trial to Improve Care for Seriously Ill Hospitalized Patients: The Study to Understand Prognoses and Preferences for Outcomes and Risks of Treatments (SUPPORT), 274 JAMA 1591 (1995).

53. See Dame Cicely Saunders, In Britain, Fewer Conflicts of Conscience, 25 HASTINGS CENTER REP. 44 (1995) (stating that good hospice care practically eliminates patients' requests for death hastening); MARGARET P. BATTIN, THE LEAST WORST DEATH: ESSAYS IN BIOETHICS ON THE END OF LIFE (1994). The Institute of Medicine of the National Academy of Sciences (Washington, DC) is conducting a project entitled Care at the End of Life, which is scheduled to produce a report in early 1997.

54. American Geriatrics Society Ethics Committee, Physician-Assisted Suicide and Voluntary Active Euthanasia, 43 J. AM. GERIATRICS SOC'Y 579 (1995).

55. Council on Scientific Affairs, American Medical Association, Good Care of the Dying Patient, 275 JAMA 474, 476 (1996).

56. Greg A. Sachs et al., Good Care of Dying Patients: The Alternative to Physician-Assisted Suicide and Euthanasia, 43 J. AM. GERIATRICS SOC'Y 553 (1995).

For many persons, the most compelling argument for assisted suicide is the avoidance of pain during the last stages of an incurable illness. Some persons would opt for a physician-assisted hastened death rather than endure intense pain. However, the choice may not be whether to endure pain or to hasten death. It is generally accepted that many physicians fail to treat patients' pain as effectively as modern medicine would allow. Perhaps if patients had more confidence that they would not suffer pain, they would not desire assisted suicide. Still, not all pain can be alleviated, and there are other indignities and suffering that cause dying patients to request a hastened death: the apparent futility of wasting away, the loss of control over bodily functions, the emotional toil of a prolonged death on loved ones, the loss of hope, and the desire to reach an ending point.

Part VI

Long-Term Care

Older persons suffer from chronic illnesses at much higher rates than the younger population as the risk of heart disease, arthritis, and cancer rises dramatically with age. The elderly are also subject to dementia, which is almost exclusively an affliction of growing older. In addition, some older persons, though mentally alert and not affected by chronic illness, become so frail that they can no longer care for themselves without help. (It should be noted that extreme frailty may not be part of normal aging but may itself represent a chronic condition or pathology.)

The term "long-term care" is a generic term referring to the provision of services for individuals who are unable to care for themselves due to chronic illness or condition, loss of mental capacity, accident, or injury. Gerontologists divide individual's life skills into those called Activities of Daily Living (ADL) and Independent Activities of Daily Living (IADL). ADLs consist of eating, dressing, toileting, bathing, and ambulating (getting in and out of a chair or bed). Independent activities of daily living consist of preparing food, using the telephone, purchasing food, and going out into the community for other activities. Individuals who have ADL deficits (jargon for "inability") usually need long-term care, possibly in a nursing home. Individuals with IADL deficits do need help, but they are usually not considered to be in need of long-term care.

Because ADL deficits vary from individual to individual, so must long-term care. No one pattern of long-term care fits all those in need. The term "long-term care" encompasses a host of different kinds of care and degrees of assistance for different persons. For example, long-term care for one person might mean buying and preparing her meals, while for another it might include feeding her. Although the degree of need is greatly different, both would be considered in need of long-term care.

Long-term care can be delivered in a variety of settings and a variety of ways. One common delivery system is the nursing home. Today, over a million and a half people currently reside in nursing homes, 90 percent of whom are age sixty-five or older. While that number is large, at any one time it is less than 5 percent of all individuals who are age sixty-five or older. Less than half of the individuals in nursing homes stay for six months or longer. For many, a nursing home is a place to go for post-hospitalization recovery (or post-hospitalization death) while others live there for several years until they die.

Although they are the most visible means of long-term care delivery, nursing homes serve only a minority of older individuals who need assistance. Undoubtedly the largest form of long-term care is that provided by spouses, and, in particular, older wives helping older husbands. Although often not thought of as being long-term care, it indeed is. For example, a wife preparing her husband's food; helping him eat; and helping him with his bathing, dressing, and toileting is prototypical long-term care.

Next to spouses, other family members provide the greatest amount of long-term care. For many families, long-term care begins with assistance in the independent activities of daily living. A daughter, for example, may run the errands for her aged, widowed mother who can no longer drive because of declining eyesight. Or a son may do all the household repairs and take care of his mother's finances, almost as if he were her guardian.

In addition, many adult children have their aging parents move in with them. We all know of individuals who have adapted a spare room or even turned their dining rooms into a bedroom for an older parent who can no longer live alone. Sometimes this care is only for a brief period because of the individual's failing health or because the family decides in the end that a nursing home is more appropriate. But in many cases the family will have an older person live with them for years, over time increasing the degree of help they provide for the older relative.

Beyond the largely unpaid family form of assistance there are, of course, many commercial types of home health care designed to assist people who remain at home. These consist of such services as visiting nurses, Medicare home health care, and paid social workers who regularly visit clients. Not to be overlooked are the millions of volunteers who help friends, neighbors, fellow church members, or even complete strangers.

There is nothing controversial about long-term care as such. That is, it is hard to be against the concept of helping those who need it. Controversy arises, however, over how long-term care should be provided and who should pay for it. There is a continuing argument about whether long-term care is best provided in formal institutions, such as nursing homes or assisted living units, or whether our goal as a society should be to keep people at home and bring the long-term care to them. Similarly, a debate rages as to who should pay for long-term care, with some arguing that long-term care should be considered a health care need no different than acute care paid for by Medicare or Medicaid. Others contend that the costs of long-term care are primarily the obligation of individuals or their families.

CHAPTER 29

Home Health Care

One of the reasons for the debate about where long-term care should be provided is the reluctance of people to see either themselves or their relatives enter a nursing home. With good reason, nursing homes are viewed as a significant imposition on an individual's freedom and autonomy. By definition, nursing homes are institutional settings in which individuals must adapt to the needs of the institution rather than the institution adapt to the particular needs of the individual. Moreover, nursing homes are too often seen as places to go to die. Of course, some residents do leave nursing homes in good health, but it is true that many older persons do die in nursing homes. Finally, there is the expense of nursing homes. The annual cost of a nursing home can run anywhere from $35,000 to $60,000 a year. To pay so much for something that is undesired is difficult for many Americans to accept. Instead, they argue that health care should be community-based; that is, long-term care should be brought to the individual, not the individual to the care.

A. What is Home Health Care?

The following article by Professors Barnes addresses the issue of community care for the frail elderly.

Alison Barnes

The Policy and Politics of Community-Based Long-Term Care

* * *

One of the most problematic aspects of health care reform is the absence of well-developed and funded plans for providing long-term home and community-based care to aged and disabled persons.[1] Changes in medical technology and life expectancy have caused a dramatic increase in the number of individuals with chronic illnesses,[2] which limit their ability to care for themselves.[3] Though many persons with disabilities from chronic conditions or advanced age[4] are unable to afford appropriate care, existing public benefits fail to meet their needs, and private insurance coverage for long-term care is relatively costly and rare.[5] Restrictions on acute care benefits are increasing the demand for home and community-based care[6] and contribute to the change in provider organizations from small nonprofit providers to minor components of large, for-profit corporations.[7] In addition, the highest inflation rate in service costs has moved from acute care to long-term care.[8]

* * *

II. The Need for Long-Term Care Coverage

The meaning of "long-term care" varies from state to state and program to program. At its most comprehensive, long-term care includes a wide array of health and social services, institutional care, and adapted or dedicated housing to meet the needs of persons who have lost some capacity for self-care. Long-term care services are usually differentiated by the settings in which they are provided: either in nursing homes and other institutions or in home and community-based settings. Two adult populations, traditionally considered separately in policy and programs, utilize community-based long-term care: adults with impairments from injury or chronic illness, and aged persons with chronic impairments or the general frailty of extreme old age.

A. Defining Community-Based Long-Term Care

Community-based long-term care includes congregate living arrangements with supportive services and community-based assistance such as home health care, congregate and home delivered meals, transportation, and shopping assistance.[9] Other long-

Nova Law Review, Vol. 19, 487–531 (1995). Reprinted by permission.

term care services, such as respite care[10] and adult day care,[11] help family caregivers cope with their continuous responsibilities.[12] The great majority of persons needing long-term care reside in the community.[13]

Formal long-term care is a relatively recent innovation, defined primarily by government programs intended to extend or substitute for caregiving families. The need for government assistance arises from a combination of demographic, technological, philosophical, and sociological changes in American society. Perhaps most important are longer life spans resulting in extended old age and unprecedented survival rates from disabling illnesses due to new medical technology.[14] Simultaneously, families are less likely to be available as caregivers; they tend to live far away, and women, the traditional caregivers, have entered the work force and are no longer available to provide care.[15] Nevertheless, most assistance is still provided informally by family members and others.[16]

Appropriate housing is also critical to the well-being of disabled and elderly persons living in the community, although housing has traditionally been funded separately from services. Factors which distinguish a home from a prison for incapacitated residents may include: access to transportation and shopping; neighborhood safety; availability of informal help and oversight by concerned neighbors, relatives, and friends; access to formal services, such as home health care and home delivered meals; and user-friendly design of entrances and in-home facilities.[17] Some older people, who stayed in their homes while their neighborhoods deteriorated, are isolated from assistance. Appropriate housing must also be affordable housing, taking into account the fact that many elderly and disabled persons have limited resources to finance the extra services that enable them to live as independently as possible.[18]

Because many persons with disabilities can manage most of their life activities with only occasional assistance and/or watchful oversight, and because it is natural for many to prefer the company and informal help of individuals with similar concerns, housing for persons with disabilities has often gravitated toward group living. Visiting services, such as homemaking, home health care, and home delivered meals, are also provided more efficiently where a number of recipients live in close proximity.[19]

* * *

The second population of long-term care users, age sixty-five and older, raises significant concerns because it is expected to double by the middle of the next century.[20] In 1990, thirty-one million Americans, or nearly thirteen percent, had reached the age of sixty-five.[21] Over the next twenty years, the elderly population will increase steadily but unspectacularly, due to low birth rates during the Depression. After 2010, however, the number of people reaching their sixty-fifth birthday each year will soar and remain high until around 2030, when the last baby boomer reaches the threshold of old age.[22] By then, people age sixty-five or older are expected to make up 20 percent of the population.

Dramatic demographic growth is already occurring in that portion of the population age eighty-five and older, due to increasing life expectancies.[23] In 1990, there were approximately three million people age eighty-five and older.[24] By the year

2010, it is estimated that this number will double to 6.1 million. By 2030, given current trends, there will be over eight million people age eighty-five and over.[25]

Older people are more likely to suffer from chronic conditions which limit their ability to care for themselves.[26] Multiple impairments and longer recovery periods from acute illnesses contribute to longer hospital stays. As a result, it is estimated that people age sixty-five and older (comprising 12.6 percent of the United States's population) account for one-third of the nation's annual health care expenditures, or about $300 billion out of a total $900 billion in 1993.[27] It is not widely doubted that growth in the aging population contributes substantially to rising health expenditures,[28] though one analysis indicates that other factors, including medical inflation and greater volume of services, have been more significant causes since 1970 and will account for most of the increase until 2005.[29] After that time, the aging of the population is likely to cause rapid acceleration in health care spending unless effective cost containment is implemented.[30]

* * *

III. A Right to Long-Term Care?

Given the need for community-based care, it is remarkable that such assistance is not readily available for a modest cost, like public utilities. To determine why, a good starting point is an examination of the societal values that have impeded development of long-term care programs, or of reasons society is reluctant to invest in the task of care for impaired members. Further, it is reasonable to consider whether the obligations of society to less capable persons, or an interest in social order through individual well-being, warrant the implementation of long-term care programs.[31]

* * *

Social forces in favor of long-term care might also lack power to implement change because of the predisposition of the American national character toward decisive individual action and swift resolution.[32] The incompatibility of such a view with long-term care is distinctly apparent when the methods and results of services delivery are contrasted with those of the current health care culture of scientific, high technology medicine. Physicians are trained in dedication to decisive intervention and cure, resulting in an inclination toward aggressive and invasive treatment and to heroic measures in attempts to defeat the effects of ill health or injury. The culture of long-term care delivery, by contrast, suggests ambivalence regarding the usefulness of many repetitive acts of assistance, any of which are of debatable significance to the ultimate well-being of the person receiving care. Persons with chronic disabilities by definition are not cured, though symptoms might be alleviated. Generally, the goal of care is to maintain capabilities and mental health. Sometimes, the goal is to alleviate suffering and fear from inevitable decline. There is little opportunity for technological heroism. Even the site of care has an ambivalent quality, a quality of compromise to accommodate conflicting interests and values, in contrast with the institutional settings of acute care in which professional opinion and goal orientation dominate.[33] Home and community-based care are provided in all-purpose, sometimes inconvenient environments, in which the needs and wishes of the person with chronic impairment coexist with the needs and wishes of caregivers. As a result, the care itself must represent a compromise between caregiver and care receiver regarding the choice and timing of assistance.[34]

Viewed in the context of health care in the late twentieth century, the narrow focus of acute care on physical improvement has failed to provide a sense of well-being for many. That viewpoint has never been monolithic and currently is yielding to more humane values, which would make health care more personalized and would better accommodate the unique needs of individual patients.[35] Such values are more suitable than traditional American values to the provision of effective long-term care, and their growing authority is compatible with the enactment of national publicly-funded long-term care.

Although prejudice against persons who are aged or have chronic disabilities may be pervasive, it is difficult to argue convincingly for such a basis for public policy. Even those who advocate age-based discrimination for health care cost containment are referring to acute care, not comfort care.[36] Rather, it appears the idea is widespread that basic home care represents values that society would like to cultivate, values neglected by the health care system to the dissatisfaction of its patients.

Despite the volume of long-term care legislation and programs,[37] there is no constitutional right to assistance for persons who are aged or disabled and living in the community. Government programs provide only a small fraction of assistance,[38] and the right to equal protection generally does not extend to appropriations from public funds without statutory authorization. Nevertheless, programs create standards which do attach once services are available. These standards generally tend to assure the fair determination of eligibility, the opportunity to object to a denial of services, and the right to appeal a denial to an impartial decision-maker. The existence of service programs tends to drift in the direction of a right to receive care.[39] A statute providing a benefit may imply action in good faith on the part of government to assure that eligible persons can receive it. As a result, an individual may have an enforceable legal claim, based on the right to a minimum quality of life which is unavailable without state assistance.

B. The Least Restrictive Alternative

* * *

2. Family Responsibility Many would hesitate to provide formal long-term care assistance on the assumption that informal care providers would abandon their roles when formal help becomes available.[40] Limiting formal assistance to needs that cannot be met by family or friends also limits the dreaded "woodwork effect," a metaphor for the number of persons in need who are expected to appear with the creation of a public long-term care benefit. Certainly, the existence of family or other social support is relevant to an individual's ability to live at home because the existence of social supports is the most significant factor in determining whether an individual will be institutionalized.[41] The actual effect of adding formal care is difficult to measure and explain, as is the balance of social and economic issues which make family withdrawal from care such a sensitive issue.[42] Possibly, formal services would partially replace informal care at increased public expense, but the lives of caregivers and care receiver would be enhanced. Also, formal services might primarily enable informal caregivers to carry on longer, resulting in a public savings.

The consensus of studies is that some informal caregivers do stop.[43] The extent is small, and the substitution appears to be primarily in IADLs, such as making and driving to appointments. The caregivers most likely to reduce their participation were those who were not closely related to the care recipient, such as friends or neighbors, and relatives other than spouses and children. It is unclear whether caregivers overall provide more or less care when formal care is available.[44]

* * *

Notes

1. Community-based chronic care encompasses such medical and social services as home health, housekeeping, congregate and home delivered meals, and transportation. In addition, it includes housing, with or without services. Services for aged persons with disabilities have more often been termed "long-term care," while services to younger adults have been called "chronic care." The reasons for and results of this split in terminology, funding, and delivery are discussed in this article. *See infra* notes 10–31 and accompanying text [some text and footnotes omitted]. With a growing recognition among policy makers that such a division poses obstacles to enacting legislation for effective services programs, there is a trend to include all ages in proposals for home and community-based care initiatives. In accord with that view, this article will use the terms interchangeably, preferring "long-term care" as the term most often heard in the health reform debates. *See generally* A.E. Benjamin, *An Historical Perspective on Home Care Policy,* 71 MILBANK Q. 129 (1993) (labeling home care a re-discovered type of assistance).

2. STEVEN A. SCHROEDER, ROBERT WOOD JOHNSON FOUND., ANNUAL REPORT 1993: CHRONIC HEALTH CONDITIONS 1, 1 (1993) (citing the number of American with disabilities as over 35 million). Figures vary widely according to the criteria of disability. *See* FAMILIES USA FOUND., THE HEAVY BURDEN OF HOME CARE 10 (1993) [hereinafter HOME CARE STUDY] (noting that 8.1 million persons living in the community have disabilities).

"Disability" refers to a limitation in function or activity resulting from a physical or mental impairment. Chronic condition refers to the presence of a specific diagnosed impairment that may or may not result in a functional or activity limitation. Since both people with disabilities and people with chronic conditions, as groups, have difficulty gaining access to an adequate range of health-related services, they are considered together in this article. A full consideration of programs and policies on mental impairments is beyond the scope of this article.

3. Major activities include both self-care activities of daily living ("ADL") and instrumental activities of daily living ("IADL") such as meal preparation, shopping, managing money, using the telephone, and doing housework. CYNTHIA M. TAEUBER, U.S. DEP'T OF COM., SIXTY-FIVE PLUS IN AMERICA 3–11 (1992); *see* [ROBERT B. FRIEDLAND, EMPLOYEE BENEFITS RESEARCH INST.,

FACING THE COSTS OF LONG-TERM CARE . . . (1990)], at 54. Functional status based on an evaluation of ADLs and IADLs was developed in the 1960s by Sidney Katz. *See* Sidney Katz et al., *Studies of Illness in the Aged, The Index of ADL: A Standardized Measure of Biological and Psychosocial Function,* 185 JAMA 914 (1963); Sidney Katz et al., *Progress in the Development of the Index of ADL,* GERONTOLOGIST, Spring 1970, at 20].

4. Most chronic conditions are caused by a disease, such as diabetes, asthma, arthritis, epilepsy, arteriosclerosis, or muscular dystrophy. Some are caused by injury or a condition such as congenital heart disease. While chronic illness is not synonymous with advanced age, incidence increases with age and is more prevalent among older women. TAEUBER, *supra* note 3, at 3–11. For example, among those 80 years of age and older, 70% of women and 53% of men had two or more of the nine common conditions of arthritis, hypertension, cataracts, heart disease, varicose vein, diabetes, cancer, osteoporosis or hip fracture, and stroke. *Id.*

5. Sales of long-term care insurance policies totaled 2.9 million at the end of 1992, an increase of about 500,000 policies in one year. The number of policies has increased an average of nearly 30% annually since 1987. *Sales of Long Term Insurance Increase,* 3 Health Law Rep. (BNA), at 291 (Mar. 3, 1994) (citing survey results from the Health Insurance Association of America, Washington, D.C.).

6. Barbara Bronson Gray, *Geriatric Nursing Is Becoming a Key Field,* AGING TODAY, Sept.–Oct. 1994, at 5.

7. Carroll L. Estes, *Crisis in Health Care Reform and the Culture of Caring,* AGING TODAY, May–June 1994, at 3.

8. *See* Dan Morgan, *Nursing Homes: The "Sleeping Giant,"* WASH. POST WKLY., Feb. 14–20, 1994, at 9.

9. CONGRESSIONAL RESEARCH SERV., LONG-TERM CARE FOR THE ELDERLY 1 (1993). Long-term care also includes legal services for adult protective services, guardianship, and other forms of surrogate decision making, which are beyond the scope of this article.

10. *See* [LAWRENCE A. FROLIK & ALISON P. BARNES, ELDERLAW 300–02 (1992)] (short-term, substitute care either inside or outside the home, in the absence of the primary caregiver).

11. "Adult day care is a community-based group program designed to meet the needs of functionally impaired adults through . . . a variety of health, social and related support services in a protective setting during any part of a day but less than 24-hour care." NAT'L COUNCIL ON THE AGING, STANDARDS FOR ADULT DAY CARE 20 (1984).

12. *See* ALISON P. BARNES, INTERGOVERNMENTAL HEALTH POL'Y PROJECT, GEO. WASH. U., CHRONIC CARE: AN OVERVIEW OF 1992 STATE LEGISLATIVE ACTIVITY 21 (1993).

13. "Contrary to popular belief, less than one-half of chronically disabled persons living in the community . . . [are] elderly." ROBERT B. FRIEDLAND, EMPLOYEE BENEFITS RESEARCH INST., FACING THE COSTS OF LONG-TERM CARE 54 (1990).

14. [*See* LAWRENCE A. FROLIK & ALISON P. BARNES, ELDERLAW 300–02 (1992).]

15. HOUSE SELECT COMM. ON AGING, PUB. NO. 99-611, EXPLODING THE MYTHS: CAREGIVING IN AMERICA 11–12 (1987) [hereinafter EXPLODING THE MYTHS].

16. HOME CARE STUDY, *supra* note 2, at 10 (noting that two-thirds of persons with disabilities relied exclusively on informal, unpaid caregivers in 1992).

17. Jon Pynoos, *Housing the Aged: Public Policy at the Crossroads in* HOUSING THE AGED: DESIGN DIRECTIVES AND POLICY CONSIDERATIONS 7 (1987).

18. *See* ELIZABETH D. HUTTMAN, HOUSING AND SOCIAL SERVICES FOR THE ELDERLY 52–53 (1977).

19. [*See* LAWRENCE A. FROLIK & ALISON P. BARNES, ELDERLAW 300–02 (1992).]

20. TAEUBER, *supra* note 3, at 2-1.

21. *Id.* at 2-3.

22. *Id.* at 2-4 to 2-5.

23. *Id.* at 2-4.

24. *Id.* at 2-3.

25. TAEUBER, *supra* note 3, at 2-2.

26. UNITED STATES SENATE SPECIAL COMM. ON AGING, AM. ASS'N OF RETIRED PERSONS, FED. COUNCIL ON THE AGING, & U.S. ADMIN. ON AGING, AGING AMERICA: TRENDS AND PROJECTIONS 112 (1991) [hereinafter AGING AMERICA].

27. [Sally T. Burner et al., *National Health Expenditures Projections Through 2030,* 14 HEALTHCARE FINANCING REV. 1, 29 (1992).]

28. *But see* Robert H. Binstock, *Healthcare Costs Around the World: Is Aging a Fiscal 'Black Hole'?,* GENERATIONS, Winter 1993, at 37 (arguing that the impact is overstated).

29. Daniel N. Mendelson & William B. Schwartz, *The Effects of Aging and Population Growth on Health Care Costs,* HEALTH AFF., Spring 1993, at 119, 120.

30. *See id.* at 120–23.

31. *See* Jeffrey Merrill, *A Test of Our Society: How and for Whom We Finance Long-Term Care,* INQUIRY, Summer 1992, at 176–77.

32. Many have observed that the American view is predicated on individualism, rather than the good of society. *See e.g.,* David Brown, *Darwin's Theory of Health Care: Coverage for All Means Less Care for Many,* WASH. POST WKLY., Sept. 19–25, 1994, at 24. "In American medicine, the ascendancy of the individual exists in nearly pure form. American physicians are taught (and believe) that the 'good of the patient' is the one consideration that trumps all others." *Id.*

33. The doctrine of informed consent is law's effort to balance the power of the physician to control the course of treatment by providing the patient with the ultimate trump card of refusal. *See* [LAWRENCE A. FROLIK & ALISON P. BARNES, ELDERLAW 300–02 (1992).]

34. Bart Collopy et al., *The Ethics of Home Care: Autonomy and Accommodation,* HASTINGS CENTER REP., Mar.–Apr. 1990, at 1, 2.

35. *See, e.g.,* Bruce Jennings et al., *Ethical Challenges of Chronic Illness,* HASTINGS CENTER REP., Supp. Feb.-Mar. 1988, at 6–8. The authors note that the distinction between "person" and "patient" goes to the heart of a new bioethics, challenging the concept of patient, the nature of the relationship between physician and patient, and the basis of medical decisionmaking. *Id.*

36. *See* Daniel Callahan, *What is a Reasonable Demand on Health Care Resources? Designing a Basic Package of Benefits,* 8 J. CONTEMP. HEALTH L. & POL'Y 1, 9 (1992) (advocating care over cure and public good over personal health as rationale for defining a health care benefits package).

37. More than 80 federal programs support long-term care, if retirement and disability income benefits are included with social services and housing programs. CONGRESSIONAL RESEARCH SERV., FINANCING AND DELIVERY OF LONG-TERM CARE SERVICES FOR THE ELDERLY CRS-6 (May 25, 1988).

38. *See* EXPLODING THE MYTHS, *supra* note 16, at 4 (indicating that "the bulk of long-term care is provided by informal caregivers").

39. Regarding rights to housing derived from benefits, see Frank I. Michelman, *The Advent of a Right to Housing: A Current Appraisal,* 5 HARV. C.R.-C.L. L. REV. 207, 209 (1970) (noting that a "movement in the general direction of a . . . right to be housed" was justified by the policy that every American family should have a decent home).

40. *But see* LEONARD HEUMANN & DUNCAN BOLDY, HOUSING FOR THE ELDERLY 19 (1982) (the family is not abandoning in large numbers its role as primary housing and support provider to the functionally impaired elderly, but fewer family members are available on a 24-hour basis). *See generally* Susan L. Ettner, *The Effect of the Medicaid Home Care Benefit on Long-Term Care Choices of the Elderly*, ECON. INQUIRY, Jan. 1994, at 103 (indicating that home care subsidies reduce the probability of at-risk elderly entering nursing homes, but also increases the substitution of formal for informal care, thus raising costs).

41. *See* Lawrence A. Frolik & Alison P. Barnes, *An Aging Population: A Challenge to the Law*, 42 HASTINGS L.J. 683, 700–03 (1991).

42. Martin B. Tracy, *Government Versus the Family: The False Dichotomy*, GENERATIONS, Winter 1993, at 47, 48.

43. Peter Kemper et al., *Community Care Demonstrations: What Have We Learned?*, HEALTH CARE FIN. REV., Summer 1987, at 87, 94.

44. *Id.*

Joel F. Handler

Community Care for the Frail Elderly: A Theory of Empowerment

* * *

The powerlessness of nursing home residents has significant effects on regulation. While there are many reasons for the development of strict, legalistic, command-and-control regulation,[1] an important one is that nursing home regulatory agencies have the full burden of generating all of the information on quality of care issues. Because of the nature and complexity of the institutions and the long-term care task, and the characteristics of the residents, the regulatory task is exceedingly difficult. Other than the occasional disgruntled worker or family member, or visible scandal, there is no other information on how patients are, in fact, personally treated. Residents are too dependent, too vulnerable to complain. Under the best of circumstances, it is hard to know whether dependent people are exercising free choice, are aware of alternatives, are participating in decisions, and are receiving proper care. The regulatory agency has to conduct frequent, burdensome inspections, and if necessary, impose legal sanctions. Along with the failure of legal rights, the failure of nursing home regulation is also well-documented.[2]

This is the context in which the new code of residents' rights has been enacted. For the vast majority of old, sick, and alone residents, it is a cruel hoax.

Originally published in 50 *Ohio State Law Journal* 541 (1989). Reprinted by permission.

II. A Theory of Empowerment

How would a theory of empowerment address the two problems of the legal rights regime: asymmetrical power and the continuing relationship? If social work practice is viewed as the exchange of resources, then power relationships are altered by increasing client resources. Empowerment means the ability to control one's environment; thus, clients must have sufficient resources (including alternatives) to be able to make choices and to negotiate more favorable outcomes.[3] Client-worker practice has to shift from its individual orientation to a more structural approach to help people connect with needed resources. Professor Yeheskel Hasenfeld argues that empowerment must occur at all levels in the organization—between the worker and the client, and at the organizational and policy levels. Strategies include increasing client information, improving personal skills, increasing collective strength, and improving links to alternatives. There must be empowerment-based practice technologies and accountability measures that stress empowerment rather than social control. There must be an increase in client control over resources (e.g., vouchers) and the availability of alternative services. The workers must change the definitions of their professional norms and tasks.[4]

While these empowerment strategies are primarily addressed to situations where clients perceive grievances or conflicts and lack the resources to complain and negotiate, they may have deeper possibilities. The structural changes that Hasenfeld advocates may affect the cultural contexts of the participants. The destabilization of power relationships, structures, and roles will produce changes in ideologies and beliefs. The participants will view themselves and their relationships differently.[5]

* * *

III. Redefining the Population

For historical reasons, we have defined long-term care for the frail elderly in medical terms and have confined residents in hospital-like facilities. Instead of starting with the most difficult situation—old, sick, alone people confined in a total institution, in an industry under siege—why not transcend the institution? Perhaps we can untie this Gordian knot by redefining the population.

The health and disability characteristics of people inside and outside of nursing homes, controlling for age, are not much different; that is, both groups need varying amounts of care, mostly of a custodial nature (e.g., assistance with transportation, nutrition, toileting, bathing, and chores). What is different are their social characteristics; the vast majority of those outside of nursing homes have someone to help them, usually a spouse or an adult daughter.[6]

The elderly should be viewed in terms of a continuum. There are many who are fully capable of functioning in regular activities, there are some with varying degrees of disability who are able to get along with varying amounts of assistance, there are some who are disabled but have no help, and there are some who are very sick. Accordingly, various commentators have called for a continuum of services rather than our present sharp institutional demarcation dictated by public funding mechanisms.[7]

Once it was demonstrated that the reason large numbers of frail elderly were in nursing homes was that they had no one to help them in their activities of daily living, the idea was born that better care could be provided at a lower cost through community-based services. If community-based services were available, the frail elderly would not have to go into nursing homes in the first place, and further, many of those now in nursing homes could be discharged back into the community. As a result, there have been several community-based or alternative care demonstration projects and a growing home-care industry designed to supplement or provide custodial and health care so that the frail elderly can remain in their communities; that is, they can live and function like the large number of disabled elderly who have informal support.

So far, government has been reluctant to take this path. The regulatory problems are daunting. The population is very vulnerable and frequently falls prey to commercial victimization. Policymakers see the prospect of hordes of private entrepreneurs hawking home help, transportation, therapy, health, respite, nutrition, and who knows what other services. The case managers themselves are the gate-keepers. The sites are dispersed throughout the community, making it difficult to evaluate these services: how can one tell whether the therapist was rough or gentle, the driver courteous or abrupt, or the home help pleasant or lazy or nasty? These are not trivial matters when dealing with the dependent elderly. Those who have worked with them know how difficult it is to get them to use services or to complain. They are often afraid, or confused, or have a counterproductive sense of independence.[8]

Nevertheless, despite the problems in home care, it would seem that if progress is to be made on the issue of residents' rights, then this is the place to start rather than the total institution. Various demonstration projects and other kinds of activities indicate possibilities.

* * *

Notes

1. E. Bardach & R. Kagan, Going by the Book: The Problem of Regulatory Unreasonableness 34–39 (1982).

2. *See, e.g.*, [The Institute of Medicine Report is Committee on Nursing Home Regulation, The Institute of Medicine, Improving the Quality of Care in Nursing Homes (1986) [hereinafter Institute of Medicine]; B. Vladeck, Unloving Care: The Nursing Home Tragedy (1980).

3. [*See, e.g.*, Hasenfeld, *Power in Social Work Practice*, 61 Soc. Serv. Rev., at 469 (1987).]

4. *Id.*

5. *See, e.g.*, Merry, *Everyday Understanding of the Law in Working Class America*, 13 Am. Ethnologist 253 (1986).

6. *See, e.g.*, E. Abel, Love Is Not Enough: Family Care of the Frail Elderly 3–8 (1987).

7. *See, e.g.*, *id.* at 52–53; B. Vladeck, *supra* note 2, at 210–42. There are examples of where institutions have been combined, e.g., short-stays in nursing homes as respite care. *See* Bernan,

Delaney, Gallagher, Atkins & Graeber, *Respite Care: A Partnership Between a Veterans Administration Nursing Home and Families to Care for Frail Elders at Home*, 27 GERONTOLOGIST 581 (1987).

8. *See, e.g.*, E. ABEL, *supra* note 6, at 28–51; R. Kane & R. Kane, *The Extent and Nature of Public Responsibility for Long-Term Care in* POLICY OPTIONS IN LONG-TERM CARE 78 (J. Meltzer, F. Farrow & H. Richman eds. 1981); Hedrick & Inui, *The Effectiveness and Cost of Home Care: An Information Synthesis*, 20 HEALTH SERV. RES. 851 (1986); Lave, *Cost Containment Policies in Long-term Care*, INQUIRY, Spring 1985, at 7; Weissert, *Seven Reasons Why It Is So Difficult to Make Community-Based Long-Term Care Cost-Effective*, 20 HEALTH SERV. RES. 442 (1985).

B. Paying for Home Health Care Programs

For private-pay patients, home health care in form of personal care aids, visiting nurses and other at-home support is a viable—though expensive—alternative to a nursing home. For those who cannot afford private-pay home care, the publicly funded Medicare and Medicaid programs do provide a limited amount of home care, but these programs are neither designed to provide nor do they provide a substitute for nursing home care. In the following material, Mr. Berquist explains the home health care provisions of Medicare and Medicaid.

Meris L. Bergquist

Home Health Care: What It Is and Who Pays for It

Most elderly individuals dread being placed in a nursing home. According to a survey by the American Association of Retired Persons, 86 percent of the elderly want to live out the remainder of their lives in their own homes.[1] This is not surprising. A profound loss of autonomy accompanies placement in a nursing home.[2] In the words of one individual, staying at home instead of in a nursing home means: "Anything from smoking a cigarette when I please to putting out the light when I please to making a meal when I please."[3] Some old people even think of nursing homes as jails.[4]

Vermont Law Journal and Digest, Vol. 17, 35 (December 1991). Reprinted by permission.

A comprehensive home health care program can provide a humane alternative to nursing home placement. Home health care services include nursing services; homemaker services; chore and personal services; occupational, physical and speech therapy; and nutritional and health education.[5] In addition, in many communities, the following supplemental programs may be available: meals-on-wheels, adult day-care and respite care, transportation service, companion service, and telephone safety service.[6]

There is little doubt that on a per capita basis home health care costs considerably less than nursing home care.[7] However, health care analysts believe that if home health care benefits were made more available, the utilization rate would be so much higher than for nursing homes that the aggregate cost of providing home health care would exceed the costs of institutionalization.[8] This fear probably accounts for the federal government's failure to develop a comprehensive and unified approach to the home health issue,[9] and for the fact that far more federal money is spent on nursing home care than on home health care.[10]

Presently most federal funding for home health care is channeled through our two major health care programs: Medicare and Medicaid.[11] Medicare is the largest source of public funding for home health care.[12] It is a national health insurance program that covers almost all Americans age sixty-five and over and certain individuals under sixty-five who are disabled or have end-stage renal disease. The Medicare program is administered by the Health Care Financing Administration (HCFA). It is divided into two parts. Part A covers inpatient hospital services, some posthospital care in skilled nursing homes, and home health care. Part B primarily covers physician services. Home health care is financed under Part B when no Part A coverage exists, though nearly 98 percent of the home health care is actually paid under Part A.

Medicare home health benefits are not easy to get. The rules defining eligibility are strict.[13] To establish eligibility all of the following conditions must be satisfied. A person must be homebound,[14] under a doctor's care,[15] and need part-time or intermittent skilled nursing care and/or physical or speech therapy.[16] Finally, as is true for all Medicare coverage, the services must be reasonable and necessary for the diagnosis or treatment of illness or injury.[17] These rules create a very small class of eligible patients. As one advocate put it, in order to qualify for the benefit, "the patient must be 'sick enough' but not 'too sick.'"[18]

For those who do manage to qualify, the following services are available: (1) part-time or intermittent skilled nursing, (2) physical therapy, (3) speech therapy, (4) occupational therapy, (5) medical social services, (6) home health aide services,[19] and (7) medical supplies and equipment other than drugs. The beneficiaries of the home care benefit can receive an unlimited number of home visits, and they do not have to pay deductibles or copayments.

Medicaid is a federal-state entitlement program which helps the poor obtain medical care. Medicaid, like Medicare, is administered by HCFA. Federal law requires that each state participating in the Medicaid program provide certain defined Medicaid services. However, states are given much latitude in choosing which additional medical services to provide. Under federal regulations, states participating in the Medicaid program must provide home health care for anyone entitled to skilled nursing facilities under the state plan.[20]

Medicaid home health services must include nursing, home health aide services, and medical supplies and equipment for use in the home.[21] States are given the option of covering physical, occupational, and speech therapy.[22] Vermont has elected to provide these services.[23]

There are some major differences between the home health care benefit available under Medicare and that available under Medicaid. Medicaid does not require patients to be homebound or to require skilled nursing care.[24] However, this does not translate into more extensive home health care coverage under Medicaid. Because the Medicaid program is means-tested, only the very poorest are eligible.[25] Furthermore, for individuals enrolled in both the Medicare and Medicaid programs (the poor, who are elderly or disabled), Medicare is the primary payor. This means Medicare must pay for the home health care services received by these dual eligibles.[26]

In an effort to provide a limited alternative to nursing home care, Congress in 1981 authorized the Department of Health and Human Services to approve state requests for "waivers" to provide home and community-based services for Medicaid-eligible individuals, who would otherwise require institutionalization.[27] A much wider array of services is available under "waiver" programs than under the regular Medicaid home health program. For example, a state which had been granted a waiver could receive federal funding for providing case management, homemakers, home health aides, personal care, adult day care, and respite care.[28] Vermont has been granted a waiver to provide the following services to the aged and disabled: case management, home care, adult day care and respite care.[29]

Home health care under the Medicare and Medicaid programs is carried out by home health agencies. There are seventeen Medicare-certified home health agencies in Vermont. All of them are nonprofit. According to a statistical report prepared by the Vermont Assembly of Home Health Agencies, in 1989 (the last year studied) Medicare paid for 40.6 percent of all home health care in Vermont and Medicaid paid for 14.7 percent. The Medicaid waiver program paid for only .5 percent. Agencies received the rest of their funding from a variety of sources, including private insurance, self pay, grants, Town Funds, the Veteran's Administration and the United Way. Most new patients are referred to a home health agency by a hospital. This appears to be changing, however, and increasing numbers of new patients are referred by doctors, patients themselves, and the Area Agency on Aging.[30]

* * *

Notes

1. New York Times, "The Best Home for Older Adults," 8/17/91, p.A20.

2. See, "Time to Rethink the Nursing Home," New York Times, August 18, 1991. ("At best life in a nursing home is a drab affair. A 'plan of care' governs every waking and sleeping hour

and every morsel of food consumed. The three R's of nursing homes—routines, regulations and reimbursement rates—compromise residents' privacy and autonomy. Residents cannot have control over their medications or even some toilet articles. They must live with strangers, and get up and go to bed on schedule. They are crowded into hospital-like double rooms where they can hardly seat two guests, let alone offer visitors a cup of tea. . . . For these losses in quality of life, they get limited nursing and personal care.")

3. Stephen Crystal, America's Old Age Crisis, (New York: Basic Books, 1982), p. 94.

4. Id. p. 93.

5. Although this article will focus on publicly-funded sources of home health care, it is very important to note that about 75% of the disabled elderly population living in the community relies exclusively on unpaid sources of home and community health care. This care is provided mostly by women—wives, daughters, and daughters-in-law. It is estimated that these informal caregivers provide more than 27 million unpaid days of care each week. Senate Special Committee on Aging, "Developments in Aging: 1989, Vol. 1," supra, at 238–239.

6. For more information about the availability of these services in Vermont, contact the Senior Access Line, 1-800-642-5119.

7. Crystal, America's Old Age Crisis, supra, at 92. See also, Senate Special Committee on Aging, "Developments in Aging: 1989, Volume 1," Sen. Rep. No. 101-249, 101st Cong., 2d Sess., p. 239. "(M)any frail elderly persons need only intermittent care and assistance, which can be provided less expensively than nursing home care. Further, as the patient's needs for care and assistance change over time—as his or her health improves or worsens—home and community-based services are more flexible in adjusting the level of care needed by the patient."

8. Crystal, America's Old Age Crisis, supra, at 92.

9. "(H)ome care is perhaps the most unevenly available and varied of all the major services for the aged." Crystal, America's Old Age Crisis, supra at 170.

10. Most of the public sector's expenditures for long term care services, . . . are for institutional care—primarily for nursing homes." Senate Special Committee on Aging, "Developments in Aging: 1989, Vol. 1," supra, at 239. (Emphasis added.)

11. The Veteran's Administration also provides home health services where necessary for the effective and economical treatment of a disability. 38 U.S.C. § 617(a)(1). They will also provide up to $2500 for improvements and structural alterations in the home to assure continuation of treatment for the disability or to provide access to the home or bathroom. 38 U.S.C. § 617(a)(2). Finally, veterans may be eligible for increased monthly pensions if they need "aid and attendance" or if they are "homebound." 38 C.F.R. §§ 3.351; 3.352. To ascertain eligibility for any of these veteran's benefits, consult 38 U.S.C. § 101 et seq. and call the Veteran's Administration in Vermont at 295-9363.

12. In relationship to the entire Medicare program, the Medicare home health care benefit is minuscule. Medicare payments for home health care comprise a relatively small 3% of total program outlays. Senate Special Committee on Aging, "Developments in Aging: 1989, Vol. 1," supra, at 164.

13. In addition to the strictness of the rules themselves, HCFA's overly restrictive application of the rules further reduces the scope of the benefit. "Since (1983) HCFA has targeted the home health benefit for continual cutbacks, lower payment levels, and narrower interpretation of the scope of the benefit. As a result, more Medicare beneficiaries need home health care at a time when less care is available." Senate Special Committee on Aging, "Developments in Aging: 1989, Vol. 1," supra, at 190–191.

14. 42 U.S.C. § 1395f(a)(2)(C).

15. 42 C.F.R. §§ 409.42(d) and 410.80.

16. 42 U.S.C. §§ 1395(a)(2)(d) and 1395x (m)(1); 42 C.F.R. §§ 409.40(a), 409.40(d), 409.42(b)(3) and 410.80.

17. 42 U.S.C. § 1395y(a)(1)(A).

18. Peter Komlos-Hrobsky, An Advocate's Guide to Home Care for the Elderly, Chicago: National Clearinghouse for Legal Services, 1988, p. 23.

19. Home health aides help patients with some of their activities of daily living like bathing, getting in and out of bed, using the toilet, and taking medication.

20. 42 U.S.C. § 1396(a)(10)(D).

21. 42 C.F.R. § 440.70(b).

22. Id.

23. Section M710 of the Vermont Medicaid Manual.

24. 42 C.F.R. § 440.70(b)(1).

25. Medicare, on the other hand, is a "quasi-insurance" program, and recipients do not have to meet any income or resource tests. Komlos-Hrobsky, An Advocate's Guide to Home Care for the Elderly, supra, at 10.

26. 42 U.S.C. § 1396a(a)(15).

27. 42 U.S.C. § 1396n(C)(1). This federal initiative is thought to represent a compromise between Congress, which wanted to increase the availability of home health care and HCFA, which feared the waiver program would increase federal expenditures. Accordingly, HCFA is said to have implemented the program "reluctantly." See, Komlos-Hrobsky, An Advocate's Guide to Home Care for the Elderly, supra at 61. The program, however, remains popular with Congress, and the states. It has been strengthened by Congress in 1986 and 1987. Senate Special Committee on Aging, "Developments in Aging: 1989, Vol. 1," supra at 268.

28. 42 U.S.C. § 1396n(c)(4)(B). Vermont provides the following "waiver" services to the aged and disabled: case management, home care, adult day care and respite, Medicare and Medicaid Guide, Commerce Clearing House ¶ 14,625. However, according to a Memorandum dated 7/2/91 from the Commissioner of the Department of Aging and Disabilities, there is currently a waiting list of more than 100 individuals for Medicaid waiver services in Vermont.

29. Medicare and Medicaid Guide, Commerce Clearing House ¶ 14,625.

30. For more information about home health agencies in Vermont, contact the Vermont Assembly of Home Health Agencies, 52 State Street, Montpelier, Vermont 05602, 802-229-0579.

Home health care is not without its drawbacks. Professor Ferrara explains how the current system of providing home health care can seriously erode the autonomy of the older recipient. He then presents a series of different proposed reforms designed to expand patient autonomy.

Peter J. Ferrara

Expanding Autonomy of the Elderly in Home Health Care Programs

I. Introduction

One of the greatest fears of advancing age is the loss of autonomy, a loss of control over one's own living conditions and the activities of life due to sickness and disability. The elderly and their advocates generally favor home health care over institutionalization in a nursing home, because home health care purports to provide greater opportunity to maintain the autonomy of the elderly care recipients. Increased autonomy is one reason federal and state programs provide substantial resources to finance home health care services.

Many elderly persons, advocates of the elderly, and analysts, however, note a troubling lack of autonomy in home health care programs. While autonomy in home care settings may be greater than in institutions, home care programs do not seem to be designed and operated to maximize the autonomy, choice, and control of the care recipients.

* * *

III. Autonomy in Home Health Care

On the surface, to speak of autonomy in home health care may seem anomalous because recipients are physically and sometimes mentally disabled and cannot perform some of the basic activities of daily living. However, physical disability and dysfunction, even partial mental disability, do not mean that the recipient has no preferences regarding any aspect of his or her life, or no desire to exercise any control over some or all of those aspects. A study of recipients of home attendant services in New York City revealed that about 90 percent were always or sometimes able to give directions to the home attendant regarding their care, and over 70 percent were at least sometimes able to manage their affairs.[1] Also, numerous studies have shown that a loss of autonomy by the elderly negatively affects their emotional, physical, and behavioral well-being, and ultimately undermines their health over the long run.[2]

The issue of autonomy in home health care can arise in regard to even the most mundane matters. For example, if the home attendant is needed for cooking, the issue arises as to what will be cooked and how. Loss of autonomy in particular may arise

New England Law Review, Vol. 25, 421 (1990).

when a doctor recommends a restricted diet and the attendant feels constrained to follow the doctor's orders. When the recipient is dependent on the attendant for shopping as well, autonomy and choice may be even more restricted. The recipient may lose control over the ability to purchase and consume favored foods, snacks, or other items such as cigarettes. The attendant's style of cooking, culinary tradition, or cooking ability may also restrict the recipient's control over how the food is prepared and what he or she eats. If an attendant is required for feeding, there may be an issue over when the recipient eats. The attendant may have preferences or schedule demands which may take precedence over the recipient's preference as to when to eat.

Similarly, if an attendant is required for dressing and laundering, the care recipient may lose the choice of attire. Dependency for bathing also raises the question of whether the recipient has control over when to bathe, or whether the preferences and schedule demands of the attendant take precedence. The recipient may prefer to watch a favorite TV show, listen to a ball game, read, or sit in a garden at the time an attendant has scheduled bathing. Household cleaning services also raise the question of what will be cleaned and how, and whether the attendant is attentive and responsive to the recipient's preferences in this regard.

Home care services may lead to a further loss of autonomy and control over living conditions in the home. The home care providers may seek to rearrange furniture or remove certain articles for the safety of the recipient. Favored area rugs which may cause a frail elderly individual to slip may be removed, or furniture may be cleared to reduce barriers to mobility. The bed, if not the entire bedroom, may be moved closer to the bathroom, or rugs may be removed from areas where attendants must move and transfer recipients. These changes may be sought by the attendant to ease cleaning and cooking duties as well as to better enable the attendant to perform services efficiently and safely.

The issue of autonomy also arises in regard to the recipient's control over medical care and treatment. Therapy and exercise schedules raise the question of control over the time of the treatment and whether the preferences and convenience of the provider or the recipient take precedence. The question of whether the recipient will be allowed to choose to reject medical treatments or medications also arises. Rejection of services often leads to doubts about the recipient's mental competence, particularly where traditional medical treatment is involved. These doubts may lead to further loss of autonomy and control for the recipient. A recipient may also be restrained from taking actions thought harmful to him or her. For example, if an elderly patient repeatedly attempts to move himself from his wheelchair to his bed under his own power and repeatedly falls, the attendants may eventually tie him to the wheelchair.[3]

Another autonomy concern is whether the recipient will be allowed to choose and hire his or her own attendant, or reject a disfavored attendant, or choose others to provide some of the care. Elderly recipients may fear that complaining about an attendant may cause them to be labeled troublemakers and ultimately cause further loss of control, or loss of the availability of an attendant altogether. The most serious infringement of autonomy occurs in those cases where the attendant physically or emotionally abuses the recipient.

Autonomy ultimately involves more than just the question of whether the recipient can control details of care or reject care. Autonomy involves a positive as well as a negative dimension.[4] The positive dimension concerns the question of whether services will be structured to expand and maximize the choices and control of the recipients and the opportunity for them to participate in favored activities and social events. Taking into account this positive dimension would require a focus on providing services to enhance the recipient's ability to interact with family, neighbors, and friends, and to participate in church, club, community activities, or other social events. It would require greater control by the recipient over transportation services, perhaps requiring family, neighbors, or friends to be brought to the recipient. It would also require scheduling other services around these activities based on the preferences of the recipient. The attendant may also have to follow the recipient and assist him or her in participating in outside activities.

While respect for patient autonomy is a central norm in acute care treatment, patient accommodation to the interests of neighbors, providers, and other residents in the home, as well as to the practicality of limited funding, may be more appropriate and realistic in home health care.[5] However, patient autonomy should probably play a greater role in home health care, as opposed to less. The choices in home health care are more subjective and personal, involving more private matters. Objective medical evaluation is much less of a factor in the services provided. The treatment is for a longer term and often permanent, and therefore loss of autonomy and control will be a much greater burden on the life of the patient than in a short-term, acute care setting. Finally, in home health care the providers are guests in the patient's home, where the patient has a legitimate interest in maintaining control and autonomy. In acute care facilities, by contrast, the patient is a guest in the provider's facility and can legitimately be asked to accommodate to the practical needs of the provider's operations.

* * *

V. Possible Reforms

A. Strengthened Legal Protections for Autonomy

One approach to overcoming barriers to autonomy in home health care is to specify stronger recipient rights in the governing statutes and regulations. The rights for home health care could be strengthened to reflect the rights given residents in a skilled nursing facility. Federal and state statutes could mandate that home health care services be structured (1) "to accommodat[e] . . . the individual needs and preferences" of each recipient[6] and (2) to enable each recipient "to attain . . . the highest practicable physical, mental, and psychosocial well-being. . . ."[7] The statutes could also require that each recipient is "treated with consideration, respect, and full recognition of his dignity and individuality."[8] Statutes could mandate that service providers "identif[y] the . . . social and emotional needs of the [recipient]."[9] Providers could be required to structure services "to [enhance participation] in social, religious, and community activities"[10] of the recipient's choice. Providers could be required to accommodate and support activities within the home, such as visits from friends and relatives. The right to privacy in the home, the right to refuse services, and the right to schedule services could also be granted to recipients.

Statutes could also require that the provider is supervised and directed by the recipient. The statutes could specify that the recipient has ultimate authority and control over all services and activities in the home.

However, whether specifying yet more statutory rights will be effective is highly questionable. This approach does not change the incentives to providers to ensure that they will be responsive to recipients' desires. Such statutory rights depend upon strict enforcement. Such enforcement in turn depends on monitoring activities, detecting and proving violations, and exacting effective penalties. The nature of home health care makes such enforcement difficult. Since services take place in the privacy of each recipient's home, monitoring activities and detecting violations is especially difficult. Proving a violation would be difficult because the statutory rights are inherently subjective. Since providers are generally nonprofit organizations, regulators may not be willing to impose stiff penalties. Also, elderly, disabled recipients would not aggressively pursue enforcement. Substantial resources are necessary for enforcement, and these resources may not be available. The administering bureaucracy has no economic incentive to vigorously pursue enforcement. The current rights have not been effective in expanding autonomy, probably for these reasons. This indicates that more regulation would not make any substantial change.

B. Economic Power Approaches

If recipients had economic clout and market power, they could force providers to be responsive to their individual needs and preferences. This approach seeks to change the economic incentives that influence provider behavior. Under this approach, a range of alternative options is available.

1. Economic Rights The simplest approach is to grant the recipients' rights over the key economic decisions within the structure of current programs. Recipients could be allowed to choose who would be employed as their attendants. They could be allowed to find their own personal care attendants and refer them to the provider agency for approval and employment.

Training and testing requirements could be dismissed, and the provider could interview the chosen attendants to determine if they are capable of performing their assigned duties. The recipient could have a right of appeal to the local government agency financing the services if a provider agency rejected a recipient's choice.

Recipients could also have the right to interview and choose among available personal care attendants from the provider agency. Recipients could also have the power to dismiss an attendant and resume the hiring process again. Recipients would also be given the right to conduct semiannual reviews of their attendants, and determine their salary.

2. *Vouchers* A step beyond the first option would be to replace current programs with a voucher system. First, local government agencies would evaluate the amount of care each recipient needed. Second, the agency would grant each recipient a voucher to purchase the needed hours of home health care services from a private provider of the recipients choice, instead of granting each recipient a certain number of hours of specific services as under the current system. The recipient could be allowed to choose to purchase any available home health service with the specified voucher amount, in the mix preferred.

The available provider agencies would discuss with recipients possible services and attendants, and the recipient would then designate which agency should provide the chosen services. The recipient could fire the provider agency or change the purchased services. Licensing authorities should seek to maximize the number of provider agencies to create competition and increase the quality of care. All requirements for providers to show need for their services before obtaining a license should be abolished.

3. *Cash* A step further than the proposed second option is to provide recipients cash instead of vouchers. Local government agencies would evaluate the care needed by each recipient but instead of granting a voucher, the agency would provide each recipient the equivalent in cash. The recipient could then use the cash to purchase the care from private providers. The recipient would, however, have the option of using some or all the money to purchase other services or items which the recipient values more highly.

4. *Savings Accounts* Under this option, workers and their employers would contribute to workers' individual savings accounts, and the resulting funds would be available only at retirement. The contributions would be tax deductible and the returns over the years tax free. Use of the funds could be limited to long-term nursing home and home health care, or to health expenses in general, or the funds could be available for any use chosen by the retiree. The broader the potential uses, the more attractive saving through the accounts would be, and the more effective the accounts would be in expanding choices in retirement. Funds used for nursing home, home health care, or other urgent health purposes would remain tax free, and each withdrawal for other purposes would be subject to standard income taxation. Retirees could use the funds to purchase nursing home and home health care insurance, and also to supplement those policies. The funds could also provide a cash annuity that could be used

to purchase home health services. The funds could be held in reserve and the annuity exercised when the retiree felt the need for home health services.[11]

Going down this list of options, each seems to provide recipients with more choices than the last, and seems to be more likely to overcome the barriers to autonomy. Granting rights to hire, fire, and determine wage increases would not only provide recipients with the choice of attendants, but it would also induce the hired attendants to be responsive to the needs and preferences of their recipients. But, this reform would do little to change the incentives of the provider agencies. Currently, these agencies are responsive to the state and local bureaucracies which provide their funding.

Vouchers would alter providers' incentives as well. The provider would be compensated as a direct result of the choice made by the recipient rather than the government bureaucracy. The provider organizations would consequently shift their concern to the recipient's needs and preferences. This option induces the fundamental change in incentives which is necessary to overcome the institutional bias against autonomy. It also expands choice by allowing recipients to choose the provider organizations, the preferred services, and the individual home attendants. As agencies compete to draw recipient vouchers, they are likely to develop a broader array of services and innovations which would further expand recipient choice.

Unlike the specified economic rights, vouchers address the issue of efficiency. Recipients with vouchers must consider the opportunity cost of purchasing one available service over another, resulting in an efficient mix of home health services. Yet, this is not a complete solution because the cost of the voucher is still borne by the taxpayer rather than the recipient. The recipient thus may purchase home health services with the voucher where the benefit does not exceed the cost.

The cash option affords more choice, since recipients can opt to purchase urgent or preferred services and goods instead of health care. Otherwise, the cash option would provide recipients with the same range of choices and improved provider incentives which vouchers provide.

The cash option would completely remove any efficiency problem. Recipients with cash grants would weigh the opportunity cost of all possible goods and services that could be purchased with the cash. Recipients would only purchase home health services when the benefits of these services exceeded their costs, because recipients would not want to waste cash that may be used for other purposes. The added costs to providers for any choices the recipients may make would be incorporated into the service price, and this would consequently force recipients to recognize the cost of their choices.

The cash option also eliminates the potential problem of abuse by recipients. The recipient is free to spend the cash on anything he or she prefers; therefore, there is no possibility of unauthorized uses. The possibility that the recipient may spend the funds on items other than home health care is built into the program. Recipients are chosen and funding and benefit levels are set with that possibility in mind. Since the recipient is provided a set amount of cash and goes into the market to obtain services, the choices provided by that cash do not create an opportunity for the recipient to abuse the government program to obtain additional services or resources for himself or others.

Allowing recipients to use cash for items other than home health care services may appear as just eliminating efforts to avoid diversion of resources and accepting such diversions. The cash option, however, contains a key aspect that vitiates this view. The cash option maximizes efficiency, with the recipient recognizing the costs and benefits of each decision. Consequently, under the cash option, policymakers can be confident that funds will be used for purposes other than home health care only when the recipient views those purposes as more urgent and beneficial. Policymakers may learn more about recipients' needs by monitoring their choices made with the additional funds. Under alternative systems, however, when incentives to ensure efficient decisions are not present, diversion of services and resources is more likely to create waste and inefficiency of taxpayer resources.

Unrestricted use of the funds in the savings account option would yield all of the benefits of the cash option, since the savings accounts would effectively provide cash to finance services. But the savings accounts would also provide recipients with more control over the financing of that cash, and afford them more choices. Recipients would have more control over the amount of cash payments, by saving funds during working years and varying the amount of payments in retirement. Recipients would also have greater control over the timing of payments. They could determine for themselves when they are in need of services rather than depend on a bureaucratic determination of eligibility. Recipients could also choose to leave some or all of their saved funds to their children or other heirs. The more restricted the use of the funds is, the more the advantages of the accounts parallel the advantages of the voucher option rather than the cash option.

* * *

Each of these four options would harness the market in greater or lesser degrees to work for recipient choices and autonomy. Placing the power of the market behind these goals is likely to be the most successful means of advancing them.

* * *

Notes

1. *See* [UNITED HOSP. FUND OF N.Y., HOME CARE IN NEW YORK CITY: PROVIDERS, PAYERS, AND CLIENTS 15, 33–34 (Mar. 1987) (hereinafter UNITED HOSP. FUND)], at 28.

2. [Hofland, *Autonomy in Long Term Care: Background Issues and a Programmatic Response,* 28 THE GERONTOLOGIST 3 (June 1988) (Supplement).]

3. [Collopy, *Autonomy in Long Term Care: Some Crucial Distinctions,* 28 THE GERONTOLOGIST 10 (1988) (Kime Supplement).]

4. [Collopy, *Autonomy in Long Term Care: Some Crucial Distinctions,* 28 THE GERONTOLOGIST 10 (1988) (Kime Supplement). *See also* Hofland, *Autonomy in Long Term Care: Background Issues and a Programmatic Response,* 28 THE GERONTOLOGIST 3 (June 1988) (Supplement); Cohen, *The*

Elderly Mystique: Constraints on the Autonomy of the Elderly with Disabilities, 28 THE GERONTOLOGIST 24 (June 1988) (Supplement).]

5. [N. Dubler, The Moral Mapping of a Home Care Client's Rights and Interests (Nov. 1988) (paper presented at meeting of Gerontological Society of America, San Francisco, CA).]

6. *See* [[42 U.S.C.] § 1395i-3(c)(1)(A)(v)(i) (1988)].

7. *See* [[42 U.S.C.] §§ 1395i-3(b)(2), 3(b)(4)(A)(i), 3(d)(1)(A) (1988)].

8. *See* [[N.Y. COMP. CODES R. & REGS. tit. 10], §§ 764.1(a)(8), 767.1(a)(8) (1989)].

9. *See* [[42 C.F.R.] § 405.1130 (1989)].

10. *See* [[42 U.S.C.] § 1395i-3(c)(1)(A)(v)(viii) (1988)].

11. The Health Care Saving Accounts (H.C.S.A.) proposed by Rep. French Slaughter (R.-VA) in H.R. 955, 100th Cong., 1st Sess. (1987), would also perform this function. Workers and employers contributing to these accounts would receive substantial income tax credits with the funds in the accounts used to replace some Medicare benefits in retirement. Excess funds would likely be available in the accounts to pay for nursing home and home health care benefits. The wide ranging benefits of the HCSA, including the substantial income tax credits, would likely induce contributions to the accounts by far more workers than would a simple tax deductible account aimed at long term care benefits in retirement.

C. *Regulation of Home Health Care*

Home health care providers are heavily regulated by both federal and state law. Almost all states require the licensure of a home health care agency as a precondition for operating. In order to be reimbursed by Medicare and Medicaid, home health care agencies must comply with the federal regulatory laws as well as state licensure requirements. In addition, many home health care agencies have elected to be accredited by volunteer organizations such as the National Home Care Council or the National League of Nursing's Community Health Accreditation Program.

In addition to home health care agencies, there are tens of thousands of individual personal care aids, nurses, attendants, and so forth who privately contract with individuals to provide personal care or health care in the home. If they are paid by the individual receiving care, these care providers have no need to meet the federal regulations and, depending on state law, may be under no obligation to meet any state requirements. If they provide only personal care, as opposed to health care, they probably are free to seek employment without any state licensure.

Naturally, having caregivers in the patient's home raises issues of legal liability. First, there is possible tort (negligence) liability to the persons for whom they provide care. Next, there is the liability of patients to caregivers for injuries suffered by the caregiver. And finally, there exists possible liability to third parties for injuries to persons or property caused by the actions of the caregiver.

In addition to tort liability, there is also potential contract liability. Generally, the patient's only obligation is to provide a safe working environment and to pay the employee as provided. Caregivers, on the other hand, make representations about certain abilities and knowledge. Caregivers who fail to either possess the claimed knowledge or ability, or fail to meet their responsibilities to show up and provide a certain minimum care, may be liable for injuries suffered by their clients.

Because home health care is provided in the isolated setting of the patient's home, it presents a risk of abuse or criminal exploitation of the patient. Even though the agency that contracts to provide the home health care service must be duly licensed, the background of the individual who performs the service may not be thoroughly checked. The following material from the federal Government Accounting Office discusses the problem of trying to protect vulnerable elderly from abusive home health care workers.

GAO Report: "Long-Term Care: Some States Apply Criminal Background Checks to Home Care Workers"

Letter Report, Sept. 27, 1996, GAO/PEMD-96-5

* * *

By 1989, an estimated 5.3 million of the noninstitutionalized persons age sixty-five and older, or about 17 percent of the thirty-one million elderly Americans, needed some regular assistance with a basic or instrumental activity of daily living. Just over one million of these persons were severely disabled and required assistance in several areas. Moreover, the need for such assistance is projected to accelerate as the elderly population surges to 80 million by the middle of the twenty-first century.

Elderly persons generally prefer home and community-based services to nursing homes, and a variety of economic and demographic trends make it likely that increasing numbers of elderly and disabled persons will eventually turn to paid home care workers for these services. Such home care workers have frequent, unsupervised access to potentially vulnerable adults and their property.

* * *

Assessing the extent of problems with abuse, neglect, or misappropriation in the home care industry is a difficult task. Formal safeguards for home care consumers vary widely across political jurisdictions, public programs, and types of providers; and in some instances, few safeguards exist.

We have three key results of our evaluation to report. Few states have licensure requirements for types of workers that are among the most common providers of home care services. However, the vast majority of states license or otherwise regulate some types of home care organizations or professionals, and some states indicate that all types of home care organizations are subject to a state licensure requirement.

While all states must maintain a registry for nursing home aides in accordance with federal law, only about a quarter have incorporated home care workers into it or have developed a separate registry for home workers.

Finally, we found that slightly over a quarter of the states require criminal background checks on some types of home care workers, though these checks are generally limited to a state's own criminal records. States with a statute requiring such checks may access Federal Bureau of Investigation (FBI) data for this purpose, but few states have made use of this capacity with respect to home care workers. Although there is no charge for checking these data for criminal justice purposes, fees are charged for checks for employment screening, and some state officials have cited these fees as a factor in reluctance to make greater use of the FBI data.

* * *

Fortunately, many older persons have family members who care for them either in the older person's home or in the home of the family member. Often family members supplement and supervise paid health care attendants. Although family caregivers save money and may provide more sympathetic care, they are under great emotional and even physical stress. As a result they may falter in their duties. In time, many family caregivers decide that the older person must be relocated, usually to a board and care home or a nursing home.

CHAPTER 30

Board and Care Homes

Many older persons of moderate means need assistance but cannot afford a personal care giver. If they have no family to help them and yet cannot live alone, lower income elderly often move into board and care homes. Also called personal care homes, boarding houses, group homes, rest homes, and old age homes, these facilities are nonmedical residential facilities that provide room, board, and some degree of personal care. The following material from hearings held by the Senate Special Committee on Aging describes these homes and the problems associated with them. Though the material dates from 1989, little has changed.

Board and Care: A Failure in Public Policy

* * *

Appendix

* * *

A staff briefing paper prepared for the U.S. Senate Special Committee on Aging for a joint hearing before the Special Committee on Aging of the United States Senate and the Select Committee on Aging House of Representatives, 101st Congress, First Session, March 9, 1989

Senate Special Committee on Aging, Serial No. 101-1; House Select Committee on Aging, Pub. No. 101-714

* * *

Introduction

In addition to providing important housing options for the poor and disabled, board and care homes have come to occupy a key niche in the American long-term health care system. In this role, board and care operators provide less intensive nursing care than a nursing home, but more monitoring and supervision than is feasible for many elderly and disabled persons living independently at home. The importance of board and care homes to the continuum of long-term care, particularly, has grown as governmental reimbursement strategies have shifted care of the elderly out of expensive institutions and into nursing homes and community-based care settings.

Remarkably, board and care facilities evolved this key role almost entirely in the absence of governmental monitoring and reimbursement. As a result, a situation has developed which is both ripe for abuse and exploitation of isolated and vulnerable adults, and fraught with frustration for the well-intended, but overwhelmed, caregiver. Problems will worsen under current trends. In addition to the pressures brought by a steadily growing elderly population, implementation of the nursing home preadmission screening provisions of the 1987 Omnibus Budget Reconciliation Act is likely to increase the reliance of chronically ill, mentally ill, and mentally-retarded nursing home residents on board and care providers in the United States.

Background

"Board and care" is a catch-all term used to describe a wide variety of nonmedical residential facilities, including group homes, foster homes, personal care homes, and rest homes. The General Accounting Office (GAO) found that they are typically located in cities, have an average of twenty-three beds or less, and are privately operated.

Board and care homes are an important and often overlooked component of the continuum of long-term care. Board and care homes provide care for poor and disabled individuals—often mentally ill—who reside in board and care homes because they can no longer take care of themselves and frequently because they have no place else to go. State surveys show that 90 percent of residents remain over six months, and two-thirds stay for over twelve months, in these facilities. As in nursing homes, residents are unlikely to have friends or relatives who visit them on a regular basis. The needs of board and care residents range from needing assistance with shopping, housekeeping, and/or repairing meals (30% to 56%), to needing assistance with bathing, dressing, eating and/or taking medications (27% to 43%).

While board and care homes provide essential long-term care to thousands of older and disabled Americans, generally neither private nor public health insurance—including Medicaid—pays for care received in these facilities. As a result, to an even greater extent than in nursing homes, out-of-pocket payments are the primary method of paying for the personal care provided in board and care homes.

The burden of financing board and care falls heavily upon the predominately poor residents of these facilities: 51% of the elderly, 64% of the mentally ill, and 78% of the mentally retarded living in board and care homes pay for their care with their meager income ($368/month for a single person in 1989) from the federal Supplemental Security Income (SSI) program. About half of the states provide a supplement payment to SSI recipients, averaging about $200/month for a single person.

In 1976, in response to concern about problems in board and care homes, Congress enacted the Keys Amendment to the Social Security Act. It required states to certify to the Department of Health and Human Services (HHS) that all facilities with SSI recipients as residents meet certain general standards. A 1987 survey of licensed facilities identified about 41,000 licensed homes, with about 563,000 beds serving the elderly, mentally ill and mentally retarded. Of this amount, about 264,000 beds were identified as serving only the elderly. Data are not available on the number of unlicensed homes, although it is generally acknowledged that a greater number of homes are unlicensed than licensed. For example, in its investigation, GAO estimated that 3,500 unlicensed facilities—compared to 330 licensed homes—are operating in Texas and Ohio.

Problems in Board and Care Facilities:

PROBLEM #1. Despite previous congressional hearings to bring board and care homes into compliance, homes still lack adequate fire escapes, cleanliness, and nutrition standards. Examples:

- According to one veteran board and care home inspector, residents are routinely locked into their rooms.
- Nonambulatory residents have been found living on the second floor and in the cellar of some facilities. In one unlicensed facility in Ohio, a double amputee was found tied into his wheelchair, with his fire escape route locked.
- GAO reported that inspectors in one facility found trash, dirty carpets, urine odor, insufficient and improperly labeled and stored food and medications, a dirty and inoperable stove, no toilet paper, flies, and no heat.

PROBLEM #2: Board and care providers overuse and misuse medications, and inadequately supervise the dispensing of medications.

- An Ohio inspector observed "multiple antipsychotic drugs administered to keep residents sedated so that the caregiver will not be bothered. Many of such residents do not even have a primary or secondary diagnosis of mental illness."
- In Pennsylvania, a provider was found using residents' prescription sleeping pills and sedatives interchangeably among residents, without regard to whether a doctor had prescribed a particular medication for a resident.
- At an unlicensed facility in Ohio, a female resident was receiving twenty-seven medications each day, including a triple dose of a powerful dehydrating agent.

- In Philadelphia a mentally retarded resident in a board and care home was repeatedly hospitalized after she received high doses of medication that was not prescribed for her condition—a mentally ill resident had been allowed to dispense her medications.
- A study of North Carolina board and care homes found an average of 5.8 drugs being taken by those residents with at least one prescribed medication. The antipsychotic agent haloperidol (Haldol) was the most frequently used prescription drug in these homes.
- A study of Massachusetts board and care homes found 39 percent of residents received at least one powerful antipsychotic drug. About half of residents had "no evidence of participation by a physician" in decisions about their drug therapy, while facility staff "revealed a low level of comprehension of the purpose and side effects" of these drugs.

PROBLEM #3: Many board and care home residents' basic personal care needs are neglected.

- A resident of a Florida board and care home was admitted to a hospital weighing 54 pounds—52 percent of her ideal body weight. It was found that the resident required assistance eating and the provider neglected to help her.
- In Ohio, a veteran inspector noted, "I have observed elderly with multiple bedsores which had not been under the care of a physician. In one instance I counted 32 bedsores on one small woman. These sores were infected and draining purulent material. In another instance I observed a bedsore that measured 14 inches. This sore was down through all the muscles to the bone."
- A California inspector noted: "An elderly woman, who was lying on a bed in a room at the back part of the facility, had her genitals exposed, she had a decubitus [bedsore] stage 3 and 4 on each hip, she was dehydrated, she was unable to swallow. . . . Her arms and legs were drawn up tightly to her frail body. She was unable to speak, eat or move. . . . She had no diaper on and she was lying in feces and urine. Her fingernails had not been cut or cleaned for some time."
- Control of incontinence is often done inappropriately by use of indwelling catheters. All catheters observed in unlicensed board and care homes in Ohio showed "purulent mucous plugs [and] tubing encrustation . . . which are signs of infection of the lower urinary tract."

PROBLEM #4: Many board and care residents require more care than the operator is competent to provide.

- Residents requiring 24-hour nursing care are sometimes not discharged to a hospital or nursing home for care, resulting in suffering and preventable deaths.
- In Alabama, a homeless man who was hospitalized after being injured in an automobile accident was found to have a decubitus ulcer, and to be suffering from dementia and malnourished. Though eligible for Medicaid-paid nursing home care, he was refused by the nursing home and instead placed in a board and care home.

PROBLEM #5: Residents with special care needs, such as Alzheimer's disease victims and the mentally ill, often do not receive appropriate supervision and care. For example:

- In Pennsylvania, some board and care operators do not allow mentally ill and retarded residents out to attend community programs designed for their needs.
- Young mentally ill residents have physically and verbally abused elderly residents, according to an official in Florida.

PROBLEM #6: Board and care residents are often financially exploited.

- In Vermont, an elderly resident suffering from Alzheimer's disease would pay the board and care home rent each time the owner told the resident that rent was due. The owner collected rent from the resident 2–3 times a month by saying rent was due when it had already been paid.
- In Florida, a board and care home operator stole $85,000 from a ninety-four-year-old resident after promising to invest it for him in a pension fund.
- In Arkansas, a board and care provider convinced an elderly woman to delete her husband's name from over $300,000 in securities and replace his name with the provider's, resulting in losses to husband in excess of $100,000. The same provider allegedly stole over $100,000 from another resident.

PROBLEM #7: Some board and care operators evidence such poor character that they are clearly unqualified to care for the elderly and disabled.

- A Pennsylvania board and care operator physically and verbally abused residents. On one occasion the operator verbally abused a male resident who had lost control of his bowels, while the resident lay on the floor, helpless and unable to resist.

Causes of Current Problems in Board and Care Homes:

CAUSE #1: States have failed to establish adequate licensing, inspection, and enforcement standards for board and care homes.

- GAO estimates that anywhere from 500,000 to 1.5 million boarding home residents are living in homes that should be licensed as board and care homes.
- States assign up to 200 licensed homes to one inspector, for annual and, in some states, semiannual inspections.
- States rarely punish substandard providers as provided under federal law—reduction of the SSI benefits of recipients living in a substandard board and care home—because this unduly penalizes residents. But half of the States GAO examined have yet to enact an alternative enforcement authority, such as the power to impose civil monetary penalties.
- There is no federal requirement that state licensure programs must be equipped

with authority to impose civil fines and other basic powers possessed by state nursing home licensure programs.

CAUSE #2: The Department of Health and Human Services has failed in its statutory responsibility to monitor state enforcement of quality standards in board and care facilities.

- The 1976 Keys Amendment requires states to establish and enforce board and care standards, and requires HHS to monitor state compliance, but HHS currently allocates only one-eighth of one person's time to check that states have mailed in their certifications.
- Some states have failed to file the required annual report with HHS, and others have falsely reported full compliance with federal law, without adverse action by HHS.

CAUSE #3: The absence of public or private insurance to reimburse the cost of personal care services in board and care homes jeopardizes access to quality care for the low-income elderly and disabled.

- Over half of all residents of board and care homes are dependent upon federal low-income support payments under the Supplemental Security Income (SSI) program to pay for room, board and personal care services in board, and care homes.
- SSI payments make no allowance for the cost of personal or nursing care required by recipients. SSI recipients are eligible for Medicaid, but this program seldom pays for board and care home services.
- GAO found that home serving predominantly SSI recipients had about twice as many violations as homes serving predominantly private-pay residents.
- Twenty-two states provide no supplements to SSI recipients in board and care homes. Where supplements are paid, supplements are available only to residents of licensed homes, and they may be inadequate to cover the cost of personal care:
  - Florida provides SSI residents with $694 a month, including a state supplement, but Florida board and care homes charge an average of $790/month.
  - A 1987 New Jersey survey revealed that SSI payments, including a state supplement, fell $200 dollars short of the average monthly cost of caring for residents.
  - Pennsylvania board and care residents receive $650/month in combined state and federal SSI payments, but the average board and care facility charge in 1988 was over $760/month.

CAUSE #4: There is a lack of training and education among care providers in board and care facilities, often leaving providers ill-prepared to care for the needs of frail elderly or chronically mentally-ill residents.

- Some providers are unable to recognize when patients need a higher level of care, resulting in inadequate care. This is a particular problem for those who care for older residents who are "aging in place"—becoming increasingly frail and in need of nursing care.

CAUSE #5: In an effort to control costs, the Medicare program and various States' Medicaid programs have attempted to move patients into the lowest possible level of care at the earliest opportunity.

- Board and care home providers report hospitals discharging patients in need of skilled rehabilitation care directly to the board and care setting.
- Pennsylvania's legislature has just passed a law that will allow nonambulatory residents to remain in board and care homes—whereas previously such patients required nursing home care.

CAUSE #6: In the absence of any case-management and coordination of long-term care, decisions about where a person receives care are left up to providers. Resulting conflicts of interest impede access to appropriate nursing and medical care.

- Nursing home bed shortages, coupled with nursing home operators' preference for private paying patients, make it very difficult for board and care operators to transfer more seriously ill SSI recipients to nursing homes.
- Some providers are unwilling to discharge residents who need more care for fear of losing a paying resident.

CAUSE #7: Board and care residents are often isolated and vulnerable without the protection offered by family, friends, ombudsmen, or state regulatory oversight.

- Many residents do not have family or friends who visit them regularly; as a result, they are often isolated and without a "watchdog" for their rights.
- Although long-term care ombudsman advocates are charged with the responsibility to visit board and care facilities, many find that their limited funds only permit them to focus on the nursing homes in their jurisdiction.

Policy Options for Reforming Board and Care Homes:

Financing Board and Care:

OPTION #1: Include personal care services (assistance with bathing, dressing, eating, ambulation/transferring, etc.) provided in licensed board and care homes in the array of services reimbursable under any federal long-term care program enacted by Congress.

OPTION #2: Add personal care services provided in licensed board and care homes to the list of mandatory State Medicaid services.

Monitoring and Enforcement of Standards in Board and Care:

OPTION #3: Specify minimum enforcement powers states must enact and use on substandard board and care operators. If a state fails to enact and/or use these powers, the Secretary would withhold up to 5 percent of federal matching funds for the state Medicaid agency's administrative costs. The minimum enforcement authority includes:

- Power to conduct unannounced onsite inspections of both licensed and suspected board and care providers.
- Licensure required for all facilities where unrelated residents require personal care (with sliding fee scale).
- Power to impose directed plan of correction.
- Civil monetary penalty authority.

OPTION #4: Require states to establish minimum health, safety, and security standards for licensed board and care operators. A state failing to enact and enforce standards at least as demanding as the federal minimums would be subject to the administrative penalty described above. Federal law would specify minimum standards in the following areas:

- Structural safety, such as fire/emergency preparedness.
- Sanitation, such as safe disposal of infectious waste.
- Safe and appropriate provision of personal care, when provided to a resident.
- Safeguards against providing services the board and care operator is not competent to provide (such as nursing, rehab).
- Code of residents' rights.

OPTION #5: Increase funding to states for expanded inspections, including:

- Annual inspections.
- Complaint inspections within 10 days of receipt of complaints.
- Crash program to identify unlicensed board and care homes.

OPTION #6: Expand resources of Long-Term Care Ombudsman program for board and care home monitoring and resident advocacy; clarify right of access to residents of ombudsman advocates.

Support for Board and Care Operators:

OPTION #7: Make federal loan guarantees available to licensed operators to help them obtain funds for upgrading the physical plant of board and care facilities.
OPTION #8: Direct the Secretary to enter into contracts to provide training and support for providers:

- Contract with one or more national organizations to develop a training curriculum including first aid, basic CPR, and personal care skills, for use in preparing caregivers to become board and care operators.

CHAPTER 31

Nursing Homes

When people refer to long-term care they are usually thinking of nursing homes. In 1995, there were approximately 16,700 nursing home facilities housing over 1.5 million residents, 90 percent of whom were age sixty-five or older. Although these facilities are not exclusively for long-term care of the chronically ill elderly (they also house post-hospitalization recovering acute-care patients), they conjure up the image of frail, sick older persons living out the last days of their lives. Unfortunately, for many residents that image is all too true. Nursing homes have become the repository for the sick, elderly patients who cannot afford the cost of round-the-clock home health care or whose families cannot or will not care for them. The very rich may be able to afford private home health care, but most older persons rely on free, volunteer assistance from family members. If that assistance is not forthcoming, a move to a nursing home may be unavoidable. Though often criticized as being poor substitutes for home care, the reality is that nursing homes exist because they are the only economical way of providing care for chronically ill or mentally incapacitated older persons. "Economical," of course, is a relative term. Nursing homes typically cost $35,000 to $60,000 a year. For most older persons, however, comparable home care would be even more expensive. While some nursing home patients could live at home for less cost, for the older sicker or more demented patients, the economics of scale (one attendant can care for several patients) make a nursing home the only economically viable alternative.

A. Profile of Residents

Vicki A. Freedman

Family Structure and the Risk of Nursing Home Admission

* * *

As the population continues to age, curbing the costs of long-term care services is likely to remain a policy focus. Nursing home care is of particular interest because it is the most expensive form of long-term care—both in terms of total ($70 billion in 1993) and per resident costs (about $3,200 per month) (Levit et al., 1994). Government programs—primarily Medicaid—pay for more than 60 percent of nursing home expenditures; the remainder is paid for out-of-pocket by nursing home residents and their families.

Given the high costs associated with institutionalization, there has been much interest in understanding the factors related to nursing home admissions and in identifying possible substitutions for such care. The family is particularly relevant to a discussion of nursing home admission, since numerous studies have demonstrated the critical role of family members in providing care, co-residential arrangements, and social and financial exchanges to older disabled persons (Sangl, 1985; Shanas, 1979; Soldo, Agree, and Wolf, 1989; Stone, Cafferata, and Sangl, 1987) and the importance of these familial activities in reducing an older person's risk of admission (Freedman et al., 1994; Newman and Struyk, 1990; Pearlman and Crown, 1992; Steinbach, 1992). Because of the active role of kin in the lives of older relatives, and the fact that family members are not interchangeable with respect to participation in exchange activities, an older person's risk of nursing home admission depends in part upon family structure. We use the term "family structure" in the demographic sense; that is, a given person's constellation of living relatives as defined by their genealogical relationships.

Interest in the consequences of family structure for long-term care in general has been sparked in part by concerns about impending demographic changes that will shift family availability for future cohorts of elderly. In the near future, such shifts will work in favor of expanding familial availability: among women aged eighty-five and older, for example, a group particularly vulnerable to nursing home entry,

Journal of Gerontology: Social Sciences, Vol. 51B, No. 2, S61–S69 (1996). Reprinted by permission from the Gerontological Society of America.

the proportion of unmarried, childless women is projected to decrease from about 20 percent in 1990 to less than 10 percent in 2020 because of sharp increases in fertility following World War II (Himes, 1992; Preston, 1992). After 2020, as the bulk of the baby boom generation reaches old age, these trends in family availability will reverse. For this younger cohort, continued high rates of divorce, coupled with low remarriage rates, are likely to reduce the availability of spouses in old age; at the same time the average number of children ever born is expected to slowly decline while the proportion with no living children will rise substantially. Given these expected trends, interest in the relationship between family structure and risk of nursing home admission is warranted.

* * *

Background

Because older persons prefer to remain in the community (Kerckhoff, 1965), institutional care is generally initiated only when the balance between an older person's physical and mental capacity and the available sources of community care is upset. As a result of this disequilibrium, more than one million elderly persons are institutionalized in nursing home facilities each year (Liu and Manton, 1983).

Interest in understanding the role of family structure in the risk of nursing home admissions has been longstanding. Three decades ago, Townsend (1965) first showed that persons who enter institutions are far less likely than the general community to have either a spouse or living children. Since then, longitudinal analyses of nursing home admission have repeatedly shown that having a spouse greatly reduces an older person's risk of nursing home entry. Findings with respect to children have been less consistent, however, possibly due to the lack of distinction between sons and daughters (see, for example, Freedman et al., 1994; Garber and MaCurdy, 1989; Greene, Lovely, and Ondrich, 1993; Headen, 1993; Palmore, 1976; Pearlman and Crown, 1992; Salive et al., 1993). To date, the role of other relatives (e.g., siblings) has been largely overlooked.

At least three interrelated pathways can be identified through which family structure might have an impact on the risk of nursing home admission. First, and most salient, kin can provide personal care directly to an older relative, often as part of a co-residential arrangement, thereby directly substituting informal care services for institutional care. Although the responsibility for an older relative's care is often shared among family members (Horowitz, 1985), a spouse or child typically will assume the role of "primary caregiver"; wives and daughters constitute the bulk of these primary caregivers.

Second, kin can provide assistance with obtaining formal home and community-based services instead of institutional care, by arranging for services or making financial transfers to pay for such care. Several studies suggest that sons are more likely to assist with bureaucratic matters or provide financial resources than to provide informal care directly to a frail parent (Horowitz, 1985; Litwak, 1985; Stoller and Earl, 1983).

TABLE 1 Family Structure Effects on First Nursing Home Admission, by the Older Person's Marital Status and Gender

	Marital Status		*Gender*	
	Not Married	*Married*	*Male*	*Female*
Living spouse	—	—	0.56	0.60
Living son(s)	0.92	1.01	1.18	0.83*
Living daughter(s)	0.70	0.90	0.75	0.72
Living sibling(s)	0.85	0.58	0.83	0.78

*$p < .05$ for test of difference in family structure effects between males and females.

Third, mounting evidence suggests that family ties may have a beneficial impact on the health and well-being of older persons, and thus an indirect effect on the volume of nursing home care demand (Cohen and Syme, 1985). Such indirect effects may accrue from both tangible and emotional support. For example, a recent study by Freedman et al. (1994) suggests that regular contact with a family member of any relationship reduces the risk of nursing home admission for women.

* * *

Prior research suggests that the effect of family structure on the risk of nursing home admission may vary depending on characteristics of the older person. Cantor (1979) has argued, for example, that older persons have hierarchical preferences for primary caregivers, with spouses preferred over other types of kin. This suggests that older unmarried persons are more likely than married persons to have children and siblings serve as caregivers. More recently, Lee et al. (1993) asserted that there is a tendency toward gender consistency between caregivers and recipients of care, with daughters more likely than sons to care for mothers.

* * *

Findings with respect to marital status are consistent with previous studies: even after controlling for health, demographics, and economic differences, married older persons have about half the risk of nursing home admission of unmarried persons. In addition, our analysis supports a protective role of other relatives against the risk of nursing home admission: Having at least one daughter or sibling reduces an older person's chances of admission by about one-fourth. In contrast, having living sons does not affect the risk of nursing home entry appreciably.

* * *

We also explored whether family structure effects varied by characteristics of the older person. We found only limited evidence of differential effects of family structure by marital status and gender. The one statistically significant finding was that sons appear to reduce the risk of admission for mothers but not for fathers. This may be due in part to the fact that sons typically do not supply care directly to a frail parent, but instead offer financial assistance or handle bureaucratic tasks. It may be that father-son relationships are less conducive to these types of transfers than mother-son relationships.

* * *

References

Cantor, M. 1979. "Neighbors and Friends: An Overlooked Resource in the Informal Support System." *Research on Aging* 1:434–436.

Cohen, S. and S.L. Syme. 1985. "Issues in the Study and Application of Social Support." In S. Cohen and S.L. Syme (Eds.), *Social Support and Health*, Orlando, FL: Academic Press.

Freedman, V.A., L.F. Berkman, S.R. Rapp, and A.M. Ostfeld. 1994. "Family Networks: Predictors of Nursing Home Entry." *American Journal of Public Health* 84:843–845.

Garber, A.M. and T. MaCurdy. 1989. "Predicting Nursing Home Utilization Among the High-Risk Elderly." National Bureau of Economic Research Working Paper No. 2843.

Greene, V., M. Lovely, and J. Ondrich. 1993. "Do Community-Based Long-term-care Services Reduce Nursing Home Use? A Transition Probability Analysis." *Journal of Human Resources* 28:297–317.

Headen, A.E. Jr. 1993. "Economic Disability and Health Determinants of the Hazard of Nursing Home Entry." *Journal of Human Resources* 28:81–110.

Himes, C.L. 1992. "Future Caregivers: Projected Family Structures of Older Persons." *Journal of Gerontology: Social Sciences* 47:S17–S26.

Horowitz, A. 1985. "Sons and Daughters as Caregivers to Older Parents: Differences in Role Performance and Consequences." *The Gerontologist* 25:612–617.

Lee, G.R., J.W. Dwyer, and R.T. Coward. 1993. "Gender Differences in Parent Care: Demographic Factors and Same-Gender Preferences. *Journal of Gerontology: Social Sciences* 48: S9–S16.

Levit, K.R., A.L. Sensenig, C.A. Cowan, H.C. Lazenby, P.A. McDonnell, D.K. Won, L. Sivarajan, J.M. Stiller, C.S. Donham, and M.S. Stewart. 1994. National Health Expenditures, 1993. *Health Care Financing Review* 16:247–294.

Litwak, E. 1985. *Helping the Elderly: The Complementary Roles of Informal Networks and Formal Systems.* New York: Guilford Press.

Liu, K. and K.G. Manton. 1983. "The Characteristics and Utilization Pattern of an Admission Cohort of Nursing Home Patients." *The Gerontologist* 23:92–98.

Newman, S. and R. Struyk. 1990. "Overwhelming Odds: Caregiving and the Risk of Institutionalization." *Journal of Gerontology: Social Sciences* 45:S173–S183.

Palmore, E. 1976. "Total Chance of Institutionalization Among the Elderly." *The Gerontologist* 16:504–507.

Pearlman, D. and W.H. Crown. 1992. "Alternative Sources of Social Support and Their Impacts on Institutional Risk." *The Gerontologist* 32:527–535.

Preston, S.H. 1992. "Cohort Succession and the Future of the Oldest Old." In R. Suzman, D.P. Willis, and K.G. Manton (Eds.), *The Oldest Old.* New York: Oxford University Press.

Salive, M.E., K.S. Collins, D.J. Foley, and L.K. George. 1993. "Predictors of Nursing Home Admission in a Biracial Population." *American Journal of Public Health* 83:1765–1767.

Sangl, J. 1985. "The Family Support System of the Elderly." In R.J. Vogal and H.C. Palmer (Eds.), *Long Term Care: Perspectives for Research and Demonstrations.* Washington, DC: Health Care Financing Administration.

Shanas, E. 1979. "The Family as a Social Support System in Old Age." *The Gerontologist* 19: 169–174.
Soldo, B.J., E.M. Agree, and D.A. Wolf. 1989. "The Balance Between Formal and Informal Care." In M.G. Ory and K. Bond (Eds.), *Aging and Health Care: Social Science and Policy Perspectives.* London: Routledge.
Steinbach, U. 1992. "Social Networks, Institutionalization, and Mortality Among Elderly People in the United States." *Journal of Gerontology: Social Sciences* 47:S183–S190.
Stoller, E.P. and L.L. Earl. 1983. "Help With Activities of Everyday Life: Sources of Support of the Noninstitutionalized Elderly." *The Gerontologist* 23:64–70.
Stone, R.G., G. Cafferata, and J. Sangl. 1987. "Caregivers of the Frail Elderly: A National Profile." *The Gerontologist* 27:616–626.
Townsend, P. 1965. "The Effects of Family Structure on the Likelihood of Admission to an Institution in Old Age." In E. Shanas and G.F. Streib (Eds.), *Social Structure and the Family.* Englewood Cliffs, NJ: Prentice-Hall.
Wolinsky, F.D., C.M. Callahan, J.F. Fitzgerald, and R.J. Johnson. 1993. "Changes in Functional Status and the Risks of Subsequent Nursing Home Placement and Death." *Journal of Gerontology: Social Sciences* 48:S93–S101.

B. Mechanisms for Monitoring Care

Once admitted to the nursing home, the patient or the patient's family may be dissatisfied with the quality of care provided. There are mechanisms in place to help resolve disputes between the patient (or the patient's family) and the facility.

Erica Wood and Naomi Karp

"Fitting the Forum to the Fuss" in Acute and Long-Term Care Facilities

* * *

G. Long-Term Care Mechanisms

1. Nursing Home Resident Assessment and Care Planning Process The Nursing Home Reform Amendments of the Omnibus Budget Reconciliation Act of 1987 (OBRA-87) require that residents participate in decisions about their care and that, to the extent

Clearinghouse Review, Vol. 29, No. 6, 621–628 (October 1995). Reprinted by permission.

possible, residents or their families be included in care planning.[1] The Health Care Financing Administration has developed a "minimum data set" of core elements and common definitions for resident assessments and guidelines for their use. "Resident assessment protocols" provide additional information about resident strengths, preferences, and needs. OBRA-87 requires that residents be assessed upon admission, annually, and whenever there is a significant change in the resident's physical or mental condition.[2]

The care planning process should be interdisciplinary, involving not only medical staff but also social work, activities, dietary planning, therapy, and nursing assistants, as well as residents and their representatives. Care planning is a means for staff to learn about a resident's particular needs and customary routines and to frame responses that maximize independence. Care planning provides an ideal forum for addressing care disputes. Advocates can help residents and families prepare for the meetings, identify issues for discussion, and provide support. Advocates also can monitor care planning implementation.

2. *Long-Term Care Ombudsmen* Initiated in 1972, the long-term care ombudsman program operates in each state under Title VII of the Older Americans Act.[3] The Title VII program on Vulnerable Elder Rights Protection requires states to establish an office of the state long-term care ombudsman to investigate and resolve problems on behalf of residents of nursing homes and board-and-care facilities and to advocate for systemic change to improve the long-term care system. Many states operate local or regional ombudsman projects as well. Ombudsman programs use trained staff and volunteers to visit facilities and respond to resident and family concerns. In 1993, the long-term care ombudsman program received more than 197,000 complaints lodged by over 154,400 people.[4]

The long-term care ombudsman program is flexible and differs in each state, with "52 distinctive approaches" to implementation.[5] Moreover, local projects and individual ombudsmen differ; some assume an adversarial posture while others take a more neutral or collaborative stance.[6] In some instances, ombudsmen may serve as mediators in conflicts involving residents, family, facility staff, physicians, and/or government agencies. Ombudsmen often provide needed information and support to aid residents and families in resolving disputes. An ombudsman also may negotiate with an administrator on behalf of a resident, file a complaint with a government agency, work with residents' councils, or play a role in facility licensing and certification. Complaints could involve abuse, access to information, admission, transfer, discharge, exercise or rights, quality of care, physician services, financial disputes, rehabilitation, restraints, activities, diet, the physical facility, administrative policies, staffing, or other areas.[7]

H. Courts

Most treatment and care decisions are best resolved in the health/long-term care setting by patients/residents, families, physicians, and other care providers. There is widespread agreement among courts and commentators that the judicial process usually is the least effective channel for addressing bioethical disputes and should be used only as a last resort.[8] The judicial process is slow, cumbersome, public, expensive, and removed from the expertise of the clinical setting. Additionally, it often erodes relationships among providers, patients/residents, and families.

However, in some instances it is important to clarify legal issues through reasoned judicial opinions and to establish precedents. Or there may be a need to seek guardianship for "unbefriended elderly" patients or residents without family or other surrogate decision-makers. Finally, some disputes are intractable and not amenable to resolution through other channels.

III. Cutting-Edge Projects: Mediating Care Disputes

In the past few years, providers and patient advocates have begun to focus more intensively on the process of resolving disputes that arise in health and long-term care institutions. Several landmark projects demonstrate mediation as a means of empowering patients, families, and staff members to resolve difficult decisions.

Mediation is a voluntary, nonbinding process in which a trained neutral facilitator helps parties reach a negotiated agreement that reflects their best interests. The mediator attempts to improve communications, unlock rigid positions, expand options for settlement, find common ground, and move toward consensus. The solutions that emerge can be more creative and more suited to individual needs than might be possible through traditional legal channels. The solutions are not imposed by the mediator but fashioned by the parties, thus fostering a sense of "ownership" in the decision and commitment to its implementation.

Mediation is not always the appropriate channel for dispute resolution. Parties in conflict may not agree to come to the table. Power imbalances may be too great to overcome. Law reform through precedent-setting cases may be desirable. But mediation offers welcome possibilities for collaborative problem solving in selected cases.

* * *

Notes

1. Omnibus Budget Reconciliation Act of 1987 (OBRA-87), 42 U.S.C. §§ 1395r(i)(3)(a)-(h), 1396r(a)-(h).
2. 42 U.S.C. § 1395i-3(b)(3). *See* National Citizens' Coalition for Nursing Home Reform, Nursing Home Reform Amendments of OBRA-87 at 52–66 (1993).
3. Title VII of the Older Americans Act, 42 U.S.C. § 3058(f)-(h).
4. Institute of Medicine, Real People, Real Problems: An Evaluation of the Long-term Care Ombudsman Programs of the Older Americans Act 4, 65 (1995).
5. *Id.* at 3.
6. *Id.* at 63.

7. Form for Long-Term Care Ombudsman Program State Annual Report to the Administration on Aging.
8. National Center for State Courts, Guidelines for State Court Decision Making in Life-sustaining Treatment Cases (1992).

Residents of nursing homes—frail, chronically ill, often suffering from mental incapacity, living in an isolated environment, almost totally dependent upon their institutional caregivers—are very vulnerable and usually unable to protect themselves from exploitation, poor-quality care, neglect, and financial and physical abuse. As a result, there are federal and state laws and regulations that provide for civil and criminal sanctions against those who abuse, neglect, or exploit nursing home residents. The following article describes those protective laws, regulations, and rights of private action and points out their shortfalls in protecting vulnerable institutionalized older persons.

Jeffrey Spitzer-Resnick and Maya Krajcinovic

Protecting the Rights of Nursing Home Residents: How Tort Liability Interacts with Statutory Protections

* * *

Nursing homes are highly regulated institutions. A significant portion of those regulations are designed to protect the vulnerable nursing home resident from abuse, neglect, or mistreatment while in the nursing home. The regulations are found in both state and federal law and have as their root the Nursing Home Reform Amendments Act, which was contained within the Omnibus Budget Reconciliation Act of 1987 (OBRA '87).[1] Though passed in 1987, the law did not truly become effective until the United States Department of Health and Human Services (HHS) implemented regulations on September 26, 1991.[2]

* * *

The federal law does not give nursing home residents an explicit private right of action. However, in dealing with the enforcement provisions of OBRA '87, Congress explicitly stated that any state or federal remedies[3] "shall not be construed as limiting such other remedies, including any remedy available to an individual at common

Nova Law Review, Vol. 19, 629 (Winter 1995). Reprinted by permission.

law."[4] The House Energy and Commerce Committee Report on the provision specifically states that the law was not meant to "limit remedies available to residents at common law, including private rights of action to enforce compliance with requirements for nursing facilities."[5]

* * *

Whether or not one can fashion a private cause of action based on the federal or state regulations which control nursing homes should not be the end of an attorney's inquiry into whether an abused or mistreated nursing home resident can maintain an action in court. Indeed, the inquiry should always include consideration of whether or not there are common law causes of action based on the mistreatment. The following examination of how the *Snow* case played out at trial, as well as how the reported decisions present both openings and barriers to common law tort actions, will demonstrate both the availability of, and barriers to, common law actions in the nursing home residents' rights context.

In *Snow*, a federal jury trial, the plaintiffs brought an action that raised a number of common law issues, including breach of contract and negligence resulting in the wrongful death of Edna Snow, as well as her conscious pain and suffering prior to death. Although examination of the nursing home admissions agreement regarding the contract claim should not be overlooked in cases such as these, the legal team in *Snow* concentrated on the negligence claim.

The plaintiffs claimed that the defendant had a history of operating the Glenfield Health Care Center in a deficient manner. For example, during the two years prior to Snow's admission to Glenfield, the nursing home routinely failed to document its patients' dietary and rehabilitative needs and progress. Less than one month after her admission to Glenfield for post-stroke recuperative care, Snow's condition deteriorated to the extent that she was hospitalized, where she died eight days later.

The plaintiffs sought to use annual surveys conducted by Wisconsin's Bureau of Quality Compliance to demonstrate the nursing home's knowledge of its care deficits prior to, and during, Snow's stay at Glenfield. The court refused to admit these surveys into evidence, ruling that they did not specifically apply to the cause of action for negligence regarding Snow. As a result, the plaintiffs were unable to present a strong case for punitive damages based on the willful disregard of Snow's needs while she was in the nursing home. Ultimately, the court ruled against allowing the issue of punitive damages to go to the jury.

Without evidence pertaining to punitive damages, the jury based its $125,000 award on the following evidence. Snow's therapeutic goals were not achieved when the nursing home failed to put her lap and shoulder brace in place. Further, the nursing home failed to toilet Snow every two hours to help her reestablish her continence. On one occasion, she was left to lie in her own feces for more than an hour while family members tried, with great difficulty, to obtain staff assistance to clean her. The jury concluded that the lack of care and the rough way in which she was finally cleaned added significantly to the loss of dignity suffered by Snow prior to her death.

Perhaps most important to the jury was the nursing home's failure to meet Snow's nutritional needs. Snow's chart was replete with instances where little or no food intake was recorded. As a result of a stroke, Snow was paralyzed on her left side and thus needed assistance to make sure that she had sufficient dietary intake. Despite this left-side deficit, nursing home personnel regularly placed food on her left side. The jury concluded that these nutritional deprivations ultimately led to Edna Snow's untimely death.

V. Establishing a Standard of Care—Negligence Per Se

If there is no clear private right of action to enforce nursing home residents' rights, these rights and regulations may be used to establish negligence per se. In *Snow*, the plaintiffs attempted to utilize this concept under Wisconsin law. To establish negligence per se in Wisconsin, the nursing home regulations must have a purpose, exclusively or in part, to protect: (1) a class of persons which includes the plaintiff, (2) the interests of the plaintiff that were invaded, (3) the plaintiff's interests against the kind of harm that resulted, and (4) the plaintiff's interests against the particular hazard from which the harm results.[6]

Although the court in *Snow* did not instruct the jury on negligence per se, the residents' rights regulations still proved valuable. In *Snow*, the plaintiffs were able to use the nursing home regulations to establish the standard of care that the defendant nursing home was required to meet. Moreover, the court allowed the nursing home regulations to be used by the jury as further guidance in deciding whether the nursing home breached its duty to Edna Snow.

* * *

B. Expert Testimony

A standard tool used to demonstrate whether a nursing home breached its duty of due care is the employment of expert testimony. Both parties may attempt to use doctors, nurses, and nursing home administrators for this purpose. Under a negligence cause of action, expert testimony provides the trier of fact with a reasonable understanding of the nature of the standard of care required by the nursing home, and information to determine whether there was a deviation therefrom.[7] If, however, the trier of fact is fully capable of determining the applicable standard of care through use of common knowledge, the court may exclude the proffered expert testimony.[8]

* * *

Notes

1. *See* 42 U.S.C. § 1395i-3 (1988) (Medicare provision); *see also id.* § 1396r (1988 & Supp. IV 1992) (Medicaid provision).
2. 42 C.F.R. § 483 (1993).
3. Such remedies include administrative enforcement through survey and certification.

4. 42 U.S.C. § 1396r(h)(8) (Supp. IV 1993).

5. H.R. Rep. No. 100-391(I), 100th Cong., 1st Sess. 453, 472 (1987), *reprinted in* 1987 U.S.C.C.A.N. 2313–273, 2313–292.

6. Fortier v. Flambeau Plastics Co., 476 N.W.2d 593 (Wis. Ct. App. 1991).

7. Juhnke v. Evangelical Lutheran Good Samaritan Soc'y, 634 P.2d 1132 (Kan. Ct. App. 1981).

8. *Id.* at 1136.

CHAPTER 32

Financing Long-Term Care

Paying for long-term care is complicated and will be covered as a separate topic in Part VII. Briefly, however, individuals pay for less than half of the out-of-pocket costs of long-term care. Medicare covers less than 5 percent of the cost of nursing home care, while Medicaid pays approximately 48 percent, though Medicaid only pays after the individual's assets are reduced to less than $2,000. (Couples are allowed to retain greater amounts for the noninstitutionalized spouse.) Much of the long-term care is provided for free by spouses, companions, families, and friends, often in the older person's home and frequently in the home of the provider. Another alternative for paying for long-term care is long-term care insurance, but it is expensive and to date is not widely used. It is estimated that long-term care insurance pays for only 1 percent of long-term care costs.

In years past, before Medicaid, families were expected to provide for their elderly relatives. In particular, states required adult children to support their impoverished parents. Though the passage of Medicaid ended the responsibility of children to pay for the health care of their parents, many nursing homes still attempt to have the children sign a contract agreeing to pay for a parent's care, should the parent be unable to afford the cost of the nursing home. The legality of these so-called financial responsibility contracts is the subject of the following article.

Eric Carlson

Illegal Guarantees in Nursing Homes: A Nursing Facility Cannot Force a Resident's Family Members and Friends to Become Financially Responsible for Nursing Facility Expenses

* * *

I. Introduction

Federal law prohibits a nursing facility[1] from requiring a third party to guarantee payment as a condition of a resident's admission.[2] Nonetheless, nursing facilities across the country continue to obtain third-party guarantees by both ignoring and evading federal law.

* * *

II. Vulnerability During Admission to a Nursing Facility

Admission to a nursing facility is a traumatic event. To an incoming resident, the admission may be perceived as a prelude to death. The resident's family members and friends likely despair over the resident's worsening condition and feel guilty for their own inability to keep him or her at home.

More often than not, the fundamental trauma of nursing facility admission is exacerbated by personal and practical problems. A resident often enters a nursing facility soon after suffering an unexpected and debilitating illness—a stroke, for example. As a result, the resident and his or her family members and friends likely will not have an opportunity even to think about nursing facilities, much less to make advance plans for nursing facility admission. Their relevant knowledge may consist solely of a stark minimum: the list of local facilities from a hospital discharge planner and information that the hospital intends to discharge the resident *right now.*

Due to these circumstances, a nursing facility has extraordinary power over an entering resident and his or her family members and friends. The resident, family, and friends likely have little ability to choose among facilities or to make demands upon a particular facility. Above all, they cannot risk not being admitted by a poten-

Clearinghouse Review, Vol. 30, No. 1, 33–44 (May 1996).

tial facility. They understand that the would-be resident no longer can remain in the family home or in the hospital and feel that his or her health and safety will be endangered unless he or she immediately is admitted to a nursing facility.

III. Federal Law Prohibition of Nursing Facility Guarantees

Nursing facilities have taken advantage of this overwhelming leverage. As Charles Sabatino of the Commission on Legal Problems of the Elderly, American Bar Association, has pointed out, "It has been a common practice for [nursing] facilities to require someone, usually a family member, to cosign the contract and to assume joint and several personal financial liability."[3] A nursing facility can use such a financial guarantee to collect tens of thousands of dollars from a friend or family member if, for example, a resident's Medicaid application was mishandled and denied.[4] Also, as noted by a U.S. Senate Committee, a nursing facility can use such a guarantee in order to double-bill, by forcing a resident's friend or family member to make a separate payment for an item or service already covered by the Medicaid per-diem rate.[5]

In 1987, Congress banned these nursing facility guarantees. In the Nursing Home Reform Law of 1987,[6] Congress stated that a "nursing facility must . . . not require a third party guarantee of payment to the facility as a condition of admission (or expedited admission) to, or continue stay in, the facility.[7]

This legislation's intent is self-evident. Due to the enormous expense of nursing facility care,[8] Congress decided that only the resident should bear financial responsibility.[9] Neither should the resident's family member or friend be threatened with the potentially catastrophic expenses for which the resident is responsible.

IV. Violation of Law by Nursing Facilities

Despite the clear intent of Congress, passage of this federal law has not eliminated the use of broad nursing facility guarantees. By and large, the nursing facility industry, ignoring and/or evading federal law, continues to seek and obtain financial guarantees from residents' family members and friends. In one believe-it-or-not example, a Georgia nursing facility filed a lawsuit for $20 million against a man solely because he refused to sign as a financially responsible "sponsor" for his father.[10]

A nursing facility guarantee generally takes one of two forms: (1) a guarantee required for the admission of any nursing facility resident who is not eligible for the Medicaid Program or (2) a guarantee obtained by deceiving a resident's family member or friend into signing an admission agreement as a "[financially] Responsible party." As explained below, both forms of guarantee are illegal and/or unenforceable.

* * *

B. Guarantee Obtained by Deceiving Family Member or Friend into Signing Admission Agreement as "Responsible Party"

The majority of nursing facilities currently obtain guarantees through deception. Specifically, these facilities have a resident's family member or friend sign an admission agreement on a signature line designated for a "responsible party." By signing, the family member or friend purportedly is "volunteering" to become liable for all nursing facility charges, although he or she likely signs the admission agreement under the assumption that a "responsible party" is simply a contact person for the resident.

In the 1994 survey of Los Angeles County nursing facilities, 78.5 percent of the surveyed facilities used such "responsible party" provisions.[11] In each of those facilities, the admission agreement's definition of "responsible party" was located several pages from the "responsible party" signature line and was convoluted and confusing.

* * *

Such a "responsible party" provision is unenforceable, for at least five reasons. A "responsible party" provision (1) can be used by a nursing facility to force a resident's family member or friend into becoming a guarantor; (2) provides no consideration to a resident, family member, or friend; (3) imposes unconscionable terms; (4) violates public policy; and (5) violates consumer protection statutes.

1. Is Used to Require Guarantor Although "responsible party" provisions purportedly are voluntary, they often are used by nursing facility staff to obtain a guarantee as condition of admission. During the admission process, facility employees often place an "X" in front of a "responsible party" signature line, essentially directing a resident's family member or friend to become a "responsible party."[12] In other instances, a nursing facility overtly requires a "responsible party" signature, despite the contractual language claiming that such a signature is "voluntary." For example, one nursing facility administrator in Los Angeles County chased a resident's son across the parking lot after he declined to sign as a "responsible party."[13]

If a nursing facility admission agreement had no signature line for a guarantor or a "responsible party," the facility never would be able to get the signature of a financially-responsible third party. By using "responsible party" provisions, nursing facilities give their staff a means of requiring a guarantor as a condition of admission, even if the "responsible party" provisions by their terms are voluntary.

2. Provides No Consideration to Resident, Family Member, or Friend As discussed, admission to a nursing facility cannot be conditioned on the provision of a guarantee. If a nursing facility nonetheless obtains a guarantee, that guarantee provides no consideration to the resident, whose admission should be independent of the provision of a guarantee.[14] Likewise, such a guarantee provides no consideration to the guarantor: the admission of the resident (the guarantor's family member or friend) is independent of the guarantee, and the guarantor certainly does not benefit by becoming liable for potentially tens of thousands of dollars.

Fortunately for the advocate, this absence of consideration is emphasized by the language of most "responsible party" provisions. In the above-quoted provision, for example, the nursing facility promises nothing in return for the "responsible party" signature. In fact, the provision essentially certifies that the nursing facility is providing no consideration—by the admission agreement's own terms, a "responsible party" acts "voluntary."

This strange disavowal of consideration reflects nursing facilities' efforts to evade the federal law stating that a "nursing facility must . . . not *require* a third party guarantee of payment to the facility as a condition of admission" (emphasis added).[15] In response, facilities use admission agreements which claim that the facilities do not *require* a financial guarantee and that any guarantee is voluntary. In doing so, however, the facilities acknowledge that their purported guarantees provide no benefit to residents or to their family members and friends. As a consequence, the purported guarantees lack consideration and, if challenged, are unenforceable.

* * *

Notes

1. "Nursing facility" is the term given by federal law to a facility commonly known as a nursing home or convalescent hospital. *See* 42 U.S.C. § 1396r(a).

2. *Id.* §§ 1395i-3(c)(5)(A)(ii), 1396r(c)(5)(A)(ii); 42 C.F.R. § 483.12(d)(2).

3. Charles Sabatino, *Nursing Home Admission Contracts: Undermining Rights the Old-Fashioned Way*, 24 CLEARINGHOUSE REV. 553, 554 (Oct. 1990); *see also* DONNA AMBROGI & LENORE GERARD, AUTONOMY OF NURSING HOME RESIDENTS: A STUDY OF CALIFORNIA ADMISSION AGREEMENTS D-7 (1986) (77 of 105 nursing facility admission agreements requiring financial guarantor as condition of admission).

4. *Rights and the Affirm*, LOS ANGELES TIMES, May 11, 1995, at B-1 (man signed nursing facility admission agreement as "[financially] responsible party" for entering resident, who was a neighbor and fellow church member; man subsequently sued by nursing facility after resident's Medicaid coverage improperly terminated).

5. STAFF OF SENATE COMM. ON AGING, 99TH CONG., 2D SESS., NURSING HOME CARE: THE UNFINISHED AGENDA 9 (May 1986) (facilities requiring that every Medicaid patient have a "'guarantor' to pay for items or services provided by the facility to the patient, but not [separately] reimbursed under the Medicaid program").

6. Omnibus Budget Reconciliation Act of 1987, Pub. L. No. 100-203, 101 Stat. 1330 (amendment 42 U.S.C. §§ 1395i-3(a)-(h) (Medicare) and 1396r(a)-(h) (Medicaid). The Nursing Home Reform Law, like most other Medicaid-related legislation, was threatened with repeal during the 1995 session of Congress, and at this writing the law remains wholly in effect.

7. 42 U.S.C. §§ 1395i-3(c)(5)(A)(ii), 1396r(c)(5)(A)(ii); *see also* 42 C.F.R. § 483.12(d)(2) (statutes restated in regulation). With few exceptions, sections 1395i-3 and 1396r contain identical provisions. Sections 1395i-3 applies to any nursing facility certified for participation in the Medicare program; section 1396r applies to any facility certified for participation in the Medicaid program.

8. E.g., the California Department of Health Services calculates that nursing facility care

costs on average over $39,000 per year. All-County Welfare Directors Letter #96-11, Cal. Dep't of Health Servs. (Feb. 9, 1996).

9. If the nursing facility resident is indigent, the Medicaid program makes or supplements the resident's payment to the nursing facility. *See* 42 U.S.C. §§ 1396a(a)(10), 1396d(a)(4)(A), 1396r.

10. Ansley Pavilion Nursing Home v. Benedit, No. 93-1663, Order Granting Summary Judgment (Ga. Super. Ct Walton County May 5, 1994).

11. [ERIC CARLSON, "IF ONLY I HAD KNOWN": MISREPRESENTATIONS BY NURSING HOMES WHICH DEPRIVE RESIDENTS OF LEGAL PROTECTION 26 (Bet Tzedek Legal Services May 1995).]

12. *See, e.g.*, Podolsky v. National Medical Enters., No. BC 049776 (Cal. Super. Ct. Los Angeles County Aug. 20, 1993) (Clearinghouse No. 48,003) (declarations of Darlene Brozovich et al.). In *Podolsky* I represent nursing facility residents in a challenge to the business practices of the Hillhaven chain of nursing facilities.

13. *Id.* (declaration of Gerald Tietz; nursing home administrator running across parking lot to seek "responsible party" signature after resident's son declined to sign).

14. RESTATEMENT (SECOND) OF CONFLICTS, § 73 (1981); *see, e.g.*, County of San Diego v. Viloria, 80 Cal. Rptr. 869 (1969) (guarantee unenforceable by hospital when hospital obligated by law to provide services regardless of guarantee).

15. 42 U.S.C. §§ 1395i-3(c)(5)(A)(ii), 1396r(c)(5)(A)(ii); 42 C.F.R. § 483.12(d)(2).

Older persons, desperate to stay in their homes and not move to a nursing home, try to make financial arrangements to be cared for in their homes. This is not necessarily a wise idea.

Clifton B. Kruse, Jr.

Contracts to Devise or Gift Property in Exchange for Lifetime Home Care—Latent and Insidious Abuse of Older Persons

I. Introduction—The Problem

A promise to execute a will, not to revoke a will, or to die intestate, such that a relative or home care provider benefits at the time of an elder's death, appears attractive to many older persons. The option of receiving personal care services in one's own home

Probate Law Journal, Vol. 12 (1994). Reprinted by permission.

in exchange for an agreement to devise property to the person promising care appears to many older persons to be preferable to living and dying in an institution.

Agreements to provide end-life care in elders' own homes in exchange for contracts to devise property have resulted in a significant amount of litigation throughout the country. Case law discloses that disquieting consequences sometimes result from such arrangements.

The *Boston Globe* addressed this issue in a three-part series appearing May 17–19, 1992. The first part, entitled "Elderly Face Peril in Trading Homes for Care,"[1] gave the following example of some problems that can result from home-care agreements for the elderly:

> The policeman standing in the bedroom doorway thought she was dead, she lay so still. At the bedside, her niece pleaded with her to wake up, shouting and then shaking her. Finally, Jane Rood stirred under heavy blankets drawn up to her chin. "Hot, hot," she murmured.

The ninety-one-year-old widow was found comatose and all alone on a sweltering day last summer because she had trusted a home care worker with her life.

Only a few years ago, Rood had a fat bank account, a monthly income to meet her needs, and a large picture window that looked out on a groomed yard with her signature parked in the driveway: a 1952 gray Buick, a big old car that she drove—barely seeing over the steering wheel—to the post office most days until her stroke in 1988.

Yet this self-assured patrician, who grew up on Fifth Avenue in New York City, wound up a penniless prisoner in her Lincoln home. One day last spring, a cleaning woman found her alone and crying because she had not been cared for all day and had soiled her bedclothes.

How did it happen?

How did a refined, educated, well-to-do widow wind up broke and abandoned in a house no longer her own?

Ironically, like many other widows in similar predicaments, she lost control of her beloved house through a desperate attempt to stay there forever. She gave it away to a health aid worker in exchange for daily care that she could no longer afford from a full-time nursing service costing $72,000 a year.

Unfortunately, the home care worker, Linda Douglas of Sudbury, did not have enough money to make the deal work, either.

Struggling financially, Douglas began farming out Rood's care to part-time help so she could work as a real estate broker during the day—even though she had contracted to be with Rood while she was "awake." One of the workers blew the whistle on Douglas last June out of fear that Rood was dying of starvation.

Specialists in elder care say that it is an increasingly common sign of the times, especially in suburban settings: infirm widows with mortgage-free houses and dwindling funds trade their homes for care and wind up with neither.[2]

* * *

II. Validity of Lifecare Contracts—Contractual and Testamentary Principles

A. Validity

A contract to will property to another in exchange for future services is valid and enforceable. "A person may agree to, and . . . may validly bind himself or herself to make a particular reasonable testamentary disposition in exchange for services."[3]

Absent wrongful behavior, persons who rely upon a promise to be given property by will in exchange for living with and assisting the promisors for the remainder of their lives may enforce the agreement. Such an arrangement is not contrary to public policy.[4] The Georgia Supreme Court wrote that contracts under which one of the contracting parties agrees with the other, for a valuable consideration, that he or she will make a will giving property to the other . . . either real or personal, have been sustained and enforced in America from the earliest times, and the validity of such contracts seems now to be beyond all doubt.[5] Such contracts may or may not serve a useful purpose for aged people.[6]

* * *

Abuse of older persons occurs in a variety of ways. Where caregivers provide for them in the elders' own homes, a confidential and intimate relationship results, as does dependency. Advanced age, contributing to physical and mental disabilities, results in a servient relationship for the elder. Importunity may result in the caregiver's benefitting in a way which was not contemplated at the time the contract for services was arranged and which is neither beneficial to nor appropriate for the elder. Numerous cases evidence wrongful influence, duress, and fraud by those who live with and hold themselves out to serve the elder population. Agreements make it possible for caregivers to leverage their deficient promisors in order to take advantage of them, to be divisive of their families, and to receive unfair benefits by gift or will. No court supervises, and often no relative inquires into, the milieu that evolves. Where, however, undue influence, fraud, or duress can be shown, the advantage taken by the provider can be set aside.

IV. Remedies for Wrongful Behavior by Caregivers of Older Persons

A. Constructive Trusts of Property Wrongfully Acquired by Caregiver Beneficiaries[7]

One cannot retain property acquired by wrongdoing. Where elder patients are wrongfully induced by caregivers to gift or devise property to those providing care, courts in equity may impose constructive trusts on the property in favor of the elders' intended beneficiaries. A constructive trust is a trust created by operation of law against one who by actual or constructive fraud, duress, abuse of confidence, commission of wrong, or any form of unconscionable conduct or other questionable means, has obtained or kept a legal right to property which he or she should not, in equity and good conscience, hold and enjoy.[8] It is a relationship which subjects the person holding title to property to an equitable duty to convey it to another on the ground that the title holder's acquisition or retention of the property is wrongful and that he or she would be unjustly enriched if permitted to retain it.[9] Wrongful behavior by the beneficiary inducing a will may not be a ground for refusing probate, but is a ground for imposition of a constructive trust on the property received by wrongdoing.[10]

Where an equitable remedy is requested, the party seeking to enforce the contract must demonstrate that the contract is fair and just. Fairness is normally determined as of the date the contract was made.[11] Service contracts where a decedent has agreed to devise property in exchange for a life care arrangement will not be enforced if they are harsh and inequitable.

A constructive trust will be erected whenever necessary to satisfy equity. . . . A constructive trust is merely "the formula through which the conscience of equity finds expression." . . . Its applicability is limited only by the inventiveness of persons who find new ways to enrich themselves unjustly by grasping what should not belong to them.[12]

* * *

In a recent case, *Herston v. Austin*,[13] a seventy-three-year-old woman, not in good health, transferred her home and savings to her son in response to his promise to support her. For several years, the son made the promised support payments—the income from the transferor's savings. Then, following an argument with his mother, he stopped making the payments. The Alabama court found that the son had indeed promised to provide for his mother, and that his promise was consideration for delivery of her property to him. The court imposed a constructive trust on the property. The case was decided under an Alabama statute that allows a grantor to void a contract for support without cause except as to bona fide purchasers and lienors.

* * *

C. Presumption that Services by Persons in Close Consanguinity are Rendered Gratuitously

Where services are performed by those in a close family relationship to the beneficiary, they may be legally presumed gratuitous.[14] The burden of proof is on the relative-claimant seeking compensation for services rendered to prove the agreement. A claimant's eleven and a half years of uncompensated services for her mother and brothers went unrewarded because this burden could not be met and the presumption overcome.[15]

* * *

The presumption may be overcome by evidence that the beneficiary of the services intends payment. Thus, a decedent's writing that "I want all personal property and real estate to go to my sister, Ethel, at my death according to our contract wherein she agreed to nurse and wait on me as long as I live. signed W. M. J. Moore," though not a will, was adequate evidence of the agreement for nursing service.[16]

Where a long-term social companionship changes to a relationship of patient and nursemaid, the presumption that services are rendered gratuitously will not apply. In *Estate of Zent*,[17] the decedent and the claimant enjoyed a social relationship for approximately ten years. They saw each other each day but maintained separate residences. For the last several years of the decedent's life, he suffered from Alzheimer's disease and required nursing attention. The relationship between the decedent and his companion changed from a social relationship to one of patient and caregiver. The decedent's companion provided personal services for him. She took care of his household needs and his personal hygiene, including problems resulting from his incontinence. The court determined that the services were not provided gratuitously. The presumption of gratuitous services did not apply since the caregiver was not a family member and the couple did not live together as husband and wife.[18]

D. Tortious Interference with the Rights of Family to Inherit

A caregiver who by fraud, duress, undue influence, or other tortious activity purposefully prevents another from receiving an inheritance (or gift) that such person would otherwise have received has interfered with an advantageous relationship. The injured party's loss may be recoverable in tort for wrongful interference with an expectation to inherit.[19]

Injury to an expectancy to inherit can occur when a caregiver benefits himself or herself by procuring a will from an elder, preventing a change in an existing will, causing an elder to revoke or amend a will, destroying a will, or obtaining inter vivos conveyances of an elder's property.

To plead a cause of action for tortious interference with the expectancy to inherit, five elements are commonly viewed as essential:

(a) existence of an expectancy;
(b) intentional interference with the expectancy by another;
(c) conduct by another which is tortious in itself (e.g., involving fraud, duress, or undue influence);
(d) reasonable certainty that the expectancy would have been received but for the interference; and
(e) actual loss.[20]

* * *

In *Davison v. Feuerherd*,[21] Elizabeth Davison, the stepdaughter of the decedent, Delia Obrig, alleged that Obrig's personal care providers engaged in tortious interference with Davison's expected inheritance. The decedent had helped rear Mrs. Davison. Delia Obrig died on December 3, 1977, leaving an estate of $160,000. The decedent's historical estate plan, structured in a revocable trust, had left most of her trust estate to her stepdaughter.

In the late summer of 1977, when Mrs. Obrig was eighty years old, the Davisons began to care for her. She was lonely, drinking alcohol daily, and was in poor physical health. The Davisons visited her each day, prepared her meals, cleaned her house, did her laundry, and took her to the doctor. . . . Mrs. Obrig was easily influenced and guided by any person upon whom she was dependent and with whom she was closely associated. She was hardly capable of exercising independent judgment . . . and Mrs. Obrig became dependent upon the Feuerherds.[22]

After the Feuerherds began caring for her, Mrs. Obrig instructed her lawyer to revise her trust; all property was to pass to her stepdaughter. Upon learning of this, the care providers "falsely persuaded her that her stepdaughter did not love her, was not concerned about her, and was not worthy of receiving her estate."[23] They told her that they were the only ones who cared for or looked after her, that they should be rewarded by being left her estate, and that they would withdraw the care and comfort upon which she had become dependent if she did not amend the trust to leave her estate to them.

Elizabeth Davison alleged that the Feuerherds tortiously interfered with her expected inheritance. The five elements commonly found necessary to satisfy the tort were present:

(a) since Elizabeth Davison was the nearest relative and a beneficiary in the Obrig estate plan for most of her life, the expectancy of inheritance was real;
(b) the Feuerherds interfered with that expectancy by making false statements about her;
(c) the Feuerherds' conduct was itself tortious, fraudulent, and wrongfully influential;
(d) Mrs. Obrig's intent to execute a revised trust benefitting her stepdaughter at the time of the Feuerherds' wrongful, intentional, and self-interested persuasion evidenced the reasonable certainty of the expectancy; and
(e) the Feuerherds' influence and fraud resulted in the stepdaughter's loss.

The case was remanded by the appellate court. The cause of action in tort was validated.

* * *

Where home care providers have abused their elder patients by wrongfully arranging to receive disproportionate gifts or inheritance in exchange for services, the elder charge, family members, and beneficiaries who would otherwise receive the elders' estates are not without remedies. Constructive trusts, a response of equity, are available; claims filed in the deceased promisors' estates may be resisted; and the relatively new tort of interference with the right to inherit may be available to injured parties. Beyond that, relief may be available under criminal statutes where a state recognizes the wrongdoing as egregious.

* * *

Notes

1. Gerard O'Neil, Elderly Face Peril in Trading Homes for Care, Boston Globe, May 17, 1992, at 1.

2. *Id.*; see also 4 ElderLaw Rep., Feb. 1993, at 5 (discussing lawsuit against Jane Rood's attorneys for failing to exercise reasonable care in protecting her interests when it was foreseeable that injury to her and plaintiff, her relative, would result). Cf. Lawrence A. Frolik, Elder Law 1122 (1992) ("The great majority of incidents of elderly abuse and neglect are caused by caregivers . . . ").

3. 4 ElderLaw Rep., July/Aug. 1993, at 6 (discussing Robitaille v. Robitaille, 613 N.E.2d 933 (Mass. App. Ct. 1993)). See also 1 Page on Wills § 10.1 nn.2 & 2(a) (Bowe & Parker, eds., 1992 Cum. Supp.) (collecting numerous cases); 79 Am. Jur. 2d Wills § 327, et seq. (1993). Regarding the validity of mutual wills, but not in the context of an exchange for services, see Estate of Aimone, 590 N.E.2d 94 (Ill. App. Ct. 1992); Wright v. Wright, 832 S.W.2d 542 (Tenn. App. 1992). The benefit the caregiver receives in exchange for services is taxable income. Metz v. United States, 933 F.2d 802 (10th Cir. 1991), aff'g 1989—2 U.S. Tax Cas. (CCH) P 13,822 (D. Kan. 1989), discussed in 3 Prob. Prac. Rep., Aug. 1991, at 12.

4. Estate of Beauchamp, 564 P.2d 908, 910 (Ariz. Ct. App. 1977); Cagle v. Justus, 28 S.E.2d 255, 258 (Ga. 1943).

5. Mann v. Moseley, 67 S.E.2d 128, 129 (Ga. 1951).

6. 79 Am. Jur. 2d, *supra* note 3, § 328.

7. For an insightful analysis of constructive trusts for the benefit of the caregiver where the promisor, now deceased, has alienated the promised devise, see Daniel S. Field, Will Contracts for Personal Services and Real Property During the Lifetime of the Aging Devisor: Resolving the Continuing Dilemma, 11 Prob. L.J. 57, 59 n.8 (1992).

8. Davis v. Howard, 527 P.2d 422, 424 (Or. Ct. App. 1974).

9. [Restatement (Second) of Trusts], § 1(e) t. c (1959).]; 5 Scott on Trusts, §§ 488, 489 (Fratcher, 4th ed. 1991).

10. *Id.* § 489.2. Restatement of Restitution, § 184, cmt. i (1937); 1 Pomeroy, Equity Jurisprudence, ... See also 66 A.L.R. 156 (1930) (collecting early cases); 155 A.L.R. 106 (1945) (collecting early cases).

11. See Mann v. Moseley, 67 S.E.2d 128, 130 (Ga. 1951).

12. Latham v. Father Divine, 85 N.E.2d 168, 170 (N.Y. 1949), reh'g denied, 86 N.E.2d 114 (citing Beatty v. Guggenheim Exploration Co., 122 N.E. 378, 380 (N.Y. 1919)). See also Estate of Beauchamp, 564 P.2d 908 (Ariz. Ct. App. 1977); In re Nutt's Estate, 185 P. 393 (Cal. 1919); Baltimore Humane Impartial Socy. v. Pierce, 60 A. 277 (Md. 1905); Pope v. Garrett, 211 S.W.2d 559 (Tex. 1948).

13. 603 So. 2d 976 (Ala. 1992).

14. There is a strong public policy favoring a marital support duty. Borelli v. Brusseau, 16 Cal. Rptr. 2d 16, 19 (Ct. App. 1993). See Clifton B. Kruse, Jr., The Effect of Relational Intimacy on Estate Claims, 21 Colo. Law. 699 (1992). For an analysis of the income tax consequences of contracts made in exchange for services by caregivers, see Metz v. United States, 933 F.2d 802, 802 (10th Cir.), cert. denied, 112 S. Ct. 416 (1991). The family member rule was not applied where the sibling-caregiver resided in a separate household three doors away from the elder. Kroeger v. Ryder, 621 N.E.2d 534 (Ohio Ct. App. 1993).

15. Haddix, 320 N.W.2d at 745. Cf. Craddock v. Berryman, 645 P.2d 399 (Mont. 1982).

16. Rose v. Reese, 160 S.W.2d 614 (Ky. Ct. App. 1941). Cf. In re Estate of Clausen, 366 N.E.2d 162, 163 (Ill. App. Ct. 1972).

17. 459 N.W.2d 795 (N.D. 1990).

18. *Id.* at 800. See also In re Napoli's Will, 110 N.Y.S.2d 406 (Sur. Ct. 1952) (housekeeper-

employer relationship was rebutted by showing that the caregiver and testator cohabited and that cohabitation resulted in the birth of two children). A daughter-in-law recovered for services rendered to her mother-in-law in Schaeffer v. Shenton, 1992 Ohio App. LEXIS 5702 (Nov. 12, 1992); but see Krichau v. Jacobsen, 501 N.W.2d 722 (Neb. 1992), (denying claim by daughter-in-law for services rendered to her father-in-law).

19. See [Restatement (Second) of Torts . . . cmt. (1965)], § 774B; 1 Page on Wills, *supra* note 3, § 24.4; Alvin E. Evans, Torts to Expectancies in Decedents' Estates, 93 U. Pa. L. Rev. 187 (1944); 2 Prob. Prac. Rep. 1, 1–4 (March 1990); Sonja A. Soehnel, Annotation, Liability in Damages for Interference with Expected Inheritance or Gift, 22 A.L.R.4th 1229 (1983); Peffer v. Bennett, 523 F.2d 1323 (10th Cir. 1975) (applying Colorado law); McGregor v. McGregor, 101 F. Supp. 848 (D. Colo. 1951); Allen v. Leybourne, 190 So. 2d 825 (Fla. Dist. Ct. App. 1966); In re Estate of Knowlson, 507 N.E.2d 28 (Ill. App. Ct. 1987); Harmon v. Harmon, 404 A.2d 1020 (Me. 1979); Neill v. Yett, 746 S.W.2d 32 (Tex. Ct. App. 1988); King v. Acker, 725 S.W.2d 750 (Tex. Ct. App. 1987); Teague v. Stephens, 564 S.W.2d 437 (Tex. Ct. App. 1978). See also Estate of Hann v. Hann, 614 N.E.2d 973 (Ind. Ct. App. 1993). In Hann, the decedent made an agreement with her brother-in-law, with whom she lived following the death of her husband. Since the arrangement was for their mutual benefit no presumption arose of a contract to pay for services. There was no promise to pay for services and the court would not imply such a contract where the parties had lived together for many years and were "close."

20. See 39 Am. Jur. Proof of Facts 177, § 4 (1984); 2 Prob. Prac. Rep., 1, 1–4 (March 1990). See also In re Estate of Knowlson, 562 N.E.2d 277 (Ill. App. Ct. 1990); In re Estate of Knowlson, 507 N.E.2d 28 (Ill. App. Ct. 1987); Greene v. First Nat'l Bank, 516 N.E.2d 311, appeal denied, 522 N.E.2d 1244 (Ill. App. Ct. 1987); Nemeth v. Banhalmi, 425 N.E.2d 1187, 1188 (Ill. App. Ct. 1981); Pope v. Garrett, 211 S.W.2d 559, 559 (Tex. 1948) (elements of the tort expressed generically as duty, breach of duty, injury and proximate cause); Soehnel, *supra* note 19, at 1233.

21. 391 So. 2d 799 (Fla. Dist. Ct. App. 1980).

22. *Id.* at 800.

23. *Id.*

Part VII

Health Care Finance

Unlike life insurance, health care insurance is not something most people are used to buying. Younger persons generally obtain health care insurance as an employment related benefit, sometimes paid for at least in part by the employer. Upon retirement, however, most Americans lose their health care insurance. For older individuals, paying for health care is perhaps the single greatest financial concern. Without adequate insurance the cost of health care is prohibitive. Some retirees are covered by union contracts that call for the continuation of health care benefits, but for most workers retirement means the termination of health care insurance. Thus arises the need for Medicare, the federally subsidized health care insurance program.

CHAPTER 33

Medicare

A. Introduction

Before Medicare was passed in 1965, over half of the elderly had no health insurance. By the mid-1990s Medicare provided health care insurance for over 97 percent of all individuals over sixty-five. Although Medicare has no means test for eligibility, the great majority of Medicare expenditures aid lower income older persons. In 1992, 83 percent of Medicare spending was on behalf of beneficiaries with annual incomes of less than $25,000.

Medicare has an enormous impact on health expenditures in general. Because of its size, and particularly because of these supplemental payments, any change in Medicare payment plans or rights to beneficiaries has a profound effect on the shape and character of the delivery of health care.

For example, in 1993 Medicare accounted for 28 percent of all hospital expenditures; 20 percent of physician expenditures; the great preponderance of income for home health care agencies, hospices, and renal dialysis facilities; and a significant share of the revenues of clinics, laboratories, ambulances services, and the like. In addition, to ensure adequate hospital availability for the older, insured population, Medicare provides special financial support to hundreds of hospitals across the country. A number of these hospitals might well have closed without this additional support payment. (The support payments began in the mid-1980s when Congress became concerned about the survival of rural hospitals and hospitals with a disproportionate share of Medicare patients.) Medicare also makes supplemental payments to hospitals that have a disproportionate share of low income individuals and teaching hospitals (because of the extra cost associated with medical education). By 1995 over 12 percent of the $65 billion Medicare bill were payments for these additional purposes.

Medicare has been greatly criticized for its apparently unending increase in costs, even though Medicare spending per enrollee increased less rapidly than private health care spending from 1981 through 1993. However, because Medicare is an insurance program aimed at the oldest and sickest members of society, it is not surprising that its costs have risen precipi-

tously. Certainly Medicare does not spend unduly on administrative overhead, which runs at less than 2 percent for Medicare compared to an average of around 17 percent for private health care insurance companies.

Medicare did not "just happen." It was a political solution to how to pay for health care for older, retired individuals. As part of a larger article, Professor Crimm describes the context of the current health care financing system for those age sixty-five and older.

Nina J. Crimm

Tax Plans for the Twenty-First Century: Medical Incentive Vouchers Address the Needs of Academic Health Centers and the Elderly

* * *

2. Effects of Aging on Health Care Costs and Expenditures

Health care expenditures for older persons are dramatically higher than for the population in general and account for a disproportionately high share of Americans' overall health care costs.[1] Health care expenditures for the elderly are projected to increase tremendously in the future due in large part to the anticipated growth in population of the oldest old.[2] This projection reflects the fact that the older and oldest old use substantially more health care resources than do younger elderly persons.[3] The high level of medical costs for the elderly is attributable to the final few years of life.[4] Nearly 30 percent of Medicare expenditures are used to treat people in the last year of life, with the greatest portion of such costs arising in the last month.[5] While some researchers have connected these costs to the medical care given to those dying in hospitals,[6] others have suggested that the majority of these expenses are associated with nursing-home care.[7] In either case, as older Americans continue to comprise a steadily increasing proportion of the overall population, health care costs for both acute and long-term care will escalate.[8]

Health care costs for the elderly are paid through a patchwork of funding vehicles. Less than 60 percent of such costs are covered by government programs such as

Originally published in *Tulane Law Review*, Vol. 71, No. 3, 653 (February 1997), the Tulane Law Review Association.

Medicare and Medicaid.[9] The remainder is paid by private insurance or out of pocket, often leaving the elderly with an overwhelming financial burden.[10] These out-of-pocket payments by older persons have grown substantially in recent years.[11]

a. Acute Care

In the acute care sector, the rate of growth of hospital costs has reached near-historic levels.[12] Population aging has an effect on health care expenditures that can be related to some extent to hospital care.[13] Within the next forty years, the aged could account for 56 percent of hospital expenditures while the share for the young could comprise only 6 percent.[14] Approximately two-thirds of patients at acute care hospitals are over sixty-five years of age, and stays for these patients may last several months.[15] When young and elderly patients are compared, the differences in their acute care charges are attributable both to the elders' lengthier hospital confinements and the greater severity of their illnesses.[16]

b. Long-Term Care

Although one of the primary goals of our public health care system, especially Medicare, has been to safeguard the elderly against financial ruin in their later years, senior citizens personally spend more on health care now than they had prior to the enactment of Medicare.[17] This sobering fact is attributed in large part to tremendous increases in both the cost of and spending for health care.[18] Another significant factor is Medicare's lack of coverage of long-term care expenses.[19] Inadequate public health care funding for the elderly is troublesome because long-term care comprises an increasingly large share of health care expenditures for the elderly.[20]

* * *

As the number of elderly in need of long-term care rises, the costs of long-term care will increase as well. Research estimates current expenditures for nursing-home and home-care services for the elderly at approximately $42 billion.[21] These costs could nearly triple by 2018 and might roughly triple again by 2048.[22] During the 1960–1990 period, spending for nursing-home care services alone increased at an annual average rate of 14.2 percent[23] and more than doubled as a percentage of national health care expenditures.[24] By 2030, nursing-home care expenditures may be twice that in 1990.[25]

Nursing-home care services generally are not covered by private health insurance or by Medicare, and Medicaid coverage is contingent on need.[26] As a result, out-of-pocket expenditures are substantial for these services, comprising more than 50 percent of the per capita health care spending for persons over sixty-five years of age.[27]

Not surprisingly, the cost of long-term care can result in financial catastrophe for some older persons.[28] As a result of out-of-pocket expenditures for health care, the retirement incomes of many elderly persons are threatened.[29] As the large population of baby boomers enter the elderly cohort during the early- and mid-twenty-first century, their security may be imperiled if, as predicted, their retirement savings are insufficient to cover health care costs.[30] Thus, demographic trends and the anticipated health status of the future elderly, coupled with the rising cost of health care and the intensity of services required, will increase substantially the need for society to contribute financial resources to long-term care services for the elderly.[31]

* * *

Notes

1. Personal health care expenditures (PHCE) for the overall population have risen steadily since the 1960s—with growth at a fairly consistent 10.5% annually between 1960 and 1970, 13% annually between 1970 and 1980, and 10.3% annually between 1980 and 1990. *See* Katharine R. Levit et al., *National Health Expenditures, 1990*, 13 HEALTH CARE FIN. REV. 29, 30–32 (1991). For the elderly, PHCE grew at an annual rate of 13.5% during the 1977 to 1987 period. *See* [Daniel R. Waldo et al., *Health Expenditures by Age Group, 1977 and 1987*, 10 HEALTH CARE FIN. REV. 111, 112–14 (1989) (hereinafter Waldo et al., *Health Expenditures by Age Group*)]. In 1987, the elderly comprised 12% of the population but accounted for over 36% of all health care expenditures. [CONGRESSIONAL BUDGET OFFICE, TRENDS IN HEALTH SPENDING: AN UPDATE 14 (1993) (hereinafter TRENDS IN HEALTH SPENDING)] (indicating households headed by elderly directly spent approximately three times more for medical services than those households not headed by the elderly). However, the extent to which rising per capita health care expenditures are attributable to the changing age composition of the population has been questioned. [Thomas E. Getzen, *Population Aging and the Growth of Health Expenditures*, 47 J. GERONTOLOGY S98, S98–104 (Supp. 1992) (finding that population aging is associated with higher health spending only if no other variables are permitted in the equation, but that such an outcome is due to secondary association of aging with rising per capita income and other omitted variables, which, when controlled, indicate no discernible association between age and health care costs)].

While statistical projections regarding the expected growth of the elderly population are cited throughout this Article, it should be noted that several factors can skew these predictions. For example, projections by the Census Bureau show that the total elderly population will increase to over 65 million by 2050 under a middle mortality assumption. *See* [GREGORY SPENCER, U.S. DEP'T OF COMMERCE, PROJECTIONS OF THE POPULATION OF THE UNITED STATES BY AGE, SEX, AND RACE: 1988 TO 2080, at 7–8 (1989) (hereinafter 1989 CENSUS) (projecting the elderly population will exceed 65 million by 2050)]. If future mortality rates are higher or lower than expected, the projected elderly population by 2050 could range anywhere from over 57 million to nearly 87.5 million. *See id.* [Remainder of note omitted.]

The expected growth in health spending is also subject to fluctuation due to changes in economic conditions. For example, the CBO lowered its projections of overall inflation through the year 2000. As a result, health spending is expected to be $66 billion less in the year 2000 than the 1992 published projection for the year 2000. *See* [CONGRESSIONAL BUDGET OFFICE, PROJECTIONS OF NATIONAL HEALTH EXPENDITURES: 1993 UPDATE 2 (1993) (hereinafter HEALTH EXPENDITURES PROJECTIONS: 1993 UPDATE) (stating that federal spending on health care will grow to over 20% by 2003)]. The bottom line, however, remains the same—while varying slightly in degree, all statistics have indicated a tremendous increase in the growth of the elderly population and a concomitant surge in health care costs.

2. [*See* Edward L. Schneider & Jack M. Guralnik, *The Aging of America: Impact on Health Care*

Costs, 263 JAMA 2335, 2335-36 (1990) (citing Census Bureau statistics); *See* [HUMAN RESOURCES DIV., U.S. GEN. ACCOUNTING OFFICE, LONG-TERM CARE: PROJECTED NEEDS OF THE AGING BABY BOOM GENERATION, H.R. DOC. NO. 91-86, at 2 (1991) [hereinafter PROJECTED NEEDS]]. The report predicts the next century will see unprecedented growth in the elderly population. As of 1992, 12.4% of the population was 65 years of age or over. See id. By 2015, that figure is expected to rise to 14.6%, reflecting the entrance of the baby boom generation into the elderly category, and by 2030, the baby boomers will enter their seventies and eighties, and the elderly will comprise 20.1% of the overall population. *See id.*]

3. See [Dennis W. Jahnigen & Robert H. Binstock, *Economic and Clinical Realities: Health Care for Elderly People, in* Too Old for Health Care? *13, 18–19 (Robert H. Binstock & Stephen G. Post eds., 1991)]. For example, in a recent year persons aged 65 and older reportedly accounted for 40.5% of the days of care in "short-stay" hospitals (as opposed to those specializing in caring for chronic-disease patients) in the United States. See id.* Within that aggregate, those aged 85 and older used hospitals at a rate that is 12% higher than that of those aged 65 to 74, and persons aged 75 to 84 used hospitals at a rate 69% higher than persons aged 65 to 74. *See id.*

As a group, the elderly are relatively more passive than younger generations in their use of health care services and, further, less likely to take cost into account when deciding to seek care. *See* Edward C. Weeks & Judith H. Hibbard, *Consumer Cost Conscious Behavior, Utilization, and Health Care Expenditures among an Elderly Population,* J. HEALTH & HUMAN RESOURCES ADMIN. 340, 341 (1992) (citing Judith H. Hibbard & Edward C. Weeks, *Consumerism in Health Care: Prevalence and Predictors,* 25 HEALTH CARE 1019 (1987)).

4. *See* ROBERT P. RHODES, HEALTH CARE POLITICS, POLICY, AND DISTRIBUTIVE JUSTICE 91 (1992).

5. *See* Gerald F. Riley & James D. Lubitz, *Longitudinal Patterns of Medicare Use by Cause of Death,* 11 HEALTH CARE FIN. REV. 1, 9–10 (1989); Noralou P. Roos et al., *Health Care Utilization in the Years Prior to Death,* 65 MILBANK Q. 231, 231 (1987).

6. *See* [Victor R. Fuchs, *"Though Much Is Taken": Reflections on Aging, Health, and Medical Care,* 62 MILBANK Q. 143, 146–47 (1984)].

7. *See* RHODES, *supra* note 4, at 91; Charlene Harrington, *The Nursing Home Industry: A Structural Analysis, in* CRITICAL PERSPECTIVES ON AGING: THE POLITICAL AND MORAL ECONOMY OF GROWING OLD 153, 155 (Meredith Minkler & Carroll L. Estes eds., 1991) (stating that in 1990 the cost of nursing home care was third highest in the health care sector after hospital and physician costs, due in part to use of high technology).

8. Public sources such as Medicare and Medicaid pay for a significant portion of health care consumption for the elderly (63% during the period 1977–87). By contrast, private sources pay for much of the care for persons under 65 (74% during the period 1977–87). *See* [Daniel R. Waldo et al., *Health Expenditures by Age Group, 1977 and 1987,* 10 HEALTH CARE FIN. REV. 111, 112–14 (1989) (hereinafter Waldo et al., *Health Expenditures by Age Group*)]. As a result, public spending on health care will spiral as the elderly population grows. *See* [Edward L. Schneider & Jack M. Guralnik, *The Aging of America: Impact on Health Care Costs,* 263 JAMA 2335, 2335–36 (1990) (citing Census Bureau statistics)]. Medicare expenditures should reach nearly $175 billion by 2040, a figure more than double that spent in 1987. *See id.* at 2338 fig.4. Additionally, the cost of nursing home care will increase from $31.1 billion in 1985 to nearly $110 billion (in 1985 dollars) by 2040. *See id.* at 2338 fig.5.

9. *See* [SPECIAL SENATE COMM. ON AGING, DEVELOPMENTS IN AGING: 1993, S. Rep. No. 103-403, at 132, 134 (1993), (hereinafter DEVELOPMENTS IN AGING)] (stating Medicare accounted for

57% of all federal health spending in 1990 and for 17% of national health expenditures in 1990); [CONGRESSIONAL BUDGET OFFICE, TRENDS IN HEALTH SPENDING: AN UPDATE 14 (1993) (hereinafter TRENDS IN HEALTH SPENDING)] (indicating that between 1980 and 1991, the federal government paid for 29%–31% of all PHCEs and state and local governments paid 10%–13%); [Dennis W. Jahnigen & Robert H. Binstock, *Economic and Clinical Realities: Health Care for Elderly People, in* TOO OLD FOR HEALTH CARE? 13, 18–19 (Robert H. Binstock & Stephen G. Post eds., 1991)] (indicating that Medicare pays 40% and Medicaid and other governmental programs pay 18%).

10. The aged spend over 25% out-of-pocket for personal health care, while private insurance covers only about 7%. *See* [SPECIAL SENATE COMM. ON AGING, DEVELOPMENTS IN AGING: 1993, S. Rep. No. 103-403, at 132, 134 (1993), (hereinafter DEVELOPMENTS IN AGING). Currently, the costs of home health care and nursing home care are not covered by Medicare, which generally places this financial burden on the elderly themselves and on their families. See Roxanne Jamshidi et al., *Aging in America: Limits to Life Span and Elderly Care Options,* 2 POPULATION RES. & POL'Y REV. 169, 173 (1992); see also infra note 11 and accompanying text]; *cf.* STAFF OF HOUSE COMM. ON WAYS AND MEANS, 102D CONG., HEALTH CARE RESOURCE BOOK 96 (Comm. Print 1991) [hereinafter HEALTH CARE RESOURCE BOOK] (stating that approximately three percent of the elderly rely on health insurance coverage from nonMedicare sources but that 76% have supplemental coverage). Moreover, on a per capita basis the elderly spend over 50% out-of-pocket for nursing home care. *See id.* Most health care costs for the elderly which are not covered by Medicare or Medicaid likewise are not covered by private insurance. *See supra* note 30. This is due in part to the failure of the private insurance market to offer affordable nursing home or other long-term elder care insurance. *See* [RICHARD A. POSNER, AGING AND OLD AGE 46 (1995)], at 285. One explanation for the lack of affordable long-term health care insurance is poor demand for such insurance. Rather than purchase such coverage, many elderly persons spend down their assets in order to qualify for Medicaid-supported, state-provided, free nursing home care. *See* Mark V. Pauly, *The Rational Nonpurchase of Long-Term-Care Insurance,* 98 J. POL. ECON. 153, 154 (1990). Other factors contributing to private insurers' reluctance to enter the long-term care market include the risk that claims costs will exceed premium revenues because only those likely to use services will buy insurance; the risk that, once insured, people will overstate their disability to take advantage of additional services; and the risk that the cost of services will increase between the time insurance is purchased and the time it is used. *See* Judith Feder, *Health Care of the Disadvantaged: The Elderly,* 15 J. HEALTH POL. POL'Y & L. 259, 267 (1990).

For an in-depth analysis of the underlying causes for and attitudes toward consumer demand for long-term care insurance, *see* Marc A. Cohen et al., *Who Buys Long-Term Care Insurance?,* 11 HEALTH AFF. 208, 208–23 (1992).

11. For example, these payments more than tripled between 1977 and 1988. *See* [Dennis W. Jahnigen & Robert H. Binstock, *Economic and Clinical Realities: Health Care for Elderly People, in* TOO OLD FOR HEALTH CARE? 13, 18–19 (Robert H. Binstock & Stephen G. Post eds., 1991)]; *see also* infra notes 26–30 and accompanying text; Peter J. Strauss, *Legal and Financial Issues in Long-Term Care Planning, in* PLANNING FOR AGING OR INCAPACITY 1993, at 208 (1993) (noting that today's elderly pay more out-of-pocket for personal health care than in 1965).

12. *See* Larry M. Manheim & Joe Feinglass, *Hospital Cost Incentives in a Fragmented Health Care System,* 21 TOPICS HEALTH CARE FIN. 24, 25 (1994).

13. For example, in 1987, the aged accounted for 39% of hospital expenditures while comprising 12% of the population whereas the young accounted for only 11% of such expenditures

and comprised 29% of the total population. *See* [Daniel R. Waldo et al., *Health Expenditures by Age Group, 1977 and 1987,* 10 HEALTH CARE FIN. REV. 111, 112–14 (1989) (hereinafter Waldo et al., *Health Expenditures by Age Group*)]. Hospital usage rises sharply for those 85 and above when their usage is compared to that of 65- to 74-year-olds. *See* [Ira Rosenwaike, *A Demographic Portrait of the Oldest Old,* 63 MILBANK MEMORIAL FUND Q. 187, 188 (1985)].

14. *See* [Daniel R. Waldo et al., *Health Expenditures by Age Group, 1977 and 1987,* 10 HEALTH CARE FIN. REV. 111, 112-14 (1989) (hereinafter Waldo et al., *Health Expenditures by Age Group*)].

15. *See Not a New Business, but New Dynamics,* 23 LONG TERM CARE MGMT., 1994 WL 2616594, at *1 (Special Report, Jan. 12, 1994) [hereinafter *Not a New Business*]. In 1985, per capita hospital expenditures for the elderly were 252% greater than such expenditures for persons under 65-years-old. *See* Robert H. Binstock, *The Oldest Old: A Fresh Perspective or Compassionate Ageism Revisited?,* 63 MILBANK MEM. FUND Q. 420, 440 (1985). Use of hospital services by the oldest old in 1985 was 77% greater than that of persons 65- to 74-years-old and 23% higher than individuals 75- to 84-years-old. *See id.* (citing U.S. Senate Special Comm. on Aging 1984); *see also supra* note 13 for statistics on hospital stays of the elderly.

16. *See* U.S. DEP'T OF HEALTH AND HUMAN RESOURCES, PUBLIC HEALTH SERVICE, VITAL AND HEALTH STATISTICS, NATIONAL HOSPITAL DISCHARGE SURVEY: ANNUAL SUMMARY, 1993, at 4, 20–21; Gary E. Rosenthal & Seth Landefeld, *Do Older Medicare Patients Cost Hospitals More?,* 153 ARCHIVES INTERNAL MED. 89, 90–92 (1993); *see also supra* notes 13–15 for statistics on hospital usage by and stays of the elderly.

17. *See* Strauss, *supra* note 11, at 208.

18. For example, the $800.2 billion spent on health care in 1992 represented a 10% increase in spending over 1991 and the fifth consecutive year that health care costs increased by double-digit percentages. *See* Strauss, *supra* note 11, at 206. Moreover, since the number of people eligible for Medicare has grown more rapidly than has the general population, Medicare spending has risen at a rate substantially higher than the rate of national spending. By 1991, federal spending for Medicare had quintupled—reaching $122.8 billion—in comparison to the $25.2 billion spent in 1970. *See* [CONGRESSIONAL BUDGET OFFICE, TRENDS IN HEALTH SPENDING: AN UPDATE 14 (1993) (hereinafter TRENDS IN HEALTH SPENDING)]. By contrast, total national health expenditures during the same period tripled from $245.3 billion to $751.8 billion. *See id.* Some of the increased cost is attributable to the use of high technology. *See* Harrington, *supra* note 7, at 154–55. Recent governmental projections anticipate that the Medicare Hospital Trust Fund will be bankrupt by the year 2001, one year earlier than previously projected. *See* David E. Rosenbaum, *Gloomy Forecast Touches Off Feud on Medicare Fund,* N.Y. TIMES, June 6, 1996, at A1.

19. Medicare is acute- and skilled-care oriented and does not cover long-term or custodial expenses. Thus, while 69% of hospital expenses for the elderly and 60% of their physicians' fees are provided under Medicare, only 2% of nursing home charges and a small fraction of home health care expenses are covered. *See* Harrington, *supra* note 7, at 155; Strauss, *supra* note 11, at 209.

20. For example, by the mid-1980s there were already more patients in nursing homes on a daily basis than in acute-care hospitals. *See* [NATIONAL INST. ON AGING, DEP'T OF HEALTH AND HUMAN SERVS., PERSONNEL FOR HEALTH NEEDS OF THE ELDERLY THROUGH THE YEAR 2020, at 17 (1987) (hereinafter HEALTH NEEDS)].

21. *See* [HUMAN RESOURCES DIV., U.S. GEN. ACCOUNTING OFFICE, LONG-TERM CARE: PROJECTED NEEDS OF THE AGING BABY BOOM GENERATION, H.R. DOC. NO. 91-86, at 2 (1991) (hereinafter PROJECTED NEEDS)].

22. *See id.*

23. *See* HEALTH CARE RESOURCE BOOK, *supra* note 10, at 54.

24. *See id.* at 58.

25. *See* [Sally T. Burner et al., *National Health Expenditures Projections Through 2030,* 14 HEALTH CARE FIN. REV. 1, 2 (1992) (comparing 1990 with 2030 and concluding that the increase in elderly as a percentage of the total population will rise from 12.4% to 20.1% during that period)].

26. Only a small fraction of nursing home expenses are covered by either private or social insurance. *See* [Sheila Rafferty Zedlewski & Timothy D. McBride, *The Changing Profile of the Elderly: Effects on Future Long-Term Care Needs and Financing,* 70 MILBANK Q. 247, 256 (1992) (citing baseline projections of the Social Security Administration and projections by the Urban Institute's Dynamic Simulation of Income Model)]. Approximately 4%–5% of the elderly carry some type of private insurance that covers long-term care, and the average premium for long-term care insurance approaches the average cost of long-term care itself by the time an individual reaches age 75. *See* [Thomas D. Cain & James R. Webster, *Health Care Delivery for the Elderly—Reform or Revolution?,* COMPREHENSIVE THERAPY 481, 482 (1994)]. Although there is a small market for long-term care insurance, benefits are limited and typically are not adequately protected against inflation. Furthermore, many policies cover only a small fraction of the catastrophic expenses incurred late in life. *See supra* note 10 and accompanying text (discussing underlying reasons for lack of private long-term care insurance). *See generally* SUSAN VAN GELDER & DIANE JOHNSON, HEALTH INSURANCE ASSOCIATION OF AMERICA, LONG-TERM CARE INSURANCE: A MARKET UPDATE (1991).

Medicare covers some post-acute care in nursing homes, but not long stays. *See* [Peter Kemper & Christopher M. Murtaugh, *Lifetime Use of Nursing Home Care,* 324 NEW ENG. J. MED. 595, 596 (1991)]. This social insurance program reportedly pays only two percent of all long-term health care costs for the elderly. *See* Laura Pedersen, *Minding Your Business: Live Long! and Prosper, Too?,* N.Y. TIMES, Nov. 12, 1995, § 3, at 7. *But see* Zedlewski & McBride, *id*,. at 247 (stating that in 1987 Medicaid paid for over 33% of nursing home care expenses for the elderly).

Medicaid covers care for those who cannot afford to pay but requires that most assets and virtually all income be exhausted in order to meet eligibility criteria. *See* Letty Carpenter, *Medicaid Eligibility for Persons in Nursing Homes,* 10 HEALTH CARE FIN. REV. 67, 71–76 (1988); Korbin Liu et al., *Medicaid Spenddown in Nursing Homes,* 30 GERONTOLOGIST 7, 9–11 (1990); Pedersen, *supra,* § 3, at 7. In fact, the financially stringent eligibility requirements under the Medicaid laws have inspired books written specifically to guide people in obtaining Medicaid benefits. *See infra* note 28 (discussing Medicaid as an option for financing long-term health care). *See generally* ALEXANDER A. BOVE, JR., THE MEDICAID PLANNING HANDBOOK (2d ed. 1996); ARMOND D. BUDISH, AVOIDING THE MEDICAID TRAP: HOW EVERY AMERICAN CAN BEAT THE CATASTROPHIC COSTS OF NURSING HOME CARE (3d ed. 1995); KEN STERN, SAFEGUARD YOUR HARD-EARNED SAVINGS (1995).

Another perceived problem with Medicaid in relation to providing long-term care is that because states determine eligibility criteria and payment levels, benefits are not uniform throughout the country. *See* MALVIN SCHECHTER, BEYOND MEDICARE: ACHIEVING LONG-TERM CARE SECURITY 79 (1993). As a result, provision of geriatric care to all poor persons who require it is erratic and thus less effective. *See id.* Nevertheless, nearly 70 cents of every Medicaid dollar is spent on nursing home care. *See id.* Medicare, which is geared toward providing health care for the elderly, by contrast spends only about one cent of each dollar on nursing home care. *See id.* at 83.

27. *See* [SPECIAL SENATE COMM. ON AGING, DEVELOPMENTS IN AGING: 1993, S. Rep. No. 103-403, at 132, 134 (1993), (hereinafter DEVELOPMENTS IN AGING); Daniel R. Waldo et al., *Health Expenditures by Age Group, 1977 and 1987*, 10 HEALTH CARE FIN. REV. 111, 112–14 (1989) (hereinafter Waldo et al., *Health Expenditures by Age Group*)] (indicating that in 1987 nursing home care accounted for only 4% of total per capita health care spending for elderly age 65–69 but accounted for 41% of health care expenditures for elderly age 85 and over); *see also* HEALTH CARE RESOURCE BOOK, *supra* note 10, at 60. In 1965, out-of-pocket payments were the dominant source of funding for nursing home services, comprising 64.6% of all nursing home spending. In 1988, they were still the largest source of payment, accounting for 48% of total nursing home spending. *See id.*

28. In 1987, the House Budget Committee's Task Force on Health concluded that the annual cost of residence in a nursing home averaged about $25,000 while the median per capita income of elderly people was only $10,000. *See* [*Budget Issues Related to Long-Term Health Care Coverage: Hearings before the Task Force on Health of the House Comm. on the Budget*, 100th Cong. 165–67 (1987), (hereinafter *Budget Issues*) (statement of Nancy M. Gordon, Asst. Dir. Human Resources and Community Dev. Div., CBO). This financial burden persists—in 1993, the average annual cost of nursing home care was estimated at $30,000. *See* [SPECIAL SENATE COMM. ON AGING, DEVELOPMENTS IN AGING: 1993, S. Rep. No. 103-403, at 132, 134 (1993), (hereinafter DEVELOPMENTS IN AGING)]. Most of this cost is paid for out-of-pocket by individuals partly because Medicaid covers nursing home care only for persons who are unable to afford such care or who have become poor as a result of exhausting all of their income and resources on nursing home care. *See id.; see also supra* note 26 (noting strict Medicaid eligibility criteria). Another government study has reported that 63% of older persons would be impoverished within 13 weeks of entering a nursing home and 83% would be impoverished after a year. *See* HOUSE SELECT COMM. ON AGING, 99TH CONG., AMERICA'S ELDERLY AT RISK VII (Comm. Print 1985). For married couples, if one spouse entered a nursing home, 37% would be impoverished within a 13-week period, 57% after a year, and 80% after two years. *See id.* By the year 2030, despite anticipated substantial growth in the incomes of the elderly, only 10% of the elderly may be able to finance the cost of nursing home care from their incomes. *See* [Sheila Rafferty Zedlewski & Timothy D. McBride, *The Changing Profile of the Elderly: Effects on Future Long-Term Care Needs and Financing*, 70 MILBANK Q. 247, 256 (1992) (citing baseline projections of the Social Security Administration and projections by the Urban Institute's Dynamic Simulation of Income Model)].

Under our present system, the elderly essentially have three options for financing long-term health care—reliance on government funding primarily by qualifying for Medicaid, the purchase of long-term health insurance, and the payment of medical expenses from personal or family income and savings. The largest proportion of long-term health care payments are by Medicaid and out-of-pocket by individuals or their families. Payments for long-term care services in 1985 came almost equally from private sources (48%) and from federal, state, and local governments (52%). *See Budget Issues, id.*, at 22; Robin Toner, *Critics Say Republican Budget Will Create Shortage of Nursing Home Beds for Elderly*, N.Y. TIMES, Nov. 12, 1995, at 30; *see also supra* notes 9–11 and accompanying text.

The first option—qualifying for Medicaid—can be perceived as undignified because qualification for Medicaid requires an individual to be categorically needy, optionally categorically needy, or medically needy. *See* 42 U.S.C. § 1396(a) (1994); 42 C.F.R. §§ 435.100-.350 (1994). In essence, the individual must have only a minimal level of income (*i.e.*, be categorically needy), must fit into a specific medically needy group, or must have income which, at least on paper, is no greater than that of categorically needy individuals when large medical expenses are taken into account. Financial qualification might be accomplished by aggressive estate planning, whereby the individual may choose to divest himself of assets to qualify. This is a Hobson's choice for some individuals, because in order to afford long-term health care they must make themselves poor in order to rely on the basic welfare mechanism of Medicaid. *See* Carpenter, *supra* note 26, at 67; Liu et al., *supra* note 26, at 7; Note, *Medicaid Estate Planning: Congress's Ersatz Solution for Long-Term Health Care,* 44 CATH. U. L. REV. 1217, 1259 n.254 (1995) [hereinafter *Medicaid Estate Planning*].

The second option—purchasing private long-term health care insurance—may be a more dignified means of securing long-term health care, but it is an underutilized method. Although the number of persons holding long-term health care policies has increased in recent years (and may further increase as a result of the enactment of the Health Insurance Portability and Accountability Act of 1996 (HIPAA), Pub. L. No. 104-191, 110 Stat. 1936, in 1990 only approximately 5% of our elderly population owned such a policy. *See* Cohen et al., *supra* note 10, at 208. This, then, is the least-used financing option. *See* STAFF OF THE HOUSE COMM. ON ENERGY AND COMMERCE, 103D CONG., MEDICAID SOURCE BOOK: BACKGROUND DATA AND ANALYSIS (1993) 59–60 (Comm. Print 1993). Since most employers do not provide long-term health care insurance and many individuals do not perceive their own need for long-term health care, often purchasing such a policy only when the need for care is imminent, its premium may be exorbitant. *See* BRIAN BURWELL, SYSTEMETRICS, MIDDLE-CLASS WELFARE: MEDICAID ESTATE PLANNING FOR LONG-TERM CARE COVERAGE 34 (1991); Cohen et al, *supra* note 10, at 217–20; *Medicaid Estate Planning, supra,* at 1236 n.98, 1259 (citing a report of the American Health Care Association and a Gallup Poll). For further discussion, see *supra* note 26 and accompanying text.

The third option—payment of long-term health care expenses from personal or family income or savings—remains the principal source of all private payments for long-term care. *See supra* notes 26–27 and accompanying text. Yet, reliance on this approach can imperil a family's financial well-being. *See infra* text accompanying note 30.

The federal income tax system has been subsidizing moderate- and high-income taxpayers upon their claiming I.R.C. § 213 medical-care expense deductions for the payment of long-term health insurance premiums and long-term health care expenditures. *See Budget Issues, id.,* at 164. However, until recently it was not clear that the § 213(d) definition of "medical care" literally included long-term care expenditures. Recognizing this lack of clarity, the HIPAA explicitly included such payments in the § 213(d) definition. *See* HIPAA §§ 321–322, 110 Stat. at 2054-62; I.R.C. §§ 7702B(c), 213(d)(1)(C) (1994). Additionally, HIPAA permits individuals to exclude from gross income amounts received under long-term insurance contracts. *See* HIPAA § 331(a), 110 Stat. at 2067-69; I.R.C. § 101(g).

29. *See* [NATIONAL INST. ON AGING, DEP'T OF HEALTH AND HUMAN SERVS., PERSONNEL FOR HEALTH NEEDS OF THE ELDERLY THROUGH THE YEAR 2020, at 17 (1987) (hereinafter HEALTH NEEDS)].

30. [*See* [HUMAN RESOURCES DIV., U.S. GEN. ACCOUNTING OFFICE, LONG-TERM CARE: PROJECTED NEEDS OF THE AGING BABY BOOM GENERATION, H.R. DOC. NO. 91-86, at 2 (1991) (hereinafter PROJECTED NEEDS). The report predicts the next century will see unprecedented growth in the elderly population. As of 1992, 12.4% of the population was 65 years of age or over. See id. By 2015, that figure is expected to rise to 14.6%, reflecting the entrance of the baby boom generation into the elderly category, and by 2030, the baby boomers will enter their seventies and eighties, and the elderly will comprise 20.1% of the overall population. *See id.*]

31. Whether society is willing to take on the responsibility of allocating major amounts of financial resources to long-term health care for an aging and aged population is an open question. This question has arisen in the context of repeated legislative efforts to increase access to health care. *See, e.g.*, Health Insurance Reform Act of 1995, H.R. 1200, 104th Cong., *Health Care Costs and Lack of Access to Health Insurance: Hearings before the Senate Comm. on Finance*, 102d Cong. (1991); *Comprehensive Health Insurance Legislation: Hearings on H.R. 3205 before the House Ways and Means Comm.*, 102d Cong. (1991). Just recently, a major step was taken in this matter. *See* HIPPA, 110 Stat. at 1936.

B. History of Medicare

Older Americans enjoy the right to participate in Medicare, the federal subsidized health care insurance program. The background, history, and outline of Medicare are detailed by Ms. Kinney.

Eleanor D. Kinney

Medicare Managed Care From the Beneficiary's Perspective

* * *

II. Background on the Medicare Program

Congress enacted the Medicare program in 1965 with the strong support of President Lyndon Johnson.[1] The program was another linchpin in the Social Security system established under the Democratic presidency of Franklin Roosevelt. In the 1940s, President Harry Truman had tried to enact health insurance for the aged and failed. President John Kennedy and Vice President Lyndon Johnson had stressed health insurance for the elderly as a major campaign theme in 1960. At that time, the problem of access to quality health care services for the aged was especially severe. In 1963,

Seton Hall Law Review, Vol. 26, 1163 (1996). Reprinted by permission.

although the aged had a greater risk of illness and far lower income than other population groups, only 56 percent had health insurance.[2] Passage of Medicare was a Democratic Party triumph. President Johnson signed the bill on the porch of President Truman's home in Independence, Missouri, stating at the time: "No longer will older Americans be denied the healing powers of modern medicine. No longer will illness crush and destroy the savings that they have so carefully put away over a lifetime so that they might enjoy dignity in later years."[3]

Over the years, the Medicare program has grown and become a linchpin in the social safety net for all Americans. The Medicare program now serves 36.3 million Americans, or just over 7 percent of the population.[4] An estimated 29 million persons were actual users of the Medicare program during 1993.[5] The average per enrollee expenditure for the Medicare program in 1992 was $3,391.[6] Over half of Medicare beneficiaries had payments of less than $500 per year, while only 9.8 percent of Medicare beneficiaries (3.5 million) incurred payments of $10,000 or more.[7]

In 1993, federal expenditures for the Medicare program were $151 billion.[8] Medicare expenditures accounted for 10 percent of the federal budget in fiscal year 1995.[9] Medicare expenditures are increasing dramatically compared to other components of health spending. The rate of increase in Medicare expenditures between 1980 and 1992 was 11.5 percent, a figure lower than in earlier decades.[10] Although substantial reforms were made in the way in which the Health Care Financing Administration (HCFA) paid hospitals and physicians in the 1980s,[11] these inflationary trends in Medicare expenditures continue to cause concern. Indeed, it is estimated that the Medicare Hospital Insurance Trust Fund, which finances Part A of the Social Security wage tax, will be exhausted in 2002.[12] These trends in Medicare expenditures are driving the push for capitated managed care for Medicare beneficiaries.

A. Medicare Benefits, Coverage and Administration

The Medicare program provides basic health insurance to the elderly, severely disabled, and people with end-stage renal disease.[13] The program is comprised of two separate programs. Part A, the Hospital Insurance Program, provides hospital and related services and is financed through a payroll tax on all workers.[14] Part B, the Supplementary Medical Insurance Program, provides physician and outpatient services and is financed by premiums from beneficiaries.[15] Medicare also pays for these services through HMOs and other capitated managed care plans as described below.[16]

Medicare is administered by the HCFA in the Department of Health and Human Services (DHHS), which in turn contracts with private insurers to handle claims, appeals, and other matters. For fee-for-service Medicare, fiscal intermediaries administer payments and claims from Part A providers; carriers administer payment and claims for Part B providers.[17] Medicare also contracts with private peer review organizations to review the quality of care accorded Medicare beneficiaries, handle beneficiary appeals arising out of hospitalization, and perform other oversight functions for the Medicare program.[18]

1. *Medicare Benefits* The benefits provided under Part A, the hospital insurance component, include ninety days of basic hospitalization for each spell of illness.[19] Part A coverage also includes a stay of one hundred days in a skilled nursing facility following a hospitalization,[20] an unlimited number of home health agency visits if the beneficiary is confined to home and in need of skilled nursing care,[21] and some limited hospice services for patients who are terminally ill.[22] When patients avail themselves of the hospital benefit, they must pay a deductible amounting to the cost of the first day of hospitalization; in addition, some coinsurance is required after the sixtieth day of a hospital stay.[23] Coinsurance is also required for skilled nursing services, but not for home health services.[24]

The benefits furnished under Part B, the supplementary medical insurance component, include physician services plus a wide variety of other medical services provided on an outpatient basis.[25] Finally, an increasingly important and costly Part B benefit is the lease or purchase of durable medical equipment.[26] There is no limitation on the number of physician services which fall under Part B coverage.[27] Enrollees pay an annual deductible of $100 and pay 20 percent coinsurance on most covered services incurred during the year.[28]

2. *Medicare Coverage Policy* Coverage is an important concept in understanding Medicare benefits, particularly the disputes over benefits that arise between beneficiaries, providers, and the Medicare program. In effect, coverage defines the type and the amount of health care benefits for which the Medicare program will pay, as well as the conditions that must be met in order to receive payment. The Social Security Act specifies certain types of services that are expressly excluded from coverage under the Medicare program.[29] For both Part A and Part B, such services include physicals, immunizations, eyeglasses, hearing aids, personal comfort items, and cosmetic surgery.[30]

One is entitled to coverage only if two conditions are met. First, the services must be "reasonable and necessary" for the diagnosis and treatment of an illness or injury.[31] Second, the services rendered must not be covered by another public insurance program.[32]

Currently, the Medicare program makes coverage policy in a fairly informal process that has generated considerable criticism over the years.[33] HCFA publishes the decisions on coverage on new technologies and other specific items and services in its *Medicare Coverage Issues Manual*[34] and other Medicare program manuals. In 1989, HCFA published a proposed rule outlining its coverage policymaking procedures.[35] HCFA has not yet officially adopted this rule. In August 1989, HCFA published a notice on its procedures for promulgating national coverage policy and included major coverage determinations.[36]

In 1986, Congress created an explicit bar to procedural challenges to Medicare national coverage determinations[37] on the grounds that current procedures for making national coverage determinations and the need to preserve the scientific integrity of national coverage policy rendered the procedures required by the Administrative

Procedure Act (APA) unnecessary.[38] Congress also required courts to remand contested national coverage policies to the Secretary of the DHHS for amplification of the record.[39] Courts have generally upheld HCFA national coverage determinations, according great deference to DHHS and its expert decision-making process.[40] However, in 1987, the Administrative Conference of the United States recommended changes regarding the procedures for making national coverage policy as well as judicial review of national coverage policy.[41]

B. Some Important History

When Congress and the Johnson administration enacted the Medicare program in 1965,[42] they deliberately maintained the fee-for-service payment system for all providers out of the concern that the health care providers in the Medicare program would otherwise be unwilling to participate in the Medicare program.[43] Indeed, the opening section of the Social Security Amendments of 1965 explicitly provided:

> Nothing in this title shall be construed to authorize any federal officer or employee to exercise any supervision or control over the practice of medicine or the manner in which medical services are provided, or the selection, tenure, or compensation of any officer or employee of any institution, agency, or person providing health services; or to exercise any supervision or control over the administration or operation of any such institution, agency, or person.[44]

Congress specified that hospitals would be paid the "reasonable cost of covered services" according to principles used by private insurance companies.[45] The Department of Health, Education and Welfare (DHEW) used the principles of cost reimbursement that Blue Cross and Blue Shield had developed for payment of hospitals under their programs.[46] The only additional requirement that Congress imposed was that hospitals conduct "utilization review" of their care of Medicare patients.[47]

Although a comparatively mild requirement by modern standards, this utilization review requirement was controversial.[48] It was imposed, however, because Congress and DHEW were concerned about the inflationary incentives in the Medicare payment system for hospitals.[49] Yet, utilization review was really the first effort of the federal government to impose some type of external "management" on the care of Medicare beneficiaries that was physician ordered.

The Medicare program had a very indirect relationship with physicians and, indeed, only paid physicians directly if patients "assigned" their claims to physicians.[50] Medicare paid for physicians' services on the basis of usual and customary charges.[51] This payment system was highly inflationary because it accorded physicians exclusive authority to determine charges for services along with the authority to control the volume of services provided to patients.

The Medicare program, along with Medicaid, generated enormous demand for health care services, and with this increased demand came sharp and continuing increases in the cost of health care services.[52] The seriousness of the cost problem surfaced shortly after the inauguration of the Medicare programs when initial DHEW inflation projections exceeded all expectations.[53] Since 1970, curbing Medicare program costs has been the predominant policy issue for the Medicare program.

Congress and DHEW took steps to curb the inflation in Medicare expenditures. In the Social Security Amendments of 1972,[54] three important cost containment measures were introduced to curb health care cost inflation. The first was an expenditure cap on allowable hospital costs.[55] The second was a capital expenditure review program, the so-called Section 1122 program.[56] The third was the Professional Standards Review Organization (PSRO) program that established independent organizations of physicians to review utilization of hospital services for Medicare beneficiaries.[57] These three programs represent the predominant regulatory approaches for controlling health care expenditures in a fee-for-services payment environment: (1) rate-setting, (2) capital expenditure review, and (3) utilization management.

These programs were extremely controversial when implemented in the early 1970s. Perhaps the most controversial—at least with physicians—was the PSRO program. Immediately upon implementation, the organized medical profession brought suit to challenge the constitutionality of the program.[58] The program was finally disbanded in the early 1980s by the Reagan administration in conformity with campaign promises that presidential candidate Ronald Reagan had made to the medical profession.[59]

Yet, in 1982, Congress enacted the Peer Review Organization (PRO) program to oversee utilization under a reformed Medicare payment system for hospitals.[60] Congress was simply concerned that imposing tightened payment methodologies on hospitals—in advance of moving toward prospective payment of hospitals without regulating utilization of services by Medicare beneficiaries—would generate costly excess services and expenditures for the Medicare program.[61] Like the PSRO program, the PRO program required the DHHS to contract with physician organizations to review hospital utilization of Medicare beneficiaries. Managed care for Medicare was unequivocally launched.

In the 1980s, the major policy initiatives and changes for the Medicare program were payment reform to address undesirable incentives in fee-for-service medicine. In 1983, Congress, with support from the Reagan administration, enacted the DRG [Diagnosis-Related Groups] prospective payment system for hospitals that paid a pre-set price based on the patient's diagnosis and medical condition.[62] Congress, with support of the Bush administration, enacted a revised payment system for physician services in 1989 that paid physicians based on the time and resources involved in treating specific conditions rather than on a charge basis.[63]

Another important policy development that augmented the development of managed care was increased emphasis on Medicare coverage policy and quality improvement strategies. In the early 1980s, health services researchers published important findings in health services research on the effectiveness or "outcomes" of specific medical procedures.[64] Responding to these findings and exhibiting an increased interest in the use of coverage policy as a means to contain Medicare program cost and improve the quality and effectiveness of care accorded Medicare beneficiaries, DHHS launched a health services research initiative to expand research on outcomes of care.[65]

In 1989, Congress charged the newly-created Agency for Health Care Policy and Research (AHCPR) to support outcomes research on outcomes of specific medical procedures, and sponsor development of medical practice guidelines based on this research.[66] Third-party payers have used outcomes research on costly and widely-used medical procedures to define the content of medically necessary and appropriate care through development of medical practice guidelines, clinical standards, and quality assurance measures. The theory behind using outcomes research in this way is that cost savings can be achieved and quality improved by limiting coverage of health care services that do not have a significant impact on health outcomes.[67] HCFA and carriers are also becoming more sophisticated in the use of medical practice guidelines, often based on DHHS funded outcomes research, to make scientifically-based coverage policy that may result in limits on coverage of certain medical procedures for Medicare beneficiaries.[68]

III. Medicare Managed Care

HCFA has long promoted managed care for its beneficiaries and, indeed, as discussed above, was in the forefront of developing managed care techniques.[69] Movement toward managed care became a central theme of the Medicare program in the early 1980s. Clearly, the major theme of the regulatory approaches to cost containment, such as payment reform as well as tighter management of utilization and coverage policy, was based on the theory that Medicare payment and coverage policies that simply affirmed physician decisions to order covered services was at the heart of the cost inflation problem in the Medicare program. Medicare program managers and Congress have viewed managed care as a major means of controlling such physician autonomy and its costly ramifications.

For reasons discussed below,[70] Congress and Medicare program managers have not acted with similar speed or enthusiasm toward moving Medicare beneficiaries into capitated HMOs or managed care plans. Such efforts were among the least developed initiatives of the current Medicare program. It is useful to speculate about the rationale for this hesitancy. It may be a belief among Medicare program managers as well as Medicare beneficiaries and their providers that HMOs may not serve well a population that has a high incidence of chronic disease and disability.

A. The History of HMOs and Capitated Health Plans for Medicare Beneficiaries

As indicated above, the Medicare program has always been and remains somewhat schizophrenic about HMOs and capitated health plans for Medicare beneficiaries. In the early years of Medicare, Congress and Medicare program managers were nervous about HMOs for Medicare beneficiaries.[71] Even after research demonstrated that

HMOs were a more efficient and cost-effective vehicle for providing medical care[72] and that Medicare was facing extraordinary cost inflation,[73] Medicare program managers and Congress were hesitant about HMOs.

In the 1960s and 1970s, congressmen from both sides of the aisle and particularly the Senate Finance Committee were concerned that the incentives for HMOs to curtail service would result in underservice to Medicare beneficiaries and enrollment of only healthy beneficiaries.[74] Indeed, for the most part, HMOs could only serve beneficiaries if they did so on a fee-for-service basis.[75]

* * *

2. *The Mixed Track Record of Medicare HMOs* The track record of HMOs under the Medicare program after 1982 has been mixed. HCFA demonstrations testing the experience of Medicare beneficiaries in HMOs with risk contracts reported generally satisfactory performance by risk-based Medicare HMOs.[76] One demonstration found little difference in the actual experience of beneficiaries in traditional fee-for-service care and Medicare HMOs, although beneficiaries in HMOs reported less confidence in the quality of HMO physicians.[77] Research also demonstrated considerable satisfaction with HMOs among Medicare beneficiaries as well as increasingly high levels of quality care.[78]

Yet, in the 1980s, Medicare beneficiaries expressed dissatisfaction with Medicare HMOs and particularly coverage decisions made by Medicare HMOs. Specifically, Network Design Group (NDG), the private contractor that handles reconsiderations of HMO determinations in grievance procedures, recently reported that a major source of beneficiary dissatisfaction was coverage disputes and noted that many enrollees who appealed coverage disputes to NDG disenrolled from Medicare HMOs shortly thereafter.[79] DHHS data reports that almost one in three Medicare beneficiaries in HMOs disenroll within two years.[80]

Also, during the late 1980s, several large HMOs exhibited serious problems with respect to quality of care and consumer satisfaction which attracted considerable media and political attention.[81] The United States General Accounting Office (GAO) expressed concern about the rapid expansion of the Medicare HMO program and the capacity of HCFA to adequately monitor Medicare HMOs.[82] During this period, Congress and HCFA were also concerned about HMO incentive payments to physicians and their effect on quality of care.[83] As noted, Congress forbade such incentive payments to physicians.[84]

In 1991, the GAO issued a report about the serious problems with large HMOs as well as continued problems with Medicare HMOs and the quality of care they provide to Medicare beneficiaries.[85] Congressional hearings and reports revealed similar concerns.[86] In 1993, the Administrator of HCFA publicly announced that HCFA was not encouraging Medicare beneficiaries to enroll in Medicare HMOs because of quality concerns.[87]

3. *Beneficiary Enrollment in Medicare HMO and Capitated Health Plans* The enrollment of Medicare beneficiaries in HMO capitated health plans over the course of the program has reflected the early ambivalence about capitated health plans for Medicare

beneficiaries as well as market trends. In 1985, fewer than one million Medicare beneficiaries had enrolled in Medicare HMOs.[88] In recent years, the number of Medicare beneficiaries enrolled in HMOs has grown considerably from 883,000 (2.9 percent) in 1984 to 2,238,000 (6.3 percent) in 1992.[89] An estimated 150 managed care organizations contracted with HCFA in 1995 which constituted a 40% increase from the previous year.[90]

It is important to appreciate that this movement of Medicare beneficiaries toward HMOs and capitated health plans is taking place without federal legislation. The movement has now taken on dramatic dimensions, and it is likely that a significant proportion of Medicare beneficiaries will receive health care through capitated health plans irrespective of federal legislation. Consequently, it is crucial to revisit the procedural protections that are now in place as well as those proposed in bills before Congress for Medicare beneficiaries.

* * *

Notes

1. Social Security Amendments of 1965, § 101, Pub. L. No. 79-97, 79 Stat. 286 (1965) (codified at 42 U.S.C. §§ 1395–1395ccc (1988 & Supp. V 1993)) (adding Title XVIII: Health Insurance for the Aged to the Social Security Act).

2. Marian Gornik et al., *Twenty Years of Medicare and Medicaid: Covered Populations, Use of Benefits, and Program Expenditures,* HEALTH CARE FIN. REV. 13, 14 (1985 Supp.).

3. Remarks at the Signing of the Medicare Bill, 2 Pub. Papers 811, 813 (July 30, 1965).

4. Katharine R. Levit et al., *National Health Expenditures,* 1993, 16 HEALTH CARE FIN. REV. 247, 263 (1994).

5. OFFICE OF RESEARCH & DEMONSTRATIONS, HEALTH CARE FIN. ADMIN., DEPT. OF HEALTH & HUMAN SERVS., MEDICARE AND MEDICAID STATISTICAL SUPPLEMENT, HEALTH CARE FIN. REVIEW 1, 24 (1995).

6. *Id.*

7. *Id.; see* Statement of Marilyn Moon, Senior Fellow, The Urban Institute, Proposed Changes in the Structure of Medicare Under the Balanced Budget Act of 1995 (Jan. 17, 1996) (discussing proposed changes and their implications); Statement of Bruce Vladeck, Administrator, Health Care Fin. Admin. to the Subcommittee on Health, House Committee on Ways and Means (Feb. 10, 1995) (addressing the subcommittee regarding the current state and future of the Medicare program).

8. Levit et al., *supra* note 4, at 262.

9. *See generally* OFFICE OF MANAGEMENT AND BUDGET, BUDGET OF THE UNITED STATES GOVERNMENT, FISCAL YEAR 1996: A CITIZEN'S GUIDE TO THE FEDERAL BUDGET (1995).

10. MEDICARE AND MEDICAID STATISTICAL SUPPLEMENT, *supra* note 5, at 16.

11. *See infra* notes 62–63 and accompanying text.

12. BOARD OF TRUSTEES OF THE SOCIAL SECURITY AND MEDICARE TRUST FUNDS, STATUS OF THE SOCIAL SECURITY AND MEDICARE PROGRAMS—A SUMMARY OF THE 1995 ANNUAL REPORTS (1996) (available via World Wide Web at http:// www.ssa.gov/policy/trustees_summary_1995.html).

13. 42 U.S.C. §§ 1395–1395ccc (1988 & Supp. V 1993).

14. 42 U.S.C. § 1395i (1988).

15. *See id.*
16. [Note omitted.]
17. 42 U.S.C. §§ 1395h & u.
18. *See infra* note 60 and accompanying text.
19. 42 U.S.C. § 1395d.
20. *Id.*
21. *See id.* § 1395x(m) (defining home health services).
22. *Id.* § 1395d(d).
23. *Id.* § 1395e.
24. *Id.* § 1395e(a)(3).
25. *Id.* § 1395k. These include services provided in hospital outpatient departments and rural health clinics; outpatient surgery; diagnostic x-ray and laboratory services; rehabilitative services; physical, occupational, and speech therapy; and services ordered by a physician but performed by physicians' assistants and nurse practitioners. *Id.*
26. *Id.*
27. *Id.* § 1395y(a)(1) (listing those items and services explicitly excluded from coverage).
28. *Id.* §§ 1395l(a)–(b) (explaining payment of benefits in terms of amounts paid and deductible provisions).
29. *See id.* § 1395y (listing exclusions from coverage).
30. *See id.*
31. *Id.* § 1395y(a)(1).
32. *Id.* §§ 1395y(a)(2)–(3).
33. *See generally* Timothy P. Blanchard, *"Medical Necessity" Denials as a Medicare Part B Cost-Containment Strategy: Two Wrongs Don't Make It Right or Rational,* 34 ST. LOUIS U. L.J. 939 (1990); Eleanor D. Kinney, *National Coverage Policy Under the Medicare Program: Problems and Proposals for Change,* 32 ST. LOUIS U. L.J. 869 (1988); *see also generally* LINDA A. BERGTHOLD & WILLIAM M. SAGE, MEDICAL NECESSITY, EXPERIMENTAL TREATMENT AND COVERAGE DETERMINATIONS: LESSONS FROM NATIONAL HEALTH CARE REFORM (Oct. 1994); Mark A. Hall & Gerald F. Anderson, *Health Insurers' Assessment of Medical Necessity,* 140 U. PA. L. REV. 1637 (1992).
34. HEALTH CARE FIN. ADMIN, MEDICARE COVERAGE ISSUES MANUAL (HCFA Pub. 6) (1995) *reprinted in* Medicare & Medicaid Guide (CCH) P 27,201 (1995).
35. Proposed Rule, Medicare Program; Criteria and Procedures for Making Medical Services Coverage Decisions That Relate to Health Care Technology, 54 Fed. Reg. 4302 (proposed Jan. 30, 1989).
36. General Notice, Medicare Program; National Coverage Decisions, 54 Fed. Reg. 34,555 (1989).
37. *See* 42 U.S.C. § 1395ff(b) (1988 & Supp. V 1993).
38. H.R. Rep. No. 1012, 99th Cong., 2d Sess. 350–51 (1986). *But see* National Coverage Determinations under the Medicare Program, 1 C.F.R. §§ 305.87–8 (1993); *see also generally* [Eleanor D. Kinney, *National Coverage Policy Under the Medicare Program: Problems and Proposals for Change,* 32 ST. LOUIS U. L.J. 869 (1988); Eleanor D. Kinney, *The Medicare Appeals System for Coverage and Payment Disputes: Achieving Fairness in a Time of Constraint,* 1 ADMIN. L.J. 1 (1987)].
39. *See* 42 U.S.C. § 1395ff(b)(3)(C) (1988 & Supp. V 1993).
40. *See, e.g.,* Fiedrich v. Secretary of HHS, 894 F.2d 829 (6th Cir. 1990) (recognizing that the DHHS is charged with establishing national standards to ensure uniformity and equality in the administration of medicare and upholding the Secretary's coverage determination);

Goodman v. Sullivan, 891 F.2d 449 (2d Cir. 1989) (recognizing that the Secretary of DHHS may regulate the Medicare program by enacting regulations concerning Medicare reimbursement); Wilkins v. Sullivan, 889 F.2d 135 (7th Cir. 1989) (deferring to the DHHS Secretary's authority to interpret Medicare statutes).

41. *See* National Coverage Determinations Under the Medicare Program, *supra* note 38, § 305.87-8 (recommending changes regarding coverage and reimbursement); *see also generally* [Eleanor D. Kinney, *National Coverage Policy Under the Medicare Program: Problems and Proposals for Change,* 32 ST. LOUIS U. L.J. 869 (1988); Eleanor D. Kinney, *The Medicare Appeals System for Coverage and Payment Disputes: Achieving Fairness in a Time of Constraint,* 1 ADMIN. L.J. 1 (1987)].

42. Social Security Amendments of 1965, Pub. L. No. 89-97, 79 Stat. 291, (codified as amended at 42 U.S.C. §§ 1395–1395ccc (1988 & Supp. V 1993).

43. *See* ROBERT J. MYERS, MEDICARE 1–84 (1970) (reviewing the legislative history of the Medicare program and the compromises with the provider community that influenced Medicare program design); JUDITH M. FEDER, MEDICARE: THE POLITICS OF FEDERAL HOSPITAL INSURANCE 1–5 (1977) (reviewing the rationale for the basic design of the Medicare program).

44. 42 U.S.C. § 1395 (1988 & Supp. V 1993)).

45. *See* 42 U.S.C. § 1395x(v) (1988 & Supp. V 1993) (defining reasonable costs with regard to covered services).

46. *See generally* DEPARTMENT OF HEALTH, EDUC., AND WELFARE, PRINCIPLES OF COST REIMBURSEMENT (1968).

47. 42 U.S.C. § 1395x(k) (1988 & Supp. V 1993).

48. *See* SYLVIA A. LAW, BLUE CROSS: WHAT WENT WRONG? 115–44 (2d ed. 1976).

49. *See* SENATE COMM. ON FINANCE, 91ST CONG., 1ST SESS, REPORT OF THE STAFF, MEDICARE AND MEDICAID—PROBLEMS, ISSUES, AND ALTERNATIVES 17–18 (Comm. Print 1970) [hereinafter MEDICARE AND MEDICAID].

50. *See* Social Security Amendments of 1965, § 101, Pub. L. No. 89-97, 79 Stat. 286 (codified as amended at 42 U.S.C. § 1395u(b)(3) (1988)).

51. 42 U.S.C. § 1395u(b)(3).

52. Gornick et al., *supra* note 2, at 35-45.

53. MEDICARE AND MEDICAID, *supra* note 49, at 3-4.

54. Social Security Amendments of 1972, Pub. L. No. 92–603, 86 Stat. 1329 (codified as amended in 42 U.S.C. §§ 1395–1395ccc (1988 & Supp. V 1993)).

55. *See* 42 U.S.C. § 1395x(v) (1988 & Supp. V 1993) (defining reasonable costs).

56. Social Security Amendments of 1972, § 221, 86 Stat. 1386 (codified at 42 U.S.C. § 1320a-1).

57. 42 U.S.C. § 1395x(k) (1988 & Supp. V 1993) (creating a utilization review plan).

58. Association of Am. Physicians and Surgeons v. Weinberger, 395 F. Supp. 125 (N.D. Ill. 1975), *aff'd,* 423 U.S. 975 (1975) (finding that the statute establishing the PSRO program did not bar physicians from practicing their profession and is not so patently arbitrary and totally lacking in rational justification as to be violative of the Due Process Clause of the Fifth Amendment to the Constitution).

59. Omnibus Budget Reconciliation Act of 1981, § 2111, Pub. L. No. 97-35, 95 Stat. 357, 793 (codified as amended at 42 U.S.C. § 1320c-4 (1988)).

60. Tax Equity and Fiscal Responsibility Act of 1982, §§ 141–50, Pub. L. No. 97–248, 96 Stat. 381 (codified as amended in 42 U.S.C. § 1320c (1988)); *see generally* Peter E. Dans et al., *Peer Review Organizations: Promises and Potential Pitfalls,* 31 NEW ENG. J. MED. 1131 (1985).

61. *Peer Review Organizations: Hearings Before the Subcomm. on Health of the Senate Comm. On Finance,* 99th Cong., 1st Sess. 2 (1985).

62. Social Security Amendments of 1983 § 601(e), Pub. L. No. 98-21, 97 Stat. 65 (codified as amended in 42 U.S.C. §§ 1395ww (1988)).

63. Omnibus Budget Reconciliation Act of 1989 § 6102, Pub. L. No. 101-239, 103 Stat. 2111, 2169 (codified as amended at 42 U.S.C. § 1395w-4(a) (1988 & Supp. V 1993)).

64. *See generally* Robert H. Brook & Kathleen N. Lohr, *Efficacy, Effectiveness, Variations, and Quality—Boundary-Crossing Research,* 23 MED. CARE 710 (1985); Mark R. Chassin, *Standards of Care in Medicine,* 25 INQUIRY 437 (1988); David M. Eddy, *Variations in Physician Practice: The Role of Uncertainty,* 3 HEALTH AFF. 74 (Summer 1984); John E. Wennberg, *Commentary: On Patient Need, Equity, Supplier-Induced Demand, and the Need to Assess the Outcomes of Common Medical Procedures,* 23 MED. CARE 512 (1985); John E. Wennberg, *Dealing with Medical Practice Variations: A Proposal for Action,* 3 HEALTH AFF. 6 (1984).

65. *See generally* William L. Roper, M.D., et al., *Effectiveness in Health Care: An Initiative to Evaluate and Improve Medical Practice,* 319 NEW. ENG. J. MED. 1197 (1988).

66. Omnibus Budget Reconciliation Act of 1989, § 6103, Pub. L. No. 101-239, 103 Stat. 2106, 2189 (1989) (codified as amended at 42 U.S.C. § 299 (1988 & Supp. V 1993)).

67. *See generally* David M. Eddy & John Billings, *The Quality of Medical Evidence: Implications for Quality of Care,* 7 HEALTH AFF. 19 (Spring 1988); John E. Wennberg, *Improving the Medical Decision-Making Process,* 7 HEALTH AFF. 99 (Spring 1988); *see also* Arnold M. Epstein, *The Outcomes Movement—Will It Get Us Where We Want to Go?,* 323 NEW ENG. J. MED. 266 (1990) (discussing the viability of using outcomes research to develop standards of medical treatment).

68. *See generally* Colleen M. Grogan et al., *How Will We Use Clinical Guidelines? The Experience of Medicare Carriers,* 19 J. HEALTH POL., POL'Y & L. 7 (1994).

69. *See supra* notes 58–65 and accompanying text.

70. *See supra* notes 52–53 and accompanying text.

71. *See generally* John K. Iglehart, *Medicare Turns to HMOs,* 312 NEW ENG. J. MED. 132, 132–33 (1985) (discussing the movement to "marry Medicare with HMOs").

72. *See generally* Sheldon Greenfield et al., *Variations in Resource Utilization Among Medical Specialties and Systems of Care: Results from the Medical Outcomes Study,* 267 JAMA 1624 (1992).

73. *See supra* notes 10–12, 52–53 and accompanying text.

74. *See generally* Iglehart, *supra* note 71.

75. *Id. See infra* note 79 ["and accompanying text" deleted].

76. *See generally* Sheldon M. Retchin et al., *How the Elderly Fare in HMOs: Outcomes from the Medicare Competition Demonstrations,* 27 HEALTH SERVICES RES. 652 (1992); Gregory R. Nycz et al., *Medicare Risk Contracting: Lessons from an Unsuccessful Demonstration,* 257 JAMA 656 (1987).

77. *See* Retchin et al., *supra* note 76.

78. *See generally* Louis F. Rossiter et al., *Patient Satisfaction Among Elderly Enrollees and Disenrollees in Medicare Health Maintenance Organizations: Results from the National Medicare Competition Evaluation,* 262 JAMA 57 (1989); Retchin et al., *supra* note 76.

79. [Susan J. Stayn, *Securing Access to Care in Health Maintenance Organizations: Toward a Uniform Model of Grievance and Appeal Procedures,* 94 COLUM. L. REV. 1674, 1685 (1994)] at 1687 & n.91 (citing DAVID A. RICHARDSON, NETWORK DESIGN GROUP, INC., A STUDY OF COVERAGE DENIAL DISPUTES BETWEEN MEDICARE BENEFICIARIES AND HMOs 2, 62 (1993)).

80. *Id.* & n.90 (citing LOUIS W. SULLIVAN, DEPARTMENT OF HEALTH & HUMAN SERVS., DISENROLLMENT EXPERIENCE IN THE MEDICARE HMO AND CMP RISK PROGRAM: 1985 TO 1988 FINAL REPORT II, 43 (1990)).

81. *See generally* John K. Iglehart, *Second Thoughts About HMOs for Medicare Patients,* 316 New Eng. J. Med. 1487 (1987).

82. *See* U.S. General Accounting Office, Experience Shows Ways to Improve Oversight of Health Maintenance Organizations, No. HRD-88-73 (Aug. 18, 1988), reprinted in Medicare and Medicaid Guide (CCH) P 37,242 (1988) (noting the rapid expansion of the Medicare HMO program and questioning the ability of the HCFA to effectively oversee the program).

83. *See* U.S. General Accounting Office, Medicare: Physician Incentive Payments by Prepaid Health Plans Could Lower Quality of Care (GAO/HRD-89-29) (Dec. 1988).

84. [*See* Omnibus Budget Reconciliation Act of 1986, § 9313(c), Pub. L. No. 99-509, 100 Stat. 1874, 2002 (codified as amended at 42 U.S.C. § 1320a-7a (1988)) (prohibiting financial incentives aimed at limiting services to program participants).]

85. *See* U.S. General Accounting Office, Medicare: HCFA Needs to Take Stronger Actions Against HMOs Violating Federal Standards (GAO/HRD-92-11) (Nov. 12, 1991), *reprinted in* Medicare and Medicaid Guide (CCH) P 39,742 (1992).

86. *See, e.g., Medicare HMOs and Quality Assurance: Unfulfilled Promises: Hearings before the Senate Special Comm. on Aging,* 102d Cong., 1st Sess. (1991) [hereinafter *Medicare HMOs and Quality Assurance*]; *Medicare HMO Risk-Contractor Program: Hearings before the House Subcomm. on Health and the Environment,* 102d Cong., 1st Sess. (1991) [hereinafter *Medicare HMO Risk-Contractor Program*]; Minority Staff of Senate Special Comm. on Aging, 100 Cong., 1st Sess., Medicare and HMOs: A First Look, With Disturbing Findings (Comm. Print 1987).

87. Robert Pear, *Medicare to Stop Pushing Patients to Enter H.M.O.s,* N.Y. Times, Dec. 27, 1993, at A1.

88. Iglehart, *supra* note 71, at 133.

89. Medicare and Medicaid Statistical Supplement, *supra* note 5, at 24.

90. Beth Freeman, *The Financial and Operational Mechanics of Medicare Risk Contract,* 2 Capitation & Risk Contracting 1, 1 (Dec. 1995); *see also* Randall S. Brown et al., *Do Health Maintenance Organizations Work for Medicare?,* 15 Health Care Fin. Rev. 7, 7–23 (1993).

Christine Cassel

The Right to Health Care, the Social Contract, and Health Reform in the United States

I want to challenge you to think about the values underlying the basic elements of health care, rather than the structures and awesome complexity of the various proposals for health care reform. Lately, people's eyes quickly begin to glaze over at the mere mention of health care reform. Unfortunately, many in the public have begun

Saint Louis University Law Journal, Vol. 39, No. 1, 53 (Fall 1994). Reprinted by permission.

to despair of any progress ever being made on the issue because opponents of reform so effectively use this complexity to obfuscate the issue. Whatever inevitable compromises occur, they should be evaluated for their effect on medical professionals, for individual patients, and for society as a whole.

The central element of true reform is universal coverage, which is important for both moral and economic reasons. Universal coverage requires cost containment. Rising costs of care are directly linked to the growing numbers of uninsured and underinsured people. It is important that providers understand this essential connection. We will NEVER be able to have universal coverage in the United States if we do not get serious about restraining rising costs. For this reason, universal coverage and cost containment are very closely linked. That reality is reflected in every major, serious proposal under consideration.

* * *

A Right To Care?

A central question remains: Is there a right to health care for citizens of the United States? This is an interesting question which has led to considerable debate. Ethics literature from the 1970s contains significant discussion on this topic.[1] That period during the 1970s was also the last time we came close to health care reform in the United States. In general, the consensus among philosophers and ethicists was that there is indeed a right to health care. Supporting arguments discuss the fact that illness strikes unevenly, that illness does not allow people to have equal opportunities to succeed in our society, and that therefore, society has a special obligation to provide health care for all of its people. Ethicists say the right to health care is basic to the rights to life, liberty, and the pursuit of happiness.

However, in the 1980s that right disappeared. There were few articles published on the subject, and the spirited discussions among ethicists ceased. The "right" to health care ceased to even be a subject for cocktail party conversations. It was not politically correct, and at best it was seen as a sentimental notion. Now, here we are in the 1990s, talking about it again. What does that mean? Does it mean that rights come and go with political parties in different elections? I would hope not. I hope that what it might mean is that if there is a right to health care, it is a different kind of right. I hope that it is a right based on a sort of social contract in which it is less an entitlement attached to a person, than it is part of the obligation of society. Those two things, which are very closely connected, nevertheless have different implications in terms of their claims on all of us and the reasons why we might decide to acknowledge a right to health care.

As we look around the world, all developed countries other than the United States have universal health care coverage of some sort for their citizens. Many even include non-citizens under their care coverage. Even in parts of the world that we might consider very different from ourselves, there is an assumption that it is the government's job to in some way provide access to health care for all of its people. This emerges from a social contract notion that interestingly has positive economic implications as well.

What is meant by a "social contract"? The fundamental idea of the social contract is that persons come together in a society and give up some liberty rights and some private property (as is the case when we pay taxes) in order to allow the state to do for people some things that they cannot do as well for themselves. In many ways these are economies of scale. Good examples include the building of interstate highways, and the maintenance of police forces, and national security. These are a few among a whole range of services we think of as public goods. We never question whether it is the appropriate role of the government to provide national security forces, interstate highways, or police and fire departments. I would also include public schools in this process because it is inefficient to think that we could educate all of our citizens to an optimal level by relying on parents individually to buy that education for their children. Although some people in the United States may currently disagree with this idea, the fact remains that we do maintain our public schools even if we do not always do a very good job of funding them. No state or city has closed its public schools. Our behavior indicates that this is still an expectation, that this is a function of the social contract. There are many services that fit in this category. Why not health care?

Health care is a set of services that is so complex and has such universal benefits that we should think of it as being more efficiently and more effectively organized around the concept of the social contract. The model we have for this is Medicare. We have thirty years or more of experience with this social contract that provides universal coverage for the elderly. Before 1965, as medical care itself was getting much more effective, and medical technology was just beginning to truly burgeon, the needs became obvious to the public. We were beginning to have intensive care units, major cardiac surgery, major new advances in all kinds of medical technology, and not surprisingly the cost of care began rising! The people who used medical care and who cost the most were the elderly because of their increased vulnerability to illness, a concomitant part of aging. As these medical costs began to rise, the families of elderly patients who needed this medical care became unable to pay those costs under traditional methods.

We had private health insurance during those years, but the health insurance companies, needing to keep their companies profitable, also realized that these elderly people were too expensive. They began experience rating. They either charged older people much higher premiums, making health insurance unaffordable for many of them, or simply denied them coverage altogether. As that situation began to worsen, pressure mounted for Congress to set up a government-funded health insurance system for the elderly.

Medicare has many flaws to be sure. One of its major flaws is that in order to overcome the political opposition mounted by physicians, hospitals, and insurance companies at the time, the government compromised by agreeing not to set limits on the fees that doctors or hospitals could charge. The plan focused almost entirely on reimbursing the costs of acute hospital care rather than outpatient or preventive care, and it allowed the private insurance companies to function as intermediaries in this so they could get their piece of the business. This seemed like a reasonable compromise at the time, but unsurprisingly it prompted dramatic inflation in health care costs. Today we are paying the price of this compromise, and physicians and the industry have reaped many benefits over the past three decades.

Nevertheless, because Medicare is a single-payer plan, there have been mechanisms to gain some control of inflationary pricing and volume. It is simply a political process of negotiating with the various health care providers about what really constitutes reasonable charges and costs that ought to be reimbursed under the system. Because it is spending public funds, the government would be irresponsible if it did not attempt to control the costs of Medicare.

Despite its problems, Medicare has been successful in many ways. It has been especially successful in spreading the risk of a large number of people under one umbrella, thereby enabling the government to provide insurance for everyone in the group.

Moreover, the benefit of Medicare was not just to the elderly. In the current debate about intergenerational equity this fact is often overlooked. Many people in Washington are great advocates for improving the status of children in our society. That is very important, but some think that the elderly have gotten too much and therefore we should reduce all the programs for the aged in order to benefit the children. It is important to remember that the most vocal advocates for Medicare were not elderly people. Instead, they were the middle-aged people who were paying the bills for their parents. The same dynamic occurred when Congress established the Social Security system. We should remember that people do not exist in horizontal generations, but rather they exist in families. What a policy can do for older people affects what middle-aged people can then do for their children and grandchildren. All these policies ought to be seen not just as benefiting a single generation within our society, but also as having effects on people in their vertical intergenerational family and horizontal community relationships.

The other thing that happened in 1965 was almost an afterthought: the establishment of Medicaid. Medicaid was intended to cover the poor who do not get insurance with their employment. The fact that Medicaid would cover long-term care was nearly an afterthought. No one ever considered that it would grow to the degree it did. Medicaid is not based on a social contract model. It is based on a welfare model that requires means testing. That is, it requires that each state establish what level of poverty is severe enough to warrant public insurance. It is therefore much more vulnerable to politics and to budget cutting. Medicaid has very few effective advocates or interest groups, and therefore is considered a failure by most policy experts. If one considers combining Medicaid and Medicare into one public program, the Medicare beneficiaries say "We don't want Medicare turning into Medicaid." You don't hear the Medicaid beneficiaries saying "We don't want to turn into Medicare." It is clear that the Medicare model for many reasons has been much more successful in maintaining standards of care, from the perspective of both beneficiaries and providers.

In 1965 we also believed that everybody not covered by Medicare and Medicaid would be covered through the workplace. What has happened instead is a replay of what happened with the elderly in the early 1960s. As health care costs continued to escalate, in part driven by the over-reimbursement of high technology by Medicare, regular people—employed people, middle-aged and middle-class people—began to not be able to afford health insurance. Increasingly, businesses started cutting back on what they would do, such as not offering insurance to certain classes of workers. Insurance companies increased their experience rating. They started charging people for pre-existing illnesses or excluding them from insurance coverage altogether. As the number of uninsured individuals proliferated, cost-shifting became a major dynamic of the way we fund hospitals and medical care in this country.

If someone who is very sick comes into the hospital without insurance, we do not send them away. We take care of them. We charge those costs to someone who DOES have insurance. And what does that do? That drives up insurance costs and then employers say "Oh, my God—our costs are going up," so fewer and fewer of them cover their employees adequately and the cycle continues, resulting in even more uninsured people and higher insurance costs. The whole mechanism—the social contract mechanism of insurance—stops working.

Health Care as an Obligation of Society

That is where we are now. We have come full cycle to where we were with the elderly in 1965. We are asking the question in a different way, not so much "is health care a right," but "is health care something that our society can provide more efficiently if we do it for everyone in more or less the same way?" We still hear the ideological debates about whether or not health care is a right. Some people say yes. Some people say no. I would argue that if we observe our behavior we have a more consistent answer. Our behavior says we ACT as if health care is a right. We may not provide the best quality care for under-insured or uninsured people, but when they get really sick and they come to our emergency rooms, we take care of them. We take care of them in the most expensive, most inefficient way imaginable. Then we charge their costs to somebody else.

Thus, it is both unfair and dishonest to say that we do not believe there is a right to health care, because we are behaving as if there is. If we really believed that health care is simply a market commodity (as some still argue), then uninsured sick people without the means to pay would be refused care regardless of the consequences to them. Indeed, this "right" to care is so imbedded in our social values that refusing to provide health care is not only viewed as unethical, but is also illegal under federal law.[2] We should uphold this right in a more efficient, more fair way where we can more evenly share the costs as well as be more cost effective in the way we provide services.

* * *

Notes

1. *See generally* MARC D. HILLER, MEDICAL ETHICS AND THE LAW 53–72 (1981); Sarah C. Carey, *A Constitutional Right to Health Care: An Unlikely Development*, 23 CATH. U. L. REV. 492 (1974); William T. Blackstone, *On Health Care as a Legal Right: An Exploration of Legal and Moral Grounds*, 10 GA. L. REV. 391 (1976).

2. *See* 42 U.S.C. § 1395dd (1994) (hospital must provide emergency care to any individual who presents with an emergency condition).

C. Medicare and Health Maintenance Organizations

Because of the rapidly growing expense of Medicare, the government has taken steps to control costs by encouraging Medicare recipients to enroll in health maintenance organizations (HMOs). To make the HMOs more attractive than traditional health care insurance, Medicare pays the HMOs an annual amount, called capitation. The HMO then provides for each enrollee a wide variety of health care services at little or no cost to the patient. Medicare pays the HMO an amount equal to approximately 90 percent of the average annual cost to Medicare of each enrollee.

In theory, HMO enrollment by Medicare participants should be a win-win situation: the government saves money, and the participant receives more care for less cost. While this may be the case for the great majority of HMO Medicare participants, some HMO participants are dissatisfied with the quality of care. Although under the Medicare statute HMOs are required to provide the same range of services that are provided for non-HMO Medicare participants, in some instances HMOs, in an attempt to reduce costs, have restricted the quantity and quality of care provided to the Medicare enrollees. Some of these Medicare enrollees have attempted to sue the HMOs seeking better care. Others have sued the federal government (Medicare) claiming that the government has abdicated its responsibility to monitor the HMOs and ensure that they provide all Medicare-covered benefits. In Grijalva v. Shalala, *946 F. Supp. 747 (Dist. of Arizona, 1996), the United States District Court of Arizona held that Medicare enrollees in HMOs could force Medicare to provide better oversight of HMOs and to provide hearings to listen to complaints of Medicare enrollees who believed that the HMO failed to provide Medicare-covered benefits.*

To date, outside the Medicare setting, HMOs have their greatest success with families, particularly families with small children. These families tend to be relatively healthy. For them limited access to providers and specialists is a small price to pay for the no-cost access to preventive health care, particularly for their children. Moreover, these young families tend to be demanding consumers. If they are not treated right, they can and will leave the HMO. Critics, however, contend that older persons are much less likely to leave a HMO even if it performs poorly. Older persons, it is contended, become dependent on their doctors and specialists and are unlikely to switch even if that care is subpar. Also, HMOs may not be appropriate because older persons are sicker and frailer. Under the traditional Medicare program, these older persons can seek out a physician or specialist who meets their particular psychological and physiological needs. Under an HMO their range of choices is much more limited.

HMOs also may not be available to many older persons, particularly those in rural areas. To date, most HMOs are found in urban and suburban areas and have shown little interest in the rural market, primarily because of the higher costs of administration associated with a spread-out population. Also, HMOs are paid a lower capitation rate for rural patients, reflecting the traditionally lower Medicare costs associated with small towns and rural areas. HMOs prefer to operate in urban areas where the capitation payments are higher. If Medicare has to pay higher capitation rates to induce HMOs to operate in rural areas, there may be little cost savings.

Possibly the most fundamental argument against HMO managed care is that it tends to save money by emphasizing preventive medicine and by forcing discounts on providers. It is not clear that preventive medicine will have the same value for older persons as it does for the young. Many of the acute and chronic care costs of the elderly are nonavoidable given their advanced age and increased frailty. As for pushing discounts on providers (such as lower payments to physicians), Medicare already does that with some success through limiting the amount of reimbursement it will provide for a variety of procedures and other kinds of medical care. It is not clear that HMOs can realize any greater savings without lowering the quality of medical care.

If HMOs are unable to significantly decrease health care utilization by their Medicare enrollees, the only way that they will be able to operate profitably is to reduce the quality of care or the amount of care provided. Critics maintain that hospital utilization and medical utilization by older persons has already been sharply decreased. There is no reason to believe that HMOs can further reduce or dramatically reduce utilization without impinging upon the health of the patients. In fact, some argue that the only real way to reduce utilization is to put financial pressure on doctors. That is, the HMO simply instructs the doctors to reduce care to patients, thereby saving money for the HMO.

Of course, the counter argument to the managed care critics is that the present system is simply unworkable. That is, the system permits Medicare enrollees carte blanche access to subsidized medical care. The current attempts for the government to cut costs by reducing payments to hospitals and doctors has had some success, but the only real success will be when Medicare enrollees are encouraged to use less medical care. What is overuse and what is needed medical care depends on the eye of the beholder. Still, it does seem probable that Medicare enrollees may well overuse health services, particularly specialists. The HMO theory, of course, is that although there is no charge for seeing the primary care physician, the individual cannot see a specialist without the primary care physician's approval. This gatekeeper role of the primary physician is thought to be one of the main cost savings. Individual patients are directed only to that level of care that they need, not to the level of care that they think that they need as they are free to do under traditional Medicare. If older persons are over-utilizing health care, HMOs may be able to provide the same quality of care at significantly less cost.

CHAPTER 34

Medicare Reform

Medicare is an expensive program whose costs are projected to rise dramatically as the baby boomers turn age sixty-five and swell the ranks of the Medicare beneficiaries. Although current "reforms" of Medicare—consisting of modest increases in premiums, restrictions on the growth of hospital and doctor reimbursements, and possible modest charges for home health care—promise to keep the Medicare fund solvent up to the year 2010, thereafter projected Medicare expenditures rise at alarming rates. In the year 2011 the leading edge of the boomers, those born in 1946, will begin to turn sixty-five. The numbers of eligible Medicare enrollees promises either to bankrupt the program or else require unprecedented tax increases. Since neither alternative is politically viable, a third alternative—that is, some combination of a reduction in benefits, higher premiums and co-pays for enrollees, and higher taxes—can be expected.

Anne E. Berdahl

The Tough Choices Commission

* * *

Spring in Washington is full of delights, but for health policy mavens it's the Season of Doom and Denial—time for the annual Medicare Trustees' report and the perennial round of sniping, posturing, and prognosticating that attends it. Recent Aprils have featured ever more dire warnings about the ill health of America's second largest social program (Social Security, with its own troubles, is first). Time marches on, but the date of projected insolvency marches inexorably backwards. This year's

Health Systems Review, Vol. 29, No. 4, 13–15 (July/August 1996). Reprinted by permission.

report warns that the Medicare Hospital Insurance (HI) Trust Fund will run dry sometime in 2001—a year earlier than was projected in 1995.

Once again, the trustees tried to conjure up as much alarm as policy wonks can: "The fact that the exhaustion would occur under a broad range of future economic conditions, and is expected to occur in the relatively near future, indicates the urgency of addressing the HI trust fund's financial imbalance." And while some have said providers can be squeezed no more in the cost containment war, the trustees indicate that "further legislation to limit payment increases to all HI providers could help reduce expenditure growth rates." Coming as it did in a highly charged election year atmosphere, this year's report sparked an unprecedented brouhaha. But are things really getting appreciably worse for the program, its providers, and its beneficiaries? Is this year's crisis any different than those in the past? Unfortunately, yes. Since 1970, the Trustees have prognosticated, off and on, that the Part A trust fund is teetering on the brink of insolvency. The years estimated to be left in the black have varied greatly, from two years in 1970 to twenty years in 1975. Political observers have little doubt that when lawmakers really have their backs to the wall, they'll stave off Medicare's approaching collapse. President Clinton and the GOP Congress favor remarkably similar proposals that are stymied almost exclusively for reasons related to politics and partisan advantage.

So why would Republican health analyst Deborah Steelman tell a Washington audience recently that "this new threat to Medicare is unique in the program's history"? She says Congress has all but exhausted its options for controlling Medicare spending, and still the program grows at ten percent per year. More important, the baby boom generation (born between 1946 and 1964), when it begins to retire in 2010, will tax the Medicare program as never before. Today there are four covered workers supporting each enrollee; by the middle of the next century there will be only two. For hospitals, this middle- to long-term picture is the walk through hell. Managed care has pinched private reimbursement so severely that "Medicare has now become the single best financial source for hospitals," according to Stuart Altman, the former chairman of the Prospective Payment Assessment Commission (ProPAC). This is bad news at a time when technology continues to prolong lives expensively and the next budget law passed in Washington is all but certain to include unbreachable Medicare spending caps.

A Political Conundrum

Thus the commonly heard refrain these days is that "tinkering" won't do and that "fundamental reform" of Medicare is imperative, now. There seems to be no getting around the fact that Medicare reform, even more than Social Security reform, will be the dominant public policy issue of the next several decades. Regrettably, even with this valuable advance warning, our public officials seem intent to put off any solutions until the next century. Politicians and interest groups have little to gain by seriously discussing real solutions to the Medicare dilemma. Seniors and the baby boomers represent powerful constituencies, one protecting a seemingly divine entitlement, the other already anxious about its economic future with or without a substantial Medicare program The trustees and other key players in the Medicare reform game have acknowledged the reluctance of our system to make tough choices and have proposed a way around it: a bipartisan commission that would develop a set of reforms that Congress would have to approve or reject, no amendments allowed.

* * *

A commission would have to confront the same list of unpopular options that Congress does today. A description of the most common follows, in no particular order. You'll notice they all share certain qualities: they are either weak and ineffectual or politically explosive. Transferring home health care from Part A to Part B: Home care is growing like a weed in Medicare's expense account, and this proposal is estimated to "save" Medicare's hospital component $ 55 billion. . . . But Representative Bill Archer (RTX), Chairman of the Ways & Means Committee, echoed the stance of many provider groups, stating that, "If we simply move obligations . . . out of the Trust Fund, we have not done anything about the (underlying) operating deficit." Dick Davidson, AHA President, calls it a "bookkeeping gimmick."

Increase beneficiaries' options for choosing private managed care plans: When conservatives talk of structurally transforming Medicare, this shift towards private plans paid on a capped basis by Medicare is the core of what they mean. They're fond of observing that Medicare's fee-for-service approach to reimbursement is hopelessly out of date and ineffectual. Steelman adds that Medicare's benefits are scant compared to most private plans. Price competition, they argue, would do more than anything in the long run to control the program's costs. But for all its seeming common sense and the apparent political consensus on the concept, Medicare's managed care experiments so far have lost money on balance and enshrined all kinds of inappropriate incentives and rewards. Attempts to remedy the gross regional inequities in risk contractor payment rates, like competitive bidding, are years away from being ready for national roll-out. Boost trust fund revenues through higher payroll contributions: Translation: increase taxes. This certainly wouldn't be sufficient on its own, but there are a few willing to go to bat for the idea as a part of a larger package of reform.

* * *

Raising the retirement age: With our health status improving, our working careers lasting longer, and our life expectancy on the rise, staving off Medicare eligibility to sixty-seven for future generations of Americans has the virtue of being both reasonable and effective. It's already been approved for Social Security, albeit decades from now. Of course, that means it's regarded as political suicide. No idea gets senior groups more upset, even though the idea wouldn't affect them. Many influential policy groups, including ProPAC, endorse raising the retirement age, again, as part of a reform package.

* * *

When asked recently if retirees might be facing fewer services or higher costs in the Medicare program, Secretary Shalala answered with a resounding "absolutely not." Herein lies our problem. Both parties know that providers have borne the brunt of most Medicare cost control efforts. Neither, however, wants to ask enough of beneficiaries (today's or tomorrow's) to truly secure the program in the long run. Lawmakers can't agree on the little things, yet conservative people like Butler believe that "no amount of fine-tuning can stave off disaster." Granted, Medicare is complicated and philosophically charged. There are no silver bullet solutions. As Stuart Altman reminds us, "a balanced approach is necessary." Unfortunately, balance hasn't been an overriding value in Washington in quite some time.

Not everyone sees the coming crisis in Medicare as a reason to radically shrink the program and either severely reduce or even eliminate the entitlement component. Professor Tiefer examines the history and logic of health care entitlement, while Mr. Dauster argues the case for Medicare as an entitlement program.

Charles Tiefer

"Budgetized" Health Entitlements and the Fiscal Constitution in Congress's 1995–1996 Budget Battle

* * *

I. Entitlements Legislation and Applicable Analytic Theories

A. Entitlements Legislation

Prior to the New Deal, government expenditures consisted almost solely of annual appropriations—a form of spending adjusted each year. The Constitution embodied the framers' understanding that limited-time appropriations, by requiring perennial renewal, subjected spending to close congressional control.[1] Numerous constitutional provisions, such as the Appropriations Clause and the Origination Clause, similarly

Harvard Journal on Legislation, Vol. 33, No. 2, 411 (Summer 1996). Reprinted by permission.

embodied the original understandings that democratic decision-making should fit particular congressional procedures on fiscal legislation. Confirming these expectations, Congress could and did react readily in the 1800s and 1900s to coordinate spending with changing conditions, such as by rapid adaptation in military spending during swings from peacetime to wartime. The fiscal constitution's elaboration further effectuated this fiscally integrated appropriation system.[2] Today, appropriations go through a process of annual enactments, reviews, and reshapings, which pit appropriation claimants against each other and against taxpayers.[3]

In contrast to appropriations, entitlements legislation does not expire at the end of a fiscal year. Hence, entitlements are not annually reviewed by Congress as part of the appropriations process. Rather, standing provisions in the United States Code determine an entitlement program's eligibility criteria and benefit levels, which remain permanently effective until the enactment of a new statute for repeal or modification.

The modern era[4] of entitlements legislation began with enactment of the Social Security Act of 1935 and its major amendments in 1939, as a system of "social insurance" income security.[5] From its inception through its many statutory adjustments, Congress attempted to bolster support for Social Security by justifying it as a social insurance program providing personal security with fiscal restraint in a manner analogous to privately purchased retirement annuities. Congress distinguished Social Security from appropriated charity by having the eligibility requirements include long-term employment and by utilizing a system of employer and employee "contributions." Congress further differentiated Social Security from appropriated charity by having the benefit levels reflect the individual's contribution history and by using dedicated "independent payroll financing" (financing by payroll taxes rather than by general revenues) paid into "trust funds." This ideological basis of fiscal isolation protected the system from congressional alteration when political majorities shifted after the New Deal.[6]

Congress also established public income assistance programs for particular groups in poverty, such as Aid to Families with Dependent Children (AFDC) in 1935, and various programs for old age assistance and assistance for the blind or disabled, which in 1972 united and expanded to become the Supplementary Security Income (SSI) program.[7] The public assistance entitlements depended on a different ideological basis of public support than the social insurance entitlements; Congress based public assistance entitlements on the worthiness of the impoverished blind, disabled, elderly, and children with single parents for receiving assistance. Similar to the social insurance entitlements, Congress protected the public assistance entitlements from the annual appropriations process by basing the model of benefits on permanent legislation, not appropriations.

When Congress created health security programs in 1965, its linking of Medicare, the program of health care for the elderly, to Social Security helped spread the social insurance umbrella over Medicare as well.[8] Medicare had two parts. Part A was hospital insurance covering hospital care, which Congress paid through employee and employer contributions to a trust fund. Part B was supplemental medical insurance covering doctor care, which Congress paid through a mix of beneficiary premiums and general taxpayer revenues. Congress also enacted Medicaid, a federal-state program of health care for the poor, as an entitlement analogous to the public assistance entitlements.[9] At the time of enactment, Congress did not foresee that Medicare and Medicaid would be particularly costly. It established these entitlements, like Social Security, outside the fiscal coordination of the annual appropriations process. Moreover, it established them on a rights-oriented basis.[10]

The high inflation of the late 1970s and early 1980s fueled both cost of living allowance (COLA)-driven increases in income entitlements[11] and also a particularly explosive rise in the cost of medical entitlements. This was in mid-swing when President Reagan came to office in 1981, eager to cut taxes for persons in top income tax brackets and for corporations. To help pay for those cuts, President Reagan used the 1981 budget process to push omnibus legislation cutting spending for the poor. These cuts targeted appropriated programs, but also curbed the Medicaid entitlement and even trimmed Social Security. In 1981–1982, President Reagan's initial backing of another round of Social Security cuts proved politically disastrous. Because the 1981 savings did not match the cost of the Reagan tax cuts and defense buildup, the budget fell into a deep, long-term imbalance. The budget process simply had not forced trade-offs between the increasing cost of entitlements and the conservative political drive to cut upper-income taxes. Moreover, even though inflation gradually decreased, the costs of health care entitlements climbed in the 1980s and early 1990s. Meanwhile, budget projections of the mid-1990s began factoring in the enormous rise in health care costs to come from the demographic shifts to an aging population.

Ultimately, the fiscal constitution will have to deal with these phenomena. Congress must coordinate the level of spending on health care entitlements with the provision of funding from either dedicated financing or general revenues. The 1995–1996 budget battle signified how Congress may do this, namely, by "budgetizing" entitlements and enhancing the processes for integrating entitlements into the annual budget process.

* * *

Notes

1. Art. I, sec. 8, cl. 12, gives Congress the power "[t]o Raise and support Armies, but no Appropriation of Money to that Use shall be for a longer Term than two Years." The "Raise and Support Clause" shows a sophisticated awareness of how limited-term appropriations foster congressional control, in this instance, over a standing army. *See* WILLIAM C. BANKS & PETER RAVEN-HANSEN, NATIONAL SECURITY LAW AND THE POWER OF THE PURSE 29, 192 n.19 (1994), *citing* Bernard Donahoe & Marshall Smelser, *The Congressional Power to Raise Armies: The Constitutional and Ratifying Conventions, 1787–1788,* 33 REV. POL. 202 (1971); 3 JOSEPH STORY, COMMENTARIES ON THE CONSTITUTION OF THE UNITED STATES § 1187-88 (Carolina Academic Press 1987) (1833).

2. Fiscal integration is the concept that fiscal decisions, such as how much to spend on any particular project, should occur in coordination with other related fiscal decisions, such as how much to spend on alternative projects or how much to raise or lower taxes in light of these spending decisions. [For an introduction to the fiscal integration of entitlements, *see* AARON WILDAVSKY, THE NEW POLITICS OF THE BUDGETARY PROCESS 273–74 (2d ed. 1992); HOUSE COMM. ON THE BUDGET, 100TH CONG., 1ST SESS., THE WHOLE AND THE PARTS: PIECEMEAL AND INTEGRATED APPROACHES TO CONGRESSIONAL BUDGETING (Comm. Print 1987) (report prepared by Allen Schick.] Regarding the fiscal constitution generally, *see, e.g.*, Charles Tiefer, *The Constitutionality of Independent Officers as Checks on Abuses of Executive Power*, 63 B.U. L. REV. 59, 70–74 (1983); Note, *Federalism, Political Accountability, and the Spending Clause*, 107 HARV. L. REV. 1419 (1994); and the sources cited in [Kenneth Dam, *The American Fiscal Constitution*, 44 U. CHI. L. REV. 271 (1977); Wm. Bradford Middlekauff, *Twisting the President's Arm: The Impoundment Control Act as a Tool for Enforcing the Principle of Appropriation Expenditure*, 100 YALE L.J. 209 (1990); Kate Stith, *Congress' Power of the Purse*, 97 YALE L.J. 1343, 1363–64 (1988); Kate Stith, *Rewriting the Fiscal Constitution: The Case of Gramm-Rudman-Hollings*, 76 CAL. L. REV. 593, 643 (1988) (hereinafter *Rewriting the Fiscal Constitution*)].

3. For a discussion of the annual appropriations process, see Louis Fisher, *The Authorization-Appropriation Process in Congress: Formal Rules and Informal Practices*, 29 CATH. U. L. REV. 51 (1979); [CHARLES TIEFER, CONGRESSIONAL PRACTICE AND PROCEDURE 848–919, 921–1010 (1989)].

4. Historically, entitlement spending dates back to 1776, when the Continental Congress established the first pension program for disabled veterans. In August 1776, the first national military pension law formally set benefits for disabled soldiers: half-pay for life or for as long as they were disabled. Before the 1930s, Congress had previously established, as entitlements, federal retirement for civilian and military employees and veterans' benefits. George Hager, *Entitlements: The Untouchable May Become Unavoidable*, 51 CONG. Q. WKLY. REP. 22, 24–25 (1993).

5. The acts created the Old Age and Survivors program and also established the unemployment compensation system. For Social Security, see Title II of the Social Security Act, 49 Stat. 622 (1935) (principally codified at 42 U.S.C. §§ 401–433 (1994).

6. It is largely for ideological reasons that Social Security survived intact the transition from the "friendly" Democratic Presidents and Congresses of the 1930s and 1940s to the new Republican President and significantly hostile Republican Congress in 1953. At that time, when the portion of the elderly population receiving Social Security benefits was small, it would not have affected a large group to replace it with the Republican proposal for an expanded old age public assistance program. However, public support for Social Security's ideology rather than its then still-narrow base of pure beneficiary self-interest kept Social Security intact. Robert M. Ball, *The Original Understanding on Social Security: Implications for Later Developments*, *in* SOCIAL SECURITY: BEYOND THE RHETORIC OF CRISIS 21, 31 n.40 (Jerry L. Mashaw & Theodore R. Marmor eds., 1988); MARTHA DERTHICK, POLICYMAKING FOR SOCIAL SECURITY 154–56 (1979).

7. For AFDC in its current form, see Social Security Amendments of 1967, Pub. L. No. 90-248, 81 Stat. 821, 877–898 (1968) (codified generally at 42 U.S.C. §§ 601–617 (1994)). For the enactment of the SSI program, see Supplemental Security Income for the Aged, Blind and Disabled Act, Pub. L. No. 92-603, 86 Stat. 1465 (1972) (codified as amended at 42 U.S.C. §§ 1381–1383d (1994)).

8. Health Insurance for the Aged Act, Pub. L. No. 89-97, 79 Stat. 290 (1965) (codified as amended at 42 U.S.C. § 1395 (1994)). [Remainder of note omitted.]

9. Grants to States for Medical Assistance Programs Act, Pub. L. No. 89-97, 79 Stat. 343 (1965) (codified as amended at 42 U.S.C. § 1396 (1994)). [Remainder of note omitted.]

10. [Note omitted.]

11. An exception is AFDC, which, lacking a COLA, does not provide beneficiaries with minimum protection comparable to Social Security and SSI.

William G. Dauster

Protecting Social Security and Medicare

* * *

IV. Budgetary Realities

A. Share of the Budget

* * *

Together Social Security and Medicare compose more than one-third of all federal spending and three-fifths of all entitlement spending.[1] Social Security accounts for 22 percent of federal spending and 39 percent of entitlement spending. Medicare constitutes 12 percent of federal spending and 22 percent of entitlement spending.[2]

* * *

D. Medicare

More complex than Social Security, Medicare consists of two federal programs of insurance: Hospital Insurance (Medicare Part A or HI) and Supplementary Medical Insurance (Medicare Part B or SMI). Unlike the Social Security Trust Fund, which is wholly supported by the payroll tax, different financing mechanisms support the two parts of Medicare. This division arose from political considerations, not a philosophical rationale.[3]

Like Social Security, a payroll tax supports the HI Fund. Thus, one can discuss the solvency of Medicare Part A in similar terms as one discusses the solvency of the Social Security Trust Fund. Solvency of the HI Fund is compromised if growth in the cost of hospitalization exceeds the growth in payroll income.

The SMI Fund, which covers doctors' and outpatient fees, is supported by premiums and general revenues from the Treasury.[4] Thus, the SMI Fund is as actuarially sound as the United States government.[5] Consequently, few debate its solvency. Figure 1[6] displays the short history of the Medicare HI Trust Fund. In its first twenty

Harvard Journal on Legislation, Vol. 33, 461 (Summer 1996). Reprinted by permission.

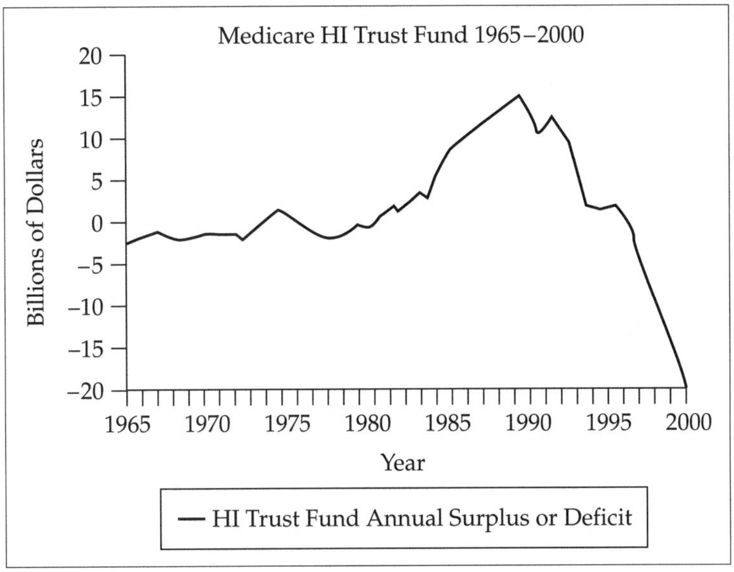

FIGURE 1

years of operation, the fund reported modest surpluses, averaging a little more than $1.5 billion per year. In the second half of the 1980s, when the government closely controlled the system, Medicare costs rose less rapidly than those for private-sector health care.[7] The Fund enjoyed a period of significant surpluses, amounting to nearly $17 billion in 1989. After 1989, however, the surpluses of the Fund decreased, and the Trustees project that they will return to deficits in 1996 and thereafter.

This deficit trend has caused the Medicare Trustees to issue the following warning:

> The Federal Hospital Insurance (HI) Trust Fund, which pays inpatient hospital expenses, will be able to pay benefits for only about seven years and is severely out of financial balance in the long range. The Trustees urge the Congress to take additional actions designed to control HI program costs and to address the projected financial imbalance in both the short range and the long range through specific program legislation as part of broad-based health care reform.[8]

Such warnings of the imminent insolvency of the HI Trust Fund are nothing new. In nine previous Trustees' reports, the warning was at least as dire as that in the current report.[9] Indeed, in 1994, the Trustees warned that the HI Trust Fund would be depleted within five years.[10] Thus, one might doubt the sincerity of politicians who warned of a Medicare crisis in 1995, if they are the same people who dismissed the idea of a crisis in 1994. In fact, prospects for the HI Trust Fund have improved since 1993, when President Clinton's first budget injected a new stream of revenues into the fund and reduced the growth in its spending.[11]

Ted Marmor of the Yale School of Management sums up the situation: "Medicare doesn't need 'saving' or 'rescuing' or any of the other hyperbolic turns of phrase the

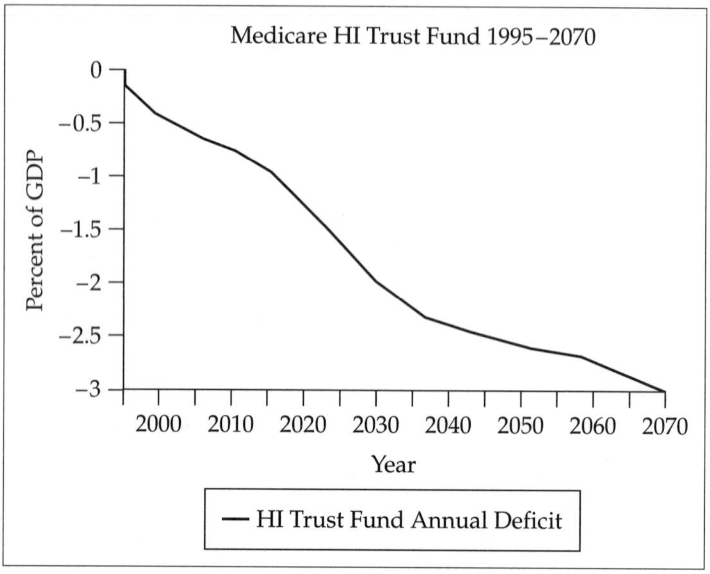

FIGURE 2

press and politicians use to discuss the program's future. To borrow from Twain, reports of a crisis are greatly exaggerated."[12]

What, after all, does the HI Trust Fund really measure? It certainly does not measure the ability of the government to fund the Medicare program. Once again, in Professor Marmor's words:

> If it chooses, Congress can appropriate more money to Medicare; it can change the tax schedule, and so on. To say that 'by law' Medicare beneficiaries will stop receiving hospital benefits in 2002 is to imply that laws are immutable. The only thing that matters is whether Congress will raise taxes to meet expenditures, or control expenditures to stay within revenues. The affordability of the program is indeed a significant issue, but to focus on the trust fund as a symbol occludes, rather than illuminates, the debate.[13]

There can be no dispute, however, that the situation Congress will face, looking at the long-term picture for the HI Trust Fund, is bleak (see Figure 2).[14] The deficits of the HI Trust Fund, even as a share of the economy, will grow dramatically and projections show no stabilization.

Thus, the impact of the baby boom generation's retirement on Social Security does not directly parallel its effect on Medicare. The Medicare HI Trust Fund is in worse condition than the Social Security Trust Fund.[15] As the Trustees advise: "A key aspect of thinking about future financing of these trust funds is recognition that under current law the timing and magnitude of the financing problems facing the programs are distinctly different."[16]

This long-run comparison merely parallels the short-run comparison. While in the short run, Social Security expenditures are currently growing at roughly the same rate as the economy, Medicare costs are growing much more quickly, reflecting the rapid growth of medical expenses.[17] The retirement of the baby boomers will add burdens to both systems, but retirement needs will stabilize for the Social Security Trust Fund.[18] Unless we get better control of the growth of health care costs, however, there will be no end in sight for the growth of HI Trust Fund deficits.

One must remember, however, that these long-term projections are like the glimpses of the future the Ghost of Christmas Yet to Come showed Scrooge.[19] They are pictures of what *might* be, not what *must* be. These projections are highly sensitive to changes in the economy, fertility, immigration rates,[20] and even small programmatic changes. Like Scrooge, we still have time—though not much time—to mend our ways.

* * *

Notes

1. *See id.* at 22, 26 (using fiscal year 1996 baseline projection data, and using all mandatory spending for entitlements, including offsetting receipts and deposit insurance).

2. Other spending is allocated as follows: Defense, 17%; Interest, 15%; Other Discretionary, 17%; Other Entitlements, 16%. *Id.*

3. *See* [Ted Marmor & Julie Beglin, *Medicare and How It Grew—To Be Confused and Misjudged,* BOSTON GLOBE, May 7, 1995, at 73].

4. The Medicare Trustees explain:

> The SMI or Part B program is financed similarly to yearly renewable, term insurance. Participants pay premiums that in 1994 covered about 30 percent of the cost; the rest is paid for by the Federal Government from general revenues. The 1995 monthly premium is $46.10.

[SOCIAL SECURITY & MEDICARE BOARD OF TRUSTEES, STATUS OF THE SOCIAL SECURITY AND MEDICARE PROGRAMS: A SUMMARY OF THE 1995 ANNUAL REPORTS 1 (1995) (hereinafter TRUSTEES' SUMMARY REPORT)]

5. The Trustees' report explains:

> The test for *SMI actuarial soundness* is met for any time period if the trust fund assets and projected income are enough to cover the projected outgo and there are enough assets to cover costs incurred but not yet paid. The adequacy of the SMI Trust Fund is measured only for years for which both the beneficiary premiums and the general revenue contributions have been set.

Id. at 4.

6. *See* [OFFICE OF MANAGEMENT & BUDGET, HISTORICAL TABLES: BUDGET OF THE UNITED STATES GOVERNMENT, FISCAL YEAR 1996, at 98 (1995) (hereinafter HISTORICAL TABLES) (for most historical data; using total mandatory spending, which includes undistributed offsetting receipts for entitlements)].

7. *See* Ted Marmor, *The Medicare Solution,* WASH. MONTHLY, Sept. 1995, at 35.

8. [SOCIAL SECURITY & MEDICARE BOARD OF TRUSTEES, STATUS OF THE SOCIAL SECURITY AND MEDICARE PROGRAMS: A SUMMARY OF THE 1995 ANNUAL REPORTS 1 (1995) (hereinafter TRUSTEES' SUMMARY REPORT).] The trustees also make the following statements regarding Medicare Part A:

> Under the intermediate assumptions, the projected year of exhaustion for the HI Trust Fund is 2002; under more adverse conditions, as in the high cost alternative, it could be as soon as 2001.

Id. at 6.

The non-administration, or "public," trustees make these further, more sweeping observations:

> There are basic questions with the scale, structure and administration of the Medicare program that need to be addressed. For example, is it appropriate to have a Part A and Part B today, or should this . . . be revised to create a unified program? Is it appropriate to combine participants' social insurance tax contributions for Part A and premium payments for approximately one-quarter of Part B with general revenues? If so, what should be the proper combination? . . . . [W]hat rights to benefits and responsibilities to pay benefits are thereby established?
>
> We feel strongly that comprehensive Medicare reforms should be undertaken to make this program financially sound now and over the long term. The idea that reductions in Medicare expenditures should be available for other purposes, including even other health care purposes, is mistaken. The focus should be on making Medicare itself sustainable, making it compatible with OASDI, and making both Social Security and Medicare financially sound in the long term.

Id. at 13.

9. *See* JENNIFER O'SULLIVAN, MEDICARE: FINANCING THE PART A HOSPITAL INSURANCE PROGRAM 6 (May 25, 1995) (CRS Rep. No. 95-650 EPW).

10. *See id.*

11. *See id.*

12. Marmor, *supra* note 11, at 36.

13. *Id.* at 36.

14. *See* [BOARD OF TRUSTEES, FEDERAL OLD-AGE AND SURVIVORS INS. AND DISABILITY INS. TRUST FUNDS, 1995 ANNUAL REPORT OF THE BOARD OF TRUSTEES OF THE FEDERAL OLD-AGE AND SURVIVORS INSURANCE AND DISABILITY INSURANCE TRUST FUNDS, H.R. DOC. NO. 57, 104TH CONG., 1ST SESS. 3 (1995) (hereinafter OASDI TRUSTEES' REPORT) (year-end 1994 data)].

15. Beginning in the year 2030, HI Trust Fund deficits are projected to reach 2% of the gross domestic product, trending upward toward 3% of the gross domestic product by the year 2070. In contrast, between 2030 and 2070, Social Security Trust Fund deficits are projected to remain between 1.5% and 2% of the gross domestic product. *See* OASDI TRUSTEES' REPORT, *id.*, at 188.

16. [SOCIAL SECURITY & MEDICARE BOARD OF TRUSTEES, STATUS OF THE SOCIAL SECURITY AND MEDICARE PROGRAMS: A SUMMARY OF THE 1995 ANNUAL REPORTS 1 (1995) (hereinafter TRUSTEES' SUMMARY REPORT).]

17. *See* [BOARD OF TRUSTEES, FEDERAL OLD-AGE AND SURVIVORS INS. AND DISABILITY INS. TRUST FUNDS, 1995 ANNUAL REPORT OF THE BOARD OF TRUSTEES OF THE FEDERAL OLD-AGE AND SURVIVORS INSURANCE AND DISABILITY INSURANCE TRUST FUNDS, H.R. DOC. NO. 57, 104TH CONG., 1ST SESS. 3 (1995) (hereinafter OASDI TRUSTEES' REPORT) (year-end 1994 data)].

18. *See id.*

19. *See* CHARLES DICKENS, *A Christmas Carol, in* CHRISTMAS BOOKS 70 (Oxford Univ. Press 1954).

20. At a Capitol Hill conference in early 1994, former Office of Management and Budget Director David Stockman expressed optimism about the long-term solvency of Social Security: to solve the problem, the United States needed merely to annex Mexico. While Mr. Stockman

spoke in jest, his remark contains a grain of truth. To the extent that the United States closes its borders to younger immigrants, who tend to have more children, it will decrease the number of future workers supporting future retirees, and add to Social Security's long-term woes.

In 1997, the General Accounting Office (GAO) issued a report on Medicare fraud and waste. Although the GAO could not state with precision how much Medicare loses each year to fraud and waste, it believed that the government could realize "large savings" if it could reduce unnecessary or inappropriate payments. It estimated that anywhere from 3 to 10 percent of the Medicare expenditures can be traced to fraud or waste, meaning that the program potentially could save anywhere from $6 billion to $20 billion a year.

The Health Care Finance Agency (HCFA) administers Medicare primarily by reimbursing claims processing contractors. These contractors, which are generally large insurance companies such as Blue Cross and Blue Shield and Travelers, in turn pay health care providers and beneficiaries. In 1996 there were about seventy of these contractors. The contractors that handle the Part A claims—that is, institutions such as hospitals, nursing homes, hospices, and home health care agencies—are called "contractors." Those who handle Part B claims submitted by physicians, laboratories, and so forth are referred to as "carriers."

As there are over 33 billion Medicare beneficiaries who generated over 800 million claims in 1996 alone, it is understandable why fraud and abuse could easily occur. For example, a contractor who reimburses a home health agency will examine the proffered billing forms to see if the agency is billing for services properly reimbursable under Medicare. Even if the forms are filled out properly, however, it is possible that no service was actually provided. Only by double checking with the alleged patient could the contractor uncover the fraud. Even if it is not fraud, there could be a misdiagnosis, and the patient could receive treatment for which there should be no Medicare reimbursement.

As for carriers who reimburse physicians and other personnel, there have been some demonstration projects trying to cut down on fraud and abuse by claims to carriers. Experience shows the best way to cut down on fraud is to give the carriers enough money so that they can run a sufficient number of audits to ensure that they are not being victimized. The GAO has recommended a number of other things that HCFA could do to minimize fraud and waste. None of the recommendations, however, will be meaningful unless HCFA is sufficiently motivated to reduce fraud and waste to a minimum. To date, HCFA seems to lack such motivation. Ferreting out fraud and waste is difficult, while merely paying the bills submitted by the contractors and carriers is relatively simple. As a result, fraud and abuse will undoubtedly continue as an aspect of Medicare for the foreseeable future.

Of course, the deeper problem is that Medicare, like any insurance program, has divorced the recipient of the goods (the payor) from the beneficiary (the patient). The patient has no reason to try to stop fraud and waste since it does not directly cost the patient anything. Intermediary contractors and carriers have no reason to try to minimize waste as long as they are reimbursed for what they pay. And the government (HCFA), which should be the ultimate watchdog, gains nothing other than a better reputation by reducing fraud and waste. If HCFA pays too much for Medicare, it merely asks Congress to ante up more tax dollars to keep the program solvent. In short, none of the players in the game have any particular reason to seriously crack down on fraud and waste.

Perhaps someday HCFA may be operated by individuals who are diligent and sincere in trying to reduce fraud and waste. But given the realities, it seems unlikely that the necessary enthusiasm and dedication will be the norm. More likely, if we want a federal Medicare program, we simply have to put up with a degree of fraud and waste.

CHAPTER 35

Rationing of Health Care

The most drastic proposals for Medicare savings involve explicit rationing of health care for older persons. While rationing has not yet been accepted as a politically viable option, it has garnered support. The following article presents the case for and against rationing.

Andrew H. Smith and John Rother

Older Americans and the Rationing of Health Care

Americans long ago dedicated themselves to the removal of social and economic barriers that unfairly burdened racial and ethnic minorities, women, and older people. Discrimination against individuals on the basis of their membership in artificially defined groups was rejected. The current crisis in health care expenditures, however, may be reviving some old prejudices and creating new ones, particularly against older people. Questions have been raised about older Americans, their place in society, and their rightful claim on resources such as health care. The way that society addresses these questions may well determine the character and quality of life in this country over the next few decades.

* * *

Originally published in *University of Pennsylvania Law Review,* Vol. 140, 1847 (1992).

II. Medical Care for the Elderly as an Alleged Source of the Health Care Expenditure Crisis

Increasing patient demand for services has been identified by proponents of rationing as a major source of rising health care costs.[1] Available empirical evidence casts some doubt on this assertion. In a study of hospital usage patterns in Boston and New Haven, researchers found (after controlling for patient differences) that Bostonians used 4.5 beds per thousand population, while the citizens of New Haven used fewer than 3 beds per thousand.[2] Boston's per capita expenditures for hospitalization were found to be consistently twice those for New Haven.[3] Most of the difference in resource use was found to be associated with medical conditions for which there is a high variation in use rates and for which physicians' clinical decision thresholds for hospitalization depend on the supply of beds.[4] Of course, patients may be more demanding than in the past, but it is difficult to reconcile the view that patient demand is of primary importance in rising health care expenditures with the findings in the Boston–New Haven use pattern study. Are the citizens of New Haven less demanding than residents of Boston, or do physicians in Boston hospitalize more aggressively? What *is* apparent is that we really know very little about patient demand, and that it may thus be inappropriate to predicate policy changes upon such an assumption.[5]

The aging of American society, with its associated increases in morbidity and health care costs,[6] is viewed by some as the most important component of a discouraging health care expenditure picture.[7] A number of commentators argue that the most appropriate place to ration care is with the elderly and propose to restrict expensive, high technology, life-sustaining care for those who have reached a certain age.[8] It is assumed that this type of care represents an investment of scarce resources with few returns, frequently involving intensive and aggressive treatment that serves only to prolong the agony of dying.[9] It is also assumed that vast resources are being expended, and are destined to be spent, on such care for the dying elderly.[10] This perception is bolstered by a study which shows that a large amount of money is expended on Medicare beneficiaries in their last year of life.[11]

Researchers examining data from 1978 found that the less than 6 percent of Medicare beneficiaries who died in that year accounted for approximately 28 percent of Medicare expenditures.[12] This proportion of expenditures may, intuitively, seem excessive. Intuition, however, is not a dependable guide. First, it is worth noting that the share of the Medicare budget devoted to elderly people in their last year of life has been nearly constant since the inception of the program.[13] Second, even if it were possible to predict with certainty which patients would die within twelve months (something which *cannot* be done), and all care were to be withheld from these beneficiaries, relatively small savings would be achieved; only 22.7 billion dollars, or 4.6 percent of health care expenditures, would have been saved in 1987.[14] Those who advocate age-based rationing do not generally propose to withhold all medical treatment from older persons, but rather, expensive, aggressive care. Researchers have found that only 3 percent of Medicare decedents incur "high costs."[15] Withholding all treatment for high-cost Medicare decedents would have produced savings of $2.8 billion in 1987.[16] This is not a negligible amount of money, but saving this sum would have produced little of economic significance in the context of health care expenditures that reached nearly one half of a trillion dollars.[17] It is also important to note that of high cost patients included in the 1984 study, over one half survived.[18] If high cost health care had been withheld from this group of once seriously ill people, a fraction of one percent in total health care expenditures could have been saved, but at the price of many lives.

Underlying the debate over rationing life-sustaining care for older persons is the image of frail, moribund, elderly patients being shocked back to life twenty or thirty times, being subjected to all the wonders of modern medical science, before finally being allowed to die.[19] This image does not, however, accurately depict how such patients are commonly treated. In fact, aggressive treatment of the elderly decreases as the level of impairment increases.[20] Frail, totally impaired patients do not routinely receive expensive, high technology medical treatment. They receive supportive care primarily, which in itself proves quite expensive.[21]

It has been argued that if we look not at the current situation, but at trends in aging, we shall see that a vastly expanded population of "older old" in the more distant future, coupled with advances in life-sustaining technology, will inevitably overwhelm and destroy our economy.[22] There is cause for concern, but the policy proposed, to set age limits for life-sustaining care, hardly exhausts the possible policy alternatives to meet the challenge of an aging society and rapidly increasing very old population. One alternative would be to increase outlays for research to prevent or effectively treat diseases of old age that create the greatest need for long-term care.[23] The incidence of Alzheimer's disease, Parkinson's disease, osteoarthritis, and osteoporosis increases exponentially with age, and each produces lengthy periods of disability requiring years of long-term care.[24] Despite the fact that current and projected costs associated with these diseases are enormous, federal research funds have been slow in coming; they are still only a small fraction of the overall spending for these diseases.[25] The prevention of these and other diseases associated with advanced age could significantly improve prospects for future health care expenditures. To suggest that these diseases cannot be conquered, or that should they be overcome they would simply be replaced by others that would similarly affect the elderly with equally high expenditures, is unfounded pessimism.[26]

III. Justifications for Age-based Rationing Proposals

Arguments in favor of age-based rationing are founded on more than economics. Medical benefit, productivity, equality, natural life-span, and intergenerational justice are just a few of the bases cited in support of age-based rationing.[27]

The medical benefit argument asserts that older people cannot, because of their physical condition, benefit from certain treatments. While it is true that advanced age is statistically associated with reduced likelihood of a favorable medical outcome, it is, as a single factor, a highly undependable clinical outcome predictor.[28] In fact, physiologic age does not correlate at all well with chronological age. Older people are extremely heterogeneous, both physiologically and psychologically—more so than younger adults.[29] For this reason, an arbitrary age-based cutoff for certain medical services is inappropriate if the goal is to target treatments to those who can benefit from them.

Some would justify the withholding of expensive medical services to older persons on the basis of the decreased productivity of the elderly.[30] Such commentators implicitly question what return society will realize from its investment in care, particularly life-sustaining care, for the older persons. Some may argue that excluding older persons from treatment could result in greater returns for society, were those dollars invested in more "worthy," productive workers. This view presents a demeaning, monetary vision of the value of human life that is not acceptable in an egalitarian society. If we believe that all human life is sacred, and equally deserving of protection, then access to care should not be determined by what society may gain from permitting an individual to regain her health.[31]

Restrictions on health care services to older Americans have been suggested to follow from application of the "principle of equality" to health care spending. This suggestion is based upon the idea that individuals should have the opportunity to live to the same age as others—that there is a prima facie right to a minimum number of life-years.[32] This perspective, as some formulate it, would support limitation of health care for the elderly to provide services that would allow all, to the extent possible, to reach at least a certain age.[33] Here persons are treated as sums of life-years, not as individual human entities; individuals' lives are not recognized as equally, but uniquely, precious.

Perhaps the most widely discussed justification for rationing life-sustaining health care for the elderly is the "natural life-span" view articulated by Daniel Callahan.[34] He argues that the cost of health care for the elderly will inevitably deprive younger generations not only of adequate health care, but of many other things they need to realize their full life experience.[35] Callahan calls for a policy-age-based rationing—that will allow young people the opportunity to become old, proceeding along the following lines.[36] The elderly know that much of their own welfare depended upon the work and contributions of earlier generations. They should not place the young in the difficult position of forcing them to make sacrifices. The elderly should lead the way, and allow the needs of the young to take precedence over their own needs. Callahan describes this state of affairs as "both gracious and fair."[37]

Callahan advances the notion of a "natural lifespan," a lifespan that is normative rather than just a statistical average.[38] He defines the natural lifespan as "one in which life's possibilities have on the whole been achieved and after which death may be understood as a sad, but nonetheless relatively acceptable event."[39] Once one has lived this natural lifespan, roughly figured to be about the late seventies or early eighties, one should not receive expensive, life sustaining medical treatment. Callahan proposes that those who continue to live on past the natural lifespan should receive only supportive and palliative care.[40]

The concept of a "natural life-span" is hard to defend in an age when so many people continue to lead active and healthy lives at age eighty and older. To attempt to establish an age at which everyone will have accomplished everything of significance is, inevitably, a hopeless enterprise.

* * *

Finally, the argument for age-based rationing as a matter of intergenerational justice, as drawn by Callahan, Lamm, and others, is unduly one-sided. As Thomasma observes, "intergenerational justice cuts both ways."[41] It is the elderly, who through their investment of "human capital," who through their sacrifices, created the vast range of resources and services younger people now enjoy.[42] Greene aptly notes that any economic analysis that takes into account the elderly's investment in human capital would find that they have received less than a competitive return on their investment.[43] We might well ask what kind of justice it is that would deprive elderly citizens of the results of medical research when their taxes financed those discoveries, and their personal sacrifices (such as those made in America's wars) preserved our opportunity to gain the rewards of a free and prosperous society.[44]

Conclusion

Rationing high technology, life-sustaining treatment for the elderly would not significantly curtail the growth of health care expenditures. There is little reason to suppose that rationing would avoid the problem of provider-generated revenue protection practices, such as increasing the volume of covered services.[45] Further, even if money were "saved," there is no reason to believe that it would be dedicated to purposes more constructive than current purposes.[46] Thus, age-based health care rationing would not achieve the practical goals articulated by its proponents. Further, the social costs of such a policy would be unacceptably high. As Levinsky observes, it would require a societal reeducation program that would excite tensions between the generations, and further devalue the status of older people.[47]

Access to health care should be considered, as it has been widely recognized to be, a right, grounded in fundamental human need.[48] It is morally unacceptable to ration beneficial health care except in the most extreme situations, and certainly unjustifiable under current circumstances. Rationing is acceptable only where real scarcity exists, where competing fundamental needs might dictate that health care services be withheld in favor of even more urgent needs. Rationing should be the very last option to be considered, and then it should be applied fairly and equitably on the basis of individualized assessment—not according to some artificial criterion such as age or social status.[49]

We must recognize, however, that the problem of rapidly rising health care costs is a threat to our society's well-being, both in the present and future. Medical care is a sector of the economy that is largely unregulated by classic market forces. No such economic sector can grow disproportionately over time without disrupting other economic sectors. It is a problem that must be constructively and expeditiously addressed.

Cost-containment to date has been a piecemeal effort that has encouraged cost shifting.[50] The general lack of success has inspired deep pessimism and cynicism about prospects for cost-containment.[51] As an empirical matter, though, we have not tried every possible way to contain health care costs on a widescale basis for a significant period of time.[52] A number of potentially useful ideas have been suggested, including promoting the widespread execution of advance directives, redoubling research efforts for diseases of old age, continuing the development and application of outcomes research, and many others. It will, however, take *comprehensive* health care reform—reform that will change both the way medicine is practiced and the way services are reimbursed—to achieve effective, long-term cost control. Only a comprehensively reformed system has the potential to eliminate system gaming efforts, to diminish inappropriate utilization of services, and to control the proliferation of medical technology. It is, therefore, comprehensive reform that should be the focus of our attention, not the ethically and economically unsound proposal to ration health care services for older Americans.

Notes

1. *See* [DANIEL CALLAHAN, WHAT KIND OF LIFE? 20–26 (1990) [hereinafter WHAT KIND OF LIFE]; Richard D. Lamm, *Brave New World of Health Care,* 52 ANNALS OF THORACIC SURGERY 369–84 (1991) (hereinafter *Brave New World*)].

2. *See* John E. Wennberg, *The Road to Guidelines,* 13 HEALTH MGMT. Q., Second Quarter, at 1, 6 (1991).

3. *See id.*

4. *See id. But see* Miron Stano, *Further Issues in Small Area Variations Analysis,* 16 J. HEALTH POL. POL'Y AND L. 573, 584 (1991) (attributing the difference in resource use to patient preferences and diffusion of information and technology which are not well understood).

5. *See* John Wennberg, *Outcomes Research, Cost Containment, and the Fear of Health Care Rationing,* 323 NEW ENG. J. MED. 1202, 1202 (1990) (noting the lack of knowledge concerning patient demand).

6. For a discussion of the aging of the population, the growth in the number of the "older old," and the resulting consequences for health care expenditures, see Dennis W. Jahnigen & Robert H. Binstock, *Economic and Clinical Realities: Health Care for Elderly People, in* TOO OLD FOR HEALTH CARE? CONTROVERSIES IN MEDICINE, LAW, ECONOMICS, AND ETHICS 13, 17–22 (Robert H. Binstock & Stephen G. Post eds., 1991) [hereinafter TOO OLD FOR HEALTH CARE?].

7. *See* [Daniel Callahan, SETTING LIMITS 15–24 (1987) (hereinafter SETTING LIMITS); Richard D. Lamm, *Columbus and Copernicus: New Wine in Old Wineskins,* 56 MOUNT SINAI J. MED. 1, 4 (1989) (hereinafter *Wineskins*)].

8. *See* SETTING LIMITS, *id.,* at 115–58; *Wineskins, id.,* at 6–8.

9. *See Wineskins, id.,* at 6–8.

10. *See id.* at 7.

11. *See* James Lubitz & Ronald Prihoda, *The Use and Costs of Medicare Services in the Last 2 Years of Life,* 5 HEALTH CARE FIN. REV. 117, 117–31 (1984).

12. *See id.* at 117.

13. *See id.*

14. *See* Jahnigen & Binstock, *supra* note 6, at 29–30.

15. *See* Lubitz & Prihoda, *supra* note 11, at 122. "High cost" in the Lubitz and Prihoda study refers to Medicare patients with reimbursements of $20,000 or more in 1978. *See id.*

16. *See* Jahnigen & Binstock, *supra* note 6, at 30.

17. *See id.*

18. *See* Lubitz & Prihoda, *supra* note 11, at 122.

19. *Wineskins, supra* note [7], at 6.

20. *See* Anne A. Scitovsky, *Medical Care in the Last Twelve Months of Life: The Relation Between Age, Functional Status, and Medical Care Expenditures,* 66 MILBANK Q. 640, 649–56 (1988).

21. *See id.*

22. *See Wineskins, supra* note [7], at 1–2. Daniel Callahan writes:

> Right now, the very old do not receive a great deal of high-technology medicine. However, the trend is clearly in that direction, with a constant upward swing in the number of treatments and procedures originally developed for younger patients being applied to elderly patients. Pursuit of that course . . . will surely divert money from the health and other needs of younger age groups.

Daniel Callahan, *Old Age and New Policy,* 261 JAMA 905, 906 (1989).

23. *See* Edward L. Schneider, *Options to Control the Rising Health Care Costs of Older Americans,* 261 JAMA 907, 908 (1989).

24. *See id.*

25. *See id.*

26. *See id.* As we look at the history of medicine in the twentieth century, we find that there is more reason for optimism than pessimism. It is a history of remarkable progress, and there is little reason to suppose that curative and preventative discoveries will not continue. Current research in genetics, for example, could produce extraordinary advances in human health and longevity. *See, e.g.,* Francesca Happe, *Aging Problem "Can be Solved,"* DAILY TELEGRAPH (London), Feb. 17, 1992, at 10 (London) (discussing the findings evolutionary biologist Dr. Michael Rase presented in a paper to the American Association for the Advancement of Science).

27. *See* ROBERT H. BLANK, RATIONING MEDICINE 189 (1988) (medical benefit); SETTING LIMITS, *supra* note 7, at 66–67 (natural life span); Raymond A. Belliotti, *Moral Assessment and the Allocation of Scarce Medical Resources,* 5 VALUES AND ETHICS IN HEALTH CARE 251, 251–62 (1980) (productivity); [Richard D. Lamm, *The Ten Commandments of an Aging Society,* 54 VITAL SPEECHES 133, 134 (1987)] (intergenerational justice); Robert M. Veatch, *Justice and Valuing Lives, in* LIFE SPAN 197, 197–224 (Robert M. Veatch ed., 1979) (equality).

28. *See* Jahnigen & Binstock, *supra* note 6, at 26.

29. *See* JAMES F. FRIES & LAWRENCE M. CRAPO, VITALITY AND AGING 108–09 (1981); NATHAN W. SHOCK ET AL., NORMAL HUMAN AGING: THE BALTIMORE LONGITUDINAL STUDY OF AGING 1 (1984).

30. *See* JOHN F. KILNER, WHO LIVES? WHO DIES? 79–80 (1990).

31. *See id.* at 90.

32. *See id.* at 83–84.

33. *See id.*

34. *See* Daniel Callahan, *Health Care Struggle Between Young and Old,* SOCIETY, Oct. 1991, at 29, 30–31 (1991).

35. *See id.* at 30.

36. *See id.*

37. *Id.* at 31.

38. *See* SETTING LIMITS, *supra* note 7, at 66 (arguing that biographical, not biological, events should be used to determine what is, or is not a "tolerable death" and therefore, when a "natural life span" has been reached).

39. *Id.*

40. *See id.* at 76–78.

41. David C. Thomasma, *From Ageism Toward Autonomy, in* TOO OLD FOR HEALTH CARE? *supra* note 6, at 146.

42. *See* Vernon L. Greene, *Human Capitalism and Intergenerational Justice,* 29 THE GERONTOLOGIST 723, 724 (1989). Greene explains that human capital embodies

> those capabilities that arise from the possession of a sophisticated stock of knowledge, skills, and accompanying attitudes that are conducive to producing wealth . . . . [I]t is called "capital" because it represents an *investment*—somebody had to sacrifice current consumption . . . in order to create it . . . . Someone then had to massively fund, both through tax payments and private purchase, the entire structure of public and private education through which this human capital is created and maintained. In short, someone had to invest massively from their incomes and opportunities in order to create the stock of human capital from which most of our current wealth arises.

Id.

43. *See id.*

44. *See* Thomasma, *supra* note 41, at 146.

45. *See* Arnold S. Relman, *The Trouble with Rationing,* 323 NEW ENG. J. MED. 911, 912 (1990).

46. As Wiener points out, the United States does not have a fixed budget for national health care spending. It is thus impossible to say where money saved through health care spending constraints would go. "[I]t is difficult to say no to additional resources for patients because there is no certainty that the funds will be put to better use elsewhere." [Joshua M. Wiener, *Rationing in America: Overt and Covert, in* RATIONING AMERICA'S MEDICAL CARE: THE OREGON PLAN AND BEYOND 12, 13 (Martin A. Strosberg et al., eds., 1992).]

47. *See* Norman G. Levinsky, *Age as a Criterion for Rationing Health Care,* 322 NEW ENG. J. MED. 1813, 1815 (1990).

48. A right to health care is recognized by a number of groups. *See, e.g., United Nations Universal Declaration of Human Rights,* Art. 25, G.A. Res. 217(III), U.N. GAOR, 3d Sess., at 71–77 ("Everyone has the right to a standard of living adequate for the health and well-being of himself and of his family, . . . including medical care . . . ."); AMERICAN ASSOC. OF RETIRED PERSONS, TOWARD A JUST AND CARING SOCIETY: THE AARP PUBLIC POLICY AGENDA 1991, at 96–97 (1991); *American Medical Association in its statement to the Subcommittee on Health, Committee on Finance,* United States Senate, July 29, 1988.

49. One ethically sound and rational basis for the allocation of truly scarce health care resources would be patient prognosis.

50. It is inaccurate to say that all cost-containment efforts have been abject failures. In 1983, the

government implemented the Medicare prospective payment system nationwide, and in recent years Medicare, as a share of national health care expenditures, has declined. *See* Robert B. Friedland, *Medicare: Meeting the Health Care Needs of the Elderly,* ISSUE BRIEF (Public Policy Institute of the AARP, Washington, D.C.), July 1991, at 13. Private employers and insurers, however, have not enacted similar tough cost containment measures. If they made a concerted effort to contain costs, it is hardly certain that their effort would fail. *See* Uwe B. Reinhardt, *Hotels and Airlines Do It: Why Not Hospitals?,* WALL ST. J., Jan. 14, 1992, at A14.

51. *See* Callahan, *supra* note 22, at 905; *Wineskins, supra* note 4, at 8.

52. *See* [Joshua M. Wiener, *Rationing in America: Overt and Covert, in* RATIONING AMERICA'S MEDICAL CARE: THE OREGON PLAN AND BEYOND 12, 13 (Martin A. Strosberg et al., eds., 1992)].

CHAPTER 36

Medicaid

In 1965, Congress created Medicaid to pay for health care of aged, blind, or disabled low-income persons. Medicaid is paid for by a combination of federal and state general tax revenues. (Individual states pay between 50 percent and 80 percent of the costs of Medicaid, called Medical Assistance in some states and Medical in California.) Originally, Medicaid for the aged was conceived as a way of paying for those elderly too poor to afford Medicare. Over time, however, more and more older persons who lived in nursing homes became eligible for Medicaid after they exhausted their savings. Once an older person has spent-down his or her savings and if her or his income is less than the monthly cost of a nursing home (which can range from $3,000 to $5,000 a month), in most states the individual becomes eligible for Medicaid. For example, if the nursing home resident has no more savings and has monthly income from Social Security and a private pension of $1,500 a month, but the nursing home costs $4,000 a month, the Medicaid program will pay the monthly short-fall of $2,500 a month.

Perhaps the main criticism of Medicaid as a payor of long-term care costs is that it works too well. That is, too many nursing home residents qualify for Medicaid assistance, thereby making the program prohibitively expensive for the states. Over 40 percent of nursing home costs are paid for by Medicaid. The use of private, long-term care insurance could reduce the dependence on Medicaid, but the cost of such insurance has discouraged its widespread adoption. Some commentators advocate governmental subsidy of long-term care premiums as a way of increasing sales. Others argue for mandatory long-term care insurance supported by a payroll tax, much like Social Security. The premiums for the insurance would be prorated on an ability-to-pay basis. None of theses ideas, however, has garnered any significant support. There is more interest in lowering the demand for long-term care nursing homes as a cost-savings measure.

Although Medicaid has its critics, it also has its supporters, such as Senator Bob Graham of Florida who attempts to justify Medicaid in the following article.

The Honorable Bob Graham

Medicaid Reform: Saving an American Success Story

* * *

I. Medicaid: An American Success Story

Medicaid was established in 1965 as a jointly funded federal-state program to provide medical assistance to low-income Americans.[1] Each state is responsible for designing and administering its own Medicaid program, subject to certain federal requirements involving issues such as eligibility, level of service provided, and health care provider payments.[2] The federal government pays a portion of whatever qualifying expenditures a state Medicaid program incurs, and the states have the option of providing any additional services.[3]

For the past thirty years, the Medicaid program has been the lifeblood of the United States' health and long-term care delivery system for millions of Americans. Indeed, over thirty-six million Americans received Medicaid benefits in 1995.[4] Medicaid is the only source of medical coverage for many Americans with diverse health care needs. It provides a medical safety net for pregnant women and children, the elderly, and disabled Americans. The program provides preventive care for low-income and moderate-income pregnant women and children, and it provides long-term care for the elderly and persons with disabilities.[5]

Through a federal-state government partnership, Medicaid provides acute-care and preventive care coverage that is similar to the employer-based coverage available to other Americans.[6] Additionally, Medicaid provides to senior citizens and disabled Americans long-term care rarely available through any other source.[7] This long-term care has also been a lifeline for America's fragile elderly. Over 60 percent of the nursing home residents in this country qualify for Medicaid,[8] many qualifying only after their life savings have been depleted by chronic medical conditions.[9] Great strides have been made in improving the quality of care for our elderly who depend upon Medicaid for their survival. For the senior citizens of our nation, Medicaid has been a tremendous success.

Medicaid also successfully provides for the needs of other segments of America. For example, the Qualified Medicaid Beneficiary program covers Medicaid premiums, deductibles, and co-payments for beneficiaries who have incomes below the federal poverty level.[10] Nearly seventeen million low-income Americans participate

Originally published in *Florida State Law Review*, Vol. 23, 917 (1996).

in this program.[11] This program has made the difference between preventive care in a doctor's office and intensive care in a hospital emergency room. The many families whose lives have been bettered through the Medicaid program all have their own stories to tell.[12] These families could have been your family, my family, or any other American family.

* * *

To tout Medicaid's successes is not to ignore its faults. There is work to be done to improve accountability, combat fraud and waste, and check growth in spending.

* * *

III. Medicaid Reform to Save America's Medical Safety Net

The only way to reform Medicaid is to restrain growing costs without jeopardizing the successful aspects of Medicaid. The Senate is not irrevocably wedded to block grants; there is a better way. The foundation of the block grant proposal—enhanced flexibility for the states—is built on shaky ground, eroding every day. Shaky, that is, unless you define "flexibility" as the freedom to raise state taxes or local property taxes, or the flexibility to pit the elderly against child beneficiaries. Otherwise, there is scant flexibility the states can receive that they cannot already get under the waiver program.[13] The Department of Health and Human Services has pioneered with willing states extraordinary demonstration projects, where statutory and regulatory requirements can be waived to permit new approaches to health care.

* * *

The best of both worlds is the "per capita cap" proposal that is gaining momentum as the "win-win" answer to the block grant's "lose-lose" proposition. The per capita cap approach provides that health care and coverage can be protected and costs controlled by disciplining the program with an annual limit in federal spending per beneficiary.

This approach maintains the individual guarantee to Medicaid coverage and creates incentives for states to maintain health care coverage. Funding would follow the patient, not some bureaucratic entity. The per capita cap approach that I presented to the Senate in November 1995 saves $62 billion over the next seven years.[14] It enhances state flexibility and reduces the rate of growth in federal Medicaid spending to a level that is sustainable for the states, the beneficiaries, and the federal government. It assures that states with innovative demonstrations already underway can continue to operate their programs and that other states wishing to innovate have the resources and ability to do so.

Let me briefly outline how the per capita cap approach would work. Federal funding would be allocated to states on a per person-in-need basis. If, hypothetically, it costs $1,000 to provide Medicaid benefits to a person in California, the federal government would allocate its share of money, or $500 in this case, for each person who qualifies for Medicaid in the state. If needs increase because of population shifts, recession, natural disaster, or public health calamity and more people become eligible for coverage, the federal partnership and contribution of $500 per person would be guaranteed—not as under a block grant where a fixed sum is allocated regardless of circumstance. The incentive is to reduce costs and not cut people off coverage because if states arbitrarily cut people off, they lose the federal match. Costs are what must be controlled. If, for example, California were to spend more than $1,000 per person cap, California would make up that difference. Again, under a per capita cap, the money follows the need and person. As a result, during economic booms, or when health needs decline, the federal government would share in the savings—also not as under the block grant system that obligates money regardless of the needs of the residents of the state or the payments made by the state.

The cap would be stated in inflation terms on an annual basis in order to protect states from potential inflation increases. The cap would be cumulative and thus allow states enough flexibility to apply savings under the cap from one year to the next. Caps would be applied separately to the elderly, the disabled, children, and their mothers. This separation into four distinct groups avoids the sinister "zero sum game" that is endemic to block grants—a game in which one group's interests are pitted against the others'.

This formula may appear complicated, but it really is a clone of the way states allocate and distribute school dollars to the districts.[15] In fact, with only four categories to consider, it is far simpler than most "per pupil" school district formulas.[16] The per capita cap idea is also one that should be familiar to many of my Republican colleagues. It is a concept that was supported in health proposals introduced by Senators Dole, Gramm, and Chafee in 1994.[17]

The Medicaid per capita cap approach permits the states to move toward managed care and other types of arrangements that save money without needing federal waivers.[18] Another advantage to the per capita cap approach is that many other detailed rules and process-oriented requirements would be phased out. States would be held accountable for performance outcomes with respect to certain quality and access measures.[19] The federal government would be interested in the outcomes of state health and long-term care delivery systems but would not be mandating how to achieve those outcomes.

Finally, the per capita cap approach would cap and retarget future growth in the DSH [disproportionate hospital share] program. The per capita cap approach would assure that children, low-income women, and disabled and elderly Americans would have continued coverage for hospital, physicians, and nursing home care services. This approach would cut costs, not people.

IV. Conclusion

The $62 billion reduction in spending achieved through the per capita cap approach amounts to a surgical cut, not the meat-ax approach of the $72 billion cut under the block grant legislation that passed the Senate in 1995.[20] Further, the per capita cap approach would continue the federal-state partnership in detecting fraud and punishing defrauders. Medicaid fraud, DSH abuse, and unconstrained spending amount to a cancer on our nation's health and long-term care delivery system. However, it is a treatable, not terminal, condition. In our zeal to cure this affliction, let's not kill the patient in the process. Let's not kill the very federal-state partnership that has served this nation so well for thirty years. After all, behind the $72 billion in cuts are human beings who will pay the price for our haste.

In addressing the Medicaid and welfare block grant debates, David Broder of the *Washington Post* wrote eloquently of the fear that under block grants, "the states will engage in a 'race to the bottom' that shreds the social safety net."[21] He predicted the likeliest scenario under block grants as follows: "What would happen when federal funding is reduced and federal standards are eliminated is that the 50 legislatures would become the arena, each year, in which the welfare population would have to compete against other claimants for scarce dollars."[22]

I share his bleak view of the future in America under block grants. You cannot have a race to the bottom without casualties along the way. Along the way in the block grant "race to the bottom" will be eyeglasses for the elderly and unfilled prescriptions formerly covered under Medicaid. Such benefits will not survive the race to the bottom, and the individual losses will be great and even overwhelming. Along the way in the block grant "race to the bottom" will be families torn apart by unnecessary nursing home placements and institutionalization. Home health care and other Medicaid waiver services will not survive the race to the bottom. Along the way in the block grant "race to the bottom" will be ugly legislative sessions in fifty state legislatures, where, among the conflicts, the elderly will be pitted against children and the mentally retarded against AIDS sufferers in a battle royal for the block-grant dollar.

Is that what we want for America? The race to the bottom has yet to begin, and it need never begin. There is another way. Per capita cap legislation is our way out of the "race to the bottom" and is our ticket to a twenty-first century that maintains an American federal-state stake in the health and welfare of its citizens.

Notes

1. U.S. CONGRESSIONAL RESEARCH SERVICE, MEDICAID SOURCE BOOK 1 (1993) [hereinafter MEDICAID SOURCE BOOK].

2. *Id.* The only state without a formal Medicaid program is Arizona, but since 1982, Arizona has been receiving federal funds through a Medicaid waiver program. *Id.*

3. *Id.*

4. Bruce C. Vladeck, Administrator, Health Care Financing Administration, Statement Before the U.S. House of Representatives Subcommittee on Human Resources and Intergovernmental Relations, Jan. 18, 1996, *available in* Federal Document Clearing House.

5. *Id.* at 2.

6. *Id.*

7. *Id.*

8. MEDICAID SOURCE BOOK, *supra* note 1, at 811.

9. *Id.* at 841.

10. *See generally* U.S. GOVERNMENT ACCOUNTING OFFICE, MEDICARE: EFFORTS TO ENHANCE PATIENT QUALITY OF CARE (1994).

11. MEDICAID SOURCE BOOK, *supra* note 1, at 11, 13–15.

12. Many of these stories are profiles in courage—the courage of families trying to deal with health setbacks and scarce resources. For instance, Yvette Elkins, of Columbus, Ohio,

> [a]fter giving birth to her first child[,] stopped working to stay home with her baby. Shortly after she resigned, she learned that she was pregnant again. Soon after, her husband left her and the baby. For the first time in her life, Yvette began receiving welfare. Two weeks after her second child was born, Yvette began interviewing for full-time jobs. She depended on Medicaid to bridge the gap between homelessness and gainful employment. Medicaid paid for prescription drugs, doctor visits, and emergency visits; all critical services since Yvette's younger child suffered from chronic ear infections. Transitional Medicaid allowed Yvette to catch up on back bills and advance far enough to obtain a job that offers benefits.

141 CONG.REC. S16,645 (daily ed. Nov. 3, 1995). Another example is the story of Donna Guyton of Nashville, Tennessee:

> A mosquito bite is irritating, but hardly ever life-threatening. After a fateful family vacation to Michigan in 1990, Donna's son, Patrick, contracted viral encephalitis, possibly from a mosquito bite. He was hospitalized for three and a half months and suffered from severe seizures. He eventually had to be placed in a drug-induced coma. Until September of 1991, he was covered under his father's medical insurance. Then his father's company was bought out, and when they re-enlisted in the plan, Patrick was not covered. Patrick was covered by COBRA for 29 months and in November 1992, he was enrolled in the Medicaid Model Waiver Program at Vanderbilt HMO so that he could receive care from the specialists he needed. But Vanderbilt's Medical director consistently denied the care that the specialists requested. As a result of the poor attention and insufficient medication, Patrick . . . has had other health and emotional problems.

141 CONG.REC. S16,646–47 (daily ed. Nov. 3, 1995).

13. As states have felt the pressures of rising Medicaid costs, they have looked for alternative strategies for providing adequate health care while limiting costs. In order to facilitate more effective methods of providing Medicaid services, states have had to deviate from the traditional Medicaid structure. David Parrelle, Statement Before the U.S. House Subcommittee on Human Resources and Intergovernmental Relations, Jan. 18, 1996, *available in* Federal Document Clearing House. One way that the federal government satisfied this need for flexibility is through waiver programs such as the section 1115 research and demonstration waiver. *Id.* This waiver allows a state to set up an experimental health care delivery program and determine whether it will meet the needs of the state. *Id.* at 4. Even though waiver programs are designed to provide flexibility, the Health Care Finance Administration reviews the waiver to ensure it meets certain criteria. *Id.* at 5.

14. This per capita cap proposal, which I proposed in November 1995, 141 CONG.REC. S16, 845–48 (Nov. 9, 1995), is quite similar to the proposal President Clinton announced in December 1995. *Medicaid Per-Capita Cap Locks in State Disparities,* WASH. HEALTH WK., Dec. 18,

1995, at 1; *see* [CONGRESSIONAL BUDGET OFFICE, THE ECONOMIC AND BUDGET OUTLOOK: FISCAL YEARS 1997–2006 74 (May 1996) (hereinafter BUDGET OUTLOOK: 1997–2006)]. The President's per capita cap proposal is estimated to save $54 billion over six years. [Diane Rowland, Executive Director of the Kaiser Commission on the Future of Medicaid, Statement Before the U.S. House of Representatives Committee on Commerce, Mar. 6, 1996, available in Federal Document Clearing House.] The National Association of Governors adopted a Medicaid budget proposal that includes a variation on the per capita cap approach. [CONGRESSIONAL BUDGET OFFICE, AN ANALYSIS OF THE PRESIDENT'S BUDGET PROPOSAL FOR FISCAL YEAR 1996 45 (Apr. 1995); Telephone Interview with Nani Coloretti, Office of Management and Budget (July 10, 1996) (hereafter Coloretti Interview).]

15. *See, e.g.*, FLA. STAT. § 361.081 (1995).

16. *Id.*

17. *See Chafee Drops Medicaid Bill; HMOs Weary of Block Grants*, INSIDE HEALTH CARE REFORM, June 1, 1995, at 1; *Chafee Medicaid Reform Alternative to Block Grants Evolving in Senate*, INSIDE HEALTH CARE REFORM, June 15, 1995, at 1.

18. GOVERNMENT ACCOUNTING OFFICE, MEDICAID: RESTRUCTURING APPROACHES LEAVE MANY QUESTIONS 6 (Apr. 1995). This provides great flexibility for states to alter state Medicaid programs to adapt to the changing needs of beneficiaries without having to go through the arduous Medicaid waiver process for each program modification.

19. Per capita caps "put states at full risk for the management of the program." *Id.*

20. 141 CONG.REC. S16,847–48 (daily ed. Nov. 9, 1995) (quoting David Broder).

21. 141 CONG. REC. S16,848 (daily ed. Nov. 9, 1995).

22. [Christina Kent, *AMA Promotes State Feasibility on Medicaid With Safety Net*, AM. MED. NEWS, Dec. 18, 1995, at 3 (hereinafter Kent, *State Feasibility*).]

CHAPTER 37

Medicaid Reform

Medicaid is a federal-state partnership: both the federal government and state governments contribute to the cost of the program. (The percentage of the state contribution varies from state to state.) So long as the Medicaid program is an entitlement program—that is, the state must provide benefits to everyone who qualifies—the states have a direct financial interest in preventing the federal government from reducing its support. In particular, state governors object strongly to any Medicaid reform that would increase their financial burden. To lower the burden on states, some commentators advocate replacement of the entitlement portion of Medicaid with a block grant program. Instead of states promising to pay the medical expenses of all eligible Medicaid participants, the state would only commit to spending a set amount of money. That is, each year the federal government would allocate a set number of dollars (a block grant) to each state to help pay for medical care for qualifying individuals. The state would match the block grant according to some formula. This arrangement would limit the state financial liability, for once the federal block grant and the state matching funds had been expended, there would be no more funding in that state for medical assistance for the poor.

Not all governors support capping Medicaid spending by the use of block grants. In their testimony before Congress, Governors Bob Miller of Nevada and Michael O. Leavitt present the case against capping Medicaid spending.

Bob Miller and Michael O. Leavitt

Testimony, March 11, 1997

It is an honor to testify before the committee today on one of the most important issues facing states—the future of the Medicaid program. Today we appear before you as members of the National Governors' Association Medicaid Task Force.

* * *

Briefly, today we will review several issues of primary concern to governors, including Medicaid cost saving strategies, children's health, and managed care quality.

Much of the discussion about Medicaid reform that has taken place in recent months has focused on producing savings to contribute to efforts to balance the federal budget. No one recognizes more clearly than governors the need to control Medicaid spending, because we continuously wrestle with the pressure Medicaid exerts on our own budgets. In fact, almost all states must cope with Medicaid costs in the context of state balanced budget requirements.

The challenges Medicaid poses to state budgets became particularly acute in the late 1980s and early 1990s. During that time, Medicaid spending increased at average annual rates in excess of 20 percent. The program grew in both absolute and relative terms, and as a result of this growth, Medicaid now is the second largest expenditure in state budgets, behind primary and secondary education.

These growth rates were unsustainable. Medicaid costs were making it difficult to fund investments in other important state priorities. To address financial pressures and to develop a more quality-oriented system, governors have begun a massive transformation of state Medicaid systems. Historically, Medicaid programs have been claims processors and bill payers. The transformation currently underway is helping states to become more sophisticated value purchasers of quality health care services and to develop integrated systems of care for vulnerable populations.

Already this transformation is producing results. Medicaid spending grew only 4.5 percent between federal fiscal years 1995 and 1996, and only 3.3 percent between 1996 and 1997. The dramatic reduction in Medicaid growth rates we have enjoyed in recent years stems in large part from aggressive state pursuit of administrative simplification, innovation, and good management.

Our successes in controlling growth rates have been recognized. In February 1997, the Congressional Budget Office (CBO) lowered its baseline projections of future growth in Medicaid spending by almost $86 billion. This recalculation follows a similar baseline revision released in December 1995 that produced $31 billion in

Statement of Governor Bob Miller (Nevada) and Governor Michael O. Leavitt (Utah) on Medicaid Reform on behalf of The National Governors' Association, before the U. S. House of Representatives, Commerce Committee, Subcommittee on Health and Environment, March 11, 1997

Medicaid savings. These reductions could not have been achieved without state cost-containment strategies.

The governors are committed to building on their record of success in controlling Medicaid costs. But this must be done very carefully. And it must be done in a way that preserves the partnership of shared financial responsibility between the federal government and the states.

Recommended Savings Level

As a starting point for Medicaid reform, we believe it is critically important that the level of Medicaid savings not be set arbitrarily to fill a hole in a deficit reduction package. Instead, governors, Congress, and the administration should agree on a package of needed Medicaid reforms. The reforms set forth will lead to a level of savings that states and the federal government will be able to achieve by taking advantage of newly expanded programmatic flexibilities. Sound policy should drive Medicaid reform decisions, not budgetary politics.

Any consideration of Medicaid's role in balancing the budget must acknowledge that even before the first decision is made regarding a reconciliation package during this Congress, Medicaid already has contributed $86 billion toward deficit reduction in this budget cycle. CBO's revised baseline projections make efforts to reach a balanced budget agreement easier by $86 billion.

The revised CBO projections reflect the transformations underway in Medicaid programs to become streamlined value-purchasers of quality health care services. Given the progress already made, there is less room in the program from which to squeeze additional savings without having a detrimental effect on the number of people served by Medicaid or the range of benefits they receive.

For that reason, the governors believe that additional Medicaid savings included in any deficit reduction package developed by Congress and the administration should be kept to a minimum. However, we agree that additional savings are possible, and we are committed to working with you to continue to eliminate all unnecessary spending from the Medicaid program.

We are confident that with the additional flexibility we will ask you for today, states will be able to produce an additional $8 billion in scorable Medicaid savings between now and 2002, very close to the net Medicaid savings included in the president's budget. As has been the case in the past, although the scorable savings may be in the range of $8 billion, our ability to actually achieve savings could exceed CBO's expectations given this enhanced flexibility. Combined with the $86 billion in savings already acknowledged by CBO, Medicaid's contribution to deficit reduction will be at least $94 billion through 2002.

This level of savings should be considered in the context of the Medicaid savings targeted in last year's Medicaid reform efforts. The original Republican reform package would have produced $185 billion in savings by 2002. By the end of the debate,

Congress supported a package including Medicaid savings of $85 billion. Throughout last year's reform discussions, the president supported a reform package that would have generated $54 billion in savings.

A $94 billion contribution to deficit reduction by 2002 fits well within these parameters. In fact, when you combine governors' recommended savings with the two baseline recalculations made by CBO within the last eighteen months, Medicaid savings have already contributed $125 billion in deficit reduction, exceeding the targets set forth by Congress and the administration at the end of last year's Medicaid debate.

The governors therefore would not support the president's proposal to produce $22 billion in gross Medicaid savings by 2002, nor would we support packages calling for even higher levels of Medicaid savings we have heard discussed by many in Congress. As we have said before, savings of that magnitude cannot be achieved without adversely affecting those who rely on Medicaid for their health care needs.

Recommended Savings Strategy

With an expectation of additional achievable savings in the range of $8 billion to add to the $86 billion in savings already realized, the question of primary importance becomes what policy choices will be needed to achieve these savings.

The governors adamantly oppose a cap on federal Medicaid spending in any form. Any unilateral cap on the Medicaid program will shift costs to state and local governments that they simply cannot afford. Once the federal spending obligation is fulfilled, all additional costs will be passed on to the states. The proposed per capita caps will help the federal government balance the budget on the backs of the states.

The governors' opposition to Medicaid caps extends to the per capita cap proposals set forth both in the president's budget package and in the budget developed by the Blue Dog Coalition. We oppose these per capita caps for a number of reasons.

First, the caps are unworkable. There would need to be four separate caps on different eligibility categories for each of the fifty states. This means two hundred separate caps, which would have to be monitored by state agencies and audited and enforced by a new bureaucracy in the Health Care Financing Administration (HCFA).

Second, caps could result in states becoming solely responsible for unexpected program costs, such as a loss in a lawsuit on reimbursement rates or the development of expensive new therapies that drive up treatment costs beyond the federally allowable rate.

Third, the cost shift resulting from a unilateral federal cap would present states with a number of bad alternatives. States essentially would have to choose between cutting back on payment rates to providers, eliminating optional benefits provided to recipients, ending coverage for optional beneficiaries, or coming up with additional state funds to absorb 100 percent of the cost of services.

It seems unnecessary to us to undertake such a disruptive and fundamental transformation of a program on which the federal government will spend half a trillion dollars over the next five years in order to achieve the $8 billion in additional savings we consider reasonable. If we consider the president's budget package, his expectations for savings attributable to a per capita cap are even smaller. Although his package includes $22 billion in gross Medicaid savings, only $7 billion of that total comes from the program cap.

The president's package also includes $15 billion in savings from the disproportionate share hospital (DSH) program. Because governors consider $8 billion to be a reasonable savings target, we oppose the magnitude of the DSH cuts included in the president's budget. We also strongly believe that DSH funds must continue to be distributed through states, not directly to providers, to ensure that the program effectively complements other federal and state sources of health care funding. Maintaining the state role in distribution will ensure that DSH is coordinated with the state's overall health systems' infrastructure.

The governors are convinced that there are better ways to achieve an additional $8 billion in Medicaid savings by 2002, and NGA's [National Governor's Association] Medicaid Task Force has developed an alternative. Our strategy sets forth a number of policy options that, when combined, will produce significant savings. We believe those savings will be scorable at $8 billion through 2002, and upon implementation will likely yield additional savings. The savings in our alternative strategy stem from a series of policy changes that would assist states in their continued transformation toward value purchasing.

In some combination, the reform suggestions we believe Congress and the administration should consider would eliminate the need to institute any unilateral cap on beneficiary spending. We can group these suggested reforms into three broad categories—reforms related to managed care, reforms tied to reimbursement policy, and other program reforms.

Managed Care Reforms

1. Managed care. Repeal of the waiver requirement for mandatory managed care will facilitate further development of the Medicaid managed care market. As Medicaid markets mature, competition between managed care entities will enable states to negotiate even more favorable rates. With the development of models to accommodate special population needs, Medicaid managed care will increasingly penetrate the more complicated and costly segments of the caseload—the elderly and disabled.

States have already achieved significant savings through Medicaid managed care. For example, Michigan will save $120 million in Medicaid costs through managed care in 1998, about 2.5 percent of the state's total program budget. Missouri's managed care program will have saved $50 million through 1997 compared to fee for service costs.

Managed care does not simply produce a one-time savings bonus for states. Between 1990 and 1996, Wisconsin has saved more than $100 million as a result of managed care. Through competitive bidding, Florida's newest round of managed care contracts include capitation rates between 87 percent and 92 percent of fee for service rates. Previous contracts included rates at 95 percent of fee for service rates.

2. Managed care for the dually eligible. The dually eligible population, which currently is 6 million people, would be enrolled in managed care, creating a more streamlined, cost-effective system of health care delivery for those elderly and disabled individuals who receive a complete, but uncoordinated, package of benefits from both Medicaid and Medicare. Managed care would produce savings for both programs while creating a more user-friendly health care experience for recipients.

Utah has conducted a voluntary managed care program for the dually eligible, operating within existing federal limitations, and has seen a reduction in costs for services of approximately 10 percent for the population enrolled in managed care. Minnesota's managed care program for the dually eligible has produced a 5 percent reduction compared with fee for service costs.

We would like to submit for the record an NGA staff working paper that begins to explore issues related to the connections between the Medicaid and Medicare programs, including dual eligibility, and the implications of those connections for the states.

3. Provider selectivity. To clarify that there is no de facto entitlement for providers to participate in the Medicaid program in the fee for service environment, HCFA should support states in their efforts to contract with a limited number of facilities so they can negotiate better rates. For example, Medicaid recipients could be directed to two out of four hospitals in a city for services, or to a particular source to have prescriptions filled. Texas and Washington each have achieved 2 percent savings in their hospital reimbursement rates through selective contracting.

Reimbursement Policy Reforms

4. Reimbursement rates for Qualified Medicare Beneficiaries (QMBs) and the dually eligible. Recent judicial interpretations have begun to force states to reimburse providers at Medicare rates for services provided to these populations. Medicaid rates, which are on average significantly lower than Medicare rates, should be sufficient to discharge state obligations until the federal government assumes full responsibility for the cost-sharing obligations associated with QMBs and until a more integrated system is developed to serve the dually eligible.

Michigan estimates that permitting the state to limit reimbursement rates to Medicaid levels for these populations would save $85 million per year in Michigan alone.

One of the fundamental arguments over Medicaid payment of long-term care is whether it should be available only after individuals have spent down all their savings and other assets, or whether older persons should be permitted to retain some of their assets to pass on to their descendants. Professor Rein considers that question in her article.

Jan Ellen Rein

Misinformation and Self-Deception in Recent Long-Term Care Policy Trends

Summary

The topic of this article is both timely and highly controversial. The fate of the federal program of long-term care assistance under Medicaid is a key issue in the clash between the Congress and the White House over the recently vetoed Balanced Budget Act which, in its Medigrant provisions, would dramatically alter long-term care policy as we know it. As this is written, the issues examined are the subject of heated debate in the White House, United States Congress, state legislatures, mayoral offices, health care agencies, and affected citizens throughout the land. The following analysis provides information and insight needed by policy makers and health care analysts from the grass roots up and from the presidency on down. No matter what happens to the Medicaid program this year, the issues raised will be debated at the community, state, and federal level for years to come.

* * *

The debate rages on about who can or should have the primary responsibility for providing or paying for long-term care.[1] In some circles, Medicaid planning (the legal use of Medicaid rules and regulations to obtain Medicaid eligibility without exhausting all personal assets) has become a dirty word.[2] Public resources for health care are not unlimited. At the same time, Americans requiring long-term care and their loved ones often face a terrible squeeze as they struggle to meet the need for long-term care without becoming modern day King Lears, bereft of that element of power and the decent quality of life that comes with it.

No one chooses to be afflicted with illnesses or disabilities requiring long-term care. Many elders who face the need for long-term care, and their loved ones, suffer an involuntary triple catastrophe.[3] First, there is the emotional pain of contemplating one's own or one's loved one's long-term disability. Next comes the shock of discovering the enormity of long-term care costs[4] and contemplating the possibility of having all or most of what the family has struggled for a lifetime to acquire and save

Journal of Law & Politics, Vol. 12, No. 2, 195 (1996). Reprinted by permission.

wiped out within a few months or years of the onset of disability.[5] The third, but not necessarily final, shock occurs when individuals and their families learn that some of their fellow Americans will view their efforts to preserve some financial cushion for themselves and their loved ones against financial ruin (and the vulnerability and helplessness that comes with it) as manifestations of selfishness, greed, or downright fraud.[6]

Doubtless, there are some cases of abuse by truly wealthy individuals (or their family members) who obtain Medicaid qualification even though private resources could easily cover their long-term care costs. But evidence of such abuse is largely anecdotal.[7] Moreover, a combination of statistics illustrating the limited amount of assets available for transfer[8] and the serious risks of irrevocable pre-death transfer of substantial amounts[9] suggest that significant abuse may be more the exception than the rule.

* * *

B. An Introduction to the Long-Term Care Financing Debate

The debate over who should pay for long-term care is but one facet of the general health care and entitlements debate. With varying degrees of purity, participants in the debate gravitate toward one of two ideological camps. One group believes that primary responsibility for securing health care rests with individuals and their families. The other believes that health care is a basic human necessity which the community is obligated to secure for all who need it regardless of station in life. Placing these opposing views in the context of the long-term care debate, one camp argues that people should privately save or buy insurance for their own long-term care, with government stepping in to help only those who are completely destitute. The opposing camp argues that, due to the historical failure of profit-driven private sector initiatives to provide universal solutions, the government should not leave its citizenry to rely primarily on the private sector but should ensure a decent modicum of long-term care for all through some form of compulsory social insurance.[10]

* * *

Are most adult children who seek Medicaid planning greedy heirs or economically beleaguered caregivers hoping to salvage something for their children's education and their own future health needs? Are institutional long-term care consumers who seek planning advice greedy geezers or grateful relatives trying to protect their loved ones and repay with a modest inheritance the enormous sacrifices made on their behalf? As Professor Lawrence Friedman wrote, "[T]he millions of caregivers, mostly family members, mostly women, who devote so much time and energy to a thankless and degrading task, and who get nothing for it most of the time" cannot be blamed for placing a loved one in an institution to gain some relief when they can no longer cope. Nor can "a sixty-year-old woman working her fingers to the bone for a ninety-year-old mother" be blamed for occasionally thinking "how nice it would be if there was some money left over when the old woman finally died."[11]

Before leaving the subject of caregivers, we should note the devastating effect that caring for a disabled spouse can have on the surviving spouse's own health and ability to provide for her own long-term care. As noted, 36 percent of caregivers are sixty-five or older. Most of them are wives caring for their husbands.[12] These women will often have their own health problems and a need to save for their own health and long-term care. Yet, relative to men, women have lower savings because "women . . . are generally lower paid and are typically the ones who take time out from work and career to care for children and elders. Child care and elder care interruptions produce significant reductions on Social Security and private pension payouts."[13] Since husbands often marry younger women, the man's health is usually the first to go.

Typically the wife cares for the husband at home, depleting resources of energy and money until the husband dies or the wife becomes too exhausted to continue and places the husband in a nursing home whereupon, with the exception of a very modest Community Spouse Resource Allowance (CSRA), the couple's resources are further depleted. By the time the husband dies, the widow is left with a severely diminished fund to see her through the remaining years of her life. "The Medicaid law's insistence that both spouses' resources be considered in the spend-down process is based on an assumption that there is a unity of interests between the spouses."[14] But the situation described above shows that this is not the case even for spouses who have been married to each other most of their adult lives. The assumption of unity is even more unrealistic as applied to senior citizen marriages with children by prior spouses, and it is further undermined by the increasing incidence of multiple marriages among the population at large.[15]

2. *The Human Costs of Spend-Down* When the time comes to enter a nursing home, the price of admission is heavy. Perhaps the greatest cost to the Medicaid recipient lies in the price in human dignity the spend-down rules extract. Recall that the vast majority of institutional Medicaid recipients are single, typically widows. The spend-down rules described earlier require them to divest themselves of all but $2,000 worth of assets except for the family home which may be taken when they die.[16] True, one can also keep a burial plot (or approved plan funds not exceeding $1,500) in value but one can do nothing with a burial plot but lie in it.[17] Thus the applicant becomes a pauper, eligible for welfare. But unlike younger, nondisabled welfare recipients, the institutional Medicaid recipient, being old and disabled, has no chance of working herself off of welfare.

* * *

The indignity to the institutional Medicaid applicant does not end upon qualification. As noted, the Medicaid nursing home recipient must contribute *all* her income, except a small personal needs allowance, to the cost of her care.[18] Since the typical monthly allowance is $30 or $40, this leaves precious little to cover the resident's personal needs like clothing, grooming and little pleasures such as television, books, newspapers, magazines and snacks. One good haircut could wipe out the allowance in many cities!

This is a bleak existence to look toward for those who have worked hard all their lives. The golden years become the grim years. The unspoken message behind this draconian divestiture policy is that the Medicaid applicant no longer needs any resources because she is already dead as far as society is concerned. The message is that you will never get out of that nursing home alive and that you do not deserve to have personal clothing or dignity-preserving services like haircuts and manicures or the little treats that make life worth living while you are there.[19]

Perhaps the worst consequence of divestment in terms of present and future well-being is that "the divested individual, whether in the nursing home or back in the community, is completely . . . defenseless against all who would impose on her."[20] This is particularly so in a society that often measures the respect due individuals according to their wealth.[21]

* * *

As an ameliorative measure pending systemic reform, spend-down requirements should be eased to permit retention of the home and a modest amount of resources. This would permit the elimination of an intricate set of exceptions and exemptions, thus simplifying the system and cutting administrative costs in the state and nursing home bureaucracy. By permitting retention of small amounts of capital, it would also permit the continued generation of income which the long-term care consumer could use to pay for his or her own long-term care financing needs. For the meagerly and modestly situated, the vast majority of us, it would eliminate many of the fears that drive some to unwise and desperate transfer attempts.

* * *

An issue of horizontal equity also plays a role in the debate. An elderly person who suffers an acute illness like a heart attack receives substantial coverage under Medicare without any spend-down requirement. Yet one stricken with a chronic illness like Parkinson's disease or Alzheimer's disease must divest herself of nearly all her assets to obtain government assistance. As Dr. Moody observed, "[t]he situation in long-term care today is as it was in 1964 before Medicare was passed. People went broke in order to have their illnesses treated."[22] Dr. Moody cites the example of "two sisters who had married at the same economic level in life, lived with their husbands on the upper and lower floors of the same house, and were approximately the same age. One husband got cancer and the other husband got Alzheimer's disease. Both faced dreadful diseases, but one was covered for the medical expenses and the other faced total impoverishment."[23] Such unequal treatment of similarly situated individuals seems unfair.

B. Post-Mortem Equity Considerations

The subject of using Medicaid planning to preserve inheritances (even modest ones) for heirs other than the surviving spouse is where the rubber hits the road in the debate on who owes what to whom.

Traditionally, the passing on of an inheritance, particularly to one's family, has been viewed as good and natural to do. Americans have come to view the ability to pass something on as almost a natural right. Indeed, although some modern theorists are moving away from this view,[24] testamentary freedom and the ability to pass on an inheritance have traditionally been justified as essential to sustaining incentives to individual "creativity, hard work, initiative, and . . . productivity."[25]

The legal rules governing family wealth transactions are designed to encourage passage of property at death to loved ones.

* * *

Income, estate, and gift tax rules are replete with rules permitting the acquisition and passage of wealth at the expense of the public treasury.

* * *

In contrast to the tax relief currently enjoyed (and perhaps to be expanded for Americans with substantial capital and income), a much grimmer picture emerges for more modestly situated individuals requiring government assistance with long-term care. The Medicaid spend-down rules are "the functional equivalent of a 100% death tax" which reduces lifetime income as well.[26] Some may argue that there is a distinction between allowing someone to avoid income taxation or to transfer assets without estate tax liability and allowing someone to receive a government benefit without first exhausting all her assets. But the logic of this argument is flawed. People do not choose to buy a bed in a nursing home the way they choose to buy a boat, a car, a good suit of clothes, a meal at a restaurant or a business investment. The decision to consume health care is not voluntary—it is forced upon one by uninvited illness, not desire. As we have seen, most middle-class Americans cannot possibly save enough—no matter how hard they try—to totally cover an extended illness. The difference between the individual who attempts to preserve some assets while obtaining long-term care and the person who passes on very substantial assets without paying any taxes on the lifetime gain or the transfer is one of form, not substance.

* * *

Notes

1. Joshua Wiener & Laurel Hixon Illston, *Options for Long-Term Care Financing Reform: Public and Private Insurance Strategies,* J. OF LONG-TERM CARE ADMIN., Fall 1993, at 46 [hereinafter, Wiener & Illston, *Options for LTC Financing Reform*] (noting the wide variety of positions taken on who should have the final responsibility for financing long-term care).

2. [Jane Bryant Quinn, *Do Only The Suckers Pay,* NEWSWEEK, Dec. 18, 1989, at 52 (claiming that children often sacrifice their parents to a welfare home in order to protect their inheritance)]; Tim W. Ferguson, *Nursing Home Operator Fights to Stop Old Shell Game,* WALL ST. J., Apr. 7, 1992, at A17 (noting that Medicaid planning has been characterized as ripping off Medicaid funds from the state). *See also* Lynn Asinof, *Medicaid Planning: Shielding Assets from Uncle Sam,* WALL ST. J., May 23, 1991, at C1.

3. I am not the first to describe this situation as a catastrophe. For instance, the term appears in the very title of a major piece of Medicaid legislation, the Medicare Catastrophic Coverage Act (MCCA), Pub. L. No. 100-360 (1988) (codified at 42 U.S.C. § 1382 (1992)). [Remainder of note omitted.]

4. [Note omitted.]

5. Under the institutional long-term care Medicaid asset testing provisions of the MCCA, a single individual may not have "available" (non-exempt) resources in excess of $2,000 to qualify. 42 U.S.C. § 1382(a)(3)(B). Since enactment of the MCCA in 1988, the eligibility rules are somewhat less draconian for married couples. In 1994, the non-institutionalized spouse was allowed to keep a Community Spouse Resource Allowance (CSRA) ranging from a minimum of $14,532 to a maximum of $72,660, depending on the level chosen by the state. 42 U.S.C. § 1396r-5. In 1991, only sixteen states chose the maximum level, while twenty-nine adopted the minimum. *See* WILLIAM H. CROWN ET AL., AN ANALYSIS OF ASSET TESTING FOR NURSING HOME BENEFITS 37–49 (1994) (This study was published by the AARP Public Policy Institute).

The financial resources of married couples, especially the community spouse, essentially would be wiped out in any state that adopts the $14,964 minimum permissible CSRA. Even in a state that adopts the maximum CSRA, a $72,820 set aside, is not, in this author's opinion, enough to assure a decent standard of living to a community spouse with a reasonable life expectancy, especially one who may incur long-term care costs of her own in the future. *See also* Joel C. Dobris, *Medicaid Estate Planning by the Elderly: A Policy View of Expectations, Entitlement and Inheritance,* 24 REAL PROP., PROB. & TRUST J. 1, 3 (1989).

6. [Note omitted.]

7. Joshua M. Wiener et al., *Nursing Home Care: Still a Routine Catastrophe, Letters to the Editor,* 30 THE GERONTOLOGIST 417 (1990) [hereinafter Wiener et al., *Letters to the Editor*]. . . . Examples of the misuse of anecdotal evidence include Bates, [Andrew Bates, *Golden Girls: Middle-Class Medicaid,* THE NEW REPUBLIC, Feb. 3, 1992 (suggesting that Medicaid is a program primarily being used to benefit a wealthy middle-class while ignoring the needs of the poor. He argues that this use of the Medicaid program is at odds with the original policy intent of the Medicaid laws)], at 18 (identifying a "trend" toward asset sheltering by the rich based on statements of Medicaid officials in one state). *See also* Brian O. Burwell, *Middle-Class Welfare: Medicaid Estate Planning for Long-Term Care Coverage,* SYSTEMETRICS REP., Sept. 1991, at 15 [hereinafter Burwell, *Middle-Class Welfare*] ("At the outset it is important to avoid a misconception. The vast majority of the elderly are not looking for free rides at taxpayers' expense. Neither are they hoarding their riches and trying to pass their nursing home bills onto taxpayers.").

8. [Note omitted.]

9. [Sometimes the steps necessary to qualify for Medicaid simply won't be worth it: Loss of step-up in basis, disqualification period due to transfers, loss of control, risk of making gifts to children who may be untrustworthy or have creditor problems, triggering capital gain by liquidating assets, and triggering penalties by liquidating time deposits early. [Janine A. Lawless, Who Will Pay for the Nursing Home, in Nat'l Academy of Elder Law Attorneys, 6th Annual Symposium, Pre-Symposium Manual 19 (1994). Additional note deleted.]

10. *See* CROWN ET AL., *supra* note 5, at 31 (containing opposing points of view in the debate); JOSHUA M. WIENER & LAUREL HIXON ILLSTON, SHARING THE BURDEN, STRATEGIES FOR PUBLIC AND PRIVATE LONG-TERM CARE INSURANCE 2–3 (1994) [hereinafter WIENER & ILLSTON, SHARING THE BURDEN].

11. [Jan Ellen Rein, *Preserving Dignity and Self-Determination of the Elderly in the Face of Competing Interest and Grim Alternatives: A Proposal for Statutory Refocus and Reform,* 60 GEO. WASH. L. REV. 1818, 1847 n.138 (1992) (hereinafter Rein, *Preserving Dignity*)] (quoting letter from Lawrence Friedman, Marion Rice Kirkwood Professor of Law, Stanford Law School, to the author (Nov. 5, 1991) (on file with author)).

12. [Note omitted.]

13. Jan Ellen Rein, *The Medicaid Morass: A Catch 22 for Elderly Disabled and Their Loved Ones*

When Law Ignores Human Needs, [INSTITUTE FOR HEALTH SERVICES RESEARCH, U. OF MINN., WHO OWES WHOM WHAT?: PERSONAL, FAMILY, AND PUBLIC RESPONSIBILITY FOR PAYING FOR LONG-TERM CARE (1994)] (hereinafter Rein, *The Medicaid Morass*). In 1992, the median annual income for women was $22,167 compared to $31,012 for men. The median income for married couple families was $42,064. U.S. Bureau of the Census, *Statistical Abstract of the United States,* (114th ed.) at 472, Tables 722 and 721 respectively, Washington, DC, 1994).

14. Rein, *The Medicaid Morass, supra* note 13, at 73.

15. *Id.* at 75 ("A second or third wife with adult children by a prior marriage is not going to have the same willingness to have her assets used for her husband's care as the spouse who has lived with her husband for forty or fifty years and raised her children").

16. [Note omitted.]

17. *See* [42 U.S.C. § 1382b(a)(2)(B) and (d)(1). These values are subject to limitation or change by the Commissioner of Social Security] for provisions regarding approved burial plans.

18. *Id.* at 72.

19. *Id.* at 68–69 (Further noting that many nursing home residents have "purely physical ailments and still have functioning minds and personalities." Moreover, many "would not even be in a nursing home . . . were [care] available to them in the community").

20. *Id.* at 69.

21. [Jan Ellen Rein, *The Medicaid Morass,* at 69–70.

22. [Harry R. Moody, *The Return of the Repressed: The Ethics of Assets and Inheritance,* in INSTITUTE FOR HEALTH SERVICES RESEARCH, U. OF MINN., WHO OWES WHOM WHAT?: PERSONAL, FAMILY, AND PUBLIC RESPONSIBILITY FOR PAYING FOR LONG-TERM CARE (1994) at 14.]

23. *Id.*

24. [Note omitted.]

25. *See* [EDWARD C. HALBACH, JR., AN INTRODUCTION TO CHAPTERS 1–4 OF DEATH, TAXES AND FAMILY PROPERTY: ESSAYS AND AMERICAN ASSEMBLY REPORT 3, 5–7 (E. Halbach ed., 1977)].

26. Dobris, *supra* note 5, at 28–29.

CHAPTER 38

Filial Responsibility for Impoverished Parents

Why, it might be asked, don't children take care of the medical and long-term care expenses of their parents? If aged parents have spent all their savings, and their income cannot cover the cost of their nursing home, perhaps their children rather than the taxpayers should pick up the shortfall. In the past, most states did have filial responsibility statutes that required adult children to support their indigent parents. The past, present, and possible future of such statutes is examined in the following note.

Robin M. Jacobson

Americana Healthcare Center v. Randall: The Renaissance of Filial Responsibility

* * *

A. History of Filial Responsibility

Parental support is a duty that extends back several thousand years to ancient Roman society.[1] When ancient Roman society changed from a militaristic to a commercial society, the obligation to provide for the family deteriorated.[2] The weakened fabric of the society led the Roman emperor to create filial responsibility laws.[3] By the third

South Dakota Law Review, Vol. 40, 518 (1995). Reprinted by permission.

century, filial responsibility laws had developed to create mutual obligations between the parent and child, resulting in the preservation of family bonds.[4] Pursuant to this development, the parental support obligation became a revered custom in Roman society.[5]

In England, a similar cultural transformation began in the fifteenth century.[6] After centuries of searching for ways to address the plight of the underprivileged, the Elizabethan Poor Laws were enacted.[7] Not having any basis in the common law, the Poor Laws were purely statutory creations.[8] The English Poor Relief Act of 1601 held parents, grandparents, and children responsible for maintaining poor family members.[9] The purpose of the Poor Laws was to relieve the general public from supporting indigent persons whose relatives had the ability to contribute to their support.[10] The basic principle underlying the Elizabethan Poor Laws was that children had a natural and moral duty to support their parents.[11] In effect, the Poor Laws merely transformed the "imperfect moral duty into a statutory and legal liability."[12]

B. Filial Responsibility in the United States

The Elizabethan Poor Laws became part of the American culture with the enactment of the Colonial Laws in New York.[13] Many other states also adopted statutes with language very similar to that of the English law.[14] By 1835, however, New York's parental support statute was narrowed, excluding grandparents and grandchildren from legal liability for the support of their relatives.[15]

The family and the corresponding responsibilities further disintegrated during the industrial age.[16] Children began to move from the country into the cites, often leaving their parents behind.[17] The increased mobility of the population aided the disintegration of the family.[18] The Social Security Act of 1935 also contributed to the shift away from family responsibility toward governmental assumption of such support obligations.[19] Yet, states were slow to drop their own filial responsibility statutes.[20]

C. Current Status of Filial Responsibility Statutes

Today, twenty-nine states have filial responsibility statutes.[21] Many of the statutes, however, limit the child's responsibility to necessities.[22] Some states impose criminal penalties for failure to provide support to indigent parents.[23]

South Dakota's filial responsibility statute dates back to 1887.[24] The earliest case involving filial responsibility in South Dakota was *McCook County v. Kammoss*.[25] In Kammoss, the county sued the children of an indigent father to recover payments made by the county for his support.[26] The county also wanted the children to provide for their father's ongoing support.[27] The court ruled the children were responsible for the past support of their indigent father.[28] The court explained that the statute "innovates the common-law rule, by imposing upon children, to the extent of their ability, the duty of maintaining their poor and helpless parents."[29] According to the court's interpretation of the statute, the child's duty to support his parents was as unequivocal as the common law duty of parents to support their children.[30] Therefore, Kammoss "elevated what in [the] past has only been a moral obligation to a statutory duty."[31]

South Dakota's current filial responsibility statute states:

> Every adult child, having the financial ability to do so, shall provide necessary food, clothing, shelter, or medical attendance for a parent who is unable to provide for himself; provided that no claim shall be made against such adult child until notice has been given such adult child that his parent is unable to provide for himself, and that such child shall have refused to provide for his parent.[32] The current statute added the requirement that notice be given to the child if his parent is unable to provide for himself.[33] The statute additionally requires that the child have the financial ability to furnish such support.[34]

* * *

D. Limitations on Children's Duties to their Parents

In interpreting filial responsibility statutes, courts have recognized limitations to the child's duty to support his parents.[35] A number of cases have considered whether children are responsible for parents who abandoned them in their minority.[36] In *Commonwealth v. Mong,*[37] James Mong was abandoned by his father when he was under sixteen.[38] The Ohio Supreme Court noted an exception to their filial responsibility statute for children who were abandoned by their parents.[39]

California has also addressed this issue in *Gluckman v. Gaines.*[40] In *Gluckman,* the father, Moses, was eighty-six years old and living in a nursing home.[41] Serious questions existed about the paternity of the alleged son, Morton.[42] Morton did not know Moses until he was twelve years old.[43] Moses often told Morton that he was not his father.[44] The court ultimately concluded Morton did not have the financial ability to support Moses,[45] and Moses had little reason to expect support from Morton.[46] In its holding, the court clarified the purpose of not requiring abandoned children to support their parents:

> Love, respect, loyalty, devotion, and the natural and inevitable desire of a child to recompense a parent for the love, service, support, and sacrifice usually lavished by a parent upon a child, cannot be legislated nor should the law force a child to make recompense for an assumed standard of upbringing, when a trial court finds on credible evidence that it never existed.[47]

While abandonment may totally relieve a child of his or her support obligation, the result may differ if the parent later returns.[48] In *Gierkont v. Gierkont,*[49] a father who had abandoned his son for over half of the son's minority sued for support.[50] By the time the son was two years old, the father and mother were separated and the father was not providing any support to the family.[51] The father later returned and resumed his relationship with the mother.[52] He subsequently wandered off and then returned, this time for somewhere between two and one-half years to four and one-half years.[53] The court noted the father was irresponsible and "was more devoted to alcohol than to his wife and family."[54] The court concluded that abandonment, coupled with later return to parental responsibilities, is a factor to be considered and may give rise to a partial support order.[55] The court held the child responsible for a percentage of the father's support equivalent to the percentage of the time the father was present during childhood.[56] Concluding the father had deserted the child for forty percent of his minority, the court assessed the support accordingly.[57]

Another factor the courts will consider in awarding support is whether the parent had good cause for abandonment.[58] In *Denny v. Public Welfare Division,*[59] the son was placed in foster care when he was a child.[60] The state statute said a child was relieved of his support obligation if the parent separated from the child without "good cause."[61] The mother sued for support from her son, arguing she had good cause for abandonment.[62] The mother claimed she placed her son in foster care so she could earn a living for both of them.[63] The court said there is no presumption of bad intentions or lack of good cause when a child is made dependent on the state.[64] Therefore, the court found the son liable for the support of his mother.[65]

An additional factor the courts have considered is the parent's past treatment of the child.[66] In *Kerr v. State Public Welfare Commission,*[67] the Commission sued the son for payments made to his father.[68] As a result of the father's job, the family frequently moved around, causing the son to miss a year of school.[69] In addition, the son alleged he was made to work at the family business at a young age without compensation.[70] Claiming the father's treatment was cruel, the son challenged the trial court's order that he support his father.[71] The court said a willful or malicious act of the parent pierces the "veil of parental immunity" if the act was done with the intention of injuring the child.[72] In this case, however, the court found the father's actions did not meet the standard for cruelty, and the son was ordered to contribute to his father's support.[73]

Another case which considered the parent's past treatment of the child was *Radich v. Kruly.*[74] In Radich, the father sued his daughter for support and maintenance.[75] The daughter was physically and mentally abused by her father.[76] The daughter also claimed her father circulated rumors in the community that she was unchaste before her marriage.[77] The court examined the father's bad behavior in light of the public policy favoring application of the filial responsibility statute.[78] The legislature enacted the filial responsibility statute "as a codification of a moral right, and primarily as a relief to the public."[79] Therefore, the daughter was held liable for the support of her father.[80] However, the "doctrine of unclean hands" was found to limit the support obligation to the father's minimum needs.[81]

One court has also considered a parent's failure to make child support payments when applying filial responsibility statutes.[82] In *Pelletier v. White,*[83] the parents were divorced when the son was eight years old.[84] The father failed to make child support payments after the divorce.[85] The court found the father had deserted his son by failing to pay child support, thereby relieving the child of any support obligation.[86]

The courts have also analyzed cases where several children can provide for their parent.[87] The court may assess each of the siblings' financial situations and distribute the support duty accordingly.[88] Siblings may also seek contribution from those siblings not ordered to provide support[89] or may seek reimbursement from the estate of the deceased parent.[90] The courts have also excluded the child's spouse as a source of support.[91]

Courts across the country have been consistent in requiring that the child have the ability to pay for the ordered support.[92] In *Mallatt v. Luihn*,[93] the State Public Welfare Commission notified the daughter that it had distributed money to her parents and that she was liable for a portion of those payments, plus an additional payment each month.[94] The Oregon Supreme Court exhibited concern for the child and his or her ability to pay "without depriving him of the means to provide for his own reasonable necessities."[95] In determining the ability to pay, the court may look at the child's overall "financial circumstances" and not just the child's income.[96] In some instances, the court may simply refuse to require a nearly destitute child to support his parent.[97]

When determining the child's ability to pay, the courts will take the child's own family support needs into consideration.[98] In *People v. Curry*,[99] the California Court of Appeals held that the child's first duty was to his or her own minor children.[100] In another case, the court held that a child's family support needs included a reasonable savings for sickness and retirement.[101]

When determining a child's ability to pay, the courts look at numerous factors, including the child's responsibilities to his or her own family[102] as well as their actual financial situation.[103] In any case, an analysis of the child's ability to pay support remains within the substantial discretion of the trial court.[104]

E. Criticisms of Filial Responsibility Statutes

The need to rely on filial responsibility statutes for parental support diminished with the adoption of the Social Security Act of 1935.[105] Filial responsibility statutes were further eroded by the 1965 Medicaid statute.[106] The Medicaid statute prohibited the states from considering the financial ability of the applicant's family, other than the individual's spouse, when awarding support.[107]

Currently, many states' filial responsibility statutes are often not enforced because modern society has become a "formal community-based welfare" system.[108] Through the welfare system, indigent parents have become the responsibility of state and local governments.[109] However, "[i]nflation, increasing health care costs, and the growing elderly population have collectively taken their toll on federal and state Medicaid budgets."[110] Consequently, filial responsibility statutes have once again arisen to combat this crisis.[111]

Critics of filial responsibility statutes insist that statutorily requiring children to support their parents is not the answer to the current crisis of the elderly.[112] The general consensus among critics is that the filial responsibility statutes "weaken family relationships and family responsibility, and are destructive to older persons and the families of their adult children."[113] In *Swoap*, the dissent noted filial responsibility statutes perpetuate poverty and destroy the family.[114] The critics say these statutes perpetuate poverty by requiring the elderly to become dependent on the extended family, thus keeping the poor classes from advancing to the middle class.[115] This situation, conclude the critics, ultimately leads to dissension and the destruction of the family.[116]

Commentators also argue that parents do not want to burden their children.[117] The elderly fear that losing their independence will result in social rejection and the loss of self-respect.[118] In addition, it is believed that dependence by the elderly on their children for their well-being may lead to depression and, ultimately, to suicide.[119]

Critics also cite economic reasons for rejecting filial responsibility statutes.[120] One critic claims the administrative costs associated with collecting the funds from relatives outweighs the money saved.[121] However, another commentator notes that in one study vigorous enforcement of filial responsibility statutes have actually reduced public support costs.[122]

Opponents have also claimed that enforcement of filial responsibility statutes would create a new bureaucracy.[123] To effectively implement recovery procedures, they say the states would have to devise entirely new bureaucracies.[124] An enforcement department would need a staff, supervisors, field workers, and an underlying superstructure, according to some critics.[125] Furthermore, many believe it is the government's duty to support the poor.[126]

Another argument against filial responsibility statutes is that it is wasteful to litigate these claims.[127] Aside from the costs of litigation, district attorneys are reluctant to bring such claims for fear of retribution at the polls.[128] In addition, the families who are required to make support payments are often too poor themselves to appeal.[129]

Although there are many criticisms of filial responsibility statutes, they are not a new development in the United States.[130] They have a long and rich history throughout the world.[131] Though objectives of filial responsibility statutes have lacked a nationwide theme,[132] states are free to decide how they will deal with the indigent and are not required to enforce a uniform act.[133] Their purpose is two-fold: to bring families closer together[134] and to relieve the public of the obligation to provide for people who have not exhausted other means of support.[135]

Filial responsibility statutes "can be used to achieve the desirable public policy objective of ensuring that the indigent elderly have at least a minimal standard of living if their children are able to provide support . . . thereby strengthening family ties by encouraging family members, rather than government, to care for one another."[136] Filial responsibility statutes also provide support to the elderly beyond what the government is able to provide.[137] One author noted, "It could be contended that a refusal to meet such a demand is immoral, being motivated by a desire to avoid one's responsibilities by casting them on the public."[138]

* * *

Notes

1. [Jean Van Houtte & Jef Breda, *Maintenance of the Aged by Their Adult Children: The Family as a Residual Agency in the Solution of Poverty in Belgium*, 12 LAW AND SOC'Y REV. 645, 649 (1978)],

at 646 (presenting the historical foundations of filial responsibility statutes). The moral duty to support one's indigent parents also has its history in the Ten Commandments: "Honor thy father and thy mother that thy days may be long in the land that the Lord thy God giveth thee." Exodus 20:12.

2. Van Houtte & Breda, supra note 1, at 647–48. The family structure "eroded from within and [crumbled] from without." *Id.* at 648. The evolution of Roman culture eroded the family and undermined their solidarity, resulting in the decrease of the obligation to provide for one's family members. *Id.*

3. *Id.* at 648. The laws were enforced somewhere between 100 A.D. and 138 A.D. *Id.* See also 1 Blackstone, Commentaries –59. Blackstone says the duty of children to parents also existed in Athenian culture, which:

> [C]arried this principle into practice with a scrupulous kind of nicety: obliging all children to provide for their father when fallen into poverty; with an exception to spurious children, to whose chastity had been prostituted by consent of the father, and to those whom he had not put in any way of gaining a livelihood. *Id.* at 453–54. Blackstone observed that the law in England followed only the first of those exceptions. *Id.* at 454.

4. Van Houtte & Breda, supra note 1, at 649.

5. *Id.* Support statutes helped to preserve the family during the Roman Empire and after its fall. *Id.*

6. *Id.* at 650.

7. [James L. Lopes, *Filial Support and Family Solidarity*, 6 PAC. L.J. 505, 512 (1975).] The Poor Laws were an addition to the pre-existing programs and the whole system was referred to as the "Elizabethan poor law system." Jacobus ten Broek, California's Dual System of Family Law: Its Origin, Development, and Present Status, Part I, 16 Stan. L. Rev. 257, 258 (1964) [hereinafter ten Broek I]. Some examples of programs in the system included: putting poor children to work, supporting hospitals and almshouses with tax revenues, punishing vagrants, sending those who refused to work to houses of correction, and encouraging the establishment of charitable organizations by benevolent persons. *Id.* at 259–60. The Poor Laws were established "[a]fter the expropriation of the monasteries by Henry VIII [because] there was a serious shortage of private funds to aid the poor." [W. Walton Garrett, *Filial Responsibility Laws*, 18 J. FAM. L. 793, 798–99 (1979) (suggesting children should provide for their parents support)], at 795.

8. Carleson v. Superior Court for County of Sacramento, 100 Cal. Rptr. 635, 643 (Cal. Ct. App. 1972). The English court said, "By the law of nature a man was bound to take care of his own father and mother; but there being no temporal obligation to enforce that law of nature, it was found necessary to establish it by Act of Parliament . . . ." Rex v. Munden, 93 Eng. Rep. 465, 465 (1795).

9. ten Broek I, supra note 7, at 283 (quoting 43 Eliz. I, ch. 2, § vi (1601)). The statute states:

> [The parents, grandparents, and the children of] everie poore olde blind lame and impotente person, or other poore person not able to worke, beinge of sufficient abilitie, shall at their owne Chardges releive and maintain everie suche poore person, in that manner and accordinge to that rate, as by the Justices of the Peace of the Countie where suche sufficient persons dwell, or the greater number of them, at their generall Quarter-Sessions shalbe assessed; upon paine that everie one of them shall forfeite twenty shillings for everie monthe which they shall faile therein. *Id.* ten Broek characterized the statute as "rambling, imprecise, and inartistic." *Id.* at 262. Prior to 1601, the statute applied only to parents and children. Daniel R. Mandelker, Family Responsibility Under the American Poor Laws, 54

Mich. L. Rev. 497, 500 (1956). The 1601 statute extended the duty to support collateral relatives. *Id.*

10. Lopes, supra note 7, at 511. See also Terrance A. Kline, *A Rational Role for Filial Responsibility Laws in Modern Society?*, 26 Fam. L.Q. 195, 197 (Fall 1992). The Elizabethan Poor Laws "reflected a desire to assume public responsibility for the poor while keeping public expenditures down." *Id.*

11. Blackstone, supra note 3, at 54.

12. People v. Hill, 46 N.E. 796, 797 (Ill. 1896) (describing the historical foundations of supporting the poor). One author noted that England spent a great deal of time in the late nineteenth century forcing children to support their parents because Poor Law assistance was drastically cut. David Thomson, The Elderly in an Urban-Industrial Society: England, 1750 to the Present in An Aging World: Dilemmas and Challenges for Law and Social Policy 55, 59 (John M. Eekelaar & David Pearl, eds., 1989) [hereinafter Thomson I]. Poverty and family bitterness resulted, and the country saw a proliferation of state-sponsored aid. *Id.* As a result, the 1601 Elizabethan Poor Law was repealed in 1948. David Thomson, 'I am not my father's keeper': Families and the Elderly in Nineteenth Century England, 2 Law and Hist. Rev. 265, 266 (1984) [hereinafter Thomson II] (explaining the history of the Elizabethan statute in England up to the late 1800's). Today, the emphasis has once again changed to minimizing state intrusion and accenting family support along with encouragement to provide for oneself by planning for the future. Thomson I, supra note 12, at 59.

13. ten Broek I, supra note 7, at 291. New York added grandchildren to the list of responsible relatives. *Id.* at 294.

14. [Terrance A. Kline, *A Rational Role for Filial Responsibility Laws in Modern Society?*, 26 FAM. L.Q. 195, 197 (Fall 1992).] Delaware, New Jersey, and Pennsylvania enacted similar statutes. *Id.* at 197 n.19. In Pennsylvania, the statute stated:

> [T]he father and grand-father, and the mother and grand-mother, and the children of every poor, old, blind, lame and impotent person, or other poor person not able to work, being of sufficient ability, shall, at their own charge relieve and maintain every such poor person, as the Magistrates or the Justices of the Peace, at their next General Quarter Sessions for the city or county where such poor persons reside, shall order and direct, on pain of forfeiting forty shillings for every month they shall fail therein.
>
> 1810 Penn. Laws ch. DCXX, § XXIX.

Compare the Elizabethan Poor Law of 1601, see supra note 7. Virginia has also had a long standing filial responsibility statute, which has evolved over the past century. [Renae Reed Patrick, *Honor Thy Father and Mother: Paying the Medical Bills of the Elderly*, 19 U. RICH. L. REV. 69, 70 (1984).] The law originally required children over 16 to support parents living in cities of 100,000 or more if they had the financial ability. *Id.* In 1922, the act was amended to require only the support of destitute parents. *Id.* A 1982 amendment inserted a provision requiring medical assistance. *Id.*

15. ten Broek I, supra note 13, at 296.

16. Leo J. Tully, Family Responsibility Laws: An Unwise and Unconstitutional Imposition, 5 Fam. L.Q. 32, 38 (1971) (describing the historical foundations of filial responsibility statutes).

17. *Id.* Tully noted the shift caused "certain equalitarian concepts in American life . . . to collide with a strict notion of filial responsibility." *Id.* See supra notes 1–5 and accompanying text for a discussion of how this shift also happened in the Roman Empire and was the impetus of the adoption of filial responsibility statutes.

18. Tully, supra note 16, at 38. One author asserted the industrial revolution ended the practice of living in an extended family. Lopes, supra note 7, at 514.

19. [George F. Indest, *Legal Aspects of HCFA's Decision to Allow Recovery from Children for Medicaid Benefits Delivered to Their Parents Through State Financial Responsibility Statutes: A Case of Bad Rule Making Through Failure to Comply With the Administrative Procedure Act*, 15 So. Uni. L. Rev. 225, 227–28 (1988) (explaining the purpose and goals of Medicaid).]

20. [Catherine Doscher Byrd, *Relative Responsibility Extended: Requirement of Adult Children to Pay for Their Indigent Parent's Medical Needs*, 22 Fam. L.Q. 87, 90 (1988).] In 1952, 38 states still had filial support statutes. *Id.* (citing Albert Schorr, U.S. Dept. of Health, Education and Welfare, Social Security Division, Filial Responsibility in the Modern American Family at 23 (1960)). By 1980, that number fell to 23. *Id.* (citing Garrett, supra note 7, at 813 n.103). That number increased to 28 in 1992. Kline, supra note 10, at 200.

21. See Alaska Stat. §§ 25.20.030, 47.25.230 (1994); Cal. Civ. Code §§ 206, 242 (West 1982); Conn. Gen. Stat. Ann. § 46b-215 (West 1986); Del. Code Ann. tit. 13, § 503 (1993); Ga. Code Ann. § 36-12-3 (1990); Idaho Code § 32-1002 (Supp. 1994); Ind. Code Ann. § 31-2-9-1 (Burns 1987); Iowa Code Ann. § 252.2 (West 1994); Ky. Rev. Stat. Ann. § 530.050 (Michie 1994); La. Rev. Stat. Ann. § 13:4731 (West 1991); Md. Code Ann., Fam. Law § 13-102 (1991); Mass. Gen. Laws Ann. ch. 273 § 20 (Law. Co-op. 1992); Minn. Stat. Ann. § 256D.15 (West 1992); Miss. Code Ann. § 43-31-25 (1993); Mont. Code Ann. §§ 40-6-214, 40-6-301 (1993); Nev. Rev. Stat. Ann. § 428.070 (1991); N.H. Rev. Stat. Ann. §§ 167:2, 546-A:2 (1994); N.J. Stat. Ann. § 44:1-140 (West 1993); N.C. Gen. Stat. § 14-326.1 (1994); N.D. Cent. Code § 14-09-10 (1991); Or. Rev. Stat. § 109.010 (1993); Pa. Stat. Ann. tit. 62, § 1973 (Supp. 1994); R.I. Gen. Laws § 40-5-13 (1990); S.D.C.L. § 25-7-27; Tenn. Code Ann. § 71-5-115 (1987); Utah Code Ann. § 17-14-2 (1991); Vt. Stat. Ann. tit. 15, § 202 (1989); Va. Code Ann. § 20-88 (Michie 1990); W.Va. Code § 9-5-9 (1990). Florida, Kansas, Texas, Washington, and Wyoming apparently never adopted filial responsibility statutes. Kline, supra note 10, at 196 n.9.

22. See Ind. Code Ann. § 31-2-9-1 (providing for "food, clothing, shelter and medical attention"); Md. Code Ann., Fam. Law § 13-102 (requiring "food, shelter, care, and clothing"); Minn. Stat. Ann. § 256D.15 (extending duty to only spouse and adult children); Mont. Code Ann. § 40-6-301 (detailing the duty to provide necessaries in addition to medical attendance and costs associated with funerals and burials); N.D. Cent. Code § 14-09-10 (providing support to the extent of the child's ability); S.D.C.L. § 25-7-27 (requesting support for "necessary food, clothing, shelter or medical attendance").

23. See Cal. Penal Code § 270c (West 1988) (providing for a misdemeanor); Conn. Gen. Stat. Ann. § 53-304 (West 1986) (requiring up to one year imprisonment); Md. Code Ann., Fam. Law § 13-102 (setting fines of up to $1,000 and one year in prison); Mont. Code Ann. § 40-6-302 (1993) (violating filial support law is a misdemeanor); Va. Code Ann. § 20-88 (fining up to $500 and 12 months in prison). In 1992, South Dakota repealed its criminal enforcement statute which made violation of the statute a class I misdemeanor. S.D.C.L. § 25-7-29 (repealed 1992).

24. [Memorandum Opinion at 3, Americana Healthcare Center v. Randall, Civ. No. 91-496 (S.D. 5th Cir. filed Oct. 7, 1992) (hereinafter Memorandum Opinion).] In 1887, the Dakota Territory adopted the following statute:

> It is the duty of the father, the mother, and the children, of any poor person who is unable to maintain himself by work, to maintain such person to the extent of their ability. The promise of an adult child to pay for necessaries previously furnished to such parent is binding.

Dak. Comp. Laws § 2612 (1887).

25. 64 N.W. 1123 (S.D. 1895).

26. *Id.* The sum sued for was $100. *Id.*

27. *Id.* The children argued there was only a moral duty to provide such support so the county had no legal means of enforcement. *Id.* The court said the duty came from the common law duty requiring a father to support his destitute minor child. *Id.*

28. *Id.* Finding no statutory authority since the statute only covered necessaries already furnished, the court said the children were not liable for the future support of their father. *Id.*

29. *Id.*

30. *Id.*

31. [Brief for Appellee at 5–6, Americana Healthcare Center v. Randall, 513 N.W.2d 566 (S.D. 1994) (No. 18186) (hereinafter Appellee's Brief).]

32. S.D.C.L. § 25-7-27. The current statute was introduced in the South Dakota Senate on January 10, 1963. State of South Dakota, Proceedings of the Senate, 38th Legislative Sess. 25 (1963).

33. State of South Dakota, Proceedings of the Senate, 38th Legislative Sess. 364 (1963); State of South Dakota, Proceedings of the House of Representatives, 38th Legislative Sess. 834 (1963).

34. State of South Dakota, Proceedings of the Senate, 38th Legislative Sess. 543. The Senate also inserted the word "financial" before the word "ability." *Id.*

35. [Catherine Doscher Byrd, *Relative Responsibility Extended: Requirement of Adult Children to Pay for Their Indigent Parent's Medical Needs*, 22 Fam. L.Q. 87, 90 (1988).]

36. Mong, 117 N.E.2d at 32 (abandoning child negates parent's ability to collect support payments); Gluckman, 71 Cal. Rptr. at 797 (expecting support and filial devotion from an abandoned child is fruitless). In Duffy, a daughter was abandoned by her mother at age six. Duffy, 84 P. at 838. The daughter was raised by an aunt whom she was already supporting at the time of the suit. *Id.* The daughter was relieved of the duty to support her mother because the mother was already being supported by other children and there was no threat of withdrawal. *Id.* at 839.

37. 117 N.E.2d 32 (Ohio 1954).

38. *Id.* The son was a resident of Ohio. *Id.* at 33. The father was a resident of Pennsylvania. *Id.* at 32. Ohio had a provision which exempted children from supporting parents who abandoned them; Pennsylvania did not. *Id.* at 33.

39. *Id.* Ohio's code § 2901.42 provided: "No person shall be required to furnish a parent with shelter, food, care or clothing, if such parent abandoned, deserted or wilfully refused or neglected to support and maintain him while an infant under sixteen years of age." *Id.*

40. 71 Cal. Rptr. 795 (Cal. Dist. Ct. App. 1968).

41. *Id.* at 799.

42. *Id.* The trial court found Moses was Morton's father. *Id.* at 800. The appellate court, however, noted the evidence of "paternity by blood . . . was scanty." *Id.* Morton testified that he did not know who his father was, where he was born or when he was born. *Id.* at 799.

43. *Id.* Morton was born in Palestine and then moved to London, where he first met his alleged father. *Id.* Morton was then brought to the United States by Moses to live with his mother. *Id.*

44. *Id.* at 801.

45. *Id.* at 798. Morton had substantial financial obligations: loan payments, child support payments, mortgage payments, and a wife to support. *Id.* He also had medical bills because he suffered from hepatitis and hypertension which required frequent hospitalization. *Id.* Morton

owned 600 acres of unimproved and non-income producing land. *Id.* The land was the family's only asset. *Id.*

46. *Id.* at 801.

47. *Id.* at 797 (quoting Radich, 38 Cal. Rptr. at 343).

48. Gierkont, 134 A.2d at 13.

49. 134 A.2d 10 (N.J. Super. Ct. App. Div. 1957).

50. *Id.* at 14.

51. *Id.* at 13. As a result, the father was arrested for non-support. *Id.* He was ordered to pay $6 per week. *Id.*

52. *Id.* A daughter was the product of that reunion. *Id.* The father left again after the daughter was 2. *Id.*

53. *Id.* There was some dispute in the testimony about how long the father was at home. *Id.*

54. *Id.* at 12.

55. *Id.* at 13.

56. *Id.* at 14. The court divided the eight and one-half years the father was present by 21 years to arrive at a weekly payment of $6.80 for the father's support. *Id.*

57. *Id.*

58. Denny v. Public Welfare Div., 483 P.2d 463 (Or. Ct. App. 1971).

59. 483 P.2d 463 (Or. Ct. App. 1971).

60. *Id.* at 464. The son was placed in a series of foster homes on several occasions. *Id.*

61. *Id.* at 464 n.1. The statute read in part:

> No liability for the support of a needy person shall be imposed . . . upon . . . [t]he child of a needy person if, during the minority of the child, such person wilfully deserted or abandoned the child, or, by expulsion or cruelty, drove the child from the parental home, or, without good cause, was responsible for the child's being "dependent." . . . *Id.* (quoting Or. Rev. Stat. § 416.030(2) (1993)).

62. Denny, 483 P.2d at 464.

63. *Id.* The evidence was uncontradicted that the mother's only motivation for placing her son in foster care was so she could earn a living for them. *Id.* When the mother and son were separated, she always contributed toward his support. *Id.*

64. *Id.*

65. *Id.* at 465.

66. Radich, 38 Cal. Rptr. at 342; Kerr, 470 P.2d at 168–69.

67. 470 P.2d 167 (Or. Ct. App. 1970).

68. *Id.* at 168. The state contributed $420 to the father's support. *Id.*

69. *Id.* Logging required travel to areas where the work was needed. *Id.* The family often lived in remote areas where transportation to school was not provided. *Id.* The court found the father violated no laws by not sending the child to school because the family lived too far away from the school. *Id.* at 168-69.

70. *Id.* at 169. The father was a gypo logger. *Id.* at 168. The son worked in the forests with his father and brother after school and during vacations. *Id.* at 169.

71. *Id.* The son did not allege that he was abandoned, deserted, unfed, or mistreated. *Id.*

72. *Id.* (quoting Chaffin v. Chaffin, 397 P.2d 771, 777 (Or. 1964)).

73. Kerr, 470 P.2d at 169. The court found no evidence of maliciousness in the father's treatment of his son. *Id.* The son was ordered to pay a total of $420. *Id.*

74. 38 Cal. Rptr. 340 (Cal. Dist. Ct. App. 1964).

75. *Id.* at 341.

76. *Id.* at 342.

77. *Id.*

78. *Id.*

79. *Id.*

80. *Id.* at 344.

81. *Id.* at 343. The court said, "[I]n our opinion the prior conduct of a parent is a relevant factor in determining the standard of support owed by a child to a parent." *Id.* at 342.

82. Pelletier v. White, 371 A.2d 1068, 1069–70 (Conn. Super. Ct. 1976).

83. 371 A.2d 1068 (Conn. Super. Ct. 1976).

84. *Id.* at 1069.

85. *Id.* The divorce decree required the father to pay $5 per week for the support of his son. *Id.* Evidence presented at trial demonstrated the father paid this sum on the average of once per month in the first year after the divorce. *Id.* The son testified his stepfather was the only "real father" to him. *Id.* The stepfather furnished complete support for the son while he was a minor. *Id.*

86. *Id.* at 1069–70. The Connecticut statute relieved children of liability "for the support of a parent who wilfully deserted such person continuously during the ten-year period prior to such person reaching his majority." *Id.* at 1069. The trial court found the father wilfully deserted the child when he failed to pay the required $5 per month support. *Id.* at 1069–70.

87. Wood v. Wheat, 11 S.W.2d 916, 918 (Ky. Ct. App. 1928) (finding children are equally liable if they have the ability to provide support); Ketcham v. Ketcham, 29 N.Y.S.2d 773, 789 (N.Y. Fam. Ct. 1941) (fixing support obligation with respect to childrens' various abilities); Mallatt v. Luihn, 294 P.2d 871, 875 (Or. 1956) (finding several siblings had sufficient incomes to contribute to their parents' support); Hansis v. Brougham, 103 N.W.2d 679, 683 (Wis. 1960) (stating the court may require more than one relative to contribute according to their ability); In re Peterson, 74 N.W.2d 148, 151 (Wis. 1956) (providing for contribution from siblings).

88. Garrett, supra note 7, at 803. One author observed that children are not obligated to provide support in equal amounts, but according to their ability. *Id.* In Ketcham, suit was brought against the children for support; one had a relatively good financial situation and the other two had lower support obligations due to other family responsibilities. Ketcham, 29 N.Y.S.2d at 789–90. No support obligation was imposed on the other two children. *Id.* The court held the child with greater financial means was responsible for a larger portion of the total support payments. *Id.* at 789.

89. Mallatt, 294 P.2d at 882. In Mallatt, the court stated a daughter had a right of contribution from her brothers and sisters who were "equally liable and equally able to pay." *Id.* Another court propounded this duty by noting, "Equality of burden results equitably in equality of payment, and one properly paying more than his proportion may recover at law by way of contribution." Manthey v. Schueler, 147 N.W. 824, 825 (Minn. 1914). The Kentucky Court of Appeals noted the burden on children who are under an obligation to support their parents cannot be shifted away from other siblings who are equally able and equally liable to share the burden. Wood, 11 S.W.2d at 918. In Iowa, a daughter agreed to care for her mother at the request of her siblings. Wyman v. Passmore, 125 N.W. 213, 214 (Iowa 1910). The court held the daughter was entitled to contribution from her siblings. *Id.*

90. Pavlick v. Teresinski, 149 A.2d 300, 302 (N.J. Juv. 1959) (finding sons who were liable for support of mother could seek contribution from mother's estate). The court observed that equity required eventual reimbursement for the childrens' contributions ordered by the court. *Id.*

The court stated that if the county could place a lien on the parent's house when seeking reimbursement for welfare payments, then children should be able to do the same. *Id.*

91. Gierkont, 134 A.2d at 12 (citing Bradley v. Zimmerman, 180 A. 241, 242 (N.J. Sup. Ct. 1935) (stating no support obligation required from son-in-law)); Commonwealth v. Goldman, 119 A.2d 631, 633 (Pa. Super. Ct. 1956) (holding earnings of child's spouse are separate property); Mangin v. Mangin, 113 So. 864, 864 (La. 1927) (declining to look to daughters' husbands for support). See also John P. Callahan, Note, Responsibility of Adult Child for the Support of Needy Parents, 33 Notre Dame Lawyer 108, 113 (1957). Callahan cited a New York case, which held the son-in-law could not be sought for support nor could his earnings be considered as evidence of his wife's assets, except in community property states. *Id.* (citing Alessandro v. Camelli, 47 N.Y.S.2d 237, 243 (N.Y. Fam. Ct. 1944)).

92. Kline, supra note 10, at 201. All states with filial responsibility statutes require courts to determine that children have sufficient assets before it will impose liability. *Id.* See also Britton v. Steinberg, 24 Cal. Rptr. 831, 832 (Cal. Dist. Ct. App. 1962) (requiring maintenance of the parent to the extent of the child's ability); San Bernardino County v. McCall, 132 P.2d 65, 66–67 (Cal. Dist. Ct. App. 1942) (stating contribution scales are to be used in conjunction with evidence of the child's ability to pay); Cherokee County v. Smith, 258 N.W. 182, 185 (Iowa 1935) (ruling that in suit brought by county, the county has the burden of proving the relative has the ability to pay); Thornsberry v. State Dep't of Public Health and Welfare, 295 S.W.2d 372, 376 (Mo. 1956) (relieving child of her duty to support her mother based on a mistaken belief about her financial situation); Gierkont, 134 A.2d at 11 (looking at child's assets, debts, employment status, and responsibilities in order to determine if support may be required).

93. 294 P.2d 871 (Or. 1956).

94. *Id.* at 875. In 1952, the Commission paid the parents $1,242. *Id.* The daughter was required to pay $180 for the initial sum plus $70 per month. *Id.* The Commission calculated the payments based on Oregon's relative contribution scale. *Id.*

95. *Id.*

96. *Id.* In Mallatt, the court said the relative's ability to pay requires consideration of more than "'net monthly income' or his 'gross annual income.'" *Id.* In Atkins v. Curtis, the court also used a contribution scale, which involved a computation of "a proportionate amount of such relative's gross income over and above an amount set by the scale affected by the number of his dependents." Atkins v. Curtis, 66 So. 2d 455, 457 (Ala. 1953). A Pennsylvania court stated the general "test for financial ability includes a consideration of the actual income, the property, assets and earning ability, as well as other attendant circumstances." Goldman, 119 A.2d at 633.

97. Gluckman, 71 Cal. Rptr. at 800.

98. Goldman, 119 A.2d at 633 (finding daughter had insufficient financial ability to support indigent parent). See also Smith v. Juras, 513 P.2d 824, 826 (Or. Ct. App. 1973) (finding trial court did not abuse discretion when lowering support obligation due to arrival of new baby in son's family); Thornsberry, 295 S.W.2d at 376 (conditioning the child's financial ability based on a duty to his or her own family); Curry, 231 P. at 360 (limiting the child's ability to pay by considering his financial situation). In Goldman, the court noted, "Public policy favored this duty to her immediate family as well as the duty to support indigent parents. But it cannot favor the latter at the expense of the former, for if there is a conflict, the duty to her husband and child is the primary one." Goldman, 119 A.2d at 633. The courts have also applied various flexible criteria for determining an adult child's ability to provide support, including the following:

99. 231 P. 358 (Cal. Dist. Ct. App. 1924).

100. *Id.* at 360. In another case, the Supreme Court of Missouri found the lower court's ruling that a daughter support her indigent mother was based on inaccurate financial statistics. Thornsberry, 295 S.W.2d at 375. The mother lived with her daughter and two grandchildren. *Id.* at 373. The mother was crippled from a paralytic stroke. *Id.* The daughter was supporting her children, one of which was in college. *Id.* The Department sought to have the mother removed from the welfare support system, claiming the daughter had sufficient income to support the mother. *Id.* The court found the Department had overestimated the daughter's salary and underestimated the actual expenses of the household. *Id.* at 375. The court said the daughter had the right to make the choice between providing for her son's college education and providing for her mother's support. *Id.* at 376. The court remanded the case for proper determination of the daughter's finances and of her ability to pay. *Id.* at 377.

101. Gierkont, 134 A.2d at 12 (quoting In re Diele's Estate, 61 N.Y.S.2d 397, 399 (Sur. Ct. 1946) (defining "sufficient needs" as "where a man has sufficient for his own needs and has something over and above")). The court also allows the child to keep a reasonable amount for his or her children's education. Gierkont, 134 A.2d at 12.

102. Juras, 513 P.2d at 826; Mallatt, 294 P.2d at 875; Goldman, 119 A.2d at 633.

103. Gierkont, 134 A.2d at 11; Mallatt, 294 P.2d at 877; Goldman, 119 A.2d at 633.

104. Carleson, 100 Cal. Rptr. at 649; Ketcham, 29 N.Y.S.2d at 788–89; Pickett, 251 N.E.2d at 687. In Ketcham, the court posited:

> "[S]ufficient ability" must depend upon the circumstances in each case, and, as the matter rests largely in the discretion of the court, it cannot depend solely upon the amount of the property the defendant owns, for in that case a child proceeded against might have a princely income and no property subject to levy. Neither can it depend solely upon the income, as his income might be small and the amount of his property large . . . . Ketcham, 29 N.Y.S.2d at 788–89. See also Woolams v. Woolams, 251 P.2d 392, 395 (Cal. Dist. Ct. App. 1952) (noting assets, future earning ability, and liabilities may be taken into consideration). Bradley v. Fenn, 130 A. 126, 127 (Conn. Super. Ct. 1925) (determining ability to pay is for the trier of fact).

105. Indest, supra note 19, at 233. The New Deal, under President Franklin Roosevelt, was the first program which addressed the problems of the indigent elderly by enacting Social Security. Kline, supra note 10, at 199. President Richard Nixon later added Supplemental Security Income and President Ronald Reagan implemented Low-Income Home Energy Assistance, which increased government assistance to the poor. *Id.*

106. Kline, supra note 10, at 199. Medicare and Medicaid were a result of President Andrew Johnson's "Great Society." *Id.*

107. *Id.* The 1965 Medicaid statute "contributed most to the decline of filial responsibility laws by prohibiting states from considering 'the financial responsibility of any individual for any applicant or recipient of assistance under the [Medicaid] plan unless such applicant or recipient is such individual's spouse . . . .'" *Id.* (quoting 42 U.S.C.A. § 1396a(a)(17)(D) (West 1992)).

108. Thomson II, supra note 12, at 265.

109. Kline, supra note 10, at 196. Family life has changed because of weakened ties within the community and the family. [Gunhild O. Hagestad, *The Aging Society as a Context for Family Life, in* AGING AND ETHICS: PHILOSOPHICAL PROBLEMS IN GERONTOLOGY 123–46 (Nancy S. Jecker, ed., 1991) (describing how families and relationships are affected by demographic

changes).] Emotional support has replaced financial support as the glue that keeps families together. *Id.* at 131.

110. Byrd, supra note 19, at 89.

111. Patrick, supra note 14, at 70. For a discussion of the growing crisis, see supra notes 5–15 and accompanying text. One author noted, "Sensible public policy may compel the enforcement of filial responsibility laws as an alternative to total public welfare for the indigent elderly." Kline, supra note 10, at 204.

112. Tully, supra note 16, at 43, 44.

113. Robert J. Levy, Supporting the Aged: The Problem of Family Responsibility in Aging World: Dilemmas and Challenges of Law and Social Policy 253, 263 (John M. Eekelaar & David Pearl, eds., 1989) (quoting the Report of the White House Conference on Aging, The Nation and its Older People 173 (1961)).

114. Swoap, 516 P.2d at 864 (Tobriner, J., dissenting). The dissent noted filial responsibility statutes "strike most aggressively and harshly at adult children occupying the lower end of the income scale." *Id.*

115. [Michael Rosenbaum, *Are Family Responsibility Laws Constitutional?*, 1 FAM. L.Q. 55, 76 (1967) (arguing for the repeal of filial responsibility statutes).] The New York State Committee on Aging suggested that filial responsibility statutes retard self-advancement: "Filial responsibility laws must . . . be considered in relation to poverty. The requirement to support is one of the network of handicaps that surrounds a poor family; it may, on occasion, be the crucial handicap that persuades a person that improvement is not in the cards for him . . . ." *Id.*

116. Tully, supra note 16, at 43. Tully stated:

> [T]he responsibility laws tend to make the poor or marginally poor live together rather than establish independent households. . . . If relatives are forced to live together rather than choosing to live together, there is apt to be an increase in emotional tensions replete with feelings of resentment at those forced upon them as well as a feeling of inadequacy and failure among those whose presence is tolerated rather than welcomed. *Id.*

117. Swoap, 516 P.2d at 864 (Tobriner, J., dissenting). In his dissent, Justice Tobriner noted, "[A]ged parents should not have to live their remaining lives facing the heartbreaking experience of being such a burden to their children. Many would prefer death but are afraid of retribution for taking their own lives. Their grief—a living death." *Id.*

118. Francis J. Braceland, Psychological Aspects of Aging 208–09 in Problems of the Aged (Clyde B. Vedder & Annette S. Lefkowitz, eds., 1965). See also Kline, supra note 10, at 206.

119. Braceland, supra note 118, at 208–09. Braceland notes that suicide is the eleventh leading cause of death in the United States, having the highest incidence rate in the elderly. *Id.* at 209.

120. Rosenbaum, supra note 115, at 59.

121. *Id.* However, Rosenbaum's research was based on a study done in 1958. *Id.*

122. Garrett, supra note 7, at 814. This study was done in Maine. *Id.*

123. Levy, supra note 113, at 265.

124. Swoap, 516 P.2d at 843. Citing a portion of the regulations in California detailing the responsibilities of the director of the County Welfare Department, the court declared:

> The director may establish a relatives' contribution scale setting forth the amount an adult child shall be required to contribute toward the support of a parent in receipt of aid . . . . Regulations of the department shall prescribe the criteria, methods of investigation and test check procedures relating to the determination of the maximum amount any adult child may be held liable to contribute . . . . *Id.* at 842 n.3.

125. Levy, supra note 113, at 265–67. Levy notes some examples of complex matrix systems for determining support levels. *Id.* at 275 n.42. The California statute says the income of an adult child includes the sum of the income of the separate property of child and the income of the child but not of his or her spouse. Swoap, 516 P.2d at 843 n.3. The formula allows a flat 25% allowance for personal income taxes, social security taxes, and necessary expenses for producing income (including meals eaten at work, the cost of transportation to and from work, and union dues). *Id.* See also Swoap, 516 P.2d at 854 (discussing California's Relative Contribution Scale which calculates support levels).

126. Ann Britton, America's Best Kept Secret: An Adult Child's Duty to Support Aged Parents, 26 Cal. W. L. Rev. 351, 368–69 (1990). Britton said, "Most older people believe it is not their children's responsibility to provide them with an adequate income; they see this as a government responsibility." *Id.* Other authors furthured this claim, "Indigent parents have been loath to claim state support for fear that the state would seek reimbursement from their children. Many have preferred to suffer in silence rather than be the cause of pressure on young, struggling families." [Martin R. Levy & Sara W. Gross, *Constitutional Implications of Parental Support Laws*, 13 U. Rich. L. Rev. 517, 524 (1979) (explaining the logic of the argument supporting an equal protection violation).] Researchers have found the elderly are more receptive to non-family and formal services. Hagestad, supra note 109, at 132. The elderly view public assistance as a right—not charity—and do not feel as guilty accepting money from the government as they do from their children. Lopes, supra note 7, at 524.

127. Levy, supra note 113, at 265.

128. Rosenbaum, supra note 115, at 61; Our Needy Aged 200 (Floyd A. Bond, et al., eds., 1954) [hereinafter Bond].

129. Tully, supra note 16, at 35.

130. Britton, supra note 126, at 351.

131. Van Houtte & Breda, supra note 1, at 646-51.

132. Levy & Gross, supra note 113, at 519. The authors noted, "In some states, [supporting an indigent parent] is a moral imperative; in other states, a sincere concern for the plight of the poor; and yet in others, a frank desire to wash state hands publicly and find a class, anywhere, anyhow, to assume an unwieldly and unwanted burden." *Id.*

133. Kline, supra note 10, at 210.

134. Mandelker, supra note 9, at 504. An Illinois statute specifically cites the family as a goal to promote: "The maintenance of the family unit shall be a principal consideration in the administration of this Code, and all public assistance policies shall be formulated and administered with the purpose of strengthening the family unit." *Id.* at n.22 (quoting Ill. Stat. Ann. § 436-1 (Supp. 1955)).

135. Duffy, 84 P. at 838 (relieving public of support for people who have other means of support is a main goal); Gluckman, 71 Cal. Rptr. at 797 (protecting the public from supporting people who have children able to support them is a central purpose).

136. Kline, supra note 10, at 203.

137. *Id.* at 207.

138. Mandelker, supra note 9, at 504.

The following case shows how a parental support statute can be invoked.

Savoy v. Savoy, 433 Pa. Super. 549, 641 A.2d 596 (1994)
Joan M. Savoy v. Marcus J. Savoy, Appellant.
Superior Court of Pennsylvania.

Mother brought action against son for support pursuant to statute making relatives liable for support of indigent persons. The Court of Common Pleas, Lycoming County, Family Division, No. 89-21269, Brown, J., directed son to financially assist mother by paying $125 per month to her medical care providers for past expenses, and son appealed. The Superior Court, No. 500 Harrisburg 1993, Johnson, J., held that mother was indigent within meaning of statute.

Affirmed.

* * *

[W]e affirm the order directing Marcus J. Savoy (Son) to pay $125 per month directly to the medical care providers of Joan M. Savoy (Mother) for her past medical care expenses.

Prior to 1986, Mother had been financially independent and regularly employed. In early 1986, Mother initially became unemployed to undergo and to recover from neck surgery. When she returned to work, Mother slipped and fell, sustaining soft tissue injuries to her head, neck, and back, and a broken right ankle. Since her fall, Mother has been unemployed due to her continuing medical difficulties. Mother received periodic payments through Workmen's Compensation, which were later commuted to a lump sum payment of $25,000, all of which has been exhausted. Mother receives Social Security disability benefits in the amount of $362 per month, and Supplemental Security Income benefits in the amount of $76.40 per month, for a total monthly income of $438.40. Mother's monthly expenses are $940. Although Mother presently has medical insurance for her continuing medical difficulties, she has unpaid medical expenses in excess of $10,000, which neither Workmen's Compensation nor any other insurance covered.

Son is an officer, shareholder, and manager in the family-owned furniture manufacturing business. Son, who has no dependents, has a net monthly income of $2,327 per month. Son's reported net monthly expenses are $2,583 per month, an amount in excess of his income.

In September 1989, Mother filed a Complaint for Support, pursuant to 62 P.S. §

1973, against Son. Son filed Preliminary Objections in the nature of a demurrer challenging the statutory basis of the support request and alleging that Mother lacked standing to bring the support action. The trial court denied Son's Preliminary Objections and ordered that a hearing be scheduled before a Master. The Master conducted hearings on April 3, April 25, and May 30, 1990. On June 26, 1990, the Master filed a proposed order directing Son to financially assist Mother by paying $125 per month to her medical care providers for past medical care expenses. Son filed exceptions to the Master's proposed order, and Mother filed cross-exceptions which she later withdrew. The parties requested that the trial court delay its decision on the exceptions to permit the negotiation of a settlement. The parties were unsuccessful in their attempt to negotiate a settlement, and after a significant lapse of time, Mother asked the trial court to enter its decision on the exceptions. On June 18, 1993, the trial court issued an order denying Son's exceptions and affirmed the Master's proposed order. Son appeals.

* * *

When we apply the above-stated definition of indigent to the facts of this case, we are constrained to conclude that Mother is indigent. Our determination of Mother's indigency rests upon the inadequacy of her Social Security benefits to meet her reasonable care and maintenance, as well as her past medical expenses, which are in excess of $10,000. Mother's monthly income is $438.40, and her monthly expenses are $940. The trial court determined that Mother's expenses were reasonable, and we observe nothing in the record to indicate otherwise. The trial court adopted the Master's conclusion that Son has the ability to financially assist Mother. We agree with this determination. In view of the disparity between Mother's income and expenses, as well as her continuing medical difficulties, and in view of Son's sufficient financial ability to assist her, we find no abuse of discretion in the trial court issuing an order directing Son to pay $125 per month to Mother's medical care providers for her past medical care expenses.

Accordingly, we affirm the parental support order.

Order affirmed.

Though filial responsibility still lives, it has only limited room in which to operate. The federal Medicare program that pays for the acute health care costs of older persons does not use a "needs" test. Thus, both rich elderly and those with rich children are equally eligible. Medicaid, which pays both the acute and chronic health care costs of impoverished older persons, will not permit states to "consider income and resources of any relative as available to an individual" (42 US Code of Federal Regulations § 435.602). Older indigent persons are therefore eligible for Medicaid even though they have well-off children who could afford to pay for their medical care.

Part VIII

Family and Social Issues

CHAPTER 39

Marriage and Family

Although most of us are aware that one out of every two marriages in America ends in divorce, what many fail to realize is how many of those divorces occur within the older population. At present, almost one fifth of all divorces occur in marriages of fifteen years or longer.

Older marriages that have endured for years may finally crumble under the pressure of retirement, when one or both partners find themselves with little or nothing to occupy their days. Other older marriages fail when underlying stresses finally seem unbearable to aging individuals who hope for at least a few more years of happiness. Not all divorces among older individuals represent the failure of a long-term marriage. Many divorces represent second and even third marriages that flounder as the parties age.

Given the almost universal application of no-fault divorce it is now possible for one partner to terminate the marriage even if the other would prefer to continue in their relationship. The party not desiring that divorce may find it very traumatic, particularly given the social attitudes among the older population about the immorality of divorce. Divorced older women may particularly find divorce a financial disaster. Being old and female makes it very difficult, if not impossible, to find employment or often even a new marriage partner. Lawyers representing older women going through a divorce must pay particular attention to ensure that the woman is adequately protected financially.

The opposite side of the coin from divorce is, of course, marriage, a common occurrence among older persons. Increasingly, however, older persons are turning to cohabitation rather than marriage. Assuming that the individuals have no moral qualms without being formally married, there can actually be a number of financial advantages to cohabitation over remarriage. For example, an older person, male or female, may be receiving Social Security benefits based on an ex-spouse's retirement benefits (possible whether they are divorced or widowed). Remarriage might cause the loss of those benefits, while cohabitation will not affect them. For others who are divorced or widowed, the ex-spouse's health care policy may be their source of health insurance. Remarriage might cause them to lose those continuing benefits. Usually, however, cohabitation would not affect coverage under the ex-spouse's medical health care plan. If an individual is receiving alimony, cohabitation probably will not terminate the ali-

mony; however, the paying party can cite cohabitation by the former spouse as a reason to reduce the amount of alimony.

Whether an older couple chooses marriage or cohabitation, they will often enter into an antenuptial agreement or a precohabitation agreement. These agreements attempt to clarify the financial arrangements between the parties and usually will cover what will happen to each party's estate upon their death or separation. Assuming that both parties have been adequately represented by independent counsel and that there has been full disclosure of assets and other relevant information, these agreements are enforceable. Specific issues that often arise upon remarriage by older couples is the problem of two houses. One party will need to sell her or his house, but what are the rights of the other party in the survivor's house? For example, Joe and Jan marry, and Jan sells her house to move in with Joe. What happens if Joe dies? Does Jan get to continue living in the house? Health care problems and long-term care expenses can pose a special problem. If parties marry, both spouses will be liable for the other's health care expenses. And although there may be insurance under Medicare for acute care, long-term care expenses may have no coverage. The parties may be well advised to purchase long-term care insurance to ensure that the survivor's assets are not eaten up in paying for the sick party's long-term care. Of course, if the parties merely cohabit there will be no liability for the other party's medical or long-term care expenses.

Older Americans will increasingly face the issue of whether to marry or to merely cohabit. While many will feel bound by tradition and morality to marry, others may decide that cohabitation with appropriate agreements is more appropriate than legally sanctioned marriage.

CHAPTER 40

Spiritual Issues

Growing old means growing closer to death. For many, the approach of death calls up questions about the meaning of their lives and about their relation with God. Dr. Blazer addresses the spiritual issues that confront many older persons.

Dan Blazer

Spirituality and Aging Well

Religion has long been thought to become more important to persons as they age, especially as they approach death. Nevertheless, religion has been studied sparsely, both in its relationship to illnesses in older adults and in its relationship to successful aging. More often than not, students of religion in late life have focused upon the role of organized religion in providing services for older adults. Religious groups are the third most important source of instrumental support to older adults, following the support of families and the federal government. Another dimension of religion—spirituality and aging—well deserves equal attention from students and practitioners of gerontology.

* * *

Though scholars and writers have not reached a consensus regarding spirituality and aging, the topic remains of much interest among elders and those who work with them. The 1971 White House Conference on Aging addressed in some detail the spiri-

Generations, Vol. 15, No. 33 (January 1991). Reprinted with permission from *Generations*, 833 Market St., Suite 512, San Francisco, CA 94103.

tual well-being of older adults from recommendations of conference participants. The National Interfaith Coalition on Aging was instituted and adopted an ecumenical definition of spiritual well-being, reflecting the views of Roman Catholic, Eastern Orthodox, Jewish, and Protestant religious leaders associated with NICA. "Spiritual well-being is the affirmation of life in a relationship with a God, self, community, and environment that nurtures and celebrates wholeness" (NICA, 1975). David Moberg (1971), who prepared background material for the 1971 White House Conference, identified six areas of spiritual need as deserving special attention: (1) sociocultural sources of spiritual needs, (2) relief from anxieties and fears, (3) preparation for death, (4) personality integration, (5) personal dignity, and (6) a philosophy of life.

These "spiritual needs" are part of the dimensions of spiritual well-being that, I believe, can and should be recognized and addressed by elders, gerontologists, and practitioners working with older adults. Some readers will disagree with my characterization of the dimensions as presented below, and others will suggest that spirituality and aging well cannot or should not be studied by the gerontological community. Yet I suspect the lack of literature on the subject is more a reflection of the difficulty of capturing the essence of spiritual well-being through usual scientific inquiries than it is of a belief that spiritual well-being is unimportant to the elderly. In the following pages I will also suggest four means by which these dimensions of spiritual well-being can be facilitated among older adults.

The Dimensions of Spiritual Well-Being

Self-determined wisdom. Personality integration and a philosophy of life are components of the construct "wisdom." According to Bateson (1972), self-determination is one aspect of wisdom, which he defines as a knowledge of the larger system in which one lives. Systems by their nature are self-correcting, and all persons, both young and old, are constantly interacting with a system—their physical and sociocultural environment. Humans have an advantage over other species, for they have the ability to transcend if not alter the environment. If their beliefs about the larger system are far removed from the reality of the environment, however, they may perceive the world as inflexible, if not hostile. The wise elder accepts the limits to which an individual can influence the environment and does not attempt to upset the balance of the system. In other words, self-determined wisdom establishes a stable person-environment fit for the older adult. "When you fall down at my age, the great secret is not to try to get up too quickly. Just lie there. Have a look at the world from a different perspective" (Dame Edith Evans, as quoted by Brian Forbes, 1977).

Self-transcendence. Growing older is accompanied by changes in physical well-being, mental acuity, and the frequency and patterns of social interaction. The changes most experienced are usually losses—of one's physical health, of one's memory, of one's social role. These losses are not inevitable, but when they do occur, they need not be experienced as negative. Many of the losses of aging can be buffered by external factors, such as planning for retirement and effective social policies to support health care for older adults. Yet adapting to loss may ultimately be a spiritual challenge or even an opportunity for older adults.

Many religions view spiritual growth as self-transcendence, that is, as crossing a boundary beyond the self.

* * *

Whitehead (1981) views self-transcendence as one of the disciplines most used by the elderly. She suggests that "the deprivations and losses of advancing age are opportunities to divest one's self of the illusionary ambitions and false securities of life which often serve as distractions from the life of the spirit; letting go of these distractions, one is able to live more fully in the present, to see life as it is."

Meaning. What is the meaning of aging? Why do we live to an age when we gradually lose physical and mental capacities? Despite our scientific advances, these are questions not easily answered by older adults and professionals who work with them. Ultimately, the answers are individual, and spirituality often provides the framework within which elders evaluate the meaning of the latter years.

* * *

Accepting the totality of life. The eighth stage of man, according to Erikson (1968), is the achievement of integrity, "the acceptance of one's one and only life cycle and of the people who have become significant to it as something that had to be and that, by necessity, permitted no substitutions." In reflecting upon one's life, there is no room for "ifs," and there is no changing the life course in retrospect. If one looks back and cannot accept the totality of one's life, despair emerges—despair that one's one and only lifetime has been squandered.

Accepting one's life is often a spiritual task. Frederick Buchner (1982:6) described this spiritual task in *The Sacred Journey* as he wrote about his past, his present, and his future. "What I propose to do now is to try listening to my life as a whole, or at least at certain key moments . . . for whatever of meaning, of holiness, of God, there may be in it to hear. My assumptions is that the story of any one of us is in some measure the story of us all."

* * *

Exit and existence. Robert Kastenbaum (1981) suggests that one of the developmental tasks of aging is "the exit from existence." He notes that, though being old has shifted to a positive rather than a negative value, dying and death have not been banished from the human condition. In fact, dying and death are more visible today than in the earlier twentieth century. This in part is due to a greater value being placed upon life in later life.

* * *

Facilitating the Spiritual Well-Being of the Elderly

Religious beliefs and spiritual experiences are by nature individualistic. Religious groups are inherently separatist, and separatism in religion appears to be increasing.

* * *

In the theology of aging and ministry to the elderly, however, there has been an amazingly cooperative atmosphere across religious groups, which has facilitated the spiritual well-being of older adults regardless of their religious orientation. Let me provide some examples:

There has been a small yet persistent investigation of the role of religion and health by gerontologists. A number of reports in the literature have identified the positive values of religion to the health and well-being of older adults (Zuckerman, 1984; Koenig et al., 1988). Other studies demonstrate the association of religion and increased life satisfaction. Blazer and Palmore (1976) found that the associations of religious activities and attitudes with personal adjustment, happiness, and feelings of usefulness were higher among older people and continued to increase over time. Usui and colleagues (1985) found a positive effect of religious attendance on the life satisfaction of older people that persisted even when health was used as a control variable. A review of textbooks in gerontology and articles in major publications reveals the interest of the gerontological community in the topic of religion and aging. The *Journal of Religious Gerontology* is devoted specifically to investigating the importance and relevance of religion in later life.

Recognition of the importance of spirituality to aging well has also precipitated programs to educate the clergy regarding aging. Following the 1971 White House Conference on Aging, the National Interfaith Coalition on Aging (NICA) obtained a grant from the Administration on Aging to train clergy in aging. This endeavor was most successful in bringing together Protestant, Catholic, and Jewish seminarians into conferences where secular experts in aging provided consultation and formal training experiences. In addition, the seminarians developed model curricula in the field of aging that could be incorporated into the educational activities of their seminaries. Most seminaries now offer at least one course in aging to improve the expertise of the clergy in facilitating the physical and psychosocial as well as the spiritual well-being of the elderly.

At a time when clergy are studying gerontology, gerontologists should study spirituality and aging well. This training need not come through professional course work or even through structured reading. Professionals who work with older adults can learn much about spirituality and aging by listening to the older people with whom they work. Encouraging older people to talk about what they wish to talk about and listening carefully can provide profound spiritual insights into the process of aging.

* * *

We can also facilitate the spiritual well-being of older adults by recognizing and encouraging the value of interfaith ministries to older adults. The Shepherd's Center in Kansas City, Missouri, begun in 1972, is an example of an ecumenical activity that serves the entire community and is derived from the cooperative effort of many religious groups. Begun by Elbert Cole, a minister at the Methodist church, the activity has provided opportunities to thousands of older adults in the area to participate in religious and secular activities. Older volunteers provide services that range from performing chores in the homes to spiritual counseling. One lesson learned from the

Shepherd's Center is that older persons are most adept at serving the physical, emotional, social, and spiritual needs of their fellow elders. The Shepherd's Center has been successful primarily because the younger ministers listened to the older volunteer ministers. . . .

* * *

References

Bateson, G., 1972. Steps to an Ecology of Mind. San Francisco: Chandler Publishing Company.

Blazer, D. G., and Palmore, E. B., 1976. "Religion and Aging." Gerontologist 16:82–85.

Buchner, F., 1982. The Sacred Journey. San Francisco: Harper and Row.

Erikson, E., 1968. Childhood and Society (2nd ed.). New York: Norton, pp. 268, 269.

Forbes, B., 1977. Dame Edith Evans. Boston: Little, Brown. As quoted in E. C. Taylor, ed., 1984, Growing On: Ideas about Aging. New York: Van Nostrand, p. 14.

Kastenbaum, R., 1981. "Exit and Existence. In C. LeFevre and P. LeFevre, eds., Aging and the Human Spirit: A Reader in Religion and Gerontology. Chicago: Exploration Press, pp. 91–116.

Koenig, H. G., Smiley, M. and Gonzales, J. P., 1988. Religion, Health and Aging: A Review and theoretical Integration. New York: Greenwood Press.

Moberg, D. O., 1971. "Spiritual Well-Being: Background and Issues." Washington, D.C.: White House Conference on Aging.

National Interfaith Coalition on Aging, 1975. "Spiritual Well-Being Definition: A Model of Ecumenical Work Product." NIC Inform 1 (August 25):4.

Usui, W. M., Feil, T. J. and Durig, K. R., 1985. "Socioeconomic Comparisons and Life Satisfaction of Elderly Adults." Journal of Gerontology 40:110–14.

Whitehead, E. E., 1981. "Religious Images of Aging." In C. LeFevre and P. LeFevre, eds., Aging and the Human Spirit: A Reader in Religion and Gerontology. Chicago: Exploration Press, pp. 156–67.

Zuckerman, D. M., 1984. "Psychosocial Predictors of Mentality Among the Elderly Poor." American Journal of Epidemiology 119:410–23.

Religion and churches play a special role in the lives of many older African Americans.

Carla T. Walls

The Role of Church and Family Support in the Lives of Older African Americans: A New Look at Families and Aging and Black Churches as Support Systems

As in most racial minority groups, the primary source of social support for older African Americans is the family (Dressler, 1985; Chatters, Taylor and Jackson, 1986; Langston, 1980). Current research, however, suggests that older African Americans have support networks beyond their family (Cantor, 1979; Langston, 1983). This research suggests that in addition to the family, older African Americans rely on friends, neighbors, and their churches for supplemental support (Langston, 1983; Taylor and Chatters, 1986b).

Consistent with Cantor's (1979) hierarchical-compensatory model, which suggests that an ordered preference exists for those selected to provide care, older African Americans seek assistance from family members first before accepting help from others (see also Chatters, Taylor and Jackson, 1986). As a second option, older blacks turn to their churches for assistance before utilizing services from some formal agencies (Ambrose, 1977; Langston, 1983). Research indicates that African American elders rely on their church for assistance more often than do elderly whites, especially when community-based services are not available (Haber, 1984; Hirsch, Kent and Silverman, 1972). The involvement of African American elders in the church supports Antonucci and Akiyama's (1987) concept of a "convoy" of social support, since these individuals' lifetime connection to the church generates a support network that provides help when needed.

* * *

Results of the Study

Most studies that examine the role of black churches as supportive networks have not considered or described how that role relates to family support and psychological well-being. In theory, when one talks about the family and the church network, the inclination is to think of them as two distinct institutions. However, these networks are not mutually exclusive. Most of the people in the networks of these African American elders were immediate family members and friends who attended their

Generations, Vol. 16, No. 3 (June 1992). Reprinted with permission from *Generations,* 833 Market St., Suite 512, San Francisco, CA 94103.

church. This finding suggests that it is important to consider the church network in relation to the family when the support networks of African American elders are studied.

One of the striking findings of this research is that family members were perceived as providing more emotional than instrumental support, compared to the perception of more instrumental than emotional support provided by church members. As expected, African American elders in this study perceived that more support overall was provided by the family than by church members; nevertheless, church support contributed to feelings of well-being.

The church and family networks were both important predictors of well-being. African American elders who received high support from either the family or the church network experienced more feelings of well-being than those who received moderate support from both networks. Additionally, older African Americans who received high levels of support from both networks scored best on well-being. Finally, the results showed that it was the perceptions the African American elders had of the church, and not the ideology (spiritual aspects) or involvement in the organizational aspects of the church, that generated feelings of well-being.

There are two possible ways to interpret these findings. One view is that in current times, black families tend to provide more emotional support, because they do not have adequate resources to provide instrumental support. In light of the fact that black churches may have more resources in comparison to what some African American families have, the churches are able to provide some instrumental support, even though it is sporadic. These findings show that older African Americans normally attend the same church as other family members, a circumstance that heightens the expectation for assistance and reciprocity, since the religious community thus becomes an extended family network (see Antonucci and Akiyama, 1987). This synthesis is beneficial for the development of supportive exchanges.

An alternative interpretation is connected to the fact that this was a sample of African American elders who were doing well physically and economically. Financial and practical assistance from the family was therefore not a necessity. Additionally, these data are dealing with people's perceptions of support—not actual supportive exchanges. This group of African American elders came from an era in which it was believed the church would provide help if needed. The perceptions of this cohort, then, may be different from the reality of what black churches actually provide. More research is needed to better understand the connection between perceptions and actual support from the church and how this differs across generations.

* * *

References

Ambrose, J. J., 1977. "The Black Church as a Mental Health Resource." In D. Jones and W. Matthews, eds., The Black Church: A Community Resource. Washington, D.C.: Institute for Urban Affairs and Research, Howard University, pp. 105–13.

Antonucci, T. C. and Akiyama, H., 1987. "Social Support Networks in Adult Life and a Preliminary Examination of the Convoy Model." Journal of Gerontology 42(5):519–27.

Cantor, M. H., 1979. "Neighbors and Friends: An Overlooked Resource in the Informal Support System." Research on Aging 1:434–63.

Chatters, L. M., Taylor, R.J. and Jackson, J. S., 1986. "Aged Blacks' Choices for an Informal Helpers Network." Journal of Gerontology 41(1):94–100.

Dressler, W.W., 1985. "Extended Family Relationships, Social Support and Mental Health in a Southern Black Community." Journal of Health and Social Behavior 26:39–48.

Haber, D., 1984. "Church-based Programs for Black Caregivers of Noninstitutionalized Elders." Journal of Gerontological Social Work 7:43–49.

Hirsch, B., Kent, D. P. and Silverman, S., 1972. "Homogeneity and Heterogeneity Among Low-Income Negro and White Aged." In D. P. Kent, R. Kastenbaum and S. Sherwood, eds., Research Planning and Action for the Elderly: The Power and Potential of Social Science. New York: Behavioral Publishers, pp. 400–500.

Langston, E. J., 1980. "Kith and Kin, Natural Support Systems: Their Implications." In E. P. Stanford, ed., Minority Aging: Policy Issues for the 80s. San Diego, Calif.: Campanile Press, pp. 124–44.

Langston, E.J., 1983. "The Family and Other Informal Supports." In E. P. Stanford and S. A. Lockery, eds., Minority Aging and Long-Term Care. San Diego, Calif.: Campanile Press, pp. 35–37.

Taylor, R. J. and Chatters, L. M., 1986b. "Patterns of Informal Support to Elderly Black Adults: Family, Friends, and Church Members." Social Work 31: 432–38.

Spiritual concerns are not strictly metaphysical issues; spiritual care plays an important role in caring for the health needs of older persons.

Ranjana Sardana

Spiritual Care for the Elderly: An Integral Part of the Nursing Process

In the preamble to the constitution of the World Health Organization, health is defined as ". . . a state of complete physical, mental, and social well-being and not merely the absence of disease and infirmity." This definition emphasizes that man is more than just an individual free from sickness. It identifies three aspects of well-

Nursing Homes and Senior Citizen Care, Vol. 39, No. 1, 15 (May 1990). Reprinted by permission.

ness—body, mind, and spirit—which can be changed by behavior or style of living. Every individual consciously or unconsciously demonstrates behavior which affects his sense of well-being.

Nurses and other members of the health care team are well able to competently take care of patients' physiological and psychosocial needs. However, spiritual healing has been often ignored or only partially undertaken, especially in the area of geriatric patient care. To provide total or holistic health care to clients and their families, we must think about the three major areas of body, mind and spirit.

Spiritual care is an integral part of the nursing process for the elderly. What is spiritual care? It involves meeting those needs of the patient that transcend but at the same time intervene his physiological and psychosocial needs. The spiritual aspect of man involves finding deeper meaning in everything, including life, sickness, and even death. Such understanding is essential for the overall well-being of the patient.

Psychologists and sociologists alike have affirmed that importance of spiritual care for the elderly. Dettmore (1984) concluded from his study on aging that the elderly will be unable to achieve contentment in later life unless they first internalize a resolution that will separate or calm the conflict between integrity and despair. Peel (1987) developed a similar theory. He stated that development in later life is only satisfactory when the elderly individual becomes less involved with superficial activities (those dealing mainly with himself and his body) and more interested in a variety of activities that ultimately serve to promote and build self worth. Since spirituality is strongly linked to physical and psychosocial care, nurses can assist in promoting enhancement of the spiritual while meeting the needs of the body and mind.

Many studies have concluded that as age increases, the importance of religion also increases. Religious beliefs in later life help the elderly to feel a greater sense of purpose and to maintain feelings of usefulness and adaptability in their lives.

Nurses have had the tendency to overlook the importance of healing in the spiritual sense. Asked if they felt they met their patients' spiritual needs, only 25 percent replied "yes." Three out of every four said they never read religious material to their patients or prayed with them (Dettmore, 1984).

Another study (Highfield and Cason, 1983) showed that nurses feel uncomfortable about giving spiritual care. They tend not to emphasize the importance of meeting those needs, but indicate that they would gladly seek education in this area.

There are many reasons why nurses may avoid their patients' spiritual needs. Most obviously, spiritual matters may be highly personal to them, and they feel that spirituality should be personal and private for others as well. They should remember, however, that if the patient is in distress, he may not wish to be left alone, and that loneliness will only add to his illness. A discussion or suggestion of support in spirituality should at least be offered, if not encouraged. Ultimately, it is up to the patient to respond, but every opportunity must be presented by the care giver.

Nurses may also avoid the spiritual realm because of a sense of vulnerability. What if the patient asks a question that the nurse has not personally resolved? Here, as in all instances, personal growth is possible. Perhaps in attempting to answer specific questions from the patient, the care giver may find something compatible with her own sense of spirituality as well, ultimately enhancing the quality of her own being. Nurses and all health professionals should study various spiritual beliefs. Subsequently, when a patient poses a difficult question, the care giver can present a number of possible answers, thereby allowing the patient to select the one most suited to his own lifestyle and beliefs.

The specific nursing process used in caring for the spiritually weak individual is the same as used with a clinically or socially weak patient. Spiritual care is not obtuse or elusive.

First, nurses must continually reevaluate their patients. Spiritual states are not static, but dynamic. As individuals grow, religious beliefs change. In the initial interview, care givers should pose direct religious questions that reveal not only any denominational affiliation or preference, but also the patients specific beliefs, customary rituals, concept of a "Higher Power," and the role all of these play in that patient's lifestyle. The nurse should also determine what the patient feels is the source of his inner strength and hope.

Baseline physical assessments provide insight to modes that might be useful in meeting spiritual needs. For example, those having mobility or auditory impairments may need special assistance to ensure their participation in spiritual enrichment programs such as worship services.

The most important assessment data comes from just listening to and observing the client during the course of care. Attentive listeners and observers can easily pick up clues and tidbits of information that tell what is important to the person spiritually. Care givers should especially note icons, religious articles, and other personal possessions kept always close at hand.

Once spiritual needs have been assessed, a care plan may be developed. In doing so, it should be remembered that many patients will not expect much in the way of spiritual care. Basically, they will expect care givers to be attentive and to have open ears, hearts, and very importantly—minds. Nurses are not only responsible for contacting religious representatives, but may also at times be asked to pray with the client, either leading in prayer or just following. In any case, the nurse should always be prepared to respond to a request to participate.

As aging individuals begin to anticipate death, they may reminisce about past experiences. Nurses can provide a large amount of support to their clients by helping them deal with these memories. By showing the patient that he has self-worth and dignity, and that he has had meaningful experiences which should be cherished, the nurse can lessen the burden of facing losses, even the end of life.

Spiritual care for the elderly is a challenging but somewhat ignored field which does not extend beyond the scope of any care giver's professional realm. In fact, accepting the challenge and subsequently meeting spiritual needs can ultimately benefit both the recipient and the donor.

The sense of values by which man lives has its roots in religious beliefs, and such beliefs, whatever they may be, constitute a significant aspect of an individual's existence. The patient who enters the nursing home or is seen in a clinic or his home brings with him his own religion and spiritual needs. Part of a nurse's responsibility is to be sensitive to such needs, and to understand and support their significance to the patient.

Although not directly responsible for religious or spiritual ministration, the nurse has certain obligations in relation to patients' religious or spiritual needs. One is respect for the patient's beliefs, regardless of what his religion might be, and contacting the clergy when the elderly person faces stressful situations.

* * *

References

Dettmore, D. (October, 1984). Spiritual care: remembering your patients' forgotten needs. Nursing, 14:46.

Highfield, M.F., and Cason, C. (June, 1983). Spiritual needs of patients: are they recognized? Cancel-Nursing, 6:187–192.

Peel, R. (1987). Spiritual Healing in a Scientific Age. Harper and Row: San Francisco.

CHAPTER 41

Social Problems

A. Alcohol

Persons of all ages have social and behavioral difficulties. Growing old does not mean the end of such problems. True, some life adjustment problems diminish with age. A retiree, for example, no longer has to deal with job stress nor do most older persons have to endure the frustration of being a primary caregiver to a young child. As individuals age, however, they confront new challenges: death of a spouse; loss of friends by moving, sickness or death; and personal physical decline. While most persons come to terms with these and other problems, some elderly persons retreat into the solace of alcohol.

Of the estimated ten million alcoholics in the United States, probably three million of them are over age sixty. Many of these older alcoholics have an early onset of alcohol abuse but have "beaten the odds" and survived into old age. Other older alcoholics were once occasional binge drinkers who become alcohol abusers as a result of the stress of aging. Finally, many individuals start drinking late in life. It is estimated that up to one-third of older alcoholics did not become problem drinkers until after age sixty-five.

Older alcoholic men outnumber older alcoholic women five to one with women more likely to start drinking heavily later in life. Single women are particularly vulnerable to alcohol abuse. For older men, retirement is often a cause of stress or social dislocation that leads to alcohol abuse. Other stress causes include death of a spouse, loss of friends, loneliness, and chronic medical conditions.

B. Suicide

Alcoholism is closely associated with suicide, a leading cause of death for persons age sixty-five or older. Although persons over age sixty-five make up only 12 percent of the population, they account for nearly 17 percent of suicides. Older persons may suffer from psychiatric disorders such as depression or psychoses or be addicted to alcohol or drugs, both of which greatly increase the probability of suicide. It is estimated, for example, that 15 percent of older persons are affected with clinical depression. The rate of suicide for older alcoholics is ten times the rate for nondrinkers. Retired, widowed males are particularly prone to suicide. The loss of both their job and their spouse seems too much for many to bear. Intervention in the form of hospitalization for the alcohol or drug addicted, prescription antidepressant drugs where appropriate, use of psychotherapy, and even electroconvulsive therapy for some depressed patients can help prevent suicide among the elderly. Providing more social support and reducing isolation and loneliness can also reduce the chance of suicide.

C. Loneliness

One of the more common assumptions about older persons, particularly the very old, is that they suffer from loneliness. Having outlived their spouses and friends, often unable to drive, seemingly isolated from the community, the very old are often objects of pity. The reality of the quality of life for the very old may be very different, however. It may well be that older persons are no more lonely than the young. What appears to be loneliness may well reflect only the older persons preference to be alone. However, even if most older persons do not suffer from loneliness, some do with very severe consequences.

Dellmar Walker and Roy E. Beauchene

The Relationship of Loneliness, Social Isolation, and Physical Health to Dietary Adequacy of Independently Living Elderly

* * *

The United States Select Committee on Nutrition and Human Needs [Todhunter, 1991] proposed that apathy and social isolation contribute to reduced food intake in the elderly especially for those who live alone. This assumption was based on the premise that the social life of many elderly adults in our society is built around food; therefore, eating is a social and psychological event as well as a biological need. Within groups of older persons, social isolation frequently is considered to be a contributing factor to development of a lack of interest in food and to dietary inadequacy [Ryan & Bower, 1989; Greene, 1981; Clancy, 1979; Clarke & Wakefield, 1975].

* * *

Loneliness may be defined as a feeling and realization of a lack of meaningful contacts with others and a lack or loss of companionship [Berg, Melistrom, Person, & Swanborg, 1981]. Living alone does not always entail loneliness. Never-married older persons have been found to be more isolated than married persons but similar to them with regard to loneliness and life satisfaction [Gubrium, 1974]. Loneliness is a subjective state that is distinguished from the objective state of social isolation and lack of social contacts. However, social isolation may contribute to loneliness by reducing opportunities for maintaining or developing meaningful relationships, and old age is potentially a time of increased risk of social isolation [Revenson & Johnson, 1984; Baum, 1982]. Feelings of loneliness often are expressed by elderly individuals who have substantial contacts with others, whereas elderly persons with minimal contacts may not perceive themselves as lonely or isolated [Heltsley & Powers, 1975]. A person surrounded by many people may still feel lonely.

* * *

Anderson [Anderson, 1982] reported that loneliness was not representative of the elderly population; however, 53 percent of persons over age seventy-five felt very lonely. In the present study, there was no relationship between age and degree of loneliness, but loneliness did appear to be related to the number of social contacts. Black participants reported a higher degree of loneliness than did white participants. Participation in group meal programs did not affect loneliness scores. Participation in other senior citizen programs was not evaluated.

* * *

The number of social contacts, which was inversely related to loneliness (r = -.35), was the most important independent variable related to degree of loneliness. Persons who were more socially active reported less loneliness, and this appeared to be related to increased nutrient intake. This result does not support the findings of Heitsley and Powers [Heltsley & Powers, 1975], who reported that loneliness was a problem for elderly individuals despite frequent contacts with others, and elderly persons with few social contacts did not necessarily perceive themselves as lonely. Revenson and Johnson [Revenson & Johnson, 1984] concluded that dissatisfaction with available relationships may be a more powerful indicator of loneliness than the number of social contacts. The quality of relationships was not measured in the present study. The trend toward incorporating congregate meal programs into senior citizen center programs appears to offer the benefit of providing both adequate diets and social interaction.

* * *

References

Anderson L. Interdisciplinary study of loneliness-with evaluation of social contacts as a means toward improving competence in old age. Acta Sociol. 1982; 25:75–80.

Berg A, Melistrom D, Person G, Swanborg A. Loneliness in the Swedish aged. J Gerontol. 1981; 36:342–349.

Baum SL. Loneliness in elderly persons: a preliminary study. Psychol Rep. 1982; 50:1317–1318.

Clancy L. Preliminary observations on media use and food habits of the elderly Gerontologist. 1979; 16:529–532.

Clarke M., Wakefield LM. Food choices of institutionalized vs independent living elderly J Am Diet Assoc. 1975; 66:600–604.

Greene JM. Coordination of Older Americans Act programs. JAm Diet Assoc. 1981; 78: 617–620.

Gubrium J. Marital desolation and the evaluation of everyday life in old age. J Marr Fam. 1974; 36:107–113.

Heltsley MC, Powers RC. Social interaction and perceived adequacy of interaction on the rural aged. Gerontologist 1975; 15:533–536.

Revenson TA, Johnson JL. Social and demographic correlates of loneliness in late life. Am J Com Psychiatry. 1984; 12:71–85.

Ryan VC, Bower ME. Relationship of socioeconomic status and living arrangements to nutritional intake of the older person. Am Diet Assoc. 1989; 89:1805–1807.

Todhunter NE. Nutrition: background and issues. The Technical Committee on Nutrition. White House Conference on Aging. Section 4. Washington, DC: 1971.

D. Mental Illness

Mental illness affects individuals of all ages. Older persons are not spared; millions suffer from mental illness. As the numbers of elderly increase, so does the number of mentally ill older persons and so does the cost of treating them. Faced with the specter of rapidly rising care costs for the mentally ill elderly, the United States Senate Special Committee on Aging held hearings in 1996 on how to reduce the frequency and cost of mental disorders in the elderly. Some of the testimony presented at those hearings is excerpted below.

Hearing, Senate Special Committee on Aging—1996

U.S. Senate, Special Committee on Aging

Washington, DC

* * *

Testimony
Dorothy P. Rice
Professor Emeritus
Institute for Health and Aging
University of California, San Francisco
The Economics of Mental Illness and the Elderly

Introduction

Thank you very much for the opportunity to testify before you today. I am a health economist at the Institute for Health and Aging at the University of California, San Francisco. I have been involved in research on the economic impact of many illnesses, including mental illness, alcohol and drug abuse, injuries, health effects of smoking and others. Today I will discuss the economics of mental illness and the elderly and how timely detection and appropriate treatment can result in savings for the health care system.

How Many Elderly People Suffer from Mental Illnesses?

The proportion of elderly people suffering from mental disorders, including dementias and the elderly in the community and in institutions, is estimated at 22 percent.[1] Applying this rate to the population aged sixty-five and over in 1994 shows that about 7.3 million elderly people suffer from mental disorders.

How Do We Measure the Costs of Mental Illness?

Mental illnesses are costly to the nation in medical resources used for care, treatment, and rehabilitation; in reduced or lost productivity; and pain and suffering of patients and their families and friends. All segments of society, including the elderly, suffer from these disorders. The economic cost to the nation of mental illness is measured in terms of the direct costs of diagnosis and treatment of patients suffering from these illnesses, indirect costs associated with loss of earnings due to reduced or lost productivity, costs to society of premature death, and other related costs.

Following are highlights of the economic consequences of these disorders for the population aged sixty-five and over. The estimates are based on the comprehensive study *The Economic Costs of Alcohol and Drug Abuse and Mental Illness: 1985*, conducted by the author and her colleagues for the Alcohol, Drug Abuse, and Mental Health Administration.[2] The 1990 estimates are based on sociodemographic and economic indices of change between 1985 and 1990.

How Much is Spent Directly on Treatment and Care of the Mentally Ill?

We estimate that the direct medical expenditures for treating mental illnesses in the United States amounted to $67 billion in 1990. Included are amounts spent for mental health care in federal, state, local, and private psychiatric hospitals, general medical hospitals, and nursing homes; for care provided by office-based physicians and other health professionals; and for drugs and support costs. This amount represents 12 percent of the total personal health care expenditures in 1990.

How Much is Spent on the Elderly?

The burden of mental health care of the elderly on the mental health system is disproportionately high. We estimate that $26.2 billion was spent in 1990 on mental health care for the elderly. This amount represents 39 percent of the total direct mental illness costs of $67 billion. Thus, the elderly comprised 12.5 percent of the total population in the U.S. in 1990, and they accounted for almost two-fifths of the total direct costs of mental illness.

These high mental care costs of the elderly are due to the large numbers of elderly persons with mental disorders that are treated by the Veterans Administration as well as in nursing homes. For example, 645,900 residents of nursing homes, 43 percent of the total, are listed with mental disorders.[3]

* * *

What Are the Prospects for the Future for Mental Illness Among the Elderly?

Looking ahead, we anticipate an explosion of the elderly population because most of the large "baby boom" cohort will be aged sixty-five and over by the year 2020. The estimated number of persons aged sixty-five and over in the United States will reach more than 50 million, a 73 percent growth since 1994.[4] Members of this cohort have high rates of emotional disorders, far exceeding the present cohort of older adults.[5] There is concern that rates may rise even higher as baby boomers reach their later years, when they may experience chronic physical illness and disability, shrinking social networks, and possible lower standards of living. This raises the question of whether our society will be able to afford the wide range of mental health services needed by elderly adults in the future.

Can Timely Detection and Appropriate Treatment Result in Savings for the Health Care System?

A body of evidence is now emerging that recognition and management of psychosocial problems can lead to substantial cost-offsets by reducing inappropriate use of other medical and surgical care.[6,7,8] A meta-analysis of fifty-eight controlled studies and analysis of Blue Cross and Blue Shield Claims files found that the reductions in use of medical services are associated with inpatient rather than outpatient utilization and tend to be larger for person over fifty-five years of age.[9] Another study concluded that psychiatric consultation in the care of patients with some somatization (patients with multiple physical symptoms but no apparent physical disease) reduced subsequent health care expenditures without inducing changes in health status or patients' satisfaction with their health care.[10]

* * *

Prepared Statement of
Ira R. Katz, M.D.,
Professor of Psychiatry and Director, Section on Geriatric Psychiatry,
University of Pennsylvania School of Medicine

Mr. Chairman and members of the committee: It is an honor to have the opportunity to share in your initiative on the mental disorders of late life. As clinical psychiatrists working with older people, my colleagues and I continually see patients with problems that illustrate the links between mental and physical health and the importance of the timely detection and treatment of mental illness. As clinical investigators, we are probing the associations between physical and mental illness both to develop more effective treatments for our patients and to elucidate the basic mechanisms underlying psychiatric disorders. Although in speaking here I will rely on depression as an example, I want to emphasize that depression is by no means the only significant psychiatric disorder affecting the elderly, and that effective treatments are available for late life psychoses and anxiety disorders and for the psychotic, affective, and behavioral symptoms of Alzheimer's disease.

My own research on late life depression was stimulated when I began doing psychiatric consultations in nursing homes and saw person after person who was profoundly depressed. Although I strongly believed that these individuals were helped through psychiatric treatment with psychotherapy and psychotherapeutic medications, I was frequently told that these patients' depressions made sense, and, therefore, that they should not be considered to be diseases. Older people enter nursing homes only when they are disabled to the point that they can no longer care for themselves and when they exceed their families' abilities to care for them. In this context, depression does make sense. Is it nevertheless a disease? To address this question, my colleagues and I conducted a placebo-controlled, double-blind study of the efficacy of a standard antidepressant medication in a group of residents, average age eighty-five, of a large urban geriatric center. We reasoned that if we saw a drug-placebo difference in the response of depressive symptoms, it would mean that depression in the frail elderly was the same disease that we see in younger and healthier patients. We did, in fact, find a robust drug-placebo difference. Thus, even though the depressions in our patients made sense, they still responded specifically to psychiatric treatment.

The importance of recognizing and treating depression in the nursing home was recognized in the nursing home reform provision of the Omnibus Budget Reconciliation Act of 1987 (OBRA 87) and the associated regulations that state "each resident must receive and the facility must provide the necessary care and services to attain or maintain the highest practicable physical, mental, and psychosocial well-being," and that a "resident who displays mental or psychosocial adjustment difficulty receives appropriate treatment and services to correct the assessed problem." Although we hope to see greater enforcement of the provisions requiring mental health treatment for those in need, I am pleased to express the strong sense of my colleagues that this legislation has improved the lives of many of the most vulnerable elderly Americans.

We now know that approximately 25 percent of cognitively intact nursing home residents have a major depressive disorder, a figure roughly tenfold greater than that for older individuals in the community. This high prevalence occurs in all kinds of facilities, public and private, for- and not-for-profit. Moreover, similar figures are observed in European, Australian, and Japanese nursing homes. They reflect the general principle that depression in late life is strongly associated with chronic disease and disability. What we saw in nursing homes was the tip of the iceberg, a reflection of a more general phenomenon operative in all patients with disabling illnesses.

At times, depression can be overlooked and symptoms attributed to medical illness. For example, approximately two years ago I saw a seventy-eight-year-old man for evaluation of depression as a possible cause of weight loss. In the previous year, since the sudden death of his son, he had lost 25 percent of his body weight. He had frighteningly low levels of plasma proteins and extensive edema. In fact, he had protein calorie malnutrition with kwashiorkor, a problem usually associated with famine in Third World countries. His primary care physicians had been convinced that only a disease like cancer could account for this degree of weight loss. Accordingly, my patient had been given an extensive array of medical tests, and, although they found nothing, psychiatric causes of his weight loss were not considered. When I saw him, it was not difficult to make the diagnosis of depression. Within days, he began a course of electroconvulsive therapy that led to his rapid and continued recovery.

Although the severity of this patient's condition was unusual, the basic observation that depression can lead to malnutrition is not. We have consistently found associations between depression and biochemical markers for protein calorie subnutrition in nursing home residents. Dr. Brant Fries of the University of Michigan has found associations between depression and weight loss in a multi-state data base on nursing home residents, and Dr. John Morley of St. Louis University has reported that depression is the most common cause of weight loss in a community nursing home.

A number of other medical symptoms can be caused or worsened by depression. Dr. Patricia Parmelee of the Philadelphia Geriatric Center has shown that depression amplifies the pain associated with the common medical conditions of late life. Similarly, Dr. Daniel Costa, now in Toronto, has shown that when women with breast cancer are depressed, they are less able to tolerate the side effects of cancer chemotherapy.

As a result of his malnutrition, my patient would have died from depression if he did not receive effective treatment. Although the mechanisms are not yet well understood, the association between depression and increased mortality is well established. Dr. Nancy Frasure-Smith in Montreal has reported that depression after a heart attack predicts decreased survival, even after controlling for the severity of the patient's heart disease. Research by Dr. Barry Rovner of Thomas Jefferson University has found that mortality is increased in nursing home residents with depression, even after controlling for coexisting medical illnesses, and Dr. Harold Koenig at Duke University has reported similar findings in medical inpatients.

Depression can also increase disability. Another patient of mine was an older woman with a history of small strokes and arthritis. She was a fiercely independent person who took pride in developing tricks to compensate for her physical impairments. As a result of her difficulty walking, she fell and fractured her hip. I first saw her when she was in the inpatient rehabilitation facility because the staff found her sullen and either unwilling or unable to participate in physical therapy. She was depressed and angry, saying that she was too worn out and in too much pain to be involved in therapy. Moreover, she accused the staff of being sadistic for asking her to do things that were beyond her abilities. She asked that she be transferred to a nursing home where, she hoped, she would be left to die. With treatment for her depression, a combination of psychotherapy and antidepressant medication, she was able to participate in physical therapy and, in fact, was able to return to walking, though slowly, using a walker. Most important, she was able to return home. For this woman, depression was acting as a barrier to rehabilitation and recovery. Untreated, it would have led to increased care needs and costs.

This patient was not unusual. A large body of research has shown that, in addition to hip fracture, depression can lead to increased disability in conditions as diverse as Alzheimer's disease, stroke, Parkinsonism, arthritis, and chronic obstructive pulmonary disease. Moreover, as Dr. Soo Borson of the University of Washington has shown in studies of patients with lung disease, the benefits of treatment for depression are not limited to its effects on mood and related symptoms; treatment can also reduce disability and improve day-to-day functioning.

Other research has confirmed the finding that depression can increase health care costs and the utilization of health care services. Dr. George Alexopolous and his colleagues at Cornell University have shown that depression leads to increased outpatient visits, laboratory tests, laboratory costs, and inpatient lengths of stay, even after controlling for the severity of medical illness. Similarly, Dr. Harold Koenig from Duke University has found that depressed medical inpatients have longer lengths of hospital stay, and that they are more likely to be readmitted to the hospital.

The most compelling consequence of depression may be suicide. Dr. Yeates Conwell of the University of Rochester has spoken of his findings from a psychological autopsy study and has described a particularly tragic story in which an older man noticed that he had rectal bleeding, and became convinced that this meant that he had cancer. Moreover, he was convinced that having cancer inevitably meant that he was destined to die a lingering and painful death. As a result of this thinking, he shot himself. When the case was reviewed, the medical examiner found that the cause of his bleeding was not cancer but hemorrhoids. The psychological autopsy based on reports from his family found that he had been depressed. In this case, it was the depression that led to his jumping to negative conclusions, and to his death.

This story, too, is not that atypical. The demographic group with the greatest risk of suicide in our country is elderly white males. While suicide in younger people can be traced to a number of conditions, in the elderly it is due almost entirely to depression. Moreover, suicide rates in the aged have been increasing significantly roughly since 1980. What makes this most tragic is the principle that suicide is a preventable cause of death. Evidence documenting the potential for prevention comes from Dr. Conwell's finding that 75 percent of older patients who killed themselves had seen their primary care doctor within a month of their deaths, and 35 percent within a week. Thus, improvements in the recognition and treatment of depression in primary care can be lifesaving.

Current barriers to mental health treatment for older adults include the stigma associated with mental disorders; lack of knowledge on the part of providers, potential patients, and families; and discriminatory co-payment provisions in health insurance. To indicate how pervasive and arbitrary they are throughout our health care system, I want to indicate that my own health insurance, obtained through the University of Pennsylvania, will reimburse me for 80 percent of the costs of medications prescribed for the treatment of general medical conditions, but only 50 percent for the costs of medications such as antidepressants that are prescribed for the treatment of psychiatric disorders.

* * *

In this testimony, I have emphasized the high rates of depression and its profound impact on older patients with significant medical illnesses. Among the relatively healthy individuals currently residing in the community who participated in the NIMH Epidemiological Catchment Area studies, the rates of major depressive disorder in the elderly were actually somewhat less than those seen in younger adults. This has been interpreted as a manifestation of a cohort effect, indicating that, for whatever reason, the current generation of older people is less vulnerable to depression than is my generation or that of my children. This phenomenon together with projected demographic trends indicates that the coming decades will expose an increasing number of more vulnerable individuals to the stresses of aging, chronic disease, and disability. We expect the magnitude of the problems discussed here to grow exponentially. Thus, it is important that we develop an effective way to deal with the interactions between mental and medical illness in late life both for the sake of the current generation of older Americans and as an investment in the future.

* * *

Medicare and Managed Care

Since the inception of Medicare in the mid-1960s, mental health treatment, as alluded to above, has been reimbursed differently than general medical interventions. For more than twenty years Medicare policy, in effect, established a $250 a year outpatient (Medicare Part B) cap on mental health treatment along with a 50 percent co-payment requirement on the part of the patient. These limits were in contrast to the typical absence of caps on most general medical outpatient interventions, and the

20 percent copayment required of patients for such treatment. In the late 1980s, steps were taken enabling the cap to be slowly removed and finally eliminated in 1990. But the copayment requirement substantially remains, imposing continuing financial hardship on elderly patients and weak links in efforts to effectively coordinate mental and physical health care.

The significance of coordinating mental and physical health care has never been greater. Research has confirmed what popular view has long perceived—the relationship between physical and mental health in later life is often inseparable, one fundamentally affecting the outcome of the other. Despite a new state-of-the-art in the understanding of mental health risk factors influencing the course of physical illness in older adults, and despite a new state-of-the-art in psychiatric treatment, the mental health co-payment lack of parity in comparison to physical health coverage remains.

While Medicare's mental health reimbursement policies have unfortunately contributed to the obstacles to utilization of mental health care, early reports on the growing managed care wave are also painting a picture of under-delivery of mental health services to elderly patients. The irony with managed care is that it has been touted as promising significant progress in approaches to prevention in health care delivery. Yet, in one of the major new domains for prevention—preventing the adverse effects of mental disorder on the course of physical illness—managed care's responses are not matching its rhetoric.

* * *

Meanwhile, Medicare's responses, too, have not matched its potential. Much attention is paid to the need to reduce the risk for institutionalization in the elderly population, especially to save societal costs. Yet, as described earlier, one of the major risk factors tilting the balance as to whether or not disease and disability can be managed at home is the excess disability toll of concurrent mental disorder, where substantial treatment is impeded because of the copayment problem.

To be sure, the present is a trying time fiscally. Hence, new approaches in health care have to be economically feasible and compatible with major principles governing policy deliberations. In this context, a *next step* is proposed in reducing the gap between mental health and general medical reimbursement for Medicare patients. What is proposed are not new or higher provider fees, nor coverage for a new treatment modality. Rather, taking a step-wise approach, *it is proposed that patients who need to receive psychiatric house calls be required only to make the same copayment that they would pay for a general medical office visit—20 percent.* Keep in mind that this is a group of patients at higher risk for institutionalization—to hospitals and nursing homes. Typically, these are patients with major physical illness (making them homebound) and concurrent mental disorder (becoming the straw that breaks their ability to remain at home out of a nursing home). Hence, this incremental approach to reducing Medicare's mental health copayment burden on older patients would better enable mental health care providers to make a major contribution in lowering the likelihood of institutionalization for a very high risk group. At the same time, this modest step (as but one example, which would need a counterpart under Managed Care) would respond in a very concrete way to public policy goals emphasizing the need to reduce the rate of institutionalization among older adults.

* * *

Notes

1. Gatz M., Smyer MA. 1992. The Mental Health System and Older Adults in the 1990s. *American Psychologist* 47(6):741–751.

2. Rice DP, Kelman S, Miller LS, Dunmeyer S. 1990. *The Economic Costs of Alcohol and Drug Abuse and Mental Illness: 1985.* Report Submitted to the Office of Financing and Coverage Policy of the Alcohol, Drug Abuse, and Mental Health Administration, U.S. Department of Health and Human Services. San Francisco, CA: Institute for Health & Aging, University of California.

3. National Center for Health Statistics. 1989. The National Nursing Home Survey: 1985 Summary for the United States. *Vital and Health Statistics.* Series 13, No. 97. DHHS Pub. Mo. (PHS) 89-1758. Washington, DC: U.S. Government Printing Office.

4. U.S. Bureau of the Census. 1995. *Statistical Abstract of the United States: 1995.* (115th Edition). Washington, D.C., Tables 14 and 24.

5. Koenig GK, George LK, Schneider R. 1994. Mental Health Care for Older Adults in the Year 2020: A Dangerous and Avoided Topic. *The Gerontologist* 34(5):674–679.

6. Eisenberg L. 1992. Treating Depression and Anxiety in Primary Care: Closing the Gap Between Knowledge and Practice. *New England Journal of Medicine* 326 (April 16): 1080–1084.

7. Mechanic D, Schlesinger, McAlpine DD. 1995. Management of Mental Health and Substance Abuse Services: State of the Art and Early Results. *The Milbank Quarterly* 73(1):19–55.

8. Fiedler JL. 1989. *The Medical Offset Effect and Public Health Policy: Mental Health Industry in Transition.* New York: Paeger.

9. Mumford E, Schlesinger HJ, Glass GV, Patrick C, Cuerdon T. 1984. A New Look at Evidence About Reduced Cost of Medical Utilization Following Mental Health Treatment. *American Journal of Psychiatry* 141(10):1145–1158.

10. Smith RG, Monson DC, Ray DC. 1986. Psychiatric Consultation in Somatization Disorder. *The New England Journal of Medicine* 314(22):1407–1413.

Part IX

Abuse, Neglect, Victimization, and Elderly Criminals

CHAPTER 42

Abuse and Neglect of Older Persons

A. Definitions and Causes

As our societal understanding of domestic violence grows, we have "discovered" child abuse and spousal abuse. More recently we have come to understand that abuse of the elderly represents the third element of the triad of family violence. The following article explains the nature and origin of the abuse, neglect and exploitation of older persons.

Sandra Baron and Adele Welty

Elder Abuse

* * *

Definition

While there is no nationwide consensus on the legal definition, most experts would agree that elder abuse consists of harm or pain that is inflicted on persons sixty years of age or older who are unable to protect themselves. This type of mistreatment consists of any behavior that causes physical pain, psychological anguish, or financial

Journal of Gerontological Social Work, Vol. 25, Nos. 1/2, 33–57 (Spring–Summer 1996). Reprinted by permission.

loss, including acts of omission that result in the neglect of a care-dependent person's essential needs for food, clothing, or shelter. Abuse and neglect are usually inflicted by a family member, caregiver, or nonrelative known to the victim. Elder abuse can be subtle, as when a caregiver berates and demeans an elderly person; or it can be extreme, as when a family member brutalizes an elder and steals possessions from the home.

* * *

One form of abuse . . . is sexual abuse, a type of abuse that is particularly tragic although studies do not show a high percentage of reported cases (Ramsey-Klawsnik, 1991). Sexual abuse is any form of sexual contact or exposure without the older person's consent.

* * *

Another category of abuse, self-neglect, is included in the elder abuse reports of certain states. Self-neglect is the failure on the part of an individual who may have mental or physical impairments to meet basic needs for food, clothing, shelter, or medical care. Self-neglecting elders who are assessed by mental health professionals and found to have the mental capacity to understand the risk of harm engendered by their impairment and who refuse offers of assistance cannot be legally forced to accept the services that health care providers and social workers believe they need. Self-neglect is the most prevalent type of abuse and often the most frustrating for case workers. Some states do not consider self-neglect a form of elder abuse.

Demography

The U.S. House of Representatives Select Committee on Aging reported in 1990 that more than 1.5 million older adults are victims of abuse or neglect every year. Another survey, conducted by the National Aging Resource Center on Elder Abuse (NARCEA), estimated 735,000 domestic elder abuse victims nationally in 1991. The NARCEA study included the experience of professionals in the field, random samples of elderly in the general population, elders served by social service agencies, and substantiated reports to state adult protective services or state and local agencies on aging (Tatara, 1993). A 1994 national study conducted by the National Center on Elder Abuse, using elder abuse reports from state adult protective services, estimated the total number of elder abuse victims annually at approximately 1.84 million persons.

Professionals believe that the number of cases of elder abuse is underestimated in all studies. National estimates are questionable because the studies suffer from methodological limitations. One such limitation is the lack of a source of complete and consistent data. For example, a study by Pillemer and Finkelhor (1988) used interview data from a random sample of 2,000 elderly people in Boston, Massachusetts, but excluded financial abuse (Tatara, 1993). Financial exploitation is a prevalent form of abuse that is usually linked to other forms of mistreatment. Most data come from reports made to Protective Services for Adults (PSA) agencies. Some survey results include only substantiated cases, and others include all reports received by PSA. While most states have mandatory reporting laws which make it incumbent upon licensed professionals to report suspected cases of elder abuse to PSA, other states have voluntary reporting or no mechanism for addressing the problem at all, and therefore do not generate data.

* * *

In addition to those abused or neglected in their homes, State Ombudsman services receive numerous reports of abuse of residents of long-term care facilities every year. This abuse ranges from theft of personal belongings to physical or chemical restraints, physical attacks including sexual assault, psychological harassment, or neglect of residents by staff. There have been no systematic national studies, thus far, concerning institutional abuse of the elderly.

* * *

Two research studies, one conducted by New York City Department for the Aging (NYC/DFTA) and one conducted by NARCEA, shed light on some important aspects of elder abuse.

* * *

Financial exploitation was the most frequently reported type of abuse, although in two-thirds of the cases, victims were subjected to a combination of neglect and financial, physical, or psychological mistreatment. Significantly, most of these cases were not reported to the police, whose involvement was usually limited to cases of physical assault.

Adult children and agency-based perpetrators, such as home attendants, were found more likely to be involved in financial abuse. Spouses were far more likely to be involved in acts of physical abuse. As for adult children, there was no difference in the types of abuse engaged in by sons and daughters. Relatives as a group comprised the overall largest category of perpetrators, and they were usually involved in more than one type of abuse.

* * *

The NARCEA study also found that over two-thirds of the victims were female, while a majority of the abusers were male. Adult children of the elder victims were the most frequent abusers.

* * *

Characteristics of The Population

Risk Factors for Elder Abuse

Domestic mistreatment of the elderly is a phenomenon with identifiable risk factors that significantly increase both the incidence and severity of abuse. If we are to prevent such mistreatment, we must be aware of some of its basic characteristics.

Dependency of the Victim

Frail older adults may be dependent on others for their care, for companionship, or financial support.

* * *

References

Pillemer, K. & Finkelhor, D. (1988). The prevalence of elder abuse: A random sample survey. *Gerontologist*, 28(1), 51–57.

Ramsey-Klawsnik, H. (1991). "Elder sexual abuse: Preliminary findings." *Journal of Elder Abuse & Neglect*, 3(3), 73–79.

Tatara, T. (1993). "Understanding the nature and scope of domestic elder abuse with the use of state aggregate data: Summaries of the key findings of a national survey of state APS and Aging agencies." *Journal of Elder Abuse & Neglect*, Vol. 5(4), 38.

Even protective arrangements such as guardianship may themselves create an opportunity for the abuse of an older person.

Lawrence A. Frolik

Elder Abuse and Guardians of Elderly Incompetents

* * *

Guardians and the Abused Elderly

Introduction

Victims of abuse and neglect rarely report it (Katz, 1980). They may be unaware that they are being victimized and have no idea that the law would protect them (U.S. Congress Select Committee on Aging, 1985). A few elderly may believe that the abusive treatment is "normal" or "deserved," or at least the best that they can expect.

Journal of Elder Abuse & Neglect, Vol. 2, Nos. 3/4, 31–56 (1990). Reprinted by permission.

For many silent victims, a fear to report stems from the possibility of retaliation or from a fear of the loss of the caregiver (even an abusive caregiver may be better than none at all) (Katz, 1980). Other victims, otherwise willing to report the abuse, do not know to whom or how to report the victimization (Katz, 1980). Still others may be so isolated or under the control of the caregiver that they have no opportunity to seek help (Katz, 1980).

For the unknowledgeable, the fearful, or the isolated victim, the only hope is detection by outsiders. These victims must rely "on the kindness of strangers." For them, state laws provide for mandatory reporting, investigatory staffs, and forceable entry.

But there are other victims for whom more is needed, much more. These are the incompetent victims of abuse and neglect. Those who do not understand what is happening to them, who no longer are able to communicate with the larger world. They are the truest victims, for they do not even know they are being abused or neglected. But they do know pain, isolation, fear, and emotional oppression. They do have financial assets at risk of theft or misuse. And they do need help.

The Incompetent Victim

Guardianship

The abused or neglected incompetent elderly get help through the guardianship system. Laws against abuse and neglect almost always provide for the appointment of a guardian as a means of assisting (rescuing?) abused victims who cannot help themselves. Of course, guardianship did not originate with the passage of anti-abuse and neglect laws. Guardianship has been a part of the Anglo American legal tradition for over five hundred years (Frolik, 1981). But only recently has it been incorporated into the scheme of protective services, which is the system by which many anti-abuse and neglect laws operate. Protective services has adopted the traditional guardianship structure as a means of protecting victims of abuse and neglect. The appointment of a guardian allows the removal of the abusive caregiver with the replacement of a "good" caregiver.

* * *

Even if no abuse or neglect has occurred, the appointment of a guardian has, as one of its objectives, the forestalling of future abuse or neglect. For surely no one is more at risk of exploitation than an incompetent individual. Guardianship is the prophylaxis that prevents abuse and neglect.

* * *

The Incompetent, the Guardian, and the Court

The court that appointed the guardian is responsible for the acts of the guardian, and only the court has the authority to supervise the performance of the guardian. While others may complain or inform the court of the shortcomings of the guardian, only the court may act to compel the guardian to modify his or her behavior. If the guardian mistreats the ward, the guardian is at fault. But ultimately, a failure of the guardian is a failure of the court. Guardians can commit a single wrong act or they can repeatedly misperform. It is not the former that concerns us or for which we would hold the court responsible. Imagine a forty-year-old woman who is the guardian for her seventy-seven-year-old aunt who suffers from early-stage Alzheimer's disease. The aunt lives with her guardian. One day the aunt is particularly difficult to deal with. The guardian in a fit of anger locks her ill-tempered ward in her room for the day to punish her. By the end of the day the guardian, now contrite, releases her aunt and never again treats her that way. (The guardian hires a practical nurse to assist in the care of her aunt.) While this might be an incident of abuse, and while the court as supervisor of the guardian is technically responsible, one is not inclined to "blame" the court on account of an isolated act of abuse by the guardian.

No, what we are after here is the repeat performer, the guardian whose pattern of performance consistently falls below the acceptable standard. The guardian who routinely misappropriates the assets of the ward, who repeatedly neglects or abuses the ward, or the guardian who has never heard of Alzheimer's and treats the stricken ward as if he or she were a willful, disobedient child. It is these chronic malperforming guardians for whom we hold the appointing court responsible. It is the abuse and neglect of their wards for whom we lay the ultimate responsibility at the feet of the court.

The Abusive Guardian

The chronic misperformance by a guardian may indicate that the court either selected an inappropriate guardian, failed to train the guardian properly, or failed to supervise the guardian effectively. In a word, the court is responsible for the selection, training, and supervision of guardians. Alternatively, the court may have performed admirably in all these functions, but the guardian nevertheless misperformed and successfully masked the malfeasance from the court. Even if that were the case, we would question the quality of the court's supervision since in most instances the court should discover a misperforming guardian.

Do courts fail in these appointive and supervisory tasks? Given the lack of human perfection, it seems safe to assume that they do. But how frequently this occurs is difficult to answer. The true test of the selection, training, and supervision of courts is in the behavior of the guardian. If the guardians perform well, it hardly seems relevant that the courts may have selected badly, trained poorly, or supervised inadequately. But if the guardians' performance is subpar, we ought to take a careful look at the performance of the appointing court.

Grading a Guardian

To determine how well guardians perform is not an easy task. Suppose that we were given the task to evaluate the performance of noninstitutional guardians.

* * *

Too many of the decisions that a guardian must make are not susceptible to easy critique. They are not black and white issues, but swirling shades of gray. The "correct" outcome is impossible to identify among the interacting and competing cultural, social, and personal values; the emotional limitations and compulsions that act upon the guardian; and the financial limitations and realities that further constrict the choices of the guardian. Given such complexity, to blandly label a guardian's behavior as "sub-par" is simplistic and misleading. At best, we might identify particular acts of the guardian as "unwise" or "of dubious merit."

* * *

[G]uardians, as with all actors, operate over a range of behavior. Certainly some guardians operate over a range that is closer to the ideal than do others. But every guardian will have the off day and will act in a manner that, in retrospective, was most unwise (perhaps even in the eyes of the guardian). And if it is difficult to "grade" any individual decision, it is much more perplexing to give a single grade to a range of behavior.

Abusive Guardians

Let us abandon, then, the apparently intractable goal of grading guardians. Instead, let us focus our attention upon a narrower, yet more critical, issue of whether guardians are guilty of abuse and neglect of their wards. Here we have a standard to guide us: the state law against abuse and neglect.

* * *

Suppose we wanted to survey guardians to discover what percent (if any) act in an abusive manner. To do so would be difficult. We cannot just ask guardians if they are guilty of abuse and neglect. Who would be so foolish as to admit it? Instead, we might ask guardians to describe how they behave. Possibly a few of the abusers would believe that their behavior was acceptable and so might reveal illegal acts. But most would probably conceal abusive behavior.

* * *

Empirical evidence of abusive guardians, therefore, will be hard to come by. The absence of direct evidence of guardian abuse does not mean we lack any evidence that guardians might abuse. We know that of those who commit elder abuse or neglect, the largest number are related to the victim. Similarly, the overwhelming majority of abusers are the victim's caregiver (Katz, 1980). We need only match those statistics with the knowledge that many, if not a majority, of noninstitutional guardians are related to their wards and many guardians act as caregivers. If some related caregivers commit abuse, it would seem probable that some related caregiver guardians also commit abuse.

* * *

Some guardians, whether voluntary or not, may abuse or neglect their ward and yet may not do so deliberately. These are guardians who are unknowledgeable about how to care for an incompetent elderly ward. They may sincerely believe that a low level of custodial care is sufficient and unknowingly allow the ward to be cared for in a manner that approaches abuse. A few may believe that it is a waste of resources to provide decent care for an elderly incompetent ward and may believe that their actions reflect the accepted societal view. Some guardians will be more negligent than culpable and commit abuse or its near equivalent out of inertia, laziness or due to the press of other responsibilities. A few noncaretaker guardians may inadvertently commit abuse by their failure to adequately supervise the actions of the caretaker of the ward.

Other guardians may be conscious that they are remiss in the manner in which they treat their ward, but believe that the incompetent ward deserves no better. We could almost say that as a cultural matter such guardians do not perceive their actions as being wrong. If questioned about the level of care that they provided, these guardians might respond defensively that they were doing nothing wrong. They lack the moral sensitivity to realize that an elderly incompetent deserves more humane treatment.

A few guardians who begin well enough may become morally desensitized over time. At the beginning of their guardianship, they may have tried to treat the ward in an acceptable manner. But gradually they permit their standards to slip as the reality of the burden of guardianship became more apparent or more burdensome (Steinmetz, 1980). The duties of guardianship, in effect, degrade them and dulls their moral sensitivity. What they would have condemned at the beginning of the guardianship by degrees becomes bearable and, at last, the norm. The deterioration of their standards is justified by the adoption of the attitude that they give the ward all he or she deserves.

Other guardians, like many abusers, may react to the difficulty of the personality of the ward and respond in kind. While the ward may not be abusive, the ward may act in a manner that is rude, provoking, or exasperating. The guardian, not trained in how to handle an incompetent ward, loses patience and loses self-control and begins to "retaliate" against the ward. The guardian justifies the abuse in the belief that the ward "deserves" it or "asked for it" (U.S. Congress Select Committee on Aging, 1985).

* * *

References

Frolik, L.A. (1981). Plenary guardianship: An analysis, a critique and a proposal for reform, *Arizona Law Review, 23*, 599.

Katz, K.D. (1980). Elder abuse. *Journal of Family Law, 18*, 711.

Steinmetz, S. (1988). *Elder abuse and family care*, pp. 564–573. Sage.
U.S. Congress Select Committee on Aging (1985). *Elder abuse: A national disgrace* (Comm. Pub. No. 99-502) Washington, D.C., U.S. Government Printing Office.

There are many reasons for the abuse of the elderly, including caregivers who were themselves abused as children, family pathology, social isolation of the victim, alcohol or drug abuse by the abuser, and the strains of being a caregiver. Typically caregivers are responsible for frail, demented, incontinent, or even bad-natured older persons. An overburdened, stressed caregiver who is helpless to reverse the waning abilities of a formerly strong, vital person, often a parent or other relative, too often expresses his or her hostility by abusive treatment of the ward. The following material discusses abuse by family caregivers.

Christine S. Sellers, W. Edward Folts, and Katherine M. Logan

Elder Mistreatment: A Multidimensional Problem

* * *

Despite the fact that the nature and extent of elder abuse are still unclear, efforts to provide theoretical explanations of physical abuse have made progress in recent years. Wolf and Pillemer (1989) assess the utility of five theories in attempting to explain the physical abuse of older adults: intra-individual dynamics, inter-generational transmission of violence, dependency, external stress, and social isolation. In their study of victims of elder mistreatment in three states, they found that physical abuse was related to intra-individual dynamics, dependency, and social isolation. The intra-individual dynamics hypothesis proposes that there is simply "something wrong" with the abuser. In their interviews, abused elders reported that their attackers had psychological or emotional problems or were identified as alcoholics. The dependency hypothesis proposes that abuse results when an impaired or frail older adult places ever greater demands on the abuser. While the study revealed that abused elders were not in poorer health and were not more functionally impaired than non-abused elders, there was evidence that the abuser was dependent on the victim, particularly for financial support. This finding has been explained by exchange theory, which suggests that abuse results as a compensatory response to the powerlessness felt by the financially dependent abuser (Pillemer, 1985; Wolf and Pillemer, 1989).

Finally, Wolf and Pillemer (1989) found that abused elders tended to be somewhat

Journal of Elder Abuse & Neglect, Vol. 4, 5 (1992). Reprinted by permission.

more socially isolated than non-abused elders. This lack of contact, however, may have been an artifact of the abuse itself: either the abuser forbade contact to further punish the victim, or the abuser's erratic behavior drove away others who may have wanted to visit the victim. What has remained unexamined, however, is the social isolation of the abuser. Drawing from the child abuse literature, isolation of the abuser reduces the resources upon which he or she may draw to relieve the stresses associated with giving care to the victim (Straus, Gelles, and Steinmetz, 1980).

Theory and research on physical abuse of the elderly point primarily to problems with the abuser: psychological problems, alcoholism, financial dependency, and possibly social isolation. Intervention strategies must focus not only on removing the elderly victim from further harm but on providing psychological counseling for the victim to overcome the abuse experience. Prevention measures should include scrutiny of caregivers who volunteer to take care of aging family members. Those displaying risk factors noted above should be provided assistance before interactions escalate into violence. Measures to prevent spouse abuse among the elderly, as revealed in the Pillemer and Finkelhor (1988) study, must also be further explored.

Psychological Abuse. Wolf and Pillemer (1989:18) also provide examples of psychological abuse: being called derogatory names; being treated as a child; and being intentionally frightened, humiliated, intimidated, threatened, or isolated. Theoretical explanations that account for physical abuse have also been employed to explain psychological abuse. Risk factors involving primarily the abuser tend to be similar: the abuser has a history of psychological problems and is often dependent upon the elderly victim (Wolf and Pillemer, 1989).

Responses to psychological elder abuse are difficult to implement. The major difficulty lies in detection: psychological abuse leaves few visible clues, yet its impact may be just as painful as if the individual had been physically attacked. Thus, intervention strategies are likely to miss a number of elderly victims. However, if prevention measures can be undertaken to provide caregivers with the personal assistance they need prior to the abusive act, then the potential for abuse may be lessened considerably.

Material Abuse. Material abuse, according to Wolf and Pillemer, involves "the illegal or improper exploitation and/or use of funds or other resources" (1989:18).

* * *

[A]lthough victims of material abuse are equally likely to be male or female, they are typically unmarried, living alone, and experiencing some problems with their ability to handle their own finances. Their exploiters are characterized as alcohol abusers and, predictably, are financially dependent on their elderly victims, often having recently experienced financial problems of their own. Typically, both victim and offender are socially isolated as well. Material abuse of the elderly appears to be a unique form of elder mistreatment not strongly related to other forms of abuse or neglect. Its causes appear to be financial in nature and may require simple solutions in the form of assistance from a neutral party to ensure that bills are paid or that funds are not diverted.

Active and Passive Neglect. Distinctions are often made between intentional and unintentional neglect. Intentional failure to give care is known as active neglect and has been defined as "refusal or failure to fulfill a caretaking obligation, including . . . deliberate abandonment or deliberate denial of food or health-related services" (Wolf and Pillemer, 1989:18). Unintentional failure to provide reasonable care is known as passive neglect, defined as "refusal or failure to fulfill a caretaking obligation . . . because of inadequate knowledge, laziness, infirmity, or disputing the value of prescribed services" (Wolf and Pillemer, 1989:18). It is important to note that many states do not have statutes requiring family members to care for adult relatives (*Tampa Tribune*, 1991). Although the sanctions for all forms of neglect tend to be less severe than for abusive situations, neglect of a family member does violate strong informal norms of filial duty.

One of the difficulties in dealing with neglect is that it can take many forms ranging from failure to provide essential physical care (e.g., food, medicine, supervision, hygiene, housekeeping, heat) to failure to provide other physical aids such as hearing aids, eyeglasses, or false teeth to more psychological needs such as companionship and support. Neglect also may be intentional or unintentional. However, the neglect of elderly relatives is becoming a problem of growing interest, in part, because all forms of neglect involve a failure to provide needed care.

In cases of both active and passive neglect, elderly victims are likely to be dependent on their caregivers. They are less able to perform usual daily activities such as meal preparation or personal care, financial and household management, general shopping tasks, or to secure transportation. Further, they are likely to have some psychological or cognitive impairments, particularly problems with memory. In short, active and passive neglect are often found when elderly victims are incompetent (Wolf and Pillemer, 1989).

Family members who unintentionally neglect their elders may be experiencing problems with their own physical health and typically may have suffered a recent loss of social support. Such problems are apparently absent in the lives of people who actively neglect older relatives. Nothing out of the ordinary in terms of stress, isolation, dependency, or individual pathology seems to explain why some caregivers intentionally choose to withhold necessary care from their elders (Wolf and Pillemer, 1989).

Intervention strategies to assist the victims of active or passive neglect should ideally focus on providing extensive care for these individuals, many of whom are incompetent to care for themselves. This strategy may involve legal intervention including a declaration of incompetency. This drastic measure may be restricted, however, to only those cases of active neglect where the caregiver intentionally fails to provide for the needs of the incompetent elderly individual. Victims of passive neglect may fare better, since their caregivers have likely neglected them out of ignorance or spent resources. Perpetrators of passive neglect would likely benefit from amelioration of their caregiving burdens while they are also being assisted to resolve their own problems, which may have been the only obstacle to proper caregiving.

* * *

References

Pillemer, K. (1985). The dangers of dependency. New findings on domestic violence against the elderly. *Social Problems*, 33(2), 146–158.

Pillemer, K. & Finkelhor, D. (1988). The prevalence of elder abuse: A random sample survey. *Gerontologist*, 28(1), 51–57.

Straus, M. Gelles, R. & Steinmetz, S. (1980). *Behind closed doors: Violence in the american family.* Garden City, NY: Anchor.

Tampa Tribune (1991). Abandoned: Elderly persons are left at the hospital door in "granny dumping." September 23.

Wolf, R. & Pillemer, K. (1989). *Helping elderly victims: The reality of elder abuse.* New York: Columbia University Press.

B. Financial Exploitation

Abuse or exploitation of the elderly takes many forms. The following article examines one manner of financial exploitation.

Clifton B. Kruse, Jr.

Contracts to Devise or Gift Property in Exchange for Lifetime Home Care—Latent and Insidious Abuse of Older Persons

I. Introduction—The Problem

* * *

Elders who seek to avoid institutional care may sometimes legitimately desire to avoid existing contracts to devise or gift property to a home care provider. Litigation concerning such contracts has included, among other issues:

1. elders' dissatisfaction with the quality of care provided to them;
2. their anxiety over unanticipated and undesired restrictions on their control, use, and disposition of the assets that are subject to the agreement;

Probate Law Journal, Vol. 12 (1994). Reprinted by permission.

3. their desire to terminate the agreement when they marry or remarry, and the resulting legal conflicts between the statutory rights of the elder's surviving spouse and the contract beneficiary; and
4. a change in attitude by the elder or caregiver making a continued relationship between the parties unbearable.

* * *

A. Validity

* * *

[I]n *In re Estate of Lamberson,*[1] . . . a will gave an elderly testator's entire estate to the elder's caregiver, whom he had known only a few weeks. The testator suffered from arteriosclerosis and had only brief periods of lucidity. The caregiver moved Lamberson and his wife into her home, did not notify his family of this move, did not inform Lamberson when his wife died, and received the elder's estate to the exclusion of his family. The caregiver personally gave her attorney instructions for preparing Lamberson's will. The court, in what appears to be an understatement, held that a jury could "possibly" conclude that the will was a product of undue influence.[2]

* * *

B. Fraud and Deceit

A conveyance or contract to give property to a caregiver will be set aside where the caregiver fraudulently received or secured it from an elder.[3]

* * *

A caregiver's taking advantage of an older person is made possible because of the often close and legally confidential nature of the parties' relationship. The deceit can occur by words, acts, conduct, concealment, or silence in situations where the caregiver has a duty to speak.[4] Because of the confidential nature of the caregiver's relationship with the one cared for and the unconscionable advantage this creates, fraud may be presumed.[5]

A physician and her husband, manager of a Long Beach sanitarium, encouraged a sanitarium patient, Carolynn Nutt, to transfer her assets to the husband in exchange for life care, including medical assistance. The attorney who had prepared Mrs. Nutt's initial will was not involved. New documents, including asset assignments, were prepared by a lawyer engaged by the husband-sanitarium manager. The lawyer spoke only to the beneficiary. He was neither requested to consult with nor given the opportunity to meet with the patient. Mrs. Nutt's physician was present when the transfer documents were executed. She even passed Mrs. Nutt the pen for signing. "Just before the execution . . . [the physician] said to her patient, apparently in response to Mrs. Nutt's discomfort, 'Never mind, Mrs. Nutt, it will be all right,' or words to that effect."[6] Mrs. Nutt was critically ill. She suffered from pellagra, a disease characterized by cracking of the skin and often resulting in insanity. Her suffering was described as intense. She was not expected to live long. Her physician, who encouraged the life care contract in exchange for the elder and critically ill person's assets, did not tell her of her probable impending death.[7] The court found that the patient's physician dominated "the mind of the weakened invalid towards whom she owed the greatest fairness by reason of her confidential relation to her patient."[8]

* * *

C. Duress

An inter vivos gift or a contract to make a will may be set aside if it is induced by duress. Freedom of will is essential to the validity of an agreement. A party who is coerced into a decision does not exercise free will but rather reflects the desires of his or her oppressor. Fear dominating the mind of a party because of pressure from another deprives the servient party of self-determination. Duress is compelling. It is the domination of another's mind. Subjectively determined, it is coercion over a person such that he or she is prevented from exercising free will and independent judgment.[9]

* * *

In a similar case, *Nemeth v. Banhalmi*,[10] an eighty-year-old in poor health who lived with his daughter and her husband

> was induced to supply the down payment for the purchase of a house, to act as a co-signatory of [a] mortgage loan, and to place [the house] title in joint tenancy with them, when told by [the daughter and her husband] that unless he did so he would have to go into a nursing home.[11]

The decedent made a will in 1976, dividing his property equally between his own daughter and his late wife's daughter. In 1977, the decedent had a stroke resulting in diminished mental powers. He was "dependent upon his daughter for food, lodging and attention to his personal needs. . . . During this period he was induced to transfer valuable personal property to [his daughter and her husband] who also commingled the income from his business investments with their own funds."[12] When the decedent died in 1978, no will could be found. The property passed by intestacy to his daughter. Wills which had provided for the stepdaughter were apparently destroyed during the period in which the daughter cared for her father.

* * *

The court . . . mentioned this malicious and coercive behavior along with other examples of self-interest; collectively, such behavior clearly constituted a breach of the fiduciary duty which the caregiver-daughter and her husband owed to their ward.

* * *

Notes

1. 407 So. 2d 358 (Fla. Dist. Ct. App. 1981).
2. *Id.* at 362 (citing Carpenter, 253 So. 2d at 702).
3. *See* 37 AM. JUR. 2D, *Fraud and Deceit*, §§ 12–19 (1968) (fraud is a question of fact. It is a tort based upon deceit where loss occurs). Actual fraud is not presumed. It must be established by clear and convincing evidence. *See* RESTATEMENT (SECOND) OF TORTS, § 525 (1965); Territorial Sav. & Loan Ass'n v. Baird, 781 P.2d 452, 458 (Utah 1989).

4. 37 AM. JUR. 2D, *Fraud & Deceit*, *supra* note 153, § 14.

5. *Id.* § 15. *See also* Harrell v. Branson, 344 So. 2d 604, 606–07 (Fla. Dist. Ct. App. 1977); Prescott v. Kreher, 123 So. 2d 721, 726-727 (Fla. Dist. Ct. App. 1960); Holland v. Lesesne, 350 S.W.2d 859, 862 (Tex. Civ. App. 1961). *See* Undue Influence, *ante*, this section, concerning caregivers as being in confidential relationships with the elders for whom they provide care. "A confidential relation may be said to exist whenever trust and confidence are reposed by one person in the integrity and fidelity of another." *In re* Arbuckle's Estate, 220 P.2d 950, 955 (Cal. Dist. Ct. App. 1950). Aged or less competent persons may recover where persons of normal intelligence would not have been misled. Wilke v. Coinway, Inc., 64 Cal. Rptr. 845 (Cal. Ct. App. 1967); Black v. J.N. Blair & Co., 302 P.2d 609 (Cal. Dist. App. 1956); International Life Ins. Co. v. Herbert, 334 S.W.2d 525 (Tex. Civ. App. 1960).

6. *In re* Nutt's Estate, 185 P. 393, 394 (Cal. 1919).

7. *Id.* at 395.

8. *Id.* at 395–96.

9. *See* [1 PAGE ON WILLS §§ 10.8, 15.2]; 17A AM. JUR. 2D, *Contracts*, § 234; Harrison v. Grobe, 790 F. Supp. 443, 454 (S.D.N.Y. 1992).

10. Nemeth v. Banhalmi, 425 N.E.2d 1187 (Ill. App. Ct. 1981).

11. *Id.* at 1188.

12. *Id.*

Uncovering elder abuse is a significant problem. Elderly victims of abuse commonly do not report it either from fear of retaliation, shame, or dependency or because they lack the physical or mental ability to communicate to others. The reporting of the abuse often occurs because of the intercession of friends or relatives. Professionals such as nurses, physicians, social workers, and home health workers also often report suspected abuse, particularly if they see the older individual on a regular basis. Reports of abuse by professionals, friends, or relatives trigger a response by the state agency, the Adult Protective Services agency, that is empowered to enforce the laws against abuse of the elderly.

Once the abuse has been reported, and if there is reasonable suspicion of abuse, the state will investigate the incident and, if abuse is determined, will attempt to protect the elderly person from further abuse. If appropriate, the abuser may be subject to criminal prosecution. States try to protect the elderly person while observing the principal of using the least restrictive alternative. Conciliation, counseling, and even material assistance will be offered as a means of stopping the abuse. However, in many instances, the older person is so vulnerable and the abuser so uncontrite that more drastic measures are required. Often the state will move for a guardianship over the abused elderly person as the initial step in removing her or him from the environment in which the abuse occurred.

Over forty states have adopted legislation that mandates the reporting of suspected abuse or neglect of the elderly by those in contact with older persons, such as physicians or caseworkers. The legislation is modeled after child abuse reporting statutes, which have had great success in attacking the problem. As with the child abuse reporting statutes, the failure to report abuses is a misdemeanor. The reporting party is shielded from liability, and the tradi-

tional privileges, such as doctor-patient confidentially, are waived. Critics of mandatory reporting object to these laws because the laws assume that older abused persons are incapable of protecting themselves. Moreover, all too often, even after a report of abuse is made, there are no available public services that will curb the underlying causes of the abuse. For example, does it help an older person who is physically abused by a caregiver to report that abuse if the older person has no choice but to live with the caregiver? Others object to mandatory reporting because elderly abuse and neglect are so ill-defined. If a caregiver routinely yells at the older ward, is this abuse or just bad manners? Essentially, critics contend that voluntary reporting will uncover serious abuse and neglect. Beyond that, the elderly can be expected to fend for themselves without excessive state paternalism and intervention.

CHAPTER 43

Abuse and Neglect in Institutions

Older individuals who live in institutional settings, such as nursing homes or board and care homes, are at special risk of abuse or neglect. Because they are isolated and physically and emotionally vulnerable, they are easily abused, neglected, and exploited by their caregivers or even systematically by the institution. The following article discusses the nature of institutional abuse.

Dorothy I. Meddaugh

Covert Elder Abuse in the Nursing Home

* * *

Most research on elder abuse has centered on the home setting. This is understandable, since only 5 percent (1.5 million) of elderly persons reside in nursing homes at any given time. Anecdotal evidence notes that abuse does occur in nursing homes. Little is known, however, about the extent or correlates of abusive behavior by staff (Pillemer and Moore, 1989). In fact, Kahana (1973) suggests that the lack of hard data on the prevalence of inhumane treatment in various institutional settings leads to the possibility of misinterpreting the isolated or occasional event as the norm. Federal and state statistics, however, provide documentation that abuse occurs in long-term care facilities (Council on Scientific Affairs, 1987).

Journal of Elder Abuse & Neglect, Vol. 5 (1993). Reprinted by permission.

Doty and Sullivan (1983) note that federal and state sources report numerous incidents of resident abuse each year. State nursing home ombudsman programs receive many complaints of staff mistreatment of residents each year (Monk, Kaye, and Litwin, 1984). Further, these authors state that a substantial amount of abuse is never reported. Early evidence regarding the extent of resident abuse in nursing homes was provided by Stannard (1973), who observed or heard about such actions as pulling a resident's hair and slapping, hitting, punching, or violently shaking a resident. However, due to the case method approach used in this study, it was unknown whether such incidents were isolated events or frequent occurrences.

One of the most critical variables in quality of nursing home care may be the relationships between residents and staff (Pillemer, 1988). Because deliberate mistreatment of residents in long-term care facilities has received so little systematic research attention, Pillemer (1988) developed a conceptual model concerning factors that could lead to mistreatment of residents and proposed a research agenda to expand our knowledge of this problem.

Pillemer's (1988) model offers a provisional guide to research and "is modeled as the outcome of staff members' and patients' characteristics that are influenced by aspects of the nursing home environment and by certain factors exogenous to the facility in question" (p. 230). The predictor variables are divided into four sets: exogenous factors, nursing home environment, staff characteristics, and resident characteristics. Exogenous factors include such examples as supply of nursing home beds and unemployment rate. Nursing home environment factors comprise custodial orientation, level of care, size, rates, cost of resident care, ownership status, staff-resident ratio, and turnover rate. Staff characteristics include education, age, gender, position, experience, and burnout; and resident characteristics, health of residents, social isolation, and gender. Pillemer (1988) further suggests that the variables under each component of the model can be used to generate hypotheses for empirical studies of elder abuse.

In a study that examined some of these variables, Pillemer and Moore (1989) looked at abuse of residents in nursing homes by surveying the staff. The 577 respondents were nursing aides (61 percent), licensed practical nurses (20 percent) and registered nurses (19 percent). Psychological abuse (81 percent) was the most frequently seen type of abuse, while physical abuse was noted by 36 percent of the sample. The findings showed that staff who reported that their personal lives were somewhat or very stressful were likely to engage in abuse, who reported that they frequently thought about quitting were more likely to engage in abuse, and who tended to view residents as childlike were more likely to be abusive. Based on their findings, the authors suggest that abuse may be a common part of institutional life.

* * *

Covert Elder Abuse

During the course of the investigation, no incidences of overt abuse such as hitting, punching, kicking, or swearing were observed. However, it was found that the staff did certain things to the subjects that represent covert forms of abuse (Podnicks, 1987). These forms of covert abuse can be categorized as psychological abuse; however, only one, isolation from others (Pollick, 1987), has been discussed as a type of psychological abuse in the literature. The subtle forms of covert abuse discovered in this investigation were in the areas of personal choice, isolation, labeling, and thoughtless practices.

Personal Choice. The loss of opportunities for personal choice was evident in the daily lives of aggressive residents. Personal choice is defined as the act of selecting (*Scribner-Bantam English Dictionary,* 1987). The aggressive resident group was physically or chemically restrained without their approval, given baths/showers at times designated by the institution, dressed by caregivers with whatever clothing was handy, and fed during times set aside by the institution more often than the non-aggressive resident group. Any attempts by these residents to do other than was determined by the caregiver or institution was met with resistance. An example of this is seen in the case of Mrs. H.

> *Case 1.* Mrs. H. frowned, cried, and moaned or groaned during one morning bath. She tried to move away from the caregiver even though she was in bed. She kicked the caregiver while a stocking was being placed on her leg and struck out twice with her fist. She sometimes looked at the caregiver and made it evident that she did not wish to be disturbed by saying, "Leave me alone, I don't like it, you dirty rat."

This behavior continued during each morning bath time observed by the investigator. However, similar activities during evening hours did not elicit the same response. Rather, Mrs. H. would accept the care without overt aggressive behavior. She might frown or moan but would occasionally smile at something said by the caregiver.

While the caregivers acknowledged that the behavior of the resident was different according to the time of day, the staff persisted in carrying out the care during the prescribed time. The staff were insensitive to the differential needs of this resident. Additionally, the shower was extremely problematic for the aggressive resident. Most (10 of the 14) aggressive residents would yell the entire time, with the harsh sound reverberating off the shower walls. It noticeably bothered the caregiver as she or he would try to tell the resident to stop yelling.

* * *

Cleanliness and daily physical assessment of each resident's body is, of course, desirable and is part of the care given in institutional settings. However, in both of the cases presented, the aggressive residents were not given choices concerning their manner of bath or bath time. It was obvious that this care had to fit into the caregiver's schedule. Further, choices were not given to aggressive residents in selection of daily dress after personal care was completed.

The findings in this study concerning personal choice confirm much of Goffman's (1961) early work which stated that institutions do not like clients to express their opinions in ways that go against the institutional milieu.

Isolation. A second aspect of covert psychological abuse uncovered in the study was the isolation of certain residents. Isolation in this study is defined as being placed alone, separated, or in a detached position (*Scribner-Bantam English Dictionary*, 1979). Staff did not include certain residents in social or rehabilitative interactions or groups because they did not behave in a manner that was acceptable to staff or the institutional milieu. Aggressive residents were isolated more often than nonaggressive residents. If a resident "acted up" one time, he or she usually was dismissed from group activities and rehabilitative efforts. One of the rare occurrences of an aggressive resident's inclusion in a group activity was documented. Mr. B. was taken to a men's coffee hour, which was charted on the record of the resident as having been successful. During the five-week period of observation, however, this was the only documented activity Mr. B. attended.

* * *

Labeling. Labeling or classifying is done in every environment. In this study, the aggressive resident was labeled as "bad" and the nonaggressive resident as "good," thus contributing to covert abuse of the elderly individual. When a resident was so classified, the isolation discussed earlier in this article would follow. Rather than discern possible reasons for the aggressive behavior, it was expected that aggressive behaviors would continue and thus the elderly individual could not be rid of the label.

* * *

References

Council on Scientific Affairs (1987). Elder abuse and neglect. *Journal of the American Medical Association* 257(7) 966–971.

Doty, P., and Sullivan, E.W. (1983). Community involvement in combating abuse neglect, and maltreatment in nursing homes. *Milbank Memorial Fund Quarterly/Health and Society* 61, 2.

Kahana, E. (1973). The humane treatment of old people in institutions. *The Gerontologist* 13, 282–84.

Monk, A., Kaye, L.W., and Litwin, H. (1984). *Resolving grievances in the nursing home: A study of the ombudsman program*, New York: Columbus University Press.

Pillemer, K. (1988). Maltreatment of patients in nursing homes: Overview and research agenda. *Journal of Health and Social Behavior*, 29, 227–238.

Pillemer, K. and Moore, D. (1989). Abuse of patients in nursing homes: Findings from a survey of staff. *The Gerontologist*, 29(3), 314–320.

Podnicks, E. (1987). The victimization of older persons. *Psychiatric Nursing*, 6–11.

Pollick, M.F. (1987). Abuse of the elderly: A review. *Holistic Nursing Practice*, 1 (2), 43–53.

Scribner-Bantam English Dictionary (1979). New York: Bantam Books, Inc.

Stannard C. (1973). Old folks and dirty work: The social conditions for patient abuse in a nursing home. *Social Problems*, 20 329–342.

Every state has addressed the problem of elder abuse by creating special penalties for abuse or neglect of older persons and by establishing adult protective services. Typically the adult pro-

tective services system includes a coordinated service delivery in conjunction with the right of the state to intervene in an older person's life if necessary to protect the older person and ensure the delivery of the needed services. (Older victims are often reluctant to seek or accept assistance). Statutes also often require mandatory reporting of abuse by professionals such as physicians and social workers, an elderly abuse "hot line," procedures for the investigation of allegations of abuse or neglect, and civil or criminal punishment for abusers.

CHAPTER 44

Sentencing of Elderly Criminals

Criminals can be and are young, middle-aged, and old. While age alone is no excuse for criminality, the age of a criminal can affect what is considered appropriate punishment. Younger criminals, for example, come under the rules of the juvenile justice system. Although there is no corresponding "elderly justice system," many question whether older criminals should be treated the same as younger ones. For example, a fifteen-year prison sentence for a sixty-five-year-old male is practically a life sentence, while a twenty-five-year-old who spends fifteen years in a prison still has a thirty-year life expectancy after he leaves prison. The following articles discuss the issues that arise when older persons are in the criminal justice system.

Molly F. James

The Sentencing of Elderly Criminals

* * *

II. Character of the Elderly and Their Crimes

The sixty-five and older population accounts for 12.4 percent (30.4 million people)[1] of the total United States population and commits about 1 percent of the crime in America.[2] The fifty-five and older population commits about 4 percent of the nation's crime.[3] Even though the number of offenses committed by the elderly is small, it is

American Criminal Law Review, Vol. 29, 1025 (Spring 1992). Reprinted by permission from publisher, Georgetown University Law Center.

growing.[4] The population of elderly criminals is likely to grow even more in the future because the elderly population in general is increasing.

* * *

Nearly 80 percent of the crimes the elderly commit are property crimes, such as shoplifting.[5] However, most of the elderly actually serving sentences are in prison for violent offenses.[6] Often they are repeat offenders.[7] One bank robber . . . had a criminal record covering seven decades.[8] Those who see the inside of a prison for the first time after their fifty-fifth birthdays are more likely than the recidivists to have been sentenced for spontaneous, interpersonal violence.[9] This violence may in part be caused by a loss of inhibitions resulting from "chronic brain syndrome,"[10] boredom, or alcohol.[11] The cost of keeping older offenders in prison can be three times more than the cost of confinement for younger offenders: $60,000 as compared to $20,000 annually.[12]

Most elderly inmates do not receive special handling by prison systems. They are not given separate facilities or lighter work assignments unless they are also infirm.[13] Three states and the District of Columbia do have specific programs for older prisoners. West Virginia has an "Old Man's Colony" where the majority of inmates over age fifty live in an open setting.[14] Similarly, the District of Columbia has special recreation facilities for older people to play checkers, play cards, or watch television.[15] Texas has a program which residentially segregates the elderly, and Virginia allows older inmates to be excluded from heavy work assignments.[16]

Special arrangements for elderly inmates can make prisons seem more like nursing homes. This raises the question of the necessity of keeping certain frail elderly people behind bars, since the infirm elderly person is least likely to commit crimes in the future.[17]

There is competing evidence on whether elderly offenders are sentenced more leniently than younger offenders. According to Professor Dean J. Champion, who conducted a study of sentencing of the elderly in the federal courts before the implementation of the Federal Sentencing Guidelines, the elderly receive less severe penalties.[18] The study examined the sentences defendants received both from the plea bargaining process and from judges after trials. It found that, on average, offenders aged eighteen to twenty-nine received sentences of 23 percent of the maximum penalty, while offenders aged sixty and up received only 10 percent of the maximum penalty.[19] Also, those over age sixty received probation in 68 percent of the cases, while younger offenders received probation in only 16 percent of the cases.[20]

Dr. William Wilbanks conducted a study of elderly sentencing in the California courts and came to a slightly different conclusion. He found that the elderly do receive less jail time overall, but not for all crimes.[21] Elderly criminals aged sixty and up were *more* likely than younger criminals to be incarcerated for aggravated assault with a weapon, negligent manslaughter with a vehicle, motor vehicle theft, dangerous drugs, molestation, disturbing the peace, and fraud.[22] Elderly criminals were *less* likely to be imprisoned for homicide, rape, robbery, simple assault, burglary, larceny, and forgery.[23] Dr. Wilbanks concluded that his study "found little evidence that the elderly are treated more leniently than younger offenders" in California.[24]

* * *

B. Specific Theories of Punishment for Elderly Criminals

There are four different approaches to sentencing of the elderly.[25] The first approach, not seriously advocated, is to punish the elderly more severely than younger criminals. According to this theory, older offenders are more culpable than younger offenders because older people are wiser and therefore "should have known better."[26] This theory is retributivist, because it bases sentence increases on moral grounds rather than utilitarian grounds. If a utilitarian believed that the elderly were "wiser," he or she may believe it takes less punishment to deter them from crime and may be easier to rehabilitate them; therefore, less punishment may be needed for the elderly rather than more.

A utilitarian argument in favor of increased sentences for the elderly can be made if one assumes that capacity diminishes with age. Older people would then need longer punishments in order to protect society from deviants who are more difficult to rehabilitate.[27]

The second approach to sentencing the elderly is to punish them less severely than younger offenders. Professor Fred Cohen explains that this approach allows the elderly defendant to show that, by virtue of age, he or she lacks the physical and psychological make-up to deal with life's stresses.[28] This focuses on aspects associated with age, rather than age itself. It is retributivist in that the moral guilt of the older criminal is thought to be diminished, leading to the need to impose a lower sentence to match this lower amount of guilt. This offers a view of the elderly as less responsible and more in need of protection than the society at large.[29]

A retributivist argument for lower sentences of the elderly can be made on the basis of age alone, rather than on the basis of a mental or physical condition associated with age. The retributivist premise that punishment should be proportionate to the offense has a particular application to elderly criminals. A long sentence is more harsh to an older person than a younger person, because it condemns the older person to spend a greater percentage of his or her remaining life in prison.[30] This disparity could be reduced by giving the elderly sentences which represent the same *percentage* of their remaining lives as those given to younger persons.[31]

For example, the average twenty-five-year-old white male can expect to live for 46.9 more years.[32] If such a person were convicted of a crime which carries a twenty-year prison term, he would spend approximately 43 percent of his remaining life behind bars. A sixty-five-year-old is expected to live 14.2 more years.[33] A twenty-year sentence would thus represent 141 percent of this defendant's remaining life, a de facto life sentence. By contrast, 43 percent of his life would be only 6.1 years. This scheme would have no effect on sentences of life imprisonment or death. Those sentences would have the same effect on a younger and an older person's remaining life.

A sentence that could be completely served by a younger person, and that would provide such a person with a chance to have some life left outside of prison, may be a life sentence for an elderly criminal. For example, in *State v. Waldrip*,[34] the judge, who reduced a sixty-seven-year-old defendant's sentence for voluntary manslaughter from five years to life to five to ten years,[35] recognized that even the minimum term of five years could theoretically be a life sentence because of the defendant's age.[36] If an older person does not have his or her sentence reduced, he or she will experience a greater punishment than a younger person sentenced for committing the same crime.

One may legitimately ask why elderly people should have special treatment in sentencing, since the elderly fight to have age disregarded in employment and guardianship issues. The Age Discrimination in Employment Act[37] prohibits employment decisions concerning individuals aged forty and older to be based on age, unless age is a "bona fide occupational qualification."[38] Guardianship is the appointment by a court of a guardian to assume decision-making of a person (often an elderly person) who has been found to be incompetent. Criteria for the determination of incompetence has sometimes included age,[39] and this has been criticized.[40]

A response to the age discrimination and guardianship analysis is that reduced sentencing for the elderly can be based on life expectancy. When age is cited as a factor in employment and guardianship decisions, age is used as a short-cut or substitute for factors *associated with* age, such as failing memory or frailty. The real problem in age discrimination and guardianship issues is that age is treated as dispositive of incompetence when incompetence is the real issue. In a reduced sentencing theory, the issue *is* age, because age is the main factor in life expectancy.[41]

From a utilitarian perspective, reduced sentences for the elderly make sense if deterrence and rehabilitation are ineffective for that population. Because punishment is not seen as an end in itself, severe punishment should not be implemented if it serves no societal purpose. If an elderly individual is not presently a threat to society, or soon will cease to be a threat because of advancing age, it would be better to release these relatively harmless individuals into society than to keep them in prison and have taxpayers incur $60,000[42] a year in their support.

The third approach to elderly sentencing refrains from punishing the elderly at all. Professor Cohen terms this approach "dubious."[43] It is a theory of total irresponsibility of the very old, similar to that of the very young[44] or the insane.[45] This theory could have a retributivist or utilitarian basis. If the aged cannot be morally guilty, it makes sense to retributivists to refrain from punishing them. If the aged are deemed to be without the mental capacity to commit crime, deterrence, important to utilitarians, would not be successful.

In the United States, there is no acceptance of the idea that the elderly can be completely exculpated merely by virtue of their age. However, in China prior to 1911, punishments were meted out according to status, and older people were given greater status by law.[46] China's Ch'ing dynasty had a statute which stated, "persons aged ninety or above . . . even though guilty of a capital offense, are not to suffer any punishment. . . . This statute does not apply to persons of ninety or above who are guilty of rebellion or treason."[47] Offenders aged seventy to eighty-nine received reduced sentences or could pay redemption to avoid further punishment of some crimes.[48] Apparently in practice, however, these rules were not absolute, and the health of an individual also could be taken into account during sentencing.[49]

The fourth approach, preferred by Professor Cohen and the United States Sentencing Commission, is age neutrality in sentencing. This theory rejects age as a factor in and of itself, but does allow "evidence of the functional impairments commonly associated with old age."[50] An individual suffering from senile dementia or "chronic brain syndrome"[51] could introduce this condition as evidence at sentencing and have it weighed in the same manner mental disturbances are weighed for defendants of any age.[52]

The Sentencing Guidelines are structured so that age is given little weight as a criterion in sentencing.[53] Section 5H1.1 allows consideration of the elderly *and* infirm, but this allowance overlaps with section 5H1.4, which allows for deviation from the Guidelines if the defendant is suffering from an "extraordinary physical impairment."[54] As such, section 5H1.1 is perhaps rendered superfluous.

Age neutrality is defensible on retributivist and utilitarian grounds using the same arguments which defend punishment in general.[55] The theory of age neutrality is based upon the view that people past age sixty vary enormously in other characteristics—making "[c]hronological age [a] very poor guide to the state of a man's mental alertness."[56] Professor Cohen criticizes other theories of punishment of the elderly because those theories "stereotype the elderly in terms of the characteristics of the least capable, least healthy, and least alert of the elderly."[57]

* * *

Notes

1. American Association of Retired Persons, *A Profile of Older Americans* 1 (1989) [hereinafter AARP].

2. [Craig J. Forsyth & Robert Gramling, *Elderly Crime: Fact and Artifact, in* OLDER OFFENDERS 3, 9 (Belinda McCarthy & Robert Langworthy eds., 1988).]

3. Ann Goetting, *The Elderly in Prison: Issues and Perspectives,* 20 J. RES. CRIME & DELINQ. 291 (1983).

4. *See* Forsyth & Gramling, *supra* note 2, at 12–13 (elderly crime increased 322% between 1965 and 1984). *See also* James J. Fyfe, *Police Dilemmas in Processing Elderly Offenders, in* ELDERLY CRIMINALS 97, 100 (Evelyn S. Newman & Donald J. Newman eds., 1984) (50% increase in arrests of elderly between 1971 and 1980).

5. Forsyth & Gramling, *supra* note 2, at 12.

6. Goetting, *supra* note 3, at 292.

7. *Id.*

8. [*Crime: Never Too Old For a Heist.* TIME, Apr. 17, 1989, at 31.]

9. See Goetting, *supra* note 3, at 292 (76.5% of those first incarcerated vs. 33.3% of recidivists).

10. Chronic Brain Syndrome is a syndrome affecting the aged in which loss of inhibitions may result in illegal sexual behavior. Other indications of the syndrome include suspiciousness, quarrelsomeness and aggressiveness. This may be caused by loss of economic and social status that comes with retiring. According to Dr. William H. Crosby this can lead to check forgery, embezzlement and other white collar crimes in an attempt to stave off feelings of despair and dependence. William H. Crosby, *Crime and the Aged,* 234(6) JAMA 639 (1975).

11. See Goetting, *supra* note 3, at 293 (these factors can work in combination).

12. *20/20: Golden Years Behind Bars* (ABC television broadcast, Jan. 19, 1990).

13. *See* Goetting, *supra* note 3, at 301 (47 states have no formal special considerations for elderly prisoners).

14. *Id.* Eighty-five percent to ninety-eight percent of older inmates are men. *Id.* at 292.

15. *Id.* at 302.

16. *Id.*

17. *ABC World News Tonight: Maximum Security Nursing Homes,* (ABC television broadcast, Oct. 8, 1990) (story on prisons in southern states which were considering releasing old prisoners).

18. Dean J. Champion, *The Severity of Sentencing: Do Federal Judges Really Go Easier on Elderly Felons in Plea-Bargaining Negotiations Compared with Their Younger Counterparts?, in* OLDER OFFENDERS 143, 155 (Belinda McCarthy & Robert Langworthy eds., 1988).

19. *Id.* at 152–53.

20. *Id.* at 156.

21. William Wilbanks, *Are Elderly Felons Treated More Leniently by the Criminal Justice System?,* 26 INT'L J. AGING & HUM. DEV. 275 (1988). Dr. Wilbanks cautions that, while his study shows differentiation in the way the elderly and nonelderly are treated, other factors, such as prior criminal record or severity or brutality of the crimes committed, were not available. Unaccounted for criteria may have played a part in sentencing outcomes. *Id.* at 287.

22. *Id.* at 282.

23. *Id.*

24. *Id.* at 286.

25. *See* Fred Cohen, *Old Age as a Criminal Defense,* 21 CRIM. L. BULL. 5, 11–17 (1985) ((1) aggravated culpability; (2) diminished responsibility; (3) no responsibility; and (4) age neutrality). Professor Cohen also discusses the option of a "geriatric court" which would entail separate procedures for the elderly, similar to the juvenile court system. *Id.* at 16. This would be one way to implement a diminished responsibility theory.

26. *Id.* at 11. Prof. Cohen extrapolates this theory from an article discussing elderly responsibilities and capacities in the labor force. *See id.* at 11 n.13 (quoting Talcott Parsons, *The Aging American Society,* 27 LAW & CONTEMP. PROB. 22, 33 (1962) (many people "actually grow in moral stature as they grow older")).

27. *Cf.* ABRAHAM S. GOLDSTEIN, THE INSANITY DEFENSE 192 (1967) (criticizing insanity defense because it puts the most dangerous people back on the street—those who cannot control themselves. If older people are of diminished capacity, they are similar to those able to use the insanity defense).

28. Cohen, *supra* note 25, at 13.

29. Robert Langworthy & Belinda McCarthy, *Police Dispositions of Arrests: An Exploratory Study of the Treatment of Older Offenders, in* OLDER OFFENDERS 110 (Belinda McCarthy & Robert Langworthy eds., 1988).

30. This rejects the argument that the life of an elderly person is similar both in and out of prison. Most prison systems do not treat older inmates specially. *See supra* note 9 and accompanying text (most prison systems do not have separate facilities for the elderly).

31. It could be argued that older people have already led a long life outside of prison, while younger people who are incarcerated are losing their prime years. The counter-argument to this is that the older person was not morally culpable until he committed a crime, so those years of freedom are in no way "owed" to the system.

32. Telephone interview with Robert Kuba, Representative of the Actuarial Dept. of Nationwide Life Insurance (Jan. 2, 1991) (discussing actuarial tables based on 1980 census data).

33. *Id.*

34. 533 P.2d 1151 (Ariz. 1975).

35. *Id.* at 1154.

36. *Id.*

37. 29 U.S.C. § 621-633a (1985 & Supp. 1990).

38. *See* Trans World Airlines, Inc. v. Thurston, 469 U.S. 111, 122 (1985) (age must relate to a "particular business").

39. *See, e.g.*, COLO. REV. STAT. ANN. § 15-14-101(1) (West 1990) (incapacitated person "means any person who is impaired by reason of . . . advanced age . . . to the extent that he lacks sufficient understanding or capacity to make or communicate responsible decisions concerning his person").

40. *See, e.g.* Christine Metcalf, *Review of Florida Legislation; Comment: A Response to the Problem of Elder Abuse: Florida's Revised Adult Protective Services Act*, 14 FLA. ST. U. L. REV. 745, 750 (1986).

41. Of course, life expectancy is also based on health, smoking, family medical history, and the like, but the fundamental starting point is age itself.

42. 20/20, *supra* note 17. If a criminal is released and enters a nursing home paid by Medicaid, the cost to the taxpayers is less than it would be for incarceration. *Cf.* telephone interview with Kathy Schey of Brooke Grove Foundation, Williamsport, Maryland Oct. 9, 1991 (private pay nursing home patients may pay $45,000 a year, and reimbursement from medicaid is less than the total cost to the nursing home).

43. Cohen, *supra* note 25, at 14.

44. *Id.* (lack of criminal responsibility for those under seven).

45. *Id.* at 21-22. *See also* GOLDSTEIN, *supra* note 27, at 197 (defendant under influence of extreme mental or emotional disturbance lacks malice aforethought).

46. Derk Bodde, *Age, Youth, and Infirmity in the Law of Ch'ing China*, 121 U. PA. L. REV. 437 (1973).

47. *Id.* at 465.

48. *Id.* at 464–65.

49. *See id.* at 451 (defendant over seventy sentenced to penal servitude even though statute allowed redemption, because he was "still 'basically flourishing'").

50. Cohen, *supra* note 25, at 15.

51. *See supra* note 10 (explaining this term).

52. See GOLDSTEIN, *supra* note 27, at 197 (mental disturbance used to explain or excuse defendant).

53. [UNITED STATES SENTENCING COMMISSION, FEDERAL SENTENCING GUIDELINES AND POLICY STATEMENTS, § 5H1.1 (1989) (emphasis in original) (hereinafter USSC).]

54. *Id.* § 5H1.4.

55. [Note omitted.]

56. *See* Cohen, *supra* note 25, at 9 (quoting ALASTAIR HERON & SHEILA CHOWN, AGE AND FUNCTION 67 (1967)).

57. *Id.* at 25 (quoting Richard Kalish, *The New Ageism & the Failure Models: A Polemic*, 19 GERONTOLOGIST 398 (1979)).

William E. Adams, Jr.

The Incarceration of Older Criminals: Balancing Safety, Cost, and Humanitarian Concerns

* * *

IV. Sentencing and Parole Standards—Should Age Be a Factor?

A. Humanitarian Concerns

The extent to which age is a factor in sentencing depends upon the weight given to each of the four theories of punishment: retribution, deterrence, prevention, and rehabilitation.[1] Retribution (also called "revenge" or "retaliation") theory imposes punishment in order to compensate for the harm to the victim.[2] Deterrence theory posits that the threat of punishment will dissuade the rational person from committing a crime.[3] Prevention is a form of deterrence theory in which the punishment is meant to incapacitate the offender in order to prevent other crimes from being committed. An educational program as punishment may serve this preventive function.[4] Rehabilitation is the process through which the punishment restores the criminal so that he may return to society with skills that reduce the likelihood of further criminal activity.[5] Although these goals are not mutually exclusive, the punishment given to a criminal may vary depending upon the weight given to each.

These theories may necessitate different results depending upon the type of crime committed and the characteristics of the older offender. Some older prisoners are clearly more dangerous than others. In order to deter or prevent future crime, some would argue that the violent prisoners should stay incarcerated. Some offenders who have committed very violent crimes may no longer be physically able to commit a violent crime because of failing health. Under a retributive theory, such a person would be kept in prison if he had not served an appropriate length of time even if he were no longer dangerous. On the other hand, those who value rehabilitation strongly might approve the release of a person who had committed a particularly heinous crime once rehabilitation is demonstrated, even if the time served were so short as to not fully serve the interests of retribution. Penalties will also have a more serious effect on some persons than on others. For example, fines or economic sanctions, which may seem more appropriate for nonviolent offenses, may have a harsher effect on an elderly person who shoplifted because of economic need. The fine may worsen the economic condition of the offender, thus contravening any deterrent

Nova Law Review, Vol. 19, 465 (Winter 1994). Reprinted by permission.

effect. Further imprisoning people past a stage where they are dangerous, particularly if more dangerous criminals are released, puts society at greater risk of harm. However, releasing older prisoners into society raises special problems for probation officers, as discussed below.

B. Sentencing

The vulnerability of older inmates has led some commentators to suggest that age be considered an appropriate criminal defense under a diminished capacity theory.[6] While not all older persons suffer from functional mental impairments,[7] it is recognized that as persons get older, the likelihood of decline in mental functioning increases.[8] This decline is probably not significant in those prisoners who are in their early fifties. However, it may be a relevant factor for older offenders.[9] These physiological changes can affect behaviors which the older person was previously able to hold in check.[10] A large number of violent older offenders suffer from mental disabilities associated with aging.[11]

The fact that elderly criminals sometimes suffer from diminished mental capacities may have an impact on the way in which elder criminals are treated by the criminal justice system. Although the sentencing guidelines and case law do not require leniency toward the elderly,[12] a number of researchers have found that police and the judicial system treat elderly persons more leniently.[13] Other researchers have found, however, that older persons are less likely to be released once arrested,[14] and that judges, even older judges, are not particularly sympathetic toward older criminals.[15] A study of county court judges in Dade County, Florida, found that significant percentages of judges reported feeling generally unsympathetic toward the elderly, and they did not feel special consideration should be given to them.[16] Of even more interest, the study found that while pretrial intervention and counseling were perceived as the most ideal sanctions for elderly shoplifters, most judges imposed fines and court costs.[17] These harsher remedies were imposed even when the appropriate deterrent would seem to be a different sanction.[18] Yet another study found that although older persons may receive shorter sentences overall, this is not true for all crimes.[19] These studies may not be properly factoring all of the variables which result in arrest or other dispositions of persons suspected of criminal activity. At least one study has also found that the elderly were less likely to invoke their due process rights than younger accused, although there is a trend towards increased assertion of rights by older defendants.[20]

* * *

C. Parole and Probation

As in other areas of elderly crime, little research has been conducted on elderly probationers. One study of elderly probationers in California found a large percentage with a prior criminal record.[21] Males in this study had most commonly committed prior sex offenses, while the elderly females had most often committed welfare fraud.[22] A majority were in poor health.[23] Although those who committed welfare fraud are probably not dangerous, those who committed sex offenses may still pose a threat if released.[24] On the other hand, a review of the elderly inmates in the Federal Bureau of Prisons indicates that a majority are not considered dangerous.[25]

Many existing probation programs are not designed to provide for the needs of older persons.[26] Nevertheless, one study found that elderly convicts are much more likely to be offered probation than younger persons convicted of crimes.[27] There have been attempts to create special diversion programs for elderly offenders. The earliest models tended to focus on persons who were either first-time offenders or who committed minor crimes.[28] These programs offered individual counseling, social activities, and emotional support; some met in group sessions where members helped each other. Although proponents of these programs claimed dramatic success rates, some researchers argue that the restrictive criteria for entrance to the programs artificially increased the success rate.[29] The researchers concluded that these and similar prison programs failed to meet the inmates' needs, and they suggested the creation of special institutions for older prisoners, with programs tailored to address their problems.[30]

If disparate treatment is called for in providing parole or probation to older offenders, it is important, for prison release purposes, as with the application of sentencing guidelines, to decide what age is to be considered "older." There is a higher crime rate for the "young" elderly population.[31] Moreover, the recidivism rate for older prisoners is less than 5 percent, and it gets even lower as age increases. Many states and the federal prison system take this lower recidivism rate into account when making parole decisions.

* * *

Notes

1. [Victoria K. Kidman, *The Elderly Offender: A New Wrinkle in the Criminal Justice System,* 14 J. Contemp. L. 131, 131 (1988).] For further discussion of theories concerning incarceration of older persons, see Fred Cohen, *Old Age as a Criminal Defense,* 21 Crim. L. Bull. 5, 11–17 (1985); Molly James, *The Sentencing of Elderly Criminals,* 29 Am. Crim. L. Rev. 1025, 1039–43 (1992).

2. Kidman, *supra* note 1, at 142.

3. *Id.* at 143.

4. *Id.*

5. *Id.*

6. Cohen, *supra* note 1, at 8–10. It could also be argued that an older person could be considered more culpable because of greater life experience. *Id.* at 11; *see also* Kidman, *supra* note 1, at 146–47.

7. Such a blanket presumption would also help perpetuate negative stereotyping of the elderly which is unfair because it is untrue of a large number of older persons. Cohen, *supra* note 1, at 25.

8. *Id.* at 9.

9. Those who suddenly commit a violent offense at an older age may suffer a loss of inhibitions due to some factor like chronic brain syndrome. Kidman, *supra* note 1, at 133.

10. *Id.* at 134 (citing [William Wilbanks & Dennis D. Murphy, *The Elderly Homicide Offender, in* Elderly Criminals 79, 80–91 (Evelyn S. Newman et al. eds., 1984) (suggesting that the elderly are less sensitive to social and cultural variables than younger persons)].

11. *Id.* at 138 n.62 (citing Stephen J. Hucker, *Psychiatric Aspects of Crime in Old Age,* in ELDERLY CRIMINALS, *supra* note 10, at 68).

12. *See, e.g.,* Bevins v. Commonwealth, 712 S.W.2d 932, 936 (Ky. 1986) (holding that consideration of the 70 year old defendant's age was within the court's discretion), *cert. denied,* 479 U.S. 1070 (1987).

13. Donald J. Bachand & George A. Chressanthis, *Property Crime and the Elderly Offender: A Theoretical and Empirical Analysis, in* [OLDER OFFENDERS: PERSPECTIVES IN CRIMINOLOGY & CRIMINAL JUSTICE 14 (Belinda McCarthy & Robert Langworthy eds., 1988) (hereinafter OLDER OFFENDERS)]. One study of federal judges across six different circuits found that offenders aged 60 and over received sentences through plea bargains which were less than half as severe as those received by younger offenders. The disparity was even greater where the defendant was convicted at trial. It should be noted that this study was conducted prior to implementation of the Federal Sentencing Guidelines. Dean J. Champion, *The Severity of Sentencing: Do Federal Judges Really Go Easier on Elderly Felons in Plea-Bargaining Negotiations Compared with Their Younger Counterparts?, in* OLDER OFFENDERS, *id.*, at 154.

14. Robert Langworthy & Belinda McCarthy, *Police Disposition of Arrests: An Exploratory Study of the Treatment of the Older Offender, in* OLDER OFFENDERS, *supra* note 13, at 111–18.

15. [Gary Feinberg, *The Role of the Elderly Defendant in the Criminal Court: Full-Dress Adversary or Reluctant Penitent?,* in OLDER OFFENDERS, id., at 124.]

16. [Gary Feinberg & Dinesh Khosia, *Sanctioning Elderly Delinquents,* TRIAL, Sept. 1985, at 46.] Only 59% reported being sympathetic towards the elderly, with 22% reporting being distinctly unsympathetic and 20% reporting neutrality. *Id.* Only 38% of the judges reported that elderly misdemeanants should be accorded special consideration. *Id.*

17. While 33% reported pretrial intervention as an ideal sanction, only 6% used it. While 30% recommended counseling as ideal, only 12% used it as a sanction. On the other hand, 39% used fines, court costs, or both while only 12% characterized them as ideal. This contradiction is compounded by the fact that the judges rated psychological problems as the most common cause of elderly shoplifting with economic need ranked second. *Id.* at 49. One study challenges the belief that elderly persons shoplift for subsistence purposes. Kidman, *supra* note 1, at 135.

18. Of 31 judges who believed misdemeanant shoplifting was caused by economic need, 45% levied fines, court costs, or both, thus exacerbating the problem that they perceived triggered the offense. The judges who attributed the shoplifting to psychological problems were also much more likely to apply economic sanctions rather than counseling. Feinberg & Khosia, *supra* note 16, at 49.

19. For some offenses, such as negligent vehicular manslaughter, aggravated assault with a weapon, motor vehicle theft, fraud, dangerous drugs, child molestation, and public order offenses, the gap between age groups narrowed. Wilbanks, *supra* note 10, at 281.

20. In a study of persons aged 60 and over accused of misdemeanors in Dade County, Florida, researchers found that a higher percentage of older defendants pled guilty and a lower percentage asked to be represented by counsel or to obtain a jury trial than younger defendants. Feinberg, *supra* note 16, at 132–39. But see Champion, supra note 13, at 155 (finding that older defendants in federal courts were more likely to proceed to trial). Note, however, that the latter study involved felonies whereas the former involved misdemeanors. It may be that the disincentives for the elderly appearing in court are outweighed by the seriousness of a felony conviction. *Id.*

21. David Shichor, *An Exploratory Study of Elderly Probationers,* 32 INTL. J. OF OFFENDER THERAPY & COMP. CRIMINOLOGY 163, 165 (1988) (finding 53.8% of those placed on probation had previously committed crimes).

22. Almost one-third of the males had committed sex offenses, primarily offenses connected with minors, and 42.9% of the females had committed welfare fraud. *Id.* The level of sex offenders among males is troubling since arguably they still pose a threat to the community. The researcher notes that some of their reports stated that imprisonment would have been recommended if the offender had been younger. *Id.*

23. *Id.* at 168–69.

24. Some believe that both deterrence and retribution are served by keeping persons who committed welfare fraud in prison, but the question is whether these goals outweigh safety concerns of more dangerous inmates being released.

25. Forty-six percent were classified in the lowest security level and 71% were classified in the three lowest security levels. [Peter C. Kratcoski & George A. Pownall, *Federal Bureau of Prisons Programming for Older Inmates,* 53 FED. PROBATION 28, 30 (June 1989).]

26. [Kenneth E. Gewerth, *Elderly Offenders: A Review of Previous Research,* in OLDER OFFENDERS, supra note 13.]

27. Persons aged 60 and over received probation recommendations 68% of the time as opposed to 16% of the time for younger offenders. The researcher attempted to control other variables so as to guard against the differences being due to factors other than age. Champion, *supra* note 13, at 156.

28. One example is the Broward Senior Intervention and Education Program established in 1979 for elderly shoplifters in Broward County, Florida. The program claimed that in its first 1400 cases, there had been only a 1.5% recidivism rate. Kidman, *supra* note 1, at 148–49. A similar program, The Advocate Program, was started in Dade County in 1978. Alvin Malley, *The Advocate Program Sees the Elderly Through,* 55 FLA. B.J. 207 (1981).

29. Gewerth, *supra* note 26, at 28.

30. [Manuel Vega & Mitchell Silverman, *Stress and the Elderly Convict,* 32 INT'L J. OF OFFENDER THERAPY & COMPAR. CRIM. 153, 158 (1988).]

31. [Craig J. Forsyth & Robert Gramling, *Elderly Crime: Fact and Artifact, in* OLDER OFFENDERS, supra note 13.]

Ronald H. Aday

Golden Years Behind Bars: Special Programs and Facilities for Elderly Inmates

Most researchers and policymakers—some have suggested—deem the crimes of youthful offenders to be more serious and dangerous for society than the crimes committed by older people (Carlie, 1970). However, in recent years, crime and the elderly

Federal Probation, Vol. 58, 47 (June 1994). Reprinted by permission.

has emerged as an issue of increasing importance. While we are more accustomed to seeing the elderly as victims, attention has begun to shift to how the elderly are increasingly the perpetrators of crime (Aday, 1988; Alston, 1986; Cullen, Wozinak, and Frank, 1985; Goetting, 1992; Kratcoski, 1990). A common portrayal of the elderly offender has been the "victimless" felon writing bad checks or the senior citizen who shoplifts in order to survive or provoke some attention. The elderly are not only committing more crimes, however, but also more serious offenses which at one time were reserved more exclusively for the young. As a result, elderly offenders are presenting complex challenges to our nation's prison systems (Aday, 1994; Anderson and Morton, 1989).

Approximately 381,000 persons ages fifty and older are arrested annually in the United States (Uniform Crime Reports, 1990). Of these, 15 percent are arrested for serious felonies such as murder, forcible rape, robbery, aggravated assault, burglary, larceny, motor vehicle theft, and arson. As more of the older population commits violent offenses, the likelihood that they will become incarcerated becomes apparent. The Corrections Yearbook reported in 1992 that 709,587 inmates were confined to state prisons nationwide, including the District of Columbia. Of these prisoners, 35,032 were over the age of fifty, representing a 50 percent increase in four years. This age group comprises approximately 5 percent of the total inmate population.

The Corrections Yearbook further reported that the Federal Bureau of Prisons housed 66,472 prisoners, of which 6,554 or about 10 percent were fifty years of age or over. By the year 2005, this prison population over fifty is expected to increase to 16 percent. Of course, as our state prison systems expand, so will our federal prisons. The number of inmates will continue to increase and will exceed 100,000 by 1995. By the year 2000, a projected 137,000 inmates will be in the federal system (Roth, 1992).

It appears that the population of older prisoners will continue to increase well into the twenty-first century. For example, Virginia currently has 15,000 prisoners in the general population, and 2,500 of these have special needs. This sector of the prison's population includes over 800 elderly inmates. By the year 2000, the prison population is expected to total 32,000 with 8,532 exhibiting special needs. Again, it is projected that approximately one-third in the special needs category will be those classified as geriatric. Numerous other states are also faced with similar increases (Aday, 1993).

Chaneles (1987) has estimated that by the year 2000, if present trends continue, the number of long-term prisoners over fifty will be approximately 125,000 with 40,000 to 50,000 over sixty-five years of age. This projection is based on new admissions and the fact that there are currently 13,937 natural lifers (life without parole), 52,054 lifers (parole possibilities), and 125,996 inmates serving twenty years or more. In addition, another 2,214 prisoners are currently serving time on death row. These groups comprise 22 percent of all inmates in state and federal prisons (The Corrections Yearbook, 1992).

Research Rationale

While the number of older prisoners is now manageable in most states, the trend toward an aged inmate population is raising questions that will significantly affect correction programs in the coming decades. Older offenders pose unique and costly problems for corrections departments already struggling to cope with outdated and overcrowded facilities. Many states are faced with an increased number of aging prisoners who are in need of acute or chronic medical care. It is estimated that elderly prisoners suffer from an average of three chronic illnesses (McCarthy, 1983). Many older offenders need corrective aids and prosthetic devices including eyeglasses, dentures, hearing aids, ambulatory equipment, and special shoes (Wilkberg, 1988). Correctional systems are faced with making necessary adjustments to accommodate the special needs of aging inmates. Issues such as providing special diets and round-the-clock nursing care, building new facilities or altering old ones, and restructuring institutional activities are becoming more frequent topics of discussion.

Older prisoners differ from younger inmates not only in their need for medical care, but also in their psychosocial needs. Walsh (1989) found that older male inmates expressed a greater need for privacy and for access to preventive health care and legal assistance than younger men. Older inmates are often unable to cope with the fast pace and noise of a regular facility (Anderson and Morton, 1989). Studies have also found that older inmates reported feeling unsafe and vulnerable to attack by younger inmates and expressed a preference for rooming with people their own age (Aday and Webster, 1979; Krajick, 1979; Walsh, 1989; Williams, 1989). Vega and Silverman (1988) also reported that abrasive relations with other inmates were the most disturbing incidents elderly prisoners had to cope with while incarcerated. Fifty-five percent of their respondents indicated that abrasive situations occurred daily. These factors, among others, often result in increasing stress for the older inmate.

The physical condition and structure of the institution also create significant problems for the elderly inmate. Prison systems are primarily designed to house young, active inmates. Older, frail offenders often find the prison environment cold and damp and the stairs and distance to the cafeteria difficult to cope with. Inmates with limited mobility may find many prisons' physical designs too stressful to negotiate, and they simply withdraw into an isolated state.

* * *

Policies and Programs

A shortcoming of the studies of older prisoners is the failure of both researchers and correctional officials to agree on what constitutes "elderly." Some authors define "elderly" as sixty-five years of age and older, some suggest sixty years, while others have reported fifty-five years, and many use fifty years of age or older. Likewise, states reporting special programs for aging inmates use a variety of ages to indicate special need. However, fifty years of age and older is the most common definition found in this study. Several correctional officials suggested that the typical inmate in his fifties has a physical appearance of at least ten years older. In addition, the declining health of many inmates contributes to them being "elderly" before their time.

From responses to this survey, it is evident that most states do not have any specific written policies which address aged or infirm inmates. In practice, however, the needs of older inmates are addressed, to the extent possible, in the course of the classification process. Typically, all inmates including the elderly are screened in the admission process. Generally, housing and work assignments are made with regard to the inmate's health, security level, and location of family. In this regard, older inmates who possess numerous chronic health problems are granted special treatment based on their inferior health status.

For example, in the State of Washington, inmates with infirmities related to old age are likely to be transferred to the state penitentiary, where a number of cells in one unit have been designated for use by such inmates. Older inmates who require long-term inpatient care would be considered for transfer to the state reformatory, which has the largest inpatient unit in the system. Those who require special services, other than inpatient care, are transferred to the Special Needs Unit at Washington Correction Center.

A few states such as Texas, Alaska, Mississippi, and South Carolina make some policy decisions based solely on age. In Texas, the inmate is medically classified according to medical history, general health, physical findings, and age. Inmates fifty to fifty-five years of age receive a classification requiring lighter, slower duties. Inmates fifty-five and over are provided a classification which restricts the inmate from harder, heavier work and may allow for reduced work hours. Alaska reports occasionally providing a modification in sentencing for disease onset in the elderly. In Mississippi, inmates over fifty years of age are housed in geriatric units if their security classification permits. In South Carolina, inmates may retire from work at age sixty-five. Numerous states also provide physicals annually for inmates over the age of fifty, rather than every other year as they do for the general prison population.

Although most states do not have a policy based strictly on age, they do provide compassionate leave for those inmates who are terminally ill or not capable of physically functioning in the correctional system. Generally, the prognosis is six months or less to live, and specific criteria with regard to custody classification and medical requirements must be fulfilled. In some states, nursing home placement is a practical alternative. However, nursing home administrators may not be favorable to the notion of accepting ex-prisoners who have life histories of crime and violence, even if they are quite ill.

When compassionate leave is impossible due to the nature of the crime, correctional policy, or lack of available alternatives, prisons are developing policies and programs to better serve the terminally ill.

* * *

Some states are developing "nursing home-like settings" within the prison environment, which provide a greater degree of shelter. For example, Mississippi has a geriatric unit which houses eighty-five offenders. In 1987, the old hospital was remodeled and specifically designed as a nursing home in a correctional setting. In this type of unit, 24-hour nursing care is provided and sick call is available weekly. A physician checks with the unit daily. In addition to the nursing staff, a psychiatric assistant provides recreational activities, and a case manager is also assigned to the unit.

Special Concerns

Rising medical costs in conjunction with health care mandates are having a tremendous impact on a significant number of states. Thirty percent of the states listed rising costs as the most pressing concern. An important issue for 26 percent of the state units is meeting the special needs of older inmates who are "aging in place" with numerous chronic health problems and limited Activities of Daily Living (ADL) functions. As one correctional health official stated, "A significant number of prisoners fifty years and over have a number of chronic illnesses that require long-term care. Another problem is lack of previous dental care requiring the provision of dental prosthesis and long-term dental care." Other problems listed by some states included a lack of community support and appropriate programming for the older inmate, in addition to the victimization of frail, aged inmates.

* * *

Policy Implications

* * *

Although studies have found that older inmates express a preference for being housed with people their own age (Aday, 1984; Krajick, 1979; Walsh, 1989; Williams, 1989), opposing views still exist regarding the arguments favoring special treatment of elderly inmates (Cavan, 1987). Some correctional officials feel no need or responsibility to provide special consideration to older offenders. Others feel older inmates provide a sense of stability to the general prison population and should not be housed separately. From this perspective, older inmates should be given housing and work assignments based on their health and the type of custody they require. Other considerations in placement should be work skills and family status. Placing an inmate in a special unit for the elderly hundreds of miles away from family could be detrimental to the inmate.

The older offender may also have a difficult time being assigned to facilities providing special needs because slots are limited. In particular, those states converting a small wing for older inmates may have a long waiting list. Also, there is still disagreement regarding the ethical obligation to provide inmates with such acute care as heart by-pass surgery or kidney transplants when others in society may not have access to or the money for the same level of care. Thus, due to lack of space, philosophy, or costs, some elderly inmates may not especially benefit from specialized programming. Of course, health access and care may vary from state to state.

A major problem in meeting the special needs of older inmates is that, in many states, there is still a very small number of aging inmates. For example, in Vermont, North Dakota, South Dakota, Hawaii, and Maine, where there are few elderly inmates, separate facilities or programs cannot be justified. In states such as these, correctional units have little choice but to mainstream elderly inmates in the general prison system. This is particularly true for aging female inmates, as they typically make up a very small portion of the total female population.

Another barrier in responding fully to the special needs of the aging inmate is the lack of adequately trained prison staff. As one prison official confessed, "I know how to run prisons, not old-age homes" (Malcolm, 1988, p. 6). Moreover, not everyone who works in a correctional environment may have the aptitude or the essential skills needed to manage elderly people. Careful selection for sensitivity to the unique requirements of geriatric inmates should be an important consideration. Training, involving administrative personnel, line security staff, and health providers, should include an increased knowledge of growing old and how this knowledge specifically affects the elderly in a prison environment. Prison staff needs to be specifically trained to understand more fully the social and emotional needs of the elderly, dynamics of death and dying, procedures for identifying depression, and a system for referring older inmates to experts in the community.

While states are responding by providing special units for older inmates, programming for elderly inmates has not kept pace. Although older inmates may be grouped together in a special needs facility, they often have nothing to do to pass the time. Physical activities popular with younger inmates may not be well-suited to many elderly inmates. Vocational training programs, a primary activity for much of the prison population, serve no purpose for long-term older offenders who are unlikely to return to the workforce. In most prisons, counseling is geared to rehabilitating younger inmates rather than coping with issues such as chronic illness or death. Instead of preparing the inmate for reentry as a productive member of society, wellness programs which aim to keep the individual alert and active are needed. Walking, gardening, woodworking, ceramics, low impact exercises, prison support groups, and other more passive recreational activities can prove successful among older inmates (Aday and Rosefield, 1992).

* * *

References

Aday, R.H. (1994). Aging in prison: A case study of new elderly offenders. International Journal of Offender Therapy and Comparative Criminology, 38, 79–91.

Aday, R.H. (1993). Old and in prison. Unpublished report. Department of Sociology, Middle Tennessee State University, Murfreesboro, TN.

Aday, R.H. (1988). Crime and the elderly. Westport, CT: Greenwood Press.

Aday, R.H. (1984). Old criminals. In E. Palmore (Ed.), Handbook on the aged in the United States. Westport, CT: Greenwood Press.

Aday, R.H., and Rosefield, H.A. (1992, Winter). Providing for the geriatric inmate: Implications for training. The Journal of Correctional Training, 14–16.

Alston, L.T. (1986). Older deviants. In L. T. Alston (Ed.), Crime and older Americans. Springfield, IL: Charles C. Thomas.

Anderson, J.C., and Morton, J.B. (1989). Graying of the nation's prisons presents new challenges. The Aging Connection, 10, 6.

Carlie, M.K. (1970). The older arrestee: Crime in the later years of life. Unpublished dissertation, Washington University, St. Louis, MO.

Cavan, R.H. (1987). Is special treatment needed for elderly offenders? Criminal Justice Policy Review, 2, 213–224.

Cullen, F.T., Wozinak, J.F., and Frank, J. (1985). The rise of the elderly offender: Will a "new" criminal be invented? Crime and Social Justice, 23, 151–165.

Kratcoski, P.C. (1990). Circumstances surrounding homicides by older offenders. Criminal Justice and Behavior, 17, 420–430.

Krajick, K. (1979). Growing old in prison. Corrections Magazine, 5, pp. 32–46.

Malcolm, A.H. (1988, December 24). Aged inmates pose problem for prisons. New York Times, p. 1.

McCarthy, M. (1983, February). The health status of elderly inmates. Corrections Today, pp. 64–65, 74.

Roth, E.B. (1992, July-October). Elders behind bars. In Perspective on aging. Washington, DC: The National Council on Aging, 25–30.

The Corrections Yearbook (1992). South Salem, NY: Criminal Justice Institute.

Uniform Crime Reports (1990). Washington, DC: Federal Bureau of Investigation, U.S. Department of Justice.

Vega, M., and Silverman, M. (1988). Stress and the elderly convict. International Journal of Offender Therapy and Comparative Criminology, 32, 153–162.

Walsh, C.E. (1989). The older and long term inmate growing old in the New Jersey prison system. In S. Chaneles and C. Burnett (Eds.), Old prisoners: Current trends. New York: The Haworth Press.

Wilkberg, R. (1988). The longtermers. The Angolite, 13, 19–58.

Williams, G.C. (1989). Elderly offenders: A comparison of chronic and new offenders. Unpublished thesis. Middle Tennessee State University, Murfreesboro, TN.

Part X

Legal Representation and Ethical Considerations

CHAPTER 45

Introduction

Lawyers are expected to practice their profession in an ethical manner. They are subject to state rules of professional behavior and to court procedures and rulings that create ethical obligations, such as duties of loyalty and confidentiality, to the client. When dealing with older clients, lawyers face additional ethical issues, many of which arise from questions as to the older client's possible lack of capacity. The following article presents an overview of these ethical issues.

Mark Falk

Ethical Considerations in Representing the Elderly

* * *

As Americans continue to live longer lives,[1] certain themes recur when an elderly person seeks legal representation. Frequently, the elderly person comes to the attorney's office accompanied by a relative, such as a son, daughter, or other significant person. The relative acts as the spokesperson and tells the attorney about the elder's needs and desires for representation.[2] The elder and the relative, however, may have different opinions on the legal needs of the elder. The attorney also may receive confidential information from the elder, and then be asked to reveal that information to the relative. The attorney must consider an elder's capacity to sign documents and make decisions, as well as how to document that capacity. The attorney may be asked

South Dakota Law Review, Vol. 36, 54 (1991). Reprinted by permission.

to be both a guardian as well as the attorney for an elderly client. These, and other issues, challenge the ethical responsibilities of all attorneys who work with the elderly.

When an elder and his relative approach the attorney, the request for assistance can encompass a broad range of legal problems. For example, the elder may need a will or a codicil. The elder may request that the relative be appointed as the elder's guardian. The relative may tell the attorney that the elder wishes to execute a power of attorney, a durable power of attorney, or even a living will. The relative or the elder may request that the elder's property be transferred by deed to a joint tenancy. The parties may seek help on numerous estate planning and health planning issues.

Depending on the problems to be addressed, and other factors, an attorney is faced with numerous questions. For example, when a relative speaks on behalf of the elder, or offers to pay the elder's bill,[3] who is the client: the elder or the relative?[4] Can the attorney represent both the elder and the relative? What happens if the elder's desires[5] are not consistent with what the relative[6]—or even the attorney—believes to be in the elder's[7] best interests?[8] To whom is the attorney's duty of confidentiality owed—the elder or the relative? How is an attorney to judge the elder's capacity to make decisions? May an attorney be both the elder's lawyer and guardian? These and many other questions reveal a need for guidance to direct the attorney who works with the elderly.

* * *

A. Who is the Client, the Elder or the Relative?

When an attorney is approached by an elder and a relative, it is not always clear whether the elder, the relative, or both will be the attorney's client. Such relationships create complex triangles.[9] In these circumstances, the elder and the relative may have special relationships with each other that will modify the attorney's "normal" professional responsibility toward whoever is accepted as the client. The first and most critical question that must be resolved by the attorney, elder, and relative is who will be the client.

The Rules of Professional Conduct provide some guidance to help a lawyer determine who his client is when two persons simultaneously ask for assistance. Rule 1.7,[10] the general conflict of interest provision, provides a network of considerations. The rule specifically prohibits representation of one client in the event that such representation would be directly adverse to another client. This means, of course, that if the elder's interests are not aligned with the relative's interests, Rule 1.7 would prohibit a joint representation. Likewise, Rule 1.7 prohibits the lawyer from representing a client if such representation materially limits the lawyer's responsibility to the other client. Therefore, although Rule 1.7 does not specifically identify the client for the attorney, its provisions make it crystal clear that the attorney and both parties, the elder and his relative, must consider and resolve any issue about who is the client at the outset.[11] The choices available to the parties include having the attorney represent the elder alone, the relative alone, or the elder and the relative together.[12]

If the attorney prefers to represent either the elder or the relative alone, counsel must consider whether he or she has had a prior relationship with the nonrepresented party. If so, Rule 1.9[13] requires the lawyer to disclose to the new client the existence of the prior relationship and obtain consent from both the new client and the former client for such representation. If there has been no prior relationship, the matter is greatly simplified. Once the parties decide who the client will be,[14] the Rules of Professional Conduct clearly delineate the attorney's obligation to that client.

A key element in an attorney's relationship with his client is loyalty.[15] The common theme running throughout the Rules of Professional Conduct is that a lawyer owes the utmost loyalty to his client in all facets of representation. The loyalty obligation underlies and permeates the attorney's duties of competence, diligence, communication, fees, and confidentiality of information, as an advisor, and as an advocate.[16] If the attorney chooses to represent the elder,[17] and there is a difference in interest between the elder and his family, the attorney clearly must advocate for the elder's position.[18] On the other hand, if the attorney represents the relative or the family member rather than the elder, the attorney must advocate for the relative.[19] Any dispute or conflict or difference in interest between the elder and the family, therefore, would be resolved in favor of that party who had become the client.

The elder and the relative may insist that the attorney represent them both as clients. The attorney must then consider whether to represent both.[20] Such representation is permitted under the Rules of Professional Conduct in certain circumstances as long as appropriate disclosures are made and prior consent is obtained from both individuals.[21]

For example, the lawyer must reasonably conclude that dual representation will not adversely affect the lawyer's relationship with either client.[22] In other words, if it is foreseeable that the clients' interests may become substantially different, the attorney should not represent both parties.[23] If, however, the attorney is able to ascertain that there is little likelihood of differing interests in the future, he may represent both. If the attorney cannot predict whether interests will differ, the attorney should explain this possibility to the two potential clients and only proceed with their mutual consent.[24] Such consent may be obtained only after full disclosure and consultation.[25]

* * *

Even though both the elder and the relative wish to consent to joint representation, an additional problem may arise.

When more than one client is involved, the question of conflict must be resolved as to each client. Moreover, there may be circumstances where it is impossible to make the disclosure necessary to obtain consent.[26]

For example, if the lawyer has knowledge about the elder's disability or possible incapacity and the elder is not able to competently consent to a disclosure of such information, the attorney could not make the necessary disclosures to obtain consent. Similarly, if the attorney has knowledge of prior actions by the elder or the relative that were clearly adverse to the other's interests or goals of the dual representation, but that party refuses to authorize disclosure of such information, the attorney may not disclose such information without violating the duty of confidentiality.

* * *

B. How Does an Attorney Resolve the Differences Between an Elder and His Family Members?

The next consideration involves an attorney's attempts to resolve disputes or differing interests between the elder and family members once representation is undertaken. Under certain circumstances and conditions an attorney may attempt to mediate disputes between two clients.[27] Although such a course is somewhat risky, in many cases the clients may benefit from an attorney who acts as a mediator. The alternative may be that each party will have to obtain separate representation, which could lead to additional costs, complications, or even litigation. For these reasons, the clients may prefer that the lawyer act as intermediary.[28]

There are, however, considerations that affect the decision to act as an intermediary. First, each client has the right to the attorney's loyal and diligent representation.[29] Further, the mediation process presupposes that each client has an equal ability to represent his or her own position. In fact, "where the lawyer is [an] intermediary, the clients ordinarily must assume greater responsibility for decisions than when each client is independently represented."[30] If, by reason of infirmity, a particular elder client was not able to fully advocate and protect his or her own interests, attempts at mediation may result in an unfair advantage for the relative.

The degree of contentiousness between the elder and his relative must be considered. A lawyer should not attempt common representation of clients when contentious litigation is imminent or when the clients contemplate contentious negotiations.[31] Likewise, when the relationship between the parties has reached a definite antagonism, it is unlikely that the client's interests can be adjusted by intermediation.[32]

* * *

One final danger exists. If either client asks the attorney to stop participating in the mediation, the attorney must not only stop, but must also withdraw from representation of both clients.[33] Consequently, if differences arise between the elder and his family or relatives, the attorney is permitted to try to resolve those differences, but must use considerable care.

C. To Whom is the Duty of Confidentiality Owed?

Occasionally, an attorney will be asked to disclose confidential information about an elder or about the elder's situation. When the attorney represents the elder alone, the attorney owes the elder a duty of confidentiality, and may not disclose the elder's confidences without the elder's consent. In the case of dual representation, however, the question becomes more complicated.

Rule 1.6 allows the lawyer to disclose only information that would advance the client's cause, is necessary to prevent the commission of certain crimes, or is needed to defend lawsuits or grievances against the attorney.[34] No express exception allows for the disclosure of confidential information to family members or co-clients. On its face, then, Rule 1.6 prohibits disclosure of confidential information about an elderly person to the family[35] just as to non-family members.[36]

This principle begins to cloud in certain circumstances where the elder's safety is in jeopardy[37] and in those cases where the attorney acts as an intermediary between the relative and the elder.[38] The complex situation where an attorney represents two parties and tries to act as an intermediary between the two parties requires a "delicate balance."

A particularly important factor in determining the appropriateness of intermediation is the effect on client-lawyer confidentiality and the attorney-client privilege. In a common representation, the lawyer is still required both to keep each client adequately informed and to maintain confidentiality of information relating to the representation. . . . Complying with both requirements while acting as intermediary requires a delicate balance. If the balance cannot be maintained, the common representation is improper. With regard to the attorney-client privilege, the prevailing rule is that as between commonly represented clients the privilege does not attach. Hence, it must be assumed that if litigation eventuates between the clients, the privilege will not protect any such communication, and the client should be so advised.[39]

Although the attorney may arguably be required to keep confidences and secrets from each client in mutual representation cases, there is no attorney-client privilege that is protectable in litigation because of the unusual characteristics of the mutual representation. Whether the right of confidentiality attaches, then, is an important consideration for the clients as well as the attorney when contemplating dual representation.[40]

Finally, there is a third exception to the principle of confidentiality where a lawyer represents a guardian but becomes aware of the guardian's improper actions. If the lawyer becomes aware that the guardian is acting adversely to the ward's interests, the lawyer should take steps to prevent or rectify the guardian's misconduct.[41] This obligation may require the disclosure of confidential information. A lawyer is prohibited from counseling or assisting a client in conduct that "the lawyer knows or reasonably should know is criminal or fraudulent."[42] The guardian and ward relationship is a delicate relationship that imposes this additional duty on the attorney.[43]

D. How Does an Attorney Determine an Elder's Capacity to Make Decisions?

Another recurring problem is whether an elderly client possesses the legal capacity to make binding decisions. When will a particular infirmity of an elderly client[44] invalidate his actions, and what duties does the attorney have to ascertain the extent of the elder's disability? How can the attorney assure that the client has the full capacity to make necessary decisions and execute documents that the client wishes to execute?[45] The Rules of Professional Conduct specifically address the situation where a client is under a disability.[46] The attorney's duty to the client is not impaired by the client's disability.

An attorney may represent an elderly individual even where it appears the elder suffers from a mental disability, so long as the elder has the capacity to enter into a contract for attorney-client services.[47] The attorney's duty is to maintain as reasonably normal a relationship as possible and advocate on behalf of the elder. Even though an incapacitated person may not have the power to make legally binding decisions, nevertheless a client lacking legal competence often has the ability to understand, deliberate upon, and reach conclusions about matters affecting the client's own well-being. Furthermore, to an increasing extent the law recognizes intermediate degrees of competence. . . . [I]t is recognized that some persons of advanced age can be quite capable of handling routine financial matters while needing special legal protection concerning major transactions.[48]

If the lawyer reasonably believes that an elder cannot adequately act in his own interests, the attorney then may petition for a guardianship.[49]

The attorney should start with the presumption that the client has the necessary capacity to make decisions on his own behalf.

In the law's view, all persons are presumed competent unless and until the contrary is proven in a court of law. Much like the presumption of innocence in criminal law, this presumption of competency is a legal doctrine that guarantees personal freedoms against unwarranted restrictions. The import of this doctrine is that all individuals retain full control of their own bodies and are free to make all personal decisions in accordance with their own judgment, unless determined to be incompetent by judicial proceedings.[50]

An attorney, then, under normal circumstances, should not try to second guess a client regarding the client's capacity to sign documents or make decisions.

* * *

The Rules of Professional Conduct honor the right to self-determination by encouraging the development of attorney-client relationships despite limitations on a client's capacity, thus limiting interference with a client's autonomy. Therefore, since there is no one test to determine an elder's capacity to make decisions, the attorney must be guided by the goals the elder wishes to accomplish, as well as the principle that the elder is presumed competent.[51] It is only when the elder begins to demonstrate that he is somehow dangerous or harmful to himself in the decision-making process, and has lost the ability to focus on the reality of the surrounding circumstances, should the attorney begin to seriously question and doubt the elder's competence. On the other hand, simply because a personal decision "causes harm or risk, or . . . is otherwise ill-advised," does not mean that the person making the decision lacks legal competency.

The law permits us to smoke, to drink, and to overeat; it allows us to make foolish purchases and imprudent investments. It has allowed a committed mental patient to refuse hip surgery urged by her physician. It has upheld an elderly derelict's choice to risk gangrene rather than lose his leg. And, with few exceptions, it allows mental-health clients to reject medication prescribed by their psychiatrist.[52]

* * *

A common difficulty faced by attorneys with incapacitated or disabled clients is whether to advocate for the expressed wishes of the clients or the "best interests" of the client as perceived by the lawyer. Several solutions have been proposed. Some commentators argue that the lawyer cannot or should not judge the "best interests" of his client.

> [T]o allow counsel to act in the 'best interests' of the client would allow attorneys to make decisions concerning the mental capacity and well-being of their client: decisions that attorneys are totally unqualified to decide. Attorneys . . . are not equipped to independently determine the physical and psychological needs of their clients.[53]

Rather, they argue that the attorney's duty is to effectively present the client's side of the case, and leave it to the court to make an informed judgment on the client's best interests.[54] Others have argued that the lawyer ought to exercise his independent professional judgment on behalf of the disabled client under a theory of "justified paternalism."[55] Another commentator proposes a solution somewhere in the middle.

> [T]he lawyer [should] consider the client's wishes, present all alternatives to the client, and attempt to persuade the client that the lawyer's conception of the client's best interest is correct. If this fails to resolve the conflict, the lawyer should indicate to the court that the lawyer is representing the client's desires, and not necessarily an expert recommendation as to what should happen to the client. Ultimately, the decision is for the court.[56]

* * *

As a practical matter, when an attorney is considering his client's competence, the attorney must consider that question of competence in relationship to the goals that the client wishes to accomplish. The basic focus of the attorney is not whether the client's decision is wise or prudent. Rather, the attorney ought to examine whether the elder is oriented toward reality,[57] and knows who he is, where he is, and what the decision he intends to make implicates for him. Certainly, an elder needs full and complete advice and information prior to making a decision that may result in harm to him. The degree of potential harm must be considered, but considerable leeway should be given to the elder. For example, an elderly person can choose to risk gangrene rather than lose his leg,[58] and certainly would have the right to make an unwise or eccentric distribution of property. On the other hand, the attorney cannot defer to the elder who wishes to commit suicide.[59] Determining an elder's competence is neither easy nor in all cases determinative of the attorney's conduct toward the elderly person. Nonetheless, such considerations must frequently be faced.

* * *

Notes

1. In 1980, there were 25.9 million people over age 65, 11.1 percent of the population. By the year 2000, it is predicted that there will be 36.3 million Americans over age 65, or 13.2 percent of the population. By 2040, it is predicted that there will be 67.3 million or 20.5 percent of the population over the age of 65. Meanwhile, those age 75 or older are also increasing. In 1975, 38 percent of the elderly were 75 or older. By the year 2000, it is estimated that 45 percent of the elderly will be over the age of 75. Kayser-Jones, Advocacy for Mentally Impaired Elderly: A Case Study Analysis, 14 AM. J. LAW & MED. 353, 354 (1989). In California, by the year 2021, one in every four Californians will be over age 60. Gilfix, Advising Aging Clients, 6 CAL. LAW. 51 (1986). Historical growth in the population of the elderly has been significant. At the turn of the century, only 4.1 percent of the American population (3.1 million people) were 65 years of age or older. Further, more substantial growth is anticipated between 2010 and 2030 as the "baby boom" generation enters old age. Rosoff, Preserving Personal Autonomy for the Elderly, Competency, Guardianship, and Alzheimer's Disease, 8 J. LEGAL MED. 1, 5–6 (1987).

2. One author describes this problem as follows: "Establishing who the client is . . . may be difficult. 'Grandpa' may come into the office with four relatives and insist that everyone remain in the room. Or a family member who is paying the attorney's fees may insist on staying." Gilfix, *supra* note 1, at 52.

For the purpose of this article, "elder" means a person of advanced age. "Relative" means any person who appears to be in a close or caretaker type relationship with the elder. These terms are generic expressions intended to describe general relationships rather than specific chronological age or pedigree.

3. See SOUTH DAKOTA RULES OF PROFESSIONAL CONDUCT Rule 1.8(f) (1990) [hereinafter Rule], which limits the lawyer's ability to accept compensation from someone other than the client.

4. Where it is agreed that the elder is the client, the attorney's duty is clear. See Rule 5.4 ("A lawyer shall not permit a person who recommends, employs, or pays the lawyer to render legal services for another to direct or regulate the lawyer's professional judgment in rendering such legal services."). The courts have consistently held that an attorney's duty is always to the client, regardless of who is paying the bill. "An attorney is under a duty to represent his client. He shall not permit a person who pays him to render legal services for another to direct or regulate his professional judgment in rendering those services." People v. White, 338 N.W.2d 556, 557 (Mich. Ct. App. 1983); see also Maryland State Bar Association, Op. 80-20 (1980) (once representation is undertaken, the person paying the bill has no authority to fire the attorney).

Issues about who controls litigation and to whom a duty is owed by the attorney arise in cases where an insured is represented by an attorney, while the insurance company pays the bill. Case law recognizes that the attorney owes a fiduciary duty to both the insurance company and the insured, but may not compromise the fiduciary duty owed to the insured for the benefit of the insurance company. "We emphasize that the attorney who represents the insured owes him an undeviating allegiance whether compensated by the insurer or the insured and cannot act as an agent of the insurance company by supplying information detrimental to the insured." Farmers Ins. Co. of Arizona v. Veagnozzi, 675 P.2d 703, 708 (Ariz. 1983); accord Bogard v. Employers Casualty Co., 210 Cal. Rptr. 578, 582 (Cal. Dist. Ct. App. 1985). Furthermore, when the interests of the insurer and the insured are in direct conflict, the insurance company has a duty to pay for an independent attorney for the insured. Nandorf, Inc. v. CNA Ins. Cos.,

479 N.E.2d 988, 992 (Ill. App. Ct. 1985). Other courts have pointed out that the attorney hired by the insurer may even be required to advocate to the detriment of the insurer on behalf of the insured. Point Pleasant Canoe Rental v. Tinicum Township, 110 F.R.D. 166, 170 (E.D. Pa. 1986).

5. On occasion, an elder will take up with a younger friend or lover. Many times, the elder's relatives see this as a threat and a potential wasting of the elder's financial estate. See Alexander, On Being Imposed Upon by Artful or Designing Persons—The California Experience With the Involuntary Placement of the Aged, 14 SAN DIEGO L. REV. 1083 (1977) (The author suggests that the idea of protecting the elder from his new friend by depriving the elder of his autonomy may not always be a benefit to the elder.).

6. "Health care professionals often assume, logically, that family members are the most concerned about the patient and the most knowledgeable about the patient's values, wishes, and preferences. In some instances, however, this is not true." Kayser-Jones, *supra* note 1, at 355. A family member's "financial or emotional interests may conflict—consciously or subconsciously—with the preferences and best interests of the [elderly nursing home] resident. . . . [Such] potential conflicts of interest lead some to question the propriety of designating the family as substitute decision-maker for an incapacitated [nursing home] resident." *Id.* at 365.

7. Some elders are becoming more vocal and insistent upon their own autonomy and self-direction. These "wrinkled radicals" formed groups called the "gray panthers" and have taken an active role in shaping government policies in the 1970s and 1980s. See, e.g., [Kuhn, *What Old People Want for Themselves, in* ADVOC. & AGE 87 (1976).]

8. There can be a significant conflict between the need to protect an elder and the need to preserve the elder's freedom.

> Caught in the middle of this conflict is the attorney who is asked to represent the elder person. What is his or her role to be? The attorney must decide if it is to be that of a strong advocate for the "legal rights" of the client, or that of a "guardian" offering representation within the attorney's perception of the client's "best interests." The trial attorney who sees her or his selection to represent an elderly person as an opportunity to preserve or vindicate individual rights has a growing body of law and services with which to work.

Krauskoph, The Elderly Person, When Protection Becomes Abuse, 19 TRIAL 60, 61 (Dec. 1983).

9. See Hazard, Triangular Lawyer Relationships: An Exploratory Analysis, 1 GEO. J. LEGAL ETHICS 15 (1987) for a discussion of such relationships. Professor Hazard focuses on two types of triangular relationships:

> The first involves a client in a fiduciary relationship to a third party. The classic example is that of a lawyer representing a guardian in matters relating to the guardian's responsibilities to a ward . . . . The second type of triangular relationship involves a third party who owes fiduciary duties to the lawyer's client, and the third party rather than the client is the one with whom the lawyer deals ordinarily. The classic situation is that of a lawyer who represents a corporation but who, in the ordinary course of professional service, deals with the corporation's officers, directors, and employees.

Id. at 15–16.

One court has also described a relationship between an insurer, an insured, and counsel as a triangular relationship with both common and conflicting interests. San Diego Navy Fed. Credit U. v. Cumis, Ins., 208 Cal. Rptr. 494, 498 (Cal. Dist. Ct. App. 1984).

10. Rule 1.7. Conflict of Interest: General Rule.

> (a) A lawyer shall not represent a client if the representation of that client will be directly adverse to another client, unless:

(1) the lawyer reasonably believes the representation will not adversely affect the relationship with the other client; and
(2) each client consents after consultation.

(b) A lawyer shall not represent a client if the representation of that client may be materially limited by the lawyer's responsibilities to another client or to a third person, or by the lawyer's own interests, unless:

(1) the lawyer reasonably believes the representation will not be adversely affected; and
(2) the client consents after consultation. When representation of multiple clients in a single matter is undertaken, consultation shall include explanation of the implications of the common representation and the advantages and risks involved.

Rule 1.7.

11. Some courts have stated that an attorney violates a conflict of interest prohibition by assuming dual representation in cases even where a potential conflict is not obvious or actual. "A conflict of interest, moreover, need not be obvious or actual to create an ethical impropriety. The mere possibility of such a conflict at the outset of the relationship is sufficient to establish an ethical breach on the part of the attorney." Haynes v. First Nat'l Bank of New Jersey, 432 A.2d 890, 900 (N.J. 1981) (Troubles arose when an attorney represented beneficiaries under a will as well as the elder who drafted the will.).

12. Another potential scenario is where a relative alone approaches the attorney and requests the attorney to represent the non-present elder. The relative then pays the fee for the representation. The question arises whether the attorney may perform legal services for the elder, and if so, what steps the attorney should take. Again, Rules 1.8(f) and 5.4(c) set out restrictions on such an arrangement. In a similar situation, the American Bar Association identified some practical steps the attorney should take when asked to represent an absent client.

It seems to us that the lawyer-client relationship should be promptly established; and that in writing [the non-present client] you should advise her of the request that has come to you through [her friend] to make the investigation and perform certain legal services, and ask her to confirm this request. You should also advise [the non-present client] that [her friend] has asked you to send [the friend] a statement of your fee in the matter and ask if [the non-present client] approves this procedure and the payment of your fee by [the friend]. Incidentally, it would seem to the committee that you should have a clear understanding with [her friend] that she is to pay the fee, if this is the arrangement made.

ABA Comm. on Ethics and Professional Responsibility, Informal Op. 679 (1963).

13. Rule 1.9. Conflict of Interest: Former Client.

(a) A lawyer who has formerly represented a client in a matter shall not thereafter represent another person in the same or a substantially related matter in which that person's interests are materially adverse to the interests of the former client unless the former client consents after consultation.

(b) A lawyer shall not knowingly represent a person in the same or a substantially related matter in which a firm with which the lawyer formerly was associated had previously represented a client whose interests are materially adverse to that person and about whom the lawyer had acquired information protected by Rules 1.6 and 1.9(c) that is material to the matter, unless the former client consents after consultation.

(c) A lawyer who has formerly represented a client in a matter or whose present or former firm has formerly represented a client in a matter shall not thereafter:

(1) Use information relating to the representation to the disadvantage of the former client except as Rule 1.6 or Rule 3.3 would permit or require with respect to a client or when the information has become generally known; or
(2) Reveal information relating to the representation except as Rule 1.6 or Rule 3.3 would permit or require with respect to a client.

Rule 1.9.

14. In the types of cases that most frequently arise, generally the attorney will opt to represent the elder if possible. In such cases, to guard against dissenting family members or improper influences, the attorney should "[m]eet alone with the elderly client and talk directly with him about his wishes. The attorney should not rely exclusively on conversations with the client's family members, who may have different agendas. It is important to ask the client open-ended questions, not only ones that can be answered yes or no." Gilfix, *supra* note 1, at 52.

15. See Rule 1.7 comment.

16. See Rules 1.1, 1.3, 1.4, 1.5, 1.6, 2.1, & ch.3, respectively.

17. Attorneys who represent and advise elders are strongly encouraged to practice "elder law," a new legal specialty that covers the entire spectrum of legal issues that may face older Americans. It is very important to engage in preventative planning, and be aware of the beneficial uses of durable powers of attorneys, revocable trusts, as well as know the requirements of medicare and other public benefits. Gilfix, *supra* note 1, at 50.

18. This is so even when the elder's mental capacity may be somewhat diminished. Indeed, not only is the elder's right to make legal decisions entitled to deference, the same holds true for health care decisions. Authorities recognize that nursing home residents who suffer some degeneration of mental capacity still "remain capable, to differing degrees, of making, expressing, and effectuating medical treatment choices." Kayser-Jones, *supra* note 1, at 374. Attorneys must be very careful once they agree to represent the elder rather than the relative.

Children and families of older clients may hold ageist stereotypes. It is important that attorneys remember who the client is and not allow children, spouses, or others to speak for the older client. Interview the client privately and try to be sure the client is expressing his/her own wishes and has not been pressured by others. Be aware that a paternalistic attitude may lead to an attorney telling clients what they should or should not do and listening more to the family than the client.

Hommel, Counseling and Interviewing Techniques, 1986 ADVISING THE ELDERLY CLIENT at I-3 (Produced by the Committee on Continuing Legal Education of the State Bar of South Dakota).

19. Relatives do not always agree on the needs of the elder. See, e.g., Guardianship and Conservatorship of Sim, 403 N.W.2d 721 (Neb. 1987) (Certain relatives hid the elder from other relatives in direct violation of a court order. Each group of relatives asserted that it was acting in the elder's best interests.).

20. An attorney encounters special problems when he attempts to represent two entities or more at the same time. For example, where an attorney for a corporation enters into an attorney-client relationship with an employee of the corporation, and then attempts to represent the corporation in a later dispute against the employee, an impermissible conflict of interest arises and prohibits the attorney from representing the corporation against the employee. Humphrey v. McLaren, 402 N.W.2d 535, 540 (Minn. 1987).

21. See Rule 1.7. For example, if full disclosure is made to both parties, both parties agree to joint representation and both parties' interests are and remain aligned, then a lawyer may rep-

resent both an estate and a beneficiary of a conveyance from the estate against a creditor who alleges fraudulent conveyance. Ethics Committee of the State Bar of South Dakota, Op. 88-5 (1988).

The South Dakota Supreme Court also has addressed this issue.

> Thus, when an attorney represents more than one party to a lawsuit and obtains their consent after fully disclosing the applicable facts and consequences concerning the dual or multiple representation, no professional misconduct is involved.... The court may and should disqualify an attorney, however, from appearing in a case, or permit him to voluntarily withdraw, if he attempts to simultaneously represent clients with adverse interests.

Arcon Constr. Co. v. State, 314 N.W.2d 303, 307 (S.D. 1982).

22. See Rule 1.7. The reasons for the rule that prohibits attorneys from representing individuals with conflicting interests go to the heart of the attorney-client relationship, as well as the legal system.

> The duty not to represent conflicting interests . . . is an outgrowth of the attorney-client relationship itself, which is confidential, or fiduciary, in a broader sense. Not only do clients at times disclose confidential information to their attorney; they also repose confidence in them. The privilege is bottomed only on the first of these attributes, the conflicting-interest rule, on both.

Schmidt v. Pine Lawn Memorial Park, Inc., 198 N.W.2d 496, 498 (1972) (citing E.F. Hutton & Co. v. Brown, 305 F. Supp. 371 (S.D. Tex 1969)). The duty goes beyond protecting confidences, it goes to safeguarding the attorney-client relationship itself. The court recognized that if only confidential disclosures were protected, and courts failed to safeguard "the attorney-client relationship itself—a relationship which must be one of trust and reliance—they can only undermine the public's confidence in the legal system as a means for adjudicating disputes." *Id.* at 499 (citing E.F. Hutton).

23. "A lawyer cannot serve two masters in the same subject matter if their interests are or may become actually or potentially in conflict." Haynes, 432 A.2d at 899.

24. One court has recognized, however, that even where the parties do consent, there may still be problems in such representation. When two parties rely on one lawyer, trouble is ahead.

> [N]o matter how careful [the attorney] may be to explain [his or her] relationship to each of the parties, [the attorney is] advancing at [his or her] own peril. Where there is a potential conflict of interest between the parties, as is true in every domestic dispute, it is inappropriate to attempt to represent them both. This is true even where the parties appear to be in full accord at the time.

Blum v. Blum, 477 A.2d 289, 296 (Md. 1984).

With some legal problems, such as obtaining a guardianship over an elder, the inherent potential for conflict of interest is similar to the typical domestic relations case. Although the parties may initially agree, their perceptions can change as the proceedings progress. What initially seemed a simple and appropriate arrangement for care of the elderly person may metamorphose into a threat to the elder's autonomy and independence.

25. The failure to make a full and fair disclosure to all parties where a conflict of interest exists has resulted in a finding that an attorney is "an unfit person to be permitted to practice law" in South Dakota. In re Morrison, 178 N.W. 732, 733 (S.D. 1920).

26. Rule 1.7 comment (Consultation and Consent). The comment gives the example of a situation where one client refuses to consent to the disclosure necessary to permit the other client to make an informed decision.

27. Rule 2.2 provides:

(a) A lawyer may act as intermediary between clients if:

(1) the lawyer consults with each client concerning the implications of the common representation, including the advantages and risks involved, and the effect on the attorney-client privileges, and obtains each client's consent to the common representation;
(2) the lawyer reasonably believes that the matter can be resolved on terms compatible with the client's best interests, that each client will be able to make adequately informed decisions in the matter, and that there is little risk of material prejudice to the interests of any of the clients if the contemplated resolution is unsuccessful; and
(3) the lawyer reasonably believes that the common representation can be undertaken impartially and without improper effect on other responsibilities the lawyer has to any of the clients.

(b) While acting as intermediary, the lawyer shall consult with each client concerning the decisions to be made and the considerations relevant in making them, so that each client can make adequately informed decisions.

(c) A lawyer shall withdraw as intermediary if any of the clients so request, or if any of the conditions in paragraph (a) is no longer satisfied. Upon withdrawal, the lawyer shall not continue to represent any of the clients in the matter that was the subject of the intermediation.

Rule 2.2.

28. Rule 2.2 comment.

29. Rule 2.2 comment (Withdrawals).

30. Rule 2.2 comment (Consultation).

31. Rule 2.2 comment.

32. *Id.*

33. Rule 2.2(c). Again, the attorney would have to take steps to protect the interests of both parties prior to withdrawing. Rule 1.16(d) requires "[u]pon termination of representation, a lawyer shall takes steps to the extent reasonably practicable to protect a client's interests, such as giving reasonable notice to the client, allowing time for employment of other counsel, surrendering papers and property to which the client is entitled and refunding any advance payment of fee that has not been earned." Moreover, as noted previously when dealing with an elder who may be particularly dependent on the attorney, the attorney must take special steps to protect that individual's interests. Alaska Bar Association, Op. No. 87-2; In re Fraser, 523 P.2d 921.

34. The text of Rule 1.6 provides:

(a) A lawyer shall not reveal information relating to representation of a client unless the client consents after consultation, except for disclosures that are impliedly authorized in order to carry out the representation, and except as stated in paragraph (b).

(b) A lawyer may reveal such information to the extent that the lawyer reasonably believes necessary:

(1) to prevent the client from committing a criminal act that the lawyer believes is likely to result in imminent death or substantial bodily harm; or
(2) to established a claim or defense on behalf of the lawyer or the lawyer's employees in a controversy between the lawyer or the lawyer's employees and the client, to estab-

lish a defense to a criminal charge or a civil claim against the lawyer or the lawyer's employees based upon conduct in which the lawyer was involved, or to respond to allegations in any proceeding concerning the lawyer or the lawyer's employees' representation of the client; or

(3) to the extent that revelation appears to be necessary to rectify the consequences of a client's criminal or fraudulent act in which the lawyer's services had been used.

Rule 1.6.

35. Hazard, *supra* note 9, at 22 (The duty of confidentiality prohibits the lawyer from revealing anything about the client's affairs to anyone else—even the client's family—except as necessary to carry out endeavors on the client's behalf.).

36. One commentator recognizes a significant dilemma in this regard. "Another dilemma may arise if the attorney believes his client is quickly losing his mental capacity and may endanger both his assets and health. How much of the confidential conversation with a client should the attorney relay to other family members?" Gilfix, *supra* note 1, at 52.

37. A particularly touchy area relates to an elder's intent to commit suicide. If suicide is not a crime in the state, then there is no ethical requirement that explicitly requires the attorney to disclose the elder's intent. In South Dakota, for example, attempted suicide is no longer a crime, but aiding and abetting suicide is a crime. See S.D.C.L. §§ 22-16-36 to 40 (1988). Nonetheless, the attorney must disclose the client's intent to commit suicide. ABA Comm. on Ethics and Professional Responsibility, Informal Op. 83-1500 (1983). The ABA relies upon the Model Rules of Professional Conduct, which provide that "a lawyer may seek the appointment of a guardian or take other protective action with respect to a client, only when the lawyer reasonably believes that the client cannot adequately act in the client's own interests." *Id.* at 2. Similar ethical opinions have been issued by the New York State Bar Association and the Massachusetts Bar Association. *Id.* at 1–2.

38. According to one commentator, "[c]ommunications and confidential information concerning [joint clients] would be governed by the rule as to 'confidences and secrets' among multiple clients. In general, a lawyer engaged in multiple representation may not withhold from one of the clients confidences and secrets that have been obtained from or on behalf of the other." Hazard, *supra* note 9, at 27–28.

39. Rule 2.2 comment (Confidentiality and Privilege).

40. Although the duty of confidentiality is of critical importance, the considerations that a lawyer must weigh before agreeing to assist both family members transcend the mere duty of confidentiality. Assuming, arguendo, that confidentiality does not become an issue, the attorney must consistently face the question whether the attorney-client relationship, itself a relationship that must be one of trust and reliance, is undermined by dual representation. See Schmidt, 198 N.W.2d 496.

41. Rule 1.14 comment.

42. Rule 1.2(d).

43. For an interesting and careful analysis of the duties flowing between guardian, ward, and the attorney representing the guardian and/or ward, see Hazard, *supra* note 9. In this article, Professor Hazard discusses the nature of the duty owed to a ward by the attorney for the guardian. Analysis is focused on the result of the case Fickett v. Superior Court, 558 P.2d 988 (Ariz. 1976), in which it was held that an attorney was liable for failing to use reasonable care to discover misappropriation, conversion, and improper investment by a guardian. Hazard, *supra* note 9, at 17. Consequently, the duty of confidentiality owed to a guardian is ob-

scured by the guardian's duty to the ward and the lawyer's duty to the institution of "guardianship" as opposed to the individual who acts as a guardian.

44.

> Dementia, a general mental deterioration of psychobiologic etiology, is the major psychiatric disorder of older age. Some form or severity of dementing illness affects approximately 10–15 percent of older adults. Chronic organic brain syndromes, presumably secondary to senile dementia, in most cases, affect 58 percent of the more than one million Americans in nursing homes. Approximately 50–60 percent of older people with dementia are thought to suffer Senile Dementia of the Alzheimer's Type (SDAT).

Rosoff, *supra* note 1, at 6.

45. It is extremely important that an attorney's considerations about an elderly client's potential capacity not be tainted by stereotypes or the attorney's own attitudes about aging and motivation. "Examination of one's own attitudes about aging and motivations and interactions with older clients is an important first step in being able to work effectively with older persons." Hommel, *supra* note 18, at I-2. Ms. Hommel identifies "a number of commonly-held myths and stereotypes based on the presumptions that old people are alike." *Id.* These stereotypes include:

- that chronological aging determines physical, mental, and emotional status;
- that the old are unproductive;
- that they prefer to disengage from life;
- that they are inflexible;
- that they are senile and forgetful; and
- that old age is a sign of senility.

Id.

According to Ms. Hommel, however,:

> there appears to be no such thing as a typical experience of old age, nor the typical older person. At no point in one's life does a person stop being himself and suddenly turn into an old person . . . . The reality is that, in the absence of disease or accident, older persons do not differ significantly from their younger cohorts. Also, in the absence of disease, older people continue to maintain a high level of intellectual functioning, do not become forgetful and do not have reduced attention spans. Often behavior that may be labeled 'senile' is merely the manifestation of such things as over-medication or inappropriate combination of medications, malnutrition, unrecognized physical illness, or emotional anxiety or depression.

Id. at I-2 & I-3.

46. Rule 1.14. Client Under A Disability.

> (a) When a client's ability to make adequately considered decisions in connection with the representation is impaired, whether because of minority, mental disability or for some other reason, the lawyer shall, as far as reasonably possible, maintain a normal client-lawyer relationship with the client.
>
> (b) A lawyer may seek the appointment of a guardian or take other protective action with respect to a client, only when the lawyer reasonably believes that the client cannot adequately act in the client's own interests.

Rule 1.14.

47. "A lawyer sometimes must determine whether an older person seeking legal assistance is competent to enter into the client-lawyer relationship. Most lawyers have the burden of making this determination without the benefit of special training or qualifications.

It has been suggested that where a prospective (or existing) client's competence is questioned, the lawyer might look to definitions of competence used by the medical profession in its determination of a patient's ability to provide informed consent to medical care." Kogut, Professional Responsibility and Representing Older Persons With Diminished Competence, 67 MICH. BAR. J. 1118, 1120 (1988).

48. Rule 1.14 comment. Not all dementia is immediate. For example, "Alzheimer's Disease may impose a slow process of deterioration, first impairing only short-term memory and concentration while sparing long-term memory, values, convictions, and personality." Rosoff, *supra* note 1, at 7. Because of the differing degrees of illness and stages of illness, "the process of removing one's legal autonomy must be closely scrutinized." *Id.*

49. Guardianship-type assistance for the mentally incapacitated begin formally "with the enactment of the statute de Praerogativa regis sometime between 1255 and 1290. This statute dealt with the mentally ill, classified as idiots (those who were born with 'no understanding') and lunatics (who had been born with understanding but had 'lost the use of reason')." Regan, Protective Services for the Elderly: Commitment, Guardianship, and Alternatives, 13 WM. & MARY L. REV. 569, 570 (1972). The English system only protected the mentally disabled elderly who were wealthy. The poor were left to their own families' resources. *Id.* at 571. Early Colonial America followed the same pattern of laws. Individuals who lacked assets and families "joined with the itinerant poor to form transient bands drifting from town to town . . . . The mentally disabled and elderly who could not work wandered aimlessly about the countryside seeking out an existence by begging." *Id.* In early America, those mentally ill persons who became violent were generally sent to a "public jail, workhouse, poor house, or to a private pen, cage, or strong room." *Id.* at 571–72. The first mental hospital in America was erected in 1773 at Williamsburg, Virginia. The second mental hospital was not erected until 1824 at Lexington, Kentucky. *Id.* at 572. The procedure to obtain a guardianship was "frighteningly simple." "All that was necessary was for a relative, a friend-or perhaps an enemy-to apply to one of the managers or physicians for an order of admission. A few words hastily scribbled on a chance piece of paper (such as Jas Sproul is a proper person for the Pennsylvania hospital), and signed by one of the physicians, and the deed was done." *Id.*

50. A.B.A. YOUNG LAWYERS DIVISION, COMMITTEE ON DELIVERY OF LEGAL SERVICES, COMPETENCY AND CONSENT TO MENTAL HEALTH TREATMENT (1988) [hereinafter COMPETENCY AND CONSENT].

51. Elder law specialists recommend that an attorney focus on "the client's remaining competence" and not solely on the client's obvious limitations. For example, the attorney should plan to schedule meetings with elderly clients at times when the client appears to be most cognizant, not at a time of the day when the elderly client may be tired or unable to concentrate. Gilfix, *supra* note 1, at 51–52.

52. COMPETENCY AND CONSENT, *supra* note 50, at 6.

53. [ABA/BNA LAWYERS MANUAL ON PROFESSIONAL CONDUCT 31:602 (1984) (hereinafter MANUAL)] at 605 (citing Frolick, Plenary Guardianship: An Analysis, a Critique, and a Proposal for Reform, 23 ARIZ. L. REV. 599, 633–37 (1981)).

54. *Id.* (citing Blinick, Mental Disability, Legal Ethics, and Professional Responsibility, 33 ALB. L. REV. 92, 115 (1968)).

55. *Id.* (citing Luban, Paternalism in the Legal Profession, 1981 WIS. L. REV. 454, 493).

56. *Id.* at 606 (citing Genden, Separate Legal Representation for Children: Protecting the Rights and Interests of Minors in Judicial Proceedings, 11 HARV. C.R.-C.L. L. REV., 565, 588–89 (1976)).

57. In South Dakota, individuals are given a fairly broad latitude in their perception of reality when it comes to deciding competence to make a testamentary disposition of property. It is not sufficient to defeat testamentary capacity to show a belief, for example, in spiritualism. "[A] belief in spiritualism, however strong, is not in itself an evidence of insanity, and . . . an insane delusion, to be fatal to the validity of a will, must be operative in the testamentary act. Whether religious views, commonly entertained by a considerable number of persons, are true or false is not a subject for judicial inquiry." Irwin v. Lattin, 135 N.W. 759, 763 (S.D. 1912).

Likewise, the belief in an afterlife is not of itself "evidence of an insane delusion or of monomania." *Id.* On the other hand, when such a religious belief begins to result in delusions that guide and "control the testator in the disposition of property" such may constitute undue influence or show lack of testamentary capacity. *Id.* The court stated:

> [A] testator may make what others may regard as a foolish, unjust, or unusual will, and still not be vulnerable to a charge of insanity or lack of testamentary capacity, for the reason that the existence of the right to dispose of property by will is not made dependent upon judicious exercise of the right itself. But where a testator is possessed of an insane delusion which controls the testamentary act, and leads him to dispose of his property under the coercion of such delusion, the act cannot be said to be that of a sane mind. Or to put in another manner, "Law,' it is said, 'is of the earth, earthy,' and that spirit wills are too celestial for cognizance by earthly tribunals—a proposition readily conceded. And yet the courts have not assumed to deny to spirits of the departed the privilege of holding communion with those of their friends who are still in the flesh, so long as they do not interfere with vested rights, or by means of undue influence seek to prejudice the interests of persons still within our jurisdiction.'

Id. (emphasis in original).

58. COMPETENCY AND CONSENT, *supra* note 50, at 6 n.8.

59. American Bar Association Committee on Ethics and Professional Responsibility, Informal Op. 83-1500 (1983).

CHAPTER 46

Representing the Incapacitated Client

Some older clients exhibit signs of diminished mental capacity. What is the proper response for the lawyer when faced with a client whose mental ability appears to be impaired? Professor Smith considers that problem in her article.

Linda F. Smith

Representing the Elderly Client and Addressing the Question of Competence

* * *

III. Legal Standards for Representing the Client of Questionable Competence

The attorney who comes to doubt her client's competence should know the legal standards that address competence. First, there may be competence standards incorporated into the substantive law that apply to the legal action the client wishes to take. The attorney should also know the standards for appointment of a guardian or other representative for an incompetent person. Finally, the attorney with a questionably

Journal of Contemporary Law, Vol. 14, 61 (1988). Reprinted by permission.

competent client must understand the applicable code of ethics. Both the Model Rules of Professional Conduct and the Model Code of Professional Responsibility will be discussed here.

This article will argue that both the Model Rules and the Model Code fail to offer adequate guidance for the lawyer in the "unavoidably difficult . . . position" of representing a client whose competence is in doubt.[1] It will analyze the weaknesses of these ethical guides. Finally, this article will propose more specific standards for representing the questionably competent client which are consistent with both the Model Rules and Model Code and which maximize client independence and autonomy.

A. Substantive Law

The attorney must be mindful of the standards of competence incorporated in the substantive law. For instance, there are legal standards of competency for executing a will,[2] marrying,[3] entering into a contract,[4] being tried for a crime,[5] and so on. These standards will govern a client's particular legal action.

If the client's competence is open to question, the attorney should interview and advise the client with the applicable legal standard in mind.[6] She may need to gather extrinsic evidence of the client's competence to take the proposed legal action by, for example, seeking a professional opinion about the client's competence.[7] When the attorney concludes that the client is competent to undertake the proposed action, the lawyer may wish to make a record demonstrating the client's competence. The lawyer should get a signed statement or report from an expert who determines that the client is competent. The lawyer should also preserve evidence of competence from lay witnesses. It may sometimes be appropriate to make a record of the client's demonstrated competence (e.g., to obtain the client's handwritten letter describing his considerations in making his will.).[8]

If the lawyer believes that the client is not competent to undertake the action he desires, the lawyer must consult the applicable ethical guides and substantive law about protective actions. In different circumstances it may be appropriate for the attorney to advise the client about this problem,[9] delay legal action until legal competence has returned,[10] or seek appointment of a guardian *ad litem* or other representative.[11]

* * *

C. Ethical Codes

The Model Rules[12] and the Model Code[13] directly address representing the client "under a disability." Yet neither the Model Rules nor the Model Code provide clear comprehensive guidance for the attorney representing such a client. Both the Model Rules and the Model Code are exhortatory in encouraging the attorney to maintain as normal an attorney-client relationship as possible.[14] Both are permissive in allowing the attorney broad discretion to act for her client when necessary.[15]

The Model Rules explicitly permit, but do not command, the lawyer to "seek the appointment of a guardian" for her incompetent client.[16] The attorney may take such protective action "only when the lawyer reasonably believes that the client cannot adequately act in the client's own interest."[17] The Model Rules Comments go on to suggest that in some circumstances the lawyer should forego seeking a guardian for her incompetent client because to do so may cause more harm than it prevents.[18]

The Model Code and Model Rules are ultimately unsatisfying guides for the attorney representing a questionably competent client. They fail to tell the attorney how she should determine whether her client is unable to adequately act in his own interests.[19] They permit a broad range of behavior in representing the client under a disability, from seeking a guardian for the client, to acting as *de facto* guardian, to accepting the decisions of the client as one must in the normal attorney-client relationship. Yet except for the permission to seek a guardian for the apparently incompetent client who would benefit thereby, and the approval of a broad utilitarian approach, neither set of standards indicates what approach is appropriate under particular circumstance. When it may be permissible for the attorney to make decisions on behalf of her client, neither the Model Code nor the Model Rules explains how the attorney should go about doing so. For example, they make no distinction between acting on behalf of a client whose instructions are ambiguous or confused and acting contrary to the expressed wishes of a client who seems eccentric.

1. *Critique and Interpretation of the Model Code and Model Rules.* One reason that the Model Code and Model Rules are confusing is that competence to undertake particular legal actions, competence as a client, and legal disqualification are all discussed simultaneously as if they were one issue. Another confusing aspect it that the Model Code and Model Rules combine the discussion about representing the client of limited or questionable competence with directions for representing a client who is clearly and completely incompetent. It is necessary to untangle these different threads before focusing upon the most difficult issue: how to represent the client whose competence as a client is in doubt.

The Model Code and the Model Rules simultaneously discuss a client's legal competence to undertake certain actions and the client's competence as a client. The Comments to Model Rule 1.14 recognize that one risk the lawyer faces is that the incompetent client "may have no power to make legally binding decisions."[20] The Code states that "obviously a lawyer cannot perform any act which the law requires his client to perform."[21] Yet, Comments to Model Rule 1.14 also suggest that a limited client "often has the ability to understand, deliberate upon, and reach conclusions about matters affecting the client's own well-being."[22] The Ethical Considerations of the Model Code similarly suggests that a client who "is legally disqualified from performing certain acts"[23] may be "capable of understanding the matter in question or of contributing to the advancement of his interests."[24] These statements suggest that there may be a "legally disqualified" client who is not actually incompetent. Such legally disqualified but not actually incompetent clients would include minor children who are old enough to express preferences and to make considered choices about the legal issue confronting them. The attorney representing such a capable minor can and should treat him like any other client and be guided by his desires.[25] Presumably, the attorney for the elderly client should not be faced with this situation. If the elderly client is actually competent to make decisions but legally disqualified, because a guardian has previously been appointed, the attorney should seek to remove the guardian and to have the client's decision-making rights restored.

Similarly, the Model Rules and the Model Code simultaneously address the client's capacity to undertake certain legal acts and the client's ability to make adequately considered decisions in connection with the representation.[26] However, the existence of an issue of legal competence to undertake a particular transaction should have no necessary effect upon the attorney-client relationship.[27] The attorney should advise the client about the potential problem and the ways to address it.[28] The attorney should abide by the client's decision unless she concludes that the client is unable to adequately make decisions about the problem.

Finally, the Model Code and Model Rules Comments simultaneously address representing the client whose competence may be questioned[29] and representing the client who is either legally disqualified or clearly and completely incompetent.[30] Unfortunately, most of the discussion focuses upon the totally incompetent or legally disqualified client, and very little of the discussion addresses the impaired or questionably competent client. Yet the totally incompetent client (e.g., an infant, a person in a coma) presents the lawyer with few dilemmas. The totally incompetent person who is unable to act in his own interests obviously cannot initiate an attorney-client relationship. Hence the lawyer never becomes this person's lawyer. When the client does establish the relationship with the lawyer and then becomes totally incompetent, as when an existing client becomes comatose, the lawyer should not hesitate to seek the appointment of a guardian unless the client's competence might return before legal action is necessary. It is the client of questionable competence who poses the most difficult problem for the lawyer. This client is sufficiently able to act in his own interests to establish an attorney-client relationship, but then appears to act in ways which seem adverse to his interests. This causes the lawyer to doubt the client's competence. It is such a client whose interests may be harmed by the attorney raising the issue of competence and seeking a guardian for her client.[31]

2. *Proposal for Ethically Representing the Client of Questionable Competence.* Although the Model Rules and Model Code seem to sanction a range of approaches in representing the client of questionable competence, not all approaches are equally respectful of the client's independence and right to self-determination. The authoritative texts[32] of the Model Rules themselves and of the Model Code's Disciplinary Rules emphasize the client's right to direct his legal affairs[33] and the lawyer's obligation to try to maintain this "normal client-lawyer relationship" even with the impaired client.[34] This emphasis is consistent with viewing the attorney as agent and the client as principal and therefore the decision-maker.[35] It is consistent with the doctrine of informed consent which might be properly applied to lawyer-client relations and decision-making.[36] Therefore, respect for the impaired client's right to decide should be the attorney's guiding principle.

The Model Rules and Model Code should be understood to require the attorney to pursue a process of investigation and client-counseling adjusted to maximize the impaired client's decision-making abilities. The attorney should not assume the role of "*de facto* guardian" to act against the client's express wishes or instructions. Only when the client's directions are conflicting, confused, or ambiguous can the attorney be justified in making decisions on behalf of the client.

* * *

When the attorney questions the competence of such a client, she may seek assistance from mental health professionals, rely upon principles of risk analysis, and investigate the client's goals, values, and interests. She should engage in a process of "gradual counseling" to assist the client in reaching a decision or to permit the attorney to infer a decision. During this process and any period of uncertainty about the client's competence, the attorney may make any necessary decisions on behalf of her client which maximize the client's options or which can be inferred from the client's values and goals. At the conclusion of the "gradual counseling" process, the client should have made or the attorney inferred a decision. If not, the attorney will have a reasonable and informed belief that the client "cannot adequately act in [his] own interests."[37] At that point the attorney is justified in seeking the appointment of a guardian for her client.

IV. Reaching a Decision with the Limited Client

* * *

A. Expert Evaluations of Competence

When the attorney questions her client's competence to make decisions about her representation, the first impulse may be to have a medical or mental health professional assess the client's competence.[38] However, this approach has drawbacks and should generally be employed only after the attorney has attempted to understand the client's problem and goals herself.

Calling an expert may suggest to the client that he appears incompetent. This will not only harm the attorney's rapport with the client, but may well cause the client significant upset.[39] It may be possible, however, to have an expert assess the client in the normal course of that expert's dealings with the client, as when the client is hospitalized or in a nursing home. This should avoid the worst results of seeking an expert assessment.

The attorney should also realize that some mental health professionals will merely give diagnostic conclusions which may not be related to the client's functional ability.[40] Such diagnostic information will be of little help to the attorney trying to work with a limited client. If the attorney does ask an expert to evaluate her client's competence, she should be certain that the expert (and any forensic instrument that he may use) addresses relevant competencies.[41] Without a request for precise evaluation, the examiner will probably only test for general competence. While a determination of general competence also affirms a capacity to make specific decisions, test results which indicate general incompetency do not prove incompetency with respect to any specific task.[42]

* * *

It is during the counseling process when the attorney may begin to doubt her client's competence. Sometimes doubts may arise because the client chooses a course of action that seems odd, unwise, or even harmful. The client may completely change his mind about what he wants or may regularly redefine "the problem" that he wants the attorney to address. The client's choice may be at variance with strongly expressed values. The client may seem disinterested or extremely indecisive about the choice. The client may appear unduly dependent, willing to agree to anything the attorney recommends, or totally influenced by some other individual.

Whenever doubts about the competence of a client's decision arise, the lawyer should look behind the perceived "problem" to see if the decision could be rational and informed.[43] In order to do this, she will need to consider her understanding of the client's values, the client's unique life circumstances, and her own values and possible prejudices. The attorney for the limited client should engage the client in a process of gradual decision-making which will involve clarification, reflection, feedback, and further investigation.

Psychological research indicates that one should investigate values and engage in "gradual counseling" when there are questions about competency. A person's decision-making ability may be influenced by psychodynamic factors, including his relationship with the person advising him,[44] and by the method in which information is presented and choices explained.[45] When the advisor calmly discusses the problem and choices, the decision-maker is helped and perhaps even taught to make a reasoned decision.[46] If the advisor can understand and enunciate the person's underlying concerns, the person may be helped to make a difficult choice.[47]

* * *

C. Inferring a Decision Using Risk Analysis and Substituted Judgment

In some cases, the limited client may be unable to enunciate a clear choice even after "gradual counseling" by his attorney. In those cases, the lawyer is justified in making certain decisions on behalf of the client.[48] This article proposes that the attorney may make such interim decisions based upon certain risk analysis principles. The lawyer should be permitted to make even an ultimate decision as a substituted judgment for the client when a decision can be inferred from the client's expressed values. This article also reviews other models for deciding on behalf of the impaired client. Finally, it is argued that in most cases in which an attorney must decide on behalf of a client, including deciding as a court-appointed guardian, the attorney should attempt to make a "substituted judgment" based upon the client's values.

1. *Risk Analysis.* The lawyer should employ certain risk analysis principles in counseling and making interim decisions for a client of questionable competence. One

decision-making principle is "reversibility . . . [choosing] alternatives that offer some chance of benefit and no loss if the hoped-for gains do not materialize."[49] Where choosing one alternative will not preclude other avenues (e.g., an appeal of Medicaid termination can always be discontinued and initiating litigation does not preclude negotiation) the attorney is justified in pursuing the "reversible" decision where the client has been unable to decide and immediate action is required. Such action leaves the client (or his future representative) free to confirm or reject the lawyer's choice thereafter.

In order to minimize risks, many decisions should be based on the most conservative and safest interpretation rather than the most probably correct (the principle of "conservation").[50] Again, for the interim decisions which must be made before the limited client can be fully counseled, the attorney should follow this principle. The attorney may also properly present the options mandated by these principles to the client as plans he will pursue rather than choices the client must make.

2. *Substituted Judgment.* There are a variety of views about how decisions should be made in the face of the client's inability to decide. Approaches for making decisions on behalf of a client include following the client's expressed instructions, promoting what the attorney believes is in the person's "best interests," taking an "advocacy" position to retain the greatest freedom for the client, relying upon the family for direction, and making a "substituted judgment" to do what the particular client would most likely have wished. While each approach has certain merits, the attorney for the limited elderly client should engage in gradual counseling and be prepared to make a "substituted judgment" for the client who is not competent to act in his own interests.

One approach is simply to comply with any expressed decision of a client. Attorneys may be more willing to do this when the decision is merely eccentric rather than when it may be harmful. Following the client's expressed decision seems to respect the client's independence and individuality. Yet accepting that decision without understanding how and why it was made utterly fails to respect the individuality of the limited client. It is tantamount to requiring the limited client to meet the standards of the fully competent client in making and expressing decisions or live with the consequences. Accordingly, where the attorney has reason to believe that a client's decision may not encompass the client's true goals, she should not blindly accept it. Instead, the lawyer should engage in the gradual counseling process to ensure that the decision the client makes is an informed expression of the client's desires.

Some attorneys operate under a "best interests" standard[51] and pursue the remedy that they believe is best for the client. Many attorneys who are appointed to represent juveniles take this tack. They determine what custody arrangement they think is best for the child and advocate that, even ignoring the child's contrary requests.[52] The best interests approach treats the limited individual as totally dependent and does nothing to promote a normal attorney-client relationship. The "best interests" standard is most appropriate for very young children who have no capacity to make or contribute to decisions.[53] They also have no life history from which "known or reasonably presumed desires" can be inferred to arrive at a "substituted judgment."[54] The "best interests" test, which involves making a "reasonable decision,"[55] might also be the appropriate standard when one alternative carries with it severe consequences and the other alternative offers some hope and little risk.[56]

Another approach is the advocacy rule in which the attorney takes the position that gives her client the most freedom.[57] Such advocacy is required of the court-appointed attorney in a civil commitment case in many jurisdictions.[58] Similarly, some courts have indicated that an advocacy approach is appropriate in providing criminal defense to those of limited competence.[59] The advocacy approach is justified where two advocates will be representing contrary views before an impartial decision-maker. In some representation of the elderly (e.g., defense against appointment of a guardian),[60] it may be appropriate to adopt the advocacy approach when the client is incapable of giving the attorney directions. However, where one course of action will not clearly guarantee greater freedom from restraint, or where both positions are not adequately represented, the advocacy approach is difficult to justify.[61]

A variation of the advocacy approach is playing the "devil's advocate" by probing and questioning all aspects of the situation.[62] The attorney does not take one position, but presents all relevant evidence and questions the credibility of all evidence in order to assist the court. Such "devil's advocacy" avoids the worst faults of the advocacy approach. Nevertheless, its usefulness is limited to cases in litigation.

A third approach which has found support lately, emphasizes relying upon the client's family for direction.[63] In dealing with minor children the law assumes that parents act in the best interests of their children. Therefore, the fit parent has broad authority to make decisions for a minor in many spheres of life (e.g., education,[64] medical treatment,[65] mental health hospitalization).[66] Similarly, the family of an elderly person will often know his interests better than anyone else and will usually have his best interests at heart.[67]

Nevertheless, relying upon the family to make decisions for the client can create problems. In some cases, the family members may have conflicts of interests (e.g., when the appointment of one relative as a conservator or the distribution of assets to family members is at issue). In other situations, the interested family members might simply disagree about what is the best course of action.

Simply consulting family members could violate ethical rules against disclosing confidential information without the client's authorization.[68] Therefore, the attorney should ask her client for permission before consulting a relative about a decision.[69] Alternatively, it may be possible to ask the family about the client's previously expressed intent without revealing any client confidences. Finally, the attorney may be justified in revealing confidential information under Model Rule 1.14 where it is not "reasonably possible" to maintain the normal counseling relationship and when the client's interests require such disclosure.[70]

A second problem with relying upon the family is that the attorney may not ethically allow anyone other than the client to direct her handling of the case.[71] However, a client might agree that a trusted relative will know best, and consent that the attorney be guided by that relative's opinion or decision. This would be appropriate primarily where the trusted relative has no personal conflict of interest in the legal matter. Given that a client may make the informed decision to defer to his attorney's judgment in any particular matter, there should be no reason why the limited client's reasoned decision to rely upon the opinion of a trusted relative should not be respected by the attorney.

There is one final potential benefit of consulting family members to reach a decision for the limited or incompetent client. "Where close, loving, intimate relationships exist, [a relative's decisions] . . . based on her understanding of [the client's] . . . interest do embody respect for his autonomy."[72] This is so because the client's sense of self involves his belief that his loved ones will care for and do what is best for him when he is incapable of doing for himself. By deferring to the decision of such a loving relative, the attorney may come closest to what the client would have chosen. Such deference may also promote a personal relationship that is important and beneficial to the client. Thus, the strongest argument for allowing the family to decide is the same argument for making a substituted judgment. The family will be most likely to know what the client would have wanted.

Making a "substituted judgment" requires the lawyer to imagine the way in which the limited or incompetent individual would decide the issue if he were competent to decide it. Courts have applied a "substituted judgment" standard in making crucial life decisions about the medical treatment of incompetent individuals. In doing so they look to the individual's previously stated desires and values,[73] his present behavior,[74] and the opinions of loving, concerned relatives about what the incompetent's preferences would probably be.[75] The rationale behind "substituted judgment" is to carry on the individual's life plan, even though the individual is presently unable to express it.[76] In this way, the standard confirms the individual's right to be treated as unique and worthy of respect despite present incapacity. Courts have looked to this standard in some recent and thoughtful decisions involving terminating artificial life support mechanisms,[77] declining procedures to prolong but not save life,[78] permitting organ donation by a limited person,[79] and mandating medication of psychotic patients.[80]

The "substituted judgment" standard has many benefits for the attorney representing the questionably competent elderly client. The elderly client will have led a life in which certain values were promoted or respected. Often the elderly client many have spoken about issues that are relevant to the decision at hand. He may have various friends and family members who can recall his stated intentions or important values. In these ways, the elderly client is unlike the incompetent child or the never-competent retarded person who has no past life plan from which a present or future decision can be inferred.[81]

The "substituted judgment" standard was developed to make decisions for totally and permanently incompetent persons. However, making a substituted judgment is perhaps even more appropriate for the client whose competence is only questionable or who may be temporarily incompetent. If the attorney relies upon a "substituted judgment" guide when she is not certain that the client has understood and freely decided the issue, she will be more likely to handle the case in the way the client wishes. The attorney will be less likely to have to undo what she has done for the client when the client is better able to assess the situation. For the limited client, even more than for the incompetent client, applying a "substituted judgment" standard is important in order to respect the client's individuality and right to self-determination.

The "substituted judgment" standard is also the only standard that makes sense of the Model Rules and Model Code's grant of permission to act as *de facto* guardian for the client when necessary. The conflict between deciding on behalf of a limited client and trying to maintain a normal attorney-client relationship is largely eliminated when the attorney applies a "substituted judgment" standard for decision-making. Using a "substituted judgment" standard makes the Model Rules and Model Code more intelligible and appropriately deferential to client autonomy. The standard simply authorizes the attorney to continue to seek what she thinks to be the client's intended goals through what she believes to be the client's approved means, even when she is not entirely certain what the client has competently "decided."

One very important benefit of operating under a "substituted judgment" standard is that it encourages the attorney to respect her client's individuality and right to self-determination. If the attorney is free to follow an apparently incompetent decision, or to apply a "best interests" standard, there is no encouragement to try to understand the difficult-to-understand client. However, where gradual counseling and the "substitute judgment" standard are used to decide questions for the client, the attorney must spend time with the client exploring the values and goals that would make one decision better for the client than another. If the attorney practices gradual counseling to help the client decide, she may learn which goals and values are most important to the client. Even when the client cannot express a "decision," the attorney may be able to infer one from this information. The line separating an "inferred decision" from a "substituted judgment" is a very unclear one. The attorney who prepares to make a "substituted judgment" for her limited client may find that the client has made a reasoned decision himself.

Finally, the process of inquiring about the client's values and goals in order to engage in gradual decision-making or to apply an individual "substituted judgment" can have a very positive psychological benefit for the limited elderly client. One important and unfortunate aspect of aging is loss. Many elderly have lost some physical health and vitality, many have lost spouses and others important to them, many have lost some ability to care for themselves or their belongings. The limited elderly person may well miss the control that he previously exercised over his own life. Accordingly, it may be very important to help the elderly individual exercise control over his legal affairs to the maximum extent possible. Inquiring after the elderly client's preferences, values, and goals can reaffirm his validity and importance as an autonomous person. Assisting the elderly client to exercise maximum control and make decisions on legal matters can be both empowering and therapeutic.

* * *

Notes

1. MODEL RULES OF PROFESSIONAL CONDUCT Rule 1.14 comment 5 (1983) [hereinafter MODEL RULES].

2. Testamentary capacity requires a general and related understanding of "the nature and extent of . . . [one's], property, . . . [t]he persons who are the natural objects of . . . [one's] bounty, and . . . [t]he disposition which . . . [one] is making of his property, . . . [and the] format[ion of] an orderly desire as to the disposition of [one's] property." T. ATKINSON, LAW OF WILLS, § 52, at 232 (2d ed. 1953). "An insane delusion is a false belief, which is the product of a diseased mind . . . adhere[d to] against evidence and reason." *Id.* at 242. It may invalidate a will if "[i]t affects the disposition. Mere eccentricities, prejudices or unusual religious beliefs do by themselves constitute insane delusions . . . ." *Id.*

3. The test of mental competence to marry generally turns upon one's "capacity to understand the nature of the contract, and the duties and responsibilities which it creates." H. CLARK, LAW OF DOMESTIC RELATIONS § 2.15, at 96 (1968) (quoting Durham v. Durham, 10 P.D. 80, 82 (1885)).

4. A contract may be voidable if the "party does not understand the nature and consequences of his act at the time of the transaction . . . [or] if the party 'by reason of mental illness of defect . . . is unable to act in a reasonable manner in relation to the transaction and the other party has reason to know of this condition.'" J. CALAMARI & J. PERILLO, THE LAW OF CONTRACTS § 8-10, at 250–51 (2d ed. 1977) (quoting RESTATEMENT (SECOND) OF CONTRACTS § 18C).

5. A criminal defendant is competent to stand trial if he "has sufficient present ability to consult with his lawyer with a reasonable degree of rational understanding . . . and . . . has a rational as well as factual understanding of the proceedings against him . . ." W. LAFAVE & I. ISRAEL, CRIMINAL PROCEDURE § 20.4, at 802–03 (1985) (quoting Dusky v. United States, 362 U.S. 402 (1960)).

6. [Note omitted.]

7. [Omitted.] Of course, the attorney should obtain the client's permission before revealing any confidential information to others.

8. *See* Gilfix, *Advising Aging Clients,* 6 CAL. LAWYER No. 9, 50, 52 (1986). On the other hand, there may be a tactical disadvantage to creating any "special" evidence of competence in that its creation raises the issue of competence. When the ill client is called upon to demonstrate competence, as in a videotaped interview, the client may be made even more confused and appear less competent on tape than he is in actuality. *Id.*

9. For example, the attorney may need to suggest to the criminal defendant that an argument of incapacity to stand trial may be called for.

10. The attorney might delay the execution of a will until the client's competence returns.

11. The lawyer may need to seek the appointment of a guardian *ad litem* when the client becomes incompetent during the course of on-going litigation.

12. [MODEL RULES OF PROFESSIONAL CONDUCT Rule 1.14 comment 5 (1983) (hereinafter MODEL RULES).]

13. MODEL CODE OF PROFESSIONAL RESPONSIBILITY, EC 7-11, 7-12 (1980) [hereinafter MODEL CODE].

14. MODEL RULES 1.14(a) provides: "When a client's ability to make adequately considered decisions . . . is impaired . . . the lawyer shall, as far as reasonably possible, maintain a normal

client-lawyer relationship with the client." The MODEL CODE similarly suggests in EC 7-12 that when a client under a disability "is capable of understanding the matter in question or of contributing to the advancement of his interests, . . . the lawyer should obtain from him all possible aid."

15. "The responsibilities of a lawyer may vary according to the intelligence, experience, mental condition or age of a client . . . ' MODEL CODE, *supra* note 13, at EC 7-11. "Any mental . . . condition of a client that renders him incapable of making a considered judgment on his own behalf casts additional responsibilities upon his lawyer . . . . If client under a disability has no legal representative, his lawyer may be compelled in court proceedings to make decisions on behalf of the client." *Id.* at EC 7-12. "If the person has no guardian or legal representative, the lawyer often must act as de facto guardian." MODEL RULES, *supra* note 1, at Rule 1.14 comment 2.

16. MODEL RULES, *supra* note 1, at Rule 1.14(b).

17. *Id.* "'Reasonably believes' . . . denotes that the lawyer believes the matter in question and that the circumstances are such that the belief is reasonable." MODEL RULES TERMINOLOGY [8].

18. MODEL RULES, *supra* note 1, at Rule 1.14 comment 3 provides:

> If a legal representative has not been appointed, the lawyer should see to such an appointment *where it would serve the client's best interests* . . . . In many circumstances, however, appointment of a legal representative may be expensive or traumatic for the client. Evaluation of these considerations is a matter of professional judgment on the lawyer's part. *Id.* (emphasis added).
>
> Rules of procedure in litigation generally provide that minors or persons suffering mental disability shall be represented by a guardian . . . . However, disclosure of the client's disability can adversely affect the client's interests. For example, raising the question of disability could, in some circumstances, lead to proceedings for involuntary commitment. The lawyer's position in such cases is an unavoidably difficult one. The lawyer may seek guidance from an appropriate diagnostician. *Id.* at comment 5.

19. The lawyer is advised that she "may seek guidance from an appropriate diagnostician." *Id.* at comment 5.

20. *Id.* at comment 1.

21. MODEL CODE, *supra* note 13, at EC 7-12.

22. MODEL RULES, *supra* note 1, at Rule 1.14 comment 1.

23. MODEL CODE, *supra* note 13, at EC 7-12.

24. *Id.*

25. See INSTITUTION OF JUD. ADMIN., A.B.A. JUV. JUST. STANDARDS, STANDARDS RELATING TO COUNSEL FOR PRIVATE PARTIES § 3.1 (1979), which recommends that "in a delinquency or in need of supervision proceeding [counsel] should ordinarily be bound by the client's definition of his or her interests with respect to admission or denial of the facts or conditions alleged." *Id.* at § 3.1(b)(ii)[a]. In child protective proceedings where "the juvenile is capable of considered judgment on his or her own behalf, determination of the client's interests . . . should ultimately remain the client's responsibility . . . ." *Id.* at § 3.1(b)(iii)[b].

26. Under MODEL RULES 1.14, comment 3, focuses upon the legal act in advising that "effective completion of the *transaction* [sale of disabled client's property] ordinarily requires appointment of a legal representative." (emphasis added) Comment 1 focuses upon the attorney-client relationship in stating: "a client lacking legal competence often has the ability to

understand, deliberate upon, and reach conclusions about matters affecting the client's own well-being." Similarly, MODEL CODE EC 7-12 recognizes the attorney's concern with the validity of the legal transaction and advises "obviously a lawyer cannot *perform any act* or make any decision which the law requires his client to perform or make . . . ."

27. One can imagine, for example, a perfectly competent individual whose desires for his estate are eccentric and likely to provoke a challenge based upon incompetence or undue influence.

28. *See supra* text part IIIA.

29. MODEL RULES 1.14(a) and comment 1 discusses the impaired client with whom the lawyer should endeavor to carry on a normal client-lawyer relationship. MODEL RULES, *supra* note 1; EC 7-12 discusses a "client who is capable to understanding the matter in question or of contributing to the advancement of his interests" and who can "aid" his lawyer. MODEL CODE, *supra* note 13.

30. MODEL RULES 1.14(b) addresses the client who "cannot adequately act in [his own] interest" and comments 2, 3, 4, and 5 discuss circumstances where the client has or could have a guardian appointed to protect his interests and to direct his attorney. MODEL RULES, *supra* note 1. EC 7-12 addresses the client "incapable of making a considered judgment on his own behalf" and an "incompetent . . . asking through a guardian or other legal representative." MODEL CODE, *supra* note 13.

31. *See* MODEL RULES, *supra* note 1, at comments 3 & 5. For a comprehensive and sensitive discussion of the difficulties involved in seeking a guardian for one's own client, see Tremblay, *On Persuasion and Paternalism: Lawyer Decisionmaking and the Questionable Competent Client,* 1987 UTAH L. REV. 515, 559–67 (1987).

32. "The Comments are intended as guides to interpretation, but the text of each Rule is authoritative." MODEL RULES, *supra* note 1, at Scope [9].

"The Disciplinary Rules, unlike the Ethical Considerations, are mandatory in character." MODEL CODE, *supra* 13, at Preamble and Preliminary Statement.

33. "A lawyer shall *abide by a client's decisions* concerning the objectives of representation . . . and shall consult with the client as to the means by which they are to be pursued . . . ." MODEL RULES, *supra* note 1, at Rule 1.2(a) (emphasis added).

"A lawyer shall explain a matter to the extent reasonably necessary to *permit the client to make informed decisions* regarding the representation." MODEL RULES, *supra* note 67, at Rule 1.4(b) (emphasis added).

"A lawyer shall not intentionally . . . [f]ail to seek the lawful objectives of his client through reasonably available means . . . [or f]ail to carry cut a contract of employment entered into with a client . . . ." MODEL CODE, *supra* note 13, at DR 7-101(A)(1) & (2).

34. MODEL RULES, *supra* note 1, at Rule 1.14(a).

35. Tremblay, *supra* note 31, at 518 n.12.

36. *See* Spiegel, *Lawyering and Client Decision Making: Informed Consent and the Legal Profession,* 128 U. PA. L. REV. 41 (1979); Tremblay, *supra* note 31, at 515 n.1.

37. MODEL RULES, *supra* note 1, at Rule 1.14(b).

38. See MODEL RULES 1.14 comment 5 ("The lawyer may seek guidance from an appropriate diagnostician.")

39. "[T]ruly competent patients whose decisions are overridden [as the result of an erroneous finding of incompetence] can suffer substantial injury to their sense of self." Appelbaum & Roth, *Clinical Issues in the Assessment of Competency,* 138:11 AM. J. PSYCHIATRY 1462, 1466 (1981). There is ample social-psychological evidence that control is related to life-satisfaction and both

physical and psychological health. Melton, *Decision Making by Children,* in CHILDREN'S COMPETENCE TO CONSENT 21, 35 n.26 (G. Melton, G. Koocher & M. Saks eds. 1983).

40. T. GRISSO, *Evaluating Competencies: Forensic Assessment and Instruments,* PERSPECTIVES IN LAW AND PSYCHOLOGY 7 (1986).

41. *See id.* for a discussion of numerous assessment instruments which address a wide variety of competencies.

42. Researchers who studied informed consent by depressed patients warn that while general tests confirming competence are likely to indicate specific competence to make treatment decisions, the reverse is often not true. The doctor must "make additional efforts to ascertain whether, despite apparent 'general incompetency,' the patient is nevertheless 'specifically competent' to understand and does understand [the question to be decided]." Roth, Lidz, Meisel, Soloff, Kaufman, Spiker, & Foster, *Competency to Decide About Treatment or Research; An Overview of Some Empirical Data,* 5 INT'L J. OF LAW & PSYCHIATRY 29, 46–47 (1982).

43. Whenever a patient appears incompetent to make a treatment decision, Appelbaum and Roth recommend considering alternative explanations for the patient's behavior. Applebaum & Roth, *supra* note 39, at 1466.

44. *Id.* at 1462.

45. [Meisel & Roth, *What We Do and Do Not Know About Informed Consent,* 246 JAMA No. 21, 2473 (1981)]; Roth, Lidz, Meisel, Soloff, Kaufman, Spiker, & Foster, *Competency to Decide About Treatment or Research: An Overview of Some Empirical Data,* 5 INT'L J. OF L. AND PSYCHIATRY 29 (1982).

46. *Id.* Psychologists suggest that young children might be "taught to exercise competent decision making." Tapp & Melton, *Preparing Children for Decision Making,* in CHILDREN'S COMPETENCE TO CONSENT 215, 217 (G. Melton, G. Koocher, & M. Sacks eds. 1983). One study of jury interaction suggests that adults' legal reasoning may be enhanced by experience with conflict of ideas and participation in decision making. *Id.* at 225.

47. Appelbaum and Roth describe one case in which an elderly nursing home resident with a history of psychotic episodes and a paranoid delusional system was able to reach an informed decision about a biopsy and possible mastectomy. The assessing psychiatrist engaged the woman in three meetings over some period of time, and at each meeting the woman's position about the procedure and her reasoning were somewhat different. Ultimately, her underlying concerns became clear to the psychiatrist who pointed them out to her and empathized with them. At that point, the woman voluntarily agreed to the procedure. Appelbaum & Roth, *supra* note 39, at 1463–64. Whenever a patient appears incompetent, Appelbaum and Roth recommend a consideration of alternative explanations for the patient's behavior, further investigation, and reassessment of the patient at a later date in order to rule possible causes of "pseudoincompetency." *Id.* at 1466.

48. The MODEL RULES and MODEL CODE suggest that the attorney may make decisions without a guardian or representative being appointed when the decision is not absolutely reserved to the client or when the risks to the client of seeking the appointment of a representative outweigh the benefits. . . . This article has contended that the lawyer should never unilaterally overrule the client's unambiguous decision.

49. [G. Bellow & B. Moulton, THE LAWYERING PROCESS: MATERIALS FOR CLINICAL INSTRUCTION IN ADVOCACY (1978)], at 298.

50. *Id.* For example, pleadings should be filed in accordance with the most conservative interpretation of the statute of limitations, rather than in accordance with a more likely correct, liberal interpretation.

51. *See generally* Mickenberg, *The Silent Clients: Legal and Ethical Considerations in Representing Severely and Profoundly Retarded Individuals,* 31 STAN. L. REV. 625 (1979) (describing and criticizing the "best interests" standard).

52. See G. HAZARD & W. HODES, THE LAW OF LAWYERING: A HANDBOOK ON THE MODEL RULES OF PROFESSIONAL CONDUCT 272–74 (1985) (giving an "illustrative case" in which the attorney appointed to represent a nine-year-old child in a divorce case determines that the "best interests of his client require that he be placed" with the parent that he does not prefer). The authors suggest that the attorney may advocate against the child's wishes under MODEL RULES 1.14, but that the case "is close enough that competent attorneys . . . could validly come to contrary conclusions." *Id.*

53. "The 'best interests' principle is the standard ordinarily used to make decisions for children" concerning life saving treatment where medical and legal ethics intersect. J. AREEN, P. KING, S. GOLDBERG & A. CAPRON, LAW, SCIENCE AND MEDICINE 1226 (1984).

54. Momeyer, *Medical Decisions Concerning Noncompetent Patients,* in RESPECT AND CARE IN MEDICAL ETHICS 45, 53–61 (D. Smith ed. 1983), *reprinted from,* 4 THEORETICAL MEDICINE 275–90 (1983).

55. "Reasonable" could be what the "prudent person" would decide or what "most people" would want. *Id.* at 55.

56. *Id.* at 56–59.

57. Mickenberg, *supra* note 51, at 629–31; *see also* STANDARDS RELATING TO COUNSEL FOR PRIVATE PARTIES, *supra* note 25, at 3.1(b)(ii)(c)[3] (recommending that "if necessary the [juvenile's] attorney may adopt the position requiring the least intrusive intervention justified" if no guardian ad litem has been appointed and the juvenile is not capable of considered judgment on his own behalf).

58. See Quesnell v. State, 83 Wash. 2d 224, 517 P.2d 568 (1974).

59. *See, e.g.,* Overholser v. Lynch, 288 F.2d 388 (D.C. Cir. 1961).

60. See Tremblay, *supra* note 31, at 550–51.

61. See G. HAZARD & W. HODES, *supra* note 52, at 275 (discussing *Overholser,* 288 F.2d 388). In that case the client plead guilty, upon advice of counsel, rather than pursue an insanity defense. A guilty plea meant a short jail sentence, but a successful insanity defense could have led to an indefinite commitment to a mental institution. The judge rejected the client's guilty plea, intimating that the attorney was obligated to present a defense. Ultimately, the client was committed to a mental institution where, in a despondent state, he took his own life.

62. I am grateful to Professor Lee Teitelbaum for this suggestion.

63. See Comment, *The Role of the Family in Medical Decision-Making for Incompetent Adult Patients: A Historical Perspective and Case Analysis,* 48 U. PITT. L. REV. 539 (1987).

64. Wisconsin v. Yoder, 406 U.S. 205 (1972).

65. *In re* Phillip B., 92 Cal. App. 3d 796, 156 Cal. Rptr. 48 (1979).

66. Parham v. J.R., 442 U.S. 584, 602 (1970).

67. Medical personnel regularly look to the family in making treatment decisions for incompetent patients. See Rabkin, Gillerman & Rice, *Orders Not to Resuscitate,* 295 N. ENG. J. MED. 364 (1976). Courts dealing with life-or-death medical decisions for incompetence have also approved the involvement of the family in such decisions. See *In re* Quinlan, 70 N.J. 10, 355 A.2d 647 (1976); *In re* Spring, 380 Mass. 629, 405 N.E.2d 115 (1980); J.F.K. Memorial Hosp. Inc. v. Bludworth, 452 So. 2d 921 (Fla. 1984); *In re* Colyer, 99 Wash. 2d 114, 660 P.2d 738 (1983).

68. MODEL RULES, *supra* note 1, Rule 1.6 prohibits revealing "information relating to representation of a client unless the client consents after consultation, except for disclosures that are

impliedly authorized in order to carry out the representation . . . ." See also MODEL CODE, supra note 13, at DR 4-101, which prohibits an attorney from revealing "a confidence or secret of his client" without the consent of the client.

69. Although the client may be incapable of deciding a complicated financial issue, he may be quite also to decide whether he wants advice from his son about the matter.

70. G. HAZARD & W. HODES, *supra* note 52, at 272–74. The illustrative case involved representing a child in a custody dispute and the attorney's right to reveal to the court negative information about the parent with whom the child wished to live. The attorney had determined that granting custody to the other parent was necessary for the child's best interests.

71. MODEL RULES, *supra* note 1, at Rule 5.4(c) and Rule 1.8(f); MODEL CODE, *supra* note 92, at DR 5-107(B).

72. Momeyer, *supra* note 54, at 60.

73. *See In re* Storar, 52 N.Y.2d 363, 420 N.E.2d 64 (1981). Brother Joseph Fox, a member of a religious order, had engaged in formal discussions of the Karen Anne Quinlan case with his religious order and had made it known that in similar circumstances he would want a respirator removed. He again expressed the same sentiment only a few months before undergoing an operation which left him in a permanently vegetative state. The New York court held that under these circumstances his common law right to decline treatment should be honored based upon his prior express wish.

74. *In re* Spring, 380 Mass. 629, 405 N.E.2d 115 (1980). The elderly patient undergoing dialysis and in late stage Alzheimer's disease had never expressed a preference. However, the patient's wife and son were of the opinion that "if competent he would request withdrawal of the treatment." He experienced unpleasant side effects from the treatment and "on occasion he kicked nurses, resisted transportation for dialysis, and pulled the dialysis needless out of his arm." *Id.* at 118.

75. *See Id.* at 122; *see also, In re* Quinlan, 70 N.J. 10, 355 A.2d 647 (1976). The father of a young adult in a permanently vegetative state was authorized to make decisions on her behalf based upon the "high degree of familial love which pervaded the home," the entire family's involvement in the Roman Catholic Church and Mr. Quinlan's consultation with religious advisors. *Id.* at 657.

76. The doctrine originated over 170 years ago in the administration of estates of the incompetent to authorize a gift from the estate based upon the principles which would have influenced the incompetent person. *In re* Hinde, 35 Eng. Rep. 878 (1816).

77. *See In re* Quinlan, 70 N.J. 10, 355 A.2d 647 (1976); *In re* Storar, 52 N.Y.2d 363, 420 N.E.2d 64 (1981).

78. Superintendent v. Saikewicz, 370 N.E.2d 417 (Mass. 1977).

79. The removal of a kidney from a retarded man in order to effect a transplant to his brother was approved when the relationship was very close, the retarded man's own identity was closely tied to his brother's love and visits, and it was thought that the retarded man would have serious adverse reactions if his brother died and he could have acted to save his life. Strunk v. Strunk, 445 S.W.2d 145 (Ky. 1969).

80. Rogers v. Okin, 634 F.2d 650 (1st Cir. 1980) mandates an individual decision for each patient, based upon the possibility and type of violence if not medicated, the likely effect of particular drugs on a particular individual, and an appraisal of alternative, less restrictive courses of action.

81. *See generally* Momeyer, *supra* note 54.

When dealing with clients with diminished capacity, the lawyer must have some standard of values that govern his or her behavior. In the following articles, Professors Margulies and Pecora address the problem and propose several core values that should guide the lawyer.

Peter Margulies

Access, Connection, and Voice: A Contextual Approach to Representing Senior Citizens of Questionable Capacity

Introduction

Elder law attorneys enter an uncertain realm when they represent senior citizens of questionable capacity.[1] On this terrain, issues of professional responsibility are pervasive and basic issues about what it means to be a lawyer come to the forefront. Coping with these issues is challenging, even (or especially) for the conscientious practitioner. Unlike some other areas, such as avoiding the commingling of funds or refraining from communicating directly with represented adverse parties when their counsel is absent, no safe harbor exists. Indeed, along with the rewards of elder law practice, sensitive lawyers representing clients with questionable capacity will endure some lost sleep, no matter what course they choose. This article will not erase the circles beneath a good lawyer's eyes. However, it may, if it succeeds in anything, provide a more organized way of thinking about problems that keep elder law attorneys awake at night.

On the surface, much of the conflict is between autonomy and welfare. Senior citizens need freedom of action. Yet, they sometimes seem to act in ways that defeat their other needs, whether financial, medical, or legal. At what point do we use concepts of capacity to curtail freedom of action in the interest of meeting needs? Thus stated, the question seems stark. However, a central argument of this article is that there is an artificiality about this distinction between autonomy and welfare. Contrary to the above formulation, autonomy is also a need. Conversely, financial, medical, and legal welfare are essential elements of autonomy.

* * *

Fordham Law Review, Vol. 62, No. 5, 1073 (March 1994). Reprinted by permission.

I. Core Values: Access, Connection, and Voice

Consideration of the situation of senior citizens and the role of attorneys suggests three core values: access, connection, and voice. The values sometimes overlap, and sometimes conflict. Using them as a basis for analysis, however, does clarify some of the difficult questions that lawyers face.

A. Access

Access is important both in the traditions and practices of the legal profession and in the lives of senior citizens. Bar codes of conduct proclaim that lawyers have a duty to maximize the availability of legal services, and provide pro bono services for those who cannot afford market rates.[2] While cynics might observe that the ideal of service has been honored mainly in the breach, recent efforts to create meaningful pro bono programs in law schools and the practicing bar suggest that the profession has the potential to live up to its own rhetoric.

Senior citizens with disabilities, whom I will call challenged seniors, are one group for whom enhanced access is vital. Seniors are often isolated from other seniors and possessed by insecurity. Seniors often live in poverty,[3] often on meager fixed incomes. Society treats challenged seniors as little better than old furniture. At family gatherings, a challenged senior is an object of condescension, or a problem to be ignored. Chronic illness, hearing and visual impairments, cognitive impediments, and variable functioning intensify isolation and frustrate empowerment. Yet, traditional legal rules make empowerment even more difficult by stressing representation of individuals.[4] This isolation of clients is a staple of the Anglo American adversary system, which structures lawyers' duties along litigation lines and distrusts group representation. The Model Rules of Professional Conduct (the "Model Rules") partially undertake to correct this anti-group bias in legal ethics by permitting the lawyer to work as intermediary.[5] However, the collective representation sanctioned by the Model Rules creates its own problems of isolation, as it may in practice allow a lawyer subtly to take sides with one client against a challenged senior.

B. Connection

Many practitioners and commentators have recognized that the bar's stress on representation of individuals neglects elements of connection between persons that make all of us human.[6] No one stands alone; we all are part of a web of relationships that define us.[7] In addition, we have emotions and values that enter into everything we do. We make judgments about others based on these values and emotions, regardless of whether they are included in the job description of the roles we occupy at our desks.[8]

A key insight of much political and social theory is that it is meaningless to talk about autonomy solely of individuals. Apart from scientific curiosities, such as boys raised by wolves and hold-outs from World War II subsisting on remote Pacific Islands, people exist in groups. Our membership in groups, whether as family members, citizens, professionals, or others, shapes our action in the world.[9] Evidence also exists that seniors place particular value on connection with others, including peers, family, and friends.[10] The experience of seeing friends and loved ones pass away, an experience undergone by seniors with increasing frequency as they age, places a premium on connections that survive. The isolation caused by physical and mental disability increases the value of connection.

The general tendency of legal representation is to compound isolation by paying insufficient attention to groups, such as the American Association of Retired Persons (the "AARP"), that offer senior citizens support.[11] A solitary person inspires little fear or respect. By contrast, people in groups have a greater ability to influence and to persuade others. Establishing connection with the client and promoting connection between the client and other seniors facilitates autonomy in the most meaningful sense.[12] While many senior citizens are part of such peer groups, others have few group involvements. Group involvements tend to decrease with age and to be fewer for men than for women.[13] For those with mental disabilities in particular, connection is vital. Mental illness is a disease of isolation that makes people withdraw into themselves. Coaxing people out of this isolation is therapeutic.[14] Lawyers perform a valuable professional service when they integrate challenged senior citizens into support networks.

Despite the benefits of connection, the profession always has sent mixed messages on the issue of the scope of a lawyer's relationship with clients. On the one hand, the Model Rules permit the attorney to offer advice in a variety of areas that may affect the client, even if those areas are not strictly legal. On the other hand, the Anglo American vision of lawyering, with its somewhat mechanical principal-agent relation, seems to curtail nonlegal conversation between lawyer and client. Yet, elder law attorneys and commentators have felt the need to address interpersonal concerns of clients as part of their conception of competent representation. Elder law attorneys also recognize that their practice necessarily involves them with groups such as families, with all the richness and occasional ambiguity and argument that such work involves. Because much elder law involves transactional, not litigation, practice, this group dimension is enhanced.

C. *Voice*

While connection is important, sometimes involvement with others can become oppressive. A senior citizen may have a view of the world that her family or the state do not share. That difference alone is no reason to abridge the senior citizen's freedom of action.[15] Indeed, in a democracy, the efforts of subordinated groups, such as senior citizens, to make their voices heard should be cause for both attention and celebration.[16] Yet, paternalistic conceptions of capacity or more mundane motives of personal gain may spur attempts to control the senior citizen's decisions.[17] In these situations, the lawyer's traditional duty to let the client's voice be heard assumes center stage.[18] The attorney must side with the senior against a group, such as the family, that is suppressing her voice. In some cases, alliances with other groups may enhance the client's voice while coping with behavior that has caused the family's concern.[19]

II. Who Is the Client?

The values of access, connection, and voice always provide an answer to the most widely asked question in elder law: who is the client? These values require that the client be the person who is most vulnerable in the situation. Frequently, therefore, a challenged senior will be the client, even if the attorney's services are being paid for by the senior's child and even if the child was the person who initially requested the attorney's services.[20]

Under this position, lawyers who, at the instruction of a senior's child, prepare documents for the senior's signature must speak with the senior as they would with any other client. This result upholds the access principle because it gives the senior an opportunity to consult with an attorney. It also enhances voice and connection because in this situation the challenged senior citizen may have no one else but the lawyer looking out for her interests, or even taking her seriously. The child in this case may also be a client. However, and here this Article and the Model Rules part company, the attorney's first loyalty is to the challenged senior citizen.[21]

In other situations, the lawyer may learn that family members on whom a challenged senior depends are overreaching by, for example, misappropriating the senior citizen's assets. In some of these cases, the lawyer also may represent other family members. The challenged senior citizen's voice, however, is the one in danger of being smothered. Consequently, the lawyer must treat her obligation to the challenged senior citizen as paramount.

Contrary to the Model Rules, because an attorney previously has represented both the senior and other members of the family, her representation should not create a mandate for the lawyer to withdraw. On the contrary, the lawyer has a special duty to the senior in such situations, particularly where the senior is dependent on family members for care and is therefore all the more vulnerable. Even if no formal guardianship has been created, the attorney should construe her duty to the challenged senior as she would construe her duty to a ward in a formal guardianship. She should view the dominant family members as constructive fiduciaries.[22] The attorney's obligation is to disclose the overreaching of the family to both the senior and, if necessary, other authorities.[23]

The Model Rules take a different approach.[24] Generally, they favor withdrawal over disclosure, except in cases where the lawyer represents a guardian who is breaching her fiduciary duty to a ward.[25] To require that the lawyer employ exit and not voice[26] when confronted with exploitation of a vulnerable client codifies professional irresponsibility. While withdrawal in other situations might tip the victimized client that something was amiss and prompt her to take corrective action, a challenged senior citizen dependent on her exploiter may be no better able to avail herself of this course than the ward of an abusive guardian. Withdrawal in this situation exacerbates the isolation that legal representation should endeavor to prevent.[27]

Moreover, the Model Rules approach leads to anomalous results. If a lawyer represents a guardian and becomes aware of malfeasance toward the ward, she may be required to disclose it, even though she does not represent the ward.[28] However, if she represents both the challenged senior and another family member, who exerts power over the senior but is not the legal guardian, the lawyer must withdraw and cannot disclose the malfeasance.[29] As a result, under the Model Rules, a lawyer must do less for a client than for a similarly situated person who is not a client. This is particularly odd because the more powerful relative in the multiple representation context is already less accountable to courts and other agencies because he is not a guardian. Hamstringing the lawyer merely compounds this lack of accountability.[30]

* * *

Notes

1. For a pioneering analysis of the issues, see Jacqueline Allee, *Representing Older Persons: Ethical Dilemmas,* Prob. & Prop. Jan./Feb. 1988, at 37; *see also* David Luban, *Paternalism and the Legal Profession,* 1981 Wis. L. Rev. 454 (discussing the paternalistic role of attorneys in competence evaluations); Linda F. Smith, *Representing the Elderly Client and Addressing the Question of Competence,* 14 J. Contemp. L. 61 (1988) (arguing that a lawyer seeking to assess client's competence must engage in process of "gradual counseling" and, in certain circumstances, must exercise "substituted judgment" for a client); Paul R. Tremblay, *On Persuasion and Paternalism: Lawyer Decisionmaking and the Questionably Competent Client,* 1987 Utah L. Rev. 515 (discussing choices available to lawyer representing client with impaired competency). For a succinct summary of the problem, see Hon. Steven D. Pepe & Cecille Lindgren, *Ethical Dilemmas in Elder Law: Working with Questionably Competent Clients,* Elder L. Rep., May 1991, at 1–6. One common area of conflict is discussed in Margrit S. Bernstein, *Ethical Considerations in Estate Planning and Probate Practice, in* The Florida Bar Continuing Legal Education Committee and the Committee on the Elderly, *Ethical Issues in Representing the Elderly Client Seminar,* June 15, 1990, at 2.1.

2. The veneration of Louis Brandeis for his pro bono work is one manifestation of this tradition. *See* David Luban, Lawyers and Justice 169-74 (1988).

In February 1993, the American Bar Association House of Delegates adopted by a vote of 228–215 an "aspirational plea" for 50 hours of pro bono service from every lawyer. See *Fifty Hours for Pro Bono: ABA House Adopts Ethics Rule Specifying How Much Time Lawyers Should Donate,* A.B.A. J., Apr. 1993, at 32; Model Rules of Professional Conduct Rule 6.1 cmt. (1993) [hereinafter Model Rules].

3. *See* Lawrence A. Frolik & Alison P. Barnes, Elderlaw 22 (1992).

4. For an insightful reinterpretation of the history of American legal ethics norms, see Russell G. Pearce, *Rediscovering the Republican Origins of the Legal Ethics Codes,* 6 Geo. J. Legal Ethics 241 (1992). *Cf.* Bruce A. Green, *"Through a Glass, Darkly": How the Court Sees Motions to Disqualify Criminal Defense Lawyers,* 89 Colum. L. Rev. 1201 (1989) (discussing judicial attitudes

toward multiple representation in criminal defense). For a discussion of the limits of the traditional adversarial conception, see [Peter Margulies, *"Who Are You to Tell Me That?": Attorney-Client Deliberation Regarding Nonlegal Issues and the Interests of Nonclients,* 68 N.C. L. REV. 213 (1990)].

5. *See* Model Rules, *supra* note 2, Rule 2.2.

6. *See* William H. Simon, *Visions of Practice in Legal Thought,* 36 Stan. L. Rev. 469 (1984). Connection has been a special concern for feminist theorists. *See* Naomi R. Cahn, *Styles of Lawyering,* 43 Hastings L.J. 1039, 1061–68 (1992).

7. *See* Hannah Arendt, The Human Condition 22–23 (1958).

8. *See* Hannah Arendt, Between Past And Future: Eight Exercises in Political Thought (1954).

9. Feminists have explored this point with eloquence. *See* Cahn, *supra* note 6.

10. *See* [Linda F. Smith, *Representing the Elderly Client and Addressing the Question of Competence,* 14 J. CONTEMP. L. 61 (1988) (arguing that a lawyer seeking to assess client's competence must engage in process of "gradual counseling" and, in certain circumstances, must exercise "substituted judgment" for a client)].

11. For discussions of lawyers and groups, see Stephen Ellmann, *Client-Centeredness Multiplied: Individual Autonomy and Collective Mobilization in Public Interest Lawyers' Representation of Groups,* 78 Va. L. Rev. 1103 (1992); John Leubsdorf, *Pluralizing the Client-Lawyer Relationship,* 77 Cornell L. Rev. 825 (1992); Gerald P. López, Rebellious Lawyering: One Chicano's Vision of Progressive Law Practice (1992); Luban, *supra* note 2.

12. It is ironic that many individual senior citizens still are disempowered while elder law as a recognized specialty probably owes much to collective movements of senior citizens that go back almost half a century. *Cf.* Edwin Amenta & Yvonne Zylan, *It Happened Here: Political Opportunity, the New Institutionalism, and the Townsend Movement,* 56 Am. Soc. Rev. 250 (1991) (discussing dynamics of senior citizen activism in the New Deal-era).

13. *See* Lawrence A. Frolik & Alison P. Barnes, *An Aging Population: A Challenge to the Law,* 42 Hastings L.J. 683, 703 (1991).

14. See Margulies, *supra* note 4. *Cf.* David B. Wexler & Bruce J. Winick, *Therapeutic Jurisprudence as a New Approach to Mental Health Law Policy Analysis and Research,* 45 U. Miami L. Rev. 979, 981–84 (1991) (discussing "therapeutic jurisprudence" and its implications for legal practice).

15. Later in this Article, I discuss circumstances under which a lawyer or others can intervene in a client's decisions. [Remainder of note omitted.]

16. Scholars developing critical race and feminist theory argue that those who are vulnerable have special knowledge that society should absorb. *See* Deborah L. Rhode, *Feminist Critical Theories,* 42 Stan. L. Rev. 617 (1990); Patricia J. Williams, The Alchemy of Race and Rights 5–14 (1991). A similar analysis applies to people with disabilities. *See* Oliver Sacks, Seeing Voices: A Journey into the World of the Deaf xiii (1989); Joseph P. Shapiro, No Pity 3 (1993).

17. *See* Julia Spring, *Applying Due Process Safeguards, Generations,* Summer 1987, at 35.

18. For one pioneering analysis of voice compared with other approaches, see Albert O. Hirschman, Exit, Voice, and Loyalty 30–43 (1970). Recent commentators have emphasized the citizen's voice, even as they have warned that the overly legalistic perspective of attorneys can sometimes smother that voice. *See, e.g.,* Anthony V. Alfieri, *Stances,* 77 Cornell L. Rev. 1233 (1992) (discussing various modern and postmodern approaches to lawyering); Anthony V. Alfieri, *Reconstructive Poverty Law Practice: Learning Lessons of Client Narrative,* 100 Yale L.J. 2107 (1991) (examining the loss of client narratives in lawyer storytelling); Anthony V. Alfieri, *The Antinomies of Poverty Law and a Theory of Dialogic Empowerment,* 16 N.Y.U. Rev. L. & Soc. Change

659, 698–701 (1987–88) (discussing the importance of dialogue in empowering impoverished clients); Clark D. Cunningham, *The Lawyer as Translator, Representation as Text: Towards an Ethnography of Legal Discourse,* 77 Cornell L. Rev. 1298, 1331–39 (1992) (arguing that the practice of law involves translation and offering a model of mental activity composed of sensation, experience, and knowledge); Clark D. Cunningham, *A Tale of Two Clients: Thinking About Law As Language,* 87 Mich. L. Rev. 2459, 2460–61 (1989) (exploring the meaning of the phrase "representing a client"); Lucie E. White, *Subordination, Rhetorical Survival Skills, and Sunday Shoes: Notes on the Hearing of Mrs. G.,* 38 Buff. L. Rev. 1, 46–48 (1990) (discussing a client who outmaneuvered her lawyer by abandoning the lawyer's script that "fragmented her voice"). *Cf.* Robert D. Dinerstein, *A Meditation on the Theoretics of Practice,* 43 Hastings L.J. 971, 981–84 (1992) (analyzing tensions in progressive lawyering literature); Paul R. Tremblay, *Rebellious Lawyering, Regnant Lawyering, and Street-Level Bureaucracy,* 43 Hastings L.J. 947, 954–59 (1992) (same).

19. *See, e.g.,* Peter J. Strauss, *Before Guardianship: Abuse of Patient Rights Behind Closed Doors,* 41 Emory L.J. 761, 761–62 (1992) (discussing alliance with church group).

20. Margrit Bernstein has told me that she customarily tries to consider who is the most vulnerable person in a situation brought to her attention and then undertakes to represent that person.

21. A corollary of this principle is that the efficiency advantages of multiple representation, such as representation of both spouses, should be available to clients whose capacity may become questionable, if an attorney believes that they have the capacity to make particular decisions. Discriminating against persons with capacity, because of concerns about future capacity, may be a violation of the Americans with Disabilities Act, 42 U.S.C. §§ 12101–12213 (Supp. III 1991), which bars discrimination on the basis of disability.

22. This same construction of fiduciary status independent of formal arrangements typifies the constructive trust.

23. For discussion of related issues, see [Geoffrey C. Hazard, Jr., *Triangular Lawyer Relationships: An Exploratory Analysis,* 1 Geo. J. Legal Ethics 15, 21–23 (1987)].

24. For discussion of ethical issues involved in representing both spouses, see Teresa Stanton Collett, *And the Two Shall Become As One . . . Until the Lawyers Are Done,* 7 Notre Dame J. L. Ethics & Pub. Pol'y 101 (1993); Malcolm A. Moore & Anne K. Hilker, *Representing Both Spouses: The New Section Recommendations,* Prob. & Prop., July/August 1993, at 26.

25. See Model Rules, *supra* note 2, Rule 1.14 cmt. 4.

26. For the definitive analysis of these two alternatives, see Hirschman, *supra* note 18.

27. Similar disclosures have been required of lawyers in the savings and loan cases. *See, e.g., In re* American Continental Corp./Lincoln Sav. & Loan Sec. Litig., 794 F. Supp. 1424, 1452 (D. Ariz. 1992) (stating that attorneys must inform a client that its conduct violates the law and, if the client continues the wrongful activity, then the attorney must withdraw if further representation will violate the rules of professional conduct).

28. *See* Model Rules, *supra* note 2, Rule 1.14 cmt. 4.

29. *Cf.* State Bar of Michigan, Comm. on Professional & Judicial Ethics, Mich. Opinion CI-693 (Nov. 1981) (unpublished informal opinion) (attorney who learns that nephew of deceased client may have misappropriated funds may disclose this to other heirs, but may not represent any party to the transaction thereafter).

30. In cases of dominant family member malfeasance, the lawyer should be permitted not to disclose if the misfeasance is entirely rectified by the offending party. This gives the lawyer an opportunity to work informally with the client to improve the situation, rather than forcing an adversarial denouement that may be in no one's best interest.

Anne K. Pecora

Representing Defendants in Guardianship Proceedings: The Attorney's Dilemma of Conflicting Responsibilities

* * *

A guardianship proceeding involves several areas of inquiry from which a court or jury must render a decision or verdict. Is the person so mentally incapacitated as to be unable to carry out transactions necessary to provide for basic needs, and therefore requires a guardian to be appointed to make decisions?[1] If the person needs a guardian, what powers should the court grant to the guardian?[2] Who should be the guardian?[3] The answers to these questions usually depend on the testimony of expert witnesses and others regarding the degree of disability, the type of judgment affected, and the character and interest of the proposed guardian.[4] For example, a person may need a guardian to manage personal or financial affairs, but may not need confinement in a nursing home. If a guardian is needed, the court must determine who the guardian should be, after considering the person's relationship to other people and a possible guardian's willingness, ability, and motives to act as such. Thus, a court may pass over a person with a confidential relationship to the defendant where that person has interfered with the defendant's attempt to confer with counsel.[5]

In guardianship proceedings, the defendant's absolute, not conditional, liberty is at stake, necessitating appointment of counsel for the person alleged to be disabled.[6] It is the initial proceeding, when the issue of a defendant's capacity is decided by a judge or jury in a court of law, which uses formal procedures and rules of evidence.[7] Usually, the petitioner is represented by an attorney.[8]

* * *

II. Responsibilities of Attorneys

A. Investigation of Facts and Interests of the Parties

An attorney representing a defendant in a guardianship proceeding must investigate the allegations against the client and the plaintiff's motives in order to present sufficient evidence at trial to allow the court or jury to determine whether the plaintiff has any interests in conflict with those of the person alleged to be disabled. The plaintiff's motives can range from the love and concern of a friend or family member to the

Elder Law Journal, Vol. 1, 139 (Fall 1993).

greed of an opportunist, or to the need of public agencies to reduce the number of individuals seeking or receiving their services.

Although guardianship proceedings are instituted under the guise of protection for the defendant, other motives of plaintiffs must be considered.[9] In some states, state agencies otherwise responsible for providing social services to disabled individuals have statutory authority to petition a court for appointment of a guardian.[10] Guardianship may be sought to avoid a difficult or time-consuming service plan or to relieve social workers of undefined fear that the individual will come to harm.

* * *

2. *Guardianship Proceedings*

a. Considerations in Determining the Client's Competency and Best Interests Although courts charge lawyers with "the highest standard of advocacy" when representing individuals unable to comprehend the nature of the guardianship proceeding,[11] the American Bar Association's *Model Rules of Professional Conduct* and the *Ethical Considerations* give little guidance to the attorney representing such a defendant in a guardianship proceeding.

* * *

Which decisions can the lawyer make on behalf of a client? When is the lawyer prohibited from making a decision on behalf of the client because the decision can only be made by the client or by a "duly constituted representative" if the client is legally incompetent? How does this Ethical Consideration apply to the very proceeding which will determine whether the client is legally incompetent? When, if ever, does the attorney *become* a guardian ad litem rather than a traditional advocate/agent? State courts have answered some of these questions.

A guardian ad litem has been defined as "a person appointed by the court to appear and act in litigation on behalf of a . . . person under a disability. . . ."[12] Although this role is easily understood in reference to litigation involving a party who has been adjudicated disabled, the role of guardian ad litem in cases seeking to appoint a guardian for a person alleged to be disabled is not so easily ascertainable.[13] Appointing an attorney to act as guardian ad litem to make recommendations to the court leaves the defendant without a traditional attorney-advocate.[14]

Although Maine has held that a guardian ad litem/attorney should act in the best interests of the proposed ward, regardless of the latter's personal wishes,[15] the supreme courts of Missouri and New Jersey have held that upon the filing of a petition to appoint a guardian, the trial court must immediately appoint an attorney[16] who must meet with the individual to determine the individual's ability to understand and assist in the defense of the case.[17] To the extent that the individual understands what is at stake and wishes to waive or exercise a particular right, that wish must be honored even if appointed counsel disagrees with the wisdom of the client's choice.[18] The allegedly disabled person's "right to counsel becomes a mere formality, and does not meet Constitutional and statutory guarantees, absent affirmative effort to protect the person's fundamental rights through investigation and submission of all relevant defenses or arguments against the plaintiff's position."[19]

On the other hand, the court in *In re Moehlenpah* held that if the client's disability requires the attorney to make decisions for the client, the attorney must "consider all circumstances then prevailing and actively care to safeguard and advance the interests of the client."[20] The court-appointed counsel reported to the trial court what had taken place when meeting with the client before trial and gave an opinion as to her client's ability to select private counsel.[21] The attorney reported that her client did not respond to most questions, whistled on and off throughout the conversation, and was unable to hold a pen or sign his name.[22] Based on the client's inability to communicate and the attorney's review of a doctor's answers to interrogatories, the court-appointed counsel concluded that her client did not understand the nature of the action.[23]

* * *

The Supreme Court of Maine has held that a court may appoint a guardian ad litem, rather than an attorney, to represent the defendant in a guardianship proceeding, despite the defendant's objection.[24] On appeal the court held that the lower court had exercised its discretion in choosing to appoint a guardian ad litem who was ordered to assist the appellant in putting the petition to proof.[25] The court held that "the guardian ad litem continued to act, as was his duty, in the best interest of [his client] regardless of [his client's] personal wishes," even though the guardian ad litem had filed an unnecessary report to the court stating that he had met with the defendant, reviewed his record, and determined that his condition required the appointment of a guardian.[26]

Other courts, however, have defined the role of counsel differently. Assuming the fundamental nature of the liberty interest in a guardianship proceeding where the defendant's very life is at stake, the Supreme Judicial Court of Massachusetts defined the responsibilities of the court-appointed attorneys or guardians ad litem as adversarial.[27] The court found that in deciding whether to grant to the guardian the authority to decide whether to terminate or continue life-prolonging hemodialysis treatment for a disabled person, the role of the representative of the allegedly disabled person is to take the opposite position from that of the moving party.[28] In this jurisdiction, then, the attorney or guardian ad litem's responsibility is to present to the judge, after a thorough investigation, "all reasonable arguments in favor of administering treatment to prolong the life of the individual involved."[29] The court did not impose a duty to present arguments which the attorney or guardian ad litem does not believe meritorious or the obligation to take appeals in every case.[30] Thus, in this model of the role of counsel, the opinions of counsel are irrelevant. The counsel simply opposes the petition in every reasonable way, as in any other litigation.

* * *

d. The Court's Responsibility for the Attorney's Decision How can the court determine the adequacy of a client's waiver of a procedural or substantive right without determining the issue of competency?[31] If the allegedly disabled person is incapable of making a knowing and intelligent waiver, who (if anyone) can waive rights if such waiver is in the best interest of the individual?[32] How can the court ensure that a defendant, who is capable of expressing wishes regarding a particular right, has those wishes honored by counsel and presented to the court?[33] The solution to these dilemmas resides with the court and with the attorney for the person allegedly disabled.

Although one California court of appeals was willing to reestablish a conservatorship with minimal due process safeguards to the defendant, the Supreme Court of Missouri's interpretation of state conservatorship and guardianship statutes has required stricter due process protections for the defendant both from counsel for the defendant and from the trial court.[34] On appeal from an order declaring her incompetency and appointing a guardian of the person and a conservator of the estate, the appellant contended that the trial court failed to adhere to the requirements of state law by not having a jury trial, by proceeding without her, and by denying her the benefit of court-appointed counsel.[35] Upon the filing of the petitions, the court issued notice to the defendant informing her of the filing of the petitions, the date and time of the hearing, the name and address of appointed counsel, the right to a jury trial, and the right to be present at the hearing.[36] Appellant's counsel neither requested a jury nor objected to proceeding without one, so the case was tried to the court without the appellant.[37] A woman claiming to be the appellant's cousin sought to inform the court that the appellant wanted to be present.[38] When the appellant's counsel objected to the cousin's remarks, the court ruled that because the cousin was not a party, she would not be allowed to speak until she conferred with counsel.[39] Appellee's counsel requested a moment to talk with the woman, but the court ordered the hearing to proceed, and ruled that any conversation with the alleged cousin should take place during a break in the proceedings.[40] The individual was not called to testify, and the court made no further inquiry into the allegations.[41]

A witness who had business dealings with the appellant in a prior matter testified at the hearing that "appellant was competent throughout his dealings with her, and that with a little assistance she remained capable of taking care of herself."[42] This witness was not cross-examined by the appellant's counsel, and no independent evidence was introduced on behalf of the appellant.[43] Based on this scant record, the trial court found the appellant to be incapacitated and disabled by reason of Alzheimer's disease and appointed a guardian of the person and a conservator of the estate.[44]

The appellant argued on appeal that the right to a jury trial can be waived only by the allegedly disabled person and appointed counsel on the record in a manner consistent with state law regarding waiver of the right to a jury by criminal defendants.[45] The appellant further asserted that state law required that the allegedly disabled person be present at the hearing or that the trial court make a record of the reasons for absence.[46]

The Missouri Supreme Court held that the waiver of the rights to a jury trial and to be present at the proceeding had not met the requirements of the statute or the Due Process Clause of the Fourteenth Amendment.[47] The court explained that applicable statutory provisions require the court to appoint an attorney to represent the respondent in the proceedings as soon as a petition for the appointment of a guardian is filed.[48] The attorney must visit the client prior to the hearing to determine whether the client is capable of understanding the matter in question or of participating in the proceeding.[49] If the client understands the nature of the action, counsel does not have the power to waive any substantial right of the client unless expressly authorized by the client.[50] "If the disability of a client compels the attorney to make decisions for the client, the attorney shall consider all circumstances then prevailing and act with care to safeguard and advance the interests of the client."[51]

* * *

Additionally, the authority of an attorney is limited to waivers of procedural or remedial matters.[52] Unless expressly authorized, counsel does not have the power to waive a substantial right of a client.[53] If a client cannot comprehend the nature of the action, counsel must make these fundamental decisions for the client after considering all the appropriate circumstances.[54] Counsel must act with care to safeguard and further the interest of the client.[55] Counsel is authorized to waive a right granted under state law on behalf of an incapacitated client when such actions will advance the "best interest" of the individual.[56] When counsel for an alleged incompetent indicates a desire to waive a right granted under statute, the trial court must ascertain from counsel whether "the decision to waive the right is the client's own choice or a product of counsel's best judgment."[57] The trial court must determine for itself whether the individual is capable of making a knowing and intelligent waiver or is so disabled as to require counsel's acting in behalf of the individual.[58] If appointed counsel's report causes the trial court to have doubts about private counsel's ability to represent the client's rights and interest, the court may appoint counsel to serve as co-counsel or as a guardian ad litem.[59] Additionally, the court may, at any time during the proceeding, appoint other counsel to enter the case.[60]

* * *

Attorneys should not be allowed or required to determine the client's best interests regarding a guardianship proceeding. Consequently, attorneys should not waive a client's fundamental rights, such as the right to a hearing, to be present, to cross-examine witnesses, and to have the plaintiff carry the burden of proof. Certainly, judges and opposing counsel would like the attorney for the allegedly disabled person to stipulate to all the evidence and legal issues. Such an approach leaves only the attorney for the defendant open to malpractice litigation, while all others are held harmless. Defendants in a guardianship proceeding are presumed to be competent; this presumption should be maintained throughout the proceeding until a judge or jury, not the defendant's attorney, finds otherwise.

Some questions remain. When is it ever in the best interest of the client to stipulate to the admission of hearsay evidence, such as a physician's affidavit stating that the client is incompetent? Even where the attorney has privately interviewed the physician, the adversary system demands, with few exceptions, that witnesses testify and be cross-examined while under oath and in the presence of the fact finder. Stipulations between attorneys to evidence which goes to the ultimate issue may be in the best interest of the judge or the attorneys, but when are such stipulations ever in the best interest of the client? Which rights are procedural and which are substantive? Is the right to a hearing procedural, not substantive, simply because it is statutorily granted? How does an attorney determine the client's best interest?

The attorney's dilemma has not been completely resolved by the courts or by the

American Bar Association's *Model Rules of Professional Conduct* and the *Ethical Considerations.* Attorneys must be aware of their individual state statutes, judicial decisions, and professional rules of conduct before they undertake representation of defendants whose liberty is at stake in a guardianship proceeding.

Notes

1. See, e.g., MD. EST. & TRUSTS CODE ANN. § 13-705(b) (1991), which provides:

> A guardian of the person shall be appointed if the court determines from clear and convincing evidence that a person lacks sufficient understanding or capacity to make or communicate responsible decisions concerning his person, including provisions for health care, food, clothing, or shelter, because of any mental disability, senility, other mental weakness, disease, habitual drunkenness, or addiction to drugs, and that no less restrictive form of intervention is available which is consistent with the person's welfare and safety.

2. See, e.g., *id.* § 13-708(a), which states: "The *court* may grant to a guardian of the person only those powers necessary to provide for the demonstrated need of the disabled person."

3. See, e.g., *id.* § 13-707, which enumerates priorities of persons entitled to appointment as guardian of the person, including: "any other person, agency or corporation considered appropriate by the court;" and, last, the director of the local department of social services, State Office on Aging, or local office on aging.

4. *In re* Kloman, 315 A.2d 830 (D.C. 1974) (petitioner must present evidence of present inability to manage property); *In re* Keiser, 204 N.W. 394 (Neb. 1925) (person needs a guardian if unable or incapable of proper personal care or managing property unassisted); *In re* Caine, 415 A.2d 13 (Pa. 1980) (petitioner must establish that defendant is unable to manage property or is liable to dissipate it or become victim of designing persons).

5. *In re* Gessler, 419 N.W.2d 541, 543–44 (N.D. Ct. App. 1988); *see also In re* Walker, 242 Cal. Rptr. 289, 299 (Cal. Ct. App. 1981) (denial of hearing to determine who was to be conservator was an abuse of discretion).

6. Federal courts have mandated the appointment of counsel for defendants in two other types of civil proceedings when the person's physical liberty is at stake and the state is acting in *parens patriae.* In Kent v. United States, 383 U.S. 541, 555 (1966), the Supreme Court held that a juvenile is entitled to the assistance of counsel in delinquency proceedings when those proceedings can result in incarceration in a state institution. Furthermore, the right to counsel is consistent with the state's interest as *parens patriae* in assuring that minors are not arbitrarily and erroneously deprived of their personal freedom. *See also In re* Gault, 387 U.S. 1, 41 (1966).

The reasoning of *Kent* and *In re* Gault was adopted by the court in Lessard v. Schmidt, 349 F. Supp. 1078, 1085 (E.D. Wis. 1972), *vacated and remanded on other grounds,* 414 U.S. 473 (1974), when it held that defendants in proceedings for involuntary commitment to mental health facilities are entitled to the appointment of counsel because they may be deprived of their physical liberty.

In civil proceedings where the individual's liberty is at stake, it is important to have the assistance of skilled counsel to inquire into the law and the facts, to assure regularity of the proceeding, and to prepare and submit any defense which the individual may have. See *Gault,*

387 U.S. at 36, and *Lessard,* 349 F. Supp. at 1097 (quoting Heyford v. Parker, 396 F.2d 393, 396 (10th Cir.1968)).

7. [Note omitted.]

8. [Peter M. Hortsman, *Protective Services for the Elderly: The Limits of Parens Patriae,* 40 MO. L. REV. 215, 231 (1975)], at 235 & n.109 (citing a study by the National Senior Citizens Law Center).

9. George J. Alexander, *Premature Probate: A Different Perspective on Guardianship for the Elderly,* 31 Stan. L. Rev. 1003, 1007 (1979) (guardianship statutes do not "ensure that the court will recognize the conflict of interests between the petitioners and the ward").

10. *See* MD. EST. & TRUSTS CODE ANN. § 13-707(a)(9) (1991) and MD. FAM. LAW CODE ANN. § 14-201 (1991).

11. Superintendent of Belchertown v. Saikewicz, 370 N.E.2d 417, 433 (Mass. 1977); *see also* Estate of Chambers, 139 Cal. Rptr. 357, 361 (Cal. Ct. App. 1977); *In re* Jessee, 744 S.W.2d 514, 516 (Mo. Ct. App. 1988).

12. Young v. Tudor, 83 N.E.2d 1, 2 (Mass. 1949).

13. Charles H. Baron, *The Mixed Roles of the Guardian Ad Litem,* Guardianship News (Christian & Robertson, Amherst, Ma.), Apr. 1981, at 1.

14. *Id.*

15. *In re* Richard H., 506 A.2d 221 (Me. 1986). See also Mazza v. Pechacek, 233 F.2d 666 (D.C. Cir.1956), in which the court of appeals refused to reverse the appointment of a conservator on the grounds that the court-appointed guardian ad litem refused to associate himself with appellant's position in opposition to the petition seeking appointment of a conservator.

16. *In re* Link, 713 S.W.2d 487, 490 (Mo. 1986); *In re* Grady, 426 A.2d 467, 471 (N.J. 981).

17. *Link,* 713 S.W.2d at 491-92.

18. *Id.* at 496.

19. *Id.*

20. *In re* Estate of Moehlenpah, 763 S.W.2d 249, 256 (Mo. Ct. App. 1988).

21. *Id.*

22. *Id.* at 252.

23. *Id.*

24. *In re* Richard H., 506 A.2d 221 (Me. 1986). But see *In re* Wargold, 575 N.Y.S.2d 230, 233 (Sur. Ct. 1991), holding that when a court-appointed guardian ad litem believes that a conservator should be appointed, counsel should be appointed to advocate the proposed conservatee's objections.

25. *In re* Richard H., 506 A.2d 221.

26. *Id.* at 221–22. But see *In re* Thomas, 270 N.Y.S.2d 797, 800 (N.Y. App. Div. 1966), where the court reversed and remanded an order appointing a committee because of the actions of the guardian ad litem. The court held that by presenting himself as an unsworn witness as to facts bearing on the issue of incompetency, summation of the guardian ad litem was prejudicial.

27. *In re* Spring, 405 N.E.2d 115, 119 (Mass. 1980).

28. *Id.* at 123.

29. *Id.* (quoting Superintendent of Belchertown v. Saikewicz, 370 N.E.2d 417, 433 (Mass. 1977)).

30. *Id.*

31. *In re* Link, 713 S.W.2d 487, 495 (Mo. 1986).

32. *Id.*
33. *Id.* at 496.
34. *Id.* at 492–93 (interpreting Mo. Rev. Stat. § 475.075 (1992)).
35. *Id.* at 491.
36. *Id.* at 490.
37. *Id.*
38. *Id.*
39. *Id.*
40. *Id.*
41. *Id.*
42. *Id.* at 491.
43. *Id.*
44. *Id.*
45. *Id.*
46. *Id.*
47. *Id.* at 498.
48. *Id.* at 491–92, 497; *see also* MO. REV. STAT. § 475.075, subd. 3 (1992).
49. *Link,* 713 S.W.2d at 492; *see also* MO. REV. STAT. § 475.075, subds. 3, 4, 8 (1992).
50. See *Link,* 713 S.W.2d at 492.
51. *Id.; see also* MO. REV. STAT. § 475.075, subds. 3, 4, 8 (1992); MODEL CODE OF PROFESSIONAL RESPONSIBILITY EC 7–15 (1981).
52. [*Link,* 713 S.W.2d at 496.]
53. *Id.*
54. *Id.; see also* MODEL CODE OF PROFESSIONAL RESPONSIBILITY EC 7-12 (1981).
55. *Link,* 713 S.W.2d at 496; *see also* MODEL CODE OF PROFESSIONAL RESPONSIBILITY EC 7–12 (1981).
56. *Link,* 713 S.W.2d at 496.
57. *Id.*
58. *Id.; see also In re* Couch, 824 S.W.2d 65, 71 (Mo. Ct. App. 1991) (citing *Link,* 713 S.W.2d 487 (Mo. 1986)). The court of appeals held that counsel can waive statutory rights for a client who cannot comprehend the action but the trial court must have sufficient evidence in the record that such waiver is in the best interest of the individual.
59. *Link,* 713 S.W.2d at 497–98.
60. *Id.* at 498.

CHAPTER 47

Ethical Conflicts

Frequently, a lawyer is approached by both the older person and that person's family, often with the goal of preserving the assets of the older person. The obvious possible conflicts among the family members present particularly difficult problems for the lawyer.

Steven H. Hobbs and Fay Wilson Hobbs

The Ethical Management of Assets for Elder Clients: A Context, Role, and Law Approach

* * *

I. The Challenge to Finish Well

As professionals working with older clients, we need to be able to understand them: who they are, what their past experiences have been, and how they have come to see their life. The journey is a continuous process, a series of intermediate steps, according to Carlsen, consisting of having basic needs met and conquering the challenges of life.[1] Those who have entered the last phase of human development represent the stream of life at its fullest flow, carrying all the rich and varied experiences of the past into the present.[2]

Having reached this plateau, elder persons need to be free from worries about the remainder of their journey. However, more often they live in fear that their choices

Fordham Law Review, Vol. 62, No. 5 (March 1994). Reprinted by permission.

and rights will be abridged because of their advancing age.[3] They live in fear of stagnation because of a societal perception that they are uncreative and unwilling to adopt new ideas.[4] They live in fear that their control will be swept away.[5]

Jules Willing "asks us to realize that 'older people need the freedom to worry—to be challenged and involved in the conflicts and tasks of everyday life—it is part of their needed stimulation."[6] Clients need to be empowered rather than treated.[7] Too often we parent our clients, "often treating them as children, incapable of participating in the decision-making process. We must become facilitators and supportive advocates for our clients as we guide them, their families, and their caretakers to more enlightened solutions to their problems."[8] The goals of the professional "include precision, objectivity, and a perspective from which we see a person in his or her wholeness rather than with simplistic attention to one particular trait or characteristic."[9]

II. The Family Context

Whenever we discuss divestment of assets or the distribution of assets, we are discussing the family managing assets accumulated over a lifetime. The problem for the lawyer is that she must approach asset management[10] from different angles and for different tasks. She must provide assistance for the wise use of assets for basic living needs. She must engage in Medicaid planning, estate planning, and general gifting of present assets. The attorney also must assist in the decisions regarding the use and ownership of shared assets—when they exist.

The principal function of an attorney advising elderly clients is the distribution or use of assets in a manner that maximizes resources for the family unit. In this regard the needs of the family unit are analyzed and prioritized. An assessment is made of the nature and extent of the available resources—both monetary and nonmonetary (such as human resources, social services, and community resources). The lawyer's task is then to put the resources to use in a way that most efficiently and effectively meets the needs of the elder person and his family. With an understanding of available resources, the family can plan for providing the basics such as food, shelter, and medical care. The family also can determine whether supplementary insurance should be purchased, homes or other property sold, new living arrangements made, trusts established, and any other assets redistributed which aid in meeting needs. Along with a plan for asset management, including the divestment of some assets, the lawyer should see who is available to help put the plan into action and what social services can be of assistance. In this panoply of resources and moveable parts the lawyer should establish who will be the responsible party in which situations and how that may change as needs and resources change.

The dilemma arises when the decision must be made as to who gets to keep or spend the assets. Will they be gifted, or utilized for health care—especially after a catastrophic illness? How can the assets be shared among family members who usually have different interests? How do we preserve the assets for the benefit of the family member who accumulated them and dispose of those assets in a way which respects the wishes of the individual(s) who earned them?

To answer these questions, this article proposes a method grounded in a therapy model that social workers and mental health professionals use. The model's basic assumption is that an individual or a family is being presented to the therapist to solve a particular problem. The solution may require more than just the individual to implement—other family members and other resources may have to come into play. The therapist will only be aware of these broader solutions if she applies a therapy model that is designed to elicit this information.

Dr. Nancy Boyd-Franklin has developed such a model that she finds particularly useful in counseling Black families and that is adaptable equally to families with elderly members who have asset management problems to solve.[11] Boyd-Franklin calls it a multisystems approach. . . .[12]

* * *

Under the Boyd-Franklin multisystems approach, there are seven levels or systems that can be accessed for problem solving.[13] Level one is the individual, who may be sufficiently capable of solving the problem.[14] This typically is a single person, without any problems with mental or physical capacity, who is perfectly able to plan ahead for his or her senior years. Level two is composed of subsystems within the family.[15] This level includes such subunit relationships as spouse-spouse, parent-child, or siblings. Here, a spouse of an adult child may be presenting a health care or Medicaid problem to the elder-care lawyer for assistance in divesting the assets of an incapacitated elder person. Level three is the family household.[16] The elder person may be living with an adult child and that child's immediate family. The adult child in this situation has assumed the primary responsibility for caring for the elder person.

Level four goes further to include the relevant extended family organization which provides a support system for the family member.[17] Siblings, nephews, nieces, and other relatives may share the responsibilities of looking after the elder person. However, members of the extended family may not all live in the same household or even in the same locality. Level five considers the support system provided by nonblood kin and friends.[18] This support system is particularly important for the elder person who is no longer in direct contact with blood relatives. Level six explores church and community system resources.[19] This system is very important for the elder person considering gifting some assets to a religious organization.[20] Finally, level seven looks to social service agencies and other outside systems.[21] The outside systems may include residential care facilities, medical care providers, or state agencies such as a department of social services which may oversee Medicaid.

* * *

The multisystems approach can be a useful planning tool for thoughtful, competent consultation with an elder person seeking a viable plan for asset management. Many good lawyers already use this approach with initial intake questionnaires and the completion of informational documents.[22] The multisystems approach is certainly a more comprehensive approach than, for example, simply drafting a will without concern for the larger context of estate planning.

* * *

IV. Defining Ethical Boundaries

Given the premise that the attorney is providing professional services in a family coping with the aging process, an analysis of the attorney's ethical responsibility must be developed in this context. The elder person should be the focus of the attorney's loyalty. If the "client" is a couple, their joint needs should be the paramount concern of the professional. Children, who might have an interest in the outcome provided, must subordinate their interest to that of their parents. As discussed below, the children stand as fiduciaries of the parents and as beneficiaries of the services provided—not only as possible recipients of family assets but also in terms of peace of mind that their parents' fundamental needs are met as they navigate the aging passage.

* * *

Given the available legal tools to assist in the aging journey, the lawyer's role is to facilitate the trip in a manner as determined by the client. The principal task of the finishing-well process and the elder-law attorney who provides assistance should be to facilitate the establishment of financial, social, and emotional security for the parties to the greatest extent practicable.[23] The law provides for the management of assets in a way that both provides for the current and future care of the elder person and allows for the dispersal of assets to the natural objects of their affections. The lawyer should help facilitate these objectives by using his skills, expertise, and experience to marshal the assets in a way that serves the interests of the elder person. This approach helps to promote self-determination and enhances the dignity of the individuals traversing the aging process.[24]

Because lawyers give advice on the management of other people's assets, they are placed in the capacity of fiduciaries.[25] . . . The attorney should not personally profit and should protect the client's assets from waste and fraud. She should competently use her abilities to achieve the objects entrusted to her by the client.

The legal standards which provide the means for asset management inform facilitative ethics and fiduciary duties. The professional must be aware of what elder-law allows and does not allow. She must be aware of the values that are inherent in the way law has been structured by our society as it attempts to accommodate the needs of our senior citizens. She must know what the law is, enables, and requires of families as they struggle to meet the challenges of the aging process.

Professionals who provide services to elderly client must take care that their focus remains on assisting the elder person in finishing well. Lawyers are the fiduciary in which trust is reposed to ensure that assets are managed well and in accordance with their clients' wishes; that the needs of other family members are respected to the extent that these needs are secondary to the fundamental needs of the elderly person; and that in the event of failing health and diminished physical and mental capacities, right will be done by them.

From an asset management perspective, the lawyer's ethical duty is, first and foremost, not to let the assets waste away. The attorney is entrusted with the fruits of a life's work and utmost care must be exercised to maximize these resources. The attorney must follow the rules of divestiture to achieve the anticipated results. Whether this involves gifting, spend-down, or trust establishment, the work should not be subject to legal challenge for failure to follow the law competently. A lawyer must not manage the assets in a fashion which could create legal liabilities such as result from an action for fraud or a prosecution for tax code violations. A lawyer must not allow misuse or misappropriation of the assets by other family members or other persons who may influence the elder person. The family members or other connected persons are bound by the same fiduciary duty as the lawyer to take care of the assets for the benefit of the elder person. If the lawyer assists such persons in the misuse or misappropriation, she too could be subject to discipline[26] or civilly liable for breach of fiduciary duty.[27]

V. Specific Ethical Issues

In the area of management of assets, all ethical issues converge. First, who is the client when it comes to managing assets? If we provide professional services to the family as a unit, is there a principal spokesperson who speaks for all? When there is no apparent agreement on the options available, can we resort to dispute resolution mechanisms? Identification is not as important as focus. Under our analysis, the needs and desires of the elder person are the focus. Their participation in whatever manner is crucial. A spouse or significant other might also have an equally or complementary interest in the asset management process. In this case the counseling skills of the attorney can be brought to bear in the intermediation of reasonable alternatives. The key is to provide options and let the elder person make decisions to the extent practicable.

A secondary order of concern is the children or other family members who may be dependent on the elder person. They may share a present or contingent interest in an asset. Their needs should be addressed by respecting the desires of the elder person consistent with the legal rights of the other family members. The decision-making process is multimodal when considering how and when assets should pass to the next generation. We base this premise on the fact that there is a functioning family. It must be recognized that human nature (greed in particular) often pits the individual against the family. In this instance, the role of the attorney changes to that of protector of the elder person and we get back to a more traditional representational analysis. The ethical decision for the lawyer is to determine whether if you were operating as a provider of professional service, you could switch hats and become an adversarial advocate. If you are focusing on the interest of the elder person, have you advised other family members that your allegiance is to the elder? Is this disclosure with the elder person's consent sufficient protection? This is a value judgment that an individual practitioner would make unless otherwise directed by the bar.

Similarly, sometimes the client must fight the elder-care system. It may be necessary to work through the confusing maze of insurance coverage and nursing home placement process. Or creditors may be overly aggressive and unjustly attach assets. In these circumstances the lawyer must be an adversarial advocate. (Keep in mind that the conflicts issue also may have to be addressed if the lawyer was providing services to the family as a unit.)

Second, there are inherent conflicts of interest in providing services to an individual who may feel the need to take into account the needs and interests of other family members. If we assume either that the client lacks capacity or that there is a strong possibility that physical and mental incapacity may occur, the professional must consider issues of substitute judgment, the best interest of the elder person, and the decision maker who may have an ultimate stake in the residue of the assets.

Third, it is unclear to whom the duty of confidentiality is owed and in what circumstances the duty of confidentiality arises. We are not sure when the rules should be different and when exceptions to the rules should apply. Is the duty owed to the elder person, the client if it is a child of the elder person, or to a third party who is providing other services such as health care or financial advise?[28] What must be disclosed to government agencies in applications for Medicaid or other government assistance?

Fourth, the attorney who provides services in this area must have a high degree of competence and command specialized skills and knowledge. He must know the tax laws, rules for Medicaid eligibility, how to sift through the maze of issues presented by the Social Security Administration or the state department of social services, and the ins and outs of estate and trust work. Medicaid is a social safety net that is provided to individuals after they spend down their available assets. In this as well as in many other asset transfers, one must be concerned about fraudulent transfers which compromise the rights of creditors or other third parties. Trusts can be arranged in a manner to take care of the person when he is no longer capable of self-determination. In addition, trusts aid in the disposition of one's assets at the end of life. All this must be done within the parameters of appropriate estate planning and the rules of the tax code.

Fifth, the elder service professional must recognize the heightened fiduciary responsibility that is placed on him when entrusted with managing valuable assets.

* * *

The ethical framework utilized by elder law attorneys must take into account the contextual focus and the special role of counseling within a family situation. While mindful of confidentiality and conflict of interest concerns, the attorney should facilitate the elder person's goals in a manner which respects her ability to participate in the management of her affairs. The bulwark of the attorney's ethical duties is his fiduciary relationship to the client. His responsibilities are marked by the requirements of elder law and the process by which the law enables the elder person to finish well.

Notes

1. *See* [MARY BAIRD CARLSEN, CREATIVE AGING: A MEANING-MAKING PERSPECTIVE (1991)], at 79.

2. *See* Gerald A. Larue, Geroethics 23 (1992).

3. *See id.* at 107 (citing Art Linkletter, Old Age is Not for Sissies 49–50 (1988).

4. *See* Harry R. Moody, Abundance of Life: Human Development Policies for an Aging Society 21 (1988).

5. *See* Carlsen, *supra* note 1, at 79.

6. *Id.* at 109 (quoting Jules Willing,).

7. *See id.* at 78.

8. *Id.* at 110.

9. *Id.* at 113.

10. For the purpose of this Article we consider not only the divestiture of assets, but also how assets are to be managed for the benefit of the elderly.

11. *See* Nancy Boyd-Franklin, Black Families in Therapy: A Multisystems Approach (1989). Throughout the discussion of Boyd-Franklin's multisystems approach, an attempt is made to relate the theory to the asset management problems confronted by the elder-law attorney.

12. *See id.* at 133.

13. In her book, Dr. Boyd-Franklin first describes the therapeutic process and than presents a discussion of multisystems levels. See Boyd-Franklin, *supra* note 11, 133–56. We have switched the order so that we can discuss systems first and then describe how they are used in the therapeutic process. Dr. Boyd-Franklin also constructs a graph of the various levels which is a serious of concentric circles with level one being at the core and level seven being placed in the circle furthest from the core. *See id.* at 149.

14. *See id.* at 148–52.

15. *See id.* at 152–54.

16. *See id.* at 153. Dr. Boyd-Franklin notes that sometimes it is difficult for many black families to reveal who is actually in the family group, making the problem solving task more challenging:

> After the first few sessions, as trust begins to build between the therapist and the family, the therapist will inevitably begin to learn more details about the extended family network. The therapist must have some knowledge of Black cultural patterns in order to ask the questions that will help to give a true sense of the real "family." The necessity of this knowledge forces us as family therapists to take a very careful look at the intake forms we use to collect family information, the questions we ask, and the timing of these questions.

Id. at 152.

This should be equally true with the elderly and their families. The lawyer needs to know who has what interests, who tends to be most influential in making decisions, and how an asset management plan might effect the family system.

17. *See id.* at 154–55. In the management of assets process it is important to be aware of who

may be giving advice besides you. Others in the family system may be useful resources in crafting a solution.

Boyd-Franklin has some suggested questions to emphasize this point:

1. How do other family members feel about this problem?
2. To whom do you go for advice?
3. Have a lot of people tried to give you their opinion about this problem?
4. To whom would you listen for advice on this issue?
5. To whom would your child (children) listen?
6. In the past, to whom would you go when you had something serious like this to deal with?
7. Who helps you out when you have troubles?
8. Have you experienced any recent losses (deaths, moves, divorces, fights, cutoffs, etc.) within the extended family nonblood kin, or friendship network?

See id. at 154.

18. *See id.* at 154–55.

19. *See id.* at 155–56. What can be said about Black families by Boyd-Franklin can also be applicable to the elderly:

> In times of crisis, the church becomes a very important social service system for many Black families . . . . [T]he crisis of fire, homelessness, hospitalization, illness, isolation, and so forth can often be helped by the support of the church "family." For many Black clients and families who are emotionally cut off or geographically isolated from their biological extended family, helping them find a church family and address their fears about doing so can have a long-term therapeutic effect.

Id. at 155.

20.

> First, the religious or spiritual belief system is so strong in some . . . families that the therapist may find it useful to simply explore it as part of general information gathering. For those families for whom religion is of paramount importance, the therapist will quickly receive feedback regarding that importance. It may the be helpful to make reference to spiritual statements made by family members as a help in reframing family impasses.

Id. at 155.

21. See *id.* at 156.

22. The major purpose in using these forms is to obtain early in the consultation an expression by the client of what he or she desires to do with assets such as joint checking or savings accounts.

23. [*See* Steven H. Hobbs, *Facilitative Ethics in Divorce Mediation: A Law and Process Approach,* 22 U. RICH. L. REV. 325, 363–64 (1988)] at 358.

24. *See id.* at 358 (quoting J. Folberg & A. Taylor, Mediation: A Comprehensive Guide to Resolving Conflicts Without Litigation 35 (1984)).

25. *See* Peter Brown, *The Punctilio of An Honor the Most Sensitive,* Tr. & Est., April 1992, at 4.

26. *See* Model Rules of Professional Conduct Rule 1.2 (1994).

27. See *In re* Hockett, 734 P.2d 877, 883–84 (Or. 1987) (en banc) (holding attorney liable for assisting an outsider waste a client's assets).

28. The third party might even have information that must be kept confidential and may influence the professional in asset management decisions. [Remainder of note omitted.]

List of Contributors

DAVID ABROMOWITZ is Director of Goulston & Storrs and Chair of the Forum on Affordable Housing and Community Development Law.

WILLIAM E. ADAMS is Assistant Professor of Law at Shepard Broad Law Center, Nova Southeastern University, Fort Lauderdale, Florida.

RONALD H. ADAY is Professor of Sociology at Middle Tennessee State University.

ANNE ALSTOTT is Associate Professor at Columbia University School of Law.

WILLIAM M. ALTMAN is an Attorney with Lewin-VHI, Washington, DC.

ALISON P. BARNES is Professor of Law at Marquette University.

SANDRA BARON is Elder Abuse Trainer and Outreach Coordinator with the Elderly Crime Victims' Resource Center, New York City Department for the Aging.

TOM L. BEAUCHAMP is Professor of Philosophy and Senior Research Scholar at the Kennedy Institute of Ethics, Georgetown University.

ROY E. BEAUCHENE is Professor Emeritus of Nutrition at the University of Tennessee.

ANNE E. BERDAHL is Associate Editor of *Health Systems Review.*

MERIS L. BERGQUIST is a staff attorney with Vermont Senior Citizens Law Project, Springfield, Vermont.

MERTON C. BERNSTEIN is Professor of Law at Washington University.

DAN BLAZER is Gibbons Professor of Psychiatry, Director of the Affective Disorders Program, and Head of the Division of Geriatric Psychiatry at Duke University Medical Center, Durham.

ERIC CARLSON is an Attorney and Director of the Nursing Home Advocacy Project at Bet Tzedek Legal Services.

CHRISTINE CASSEL is Chief of the Section of General Internal Medicine; Director of the Center on Aging, Health and Society; and Director of the Center for Health Policy Research and Professor of Medicine and Public Policy at the University of Chicago.

NINA J. CRIMM is Professor of Law and Director of the Project for Socially Responsive Taxation, Center for Law and Public Policy, St. John's University School of Law.

WILLIAM G. DAUSTER is Democratic Chief of Staff and Chief Counsel, Committee on the Budget, United States Senate.

DAVID M. ENGLISH is Professor of Law at the University of South Dakota.

RICHARD A. EPSTEIN is James Parker Hall Distinguished Service Professor of Law at the University of Chicago.

LOIS K. EVANS is with the School of Nursing, University of Pennsylvania.

MARK FALK is Executive Director of Black Hills Legal Services, Inc., Rapid City, South Dakota.

LINDA C. FENTIMAN is Associate Professor of Law, Suffolk University Law School.

PETER J. FERRARA is Associate Professor of Law at George Mason University School of Law and Senior Fellow, Cato Institute.

LEONARD M. FLECK is Professor of Philosophy and Medical Ethics, Philosophy Department, Center for Ethics and Humanities in the Life Sciences, Michigan State University.

W. EDWARD FOLTS is Associate Professor of Sociology at Appalachian State University.

VICKI A. FREEDMAN is on the RAND Health Staff, Washington, D.C.

LAWRENCE M. FRIEDMAN is Marion Rice Kirkwood Professor of Law at Stanford University.

LAWRENCE A. FROLIK is Professor of Law at the University of Pittsburgh.

BOB GRAHAM is Senior U.S. Senator from Florida.

PETER J. GRECO is with the School of Medicine, Case Western Reserve University.

JEANE ANN GRISSO is with the Center for Clinical Epidemiology and Biostatistics, Division of General Internal Medicine, University of Pennsylvania.

THOMAS L. HAFEMEISTER is Senior Staff Attorney with the National Center for State Courts' Institute on Mental Disability and the Law, Williamsburg, Virginia;

Project Director for the National Probate Court Standards Project; and Adjunct Professor of Law at the Marshall-Wythe School of Law, College of William and Mary.

DANIEL I. HALPERIN is Professor of Law at Georgetown University.

JOEL F. HANDLER is Professor of Law at the University of California at Los Angeles.

PAULA L. HANNAFORD is a Research Associate with the National Center for State Courts, Williamsburg, Virginia.

MICHAEL C. HARPER is Professor of Law at Boston University.

FAY WILSON HOBBS is Institution Rehabilitation Counselor with the Virginia Department of Youth and Family Services.

STEVEN H. HOBBS is Professor of Law at Washington and Lee University.

GEOFFREY T. HOLTZ was a 1997 J.D. Candidate at California State University, San Diego.

HOWARD M. IAMS is with the Social Security Administration.

ROBIN M. JACOBSON is a second year law student at the University of South Dakota School of Law.

MOLLY F. JAMES is a third year law student at Georgetown University.

CHRISTINE JOLLS is Assistant Professor of Law at Harvard University and Faculty Research Fellow.

YALE KAMISAR is Clarence Darrow Distinguished University Professor at the University of Michigan Law School.

RICHARD L. KAPLAN is Professor of Law at the University of Illinois at Urbana-Champaign.

MARSHALL B. KAPP is Professor in the Department of Community Health and Director of the Office of Geriatric Medicine and Gerontology, Wright State University School of Medicine.

NAOMI KARP is Associate Staff Director of the American Bar Association Commission on Legal Problems of the Elderly.

ELEANOR D. KINNEY is Professor of Law and Director of the Center for Law and Health, Indiana University School of Law, Indianapolis.

MAYA KRAJCINOVIC is a second year law student at the University of Wisconsin, Madison.

KAROL P. KROTKI is with the Institute for Survey Research, Temple University.

CLIFTON B. KRUSE, JR. is an Attorney with Kruse & Lynch, P.C., Colorado Springs.

KARIN LAPANN is with the Center for Clinical Epidemiology and Biostatistics, Division of General Internal Medicine, University of Pennsylvania.

DEAN R. LEIMER is with the Division of Economic Research, Office of Research and Statistics, Social Security Administration.

MICHAEL V. LEONESIO is with the Division of Economic Research, Office of Research and Statistics, Social Security Administration.

BERNARD LO is Associate Professor of Medicine and Acting Chief of the Division of Medical Ethics, University of California, San Francisco.

KATHERINE M. LOGAN is Assistant Professor of Sociology at Appalachian State University.

GREG MAISLIN is with the Center for Clinical Epidemiology and Biostatistics, Division of General Internal Medicine, University of Pennsylvania.

PETER MARGULIES is Associate Professor at St. Thomas University School of Law.

DOROTHY I. MEDDAUGH is Assistant Professor in the Department of Family and Community, School of Nursing, Ohio State University.

ALAN MEISEL is Professor of Law at the University of Pittsburgh and Director of the University's Center for Medical Ethics.

VICKI MICHEL is Associate Director of the Pacific Center for Health Policy and Ethics, University of Southern California, Los Angeles.

LINDA O'BRIEN is with the Center for Clinical Epidemiology and Biostatistics, Division of General Internal Medicine, University of Pennsylvania.

ANDREA D. PANJWANI is an Attorney with Legal Services of Greater Miami, Inc.

PATRICIA A. PARMELEE is Senior Research Psychologist at Polisher Gerontological Research Institute of the Philadelphia Geriatric Center.

ANNE K. PECORA is Associate Professor at the University of Baltimore School of Law.

REBECCA PLAUT is Special Assistant to the Administrator of the Boston Housing Authority.

DAVID PRYOR is United States Senator from Arkansas.

DANIEL B. RADNER is with the Division of Economic Research, Office of Research and Statistics, Social Security Administration. Ramona C. Rains is a third year law student at Cumberland School of Law, Samford University.

JAN ELLEN REIN is Professor of Law at the McGeorge School of Law, University of the Pacific.

VIRGINIA P. RENO is with the Office of Policy and External Affairs, Social Security Administration.

ROBERT P. ROCA is Director of Geriatric Services at the Sheppard and Enoch Pratt Hospital in Baltimore and Associate Professor of Psychiatry at the Johns Hopkins University School of Medicine.

JOHN ROTHER is Director of the Division of Legislation and Public Policy, American Association of Retired Persons.

STEVEN H. SANDELL is with the Office of the Assistant Secretary for Planning and Evaluation, Department of Health and Human Services.

RANJANA SARDANA lives in Houston.

CHRISTINE S. SELLERS is Assistant Professor of Criminology at the University of South Florida.

CHRISTINE A. SEMANSON lives in Michigan.

ELISABETH A. SIEGERT is with the University of Medicine and Dentistry of New Jersey, Robert Wood Johnson Medical School at Camden.

ANDREW H. SMITH is a Research Analyst with the Public Policy Institute, American Association of Retired Persons.

LINDA F. SMITH is Clinical Program Director and Associate Professor of Law at the University of Utah.

MICHAEL A. SMYER is Professor of Human Development at Pennsylvania State University and President of the Division of Adult Development and Aging, American Psychological Association.

JEFFREY SPITZER-RESNICK is a solo practitioner in Madison, Wisconsin.

JUNE O. STARR is Associate Professor of Law at Indiana University School of Law, Indianapolis.

T. HOWARD STONE is a Consultant with the World Health Organization, Regional Office for the Western Pacific.

GEORGE J. TICHY, II is a Partner with Littler Mendelson, P.C., San Francisco.

CHARLES TIEFER is Associate Professor of Law at the University of Baltimore.

PHILIP B. TOR is a J.D. candidate at the College of Law, University of Arizona.

DELLMAR WALKER is Professor of Human Sciences at Middle Tennessee State University.

CARLA T. WALLS is a Staff Member with the Philadelphia Health Management Corporation.

SIDNEY D. WATSON is Associate Professor at Mercer University School of Law.

ADELE WELTY is with the Institute on Law and Rights of Older Adults, Brookdale Center on Aging, Hunter College, CUNY.

LINDA S. WHITTON is Associate Professor at Valparaiso University School of Law.

WILLIAM J. WINSLADE is James Wade Rockwell Professor of Philosophy in Medicine, Institute for the Medical Humanities, University of Texas Medical Branch, Galveston, and Professor of Law at the Health Law and Policy Institute, University of Houston Law Center.

KEVIN R. WOLFF is a second-year law student at the University of Georgia School of Law.

ERICA WOOD is Associate Staff Director of the American Bar Association Commission on Legal Problems of the Elderly.

BARBARA W. K. YEE is Developmental Psychologist in the School of Allied Health Sciences, University of Texas Medical Branch, Galveston, Texas.

Index